Longman Participate.com 2.0

TAKE A STAND.

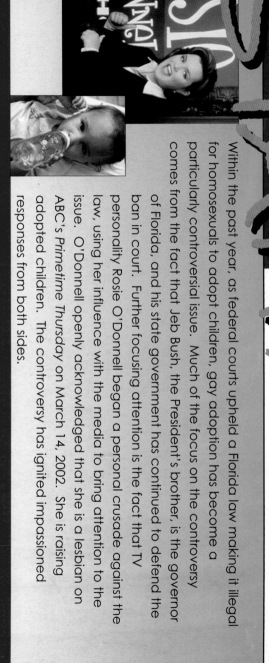

Within the past year, as federal courts upheld a Florida law making it illegal for homosexuals to adopt children, gay adoption has become a particularly controversial issue. Much of the focus on the controversy comes from the fact that Jeb Bush, the President's brother, is the governor of Florida, and his state government has continued to defend the ban in court. Further focusing attention is the fact that TV personality Rosie O'Donnell began a personal crusade against the law, using her influence with the media to bring attention to the issue. O'Donnell openly acknowledged that she is a lesbian on ABC's Primetime Thursday on March 14, 2002. She is raising adopted children. The controversy has ignited impassioned responses from both sides.

You'll be able to read both sides of this controversy and join the debate in the new version of **LongmanParticipate.com**, now with CourseCompass.

The above excerpt, from the Gay Adoption Participation Debate activity in the Civil Rights chapter, is just one example of the many interactive and dynamic activities found on **LongmanParticipate.com 2.0**.

P9-CAL-941

Are you up for the challenge?

For every chapter in your textbook, LongmanParticipate.com 2.0 offers 5 highly interactive exercises that will get you experiencing the excitement of politics firsthand....

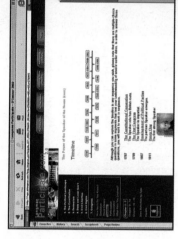

Simulations. You're given a role to play, an objective to reach, and "the rules of the game." How well you score depends on the decisions you make and your knowledge of American government! Some of your roles: police officer, member of Congress, hotshot lawyer, and big city mayor.

Timelines. Ever wondered if there were other "close calls" like the 2000 presidential election? Need to understand the evolution of our foreign policy for your next exam? These *Timelines* offer an engaging tour through the evolution of an aspect of our government.

Visual Literacy. What is the relationship between race and the death penalty? What speech is protected by the Constitution? *Visual Literacy* activities help you answer these questions through interpreting data and working with tables, charts, and graphs. Each exercise begins with an interactive primer on reading graphics to help you get started.

Participation. Bringing the importance of politics home, these activities appear in 3 types:

- **NEW** "Debates" ask you to analyze the pros and cons of a hot current issue and reach your own conclusions.
- "Surveys" get you exploring your opinions about political issues.
- "Get Involved" activities encourage you to participate in politics.

Comparative. Find out whether Britain has a bill of rights and whether Israeli citizens are allowed to marry outside their religion in these thought-provoking activities. With more visuals, more countries, and more engaging, informative, and eye-opening details, you'll compare and contrast the U.S. political system to those of other countries.

Want to get a better grade?

Developed and revised by a team of political science faculty from across the country, LongmanParticipate.com 2.0 was designed not only to be fun, but to help you learn—so you are better prepared for tests and get a better grade in the course.

Feedback and Scoring. At every step in every activity, you are given feedback so you know why you got something right or wrong. This way, you always know how you are doing and if you are understanding the material.

NEW! "Test Yourself" quizzes.
At the end of every activity, there is a 10-question, multiple-choice quiz called "Test Yourself." These quizzes allow you to see how much you've learned by doing the activity so you are better prepared for exams.

NEW! "How Much Do You Know?" surveys and "How Much Have You Learned?" post-tests. At the beginning and end of each chapter on the site, these pre- and post-tests will allow you to see how well you've grasped the chapter topic.

Other Resources to Help You Get a Better Grade...

▶ **NEW! "Politics Now" Current Events feature.** With an automatic feed from *The New York Times* Web site, you can click on headlines to read the article. A great way to keep up with the current events that your instructor will often test you on.

▶ **In the News.** A comprehensive list of news and current-events Web sites.

▶ **Writing Term Papers.** An interactive primer that gives you what you need to know to write an A+ paper or essay!

▶ **Analyzing a Debate.** Gives you the basics on how to analyze an argument so you can be a critical consumer of the issues presented on this site and in the news.

To Instructors: Easy to Integrate Into Any Course

We want LongmanParticipate.com 2.0 to be an easy-to-integrate part of every American government classroom. We have therefore developed the following features to make it as useful as possible for you:

NEW! Text-Specific Versions of LongmanParticipate.com 2.0. Each Longman textbook has its own, text-specific version of the site. Now, the content on the Web site exactly matches the table of contents of the text you are using in class, creating a seamless flow between the text and the Web.

NEW! Online Administration Features in CourseCompass. Version 2.0 has been wedded to CourseCompass' powerful online course administration features so that instructors can easily track student work on the site and monitor students' progress on each activity. The *Instructor Gradebook* provides maximum flexibility, allowing instructors to sort by student, activity, or to view their entire class in spreadsheet view.

NEW! Quick Start Guide with Access Code for Instructors. This brief guide contains your access code to LongmanParticipate.com 2.0 and CourseCompass, as well as step-by-step instructions for getting online. **ISBN 0-321-17273-6.**

REVISED! Faculty Guide for 2.0. This easy-to-use guide gives step-by-step instructions for using the site and integrating the activities into a course. Available February 2003. **ISBN 0-321-13672-1.**

Look to Longman for other outstanding new books in Political Science...

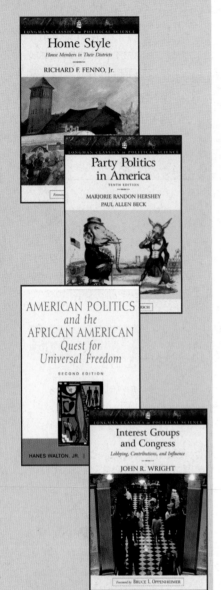

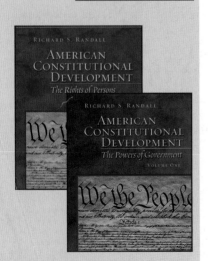

For more information about each book, including a table of contents, please visit our Web site at **www.ablongman.com/polisci**

POLITICAL INSTITUTIONS

FENNO, *Home Style: House Members in Their Districts*
(Longman Classics in Political Science Series) ISBN 0-321-12183-X

GENOVESE, *The Presidential Dilemma: Leadership in the American System,* 2/e
ISBN 0-321-10898-1

LELOUP/SHULL, *The President and Congress: Collaboration & Combat in National Policymaking,* 2/e ISBN 0-321-10041-7

PFIFFNER/DAVIDSON, *Understanding the Presidency,* 3/e ISBN 0-321-08986-3

FIORINA, *Divided Government,* 2/e
(Longman Classics in Political Science Series) ISBN 0-321-12184-8

POLITICAL PARTICIPATION

BENNETT, *News: The Politics of Illusion,* 5/e
(Longman Classics in Political Science Series) ISBN 0-321-08878-6

ERIKSON/TEDIN, *American Public Opinion,* 6/e, *Update Edition* ISBN 0-321-12734-X

HERSHEY/BECK, *Party Politics in America,* 10/e
(Longman Classics in Political Science Series) ISBN 0-321-09543-X

ROSENSTONE/HANSEN, *Mobilization, Participation and Democracy in America*
(Longman Classics in Political Science Series) ISBN 0-321-12186-4

WALTON/SMITH, *American Politics and the African American Quest for Universal Freedom,* 2/e ISBN 0-321-10479-X

WRIGHT, *Interest Groups and Congress: Lobbying, Contributions, and Influence*
(Longman Classics in Political Science Series) ISBN 0-321-12187-2

COURTS/CONSTITUTIONAL LAW/CIVIL RIGHTS & LIBERTIES

DOMINO, *Civil Rights and Liberties in the 21st Century,* 2/e ISBN 0-321-08970-7

RANDALL, *American Constitutional Development*
Volume One: The Powers of Government ISBN 0-8013-2019-4
Volume Two: The Rights of Persons ISBN 0-8013-2021-6

URBAN POLITICS

BROWNING/MARSHALL/TABB, *Racial Politics in American Cities,* 3/e
ISBN 0-321-10035-2

HARRIGAN/VOGEL, *Political Change in the Metropolis,* 7/e ISBN 0-321-09744-0

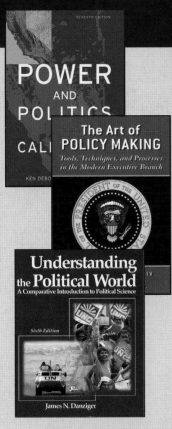

For more information about each book, including a table of contents, please visit our Web site at **www.ablongman.com/polisci**

There are 2 versions of *The Struggle for Democracy* by Greenberg and Page—contact your local Allyn & Bacon/Longman representative if you'd like to examine one of these other versions.

Comprehensive Sixth Edition

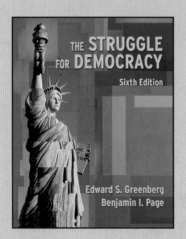

© 2003 • 656 pages • Hardcover
ISBN 0-321-09703-3
© 2003 • 656 pages • Paper
ISBN 0-321-09701-7 (Student Edition)
ISBN 0-321-10869-8 (Instructor Edition)

This version contains detailed coverage of all topic areas.

Contents

1. Democracy and American Politics.
2. The Constitution.
3. Federalism: States and Nation.
4. The Structural Foundations of American Government and Politics.
5. Public Opinion.
6. The News Media.
7. Interest Groups and Business Corporations.
8. Social Movements.
9. Political Parties.
10. Participation, Voting, and Elections.
11. Congress.
12. The President.
13. The Federal Bureaucracy.
14. The Courts.
15. Freedom: The Struggle for Civil Liberties.
16. Civil Rights: The Struggle for Political Equality.
17. Domestic Policy: The Economy and Social Welfare.
18. Foreign Policy and National Defense.
APPENDICES.

CourseCompass Edition

© 2002 • 656 pages • Hardcover
ISBN 0-321-09764-5

This edition seamlessly integrates Greenberg & Page's 5th Edition text with the unparalleled easy-to-use online course management capabilities of CourseCompass.

- A 16-page insert in the front of the text walks students through the many features of Greenberg's CourseCompass Web site.

- CourseCompass icons in the text direct students to relevant activities on the Web site, tying the text and site together. These icons direct students to one of two types of activities: Web Explorations or LongmanParticipate.com activities.

- Pincodes to the Greenberg CourseCompass Web site are automatically packaged for FREE in every new copy of the text.

The Struggle for Democracy

SIXTH EDITION

Edward S. Greenberg
University of Colorado

Benjamin I. Page
Northwestern University

Longman

New York   San Francisco   Boston
London   Toronto   Sydney   Tokyo   Singapore   Madrid
Mexico City   Munich   Paris   Cape Town   Hong Kong   Montreal

VICE PRESIDENT AND PUBLISHER:	Priscilla McGeehon
EXECUTIVE EDITOR:	Eric Stano
DEVELOPMENT DIRECTOR:	Lisa Pinto
DEVELOPMENT EDITOR:	Nancy Crochiere
SENIOR MARKETING MANAGER:	Megan Galvin-Fak
SUPPLEMENTS EDITOR:	Kristi Olson
MEDIA EDITOR:	Patrick McCarthy
PRODUCTION MANAGER:	Donna DeBenedictis
PROJECT COORDINATION, TEXT DESIGN, AND ELECTRONIC PAGE MAKEUP:	Elm Street Publishing Services, Inc.
COVER DESIGN MANAGER:	Wendy Ann Fredericks
COVER DESIGNER:	Kay Petronio
COVER PHOTO:	© Creative Concepts/Index Stock Picture Cube Southern Stock
ART STUDIO:	Elm Street Publishing Services, Inc.
PHOTO RESEARCHER:	Photosearch, Inc.
MANUFACTURING BUYER:	Lucy Hebard
PRINTER AND BINDER:	Quebecor World/Taunton
COVER PRINTER:	Phoenix Color Corporation

For permission to use copyrighted material, grateful acknowledgment is made to the copyright holders on pp. C-1–C-2, which are hereby made part of this copyright page.

Library of Congress Cataloging-in-Publication Data
Greenberg, Edward S., 1942–
    The struggle for democracy / Edward S. Greenberg, Benjamin I. Page.—6th ed.
      p. cm.
    Includes bibliographical references and index.
    ISBN 0-321-09703-3 (hc: alk. paper)—ISBN 0-321-09701-7 (pbk.: alk. paper)
    1. United States—Politics and government. 2. Democracy—United States. I. Page, Benjamin I. II. Title.
    JK276.G74 2003
    320.473—dc21   2002075443

Please visit our website at **http://www.ablongman.com/greenberg**

ISBN 0-321-09703-3 (hardcover)
ISBN 0-321-09701-7 (softcover)

1 2 3 4 5 6 7 8 9 10—WCT—05 04 03 02

Brief Contents

Detailed Contents

Note: Each chapter ends with the following sections: Summary, Suggestions for Further Reading, Internet Sources, and Notes. Gold arrows designate special features within the chapter.

List of Features

Using the Framework

How Democratic Are We?

By the Numbers

Web Explorations

Web Explorations *(continued)*

Preface

"Critical Thinking" and *The Struggle for Democracy*

This sixth edition of *The Struggle for Democracy* carries forward and strengthens the extensive changes we made in the fifth edition that contributed to its widespread popularity among teachers and students. Following the well-known adage "if it ain't broke, don't fix it," we have decided to confine major changes in this edition to those that enrich and sharpen its critical thinking focus. In addition to a general updating and freshening of materials throughout the text—including the Bush presidency; the impact of the 9/11 terrorist attacks on the United States; the 2002 midterm elections; the creation of the new office of Homeland Security; and Court rulings on federalism, the death penalty, school vouchers, and affirmative action—our most significant change in this regard is the addition of a feature we call "By the Numbers" that helps students think more critically about the official and unofficial numbers and statistics they encounter almost every day, whether they be reports about the extent of poverty in the United States, the crime rate, or voting turnout in presidential elections. We will say more about this feature later.

The watchword for the sixth edition of *The Struggle for Democracy*, much as it was for the fifth, is "critical thinking." Critical thinking has always been at the heart of this book, of course, but its sharp edge had gradually, if almost unconsciously, become blunted slightly with each revision as material was added to answer first one perceived need then another. With the fifth edition and the present sixth edition revision, we have sharpened the critical thinking edge, getting it back to where it was supposed to be. Every element in this version of *The Struggle for Democracy* is designed to serve the "critical thinking" objective. We have continued to pare away any and all materials that do not help students think critically about American government and politics and about their role as citizens. In moving in this direction, we are returning to our original vision when we first decided to write this book, responding to what we learned from a multitude of instructors and students about what they want in an introductory textbook, and conforming to what we, as experienced teachers of the introductory course, know works in the classroom. We have created a textbook that treats students as adults, engages their intellectual and emotional attention, and encourages them to be active learners.

The critical thinking orientation of this edition of *The Struggle for Democracy*, as it was for the fifth, is organized around two principal themes: *Using the Democracy Standard* and *Using the Framework*. The first helps students come to grips with American government and politics in normative or value terms. The second helps students cut through the jumble of information about government and politics and bring some order out of the confusion, helping them make sense of why things happen. We have also created a rich set of Web Explorations in which students do assignments on the Internet where they hone their evaluative and analytical critical thinking skills and, at the same time, have some fun. New to this edition is "By the Numbers," a feature that not only helps students think more critically about published numbers and statistics but asks them to use the insights they have garnered from using this feature to think about current political problems and issues.

Using the Democracy Standard

Throughout the pages of this textbook, we help students think about the system as a whole, as well as particular political practices and institutions, using a clearly articulated, evaluative democracy "yardstick" for reaching judgments about the degree to which we have become, or are becoming, more or less democratic.

We develop this "evaluating democracy" theme in a number of places:

- Democracy is carefully defined in Chapter 1, and students learn there how they might use democracy to evaluate the performance of the American political system. The definition of democracy is broad and inclusive, built on the concepts of popular sovereignty, political equality, and liberty.

- In the opening pages of each chapter, students are reminded about the democracy "yardstick" and how it might be used to think critically about the subject matter to follow.

- Discussion of the relative democratic performance of the American political system, using the Chapter 1 definition as the yardstick, is laced throughout the text narrative.

- A chapter-ending box, "How Democratic Are We?," helps students think through the democracy issue once again, only this time they have the capacity to bring information and insights to bear that they have gained from reading the chapter, attending class and joining its discussions, and doing the Web Explorations. This feature is organized in the following way. It opens with a strongly stated proposition about the relative democratic character of the particular political or governmental institution under consideration in the chapter. The proposition is answered by two opposing views, brief but fairly stated "agree" and "disagree" statements. Finally, we the authors respond to the proposition, sometimes aligning with the "agree" position, sometimes with the "disagree" position, but usually incorporating elements of each into a more subtle and balanced argument. This feature helps students to understand the complexity of many of the issues addressed in the book and to learn how to formulate intellectually compelling arguments.

Using the Framework

In Chapter 1 we also provide a simple but powerful analytical framework that helps students understand how our complicated political system works. The framework makes clear that government, politics, and the larger society are deeply intertwined in recognizable patterns; that understanding what is going on requires a holistic focus; and that what might be called "deep structures"—the economy, society, culture, technology, and the constitutional rules—are particularly important for understanding how our system works. These deep structures have a great deal to do with the creation of the problems to which government must attend, the level of resources that is available to solve problems, the ideas that citizens and elected officials have in their heads as they go about using government to address problems, and the distribution of political power in society among individuals, groups, and organizations.

The framework appears in *The Struggle for Democracy* in the following places:

- The framework is discussed in detail in Chapter 1, and students are shown how it can be used to organize the large amounts of material they will encounter in the course of their reading. A powerful graphic associated with the discussion makes the framework more understandable and compelling.

- In the opening pages of each chapter, students are reminded about the framework and how it can be used to understand how government and politics work in the United States.

- Chapters in Part Two examine the nature of American society, culture, and economy; the United States's position in the world; and our constitutional rules—and why these issues matter for how government and politics work.

- Concepts and insights from the framework, as well as materials from the chapters in Part Two, are used throughout the text narrative.

- A "Using the Framework" box appears in each chapter. The purpose of the box is to show students how the framework might be used to answer questions they might have about why things happen in American government and politics. Concepts and insights from the framework, as well as a graphical reminder, are used to provide the tools to answer questions that students are interested in, such as "Why is out-of-state tuition more costly than in-state tuition?" and "Why can't we seem to get big money out of politics?" Teachers and students have told us repeatedly that this feature, which first appeared in the fifth edition, made the analytical framework come alive for them and helped them appreciate how the framework can be used to understand what is going on in American government and politics.

Web Explorations

We have designed a series of what we call "Web Explorations," where students can explore and use the many riches of the Internet to put their critical thinking skills to work and have some fun at the same time. In these Web Explorations, we do not simply identify a Website for students to visit but give them a question or issue to investigate and ask that they report the results. These reports, tangible products of their investigations and analyses, may be for students' own edification, enriching their experiences in the text, or may be assigned as a class activity. The Explorations are active and interactive in nature, never passive. Students are not casual visitors, browsing a site, but investigators and analysts using their critical thinking skills.

By the Numbers

As teachers of the introductory course, we have grown increasingly concerned over the years by the inability of many students to understand the statistical information on government, politics, economy, and society that they encounter—including statistics such as the Gross Domestic Product, the crime rate, voting turnout in presidential elections, and the level of poverty in the United States—or to distinguish between good and bad statistical information. Partly, this is the result of their general discomfort with statistics and numbers. Partly, this is the product of the failure of statistical reporting agencies and organizations to openly describe their operating assumptions and methods. All too often, moreover, interest and advocacy groups use statistics as instruments of political combat, leaving the impression that all statistics are "lies and damn lies," with one statistic no better than another. The news media are not all that helpful either, with their tendency to report social, economic, and political statistics in a haphazard, noncritical, and out-of-context fashion. Finally, statistics from the federal government, though generally more reliable and sensible than those calculated by interest groups, are themselves often the product of political negotiation and compromise—the poverty-line calculation is a good example. Although government statistics are incredibly useful, the consumer of such statistics must remain alert.

The "By the Numbers" boxed feature appears throughout the text. The goal of the feature is to help students become better consumers of statistical information and more analytical readers of social, economic, and political statistics reported by government, interest and advocacy groups, and academic researchers. Each box describes a particular statistic and tells why the statistic is important—examples include voting turnout, the poverty line, the crime rate, the size of the federal government, interest group scoring of the performance of senators and representatives, and more. We then tell the story behind the statistic—why the statistic was first calculated, let us say, or what assumptions are embedded in it. We then show how the statistic is calculated and examine what critics and supporters say about its usefulness and validity. Finally, we ask students "What do you think?" encouraging them to think in more depth about issues addressed by the statistic, whether it be poverty, voting turnout, or how the U.S. Census Bureau goes about doing the decennial census. If the "By the Numbers" feature works as we hope it does, students should become more sophisticated users of statistical information, but not cynical ones. We believe that in a world increasingly described by numbers, students who are armed with these skills can be better and more effective citizens.

Organization and Coverage

Part One contains the introduction to the textbook and focuses primarily on describing the critical thinking tools to be used throughout: democracy and the analytical framework. Part Two covers the structural foundations of American government and politics and also addresses subjects such as the economy, culture, and international system; the constitutional framework of the American political system; and the development of the federal system. Part Three focuses on what we call *political linkage* institutions, such as parties, elections, public opinion, social movements, and interest groups, that serve to convey the wants, needs, and demands of individuals and groups to public officials. Part Four concentrates on the central institutions of the national government, including the presidency, Congress, and the Supreme Court. Part Five describes the kinds of policies the national government produces and analyzes how effective government is in solving pressing social and economic problems.

Although all of the standard topics in the introductory course are covered in the text, our focus on using democracy as a measuring rod to evaluate our system of government, and on using an analytical framework for understanding how things work, allows us to take a fresh look at traditional topics and to pay attention to topics that are not covered in detail in other textbooks.

● We pay much more attention to *structural factors*, which include the American economy, social change in the United States, technological innovations and change, the American political culture, and changes in the global system, and examine how they affect politics, government, and public policy. These factors are introduced in Chapter 4—a chapter unique among introductory texts—and are brought to bear on a wide range of issues in subsequent chapters. For example, our discussion of interest group politics includes relevant information about how the distribution of income and wealth affects the ability of different groups to form effective lobbying organizations.

● We attend very carefully to issues of *democratic political theory*. This follows from our critical thinking objective, which asks students to assess the progress of and prospects for democracy in the United States, and from our desire to present American history as the history of the struggle for democracy. For instance, we examine how the evolution of the party system has improved democracy in some respects in the United States but hurt it in others.

● We also include more *historical information* than is common among introductory texts, because the best way to understand the struggle for democracy and evaluate the progress of democracy in the United States benefits from a historical perspective. We show, for example, how the expansion of civil rights in the United States has been associated with important historical events and trends.

● We also include substantial *comparative information*, because we believe that a full understanding of government and politics and the effect of structural factors on them is possible only through a comparison of developments, practices, and institutions in the United States with those in other nations. We understand better how our system of social welfare works, for example, when we see how other rich democratic countries deal with the problems of poverty, unemployment, and old age.

● Our approach also means that the subjects of *civil liberties* and *civil rights* are not treated in conjunction with the Constitution in Part Two, which is the case with many introductory texts, but in Part Five, on public policy. This is because we believe that the real-world status of civil liberties and civil rights, while partly determined by specific provisions of the Constitution, is better understood as the outcome of the interaction of structural, political, and governmental factors. Thus, the status of civil rights for gays and lesbians depends not only on constitutional provisions but also on the state of public opinion, degrees of support from elected political leaders, and the decisions of the Supreme Court. (Instructors who prefer to introduce their students to civil liberties and civil rights immediately after considering the Constitution can simply assign the liberties and rights chapters out of order.)

What's New in This Edition

A number of important changes have been made in this edition. They include the following:

● To reiterate a point already made: The most important change in this sixth edition of *The Struggle for Democracy* is the extension of the focus on critical thinking as the central organizing template. To get there, we have further refined and strengthened our discussions of democracy as a tool of evaluation and of the framework as a tool of analysis and understanding, paid special attention to drawing out these themes in every chapter, and included a series of Web Explorations to enable students to be active critical thinkers.

● This edition of *The Struggle for Democracy* includes a new "By the Numbers" feature, described earlier in more detail. This feature is unique among introductory American government and politics textbooks and adds to the critical thinking tools available to students.

● This edition pays more attention to "marginalized" groups in American society, including Hispanics and gays and lesbians. Combining this enhanced attention to marginalized groups with *The Struggle for Democracy*'s traditionally strong coverage of African-Americans and women means that the current edition of this textbook reflects much of the cultural richness, diversity, and complexity of American society itself. These new materials are found throughout in the text narrative, in chapter-opening vignettes, and in boxed features. For example, Chapter 15 considers the status of Arab-Americans in the United States in the aftermath of 9/11. Chapter 16 discusses the current status of gay rights legislation in the states.

● We have expanded our coverage of Websites in the Internet Sources sections and integrated them even more tightly with *The Struggle for Democracy* home page. This is in addition to the very strong Internet presence found in the Web Exploration features distributed throughout. Together, these will allow both students and instructors to have better access to timely information and alternative perspectives.

● In addition to expanded coverage of Websites and the Web Explorations feature, we have made further strides to integrate the Web. Throughout the text, icons can be found in the margins referring readers to *LongmanParticipate.com, Version 2.0,* Longman's interactive Website for American government. Each icon appears next to a particular topic and indicates that a simulation, visual literacy exercise, interactive timeline, participation activity, or comparative government exercise related to that topic exists on the site. Each activity provides feedback, helps the reader better understand the concepts presented in the text, and makes learning fun. See the insert at the front of this text for more information.

● Information has been updated throughout. There is not a single page in the text without fresh information. Timely subjects, such as the 2002 congressional elections; the actions and policies of the George W. Bush administration; the continuing impact on American politics of the September 11, 2001, terrorist attacks on the United States (which we sometimes refer to as 9/11 or Nine-Eleven); the creation of the new Department of Homeland Security; the public and governmental responses to the accounting scandals in the corporate world; important Court decisions involving federalism, civil liberties, and civil rights; emerging foreign policy problems in the Middle East, and more, are covered throughout. In addition, topics such as the affirmative action controversy, changing party alignments, and the effect of global economic and technological change are given even greater attention than in the fifth edition.

- We have continued our effort to make the text more user-friendly for students by paying more attention to the layout of text and the highlighting of key points, better defining technical terms, presenting more detailed captions that explain tables and graphs, and providing more information in photo captions. Most importantly, we have tied the chapters together with critical thinking guideposts, exercises, and concluding observations.

Supplements

Longman Publishers provides an impressive array of text supplements to aid instructors in teaching and students in learning. Each item in this extensive package works together to create a fully integrated learning system. Great care was taken to provide both students and professors with a supportive supplements package that accurately reflects the unique spirit of *The Struggle for Democracy*.

Instructor Supplements for Qualified College Adopters

American Government Presentation Library CD-Rom This complete multimedia presentation tool provides a built-in presentation maker, 20 video clips, 200 photographs, 200 figures and graphs from Longman texts, 20 minutes of audio clips, and links to more than 200 Websites. Media items can be imported into *PowerPoint®* and *Persuasion®* presentation programs.

The Struggle for Democracy Companion Website (http://www.ablongman.com/greenberg) Designed to support instructors and students who are using *The Struggle for Democracy*, this Website includes summaries, Web Explorations, and practice tests for each chapter for students. For instructors, there is a *PowerPoint®* presentation, created by Terri Wright of California State University, Long Branch, and Mary Carns of Stephen F. Austin State University, to support and enhance lectures; downloadable art and images for each chapter; the *Instructor's Manual;* and a group of teaching links.

Instructor's Manual Written by Todd M. Schaefer of Central Washington University and Mary Carns of Stephen F. Austin State University, this comprehensive manual is designed to help instructors prepare lectures, classroom activities, and assignments. The manual features chapter outlines and summaries, a broad range of teaching suggestions, ideas for student research, and suggestions for discussion that complement text themes.

Test Bank Prepared by Robert Yowell of Stephen F. Austin State University, this manual is designed to reinforce and test students' knowledge of the themes and concepts of the text. The test bank contains hundreds of multiple-choice, short-answer, true/false, and essay questions with an answer key.

Test Gen EQ Computerized Testing System This flexible, easy-to-master computerized test bank includes all the test items in the printed test bank.

The software allows professors to edit existing questions and to add their own items. Tests can be printed in several different formats and can include features such as graphs and tables. It is available for Windows and Macintosh computers.

PowerPoint® **Presentations**   Available to download on the textbook's Companion Website at: **www.ablongman.com/greenberg**. Written by Mary Carns at Stephen F. Austin State University and Terri Wright of California State University, Long Beach, these slides can also be easily modified using *PowerPoint*® software.

Transparencies   This acetate package is comprised of 40 images drawn from the text.

Faculty Guide to Accompany LongmanParticipate.com Version 2.0 Website   Contains chapter-by-chapter detailed summaries for each of the site's interactive activities, as well as a list of concepts covered, recommendations about how to integrate the site into coursework, and discussion questions and paper topics for every exercise. Instructors may use the table of contents in the front of the guide to locate information on a given activity icon that appears in the margin of this textbook. This guide also provides instructors with detailed instructions and screen shots showing how to register on the site and how to set up and use the administrative features. The introductory chapter describes the numerous additional resources included on the Website. Written by Scott Furlong of the University of Wisconsin.

Quick Start Guide to Accompany LongmanParticipate.com Version 2.0   Contains instructor access code and step-by-step instructions for using LongmanParticipate.com Version 2.0's dramatic new administrative features, now found in the Course Compass course management system. To order, contact your local Allyn & Bacon/Longman representative and request a copy using **ISBN 0-321-17273-6.**

Interactive American Government Video   Contains 27 video segments on topics ranging from the term limit debate, to Internet porn, to women in the Citadel. Critical thinking questions accompany each clip, encouraging students to "interact" with the videos.

Politics in Action **Video**   Eleven "lecture launchers," covering broad subjects such as social movements, conducting a campaign, and the passage of a bill, are examined through narrated videos, interviews, edited documentaries, original footage, and political ads.

Longman Political Science Video Program   Qualified adopters can peruse our list of videos for the American government classroom. Contact your local Allyn & Bacon/Longman representative for more information.

Active Learning Guide   This guide is designed to get students actively involved in course material and encourage them to evaluate and defend viewpoints. Included in this guide are role-playing exercises, debates, and Web-based group projects.

Student Supplements for Qualified College Adopters

LongmanParticipate.com, Version 2.0   FREE student subscription in every new copy of *The Struggle for Democracy.* LongmanParticipate.com, Version 2.0, the most interactive and comprehensive Website for American government, retains the strengths of the first version with five types of highly interactive activities (Simulations, Visual Literacy, Timelines, Participation, and Comparative) for every chapter in the text. Version 2.0 offers dramatic enhancements including a text-specific version of the site, a stunning new look, new and revised activities, better scoring and feedback, and more powerful instructor administration features. See the front of this book for more information!

Companion Website (www.ablongman.com/greenberg)   This text-specific, online study guide includes: practice tests with feedback (multiple choice, true/false, fill-in-the-blank, and essay questions), Web exploration exercises, chapter summaries, and more.

Multimedia Edition CD-ROM   This CD-ROM contains the full text of *The Struggle for Democracy,* Sixth Edition, on CD with hyperlinks to video clips, interactive practice tests, Web links, figures, photos, and more! (Publishing April 2003 for summer and fall classes)

Study Wizard CD-ROM   This interactive tutorial program helps students master concepts in the text through practice tests, chapter and topic summaries, and an interactive glossary. Students receive immediate feedback in the form of answer explanations and page references in the text to go to for review.

Study Guide   Written by George Gonzalez of the University of Miami and Mary Carns of Stephen F. Austin State University. The printed study guide includes chapter outlines, key terms, practice tests, and critical thinking questions.

iSearch Guide for Political Science   This brief yet complete online research guide offers step-by-step instructions for using the Internet to do research, critical thinking exercises, and information about evaluating sites for academic usefulness. The guide also includes a FREE access card to the Research Navigator Online research Database.

ResearchNavigator.com   This complete online research resource features the *New York Times* Search-by-Subject database of articles; ContentSelect, a customized, searchable collection of 25,000+ discipline-specific articles; the *New York Times* "Themes of the Times" collections; Link Library; and more. Access codes come in the iSearch Guide described above.

***New York Times* Discount Subscription**   A 10-week subscription for only $20! Contact your local Allyn & Bacon/Longman representative for more information.

***American Government in a Changed World: The Effects of
September 11, 2001***   To help students understand how the September 11,
2001, terrorist attacks have affected American government and our way of life,
Longman has published a compendium of original essays by our renowned
roster of American government authors. Each essay begins with a "Headnote"
and concludes with discussion questions, Websites, and suggested readings.
Free when ordered packaged with this text.

***Voices of Dissent: Critical Readings in American Politics,* Third
Edition**   Edited by William F. Grover, St. Michael's College, and Joseph G.
Peschek, Hamline University, this collection of critical essays goes beyond the
debate between mainstream liberalism and conservatism to fundamentally
challenge the status quo. Available at a discount when ordered packaged with
the text.

Ten Things That Every American Government Student Should Read
Edited by Karen O'Connor, American University. We asked American government instructors across the country to vote for 10 things beyond the text that
they believe every student should read and put them in this brief and useful
reader. Free when ordered packaged with the text.

Choices: An American Government Database Reader   This customiz-
able reader allows instructors to choose from a database of more than 300
readings to create a reader that exactly matches their course needs. Go to
www.pearsoncustom.com/database/choices.html for more information.

Discount Subscription to *Newsweek* Magazine   Students receive 12
issues of *Newsweek* at more than 80 percent off the regular price. An excellent way for students to keep up with current events.

Penguin–Longman Value Bundles   Longman offers 25 Penguin
Putnam titles at more than a 60 percent discount when packaged with any
Longman text. A totally unique offer and a wonderful way to enhance students' understanding of concepts in American government. Please go to
www.ablongman.com/penguin for more information.

***Writing in Political Science,* Second Edition**   Written by Diane
Schmidt, this guide takes students step-by-step through all aspects of writing
in political science. Available at a discount when ordered packaged with any
Longman textbook.

Getting Involved: A Guide to Student Citizenship   Written by Mark
Kann, Todd Belt, Gabriela Cowperthwaite, and Steven Horn. A unique and
practical handbook that guides students through political participation with
concrete advice and extensive sample material—letters, telephone scripts, student interviews, and real-life anecdotes—for getting involved and making a
difference in their lives and communities.

***Texas Politics Supplement,* Second Edition**   Written by Debra St. John.
A 90-page primer on state and local government and issues in Texas. Free
when shrink-wrapped with the text.

***California Politics Supplement,* Second Edition** Written by Barbara Stone. A 70-page primer on state and local government and issues in California. Free when shrink-wrapped with the text.

Florida Politics Supplement Written by John Bertalan. A 50-page primer on state and local government and issues in Florida. Free when shrink-wrapped with the text.

Acknowledgments

Writing and producing an introductory textbook is an incredibly complex and cooperative enterprise in which many people besides the authors play roles. We would like to take the opportunity to thank them, one and all. We start with the many wonderful people at Longman who worked on this edition, including development editor Nancy Crochiere, production manager Donna DeBenedictis, Sue Nodine and her colleagues at Elm Street Publishing Services for design and production work, photo researcher Sherri Zuckerman, and marketing manager Megan Galvin-Fak. Special thanks go to Eric Stano who has always believed in this book project and in us, and whose guidance helped make the fifth edition the most successful one yet. We hope that his wise counsel on revisions for the sixth edition will have a similar result.

Ed Greenberg would like to thank Colorado graduate student Andy Thangasamy for his expert research assistance and Jay Zarowitz of Muskegon Community College for supplying mountains of information for chapter revisions and for testing and giving advice on the Web Exploration features. David Olson of the University of Washington, Neal Milner of the University of Hawaii, and Art Paulson of Southern Connecticut State University advised on the content and form of the "By the Numbers" feature. As always, our students in the introductory courses in American government and politics at the University of Colorado and at Northwestern University had much to say about what they liked and didn't like in the book and were more than willing to tell us how it might be improved.

Over the years, Longman enlisted the help of many political scientists on various aspects of this project. Their advice was especially valuable, and the final version of the book is far better than it would have been without their help. We would like to extend our appreciation to the following political scientists, who gave so generously of their time and expertise through the editions of *The Struggle for Democracy* and its supplements:

Gordon Alexandre, Glendale Community College

John Ambacher, Framingham State College

Sheldon Appleton, Oakland University

Jeffrey M. Ayres, Lake Superior State University

Ross K. Baker, Rutgers University

Manley Elliott Banks II, Virginia Commonwealth University

Ryan Barrilleaux, University of Miami

Stephen Bennett, University of Cincinnati

Bill Bianco, Duke University

Melanie J. Blumberg, University of Akron

Joseph P. Boyle, Cypress College

Evelyn Brodkin, University of Chicago

James Bromeland, Winona State University

Barbara Brown, Southern Illinois University–Carbondale

Charles R. Brown, Jr., Central Washington University

Joseph S. Brown, Baylor University

David E. Camacho, Northern Arizona University

Mary Carns, Stephen F. Austin University

Jim Carter, Sam Houston State University

Gregory Casey, University of Missouri

Carl D. Cavalli, North Georgia College and State University

James Chalmers, Wayne State University

Paul Chardoul, Grand Rapids Community College

Alan J. Cigler, University of Kansas

David Cingranelli, State University of New York at Binghamton

Natale H. Cipollina, CUNY Baruch College

Dewey M. Clayton, University of Louisville

John Coleman, University of Wisconsin

Ken Collier, University of Kansas

Lee Collins, Monmouth College

Edward Collins Jr., University of Maine

Richard W. Crockett, Western Illinois University

Lane Crothers, Illinois State University

Landon Curry, University of Texas

Paul B. Davis, Truckee Meadows Community College

Christine Day, University of New Orleans

Alan Draper, St. Lawrence University

Euel Elliott, University of Texas

Bob England, Oklahoma State University

Robert S. Erikson, University of Houston

Thomas Ferguson, University of Massachusetts, Boston

M. Lauren Ficaro, Chapman University

John Geer, Arizona State University

Scott D. Gerber, College of William and Mary

Thomas Gillespie, Seton Hall University

Gregory Goldey, Morehead State University

Doris A. Graber, University of Illinois

John Green, University of Akron

Daniel P. Gregory, El Camino Community College

Eric E. Grier, Georgia State University

Mark F. Griffith, The University of West Alabama

Bruce E. Gronbeck, University of Iowa

Maria Guido, Bentley College

Russell L. Hanson, Indiana University

Valerie Heitshusen, University of Missouri

Richard Herrara, Arizona State University

Roberta Herzberg, Indiana University

Seth Hirshorn, University of Michigan

Eugene Hogan, Western Washington University

John W. Homan, Boise State University

Marilyn Howard, Cols State Community College

Ronald J. Hrebnar, University of Utah

David Hunt, Triton College

Jon Hurwitz, University of Pittsburgh

James Hutter, Iowa State University

Gary C. Jacobson, University of California at San Diego

William Jacoby, University of South Carolina

Willoughby Jarrell, Kennesaw State College

Jodi Jenkin, Fullerton College

Christopher B. Jones, Eastern Oregon State University

Mark R. Joslyn, University of Kansas

William Kelly, Auburn University

Fred Kramer, University of Massachusetts

Richard Lehne, Rutgers University

Jan E. Leighley, Texas A&M University

Joel Lieske, Cleveland State University

R. Philip Loy, Taylor University

Stan Luger, University of Northern Colorado

Dean E. Mann, University of California

Joseph R. Marbach, Seton Hall University

Michael D. Martinez, University of Florida

Peter Mathews, Cypress College

Louise Mayo, County College of Morris

Steve Mazurana, University of Northern Colorado

Michael W. McCann, University of Washington

Carroll R. McKibbin, California Polytechnic State University

William P. McLauchlan, Purdue University

Michael E. Meagher, University of Missouri

Charles K. Menifield, Murray State University

Norma H. E. Miller, South Carolina State University

Neil Milner, University of Hawaii

Kristen R. Monroe, Princeton University

Mike Munger, University of Texas

Laurel A. Myer, Sinclair Community College

Albert Nelson, University of Wisconsin, La Crosse

David Nice, Washington State University

Charles Noble, California State University at Long Beach

Maureen Rand Oakley, Mount St. Mary's College

Colleen M. O'Connor, San Diego Mesa College

Daniel J. O'Connor, California State University at Long Beach

David J. Olson, University of Washington

Laura Katz Olson, Lehigh University

John Orman, Fairfield University

Marvin Overby, University of Mississippi

Elizabeth M. H. Paddock, Drury College

Kenneth T. Palmer, University of Maine

Toby Paone, St. Charles Community College

Arthur Paulson, Southern Connecticut State University

Joseph Peschek, Hamline University

Mark P. Petracca, University of California

Larry Pool, Mountain View College

Amy Pritchett, Cypress College

John D. Redifer, Mesa State College

Richard Reitano, Dutchess Community College

Curtis G. Reithel, University of Wisconsin, La Crosse

Russell D. Renka, Southeast Missouri State University

Richard C. Rich, Virginia Polytechnic Institute and State University

Leroy N. Rieselbach, Indiana University

Sue Tolleson Rinehart, Texas Tech University

Phyllis F. Rippey, Western Illinois University

David Robinson, University of Houston–Downtown

David W. Romero, University of California

Francis E. Rourke, Johns Hopkins University

David C. Saffell, Ohio Northern University

Donald L. Scruggs, Stephens College

Jim Seroka, University of North Florida

L. Earl Shaw, Northern Arizona University

John M. Shebb, University of Tennessee

Mark Silverstein, Boston University

Morton Sipress, University of Wisconsin, Eau Claire

Henry B. Sirgo, McNeese State University

David A. Smeltzer, Portland State University

Neil Snortland, University of Arkansas, Little Rock

C. Neal Tate, University of North Texas

James Lance Taylor, University of San Francisco

Robert Thomas, University of Houston

Richard J. Timpone, State University of New York at Stony Brook

Eric Ulsaner, University of Maryland

José M. Vadi, California State Polytechnic University, Pomona

Elliot Vittes, University of Central Florida

Charles Walcott, University of Minnesota

Benjamin Walter, Vanderbilt University

Susan Weissman, St. Mary's College of California

Nelson Wikstrom, Virginia Commonwealth University

Daniel Wirls, Merrill College

Eugene R. Wittkopf, Louisiana State University

James Woods, University of Toledo

Teresa Wright, California State University–Long Beach

Jay Zarowitz, Muskegon Community College

Michele Zebich-Knos, Kennesaw State University

Finally, we thank you, the instructors and students who use this book. May it bring you success.

Edward S. Greenberg
Benjamin I. Page

Part One

Introduction: Main Themes

In Part One, we explain the overall plan of the book, describe the main themes that you will see in each chapter, and suggest why these topics are important for the study of American government and politics. We introduce the central dramatic thread that ties the book together: the struggle for democracy. We make the point that American political life has always involved a struggle among individuals, groups, classes, and institutions over the meaning, extent, and practice of democracy. Finally, in this part, we suggest that although democracy has made great progress over the course of United States history, it remains only imperfectly realized and is threatened by new problems that only vigilant and active citizens can solve.

Chapter 1
Democracy and American Politics

In This Chapter

- An introduction to how government and politics work

- What democracy means, and how it can be used as a standard to evaluate American government and politics

Robert Moses and the Struggle for African-American Voting Rights

The right to vote in elections is fundamental to democracy. But many Americans have won the right to vote only after long struggles. It took more than 30 years from the adoption of the Constitution, for instance, for most states to allow people without property to vote. Women gained the right to vote in all U.S. elections only in 1920, and young people ages 18 to 20 did so only beginning in 1971. As the following story indicates, African-Americans in the South were not able to vote in any numbers until after 1965 despite the existence of the Fifteenth Amendment—which says that the vote cannot be denied to American citizens on the basis of race, color, or previous condition of servitude—adopted in 1870.

In Mississippi in the early 1960s, only 5 percent of African-Americans were registered to vote, and none held elective office, although they accounted for 43 percent of the population. In Amite County, Mississippi, only one African-American was registered to vote out of approximately 5,000 eligible voters; in Walthall County, not a single black was registered, although roughly 3,000 were eligible to vote.[1] What kept them away from the polls was a combination of biased voting registration rules, economic pressures, and physical intimidation and violence directed against those brave enough to defy the prevailing political and social order. In Ruleville, Mississippi, Mrs. Fannie Lou Hamer was forced out of the house she was renting on a large plantation, fired from her job, and arrested, jailed, and beaten by police after she tried to register to vote. In Mileston, after an unsuccessful attempt to register, Hartman Turnbow lost his house to a Molotov cocktail. He was later arrested for arson.[2]

The Student Non-Violent Coordinating Committee (widely known by its initials, SNCC) launched its Voter Education Project in 1961 with the aim of ending black political isolation and powerlessness in the Deep South. Composed primarily of African-American college students from both the North and the South, SNCC aimed to increase black voter registration and to challenge exclusionary rules like the poll tax and the literacy test. SNCC also wanted to enter African-American candidates in local elections. Its first step was to create "freedom schools" in some of the most segregated counties in Mississippi, Alabama, and Georgia to teach black citizens about their rights under the law and to encourage them to register to vote. Needless to say, SNCC volunteers tended to attract the malevolent attentions of police, local officials, and vigilantes.

The first of the freedom schools was founded in McComb, Mississippi, by a remarkable young man named Robert Parris Moses who quit his job as a teacher in order to work with other young people in SNCC. Despite repeated threats to his life and more than a few physical attacks, Moses traveled the back roads of Amite and Walthall coun-

ties, meeting with small groups of black farmers and encouraging them to attend the SNCC freedom school. At the school, he showed them not only how to fill out the registration forms but also how to read and interpret the constitution of Mississippi for the "literacy test" required to register to vote. Once people in the school gathered the courage to journey to the county seat to try to register, Moses went along with them to lend support and encouragement.

Moses suffered for these activities. Over a period of a few months, he was arrested several times for purported traffic violations; attacked on the main street of Liberty, Mississippi, by the county sheriff's cousin and beaten with the butt end of a knife; assaulted by a mob behind the McComb County courthouse; hit by police and dragged into the station house while standing in line at the voting registrar's office with one of his students; and jailed for not paying fines connected with his participation in civil rights demonstrations.

Despite the efforts of Bob Moses and other SNCC volunteers and the bravery of African-Americans who dared to defy the rules of black political exclusion in Mississippi, African-American voting registration barely increased in that

Discriminatory registration restrictions and intimidation heavily curbed African-American voting in the Deep South for almost a century after the end of slavery. It was not until the passage of the 1965 Voting Rights Act that literacy tests, poll taxes, and other devices designed to keep blacks away from the polls were outlawed and African-Americans were able to turn out at the polls in record numbers.

civil rights
Guarantees by government of equal citizenship to all social groups.

state in the early 1960s. Black Americans in Mississippi would have to await the passage of the 1965 Voting Rights Act, which provided powerful federal government protections for all American citizens wishing to exercise their right to vote. The Voter Education Project, however, was one of the key building blocks of a powerful civil rights movement (see Chapter 8) that would eventually force federal action in the 1960s to support the citizenship rights (or **civil rights**) of African-Americans in the South.

Robert Moses and many other African-Americans in Mississippi were willing to risk all they had, even their lives, to gain full and equal citizenship in the United States. Likewise, throughout our history, Americans from all walks of life have joined the struggle to make the United States a more democratic country. The same thing is happening in many parts of the world today. We live in an age of democratic aspiration and upsurge; people the world over are demanding the right to govern themselves and control their own destinies. Americans are participants in this drama, not only because American political ideas and institutions have often provided inspiration for democratic movements in other countries but also because the struggle for democracy continues in our own society. Although honored and celebrated, democracy remains an unfinished project in the United States. The continuing struggle to expand and perfect democracy is a major feature of American history and a defining characteristic of our politics today. It is a central theme of this book. ■

Democracy

Why should there not be a patient confidence in the ultimate justice of the people? Is there any better, or equal, hope in the world?

—ABRAHAM LINCOLN, FIRST INAUGURAL ADDRESS

When people live together in groups and communities, it is generally understood that a governmental entity of some sort is needed to provide law and order, to protect against external aggressors, and to provide essential public goods such as roads, waste disposal, and clean water. If government is both necessary and inevitable, certain questions become unavoidable: Who is to govern? How are those who govern to be encouraged to serve the best interests of society? How can governments be induced to make policies and laws that citizens consider legitimate and worth obeying? In short, what is the best form of government? For most Americans—and for increasing numbers of people in other places—the answer is clear: democracy.

The intrinsic attractiveness of democracy's central ideas—that ordinary people want to rule themselves and are capable of doing so—is only one reason democracy is so popular. For many political thinkers, democracy is simply superior to every other form of political organization. Some have argued, for example, that democracy is the form of government that best protects human rights because it is the only one based on a recognition of the intrinsic worth and equality of human beings. Others believe that democracy is the form of government most likely to reach rational decisions because it can count on the pooled knowledge and expertise of a society's entire population. Other thinkers have claimed that democracies are more stable and long-lasting because their leaders, elected by their citizens, enjoy a strong sense of legitimacy. Still others suggest that democracy is the form of government most conducive to economic growth and material well-being, a claim that is strongly supported by research findings. Others, finally, believe that democracy is the form of government under which human beings, because they are free, are best able to develop their natural capacities and talents.[3] There are many compelling reasons, then, why democracy has been preferred by so many people.

Americans prefer democracy to other forms of government, and they have helped make the nation more democratic over the course of our history. Nevertheless, democracy remains a work in progress in the United States, an evolving aspiration rather than a finished product. Our goal in this book is to help you think carefully about the quality and progress of democracy in the United States. We want to help you reach your own independent judgments about the degree to which politics and government in the United States make our country more or less democratic. We want to help you draw your own conclusions about which political practices and institutions in the United States encourage and sustain democracy and which ones discourage and undermine it. To do this, we must be clear about the meaning of democracy.

Longman
Visual Literacy
Understanding
Who We Are

Web Exploration
The Diffusion of Democracy

Issue:　Around the world, over the course of the twentieth century, democracy has both advanced and receded in a series of waves.

Site:　Go to the Historical Atlas of the Twentieth Century on our Website at **www.ablongman.com/greenberg**. In the "Web Explorations" section for Chapter 1, open the "diffusion of democracy" link, then click on "Historical Atlas." Under "General Trends," select Government, then look at each decade of the Twentieth Century.

What You've Learned:　What conclusions can you make about the spread of democracy over the course of the century? When and where were the greatest gains made? What factors do you think explain the patterns you have discovered?

HINT: World wars, the rise and fall of fascism and communism, and the spread of mass communications have all played important roles.

The Democratic Idea

democracy

A system of rule by the people, defined by the existence of popular sovereignty, political equality, and political liberty.

Many of our ideas about democracy originated with the ancient Greeks. The Greek roots of the word *democracy* are *demos,* meaning "the people," and *kratein,* meaning "to rule." **Democracy,** then, is "rule by the people" or, to put it another way, self-government by the *many,* as opposed to the *few* or the *one.*

Most Western philosophers and rulers before the eighteenth century were not friendly to the idea of rule by the *many.* Most believed that governing was a difficult art, requiring the greatest sophistication, intelligence, character, and training—certainly not the province of ordinary people. Most preferred rule by a select *few* (such as an aristocracy, in which a hereditary nobility rules) or by an enlightened *one* (such as a king or a military chieftain). In practice, most governments were quite undemocratic. The idea that ordinary people might rule themselves represents an important departure from such beliefs.[4]

Also crucial to the concept of democracy is the idea that it is the purpose of a government to serve *all* of its people and that ultimately none but the people themselves can be relied on to know and hence to act in accordance with their own values and interests. Power in any other hands will eventually lead to **tyranny,** a society where leaders abuse their power.

tyranny

The abuse of power by a ruler or a government.

Direct Versus Representative Democracy

direct democracy

A form of political decision making in which the public business is decided by all citizens meeting in small assemblies.

To the ancient Greeks, democracy meant rule by the common people exercised *directly* in open assemblies. They believed that democracy implied face-to-face deliberation and decision making about the public business. **Direct democracy** requires, however, that all citizens be able to meet together regularly to debate and decide the issues of the day. Such a thing was possible in fifth century B.C. Athens, which was small enough to allow all male citizens to gather in one place. In Athens, moreover, male citizens had time to meet and to deliberate because women provided household labor and slaves accounted for most production.

Because direct, participatory democracy is possible only in small communities where citizens with abundant leisure time can meet often on a face-to-face basis, it is an unworkable arrangement for a large and widely dispersed society such as the United States.[5] Democracy in large societies must take the representative form, since millions of citizens cannot meet in open assembly. By **representative democracy** we mean a system in which the people select others, called *representatives,* to act in their place.

representative democracy

Indirect democracy, in which the people rule through elected representatives.

Longman
Participate.com 2.0
Timeline
Major Technological Innovations that Have Changed the Political Landscape

Although representative (or indirect) democracy seems to be the only form of democracy possible in large-scale societies, some political commentators argue that the participatory aspects of direct democracy are worth preserving as an ideal and that certain domains of everyday life—workplaces and schools, for instance—could be enriched by more direct democratic practices.[6] It is worth pointing out, moreover, that direct democracy can and does flourish in some local communities today. In many New England towns, for example, citizens make decisions directly at town meetings. Some observers believe that the Internet will enable more people to become directly involved in political deliberations and decision making in the future.[7]

Fundamental Principles of Representative Democracy

In large societies such as our own, then, democracy means rule by the people, exercised indirectly through representatives elected by the people. Still, this definition is not sufficiently precise to use as a standard by which to evaluate the American political system. To help further clarify the definition of democracy, we add three additional benchmarks drawn from both the scholarly literature and popular understandings about democracy. These benchmarks are *popular sovereignty, political equality,* and *political liberty.* A society in which all three flourish, we argue, is a healthy representative democracy. A society in which any of the three is absent or impaired falls short of the representative democratic ideal. Let us see what each of them means.

Popular Sovereignty

Popular sovereignty means that the ultimate source of all public authority is the people and that government does the people's bidding. If ultimate authority resides not in the hands of the *many* but in the hands of the *few* (as in an aristocratic order), or of the *one* (whether a benevolent sovereign or a ruthless dictator), democracy does not exist.

popular sovereignty
The basic principle of democracy that the people ultimately rule.

How can we recognize popular sovereignty when we see it? The following six conditions are especially important:

Government Policies Reflect the Wishes of the People

The most obvious sign of popular sovereignty is the existence of a close correspondence between what government does and what the people want it to do. It is hard to imagine a situation in which the people rule but government officials make policies contrary to the people's wishes.

This much seems obvious. However, does the democratic ideal require that government officials always do exactly what the people want, right away, responding to every whim and passing fancy of the public? This question has troubled many democratic theorists, and most have answered that democracy is best served when representatives and other public officials respond to what might be called the "deliberative will" of the people: what the people want after they have deliberated about an issue with others.[8] We might, then, want to speak of democracy as a system in which government policies conform to what the people want over some period of time.

The essence of the classical Greek idea of democracy was face-to-face deliberations among citizens in open assemblies. This is difficult to achieve in societies with large populations where democracy depends instead on the election of representatives.

By the Numbers

Is voting turnout declining in the United States?

Commentators have been decrying the declining rate of voting in the United States for many years now. All sorts of explanations have been advanced to explain the decline; all sorts of remedies for the problem have been proposed. But what if there really hasn't been a decline in voting at all?

Why It Matters: We have argued in this chapter that widespread participation in voting and other civic activities is one measure of the health of democracy in any society. If the way we measure participation is inaccurate, we cannot do a good job of assessing the quality of democracy in the United States, or identify what problems and shortcomings in our political system need to be addressed to make it more democratic.

Behind the Traditional Voting Turnout Measure: Voter turnout in American elections is determined by a very simple calculation: the number of people who vote in a national election divided by the number of people in the United States who are of voting age,

that is, 18 years of age and older. The denominator for this equation—voting age population, or VAP—is provided by the Census Bureau. But there is a problem: The denominator may be misleading. The Census Bureau includes in its VAP numbers millions of people who are not eligible to vote at all: non-citizens, felons (some states), people with past felonies (some states), and the mentally incompetent. If we calculated voting turnout as the number of voters divided by the number of people in the United States who are eligible to vote—the voting eligible population, or VEP—turnout would always be higher than is now reported because the denominator would be smaller.

Calculating a VEP-based Measure of Turnout: Two political scientists, Michael McDonald and Samuel Popkin, have done us the great service of transforming the Census Bureau's VAP (voting age population) number to a VEP (voting eligible population) number for every national election since 1948, pulling out non-citizens, ineligible felons, and former felons. Using the voting eligible population rather than the resident population over the age of 18 as the denominator in the voting turnout equation, McDonald and Popkin found the following:

- Voting turnout is actually 4 or 5 percentage points higher in recent elections than usually reported.

Government Leaders Are Elected The existence of a close match between what the people want and what government does, however, does not necessarily prove that the people are sovereign. In a dictatorship, for example, the will of the people can be consciously shaped to correspond to the wishes of the leadership. For the direction of influence to flow from the people to the leadership, some mechanism must exist for forcing leaders to be responsive to the people's wishes and to be responsible to them for their actions. The best mechanism ever invented to achieve these goals is the election in which both existing and aspiring government leaders must periodically face the people for judgment.

Elections Are Free and Fair If elections are to be useful as a way to keep government leaders responsive and responsible, they must be conducted in a fashion that is free and fair. By free, we mean that there is no coercion of voters or election officials and that virtually all citizens are able to run for office and vote in elections. By fair, we mean, among other things, that election rules do not favor some over others, and that ballots are accurately counted.

- Voting turnout declined between 1960 and 1972 regardless of which method was used. However, voting turnout appears to decline further after 1972 only when using the traditional VAP method; the VEP method shows no decline in voting turnout over the past 30 years.

The main reason that voting turnout has declined in recent elections using the traditional VAP method is that the number of people who are residents of the United States but who are not eligible to vote in American elections has increased at every election, mostly due to the number of non-citizens living here.

Criticism of the VEP-based Measure of Turnout: Some critics suggest that the old way of calculating voting turnout has useful purposes. The Constitution does not exclude non-citizens from voting, for example; nor does it exclude felons or former felons, so a measure that includes these people as part of the voting population might tell us more about how far we have come as a democracy.

What to Watch For: When you come across voter turnout numbers, pay attention to whether the figure has been calculated based on the voting age population or on the voting eligible population. The latter will always be higher than the former. It is important to be aware that both methods of calculating turnout make sense in their own way; each has a slightly different story to tell.

What Do You Think? Do you think we can and should try to increase the rate of voting turnout in

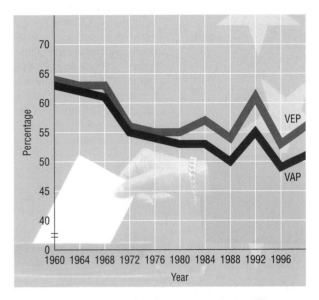

Voting Turnout in Presidential Elections, by Year

the United States, which is low in comparison to other democratic countries, regardless of which method of calculation we use? What do you think about making non-citizens—who pay taxes and are subject to U.S. laws—eligible to vote? How about former felons who have paid their debt to society?

Source: Michael P. McDonald and Samuel L. Popkin, "The Myth of the Vanishing Voter," *The American Political Science Review* (December 2001), Vol. 95, no. 4, pp. 963–974.

People Participate in the Political Process Though government leaders may be elected in a balloting process that is free and fair, such a process is useful in conveying the will of the people and keeping leaders responsive and responsible only if the people participate. If elections and other forms of political participation only attract a minority of the eligible population, they cannot serve as a way to understand what the broad public wants or as an instrument forcing leaders to pay attention to it. Widespread participation in politics—including voting in elections, contacting public officials, working with others to bring matters to public attention, joining associations that work to shape government actions, and more—is necessary to ensure not only that responsive representatives will be chosen, but that they will have continuous incentives to pay attention to the people. Because widespread participation is so central to popular sovereignty, we can say that the less political participation there is in a society, the weaker the democracy. (See "By the Numbers: Is voting turnout declining in the United States?" to get a sense of how much Americans participate.)

Most Americans believe that all ballots are counted, when, in fact, many go uncounted because of intentional or accidental mistakes by the voter or voting machine errors. Here an election official examines a ballot for "hanging chads" and "dimples" to try to determine voter intentions during the vote recount in Broward County, Florida. The recount was eventually stopped by the U.S. Supreme Court, leaving George H. W. Bush the winner of Florida's electoral college votes and the presidency.

High-Quality Information Is Available   If people are to form authentic and rational attitudes about public policies and political leaders, they must have access to accurate political information, insightful interpretations, and vigorous debate. These are the responsibility of government officials, opposition parties, opinion leaders, and the mass media. If false or biased information is provided, if policies are not challenged and debated, or if misleading interpretations of the political world (or none at all) are offered, the people cannot form opinions in accordance with their values and interests, and popular sovereignty cannot be said to exist.

The Majority Rules   How can the opinions and preferences of many individual citizens be combined into a single binding decision? Since unanimity is unlikely—so the insistence that new policies should require unanimous agreement for them to be adopted would simply enshrine the status quo—reaching a decision requires a decision rule. If the actions of government are to respond to all citizens, each citizen being counted equally, the only decision rule that makes sense is **majority rule,**[9] which means that the government adopts the policy that the *most* people want. In practical terms, what this means is that the popular will, formed in the best circumstances after careful deliberation, is discovered by ascertaining the positions on public issues of the majority of citizens. The only alternative to majority rule is minority rule, which would unacceptably elevate the *few* over the *many*.

Political Equality   The second fundamental principle of democracy is **political equality,** the idea that each person carries the same weight in voting and other political decision making. Imagine, if you will, a society in which one person could cast 100 votes in an election, another person 50 votes, and still an-

majority rule

The form of political decision making in which policies are decided on the basis of what a majority of the people want.

political equality

The principle that says that each person carries equal weight in the conduct of the public business.

Democracy requires broad citizen participation in public affairs. Special efforts have been made in recent years—much like these at the University of Texas at Austin—to increase voting registration and turnout among young people, a group with especially low participation rates in American elections.

other 25 votes, while many unlucky folks had only 1 vote each—or none at all. We would surely find such an arrangement a curious one, especially if that society described itself as democratic. We would react in this way because equality of citizenship has always been central to the democratic ideal. Democracy is a way of making decisions in which each person has one, and only one, voice.

Most people know this intuitively. Our sense of what is proper is offended, for instance, when some class of people is denied the right to vote in a society that boasts the outer trappings of democracy. The denial of citizenship rights to African-Americans in the South before the passage of the 1965 Voting Rights Act is such an example. We count it as a victory for democracy when previously excluded groups win the right to vote.

Political equality also involves what the Fourteenth Amendment to the Constitution calls "equal protection," meaning that everyone in a democracy is treated the same by government. Government programs, for example, should not favor one group over another or deny benefits or protections to identifiable groups in the population, such as racial and religious minorities. Nor should people be treated better or worse than others by law enforcement agencies and the courts.

Does democracy require substantial equality in the distribution of income and wealth? While many do not think this to be the case, thinkers as diverse as Aristotle, Rousseau, and Jefferson thought so, believing that great inequalities in economic circumstances are almost always translated into political inequality. Political scientist Robert Dahl describes the problem in the following way:

> *If citizens are unequal in economic resources, so are they likely to be unequal in political resources; and political equality will be impossible to achieve. In the extreme case, a minority of rich will possess so much greater political resources than other citizens that they will control the state, dominate the majority of citizens, and empty the democratic process of all content.*[10]

Although political equality is a cornerstone of American democracy, the nation's understanding of who is entitled to equal status has changed over the years. The right to vote was granted to all men regardless of race in 1870, although stringent registration rules made it very difficult for nonwhites to exercise that right. It wasn't until 1920 that the Nineteenth Amendment extended the right to vote to women; in 1971, a constitutional amendment lowered the voting age from 21 to 18.

In later chapters, we will see that income and wealth are distributed in a highly unequal way in the United States and that this inequality is sometimes translated into great inequalities among people and groups in the political arena. In such circumstances, the norm of political equality is violated.

political liberty

The principle that citizens in a democracy are protected from government interference in the exercise of a range of basic freedoms, such as the freedoms of speech, association, and conscience.

Political Liberty The third element of democracy is **political liberty.** Political liberty refers to basic freedoms essential to the formation and expression of the popular will and its translation into policy. These essential liberties include the freedoms of speech, of conscience and religion, of the press, and of assembly and association, embodied in the First Amendment to the U.S. Constitution.

Without these liberties (and a few more, including freedom from arbitrary arrest and imprisonment), the other fundamental principles of democracy could not exist. Popular sovereignty cannot be guaranteed if people are prevented from participating in politics or if opposition to the government is crushed by the authorities. Popular sovereignty cannot prevail if the voice of the people is silenced and if citizens are not free to argue and debate, based on their own ideas, values, and personal beliefs, and form and express their political opinions.[11] Political equality is violated if some people can speak out but others cannot.

For most people today, democracy and liberty are inseparable. The concept of *self-government* implies not only the right to vote and to run for public office but also the right to speak one's mind, to petition the government, and to join with others in political parties, interest groups, or social movements.

Over the years, a number of political philosophers and practitioners have viewed liberty as *threatened* by democracy rather than as essential to it. We will have more to say about this subject later as we consider several possible objections to democracy. But it is our position that self-government and political liberty are inseparable, in the sense that the former is impossible without the latter.[12] It follows that a majority cannot deprive an individual or a minority group of its political liberty without violating democracy itself.

Objections to Majoritarian Representative Democracy

Not everyone is convinced that majoritarian, representative democracy is the best form of government. Here are the main criticisms that have been leveled against democracy as we have defined it.

Longman
Participate.com 2.0
Simulation
How to Satisfy Aunt Martha

"Majority Tyranny" Threatens Liberty   James Madison and the other Founders of the American republic feared that majority rule was bound to undermine freedom and threaten the rights of the individual. They created a constitutional system (as you will see in Chapter 2) that was in fact designed to protect certain liberties against the unwelcome intrusions of the majority. The fears of the Founders were not without basis. What they called the "popular passions" have sometimes stifled the freedoms of groups and individuals who have dared to be different. Until quite recently, for instance, a majority of Americans were unwilling to allow atheists or communists the same rights of free speech that they allowed others, and conscientious objectors were treated harshly during both world wars. In the 1950s, many people in the movie industry, publishing, and education lost their jobs because of the anti-left hysteria whipped up by Senator Joseph McCarthy and others.[13]

Although there have been instances during our history of **majority tyranny,** in which the majority violated the citizenship rights of a minority— the chapter opening vignette is a good example—there is no evidence that the *many* consistently threaten liberty more than the *few* or the *one*. To put it

majority tyranny

Suppression of the rights and liberties of a minority by the majority.

Political hysteria has periodically blemished the record of American democracy. Fear of domestic communism, captured in this editorial cartoon, was particularly potent in the twentieth century and led to the suppression of political groups deemed threatening by the authorities.

another way, the majority does not seem to be a special or unique threat to liberty. Violations of freedom seem as likely to come from powerful individuals and groups or from government officials as from the majority.

Liberty is essential to self-government, and threats to liberty, whatever their origin, must be guarded against by all who value democracy. But we must firmly reject the view that majority rule inevitably or uniquely threatens liberty. Majority rule is unthinkable, in fact, without the existence of basic political liberties.

The People Are Irrational and Incompetent

Political scientists have spent decades studying the attitudes and behaviors of citizens in the United States, and some of the findings are not encouraging. For the most part, the evidence shows that individual Americans do not care a great deal about politics and are rather poorly informed, unstable in their views, and not much interested in participating in the political process.[14] These findings have led some observers to assert that citizens are ill-equipped for the responsibility of self-governance and that public opinion (the will of the majority) should not be the ultimate determinant of what government does.

We will see in Chapter 5, however, that this evidence about individuals has often been misinterpreted and that the American public taken collectively is more informed, sophisticated, and stable in its views than it is generally given credit for.

Majoritarian Democracy Threatens Minorities

We have suggested that when rendering a decision in a democracy, the majority must prevail. In most cases, the minority on the losing side of an issue need not worry unduly about its well-being because many of its members are likely to be on the winning side in future decisions about other matters. Thus, people on the minority and losing side of an issue such as welfare reform may be part of the majority and winning side on an issue such as educational spending. What prevents majority tyranny over a minority in most policy decisions in a democracy is that the composition of the majority and the minority is always shifting depending on the issue.

However, what happens in cases that involve race, ethnicity, religion, or sexual orientation, for example, where minority status is fixed? Does the majority pose a threat to such minorities? Many people worry about that possibility. The worry is that unbridled majority rule leaves no room for the claims of minorities. This worry has some historical foundations, for majorities have trampled on minority rights with alarming frequency. Majorities long held, for instance, that Native Americans and African-Americans were inferior to whites and undeserving of full citizenship. Irish, Eastern European, Asian, and Latin American immigrants to our shores, among others, have all been subjected to periods of intolerance on the part of the majority, as have Catholics and Jews. Gays and lesbians have been discriminated against in housing and jobs and have sometimes been violently victimized.

As Robert Dahl points out, however, there is no evidence to support the belief that the rights of minorities are better protected under alternative forms of political government, whether rule by the *few* or by the *one* (fascism, communism, authoritarian dictatorship, theocracy, and the like),[15] and that given the other benefits of majority rule democracy, it is to be preferred.

In any case, democracy, as we have defined it, requires the protection of crucial minority rights. Recall that majority rule is only one of the defining conditions of popular sovereignty and that popular sovereignty is only one of the

Longman
Participate.com
2.0
Participation
**The Debate
Over
Immigration**

three basic attributes of democracy, the others being political equality and political liberty. The position of minorities is protected in a fully developed democracy, in our view, by the requirements of equal citizenship (the right to vote, to hold public office, to be protected against violence, and to enjoy the equal protection of the law) and access to the full range of civil liberties (speech, press, conscience, and association). To the extent that a majority violates the citizenship rights and liberties of minorities, society falls short of the democratic ideal.

Democracy as an Evaluative Standard: How Democratic Are We?

After this discussion, it should be easy to see how and why the democratic ideal can be used as a measuring rod with which to evaluate American politics. We have learned that the fundamental attributes of democracy are popular sovereignty, political equality, and political liberty. Each suggests a set of questions that will be raised throughout this book to encourage critical thinking about American political life.

- *Questions about popular sovereignty.* Does government do what citizens want it to do? Do citizens participate in politics? Can citizens be involved when they choose to be, and are political leaders responsive? Do political linkage institutions, such as political parties, elections, interest groups, and social movements, effectively transmit what citizens want to political leaders? What is the quality of the public deliberation on the major public policy issues of the day? Do the media and political leaders provide accurate and complete information?

- *Questions about political equality.* Do some individuals and groups have persistent and substantial advantages over other individuals and groups in the political process? Or is the political game open to all equally? Do government decisions and policies benefit some individuals and groups more than others?

- *Questions about political liberty.* Are citizens' rights and liberties universally available, protected, and used? Are people free to vote? Can they speak openly and form groups freely to petition their government? Do public authorities, private groups, or the majority threaten liberty or the rights of minorities?

These questions will help us assess where we are and where we are going as a democracy. We do not believe that popular sovereignty, political equality, and political liberty are attainable in perfect form. They are, rather, ideals to which our nation can aspire and standards against which we can measure everyday reality.

A Framework for Understanding How American Politics Works

In addition to helping you answer questions about the quality of democracy in the United States, our goal in this textbook is to help you understand how American government and politics work. To help you do so, we describe in this section a simple way to organize information and to think about how our political system works.

Organizing the Main Factors of Political Life

If we are to understand why things happen in government and politics—for example, the passage of the 1965 Voting Rights Act that Robert Moses and his SNCC colleagues did so much to bring about—we must begin with what biologists call *taxonomy:* placing things in their proper categories. We believe that each and every actor, institution, and process that influences what our politics are like and what our national government does can be placed into four main categories: structure, political linkage, government, and government action.

- *Structure.* This category includes the economy and society, the constitutional rules, the political culture, and the international system: the most fundamental and enduring factors that influence government and politics. They form the foundation upon which all else is built. They determine, to a very large extent, what issues become a part of the political agenda, how political power is distributed among the population, what rules structure how government works, and what values Americans bring to their political deliberations.

- *Political linkage.* This category includes all of the political actors, institutions, and processes that transmit the wants and demands of people and groups in our society to government officials and that together help shape what government officials do and what policies they adopt. These include public opinion, political parties, interest groups, the mass media, and elections.

- *Government.* This category includes all public officials and institutions (Congress, the president, the federal bureaucracy, and the Supreme Court) that have formal, legal responsibilities for making public policy.

- *Government action.* This category includes the wide range of actions carried out by government: making laws, issuing rules and regulations, waging war and providing national defense, settling civil disputes, providing order, and more.

Web Exploration
Understanding What Government Does

Issue: What government does can only be understood by taking into account how government, political linkage, and structural factors interact with one another.

Site: On our Website at **www.ablongman.com/greenberg** go to the "Web Explorations" section for Chapter 1. Open the "understanding what government does" link, and look at two of the nation's leading newspapers. Select a story about some domestic federal government action (e.g., a new law, a Supreme Court decision, an action by a bureaucratic agency, an executive order, and so on) for each newspaper.

What You've Learned: See if you can organize the story of the government action you have selected according to the categories of the analytical framework explained in this section and shown in Figure 1.1. Does this help you better understand why the government action happened?

HINT: Be sure you have information for each of the categories in the framework.

This textbook is organized around these four categories. The chapters in Part Two focus on structural level factors. The chapters in Part Three are about political linkage processes and institutions. The chapters in Part Four attend to government institutions and leaders. Finally, the chapters in Part Five examine what government does.

Connecting the Main Factors of Political Life

To understand how government and politics work in the United States, we must appreciate the fact that the structural, political linkage, and governmental categories interact with one another in a particular kind of way to determine what actions government takes (see Figure 1.1). The best way to see this is to look at these categories in action, using the passage of the 1965 Voting Rights Act as an example. The main point of the exercise is to show how connecting and considering together the main factors of political life— structure, political linkage, and government—can help explain why government takes certain actions.

To understand passage of the landmark legislation, we might begin with *government,* focusing our attention on Congress and its members, President Lyndon Johnson (who was the most vigorous proponent of the voting rights legislation) and his advisers, and the Supreme Court, which was becoming increasingly supportive of civil rights claims in the mid-1960s.

Knowing these things, however, would not tell us all that we needed to know. To understand why Congress, the president, and the Court behaved as they did in 1965, we would want to pay attention to the pressures brought to bear on them by *political linkage* actors and institutions: public opinion (increasingly supportive of civil rights), the growing electoral power of African-Americans in the states outside the South, and most important, the moral power of the civil rights movement inspired by people like Robert Moses and Martin Luther King.

African-American combat service in World War II and in Korea helped transform white attitudes about racial equality in the United States and contributed to the emergence of a supportive environment for the civil rights movement. Shown here are six gunners from the 17th Bomb Wing night interdiction team that saw heavy action in Korea.

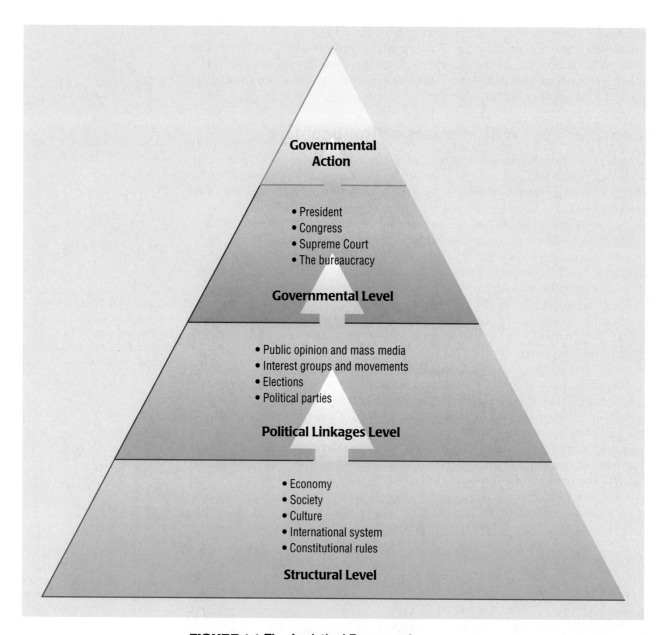

FIGURE 1.1 The Analytical Framework

Various actors, institutions, and processes interact to influence what government does in the United States. Structural factors such as the economy, the culture, the international system, and constitutional rules play a strong role in political events. They may influence the government directly, or, as is more often the case, through political linkages such as elections, parties, and interest groups. In a democratic society, the policies created by the government should reflect these influences.

Even knowing these things, however, would not tell us all that we needed to know about why the 1965 Voting Rights Act happened. Our inquiry would have to go deeper to include *structural* factors: economic, cultural, and social change; constitutional rules; and the international position of the United

States. For example, economic changes in the nation over the course of many decades triggered a "great migration" of African-Americans from the rural South to the urban North. Over the long run, this population shift to states with large blocks of **electoral college** votes, critical to the election of presidents, increased the political power of African-Americans. Cultural change increased the number of Americans bothered by the second-class citizenship of African-Americans, even as combat service in World War II and the Korean War led many black Americans to insist on full citizenship rights. Finally, the **Cold War** struggle of the United States against the Soviet Union played an important role. Many American leaders, recognizing the contradiction between asking for the support of people of color in Third World countries in the struggle against communism while treating African-Americans in the United States as second-class citizens, sought an end to the system of official segregation in the South (known as **Jim Crow**).[16]

We see, then, that a full explanation of why the 1965 Voting Rights Act happened (government action) requires that we take into account how governmental, political linkage, and structural factors interact with one another to bring about significant change in American politics.

Understanding American Politics Holistically

This way of looking at things—that what government does can only be understood by considering structural, political linkage, and governmental factors—will be used throughout this book and will help bring order to the information presented. We will suggest throughout that action by public officials is the product not simply of their personal desires (although these are important) but also of the influences and pressures brought to bear by other governmental institutions and by individuals, groups, and classes at work in the political linkage sphere. Political linkage institutions and processes, in turn, can often be understood only when we see how they are shaped by the larger structural context, including such things as the national and global economies and the political culture. This way of understanding how American government and politics work is illustrated in the "Using the Framework" feature on the next page. This feature appears in each chapter.

You should also keep in mind that, as in all complex systems, feedback also occurs. That is to say, influences sometimes flow in the opposite direction, from government to political linkage actors and institutions to structural factors. For example, federal tax laws influence the distribution of income and wealth in society, government regulations affect the operations of corporations, and decisions by the courts may determine what interest groups and political parties are able to do. We will want to pay attention, then, to these sorts of influences in our effort to understand how the American political system works.

You need not worry about remembering exactly which actors and influences belong to which of the four categories. That will become obvious because the chapters of the book are organized into sections corresponding to them. Nor do you need to worry about exactly how the people and institutions in the different levels interact with one another. This will become clear as materials are presented and learned and as you become more familiar with the American political process.

electoral college

Representatives of the states who formally elect the president; the number of electors in each state is equal to the total number of its senators and congressional representatives.

Cold War

The period of tense relations between the United States and the Soviet Union from the late 1940s to the late 1980s.

Jim Crow

Popular term for the system of legally sanctioned racial segregation that existed in the American South until the middle of the twentieth century.

USING THE FRAMEWORK: The Voting Rights Act

How was it possible to overcome Southern resistance to black political participation?

Background: The Voting Rights Act of 1965 transformed the politics of the American South. Under federal government protection, the Act permitted African-Americans to vote and run for elected office in states where a combination of violence, economic pressure, and state and local government rules made political participation difficult if not impossible prior to 1965. We can understand how such a momentous transformation happened by examining structural, political linkage, and governmental factors.

Governmental Action

The Voting Rights Act of 1965

Governmental Level

- The Supreme Court prepared the ground by steadily expanding the reach of the "equal protection" clause of the Constitution's Fourteenth Amendment. →
- A pro-civil rights majority in Congress was responsive to the voting rights issue. →
- President Lyndon Johnson pushed hard for federal protection of African-American voting rights.

Political Linkages Level

- The votes of African-Americans proved decisive in several large electoral vote states in the 1960 and 1964 presidential elections. →
- Dramatic civil rights demonstrations highlighted the denial of the vote to black Americans in the Deep South. →
- Public opinion and the mass media grew more supportive of demands by African-Americans for full citizenship. →
- Unions and business organizations endorsed voting rights legislation.

Structural Level

- Industrialization and the rise of large manufacturing corporations spurred the "Great Migration." →
- Relocation of African-Americans to large states outside the Deep South improved their political, social, and economic standing. →
- World War II generated pressures to integrate the armed forces. →
- The struggle against the Soviet Union for the "hearts and minds" of Third World peoples made segregation problematic for the United States in world affairs.

Summary

The struggle for democracy has played an important role in American history and remains an important theme in our country today, as well as in many other parts of the world. The struggle has involved the effort to make popular sovereignty, political equality, and political liberty more widely available and practiced. Because democracy holds a very special place in Americans' constellation of values and is particularly relevant to judging political processes, it is the standard used throughout this text to evaluate the quality of our politics and government.

The materials about politics and government are organized in a way that will allow us to make sense of the confusing details of everyday events and see *why* things happen the way they do. The organizing framework presented in this chapter visualizes the world of American politics as a set of interrelated *actors* and *influences*—institutions, groups, and individuals—that operate in three interconnected realms: the *structural, political linkage,* and *governmental* sectors. This way of looking at American political life as an ordered, interconnected whole will be used throughout the remainder of the book.

Longman
Participate.com
2.0
Comparative
**Comparing
Political
Landscapes**

Suggestions for Further Reading

Barber, Benjamin. *Strong Democracy: Participatory Democracy for a New Age.* Berkeley: University of California Press, 1984.
   The case for direct, participatory democracy by a leading contemporary political theorist.

Dahl, Robert A. *Democracy and Its Critics.* New Haven, CT: Yale University Press, 1989.
   A sweeping defense of democracy against its critics by one of the most brilliant political theorists of our time.

Dahl, Robert A. *On Democracy.* New Haven, CT: Yale University Press, 1998.
   A brief yet surprisingly thorough examination of classical and contemporary democracy, real and theoretical.

Guttman, Amy, and Dennis Thompson. *Democracy and Disagreement.* Cambridge, U.K.: Belknap Press, 1996.
   A compelling examination of why deliberation is so important to genuine democracy and how more deliberative processes might be incorporated into contemporary democratic societies.

Held, David. *Models of Democracy.* Stanford, CA: Stanford University Press, 1987.
   A highly accessible review of the many possible meanings of democracy.

Putnam, Robert D. *Making Democracy Work: Civic Traditions in Modern Italy.* Princeton, NJ: Princeton University Press, 1993.
   A brilliant and controversial argument that the success of democratic government depends on the vitality of a participatory and tolerant civic culture.

Internet Sources

A number of sites on the World Wide Web serve as "gateways" to vast collections of material on American government and politics. In subsequent chapters, we will indicate the location of sites on the Web to begin searches on the specific subject matter of the chapters. Here we concentrate on the general gateways, the starting points for wide-ranging journeys through cyberspace, geared to subjects governmental and political.

For most students, connections to the Internet will be through systems already in operation at most colleges and universities. For some students, connections will be through one of the commercial services such as America Online, CompuServe, or the Microsoft Network. As part of its service, each has a browser, a tool used to get around the Internet and find what one wants. University and college systems are likely to have Netscape Navigator or Microsoft Explorer. Whichever browser one uses, simply type in the addresses of the gateways listed here and the browser will do the rest. Once at the gateway, a simple click on highlighted words and phrases (hyperlinks) will take users to a particular body of information.

Here are the gateways:

Internet Public Library   **http://ipl.org/ref/RR/static/gov0000.html**

The Jefferson Project   **http://solstice.stardot.com/jefferson**

New York Times, Political Points
www.nytimes.com/library/politics/polpoints.html

Political Resources on the Web   **www.politicalresources.net**

Weblinks: A Guide to Internet Resources in Political Science
www.abacon.com/internetguides/pol/weblinks.html

Yahoo/Government   **http://www.yahoo.com/Government/**

Notes

1. William H. Chafe, *The Unfinished Journey: America Since World War II* (New York: Oxford University Press, 1986), p. 304; Howard Zinn, *SNCC: The New Abolitionists* (Boston: Beacon Press, 1964), p. 64.

2. Chafe, *Unfinished Journey,* p. 305.

3. For a fuller treatment of these claims, as well as supporting evidence for them, see Robert A. Dahl, *Democracy and Its Critics* (New Haven, CT: Yale University Press, 1989); and Robert A. Dahl, *On Democracy* (New Haven, CT: Yale University Press, 1998). Also see Benjamin Radcliff, "Politics, Markets, and Life Satisfaction: The Political Economy of Human Happiness," *American Political Science Review* (December, 2001), Vol. 95, no. 4, pp. 939–952.

4. John Dewey, *The Public and Its Problems* (New York: Holt, 1927).

5. See Robert A. Dahl, *After the Revolution: Authority in the Good Society* (New Haven, CT: Yale University Press, 1970); Dahl, *Democracy and Its Critics;* Jane Mansbridge, *Beyond Adversary Democracy* (New York: Basic Books, 1980).

6. See Benjamin Barber, *Strong Democracy: Participatory Democracy for a New Age* (Berkeley, CA: University of California Press, 1984); Peter Bachrach, *The Theory of Democratic Elitism* (Boston: Little, Brown, 1967); Robert A. Dahl, *A Preface to Economic Democracy* (Berkeley, CA: University of California Press, 1985); Edward S. Greenberg, *Workplace Democracy: The Political Effects of Participation* (Ithaca, NY: Cornell University Press, 1986); C. B. MacPherson, *Democratic Theory: Essays in Retrieval* (Oxford, U.K.: Clarendon Press, 1973); Carole Pateman, *Participation and Democratic Theory* (London: Cambridge University Press, 1970).

7. Esther Dyson, *Release 2.0* (New York: Broadway Books, 1997); Lawrence K. Grossman, *The Electronic Republic: Reshaping Democracy in the Information Age* (New York: Viking Press, 1995).

8. On deliberation and democracy, see Seyla Benhabib, "Toward a Deliberative Model of Democratic Legitimacy," in Seyla Benhabib (ed.), *Democracy and Difference* (Princeton, NJ: Princeton University Press, 1996); John Dryzek, *Discursive Democracy* (Cambridge: Cambridge University Press, 1990); Nancy Fraser, "Rethinking the public sphere," in Craig Calhoun (ed.), *Habermas and the Public*

Sphere (New Brunswick, NJ: Rutgers University Press, 1992), pp. 109–142; Amy Guttman and Dennis Thompson, *Democracy and Disagreement* (Cambridge, U.K.: Belknap Press, 1996); and Jurgen Habermas, *The Structural Transformation of the Public Sphere* (Cambridge, MA: MIT Press, 1989).

9. Kenneth May, "A Set of Independent, Necessary, and Sufficient Conditions for Simple Majority Decision," *Econometrica,* 20 (1952), pp. 680–684, shows that only majority rule can guarantee popular sovereignty, political equality, and neutrality among policy alternatives. See also Douglas W. Rae, "Decision Rules and Individual Values in Constitutional Choice," *American Political Science Review,* 63 (1969), pp. 40–53; Phillip D. Straffin Jr., "Majority Rule and General Decision Rules," *Theory and Decision,* 8 (1977), pp. 351–360.

10. Dahl, *A Preface to Economic Democracy,* p. 68.

11. Robert A. Dahl, "On Removing Certain Impediments to Democracy in the United States," *Political Science Quarterly,* 92, No. 1 (Spring 1977), p. 14; Elaine Spitz, *Majority Rule* (Chatham, NJ: Chatham House, 1984), p. 83; Dahl, *Democracy and Its Critics,* p. 170.

12. See Marc Plattner, "Liberalism and Democracy," *Foreign Affairs* (March–April, 1998), pp. 171–180.

13. David Caute, *The Great Fear* (New York: Simon & Schuster, 1978); Victor Navasky, *Naming Names* (New York: Viking, 1980); Michael Rogin, *The Intellectuals and McCarthy* (Cambridge, MA: MIT Press, 1967).

14. See Bernard R. Berelson, Paul F. Lazarsfeld, and William N. McPhee, *Voting* (Chicago: University of Chicago Press, 1954); V. O. Key Jr., *Public Opinion and American Democracy* (New York: Knopf, 1961); Herbert McClosky and Alida Brill, *Dimensions of Tolerance* (New York: Russell Sage Foundation, 1983). But see, in rebuttal, James L. Gibson, "Political Intolerance and Political Repression During the McCarthy Red Scare," *American Political Science Review,* 82 (1988), pp. 511–529; Benjamin I. Page and Robert Y. Shapiro, *The Rational Public: Fifty Years of Trends in Americans' Policy Preferences* (Chicago: University of Chicago Press, 1992). See a summary of the debate and the supporting evidence in Carroll J. Glynn, et al., *Public Opinion* (Boulder, CO: Westview Press, 1999).

15. Dahl, *Democracy and Its Critics,* p. 161.

16. Philip A. Klinkner with Rogers M. Smith, *The Unsteady March: The Rise and Decline of Racial Equality in America* (Chicago: The University of Chicago Press, 1999).

Part Two
Structure

The chapters in Part Two focus on structural influences on American government and politics. Structural influences are enduring features of American life that play key roles in determining what issues become important in politics and government, how political power is distributed in the population, and what attitudes and beliefs guide the behavior of citizens and public officials.

The constitutional rules are a particularly important part of the structural context of American political life. These rules are the subject matter of two of this part's chapters. Chapter 2 tells the story of the Constitution: why a constitutional convention was convened in Philadelphia in 1787, what the Founders intended to accomplish at the convention, and how specific provisions of the document have shaped our political life since the nation's founding. Chapter 3 examines federalism, asking what the framers intended the federal system to be and tracing how it has changed over the years.

The basic characteristics of American society also influence the workings of our political and governmental institutions, as well as the attitudes and behaviors of citizens and public officials. Chapter 4 looks in detail at the American economy, society, and political culture, as well as this country's place in the world, showing how these factors structure much of our political life.

Chapter 2
The Constitution

In This Chapter

- The enduring legacies of the American Revolution and the Declaration of Independence
- Our first constitution: The Articles of Confederation
- The Constitutional Convention
- What kind of constitution the framers created
- How the Constitution structures the rules of American politics

Shays's Rebellion

Artemas Ward, commander of American forces at Bunker Hill, a Revolutionary War hero, and a state judge, could not convince the crowd of several hundred armed farmers to allow him to enter the Worcester, Massachusetts, courthouse. For nearly two hours, he pleaded and threatened, but to no avail. Although most admired him for his achievements, they were determined that he not hold court that day in September 1786, when he was to begin legal proceedings to seize farms for nonpayment of taxes. He left Worcester in a fury, unable to convince the local militia to come to his assistance, and carried word of the rebellion to Boston. Other judges trying to hold court in western Massachusetts in the summer and fall of 1786 had no better luck.[1]

The farmers of western Massachusetts were probably not a rebellious lot by nature, but desperate times pushed many of them to desperate actions. All over the new nation, the end of the Revolutionary War in 1783 brought the collapse of prices for agricultural products and widespread economic distress among farmers. Poor farmers sought relief from their troubles from state governments, and for the most part, political leaders responded. Several states lent money (in the form of scrip, or paper money) to farmers to pay their taxes and debts. Other states passed stay laws, which postponed tax and mortgage payments for hard-pressed farmers.

In Massachusetts, however, the state legislature refused to help. Worse yet, the legislature and the governor decided that all state debts were to be paid off in full to establish the creditworthiness of the state. The state's debt, accumulated to pay the state's share of the costs of the Revolutionary War, was owed primarily to a handful of the wealthiest citizens of the state, who had bought up outstanding notes for pennies on the dollar. To make good on this debt, the legislature levied heavy taxes that fell disproportionately on farmers, especially those in the western part of the state. When taxes could not be paid—a distressingly common circumstance—money could be raised by the state only through foreclosure: the public sale of farmers' lands, buildings, and livestock. Tax foreclosures and imprisonment under harsh conditions for those who could not pay their debts became frequent occurrences. Responding to these dire circumstances, many western Massachusetts farmers took up arms to prevent courts from sitting.

By September 1786, Governor James Bowdoin had seen enough. He issued a proclamation against unlawful assembly and called out the militia to enforce it. Six hundred soldiers were sent to Springfield to ensure that the state supreme court could meet and issue the expected indictments against the leaders of the insurrection. The soldiers were met there by 500 or 600 armed farmers led by a for-

mer Revolutionary War officer, Captain Daniel Shays. After a long standoff, the militia withdrew, leaving the rebels in charge and the court unable to meet.

These events only hardened the resolve of the governor to break the rebellion. The armed forces he sent from Boston proved too much for the hastily organized and ill-equipped force under Shays. By the spring of 1787, the Boston militia had defeated the rebels in two pitched battles, one at Springfield and the other at Petersham, and Shays's Rebellion (as it was soon called) ended.

Although the insurrection was put down, most of the new nation's leading citizens were alarmed by the apparent inability of state governments under the Articles of Confederation to maintain public order. Under the Articles, our first constitution (in effect from 1781 to 1788), the national government in Philadelphia was virtually powerless. Responsibility for civil order was mainly in the hands of the states. Shays's Rebellion realized the worst fears of national leaders about the dangers of ineffective state governments and popular democracy out of control, unchecked by a strong national government. George Washington worried, "If government cannot check these disorders, what security has a man?"[2] It was in this climate of crisis that a call was issued for a constitutional convention to meet in Philadelphia to correct the flaws in our first constitution. Rather than amend the Articles of Confederation, however, the men who met in Philadelphia in the summer of 1787 wrote an entirely new constitution. ■

Thinking Critically About This Chapter

This chapter is about the founding of the United States (see Figure 2.1) and the formulation of the constitutional rules that structure American politics to this day.

Using the Framework   You will see in this chapter how structural factors such as the American political culture, economic developments, and the composition of the Constitutional Convention shaped the substance of our Constitution. You will also see how the Constitution is itself an important structural factor that helps us understand how American government and politics work today.

Using the Democracy Standard   Using the conception of democracy you learned about in Chapter 1, you will be able to see how and why the Framers were uneasy about democracy and created a republican form of government that, although based on popular consent, placed a number of roadblocks in the path of popular rule. ◄

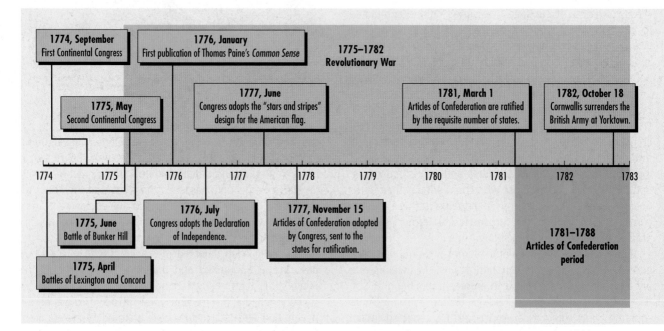

FIGURE 2.1 Time Line of the Founding of the United States, 1774–1791

The Political Theory of the Revolutionary Era

Initially, the American Revolution (1775–1783) was waged more to preserve an existing way of life than to create something new. By and large, American colonists in the 1760s and 1770s were proud to be affiliated with Great Britain and satisfied with the general prosperity that came with participation in the British commercial empire.[3] When the revolution broke out, the colonists at first wanted only to preserve the English constitution and their own rights as British subjects. These traditional rights of life, liberty, and property seemed to be threatened by British policies on trade and taxation. Rather than allowing the American colonists to trade freely with whomever they pleased and to produce whatever goods they wanted, for instance, England was restricting the colonists' freedom to do either in order to protect its own manufacturers. To pay for the military protection of the colonies against raids by Native Americans and their French allies, England imposed taxes on a number of items, including sugar, tea, and stamps (required for legal documents, pamphlets, and newspapers). The imposition of these taxes without the consent of the colonists seemed an act of tyranny to many English subjects in America.

Although the initial aims of the Revolution were quite modest, the American Revolution, like most revolutions, did not stay on the track planned by its leaders. Although it was sparked by a concern for liberty—understood as the preservation of traditional rights against the intrusions of a distant government—it also stimulated the development of sentiments for popular sovereignty and political equality. As these sentiments grew, so did the likelihood that the American colonies would split from their British parent and form a system of government more to the liking of the colonists.

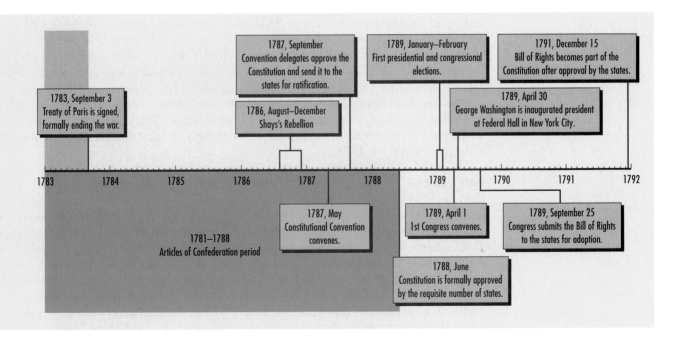

American leaders were reluctant at first to declare independence from Great Britain. One of the things that helped change their minds was Thomas Paine's wildly popular and incendiary pamphlet *Common Sense*, which mercilessly mocked the institution of monarchy.

THOMAS PAINE ESQ.ᴿ
Late Secretary for Foreign Affairs to the
American Congress.
Author of
The Rights of Man, Common Sense, &c.

COMMON SENSE;

ADDRESSED TO THE

INHABITANTS

OF

A M E R I C A,

On the following interesting

S U B J E C T S.

I. Of the Origin and Design of Government in general, with concise Remarks on the English Constitution.

II. Of Monarchy and Hereditary Succession.

III. Thoughts on the present State of American Affairs.

IV. Of the present Ability of America, with some miscellaneous Reflections.

Man knows no Master save creating HEAVEN,
Or those whom choice and common good ordain.
THOMSON.

PHILADELPHIA;
Printed, and Sold, by R. BELL, in Third-Street.
MDCCLXXVI.

The Declaration of Independence

When the Second Continental Congress began its session on May 10, 1775—the First had met only briefly in 1774 to formulate a list of grievances to submit to the British Parliament—the delegates did not have independence in mind, even though armed conflict with Britain had already begun with the battles of Lexington and Concord. Pushed by the logic of armed conflict, an unyielding British government, and Thomas Paine's incendiary call for American independence in his wildly popular pamphlet *Common Sense,* however, the delegates concluded by the spring of 1776 that separation and independence were inescapable.[4] In early June, the Continental Congress appointed a special committee, composed of Thomas Jefferson, John Adams, and Benjamin Franklin, to draft a declaration of independence. The document, mostly Jefferson's handiwork, was adopted unanimously by the Second Continental Congress on July 4, 1776.

Key Ideas in the Declaration of Independence The ideas in Jefferson's Declaration of Independence are so familiar to us that we may easily miss their revolutionary importance. In the late eighteenth century, most societies in the world were ruled by kings with authority purportedly derived from God, subject to little or no control by their subjects. Closely following John Locke's ideas in *The Second Treatise on Government,* Jefferson's argument that legitimate government can be established only by the people and can govern only with their consent seemed outrageous at the time. However, these ideas sparked a responsive chord in people everywhere when they were first presented, and they remain extremely popular all over the world today. Ideas articulated in the Declaration influenced the French Revolution of 1789, the 1991 "velvet revolution" in Czechoslovakia, and many revolutions in between. The argument as presented in the Declaration of Independence goes as follows:

- Human beings possess rights that cannot be legitimately given away or taken from them. *"We hold these truths to be self-evident, that all men are created equal, that they are endowed by their Creator with certain unalienable Rights, that among these are Life, Liberty, and the Pursuit of Happiness."*

- People create government to protect these rights. *"That to secure these rights, Governments are instituted among Men, deriving their just powers from the consent of the governed."*

- If government fails to protect people's rights or itself becomes a threat to them, people can withdraw their consent from that government and create a new one. *"That whenever any Form of Government becomes destructive of these ends, it is the Right of the People to alter or to abolish it, and to institute new Government, laying its foundation on such principles, and organizing its powers in such form, as to them shall seem most likely to effect their Safety and Happiness."*

Omissions in the Declaration   The Declaration of Independence carefully avoided several controversial subjects, including what to do about slavery. Jefferson's initial draft denounced the Crown for violating human rights

Web Exploration
The Declaration of Independence

Issue: The delegates to the Second Continental Congress in Philadelphia did not simply declare independence for the 13 British colonies in North America but gave their reasons for doing so in a document that has influenced people around the world for more than two centuries.

Site: See the Declaration of Independence as eighteenth-century Americans first saw it at the online Exhibition Hall of the National Archives on our Website at **www.ablongman.com/greenberg**. In the "Web Explorations" section for Chapter 2, open "Declaration of Independence," then "Declaration." Select "Charters of Freedom," then "the Declaration of Independence." Examine the document, then read the online essay, "The Stylistic Artistry of the Declaration."

What You've Learned: Do you agree with Lucas that "the Declaration of Independence is perhaps the most masterly written state paper of western civilization"? This is a very big claim. Has Lucas convinced you that it is true? What is most memorable and meaningful about the Declaration? What, if anything, is merely mundane and extraneous in Jefferson's document?

HINT: The most stirring and memorable parts of the Declaration come at the beginning and make universal claims about individual rights and the role of government; it is these universal claims, rather than the long list of transgressions by Great Britain that make up the latter part of the Declaration, that have been so influential.

by "captivating and carrying Africans into slavery," but this was considered too controversial and was dropped from subsequent versions. The contradiction between the institution of slavery and the Declaration's sweeping claims for self-government, "unalienable" individual rights, and equality ("all men are created equal") was obvious to many observers at the time and is glaringly apparent to us today. The Declaration was also silent about the political status of women, Native Americans, and African-Americans who were not slaves. Indeed, it is safe to assume that neither Jefferson, the main author of the Declaration, nor the other signers of the document had women, Native Americans, free blacks, or slaves in mind when they were fomenting revolution and calling for a different kind of political society. Interestingly, free blacks and women would go on to play important roles in waging the Revolutionary War against Britain.[5]

The Articles of Confederation: The First Constitution

confederation

A loose association of states or territorial divisions formed for a common purpose.

The leaders of the American Revolution almost certainly did not envision the creation of a single, unified nation. At most, they had in mind a loose **confederation** among the states. This should not be surprising. Most Americans in the late eighteenth century believed that a government based on popular consent and committed to the protection of individual rights was possible only in small, homogeneous republics, where government was close to the people and where fundamental conflicts of interest among the people did not exist. Given the great geographic expanse of the colonies, as well as their varied ways of life and economic interests, the formation of a single unified republic seemed unworkable.

Provisions of the Articles

constitution

The basic framework of law that prescribes how government is to operate.

Our first **constitution,** passed by the Second Continental Congress in the midst of the Revolutionary War in 1777 but not ratified by the requisite number of states until 1781, created a nation that was hardly a nation at all. The Articles of Confederation created in law what had existed in practice from the time of the Declaration of Independence: a loose confederation of independent states with little power in the central government, much like the United Nations today. Under the Articles, most important decisions were made in state legislatures.

The Articles provided for a central government of sorts, but it had few responsibilities and virtually no power. It could make war or peace, but it had no power to levy taxes (even customs duties) to pursue either goal. It could not regulate commerce among the states, nor could it deny the states the right to collect customs duties. It had no independent chief executive to ensure that the laws passed by Congress would be enforced, nor had it a national court system to settle disputes between the states. There were no means to provide a sound national money system. The rule requiring that all national laws be approved by 9 of the 13 states made lawmaking almost impossible. And, defects in the new constitution were difficult to remedy because amending the Articles required the unanimous approval of the states.

Shortcomings of the Articles

The Articles of Confederation did what most of its authors intended: to preserve the power, independence, and sovereignty of the states and ensure that the central government would not encroach on the liberty of the people. Unfortunately, there were also many problems that the confederation was ill-equipped to handle.

Most important, the new central government could not finance its activities. The government was forced to rely on each state's willingness to pay its annual tax assessment. Few states were eager to cooperate. As a result, the bonds and notes of the confederate government became almost worthless, and the government's attempts to borrow were stymied.

The central government was also unable to defend American interests in foreign affairs. Without a chief executive or a standing army, and with the states holding a veto power over actions of the central government, the confederation lacked the capacity to reach binding agreements with other nations or to deal with a wide range of foreign policy problems. These included the continuing presence of British troops in western lands ceded to the new nation by Britain at the end of the Revolutionary War, violent clashes with Native Americans on the western frontier, and piracy on the high seas.

The government was also unable to prevent the outbreak of commercial warfare between the states. As virtually independent nations with the power to levy customs duties, many states became intense commercial rivals of their neighbors and sought to gain every possible advantage against the products of other states. New York and New Jersey, for instance, imposed high tariffs on goods that crossed their borders from other states.

Factors Leading to the Constitutional Convention

Historians now generally agree that the failings of the Articles of Confederation led most of the leading citizens of the confederation to believe that a new constitution was desperately needed for the fledgling nation. What is left out of many accounts of the convening of the Constitutional Convention in Philadelphia, however, is the story of the growing concern among many of the most influential men in the confederation that the passions for democracy and equality among the common people set loose by the American Revolution were getting out of hand. During the American Revolution, appeals to the people for the defense of freedom and for the spread of the blessings of liberty were often translated by the people to mean their right to better access to the means of government and to the means of livelihood.[6] The common people were convinced that success would bring substantial improvements in their lives.[7]

The Republican Beliefs of the Founders

This fever for popular participation and greater equality is not what most of the leaders of the American Revolution had in mind.[8] The Founders were believers in a theory of government known as **republicanism.** Like other eighteenth-century republicans, they were interested in discovering a form of government that would be based on the consent of the governed but which

republicanism

A political doctrine advocating limited government based on popular consent, protected against majority tyranny.

The Constitution is preserved and on display at the National Archives in Washington, D.C.

would also prevent tyranny, defined as the abuse of power by rulers and the destruction of the liberty of their subjects. Tyranny, they believed, could flow from any one of three places—from the misrule of the *one* (a king), the *few* (an aristocratic class), or the *many* (the common people)—and that a properly designed constitution must protect against all three possibilities. Their solution to the problem of simultaneously gaining the consent of the governed and preventing tyranny was two-fold: to elect government leaders and limit the power of government. The election of representatives would serve to keep potentially tyrannical kings and aristocratic factions from power while ensuring popular consent. Limiting the power of government, either by stating what government could and could not do in a written constitution or by fragmenting governmental power in the very way government is organized, would prevent tyranny no matter who eventually won control of government.

Although eighteenth-century republicans believed in representative government—a government whose political leaders are elected by the people—they were quite unsympathetic to what we might today call popular democracy. For the most part, they thought that public affairs ought to be left to men from the "better" parts of society; the conduct of the public business was, in their view, the province of individuals with wisdom and experience, capacities associated mainly with people of social standing, substantial financial resources, and high levels of education.

Nor did eighteenth-century republicans believe that elected representatives should be too responsive to public opinion. Once in office, representatives were to exercise independent judgment, taking into account the needs and interests of society rather than the moods and opinions of the people.

Eighteenth-century republicans, then, did not believe in democracy as defined in Chapter 1. Most importantly, while republican doctrine allowed the common people a larger role in public life than existed in other political systems of the day, the role of the people was to be far more limited than we expect today (the differences between republican and democratic doctrines are highlighted in Table 2.1). They worried that too much participation by the people could only have a bad outcome. As James Madison put it in *The Federalist Papers*, "[Democracies] have ever been spectacles of turbulence and con-

Longman
Participate.com 2.0
Participation
Democracy and the Internet

TABLE 2.1 Comparing Eighteenth-Century Republicanism and the Democratic Ideal

Republicanism	Democracy
Government is based on popular consent.	Government is based on popular consent.
Rule by the people is indirect, through representatives.	Rule by the people may be direct or indirect.
The term *people* is narrowly defined (by education, property holding, and social standing).	The term *people* is broadly defined.
Elected representatives act as "trustees" (act on their own to discover the public good).	Elected representatives act as "delegates" (act as instructed by the people; accurately reflect their wishes).
Barriers to majority rule exist.	Majority rule prevails.
Government is strictly limited in function.	Government does what the people want it to do.
Government safeguards rights and liberties, with a special emphasis on property rights.	Government safeguards rights and liberties, with no special emphasis on property rights.

tention; have ever been found incompatible with personal security or the rights of property; and have in general been as short in their lives as they have been violent in their deaths."[9]

Why the Founders Were Worried

An Excess of Democracy in the States Worries that untamed democracy was on the rise were not unfounded.[10] In the mid-1780s, popular assemblies (called conventions) were created in several states to keep tabs on state legislatures and to issue instructions to legislatures concerning what bills to pass. Both conventions and instructions struck directly at the heart of the republican conception of the legislature as a deliberative body shielded from popular opinion.[11]

The constitution of the state of Pennsylvania was also an affront to republican principles. Benjamin Rush, a signatory to the Declaration of Independence, described it as "too much upon the democratic order."[12] This constitution replaced the property qualification to vote with a very small tax (thus allowing many more people to vote), created a unicameral (single-house) legislative body whose members were to be elected in annual elections, mandated that legislative deliberations be open to the public, and required that proposed legislation be widely publicized and voted on only after a general election had been held (making the canvassing of public opinion easier).

To many advocates of popular democracy, including Tom Paine, the Pennsylvania constitution was the most perfect instrument of popular sovereignty. To others, like James Madison, the Pennsylvania case was a perfect example of popular tyranny exercised through the legislative branch of government.[13]

The Threat to Property Rights in the States   One of the freedoms that republicans wanted to protect against the intrusions of a tyrannical government was the right of the people to acquire and enjoy private property. Developments toward the end of the 1770s and the beginning of the 1780s seemed to put this freedom in jeopardy. For one thing, the popular culture was growing increasingly hostile to privilege of any kind, whether of social standing, education, or wealth. Writers derided aristocratic airs; expressed their preference for unlettered, plain-speaking leaders; and pointed out how wealth undermined equal rights.[14] Legislatures were increasingly inclined, moreover, to pass laws protecting debtors. For example, Rhode Island and North Carolina issued cheap paper money, which note holders were forced to accept in payment of debts. Other states enacted **stay acts,** which forbade farm foreclosures for nonpayment of debts. Popular opinion, while strongly in favor of property rights (most of the debtors in question were owners of small farms), also sympathized with farmers, who were hard-pressed to pay their debts with increasingly tight money, and believed—with some reason—that many creditors had accumulated notes speculatively or unfairly and were not entitled to full repayment. Finally, Shays's Rebellion in western Massachusetts, where armed rebels tried to prevent the state courts from seizing farms for the nonpayment of debts, greatly alarmed American notables.

stay acts

Enactments postponing the collection of taxes or mortgage payments.

The Constitutional Convention

Concerned about these developments and shortcomings in the design of government under the Articles, most of America's economic, social, and political leaders were convinced by 1787 that the new nation and the experiment in self-government were in great peril. These concerns helped convince leaders in the states to select 73 delegates to attend the Constitutional Convention in Philadelphia (only 55 actually showed up for its deliberations). The goal was to create a new government capable of providing both energy and stability.

The convention officially convened in Philadelphia on May 25, 1787, with George Washington presiding. It met in secret for a period of almost four months. By the end of their deliberations, the delegates had hammered out a constitutional framework that has served as one of the structural foundations of American government and politics to the present day.

Who Were the Framers?

The delegates were not common folk. There were no common laborers, skilled craftspeople, small farmers, women, or racial minorities in attendance. Most delegates were wealthy men: holders of government bonds, real estate investors, successful merchants, bankers, lawyers, and owners of large plantations worked by slaves. They were, for the most part, far better educated than the average American and solidly steeped in the classics. The journal of the convention debates kept by James Madison of Virginia shows that the delegates were conversant with the great works of Western philosophy and political science; with great facility and frequency, they quoted Aristotle, Plato, Locke, Montesquieu, and scores of other thinkers. They were also a surprisingly young group, averaging barely over 40 years of age. Finally, they were a group with broad experience in American politics, and many were veterans of the Revolutionary War.

Judgments about the framers, their intentions, and what they produced vary widely. Historian Melvin Urofsky wrote that "few gatherings in the his-

Members of the convention sign their names to the Constitution on September 17, 1787. The Constitution did not become the law of the land, however, until the ninth state, New Hampshire, ratified it nine months later.

tory of this or any other country could boast such a concentration of talent."[15] Supreme Court Justice Thurgood Marshall, on the other hand, once claimed that the Constitution was "defective from the start" because the convention at which it was written did not include women or blacks.[16]

The most influential criticism of the framers and what they created was mounted in 1913 by the Progressive historian Charles Beard in his book *An Economic Interpretation of the Constitution.*[17] Beard boldly claimed that the framers were engaged in a conspiracy to protect their immediate and personal economic interests. Those who controlled the convention and the ratification process after the convention, he suggested, were owners of public securities who were interested in a government that could pay its debts, merchants interested in protections of commerce, and land speculators interested in the protection of property rights.

Beard has had legions of defenders and detractors.[18] Historians today generally agree that Beard overemphasized the degree to which the framers were driven by the immediate need to "line their own pockets," failed to give credit to their more noble motivations, and even got many of his facts wrong. So a simple self-interest analysis is not supportable. But Beard was probably on the mark when he suggested that broad economic and social-class motives were at work in shaping the actions of the framers. This is not to suggest that they were not concerned about the national interest, economic stability, or the preservation of liberty. It does suggest, however, that the ways in which they understood these concepts were fully compatible with their own positions of economic and social eminence. It is fair to say that the Constitutional Convention was the work of American notables authentically worried about the instability and the economic chaos of the confederation.

Consensus and Conflict at the Convention

The delegates to the convention were of one mind on many fundamental points. Most importantly, they agreed that the Articles of Confederation had to be scrapped and replaced with a new constitution.

Most of the delegates also agreed about the need for a substantially strengthened national government to protect American interests in the world, provide for social order, and regulate interstate commerce. Such a government would diminish the power and sovereignty of the states. Supporters of the idea of a strong, centralized national government, such as Alexander Hamilton, had long argued this position. By the time of the convention, even such traditional opponents of centralized governmental power as James Madison had changed their minds. As Madison put it, some way must be found "which will at once support a due supremacy of the national authority, and leave in force the local authorities so far as they can be subordinately useful."[19]

But the delegates also believed that a strong national government was potentially tyrannical and should not be allowed to fall into the hands of any particular interest or set of interests, particularly the majority of the people, referred to by Madison as the "majority faction." The delegates' most important task became that of finding a formula for creating a republican government based on popular consent but a government not unduly swayed by public opinion and popular democracy. As Benjamin Franklin put it, "We have been guarding against an evil that old states are most liable to, excess of power in the rulers, but our present danger seems to be a defect of obedience in the subjects."[20]

Virginia Plan

Proposal by the large states at the Constitutional Convention to create a strong central government with power in the government apportioned to the states on the basis of population.

New Jersey Plan

Proposal of the smaller states at the Constitutional Convention to create a government based on the equal representation of the states in a unicameral legislature.

The Great Compromise By far the most intense disagreements at the convention concerned the issue of representation in Congress, especially whether large or small states would wield the most power in the legislative branch. The **Virginia Plan,** drafted by James Madison, proposed the creation of a strong central government controlled by the most populous states: Virginia, Massachusetts, and Pennsylvania. The Virginians wanted a national legislature with seats apportioned to the states on the basis of population size and with the power to appoint the executive and the judiciary and to veto state laws. The smaller states countered with a set of proposals drafted by William Paterson of New Jersey (thereafter known as the **New Jersey Plan**), whose central feature was a unicameral national legislature whose seats were

Web Exploration
Delegates to the Convention

Issue: The Constitution was made by people who were not much like the average inhabitant of the United States in 1787.

Site: Find out more about the delegates to the Convention by going to the National Archives on our Website at **www.ablongman.com/greenberg**. In the "Web Explorations" section for Chapter 2, open "delegates to the convention," then "delegates." Select a state and read the biographies of the delegates.

What You've Learned: How would you describe the average delegate? How representative do you believe them to have been of the American people of the time?

HINT: There were no women; few artisans and small farmers; and no free blacks, indentured servants, slaves, or Native Americans at the proceedings. These groups together comprised the vast majority of the American population.

apportioned equally among the states. The New Jersey Plan envisioned a slightly more powerful national government than the one that existed under the Articles of Confederation, but one that was to be organized on representational lines not unlike those in the Articles, in which each of the states remained sovereign. The Virginia Plan, by contrast, with its strong national government run by a popularly elected legislature, represented a fundamentally different kind of national union, one in which national sovereignty was superior to state sovereignty.

Debate over this issue was so intense that no decision could be reached on the floor of the convention. As a way out of this impasse, the convention appointed a committee to hammer out a compromise. The so-called Committee of Eleven met over the Fourth of July holiday while the convention was adjourned. It presented its report, sometimes called the Great Compromise and sometimes the **Connecticut Compromise** (because it was drafted by Roger Sherman of that state), on July 5, 1787. Its key feature was a bicameral (two-house) national legislature in which each state's representation in the House of Representatives was to be based on population (thus favoring the large states), while representation in the Senate was to be equal for each of the states (thus favoring the small states). The compromise, adopted on July 16, broke the deadlock at the convention and allowed the delegates to turn their attention to other matters.

Connecticut Compromise
Also called the *Great Compromise*; the compromise between the New Jersey and Virginia plans put forth by the Connecticut delegates at the Constitutional Convention; called for a lower legislative house based on population size and an upper house based on equal representation of the states.

Slavery Despite great distaste for the institution of slavery among many delegates—it is said that Benjamin Franklin wanted to insert a provision in the Constitution condemning slavery and the slave trade but was talked out of it for fear of splintering the convention[21]—slavery was ultimately condoned in the Constitution, although only indirectly; the word "slavery," in fact, does not appear in the Constitution at all. Rather, the legal standing of "involuntary servitude" is affirmed in three places. First, the delegates agreed, after much heated debate, to count three-fifths of a state's slave population (referred to as "three-fifths of all other Persons") in the calculation of how many representatives a state was entitled to in the House of Representatives (Article I, Section 2, paragraph 3). Much harm was done by this; counting noncitizen slaves for purposes

One of the great shortcomings of the framers was their inability or unwillingness to abolish slavery in the Constitution. It would take a great and terrible civil war to rectify their mistake.

of representation in the House increased the power of the slave states in Congress as well as the number of their electoral votes in presidential elections. This imbalance would continue until 1865, when the Civil War and the Thirteenth Amendment, ratified after the war, ended slavery in the United States. Second, it forbade enactments against the slave trade until the year 1808 (Article I, Section 9). Third, it required nonslave states to return runaway slaves to their owners in slave states (Article IV, Section 2, paragraph 3).

Many Americans today are no doubt bothered by the fact that a significant number of the delegates to a convention whose goal was to build a nontyrannical republic were themselves slaveholders (although a few, including George Washington, had provisions in their wills freeing their slaves upon their death). To understand more fully why the delegates did not abolish slavery, see the "Using the Framework" feature on the next page.

It would finally take a terrible civil war to abolish slavery in the United States. At the convention, Virginia delegate George Mason had a foreboding of such an outcome when he observed about slavery that "providence punishes national sins by national calamities."[22]

The Presidency   The Virginia Plan called for a single executive, while the New Jersey Plan called for a plural executive. In the spirit of cooperation that pervaded the convention after the Great Compromise, the delegates quickly settled on the idea of a single executive. They could not agree, however, on how this executive should be selected. Both sides rejected direct election by the people of the chief executive, of course, because this would be "too much upon the democratic order," but they locked horns over and could not agree to the Virginia Plan's method of selection: by the vote of state legislatures. The compromise that was eventually struck involved a provision for an **electoral college** that would select the president. In the electoral college, each state would have a total of votes equal to its total number of representatives and senators in Congress. Members of the electoral college would then cast their votes for president. Should the electoral college fail to give a majority to any person, which most framers assumed would usually happen, the House of Representatives would choose the president, with each state having one vote (Article II, Section 1, paragraphs 2 and 3).

electoral college

Elected representatives of the states whose votes formally elect the president; the number of electors in each state is equal to the total number of its senators and representatives in the House.

What the Framers Created

What kind of government did the framers create? Let us examine the fundamental design for government laid out in the Constitution.

A Republican Form of Government   Recall that republican doctrine advocated a form of government that, while based on popular consent and some popular participation, places obstacles in the path of majoritarian democracy and limits the purposes and powers of the government in order to prevent tyranny.

Election of Government Leaders   Republican government is based on the principle of representation, meaning that public policies are made not by the people directly but by the people's elected representatives acting in their stead. Under the rules created by the Constitution, the president and members of Congress are elected by the people, though in the case of the presidency and the Senate, to be sure, they are elected only indirectly (through the electoral college and the state legislatures, respectively). The upshot, then, is that government policies at the national level are mostly made by either directly or

USING THE FRAMEWORK: Slavery in the Constitution

Why was slavery allowed in the Constitution of 1787?

Background: Slavery was allowed in the Constitution until passage, after the Civil War, of the Thirteenth Amendment, which ended involuntary servitude in the United States. Although the words "slave" or "involuntary servitude" never appear in the document, slavery is given constitutional standing in the original document in Article I, Section 2, paragraph 3; Article 2, Section 9; and Article IV, Section 2, paragraph 3. For Americans today, it seems almost inconceivable that such a thing could have happened. Taking a broader and more historical view makes the story clearer, though hardly more acceptable.

Governmental Action

The framers allowed the institution of slavery to continue in Article I, Section 2; Article II, Setion 9; and Article IV, Section 2 of the Constitution.

Governmental Level

- Slaveholders and merchants involved in the slave trade were well represented among the convention delegates. →
- Many other delegates, although personally opposed to slavery as an institution, feared that the introduction of a provision to end slavery would cause those states with high numbers of slaves to leave the convention and doom the effort to create a United States of America.

Political Linkages Level

- Slaves and free blacks played no significant political role in America during the Articles of Confederation period. Their concerns about slavery had no political weight. →
- Few private organizations—interest groups, churches, or newspapers—were actively pressing for an end to slavery at the time of the constitutional convention.

Structural Level

- The slave trade was a profitable business. →
- For the most part, individuals of European descent in America during the time of the constitutional convention did not believe that people of African descent were equal to whites in any respect, nor did they believe that they were beings who possessed basic human rights.

indirectly elected officials. This guarantees a degree of popular consent and some protection against the possibilities of tyrannical government arising from misrule by the *one* or by the *few,* given the electoral power of the *many.*

Federalism   The Articles of Confederation envisioned a nation structured as a loose union of politically independent units with little power in the hands of the central government. The Constitution fashioned a **federal** system in which some powers are left to the states, some powers are shared by the component units and the central government, and some powers are granted to the central government alone.

The powers in the Constitution tilt slightly toward the center, however.[23] This recasting of the union from a loose confederation to a more centralized federal system is boldly stated in Article VI, Section 2, commonly called the **supremacy clause:**

> *This Constitution and the Laws of the United States which shall be made in Pursuance thereof; and all Treaties made, or which shall be made, under the Authority of the United States, shall be the supreme Law of the Land; and the Judges in every State shall be bound thereby, any Thing in the Constitution or Laws of any State to the Contrary notwithstanding.*

The tilt toward national power is also enhanced by assigning important powers and responsibilities to the national government: to regulate commerce, to provide a uniform currency, to provide uniform laws on bankruptcy, to raise and support an army and a navy, to declare war, to collect taxes and customs duties, to provide for the common defense of the United States, and more. (See Article I, Section 8.) Especially important for later constitutional history is the last of the clauses in Section 8, which states that Congress has the power to "make all laws which shall be necessary and proper" to carry out its specific powers and responsibilities. We shall see later how this **elastic clause** became one of the foundations for the growth of the federal government in the twentieth century.

The Constitution left it up to each of the states, however, to determine qualifications for voting within their borders. This left rules in place in all the states that denied the right to vote to women, slaves, and Native Americans; it left rules untouched in many states that denied the vote to free blacks and to white males without substantial property. Most states removed property qualifications by the 1830s, establishing universal white male suffrage in the United States. It would take many years and constitutional amendments to remove state restrictions on the voting rights of women and racial minorities.

Limited Government   The basic purpose of the U.S. Constitution, like any written constitution, is to define the purposes and powers of the government. Such a definition of purposes and powers automatically places a boundary between what is permissible and what is impermissible. By listing the specific powers (as in Article I, Section 8) of the national government and specifically denying others to the national government (as in Article I, Section 9, and in the first ten amendments to the Constitution, known as the **Bill of Rights**), the Constitution carefully limited what government may legitimately do.

Checks on Majority Rule   Afraid of unbridled democracy, the framers created a constitution by which the people rule only indirectly, barriers are placed in the path of majorities (see Figure 2.2), and deliberation is prized over confor-

---

federal

Describing a system in which significant governmental powers are divided between a central government and smaller units, such as states.

supremacy clause

The provision in Article VI of the Constitution that the Constitution itself and the laws and treaties of the United States are the supreme law of the land, taking precedence over state laws and constitutions.

elastic clause

Article I, Section 8, of the Constitution, also called the *necessary and proper clause;* gives Congress the authority to make whatever laws are necessary and proper to carry out its enumerated responsibilities.

Bill of Rights

The first ten amendments to the U.S. Constitution, concerned with basic liberties.

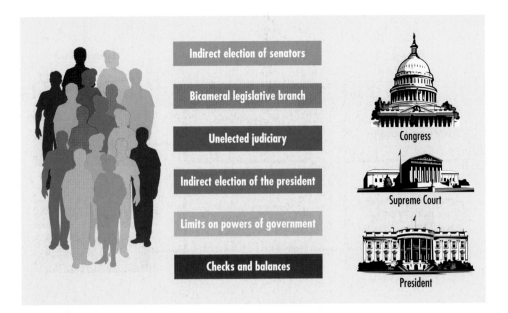

FIGURE 2.2 Limiting the Power of the Majority

The framers of the Constitution were concerned that the unreflective and unstable opinions of the majority might overwhelm the considered judgments of government leaders and lead to tyranny. One antidote was to create mechanisms in the Constitution that, while preserving "the consent of the governed," ensured that the voice of the people would be muted in the councils of government.

mity to the popular will. As political philosopher Robert Dahl puts it, "To achieve their goal of preserving a set of inalienable rights superior to the majority principle . . . the framers deliberately created a framework of government that was carefully designed to impede and even prevent the operation of majority rule."[24] Let us see what the framers did to try to dilute the power of the majority in the national government.

Of the three branches of government, only a part of one of them is selected by the direct vote of the people: the House of Representatives (Article I, Section 2, paragraph 1). As for the rest of the national government, the president is elected by the electoral college; the members of the Senate are elected by the state legislatures; and judges are appointed by the president and confirmed by the Senate. Representatives, senators, and presidents are elected, moreover, for different terms (two years for representatives, four years for presidents, and six years for senators), from different constituencies, and (often) at different times. These noncongruencies in elections were intended to ensure that popular majorities, at least in the short run, would be unlikely to overwhelm those who govern. Finally, the framers rejected the advice of radical democrats, such as Thomas Paine, Samuel Adams, and Thomas Jefferson, to allow the Constitution to be easily amended. Instead, they created an amending process that is exceedingly cumbersome and difficult (see Figure 2.3).

Thus, the framers designed a system in which the popular will, though given some play (more than anywhere in the world at the time), was largely deflected and slowed, allowing somewhat insulated political leaders to deliberate at their pleasure.

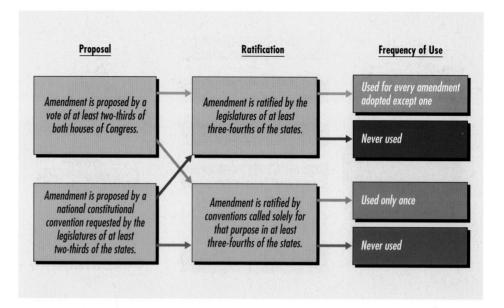

FIGURE 2.3 Amending the Constitution

With two ways of proposing a constitutional amendment and two ways of ratifying one, there are four routes to changing the Constitution. In all but one case (the Twenty-First Amendment, which repealed Prohibition), constitutional amendments have been proposed by Congress and then ratified by the state legislatures.

Longman
Participate.com
2.0
Visual Literacy
The American
System of
Checks and
Balances

Separation of Powers; Checks and Balances During the American Revolution, American leaders worried mainly about the misrule of executives (kings and governors) and judges. As an antidote, they substituted legislative supremacy in state constitutions and in the Articles of Confederation, thinking that placing power in an elected representative body would make government effective and nontyrannical. The men who drafted the Constitution, however, though still leery of executive and judicial power, were more concerned by 1787 about the danger of legislative tyranny. To deal with this problem, the framers turned to the ancient notion of balanced government, popularized by the French philosopher Montesquieu. The central idea of balanced government is that concentrated power of any kind is dangerous and that the way to prevent tyranny is first to fragment governmental power into its constituent parts—executive, legislative, and judicial—then place each into a separate and independent branch. In the U.S. Constitution, Article I (on the legislative power), Article II (on the executive power), and Article III (on the judicial power) designate separate spheres of responsibility and enumerate specific powers for each branch. We call this the **separation of powers.**

To further ensure that power would not be exercised tyrannically, the framers arranged for the legislative, executive, and judicial powers to check one another in such a way that "ambition . . . be made to counteract ambition."[25] They did this by ensuring that no branch of the national government would be able to act entirely on its own without the cooperation of the others. To put it another way, each branch has ways of blocking the actions of the others. For instance, Congress is given the chief lawmaking power under the Constitution, but a bill can become a law only if the president signs it. The

separation of powers

The distribution of government legislative, executive, and judicial powers to separate branches of government.

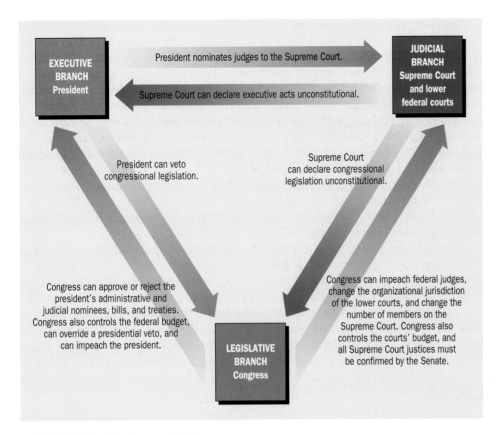

FIGURE 2.4 Checks and Balances

The framers of the Constitution believed that tyranny might be avoided if the power of government were fragmented into its executive, legislative, and judicial components and if each component were made the responsibility of a separate branch of government. To further protect against tyranny, they created mechanisms by which the actions of any single branch could be blocked by either or both of the other branches. This system of checks and balances is highlighted in this drawing.

Supreme Court, moreover, has the power (though it is not specifically mentioned) to reject a law formulated by Congress and signed by the president if it is contrary to the Constitution. What is at work here was described nicely by Thomas Jefferson: "The powers of government should be so divided and balanced among several bodies of magistracy, as that no one could transcend their legal limits, without being effectually checked and constrained by the others."[26] We call the provisions that accomplish this objective **checks and balances.** Figure 2.4 shows in detail how each separate branch of the federal government can be checked by the other two. In this constitutional scheme, each branch has power, but none is able to exercise all of its powers on its own.

checks and balances
The constitutional principle that government power shall be divided and that the fragments should balance or check one another to prevent tyranny.

The Foundations for a National Free Enterprise Economy

The framers believed that the right to accumulate, use, and transfer property was one of the fundamental and inalienable rights that governments were instituted to defend, so they looked for ways to protect property. They also believed that the obstacles to trade allowed under the Articles of Confederation were threatening to block the emergence of a vibrant national economy in which most of them were involved.

Property rights are protected in several places in the Constitution. Article I, Section 10, forbids the states to impair the obligation of contracts, to coin money, or to make anything but gold and silver coin a tender in payment of debts. In other words, the states could no longer help debtors by printing inflated money, forgiving debts, or otherwise infringing on the property of creditors, as had happened in such places as Rhode Island and North Carolina under the Articles of Confederation. Article IV, Section 1, further guarantees contracts by establishing that the states must give "full faith and credit" to the public acts, records, and judicial proceedings of every other state, which means that one could no longer escape legal and financial obligations in one state by moving to another. In addition, the Constitution guaranteed that the U.S. government would pay all debts contracted under the Articles of Confederation (Article VI, Section 1). Article IV, Section 2, paragraph 3, even protected private property in slaves by requiring states to deliver escaped slaves back to their owners.

Besides protecting private property, the framers took additional steps to encourage the emergence of a national free enterprise economy. Article I, Section 8, grants Congress the power to regulate interstate commerce (thus ending the chaos of individual states' regulations), to coin money and regulate its value (thus establishing a uniform national currency), to establish uniform laws of bankruptcy, and to protect the financial fruits of invention by establishing patent and copyright laws. At the same time, Article I, Sections 9 and 10, broke down barriers to trade by forbidding the states to impose taxes or duties on other states' exports, to enter into foreign treaties, to coin money, or to lay any imposts or duties on imports or exports.

The Struggle to Ratify the Constitution

Congress had instructed the delegates to the convention to propose changes to the Articles of Confederation. Under the provisions of the Articles of Confederation, such alterations would have required the unanimous consent of the 13 states. To follow such a course would have meant instant rejection of the new constitution, because Rhode Island, never friendly to the deliberations in Philadelphia, surely would have voted against it, and one or two additional states may well have joined Rhode Island. Acting boldly, the framers simply stated that ratification would be based on guidelines specified in Article VII of the unratified document they had just written, namely, approval by nine states meeting in special constitutional conventions. Congress agreed to this procedure, voting on September 28, 1787, to transmit the Constitution to the states for their consideration.

The battle over ratification was heated, and the outcome was far from certain. That the Constitution eventually carried the day may be partly attributed to the fact that the **Federalists** (those who supported the Constitution) did a better job of making their case than the **Anti-Federalists** (those who opposed the Constitution). Their intellectual advantages were nowhere more obvious than in the 85 articles written in defense of the Constitution for New York newspapers, under the name "Publius," by Alexander Hamilton (who wrote the most), James Madison (who wrote the best), and John Jay (who wrote only three). Collected later and published as *The Federalist Papers,* these articles strongly influenced the debate over ratification and remain the most impressive commentaries ever written about the U.S. Constitution. (Numbers 10 and 51, written by Madison, are reprinted in the Appendix, as is number 78, written by Hamilton.)

Federalists

Proponents of the Constitution during the ratification fight; also the political party of Hamilton, Washington, and Adams.

Anti-Federalists

Opponents of the Constitution during the fight over ratification.

TABLE 2.2 The Bill of Rights	
Amendment I	Freedom of religion, speech, press, and assembly
Amendment II	The right to bear arms
Amendment III	Prohibition against quartering of troops in private homes
Amendment IV	Prohibition against unreasonable searches and seizures
Amendment V	Rights guaranteed to the accused: requirement for grand jury indictment; protections against double jeopardy and self-incrimination; guarantee of due process
Amendment VI	Right to a speedy and public trial before an impartial jury, to cross-examine witnesses, and to have counsel
Amendment VII	Right to a trial by jury in civil suits
Amendment VIII	Prohibition against excessive bail and fines and against cruel and unusual punishment
Amendment IX	Traditional rights not listed in the Constitution are retained by the people
Amendment X	Powers not denied to them by the Constitution or given solely to the national government are retained by the states

Note: See the Appendix for the full text.

Anti-Federalist opposition to the Constitution was based on fear of centralized power and concern about the absence of a bill of rights.[27] Although the Federalists firmly believed that a bill of rights was unnecessary because of the protection of rights in the state constitutions and the many safeguards against tyranny in the federal Constitution, they promised to add one during the first session of Congress. Without this promise, ratification would probably not have happened. The Federalists kept their word. The 1st Congress passed a bill of rights in the form of ten amendments to the Constitution (see Table 2.2 and the Appendix), and the amendments were eventually ratified by the required number of states by 1791.

Ratification of the Constitution was a close call. Most of the small states quickly approved, attracted by the formula of equal representation in the Senate. Federalists organized a victory in Pennsylvania before the Anti-Federalists realized what had happened. After that, ratification became a struggle. Rhode Island voted no. North Carolina abstained because of the absence of a bill of rights and did not vote its approval until 1790. In the largest and most important states, the vote was exceedingly close. Massachusetts approved by a vote of 187–168; Virginia, by 89–79; and New York, by 30–27. The struggle was especially intense in Virginia, where prominent, articulate, and influential men were involved on both sides. The Federalists could call on George Washington, James Madison, John Marshall, and Edmund Randolph. The Anti-Federalists countered with George Mason, Richard Henry Lee, and Patrick Henry. Patrick Henry was particularly passionate, saying that the Constitution "squints towards monarchy." Although New Hampshire technically put the Constitution over the top, being the ninth state to vote approval, the proponents did not rest easily until approval was narrowly voted by Virginia and New York.

Longman
Participate.com
2.0
Simulation
**You Are
James
Madison**

The Changing Constitution, Democracy, and American Politics

The Constitution is the basic rule book for the game of American politics. Constitutional rules apportion power and responsibility among governmental branches, define the fundamental nature of the relationships among governmental institutions, specify how individuals are to be selected for office, and tell how the rules themselves may be changed. Every aspiring politician who wants to attain office, every citizen who wants to influence what government does, and every group that wants to advance its interests in the political arena must know the rules and how to use them to their best advantage. Because the Constitution has this character, we understand it to be a fundamental *structural* factor influencing all of American political life.

Constitutional rules, however, like all rules, can and do change over time. Their tendency to change with the times is why we sometimes speak of the "living Constitution." Constitutional changes come about in three specific ways: formal amendment, judicial interpretation, and political practices.

The Constitution may be formally amended by use of the procedures outlined in Article V of the Constitution (again, refer to Figure 2.3). This method has resulted in the addition of 27 amendments since the founding, the first ten of which (the Bill of Rights) were added within three years of ratification. That only 17 have been added in the roughly 200 years since suggests that this method of changing the Constitution is extremely difficult. Nevertheless, formal amendments have played an important role in expanding democracy in

Longman
Participate.com
2.0
Timeline
The History of Constitutional Amendments

The Constitution has evolved over the years in three ways: through the amendment process, through evolving political practices, and through the Supreme Court's changing interpretation of the Constitution's meaning. Here antiabortion protesters demonstrate in front of the Supreme Court building on the anniversary of the Court's *Roe* v. *Wade* decision to demand a reversal of that landmark decision.

the United States by ending slavery; extending voting rights to African-Americans, women, and young people ages 18 to 20; and making the Senate subject to popular vote.

The Constitution is also changed by decisions and interpretations of the U.S. Supreme Court. For instance, in *Marbury* v. *Madison* (1803), the Court claimed the power of **judicial review**—the right to declare the actions of the other branches of government null and void if they are contrary to the Constitution—even though such a power is not specifically mentioned in the Constitution. In *Griswold* v. *Connecticut* (1965), and later in *Roe* v. *Wade* (1973), to take another example, the Court supported a claim for the existence of a fundamental right of privacy even though such a right is not explicitly mentioned in the Constitution.

judicial review

The power of the Supreme Court to declare actions of the other branches and levels of government unconstitutional.

The meaning of the Constitution also changes through changing political practices, which end up serving as precedents for political actors. Political

HOW DEMOCRATIC ARE WE?

A Republic or a Democracy?

PROPOSITION: The Constitution created a republic, not a democracy.

AGREE: The framers created a republic because they were worried about the possibility of majority tyranny in the new nation. Consequently, they wrote a number of provisions into the Constitution to control the purported excesses of democracy: separation of powers, checks and balances, federalism, an appointed judiciary with life tenure, selection of the president by the electoral college, and election of members of the Senate by state legislatures. Although some of these provisions have not worked precisely as the framers intended, the American system of government remains essentially "republican" in nature, with the majority finding it very difficult to prevail.

DISAGREE: Although the framers had every intention of creating a republic and holding democracy in check, they were unable to do so. Over the years, as the nation became more egalitarian in its cultural, economic, and social life, the tide of democracy transformed the original constitutional design. By formal amendment, judicial interpretations, and changing political practices, government has been fashioned into a highly responsive set of institutions, heeding the voice of the people. Today, the national government does pretty much what the American people want it to do, even if it sometimes takes a while for it to do so.

THE AUTHORS: You will see throughout this text that the United States is far more democratic than the framers had intended it to be—with much of the credit going to the "struggle for democracy"—but that our system remains very much a republican one. Those pressing for national action to solve any number of problems soon run up against the barriers to decisive action erected by the framers. At almost every point in our system of government, it is easier to block or to veto than to act or enact. There is no denying the fact, however, that elected representatives and executives often try to be responsive to the popular will. Sometimes they are successful; sometimes they are not. There is no denying the additional fact that the framers were successful in creating a governing structure in which political liberty, an important component of democracy, is protected and allowed to flourish. We would call such a system of government a "democrat republic."

Longman
Participate.com
2.0
Comparative
**Comparing
Constitutions**

parties and nominating conventions are not cited in the Constitution, for example, but it would be hard to think about American politics today without them. It is also fair to say that the framers would not recognize the modern presidency, which is now a far more important office than they envisioned, a change that has been brought about largely by the political and military involvement of the United States in world affairs.

The story of how formal amendment, judicial interpretations, and political practices have changed the constitutional rules in the United States will be told in more detail throughout this text.

Summary

The first constitution joining the American states was the Articles of Confederation. Under its terms, the states were organized into a loose confederation in which the states retained full sovereignty and the central government had little power. Because of a wide range of defects in the Articles of Confederation and fears among many American leaders that democratic and egalitarian tendencies were beginning to spin out of control, a gathering was called in Philadelphia to amend the Articles of Confederation. The delegates chose instead to formulate an entirely new constitution, based on the principles of republicanism (federalism, limited government, the separation of powers, checks and balances, and limitations on majority rule).

The Constitution was ratified in an extremely close vote of the states after a hard-fought struggle between the Federalists and the Anti-Federalists. The Federalists were supported primarily by those who believed in a more centralized republicanism; the Anti-Federalists were supported primarily by those who believed in small-scale republicanism. Despite its "close shave," the Constitution became very popular among the American people within only a few years of the ratification fight. Because of the continuing struggle for democracy by the American people, the Constitution has become far more democratic over the years than was originally intended by the framers.

Suggestions for Further Reading

Ellis, Joseph J. *Founding Brothers: The Revolutionary Generation*. New York: Alfred Knopf, 2001.
> *An entertaining and accessible look at the intertwined lives of the men who wrote the Declaration of Independence, fought the Revolutionary War, fashioned the Constitution, and launched the new American government.*

Maier, Pauline. *American Scripture: Making the Declaration of Independence*. New York: Alfred Knopf, 1997.
> *A detailed account of the writing of the Declaration of Independence and its gradual transformation into a revered icon of American democracy.*

Rossiter, Clinton, ed. *The Federalist Papers*. New York: New American Library, 1961.
> *Classic commentaries on the Constitution and its key provisions, written by Alexander Hamilton, John Jay, and James Madison.*

Storing, Herbert J. *What the Anti-Federalists Were For*. Chicago: University of Chicago Press, 1981.
> *The most complete collection available on the published views of the Anti-Federalists. Includes convincing commentary by Storing.*

Wills, Gary. *Explaining America: The Federalist*. New York: Doubleday, 1981.
> *A fresh look at the writing of the Constitution by one of America's most provocative intellectuals.*

Wood, Gordon S. *The Creation of the American Republic.* New York: Norton, 1972.
The most exhaustive and respected source on America's changing ideas during the period 1776–1787, or from the start of the American Revolution to the writing of the Constitution.

Wood, Gordon S. *The Radicalism of the American Revolution.* New York: Knopf, 1992.
Examines and rejects the argument that the American Revolution was merely a political and not a social and economic revolution.

Internet Sources

Annotated Constitution   **www.access.gpo.gov/congress/senate/constitution**
An annotation of the Constitution in which each clause is tied to Supreme Court decisions concerning its meaning; done by the Library of Congress.

Biographical Sketches of the Delegates to the Constitutional Convention
http://www.nara.gov/exhall/charters/constitution/confath.html
Profiles of the delegates to the Constitutional Convention.

Cornell University Law School   **http://www.law.cornell.edu/**
Pathways to the full text of U.S. Supreme Court decisions and opinions, articles on constitutional issues, and much more.

Political Science Resources: Political Thought   **http://www.psr.keele.ac.uk/**
A vast collection of documents on democracy, liberty, and constitutionalism.

The U.S. Constitution On-Line   **www.usconstitution.net**
A very rich site that presents material on every aspect of the history and development of the Constitution.

Notes

1. Page Smith, *A People's History of the Young Republic: Vol. 3. The Shaping of America* (New York: McGraw-Hill, 1980), p. 25.

2. Quoted in Jackson Turner Main, *The Anti-Federalists* (Chapel Hill, NC: University of North Carolina Press, 1961), p. 62.

3. Richard Bushman, "Revolution," in Eric Foner and John A. Garraty, eds., *The Reader's Companion to American History* (Boston: Houghton Mifflin, 1991), p. 936; Gordon S. Wood, *The Creation of the American Republic* (New York: Norton, 1972), p. 12.

4. Joseph J. Ellis, *Founding Brothers: The Revolutionary Generation* (New York: Alfred A. Knopf, 2001), pp. 212–213.

5. Sarah M. Evans, *Born for Liberty: A History of Women in America* (New York: Free Press, 1997); John Hope Franklin and Alfred A. Moss Jr., *From Slavery to Freedom* (New York: Knopf, 1967).

6. See Hannah Arendt, *On Revolution* (New York: Viking, 1965).

7. Smith, *Shaping of America,* pp. 8–9.

8. Richard Hofstadter, *The American Political Tradition* (New York: Vintage Books, 1948), p. 4.

9. Alexander Hamilton, James Madison, and John Jay, *The Federalist Papers,* ed. Clinton Rossiter (New York: New American Library, 1961), No. 10. (Originally published 1787–1788.)

10. See Gordon S. Wood, *The Radicalism of the American Revolution* (New York: Knopf, 1992).

11. Wood, *Creation of the American Republic,* pp. 311–318.

12. Ibid., ch. 8.

13. Samuel Elliot Morison, *The Oxford History of the American People* (New York: Oxford University Press, 1965), p. 274.

14. See Wood, *Creation of the American Republic,* p. 400.

15. Melvin I. Urofsky, *A March of Liberty* (New York: Knopf, 1988), p. 89.

16. Quoted in *The Washington Post,* May 7, 1987. Also see Lee Epstein and Thomas G. Walker, *Constitutional Law for a Changing America* (Washington, D.C.: CQ Press, 2000), p. 6.

17. Charles Beard, *An Economic Interpretation of the Constitution* (New York: Macmillan, 1913).

18. See Robert Brown, *Charles Beard and the Constitution* (Princeton, NJ: Princeton University Press, 1956); Hofstadter, *The American Political Tradition;* Leonard Levy, *Constitutional Opinions* (New York: Oxford University Press, 1986); Robert A. McGuire and Robert L. Ohsfeldt, "An Economic Model of Voting Behavior over Specific Issues at the Constitutional Convention of 1787," *Journal of Economic History,* 66 (March 1986), pp. 79–111; James A. Morone, *The Democratic Wish* (New York: Basic Books, 1990); Forrest McDonald, *We the People: The Economic Origins of the Constitution* (Chicago: University of Chicago Press, 1958); Gordon S. Wood, *The Convention and the Constitution* (New York: St. Martin's Press, 1965); Wood, *Creation of the American Republic.*

19. Quoted in Wood, *Creation of the American Republic,* p. 473.

20. Ibid., p. 432.

21. Ellis, *Founding Brothers,* p. 110.

22. Max Farrand, *The Records of the Federal Convention of 1787* (New Haven, CT: Yale University Press, 1937).

23. "The Invention of Centralized Federalism," in William H. Riker, ed., *The Development of Centralized Federalism* (Boston: Kluwer Academic, 1987).

24. Robert A. Dahl, "On Removing the Impediments to Democracy in the United States," *Political Science Quarterly,* 92 (Spring 1977), p. 5.

25. Hamilton, Madison, and Jay, *The Federalist Papers,* No. 51.

26. Thomas Jefferson, *Notes on the State of Virginia,* ed. Thomas Perkins Abernathy (New York: Harper & Row, 1964), p. 120.

27. See Main, *The Anti-Federalists;* Wood, *Creation of the American Republic;* Smith, *Shaping of America,* p. 99; Herbert Storing, *What the Anti-Federalists Were For* (Chicago: University of Chicago Press, 1981), p. 71.

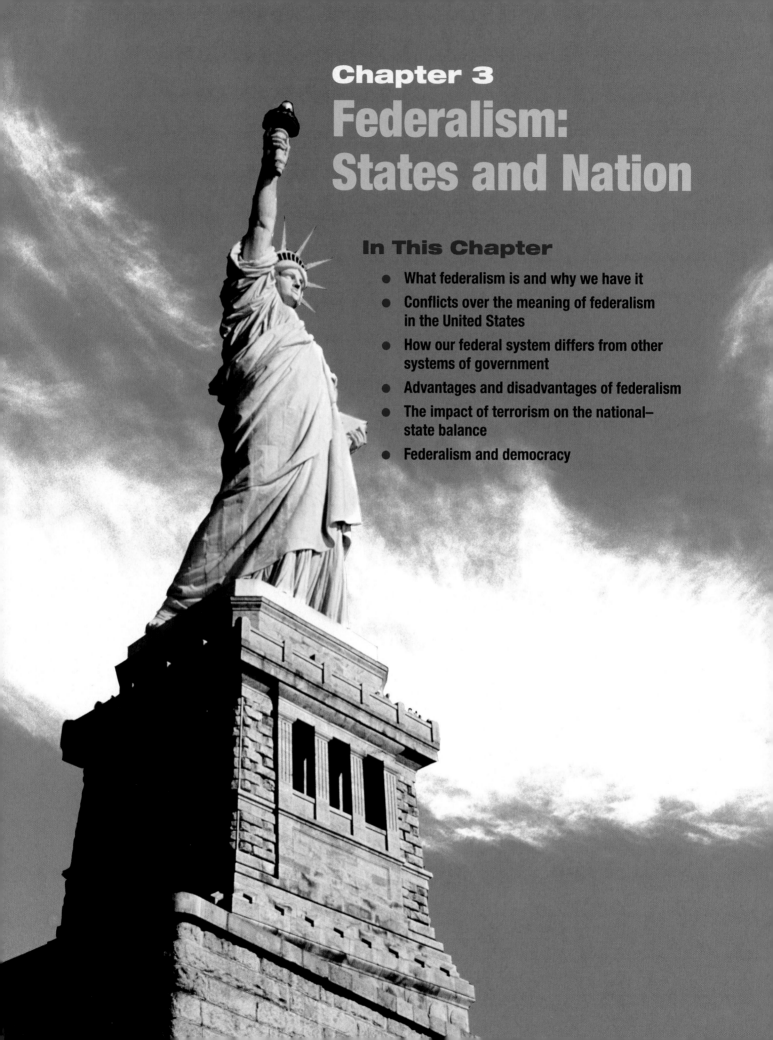

Chapter 3
Federalism: States and Nation

In This Chapter

- What federalism is and why we have it
- Conflicts over the meaning of federalism in the United States
- How our federal system differs from other systems of government
- Advantages and disadvantages of federalism
- The impact of terrorism on the national–state balance
- Federalism and democracy

Welfare Reform and the States

Bill Clinton and many Republican and Democratic members of Congress promised to "end welfare as we know it." Long before Congress and the president could agree on a specific plan, however, many state governments—with special permission from Washington—took the lead in trying out their own welfare reforms. This interplay between national and state governments illustrates the dispersion of power in our federal system.

Under the Social Security Act of 1935, the U.S. government established Aid to Families with Dependent Children (AFDC) as an entitlement program for children in poor families. The states administered the program, offering different levels of benefits from one state to another. But the national government, which provided most of the money, also made the rules about who was eligible, for how long, and under what circumstances. It guaranteed that any eligible family in the country would be entitled to benefits.

That pattern of national rule-setting began to change around the beginning of the 1990s. New, mostly Republican state governors and legislatures were elected, promising to reform welfare by encouraging work and parental responsibility. Pioneers such as Republican Governor Tommy G. Thompson of Wisconsin, who took office in 1987, came up with many different ideas: requiring efforts to find work; putting time limits on benefits; easing benefit reductions when recipients earned some money working; helping with training, day care, job placement, and community service jobs; requiring young mothers to live with their parents or other adults; paying bonuses for staying in school; and restricting payments for children born to mothers already on welfare.

The Bush administration and especially the Clinton administration granted many "waivers," exceptions to the national rules, so that states could experiment with these ideas. By 1995, 32 states had waivers, affecting about half the nation's 14 million welfare recipients. More than 30 states let recipients earn more and keep assets without losing benefits, 25 states required teenage mothers to live with adults; and more than 20 got waivers to require that welfare recipients find work or to help them do so.

Some of the results were impressive. In Wisconsin, for example, after Thompson took office and persuaded Washington to give him 179 waivers, the welfare rolls dropped by 27 percent and spending was cut by $210 million per year. The money that was poured into child care and job training seemed to pay off, saving about $2 in welfare costs for each $1 spent. Michigan, under Republican Governor John Engler, cut caseloads to the lowest point in 21 years, led the nation by steering 30 percent of its 190,000 welfare recipients into work, and saved about $100 million a year.[1]

Finally, in 1996, the president and Congress passed the Personal Responsibility and Work Opportunity Act, which made public welfare a state responsibility with federal financial support. The new law ended welfare as an entitlement program, limited recipients to no more than five years of benefits, and imposed work and work-training requirements. Within these general guidelines, states are allowed wide latitude in creating their own welfare programs. Some states remain more generous than others. California, for example, allows recipients to stay on the rolls for five years, provides some benefits for children (using state, not federal, funds) beyond the five-year limit, and only weakly sanctions (with loss of some benefits) individuals who refuse to work or train for work. Florida, by contrast, limits adult recipients to four years, is less generous to children beyond the five-year limit, and cuts off aid to the entire family if the adult fails to comply with work requirements.[2] It remains to be seen what the eventual political and social fallout will be in the states as more and more people use up their welfare eligibility years, even as jobs are harder to get in times of slow economic growth or recession. ■

Thinking Critically About This Chapter

The mixture of state and national action on this issue, and the state experimentation that affected policymaking in the nation as a whole, is characteristic of American federalism. So, too, is the conflict between national standards and local flexibility.

Using the Framework In this chapter, you will learn how and why federalism is one of the most important structural factors that affect American politics and government and shape public policy. You will learn how federalism influences our entire system: from the kinds of political parties we have and the workings of Congress to how domestic programs are affected. You will also learn how federalism itself has changed over time.

Using the Democracy Standard Using the evaluative tools you learned in Chapter 1, you will be able to judge for yourself whether federalism enriches or diminishes democracy in the United States. ◄

Federalism as a System of Government

The United States is full of governments. We have not only a federal government in Washington, D.C. (which, to avoid confusion, we will refer to in this chapter as the *national* or *central* government), but also governments in each of 50 states and in each of thousands of smaller governmental units, such as counties (about 3,000 of them), cities, towns and townships, school districts, and special districts that deal with such matters as parks and sanitation.

All these governments are organized and related to each other in a particular way. The small governments—those of counties, cities, towns, and special districts—are legal creations of state governments. They can be created, changed, or abolished by state laws, at the state's convenience. But state governments themselves have much more weight and permanence because of their prominent place in the Constitution. Together with the national government in Washington, D.C., they form what is known as a federal system. The *federal system* is part of the basic structure of U.S. government, deeply rooted in our Constitution and history. It is one of the most important features of American politics, since it affects practically everything else.

federalism

A system in which significant governmental powers are divided between a central government and smaller units, such as states.

confederation

A loose association of states or territorial divisions in which very little power is lodged in the central government.

The Nature of Federalism

Federalism is a system under which significant government powers are divided between the central government and smaller units, such as states. Neither one completely controls the other; each has some room for independent action. A federal system can be contrasted with two other types of government: a confederation and a unitary government. In a **confederation,** the constituent states get together for certain common purposes but retain ultimate

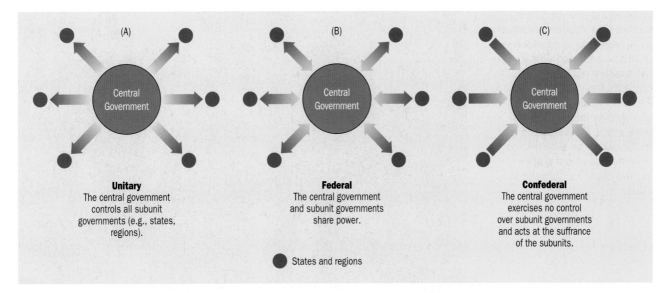

FIGURE 3.1 Types of Political Systems

A majority of countries have unitary systems (A), in which the central government controls the state and local governments, which in turn exert power over the citizens. The United States, however, has a federal system (B), in which the central government has power on some issues, while the states have power on others. In a confederation (C), the central institutions have only a loose coordinating role, with real governing power residing in the constituent states or units.

individual authority and can veto major central governmental actions. The United Nations, the European Union, and the American government under the Articles of Confederation are examples. In a **unitary system,** the central government has all the power and can change its constituent units or tell them what to do. Japan and France have this kind of government. These three different types of governmental systems are contrasted in Figure 3.1.

unitary system

A system in which a central government has complete power over its constituent units or states.

The Roots of Federalism

Some of the elements of federalism go back in history at least as far as the Union of Utrecht in the Netherlands in 1579, but federalism as it exists today is largely an American invention.[3]

Historical Origins   American federalism emerged from the particular way in which the states declared independence from Britain—becoming, in effect, separate countries—and then joined together to form a confederation and then a single nation, as discussed in Chapter 2. Recall that the framers of the Constitution turned to federalism as a middle-ground solution between a confederation form of government—which was deemed a failed model based on the experience of the United States under the Articles of Confederation—and a unitary form of government, which a majority of states, jealous of their independence and prerogatives, found unacceptable. But we can gain further insight into *why* the United States adopted and has continued as a federal system if we look at what other countries with similar systems have in common.

Role of Size and Diversity   Most federal systems around the world are found in countries that are geographically large and have regions that differ from one another in various important ways: economic activity, religion, ethnicity, and

Federations are not necessarily forever. The Yugoslav federation of republics, in which each republic was formed primarily on the basis of nationality, could not withstand the dramatic rise in ethnic tensions after the death of Yugoslav leader Marshall Tito. Here ethnic Serb soldiers and militia escort an elderly Croat from his basement shelter during the battle for Vukovar in 1991.

Longman
Participate.com
2.0
Comparative
**Comparing
State and
Local
Governments**

language. In Germany, for example, the conservative Catholics of the south have traditionally been different from the liberal Protestants of the north and east. In Canada, the farmers of the central plains are not much like the fishers of Nova Scotia, and the French-speaking (and primarily Catholic) residents of Quebec differ markedly from the mostly English-speaking Protestants of the rest of the country. Such diverse groups often want the local independence that federalism allows, rather than submitting to a unified central government.

The United States, too, is large and diverse. From the early days of the Republic, the slave-holding and agriculture-oriented South was quite distinct

Web Exploration
Regional Variation and Federalism

Issue: Federalism seems most appropriate where there is substantial variation among regions of a nation.

Site: You can examine how much variation exists in the United States by going to the *Statistical Abstracts of the United States* on our Website at **www.ablongman.com/greenberg**. In the "Web Explorations" section for Chapter 3, open "Regional Variation and Federalism," then open "states." Select "state rankings." Compare your own state with three or four others from different geographical regions of the United States on issues such as education, income, population growth, immigration, crime, and the like.

What You've Learned: Given the profile of your state compared with others, are the differences great enough to support the need for greater autonomy for your state government, or would national rule making and policies make more sense?

HINT: If the differences are significant, from your point of view, federalism would make a lot of sense. Religious differences seem especially important to many people.

from the merchant Northeast, and some important differences persist today. Illinois is not Louisiana; the farmers of Iowa differ from defense and electronics workers in California. States today also vary from one another in their approaches to public policy, their racial and ethnic composition, and their political cultures.[4] In *The Federalist Papers,* the Founders argued that this size and diversity made federalism especially appropriate for the new United States.

Federalism in the Constitution

Federalism is embodied in the U.S. Constitution in two main ways: (1) power is expressly given to the states, as well as to the national government, and (2) the states have important roles in shaping, and choosing officials for, the national government itself.

Independent State Powers

Although the Constitution makes the central government supreme in certain matters, it also makes clear that the state governments have independent powers. The **supremacy clause** in Article VI states that the Constitution, laws, and treaties of the United States shall be the "supreme law of the land," but Article I, Section 8, enumerates what kinds of laws Congress has the power to pass, and the Tenth Amendment declares that the powers not delegated to the central government by the Constitution or prohibited by the Constitution to the states are *"reserved to the states* [emphasis added] respectively, or to the people." This provision is known as the **reservation clause.**

In other words, the U.S. Constitution specifically lists what the national government can do. Its powers include authority to levy taxes, regulate interstate commerce, establish post offices, and declare war, plus make laws "necessary and proper" for carrying out those powers. The Constitution then provides that all other legitimate government functions may be performed by the states, except for a few things, such as coining money or conducting foreign policy, that are forbidden by Article I, Section 10. The reservation clause is unique to the United States. Other federal systems, such as Canada's and Germany's, reserve to the national government all functions not explicitly given to the states. The Constitution is, thus, not crystal clear on the balance of powers and responsibilities between the state and national governments, leaving ample room for the meaning of federalism to change with the times.

supremacy clause

The provision in Article VI of the Constitution that the Constitution itself and the laws and treaties of the United States are the supreme law of the land, taking precedence over state laws and constitutions.

reservation clause

The Tenth Amendment to the Constitution, reserving powers to the states or the people.

Longman
Participate.com
2.0
Participation
Explore Your State Constitution

The States' Roles in National Government

Moreover, the Constitution's provisions about the formation of the national government recognize a special position for the states. The Constitution declares in Article VII that it was "done in Convention by the unanimous consent of the *states* present" (emphasis added) and provides that the Constitution would go into effect not when a majority of all Americans voted for it but when the conventions of nine *states* ratified it. Article V provides that the Constitution can be amended only when conventions in or the legislatures of three-quarters of the states ratify an amendment. Article IV, Section 3, makes clear that no states can be combined or divided into new states without the consent of the state legislatures concerned. Thus, the state governments have charge of ratifying and amending the Constitution, and the states control their own boundaries.

The Constitution also provides special roles for the states in the selection of national government officials. The states decide who can vote for members of

By the Numbers

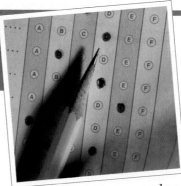

How do we know how many people there are in each of the states?

Utah officials were angry. Convinced that the counting method used for the 2000 census had undercounted the number of people residing in the state, thereby "robbing" them of a congressional seat, they sued the U.S. Census Bureau.

How can something as simple as counting people become so controversial? And why are these census figures so important to states, anyway?

Why It Matters: The Constitution specifies that every ten years, a census will be taken of the population of the United States. One purpose of the census is to determine how the finite number of seats in the House of Representatives (435) will be divided among the states, based on the size of their populations. A state's population also determines how much federal money (for example, highway money) it will get. Moreover, counts of certain categories of people, like the poor, determine how much aid (for example, Medicaid) the state will receive.

The Story Behind the Number: For most of our nation's history, the Census Bureau hired people to go door-to-door all across the United States—from isolated farms to packed apartment buildings—to conduct a direct count of the population. Many people were missed in this process. Some were not home when the census takers came by; others lived in high crime neighborhoods where census takers did not want to venture; and some had no home other than a crude shelter under a highway overpass. Recent immigrants had trouble communicating in English, and illegal aliens did not necessarily want to be found by census takers.

Indeed, the undercounted population in every recent census has been comprised mainly of racial minorities, recent immigrants, the homeless, and the undocumented. This pattern has generated complaints from a wide range of people and organizations: advocates of the poor who want more federal government monies directed to the problem of poverty in each state; civil rights organizations that believe that racial minorities are under-represented in the House of Representatives; and Democratic Party politicians who believe that a more accurate count would benefit their party (the assumption being that lower income people, racial minorities, and recent immigrants tend to vote for Democrats).

In an attempt to remedy these undercount problems, the Census Bureau wanted to use "statistical sampling" of the population to fill in the gaps. However, the Supreme Court ruled in 1999 that the Bureau could not do so for purposes of reapportioning congressional seats, and President Bush announced that sampling could not be used to determine how much federal money the states would get. As an alternative, the Bureau has increasingly relied on a statistical procedure called "imputing."

Calculating Population Size and Characteristics:

Though Census Bureau statisticians have been using "imputing" in limited ways since the 1940s to fill in the gaps left by the inevitable undercounting, they relied much more on it for the 2000 census. In imputing, estimates are made about the characteristics of people living in a household where the Bureau has been unable to collect information. The estimates are based on what their neighbors are like (whether they are poor or rich, white or African-American, and so on).

the U.S. House of Representatives (Article I, Section 2). Each state is given two senators (Article V) who were, until 1913, to be chosen by the state legislatures rather than by the voters (Article I, Section 3; altered by the Seventeenth Amendment). And the states play a key part in the complicated electoral college system of choosing a president in which each state has votes equal to the number of its senators and representatives combined, with the president elected by a majority of *electoral* votes, not a majority of popular votes (Article II, Section 1). (See "By the Numbers: How do we know how many people there are in each of the states?" to learn how state populations are determined,

In the 2000 census, using imputing, almost 6 million people who had not actually been counted were included in the nation's population total. In some states, most notably in those with large numbers of racial minorities and immigrants (including California, Arizona, New Mexico, and Texas), more than 3 percent of the state's total population was imputed.

This brings us back to the state of Utah. Utah's suit claimed that the Census Bureau had illegally imputed tens of thousands of additional people to the state of North Carolina, resulting in North Carolina receiving the congressional seat that properly should have gone to Utah. Unfortunately for Utah, the Supreme Court approved imputing in 2002.

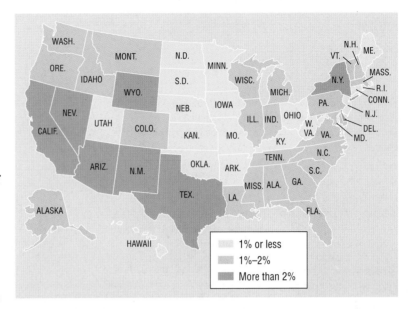

Percentage of People Imputed by the U.S. Census Bureau in Its Population Totals, by State

Source: *The Wall Street Journal,* August 30, 2001.

Imputing Criticized: Though most statisticians believe that imputing is a reasonable way to solve the problem of undercounting, the technique has its critics:

- The Utah suit claimed, and others agree, that imputing—much like more standard sampling—makes statistical inferences about parts of the population rather than counting people directly, as implied by the wording in the Constitution (Article I, Section 2).
- Imputing assumes that neighborhoods are homogenous; it is based on the assumption that a household's characteristics can be estimated from the characteristics of its neighbors. Members of several minority groups who tend to live in less segregated circumstances—Asians and Pacific Islanders, for example—may find themselves undercounted.

What to Watch For: Official statistics are often published in both "adjusted" and "unadjusted" forms. "Adjusted" means that the raw information has been corrected in one way or another. Usually, the reasons for doing so are very reasonable and defensible. You might want to look at the documentation that is associated with all government statistical information to learn how the numbers have been "adjusted."

What Do You Think? In your view, does it make sense to depend on the census for methods of enumerating that were fashioned by the framers of the Constitution? Is there a reason to keep to traditional methods? Or does the greater accuracy introduced by advances in statistical computing—either imputing or sampling—argue for a different method for conducting the census?

population being the basis for apportioning seats in the House of Representatives, electoral votes, and federal monies to the states.)

Relations Among the States

Article IV of the Constitution includes a few provisions that regulate relations among the states (see Table 3.1). For example, each state is required to give "full faith and credit" to the public acts, records, and judicial proceedings of every other state. This means, among other things, that contracts signed by

Longman
Participate.com
2.0
Visual Literacy
Explaining Differences in State Laws

TABLE 3.1 Constitutional Underpinnings of Federalism

Provisions	Where to Find Them in the Constitution	What They Mean
Supremacy of the national government in its own sphere	Supremacy clause: Article VI	The supremacy clause establishes that federal laws take precedence over state laws.
Limitations on national government powers and reservation of powers to the states	Enumerated national powers: Article I, Section 8; Limits on national powers: Article I, Section 9; Article IV, Section 3; Eleventh Amendment Bill of Rights: First through Tenth Amendments Reservation clause: Tenth Amendment	The powers of the federal government are laid out specifically in the Constitution, as are strict limitations on the power of the federal government. Powers not specifically spelled out are reserved to the states or the people.
Limitations on state powers	Original restrictions: Article I, Section 10 Civil War Amendments: Thirteenth through Fifteenth Amendments	The Constitution places strict limitations on the power of the states in particular areas.
State role in national government	Ratification of Constitution: Article VII Amendment of Constitution: Article V Election of representatives: Article I, Section 2 and Section 4 Two senators from each state: Article I, Section 3 No deprivation of state suffrage in Senate: Article V Choice of senators: Article I, Section 3 (however, see Seventeenth Amendment) Election of president: Article II, Section 1 (however, see Twelfth Amendment)	The states' role in national affairs is clearly laid out. Rules for voting and electing representatives, senators, and the president are defined so that state governments play a part.
Regulation of relations among states	Full faith and credit: Article IV, Section 1 Privileges and immunities: Article IV, Section 2	Constitutional rules ensure that the states must respect each other's legal actions

The states play a central role in the election of the president, who is selected for office not by popular vote but by the electoral college vote, assembled on a state-by-state basis. In the end, the disputed 2000 presidential election outcome depended on which candidate would win Florida's 25 electoral votes. Here election officials conduct a hand recount of ballots in Palm Beach County.

individuals or companies in one state must be honored by officials in other states and that decisions by the courts of one state must be recognized by the others. Under Article IV, moreover, the citizens of each state are entitled to all the "privileges and immunities" of the citizens in the several states. That means that whatever citizenship rights a person has in one state apply in the other states as well.

The Evolution of American Federalism

It took a long time after the adoption of the Constitution for the present federal system to emerge. There were ebbs and flows in the relative power of the states and the federal government. Eventually, however, the national government gained ground. There are many reasons why this happened.

- Economic crises and problems generated pressures on the government in Washington to do something to help fix the national economy. The Great Depression in the 1930s is the primary example, but even today, we expect the president, Congress, and the Federal Reserve to competently manage national economic affairs, something the states cannot do for themselves.

- War and the preparation for war are also important spurs to national-level actions, rather than state-level ones, for it is only the government in Washington that can raise an army and a navy, generate sufficient revenues to pay for military campaigns, and coordinate the productive resources of the nation to make sustained war possible. It is no accident, then, that each of our major wars has served to enhance the power of government in Washington: the Civil War, World Wars I and II, the Korean War, the Vietnam War, and the new war on terrorism.

- Finally, a number of problems emerged over the course of our history that most political leaders and the public believed could be solved most efficiently by the national government rather than by 50 separate state governments: air and water pollution; unsafe food, drugs, and consumer products; the denial of civil rights for racial minorities; anti-competitive practices by some large corporations; poverty; and more.

The Perpetual Debate About the Nature of American Federalism

From the very beginnings of our nation, two political philosophies have contended with one another over the nature of American federalism and the role to be played by the national government. These are generally referred to as the nationalist position and the states' rights position.

The Nationalist Position   Nationalists believe that the Constitution was formed by a compact among the people to create a single national community, pointing to the powerful phrase that opens the preamble: "We the People of the United States" (not "We the States"). Nationalists also point to the clear expression in the preamble of the purposes for which "we the people" formed a new government, namely to "create a more perfect union . . . and to promote the General Welfare." Also important in the nationalist brief are provisions in the Constitution that point toward a strong central government with expansive

nationalist position
The view of American federalism which holds that the Constitution created a system in which the national government is supreme, relative to the states, and that granted to it a broad range of powers and responsibilities.

How to control illegal immigration across the U.S.—Mexican border, and what to do about those who make it across, have become contentious issues between several states and the federal government.

necessary and proper clause

Article I, Section 8, of the Constitution, also known as the *elastic clause*; gives Congress the authority to make whatever laws are necessary and proper to carry out its enumerated responsibilities.

states' rights position

The view of American federalism which holds that the Constitution created a system of dual sovereignty in which the national government and the state governments are sovereign in their own spheres.

dual federalism

Federalism in which the powers of the states and the national government are neatly separated like the sections of a layer cake.

responsibilities, namely, the "supremacy clause " in Article VI and the "elastic" or **"necessary and proper" clause** in Article I, Section 8. Not surprisingly, proponents of the nationalist position have advocated an active national government with the capacity and the will to tackle whatever problems might emerge to threaten the peace and prosperity of the United States or the general welfare of its people. Alexander Hamilton, Chief Justice John Marshall, Abraham Lincoln, Woodrow Wilson, the two Roosevelts, and most modern liberals are generally associated with the nationalist position.

The States' Rights Position   Proponents of the states' rights position argue that the Constitution was created as a compact among the states and that the framers meant for the states to be coequal with the national government. They base their argument on a number of foundations. They note, for instance, that the Constitution was written by representatives of the states, that it was ratified by the states and not by a vote of the public, and that the process for amending the Constitution requires the affirmative votes of three-fourths of the states, not three-fourths of the people. They also point out that the Constitution mandates equal representation of states in the Senate and requires that the president be elected by the electoral votes of the states. States' rights proponents say that the prominent role of the states in our system of government is also indicated in Article IV, Section 3 (which says that states are inviolate), and in the Tenth Amendment (the "reservation" clause, discussed above).

Not surprisingly, proponents of the states' rights position have argued that the Constitution created a form of government in which the national government is strictly limited in size and responsibility and in which states retain broad autonomy in the conduct of their own affairs. Popular among states' rights proponents is the concept of **dual federalism,** which suggests that there are distinct, non-overlapping areas of responsibility for the national government and the state governments, and that each level of government is sovereign in its own sphere. Thomas Jefferson, John C. Calhoun, the New England and Southern secessionists, the southern resistors to the civil rights revolution, and many contemporary conservatives are associated with this view of federalism.

We shall see in the pages ahead that the nationalist view has prevailed over the long haul of American history (see Figure 3.2). However, the states' rights view has always been and remains today a vital position from which to oppose too much power and responsibility in the government in Washington.

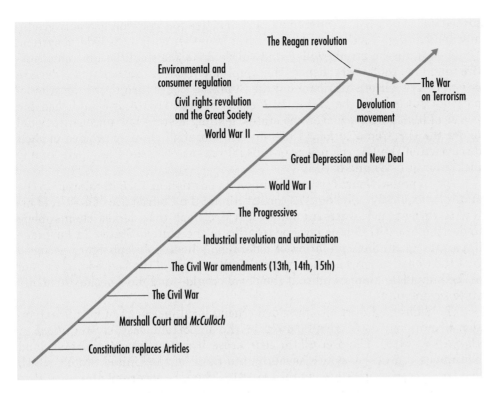

FIGURE 3.2 Landmarks on the Road of Rising Federal Power and Responsibilities

Over the course of American history, power and responsibilities in our federal system have flowed to the national government. The trend towards devolution that started in the late 1970s and 1980s may well be reversed by the events of September 11, 2001, and the subsequent war on terrorism.

Federalism Before the Civil War

In the late 1790s, during the administration of John Adams, Thomas Jefferson's Republicans deeply resented the Alien and Sedition Acts, which the Federalists used to punish political dissent by followers of Jefferson. In response, Jefferson and Madison secretly authored the Virginia and Kentucky Resolutions, which declared that the states did not have to obey unconstitutional national laws and left it to the states to decide what was unconstitutional. In this case, the Republicans, representing the more agricultural South, were advocating states' rights against a national government run by the more merchant-oriented Federalists of the Northeast. About a decade later, however, the merchants of New England used the southerners' own arguments to oppose President Madison's War of 1812 against Britain, which they felt interfered with their trade. Neither of these efforts at **nullification** prevailed. Nor did the later attempt by John C. Calhoun and other southern agriculturalists to declare null and void the "tariff of abominations," the 1833 national tariff that dramatically raised the prices of imports and hurt southern agricultural exports.

nullification

An attempt by states to declare national laws or actions null and void.

The Marshall Court One crucial question about federalism in the early years of the United States concerned who, if anyone, would enforce the supremacy clause. Who would make sure that the U.S. laws and Constitution were actually the "supreme law of the land," controlling state laws? The answer turned out to be the U.S. Supreme Court, but this answer emerged only gradually and haltingly as the Court established its power within the federal system.

Only after the strong-willed and subtle John Marshall became chief justice and, in 1803, established the Supreme Court's authority to declare *national* laws unconstitutional did the Supreme Court turn to the question of national power over the states. In *Fletcher* v. *Peck* (1810), it established the power of judicial review over the states, holding a state law unconstitutional under the U.S. Constitution.[5] Chief Justice Marshall cleverly avoided explicit discussion of the Court's power of judicial review over state laws. He simply took it for granted and used it.

The Supreme Court further solidified its position in 1816 in relation to the states by explicitly upholding as constitutional the Court's use of a "writ of error" to review (and overturn) state court decisions that denied claims made under the Constitution or laws or treaties of the United States. In language important to the interpretation of federalism, Justice Joseph Story declared that the Constitution was the creation of "the people of the United States," not of the individual states, and that the people could—and did—decide to modify state sovereignty.[6]

The Supreme Court also provided crucial legal justification for the expansion of national government power in the important case of *McCulloch* v. *Maryland* (1819). The *McCulloch* case arose because the state of Maryland had imposed a tax on notes issued by the Bank of the United States, which had been incorporated by Congress in 1816. The U.S. government argued that such a tax on a federal entity was invalid. Maryland replied that the incorporation of the bank had been unconstitutional, exceeding the powers of Congress, and that, in any case, the states could tax whatever they wanted within their own borders. But Chief Justice Marshall upheld the constitutionality of the bank's incorporation and its immunity from taxation, and in the process made a major statement justifying extensive national authority.[7]

In the Court's decision, Marshall declared that the Constitution emanated from the sovereign people. The people had made their national government supreme over all rivals within the sphere of its powers, and those powers must be construed generously if they were to be sufficient for the "various crises" of the age to come. Congress had the power to incorporate the bank under the clause of Article I, Section 8, authorizing Congress to make all laws "necessary and proper" for carrying into execution its named powers. Moreover, Maryland's tax was invalid because "the power to tax involves the power to destroy," which would defeat the national government's supremacy within its sphere. Justice Marshall's broad reading of the *necessary and proper* clause laid the foundation for an expansion of what the national government could do in the years ahead. He made it clear that states would not be allowed to interfere.

The Slavery Issue   In the second decade of the nineteenth century, the issue of slavery in the western territories began to dominate disputes about the nature of federalism. As new, nonslave states were settled and sought to join the Union, white southerners feared that their political power in Washington, D.C. (especially in the Senate)—and therefore their ability to protect their own slave system—was slipping away.

The Missouri Compromise of 1820 established an equal number of slave and free states and banned slavery in the territories above a line running westward to the Rockies from Missouri's southern border. But the acquisition of vast new territories in the Southwest through the Mexican War reopened the question of whether new states would be slave or free. The Compromise of 1850 admitted California as a free state and temporarily balanced matters (in white southerners' eyes) by enacting the Fugitive Slave Act, which compelled private citizens in the North to help return runaway slaves—legislation that many northerners bitterly resented. The 1854 decision to organize Kansas and Nebraska as territories and let them decide for themselves whether to become slave or free states (even though they were above the Missouri Compromise line and therefore supposed to be free) led to violence between pro- and anti-slavery forces in "bleeding Kansas."

In 1860, the northern and southern wings of the Democratic party split apart over the slavery issue. The old Whig party was destroyed by the issue, and the candidate of the newly formed Republican party, Abraham Lincoln (who opposed slavery in the western territories), was elected president. South Carolina seceded from the Union, soon followed by the other six states of the Deep South, and they all banded together to form the Confederate States of America. When President Lincoln decided to relieve the besieged U.S. garrison at Fort Sumter, South Carolina, the Civil War began.

The Civil War and the Expansion of National Power

The Civil War had profound effects on the relationship between the states and the national government.

Indissoluble Union The complete northern victory and unconditional southern surrender in the Civil War decisively established that the Union was indissoluble; states could not withdraw or secede. Hardly any American now questions the permanence of the Union.

Constitutional Amendments The Civil War also resulted in constitutional changes that subordinated the states to certain new national standards, enforced by the central government. The Thirteenth Amendment abolished slavery, and the Fifteenth gave former male slaves a constitutional right to vote. (This right was enforced by the national government for a short time after the Civil War; it was then widely ignored until the 1965 Voting Rights Act.)

The Fourteenth Amendment (1868) included broad language going well beyond the slave issue: It declared that *no state* shall "deprive any person of life, liberty, or property, without due process of law; nor deny to any person within its jurisdiction the equal protection of the laws." The **due process clause** eventually became the vehicle by which the Supreme Court ruled that many civil liberties in the Bill of Rights, which originally protected people only against the national government, also provided protections against the states. And the **equal protection clause** was eventually made the foundation for protecting the rights of blacks, women, and other categories of people against discrimination by state or local governments. (These matters are discussed in Chapters 15 and 16.)

due process clause

The section of the Fourteenth Amendment that prohibits states from depriving anyone of life, liberty, or property "without due process of law," a guarantee against arbitrary or unfair government action.

equal protection clause

The section of the Fourteenth Amendment that provides equal protection of the laws to all citizens.

Expanded National Activity Since the Civil War

Since the Civil War, and especially during the twentieth century, the activities of the national government expanded greatly, so that they now touch on almost every aspect of daily life and are thoroughly entangled with state government activities.

The Late Nineteenth Century to World War I During the late nineteenth century, the national government was increasingly active in administering western lands, subsidizing economic development (granting railroads enormous tracts of land along their transcontinental lines), helping farmers, and beginning to regulate business, particularly through the Interstate Commerce Act of 1887 and the Sherman Antitrust Act of 1890. The national government became still more active with Woodrow Wilson's New Freedom domestic legislation in 1913 and 1914, and with the great economic and military effort of World War I. During that war, for example, the War Industries Board engaged in a form of economic planning whose orders and regulations covered a substantial number of the nation's manufacturing firms.

The New Deal and World War II Still more important, however, was Franklin Roosevelt's New Deal of the 1930s. In response to the Great Depression, the New Deal created many new national regulatory agencies to supervise various aspects of business, including communications (the Federal Communications Commission, or FCC), airlines (the Civil Aeronautics Board, or CAB), financial markets (the Securities and Exchange Commission, or SEC), utilities (the Federal Power Commission, or FPC), and labor-management relations (the National Labor Relations Board, or NLRB). The New Deal also brought national government spending to such areas as welfare and relief, which had previously been reserved almost entirely to the states, and established the Social Security pension system.

World War II involved a total economic and military mobilization to fight Germany and Japan. Not surprisingly, directing that mobilization, as well as collecting taxes to support it, planning for production of war materials, and bringing on board the employees to accomplish all of this, was centered in Washington, D.C., not in the states.

The Post-War Period Ever since World War II, the federal government has spent nearly twice as much per year as all of the states and localities put together. Much of the money has gone in direct payments to individuals (through such items as Social Security benefits), and for national defense,

The Works Project Administration (WPA), created by Franklin Roosevelt as part of the New Deal, put many unemployed Americans to work on federal building projects during the Great Depression.

especially during the height of the Cold War and during the years of the Vietnam conflict.

Two other trends in the last third of the twentieth century enhanced the role of the national government relative to the states. The first was the civil rights revolution (discussed in Chapters 8 and 16), and the second was the regulatory revolution, especially regulation related to environmental protection (discussed in Chapter 17). With respect to both, national standards, often fashioned by bureaucrats under broad legislative mandates and watched over by federal courts, were imposed on both states and localities. The civil rights revolution also had a great deal to do with the creation of Lyndon Johnson's Great Society program designed both to alleviate poverty and politically empower the poor and racial minorities. The Great Society not only increased the level of domestic spending, but also increased the federal role in the political lives of states and localities.

The Supreme Court's Support for Nationalism For several decades, beginning in the late nineteenth century, the U.S. Supreme Court resisted the growth in national government power to regulate business. In 1895, for example, it said that the Sherman Antitrust Act could not forbid monopolies in manufacturing, since manufacturing affected interstate commerce only "indirectly." In 1918, the Court struck down as unconstitutional a national law regulating child labor. During the 1930s, the Supreme Court declared unconstitutional such important New Deal measures as the National Recovery Act and the Agricultural Adjustment Act.[8]

Longman Participate.com 2.0

Timeline
Federalism and the Supreme Court

After 1937, perhaps chastened by President Roosevelt's attempt to enlarge the Supreme Court and appoint more friendly justices, the Court became a nationalizing force, immediately upholding essential elements of the New Deal, including the Social Security Act and the National Labor Relations Act. Since that time, and until quite recently, the Court has upheld virtually every piece of national legislation that has come before it.

An important example is the Civil Rights Act of 1964, which rests on a very broad interpretation of the Constitution's commerce clause. In the 1964 act, the national government asserted a power to forbid discrimination at lunch counters and other public accommodations on the grounds that they are engaged in interstate commerce: They serve food imported from out of state. State economies are so closely tied to each other that by this standard, practically every economic transaction everywhere affects interstate commerce and is therefore subject to national legislative power.

Resurgence of the States in the 1990s

During the 1990s, there were a number of indications that the states were becoming more important in the American federal system. First, the states accounted for an ever-increasing share of public spending in the United States, suggesting that they were becoming more active in providing the wide range of government services the public demands (see Figure 3.3). Second, the states accounted for an ever-increasing share of public employees in the United States; while state (and local) government employment grew during the 1990s, federal government employment shrank, suggesting that government service delivery was shifting to the states. Moreover, according to many scholars and political observers, state governments began to capture a rising share of the talented people who enter government service, both in elected office and in state bureaucracies.[9] None of this would have happened unless the states had become increasingly important as locations for policy innovations and delivery of government services.

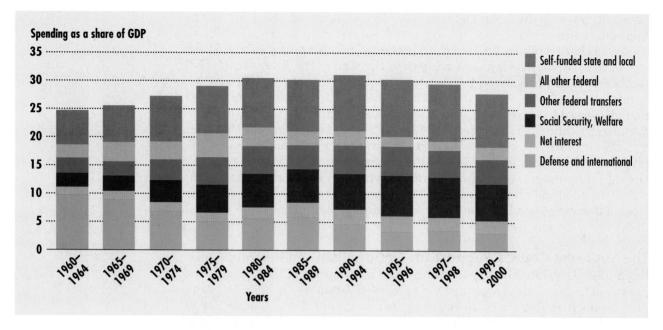

FIGURE 3.3 U.S. Public Spending, 1960–2000

A steadily increasing share of U.S. public spending is accounted for by state and local governments out of their own revenues. Most of the increase in government spending in recent years has been by the states, suggesting their increasingly important role in our federal system.

Source: Office of Management and Budget, Fiscal 2002 Budget, Historical Table 15.5.

devolution

The delegation of power by the central government to state or local bodies.

Longman
Participate.com
2.0
Simulation
**You Are a
Federal Judge**

What was behind the new vitality of the states within American federalism was the growing national consensus during the 1980s and 1990s about the virtues of **devolution.** Public opinion surveys, for example, showed that a substantial majority of Americans believed that state governments were more effective and more trustworthy than the government in Washington and more likely to be responsive to the people. And Americans said that they wanted state governments to do more and the federal government to do less.[10]

The Rehnquist Court has been especially enthusiastic about increasing the power of the states and decreasing that of the national government. It overruled a number of federal actions and laws on the ground that the federal government had exceeded its constitutional powers, reversing over half a century of decisions favoring an increased federal government role. In 1995, for example, the Court overturned federal legislation banning guns from the area around schools, and legislation requiring background checks for gun buyers, arguing that both represented too broad a use of the commerce power in the Constitution. The Court used similar language in 2000 when it invalidated part of the Violence Against Women Act and in 2001 when it did the same to the Americans with Disabilities Act. The Court also decided two cases in which it ruled that states could not be sued for violating federal rules and laws. It based the decision on a concept of "state sovereign immunity" that most constitutional scholars had never heard of and that considerably increased the autonomy of the states. In a 5-4 decision in the case *Federal Maritime Commission* v. *South Carolina* (2002), the court reaffirmed this controversial doctrine.

President Clinton was also an enthusiastic devotee of devolution, freely granting waivers from federal regulations to the states for experimenting with new forms of welfare, boasting of cuts in federal government employment, and touting the benefits of state government. And the Republican majority in the

104th Congress, working with President Clinton (but few from his party), passed legislation restricting "unfunded mandates" (about which we will have more to say later) and transferring welfare responsibility to the states.

Terrorism and the Resurgence of the Federal Government

The terrorist attacks of September 11, 2001, and the subsequent war on terrorism helped refocus the nation's attention on national leaders in Washington, D.C. As in all wartime situations during our country's history, war and the mobilization for war require centralized coordination and planning. This tendency toward nationalism during war will probably be further exaggerated by the perceived need for homeland security, with the national government in Washington playing a larger role in areas such as law enforcement, intelligence gathering, bank oversight (to track terrorist money), public health (to protect against possible bioterrorism), and more.

Changing American Federalism

Over the course of our history, there has been a perceptible shift of power and responsibility to the national government in Washington. We summarize that history in Figure 3.4. Imagine, if you will, a continuum of forms of government ranging from the pure unitary form on one end, to the pure confederational form at the other end, with the federal form as a midpoint between the two. We suggest that our original Constitution, though fundamentally federal in its design, was tilted slightly toward central government power. By 1980, we also suggest, the United States had shifted even further towards centralized government power. In the 1990s, states regained some lost ground. In all probability, the war on terrorism at home and abroad is likely to rekindle the long-term trend

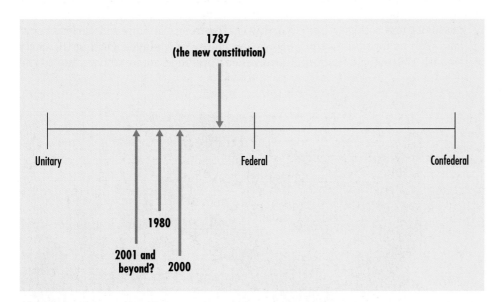

FIGURE 3.4 The Evolution of American Federalism

Over the years, American federalism has become more centralized in power and responsibilities, meaning that the nation has shifted slightly towards the unitary end of the Unitary–Confederal continuum. The war on terrorism may move the United States even further toward the unitary end.

towards national government preeminence. Note, however, that the 2001 arrow on the continuum is still placed well to the right of unitary government, suggesting that the states still play, and will continue to play, a very important role in the way Americans govern themselves.

"Marble Cake"   Today's federalism is very different from what it was in the 1790s or early 1800s. One major difference is that the national government is dominant in many policy areas; it calls many shots for the states. Another difference is that state and national government powers and activities have become deeply intertwined and entangled. The old, simple metaphor for federalism was a "layer cake": a system of *dual federalism* in which state and national powers were neatly divided into separate layers. If we stay with bakery images, a much more accurate metaphor for today's federalism is a "marble cake": a **cooperative federalism** in which elements of national and state influence swirl around each other, without very clear boundaries.[11] Much of this intertwining is due to financial links among the national and state governments, which we address in the next section.

cooperative federalism

Federalism in which the powers of the states and the national government are so intertwined that public policies can happen only if the two levels of government cooperate.

National Grants-in-Aid to the States

One of the most important elements in modern American federalism is the grant of money from the national government to state and local governments, which has been used to increase national government influence over what the states and localities do. These grants have grown from small beginnings to form a substantial part of government budgets.

Origin and Growth of Grants

National government grants to the states began at least as early as the 1787 Northwest Ordinance. The U.S. government granted land for government buildings, schools, and colleges in the Northwest Territory and imposed various regulations, such as forbidding the importation of any new slaves. During the early nineteenth century, the national government provided some land grants to the

Lyndon Johnson visits Job Corps sites. The Job Corps was part of Johnson's Great Society of the 1960s, which relied heavily on categorical grants to state and local governments.

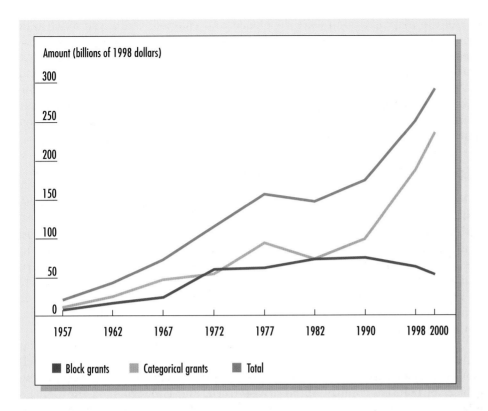

Amount (billions of 1998 dollars)

■ Block grants   ■ Categorical grants   ■ Total

FIGURE 3.5 The Growth of Federal Grants-in-Aid

Federal grants-in-aid to state and local governments grew sharply during the 1960s and peaked at the end of the 1970s. They then declined in the early 1980s during the Reagan administration but increased again in the 1990s.

Source: Budget of the United States, Fiscal Year 2001, Historical Table and U.S. Census Bureau, 2001.

states for roads, canals, and railroads, as well as a little cash for militias; after 1862, it helped establish agricultural colleges. Some small cash-grant programs were begun around 1900 for agriculture, vocational education, and highways.[12]

However, it was during the 1950s, 1960s, and 1970s, under both Republican and Democratic administrations, that federal grants to the states really took off. Such programs as President Dwight Eisenhower's interstate highway system and President Lyndon Johnson's Great Society poured money into the states.[13] After a downturn and a pause during the Carter and Reagan presidencies, grants began to increase again in the 1990s (see Figure 3.5). National grant money to the states increased because Congress sought to deal with many nationwide problems—especially interstate highways, poverty, crime, and pollution—by setting policy at the national level and providing money from national tax revenues while having state and local officials carry out the policies.

Categorical Grants

Many of the new programs were established through **categorical grants,** which give the states money but clearly specify the category of activity for which the money has to be spent and often define rather precisely how the program should work. For example, the Clean Air Act of 1970 and the Medicaid program of 1965 provided large amounts of money along with specific instructions on how to use it.

categorical grants

Federal aid to states and localities clearly specifying what the money can be used for.

As the new programs were developed and enacted, there was much talk about a new system of "cooperative" federalism. Soon, however, conflicts between the national and the state governments emerged. In some cases, when national rules and guidelines were vague, state and local governments used the money for purposes different from those Congress intended. When the rules were tightened up, some state and local governments complained about "red tape." And if state and local governments were bypassed, they complained that their authority had been undermined.

Block Grants and Revenue Sharing

block grants

Federal grants to the states to be used for general activities.

general revenue sharing

Federal aid to the states without any conditions on how the money is to be spent.

The Republican Nixon and Ford administrations eased national control, first instituting **block grants** (which give money for more general purposes and with fewer rules than categorical grant programs), then **general revenue sharing,** which distributed money to the states with no federal controls at all. President Nixon spoke of a "New Federalism" and pushed to increase these kinds of grants with few strings attached. They often provided money under an automatic formula related to the statistical characteristics of each state or locality, such as the number of needy residents, the total size of the population, or the average income level.

Disputes frequently arise when these formulas benefit one state or region rather than another. Because statistical counts by the census affect how much money the states and localities get, census counts themselves have become the subject of political conflict. Illinois, New York, and Chicago sued the Census Bureau for allegedly undercounting their populations, especially the urban poor, in the 1990 census.

grants-in-aid

Funds from the national government to state and local governments to help pay for programs created by the national government.

Block grants—and especially revenue sharing—reached a peak at the end of the 1970s, when they constituted about one-quarter of the total **grants-in-aid.** But then they fell out of favor. Increasing numbers of strings were attached to the money, and general revenue sharing was completely ended in 1987. Though block grants are still important, a good deal more of federal government money distributed to the states is in the form of categorical grants (see Figure 3.5).

Web Exploration
State-National Balance of Payments

Issue: Citizens in the states pay taxes to the federal government, and states receive back federal grants-in-aid to support a range of programs. Some states fare better in this process than others.

Site: Go to our Website at **www.ablongman.com/greenberg**. In the "Web Explorations" section for Chapter 3, open "State-National Balance of Payments," then open "taxes." Select Item 3 and look at state rankings, as well as the profile of your own state.

What You've Learned: Which states fare best in the exchange of funds between the states and the federal government? How does your own state fare? Why do you suppose that some states do better than others?

HINT: Relatively speaking, the poorest states get the most, meaning that a rough sort of regional redistribution is going on.

The states depend on federal aid, often based on formulas using census figures, to help them take care of the homeless. But when 2000 census takers failed to count a large number of homeless people, cities received less money in national grants.

Debates About Federal Money and Control

Most contemporary conflicts about federalism concern not just money but also control.

Conditions on Aid As we have seen, many categorical grant-in-aid programs require that the states spend federal money only in certain restricted ways. Increasingly, even general block grants have carried **conditions.** In theory, these conditions are "voluntary" because the states could refuse to accept the aid. But in practice, there is no clear line between incentives and coercion. Because the states cannot generally afford to give up federal money, they have to accept the conditions attached to it.

conditions

Provisions in federal assistance requiring that state and local governments follow certain policies in order to obtain federal funds.

Some of the most important provisions of the 1964 Civil Rights Act, for example, are those that declare that no federal aid of any kind can be used in ways that discriminate against people on grounds of race, gender, religion, or national origin. Thus, the enormous program of national aid for elementary and secondary education, which began in 1965, became a powerful lever for forcing schools to desegregate.

The national government uses its money to influence many diverse kinds of policies. During the energy crisis of the 1970s, all states were required to impose a 55-mile-per-hour speed limit or lose a portion of their highway assistance funds. The requirement was finally repealed in 1995. Similarly, in 1984, all states were required to set a minimum drinking age of 21 or have their highway aid cut by 15 percent.

Mandates The national government often imposes a **mandate,** or demand, that the states carry out certain policies even when little or no national government aid is offered. Mandates have been especially important in the areas of civil rights and the environment. Most civil rights policies flow from the equal protection clause of the Fourteenth Amendment to the U.S. Constitution or from national legislation that imposes uniform national standards. Most environmental regulations also come from the national government, since problems of dirty air, polluted water, and acid rain spill across state boundaries. Many civil rights and environmental regulations, therefore, are enforced by the federal courts.

mandate

A formal order from the national government that the states carry out certain policies.

Opposition to federal court-ordered busing—like this demonstration in Charlestown, Massachusetts—formed one element in a conservative turn in U.S. politics at the end of the 1970s.

Longman
Participate.com
2.0
Visual Literacy
Federalism
and
Regulations

Federal courts have, for example, mandated expensive reforms of over-crowded state prisons, most notably in Texas. National legislation and regulations have required state governments to provide costly special facilities for the disabled, to set up environmental protection agencies, and to limit the kinds and amounts of pollutants that can be discharged. The states often complain bitterly about federal mandates that require state spending without providing the money.

Cutting back on these "unfunded mandates" was one of the main promises in the Republicans' 1994 Contract with America.[14] The congressional Republicans delivered on their promise early in 1995 with a bill that had bipartisan support in Congress and that President Clinton signed into law. Because it does not apply to past mandates, however, and because it does not ban unfunded mandates but only regulates them (requiring cost-benefit analyses, for example), it is not yet clear how much effect the legislation will have.

U.S. Federalism: Pro and Con

Longman
Participate.com
2.0
Participation
Is Federalism
Dead and
Should It Be?

Over the years, from the framing of the U.S. Constitution to the present day, people have offered a number of strong arguments for and against federalism, in contrast to a more unitary system. Let us consider some of these arguments.

Pro: Diversity of Needs The oldest and most important argument in favor of decentralized government is that in a large and diverse country, needs and wants and conditions differ from one place to another. Why not let different states enact different policies to meet their own needs? (See the "Using the Framework" feature on why states can set their own tuition levels, including those for out-of-state students.)

Con: The Importance of National Standards However, the needs or desires that different states pursue may not be worthy ones. Political scientist William Riker has pointed out that, historically, one of the main effects of federalism was to let white majorities in the southern states enslave and then

USING THE FRAMEWORK: Out-of-State Tuition

I thought that attending a public university would save a lot of money, but it hasn't because I have to pay out-of-state tuition. Why do I have to pay so much money?

Background: All over the United States, students who choose to attend out-of-state public universities pay much higher tuition than state residents. Some educational reformers have suggested that the system be reformed so that students might attend public universities wherever they choose, without financial penalty. They have suggested that, over the long-haul and on average, such a reform would not have much impact on state budgets because students would randomly distribute themselves across state borders. Such proposals have never gotten very far. Taking a broad view of how structural, political linkage, and governmental factors affect this issue will help explain the situation.

Governmental Action

State legislatures decline to pass uniform tuition legislation.

Governmental Level

- Elected leaders → know that voters want access to low cost higher education for state residents.
- Elected leaders → are not subject to political pressures to change tuition policy.
- Elected leaders are concerned with short-term budget issues; high out-of-state tuition allows them to raise part of the higher education budget out of such revenues.

Political Linkages Level

- Voters in each state → insist on access for their children and the children of their neighbors to low-cost public higher education.
- There is little political → pressure on elected leaders within the states to lower or eliminate out-of-state tuition, whether from
  – Public opinion and voters.
  – Parties.
  – The mass media.
  – Interest groups.
  – Social movements.
- Out-of-state students rarely vote in the states where they go to school; politicians have no incentive to think seriously about their tuition concerns.

Structural Level

- The states are mainly responsible for education in our federal system; national tuition reform would require agreements among all the states.

discriminate against black people, without interference from the North.[15] Perhaps it is better, in some cases, to insist on national standards that apply everywhere.

Pro: Closeness to the People
It is sometimes claimed that state governments are closer to the ordinary citizens, who have a better chance to know their officials, to be aware of what they are doing, to contact them, and to hold them responsible for what they do.

Con: Low Visibility and Lack of Popular Control
However, others respond that geographic closeness may not be the real issue. More Americans are better informed about the *national* government than they are about state governments, and more people participate in national than in state elections. When more people know what the government is doing and more people vote, they are better able to insist that the government do what they want. For that reason, responsiveness to ordinary citizens may actually be greater in national government.

Pro: Innovation and Experimentation
When the states have independent power, they can try out new ideas. Individual states can be "laboratories." If the experiments work, other states or the nation as a whole can adopt their ideas, as has happened on such issues as allowing women and 18-year-olds to vote, fighting air pollution, reforming welfare, and dealing with water pollution.[16]

Likewise, when the national government is controlled by one political party, federalism allows the states with majorities favoring a different party to compensate by enacting different policies. This aspect of diversity in policy-making is related to the Founders' contention that tyranny is less likely when government's power is dispersed. Multiple governments reduce the risks of bad policy or the blockage of the popular will; if things go wrong at one governmental level, they may go right at another.

Con: Spillover Effects and Competition
Diversity and experimentation in policies, however, may not always be good. Divergent regulations can cause bad effects that spill over from one state to another. When factories in

Industrial pollution—here toxic metals seep into the soil and groundwater at an abandoned industrial site—often affects the people of more than one state and requires the participation of the national government to clean up the mess and prevent recurrences.

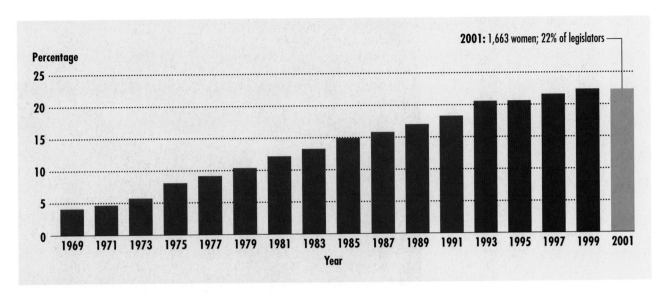

FIGURE 3.6 Women Legislators in the United States, 2001

There has been a steady increase in the number of women legislators in the United States over the past three decades or so. Wide variations exist among the states, however, on what proportion of their legislatures are made up of women.

Source: National Conference of State Legislators, 2001.

the Midwest spew out oxides of nitrogen and sulfur that fall as acid rain in the Northeast, the northeastern states can do nothing about it. Only nationwide rules can solve such problems. Similarly, it is very difficult for cities or local communities in the states to do much about poverty or other social problems. If a city raises taxes to pay for social programs, businesses and the wealthy may move out of town, and the poor may move in, impoverishing the city.[17]

Pro: Training Ground for Women and Racial Minorities It is often in politics at the local and state levels that talented women and minority group members have been identified, recruited, and trained for public office (see Figure 3.6). And it is frequently their performance on the job and the visibility provided by state and local offices that launches women and minorities into national politics. Former Congresswoman Barbara Jordan, an African-American, made her start in Texas politics. Senator Carol Moseley-Braun was a player in Illinois politics before she made her successful run for the Senate (she lost her bid for a second term, however). Loretta Sanchez was active in Orange County, California, politics before she won a seat in Congress in 1996. J. C. Watts (R–OK), an African-American, was elected Oklahoma Corporation Counsel before he won election to the House of Representatives.

What Sort of Federalism?

As the pros and cons indicate, a lot is at stake. It is not likely, however, that Americans will ever have a chance to vote yes or no on the federal system or to choose a unitary government instead. What we can decide is exactly *what sort* of federalism we will have—how much power will go to the states and how much will remain with the national government. Indeed, we may want a fluid system in which the balance of power varies from one kind of policy to another.

The balance of power between states and nation has been a very hot issue in recent years, with most Republicans favoring increasing the power of

A shift of power and responsibility from the federal level to the state level, given low voting turnout in state and local elections, may mean a decrease in the quality of American democracy.

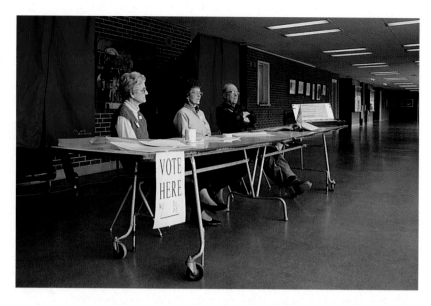

HOW DEMOCRATIC ARE WE?
Federalism, Majority Rule, and Political Equality

PROPOSITION: Federalism undermines democracy by getting in the way of majority rule and political equality.

AGREE: Federalism adds complexity to policy-making and makes it difficult for citizens to know which elected leaders to hold responsible for government actions. Also, citizens are much less informed about what goes on in state governments where many important policies are made. In state-level politics, popular participation tends to be lower, politics tends to be less visible, and interest groups may have an easier time getting their way. Because the well organized and the affluent have extra influence, political equality is impaired.

DISAGREE: Federalism promotes popular democracy rather than undermining it. It does so by allowing a majority of citizens in each state to exercise control over a range of policies that directly affect them. This is especially important in a country where the populations of the states vary as widely as they do. With diverse populations, with their diverse needs and interests, federalism allows for diverse policies.

THE AUTHORS: On balance, federalism has served the intentions of the framers by toning down the influence of democracy in determining what the national government does, while maintaining popular consent. There are four ways that federalism constrains democracy. First, many policy areas (such as education) are mainly the responsibility of the states, where policymakers are insulated from national majorities. Second, small-population states play a decisive role in the constitutional amending process. Third, small and large states have equal representation in the Senate, meaning that senators representing a minority of the population can block actions favored by senators representing the majority. Fourth and finally, state politics are much less visible to the public and are especially vulnerable to the influence of special interests. This may well be changing, however; as state governments do more, the media and the public are more likely to pay closer attention in the future.

state governments and Democrats favoring retention of national government programs and standards. Over the long term of American history, of course, the nationalist position on federalism rather than the states' rights position has generally prevailed. While some devolution of governmental power occurred in the 1990s, the terrorist attacks on the United States in 2001 and the subsequent war on terrorism may have tilted the balance once again toward the center.

It is important to keep in mind that arguments about federalism do not concern just abstract theories; they affect who wins and who loses valuable benefits. People's opinions about federalism often depend on their interests, their ideologies, and the kinds of things they want government to do.

Summary

Longman
Participate.com
2.0
Comparative
Comparing
Federal and
Unitary
Systems

Federalism, a system under which political powers are divided between the state and national governments, is a key structural aspect of American politics. Federalism is most frequently found in large, diverse countries. Arguments in favor of federalism have to do with diversity of needs, closeness to the people, experimentation, and innovation. Arguments against federalism involve national standards, popular control, and needs for uniformity.

The U.S. Constitution specifies the powers of the national government and reserves all others (except a few that are specifically forbidden) to the states. The Constitution also provides special roles for the states in adopting and amending the Constitution and in choosing national officials. The precise balance of federalism has evolved over time, with the national government gaining ground as a result of U.S. Supreme Court decisions, the Civil War, expanding national domestic programs, two world wars, and the war against terrorism.

Contemporary federalism involves complex "marble cake" relations among the national and state governments, in which federal grants-in-aid play an important part. Grants for many purposes grew rapidly for a time but have now slowed down. The national government also influences or controls many state policies through mandates and through conditions placed on aid. Federalism has mixed implications for democracy.

Suggestions for Further Reading

Donahue, John D. *Disunited States.* New York: Basic Books, 1997.
   Examines the new vitality of the states in the federal system and raises questions about the costs and benefits of the transformation.

Grodzins, Morton. *The American System.* New Brunswick, NJ: Transaction Books, 1983.
   A classic work that describes and approves of a complex intermingling of national, state, and local government functions.

Hero, Rodney E. *Faces of Inequality: Social Diversity in American Politics.* New York: Oxford University Press, 1998.
   An impressive argument with strong empirical evidence that the racial composition of states matters for patterns of state politics.

Peterson, Paul E. *The Price of Federalism.* Washington, D.C.: Brookings Institution, 1995.
   Describes modern federalism and argues that the national government is best at redistributive programs, while the states and localities are best at economic development.

Riker, William H. *The Development of American Federalism.* Boston: Kluwer Academic, 1987.
>   *An influential discussion of what American federalism is and how it came about.*

Walker, David B. *The Rebirth of Federalism,* 2nd ed. New York: Chatham House/Seven Bridges Press, 2000.
>   *Examination of the revitalization of the states and why it has happened.*

Internet Sources

Assessing the New Federalism   **http://newfederalism.urban.org/**
>   *News, essays, and research on the New Federalism and devolution.*

National Center for State Courts   **www.ncsconline.org**
>   *Links to the home pages of the court systems of each of the states.*

National Conference of State Legislatures   **http://www.ncsl.org**
>   *Information about state governments and federal relations, including the distribution of federal revenues and expenditures in the states.*

Publius   **http://ww2.lafayette.edu/~publius/**
>   *Home page of the leading academic journal on federalism.*

State Constitutions   **www.findlaw.com/**
>   *A site where the constitutions of all the states may be found.*

U.S. Federalism Site   **www.min.net/~kala/fed**
>   *As complete a site as one might wish for on the history, philosophy, law, and operation of federalism in the United States.*

Notes

1. "Michigan's Welfare System: Praise amid Warning Signs," *The New York Times* (October 24, 1995), pp. 1, 12; "Steps Taken on Michigan Welfare," *The New York Times* (November 1, 1995), p. 11.

2. Virginia Ellis, "Welfare Reform," *The Los Angeles Times* (August 22, 1997), p. 1. We examine the effects of welfare reform on the poor in Chapter 17.

3. William H. Riker, *The Development of American Federalism* (Boston: Kluwer Academic, 1987), pp. 56–60.

4. Rodney Hero, *Faces of Inequality: Social Diversity in American Politics* (New York: Oxford University Press, 1998).

5. Ibid., pp. 31–34.

6. *Martin* v. *Hunter's Lessee* (1816); see also ibid., pp. 39–42.

7. Robert G. McCloskey, *American Supreme Court,* 2nd ed., ed. Sanford Levinsonn (Chicago: University of Chicago Press, 1994), pp. 43–45.

8. McCloskey, *American Supreme Court,* pp. 97–100, 111–112.

9. Donahue, *Disunited States,* pp. 11–12.

10. Ibid., p. 13.

11. Morton Grodzins, *The American System* (New Brunswick, NJ: Transaction Books, 1983).

12. David B. Walker, *Toward a Functioning Federalism* (Cambridge, MA: Winthrop, 1981), pp. 60–63.

13. Paul E. Peterson, Barry G. Rabe, and Kenneth Wong, *When Federalism Works* (Washington, D.C.: Brookings Institution, 1986), p. 2.

14. Ed Gillespie and Bob Schellhas, eds., *Contract with America: The Bold Plan by Rep. Newt Gingrich, Rep. Dick Armey and the House Republicans to Change the Nation* (New York: Random House, 1994), p. 125.

15. William H. Riker, *Federalism: Origin, Operation, Significance* (Boston: Little, Brown, 1964), ch. 6.

16. Jack Walker, "The Diffusion of Innovations Among the American States," *American Political Science Review,* 63 (1969), p. 883.

17. Paul E. Peterson, *City Limits* (Chicago: University of Chicago Press, 1981); Paul E. Peterson, *The Price of Federalism* (Washington, D.C.: Brookings Institution, 1995).

Chapter 4
The Structural Foundations of American Government and Politics

In This Chapter

- How population size, location, and diversity affect American politics

- How the free enterprise economy shapes American political life

- Income and wealth distribution, and why they matter

- How globalization affects the United States and its people

- What Americans believe about people, politics, government, and the economy

"B-1 Bob" Learns About His District

Bob Dornan and the political establishment were stunned. The nine-term Republican member of Congress from Orange County, California's 46th district had lost his House seat to political newcomer Democrat Loretta Sanchez by a mere 984 votes. Known widely as either "B-1 Bob," because of his staunch support for increased military spending, or "sound-bite Bob," because of the former talk-show host's tendency to attack immigrants, gays, feminists, and liberals with short, savage remarks, Dornan played on his traditional themes during the 1996 congressional election. This tactic had always worked in the past. He saw no reason to change his long-term strategy in his district, especially against an opponent who had lost her only previous try for elective office.

What Bob Dornan and others learned was that the 46th district, like many others in California and in other states, had experienced enormous demographic changes, and these changes were inevitably going to play themselves out in the political arena. A bastion of the white middle class for much of the post-war period, the district by the mid-1990s had become mostly working class and minority in composition. In fact, fully 50 percent of the district was Hispanic and 12 percent was Asian. The non-Hispanic whites who remained were mainly blue collar and service workers, having migrated to the southern suburbs of Los Angeles during the previous decade. Bob Dornan's oft-repeated campaign themes—increasing military spending, banning abortion, and bashing gays and immigrants—not only failed to resonate with people more concerned about jobs, crime, and education, but actively alienated the largest ethnic group in his district.

Loretta Sanchez understood the new math, even if Dornan did not. A former Republican and business consultant, she was also the daughter of Mexican immigrants to the United States and a former Head Start child. She switched her party affiliation because she was angry with the Republican Party, as were many other Hispanics, for sponsoring state ballot initiatives attacking affirmative action, bilingual education, and immigrant rights. A moderate

Republican turned moderate Democrat, she focused her door-to-door, low-budget campaign on issues more attuned to the interests of potential voters in her district, and spent precious campaign time attending festivities in the Hispanic and Asian communities. Striking back in a way that was typical of his previous campaigns, Dornan attacked Sanchez as "the champion of homosexuals."

Dornan's defeat in 1996—and again in 1998, this time by a landslide margin—was not only the product of the transformation of his district from a predominantly white middle-class one to a working-class and minority-dominated one, but of the general mobilization of the Hispanic vote, especially in California, but elsewhere as well.[1] Dornan was smart enough to read the numbers. He surely knew that his district was changing under his feet. But in previous elections, the Hispanic population had always voted in very low numbers. The Hispanic share of the electorate was always much lower than its share in the population. In recent years, however, the intense support by Governor Pete Wilson and other Republicans of what appeared to many to be anti-immigrant and antiminority initiatives galvanized Hispanics and pushed them into politics. In Southern California between 1992 and 1996, for example, Hispanic voter registration increased by almost 30 percent, and registered Hispanics came out to vote in higher numbers than before.

The results were felt all across the state. By the end of the decade, Hispanic representation in the California legislature had increased by 40 percent, two Hispanics in a row served as Speakers of the California state assembly, and two more Hispanics were added to the state's delegation in the U.S. House of Representatives.

The demographic changes described in this story that are transforming American politics are but the tip of the iceberg of politically relevant changes that are going on in the economy and society. Tracking these many changes, and examining how they are shaping American politics and what government does, is the focus of this chapter. ■

Thinking Critically About This Chapter

Using the Framework In this chapter, you will learn about the demographic characteristics of the American population (race, ethnicity, geographical location, occupation, income, and the like), the U.S. economy and how it is evolving and changing, and the American political culture. Together with the constitutional rules you learned about in previous chapters, you will see how these structural-level factors have a great deal to do with what issues dominate the political agenda, how political power is distributed in the population, and what ideas Americans bring to bear when grappling with complex public policy issues.

Using the Democratic Standard Popular sovereignty, political equality, and liberty require a supportive economic and social environment. These include (but are not confined to) such things as a well-educated population, a sizeable middle class with access to resources allowing its members to participate in public affairs, conditions of nondiscrimination against racial and ethnic minorities, and a culture that values and protects liberty. In this chapter you will learn whether or not such an environment exists. ◄

American Society: How It Has Changed and Why It Matters

Longman
Participate.com 2.0
Visual Literacy
**Understanding
Who We Are**

The typical American today is very different from the typical American of 1950, let alone 1790, when the first census was conducted. Where we live, how we work, our racial and ethnic composition, and our average age and standard of living have all changed substantially. Each change has influenced our political life.

Growing Diversity

Ours is an ethnically, religiously, and racially diverse society. The white European Protestants, black slaves, and Native Americans who made up the bulk of the U.S. population when the first census was taken in 1790 were joined by Catholic immigrants from Ireland and Germany in the 1840s and 1850s (see Figure 4.1). In the 1870s, Chinese migrated to America, drawn by jobs in railroad construction. Around the turn of the twentieth century, most emigration was from eastern, central, and southern Europe, with its many ethnic, linguistic, and religious groups. Today most emigration is from Asia and Latin America, with people from Mexico representing the largest single component. There has also been a significant increase in the number of immigrants from the Middle East and other locations with Muslim populations.

The rate of migration to the United States has accelerated in recent decades. If estimates of illegal entrants are included in the total, from 22 to 24 million people immigrated to the United States during the 1980s and 1990s, the highest total for any two consecutive decades in American history.[2] (See Figure 4.1.) As a result, the percentage of foreign-born people resident in the United States has almost tripled since 1970, reaching 28.4 million in 2000, slightly more than 10 percent of the population. Though the foreign-born population is concentrated in a handful of states—mainly California, New York, New Jersey, Florida, and Texas—and a handful of cities and localities—mainly Miami, New York, Los Angeles-Long Beach, Orange County, Oakland, and Houston—the presence of new immigrants is being felt almost everywhere in America, including the Midwest and the Deep South. In California, fully 25 percent of the population is foreign-born.

Although immigration is substantial, it is worth noting that, in a proportional sense, the number of immigrants to the United States today does not approach historical highs. Thus, immigration as a proportion of the total population was much higher between 1840 and 1920 (see Figure 4.1). For most people, of course, it is what has been happening recently that is most important to them, not historical comparisons.

Longman
Participate.com
2.0
Participation
The Debate Over Immigration

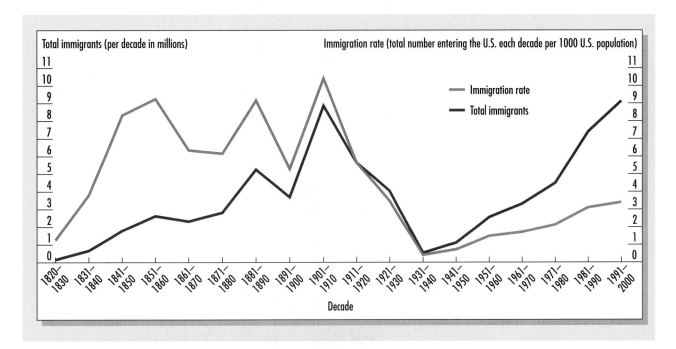

FIGURE 4.1 Immigration to the United States, by Decade

Measuring immigration to the United States in different ways gives rise to quite different interpretations of its scale. Measured in total numbers, the high points of immigration were the 1880s, the decade and a half after 1900, and the 1980s and 1990s. Measured in terms of the total U.S. population, however, immigration was an important factor in population change for much of the nineteenth century and the early part of the twentieth century, but not much after that. Recent immigration, relative to the total U.S. population, remains historically low, although it is on the rise.

Source: U.S. Bureau of the Census.

The natural outcome of this history is substantial racial and ethnic diversity in the American population. Though the U.S. is still overwhelmingly white (see Figure 4.2), its diversity is growing with every passing year. Most importantly, Hispanics (who can be of any race, with almost one-half of Hispanics categorizing themselves as white in Census Bureau surveys) have now reached population parity with non-Hispanic blacks—each group has slightly more than 35 million people out the U.S. total of almost 285 million—and should soon pass blacks, given higher rates of Hispanic birth rates and immigration to the United States.

The most recent wave of immigration, like all previous ones, has added to our rich linguistic, cultural, and religious traditions; it has also helped revitalize formerly poverty-stricken neighborhoods in cities such as Los Angeles, New York, and Chicago. But it has also generated political and social tensions. The arrival of immigrants who are different from the majority population in significant ways has often sparked anti-immigration agitation and demands that public officials stem the tide. **Nativist** (antiforeign) reactions to Irish Catholic migrants were common throughout the nineteenth century. Anti-Chinese agitation swept the western states in the 1870s and 1880s. Alarm at the arrival of waves of immigrants from eastern, southern, and central Europe in the early part of the last century led Congress virtually to close the doors of the United States in 1921 and keep them closed until the 1950s. Wars have also triggered hostile action against certain immigrant groups: German immigrants during World War I; Japanese Americans during World War II; and people from Middle Eastern and other Muslim countries after the September 11, 2001, terrorist attacks on the United States.

The current wave of Hispanic immigration has caused unease among some Americans. In 1994, for example, California voters approved Proposition 187, which barred welfare, health, and education benefits to illegal immigrants (the Proposition has since been declared unconstitutional by a federal

nativist

Antiforeign; applied to political movements active in the nineteenth century.

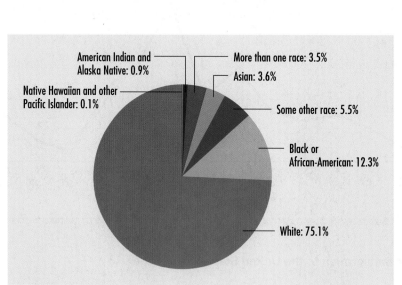

FIGURE 4.2 Racial Composition of the United States, 2000

The United States is a racially diverse society and is becoming more so every year. Whites remain a substantial majority, however, and will remain so for a long time, primarily because the Bureau of the Census classifies Hispanic origin as an ethnic rather than a racial category. Also, for the first time in 2000, the Census allowed people to identify themselves as belonging to more than one race.

Source: U.S. Bureau of the Census, 2001.

S. Kelly © 1995 *San Diego Union-Tribune*, Copley News Service.

district court). In 1998, California voters approved another proposition that banned bilingual education. In that same year, at the urging of Governor Pete Wilson, the Board of Regents ended affirmative action programs at the University of California.

Although waves of immigration often trigger an initial negative response from the native population (among all races and ethnic groups, it is important to add), politicians begin to pay attention to immigrant groups as more of their number become citizens and voters. Governor Pete Wilson of California used

Web Exploration

Immigration and Immigrants

Issue: Immigration, and what to do about it and its social consequences, has become a contentious issue in American politics.

Site: Find out what Americans want to do about immigration by going to Public Agenda On-Line. Access our Website at **www.ablongman.com/greenberg**. In the "Web Explorations" section for Chapter 4, select "Immigration and Immigrants," then "Immigrants." Under Issues, select "immigration." Then look at "people's chief concerns" and "major proposals."

What You've Learned: What are Americans most worried about when it comes to immigration? What do they want to do about it? As you look at each survey question, ask yourself what immigration policies you favor. Are your views in line with the majority of Americans, or are you an "outlier?"

HINT: Note that people seem to worry not about immigration, as such, but about illegal immigration. They strongly support policies, moreover, that rapidly assimilate immigrants, including a focus on learning English.

the anti-immigrant card as the defining theme of his effort to win the 1996 Republican presidential nomination. He not only failed to win the nomination, but his actions fueled the political mobilization of Hispanic voters in California that resulted in the loss of the legislature and the governorship to the Democratic Party, as well as the state's electoral votes in the 2000 presidential election (Gore won handily over Bush there). Today, candidates for statewide and national office in California avoid Wilson's mistake, knowing that about one-third of the state's population is Hispanic.

The growing importance of Hispanics in the United States is partly a reflection of sheer numbers and partly a reflection of their geographic concentration into states with very large blocs of electoral votes in presidential elections, including California, Texas, Florida, New Jersey, New York, and Illinois. George W. Bush has been especially conscious of the math of presidential elections and has made a number of important symbolic overtures to the Hispanic community: Hispanic cabinet appointments, weekly radio addresses in Spanish, and conspicuously warm relations with Mexican president Vicente Fox.

Though the doors to the United States have been relatively wide open for immigrants since the early 1970s, there is some evidence that these doors may be closing a bit in the wake of the terrorist attacks of 2001. A substantial majority of Americans now favors a decrease in the number of people allowed to immigrate to the United States and supports stronger efforts by the government to find and deport illegal immigrants.[3] The federal government has responded to the attacks in a number of ways that may also affect future immigration by making the United States either less attractive as a destination or a harder place to enter. For example, the government has increased the number of INS and military personnel assigned to protect American borders. It has also strengthened visa requirements for those wishing to visit the United States or study here, especially for people from Muslim countries.

Changing Location

Where the growing population of the United States is located also matters. Although we began as a country of rural farms and small towns, we rapidly became an urban people. By 1910, some 50 cities had populations of more than 100,000, and three (New York, Philadelphia, and Chicago) had more than 1 million. Urbanization, caused mainly by industrialization—the rise of large manufacturing firms required many industrial workers, while the mechanization of farming meant that fewer agricultural workers were needed—continued unabated until the mid-1940s. After World War II, a massive federal and state road-building program and government-guaranteed home loans for veterans started the process by which the United States became an overwhelmingly suburban nation (see Figure 4.3).

This shift in the location of the American population has had important political ramifications. The continued drain of population from rural areas, for instance, has diminished the power of the rural voice in state and national politics. For their part, some central cities, burdened with populations of the poor and the less well-to-do, find it difficult to provide the level of public services considered normal only a few years ago. Heavily dependent on the assistance of the federal government, poor central-city populations have become even more consistently Democratic in their voting preferences than in the past. Conversely, people living in the distant suburbs, mainly middle-class and working-class homeowners—who increasingly include among their number many members of minority and immigrant groups—have become less willing to support programs for central-city populations. They are more attuned to politicians who promise to pay attention to issues of traffic congestion and sprawl.

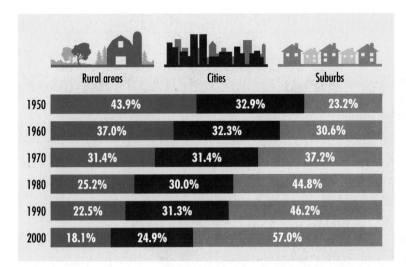

	Rural areas	Cities	Suburbs
1950	43.9%	32.9%	23.2%
1960	37.0%	32.3%	30.6%
1970	31.4%	31.4%	37.2%
1980	25.2%	30.0%	44.8%
1990	22.5%	31.3%	46.2%
2000	18.1%	24.9%	57.0%

FIGURE 4.3 Population Shift: From Rural to Urban to Suburban

In a relatively short period of time, the United States has changed from a society in which the largest percentage of the population lived in rural areas to one in which the largest percentage lives in suburbs. This development has produced several important changes in American politics and in the fortunes of our political parties.
Source: U.S. Bureau of the Census.

The U.S. population has also moved west and south over the course of time. The shift accelerated after World War II as people followed manufacturing jobs to these regions (many companies were attracted to the western and southern states because of their low taxes and anti-union policies). This population shift has led to changes in the relative political power of the states. Following each census from 1950 to 2000, states in the East and the upper Midwest lost congressional seats and presidential electoral votes. States in the West and the South—often referred to as the **Sun Belt** because of their generally pleasant weather—gained at their expense. Figure 4.4 shows the extent of change during the 1990s. Because a majority of Sun Belt states are more conservative than other states, their increasing importance in national politics may have contributed to Republican gains in Congress in the 1990s. (See "By the Numbers: Does population movement and change affect the electoral fortunes of the parties?" on pages 94–95 for more information on how population movement affects political change.)

Sun Belt

States of the Lower South, Southwest, and West, where sunny weather and often conservative politics prevail.

Changing Jobs and Occupations

At the time of the first census in 1790, almost three-quarters of all Americans worked in agriculture. Most of the remainder of the population worked in retail trade, transportation, and skilled trades closely connected to agriculture. About 80 percent of the working, male, nonslave population was self-employed, owning small farms, stores, wagons and horses, and workshops.[4]

The American occupational structure was radically transformed by the industrialization of the United States in the late nineteenth century (often called the **Industrial Revolution**). By 1910, the proportion of the labor force in agriculture had dropped to only 32 percent, and individuals working for others for wages and salaries had swelled to over 69 percent.[5] By 1940, the "typical" American was a skilled, semiskilled, or unskilled **blue-collar worker** in manufacturing.

Industrial Revolution

The period of transition from predominantly agricultural to predominantly industrial societies in the Western nations in the nineteenth century.

blue-collar worker

A skilled, semiskilled, or unskilled worker in industry.

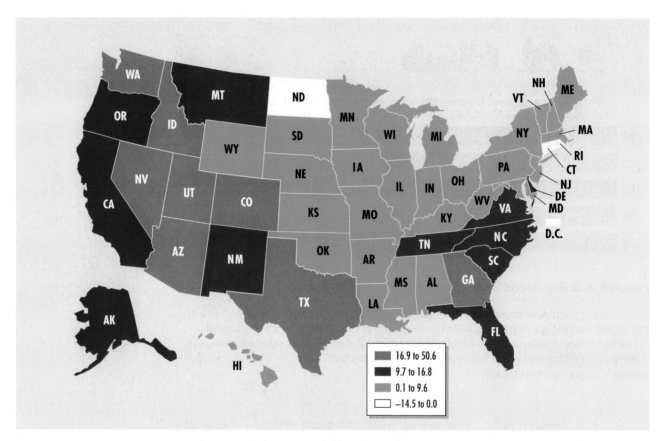

FIGURE 4.4 Percentage Population Change in the States Between
1990 and 2000

The U.S. Bureau of the Census reports that the relative population sizes of the states
changed substantially in the 1990s.
Source: U.S. Bureau of the Census.

white-collar worker

A person working at a service,
sales, or office job.

In 1950, the United States became the first nation in the world where
white-collar workers (in clerical, technical, professional, managerial, services, and sales jobs) were the majority. The recent decline of certain manufacturing industries, the disappearance of the small family farm, and the rapid
rise of the high-technology and information sectors accelerated the shift of employment from factory and farm to the office.

Occupational change matters a great deal in our politics. Displaced
workers, for example, often ask government to expand welfare and unemployment benefits, job retraining, and programs that encourage economic
development. The expansion of service, clerical, technical, and other kinds of
white-collar jobs has coincided, moreover, with a substantial expansion in
the number of gainfully employed female workers. The participation of
women in the paid workforce has passed 75 percent and is rapidly approach-
ing the participation rate of men. This massive entry by women into working
life outside the home has had enormous political consequences. For one
thing, paid work has improved women's income (although women still earn
only about three-quarters of what men earn) and has increased their influence and self-confidence in many spheres, including politics. These developments very likely contributed to the formation of the women's movement in
the late 1960s and early 1970s when women began to reenter the paid work-

Because fewer and fewer families can afford the luxury of having one parent stay home with the children, pressures on government for a longer school day and increased funding for day care are likely to increase.

force in a major way (see Chapter 8). Moreover, because women with young children are now working outside the home in unprecedented numbers—65 percent of married women with children under six years of age are in the paid workforce[6]—we might see strong pressures for government-funded child care and early education and for the extension of the school day.

The Aging of the American Population

One of the most significant demographic trends in the United States and in other industrialized countries is the aging of the population. In 1800, the median age in the United States was just under 16; today it is slightly more than 35, its highest level ever. By 2030, it will be about 38. The median age has been increasing because the proportion of the population over age 65 has been growing (though slower during the 1990s than in the 1980s), while the proportion between the ages of 18 and 44 has been shrinking. Today almost 13 percent of Americans are elderly. By 2030, this figure is projected to rise to about 20 percent. Meanwhile, the proportion of the population in the prime working years is likely to fall from 61.4 percent today to about 56.5 percent in 2030. The upshot is that an increasing proportion of Americans is likely to be out of the workforce and in need of services, and a shrinking proportion is likely to be taxpaying wage or salary earners. (It is worth pointing out that the aging of the American population is much less pronounced than in other rich democratic countries, primarily because of the high number of migrants here, many of whom are quite young.)

Because the population is slowly aging, how to finance Social Security and Medicare is likely to remain an important political question for the foreseeable future. The voting power of the elderly is likely to make it difficult for elected officials to substantially reduce social insurance programs for Americans over age 65 or to ignore demands for increased benefits such as prescription drug coverage. Meanwhile, the tax load on those still in the workforce may feel increasingly burdensome. Also, more and more middle-aged people are trying to figure out how to finance assisted-living and nursing home care for their elderly parents. How these issues will play out in the political arena in the near future will be interesting to follow.

Longman
Participate.com
2.0
Simulation
How to Satisfy Aunt Martha

By the Numbers

Does population movement and change affect the electoral fortunes of the parties?

Two-hundred seventy is the magic number for presidential candidates; it is the number of electoral college votes needed to win the presidency. In 2000, though he lost the national popular vote to Al Gore, George W. Bush won 271 electoral votes and the White House. Like any other winning presidential candidate, Bush put together a package of states with enough electoral college votes to win the only election that counts.

Why It Matters: Because of the magic number 270, presidential campaign strategists always design their campaigns around the states. For the most part, they attempt to build a majority of electoral votes by maintaining their lead in states with solid loyalties to their party, contesting states that might go either way, and generally ignoring states that are safely in the camp of the opposition. As the American population distributes and redistributes itself across the United States, campaign strategists must be alert to changes in the party leanings of the states, and constantly readjust their strategies for winning.

Behind the Number: Over the past half-century or so, the states that each party can count on to put together 270 electoral votes has changed. Much (though not all) of this can be explained by population movements:

• Many African-Americans migrated from the deep South to manufacturing centers in the Northeast, the upper Midwest, and far West, bringing their Democratic Party loyalties with them.

• Many other Americans migrated to the South and Southwest to fill jobs in non-union factories and in defense and high-tech industries, swelling GOP votes in the states of these regions.

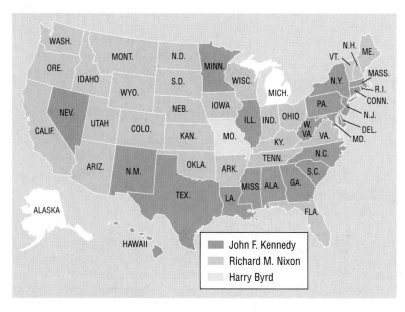

Electoral College Map, 1960

Income, Wealth, and Poverty

The United States enjoys one of the highest standards of living in the world. In terms of gross domestic product (GDP) per capita, the usual measure of a nation's living standards, the United States leads the world. On the UN's Human Development Index—which takes into account education and life expectancy as well as per capita GDP—the United States in 1999 was among the top six nations (with Australia, Canada, France, Norway, and Iceland).[7] However, the high standard of living is not shared by all Americans.

- Immigrants swelled the populations of a wide range of states, making Florida more Republican (its large number of Cuban immigrants favor the GOP), but making California, New York, and Illinois more Democratic (Asian and Hispanic immigrants lean toward the Democrats).
- A substantial number of white Americans migrated to the Mountain states, enhancing their standing as the area with the highest proportion of non-Hispanic whites, anchoring these states even more firmly in the Republican camp.

Counting to 270: We display here two electoral college maps, one showing the distribution of party victories by state in the 1960 presidential election (John F. Kennedy versus Richard M. Nixon), the other in the 2000 election. Democratic states are shown in blue, Republican states in red. Note the geographical pattern of the vote. In 1960, the geographical strength of the Democratic Party was in the South and in the large industrial states of the mid-Atlantic and the upper Midwest; by 2000, states in the South had become bastions of the Republican Party. In 1960, the GOP could count on most of New England, the farm states of the Midwest, the Mountain states, and the Pacific Coast states. By 2000, New England and the Pacific Coast were solidly in the Democratic camp (though, to be sure, the vote in Oregon in 2000 was extremely close).

What to Watch For: Pay attention to where presidential candidates make most of their campaign visits and where the parties spend the most money on advertising and getting out the vote. For the most part, they leave "hopeless" states alone, do enough to maintain their lead in states where they are strong, and focus the bulk of their activities in states that are very close and where the election could go in either direction.

What Do You Think? Do you think that the electoral college distorts political campaigns by encouraging presidential candidates to focus on particular states rather than on Americans everywhere? Or do you think there is something about the electoral college system that is important for the health of our federal system?

Final Results
December 18, 2000

Bush   Gore

Electoral College Map, 2000

Income After an almost two-decade-long period of stagnation that began in 1973, **median household income** in the United States began to rise steadily after 1994, coincident with the long economic boom of the mid- and late-1990s. In 2000, median household income reached $42,100.[8] In real dollar terms—that is, adjusted for inflation—median household income was up 25 percent from 1967 when the federal government first began to collect this statistic.

median household income

Household income number at which one-half of all households have more income and one-half have less income; the mid-point of all households ranked by income.

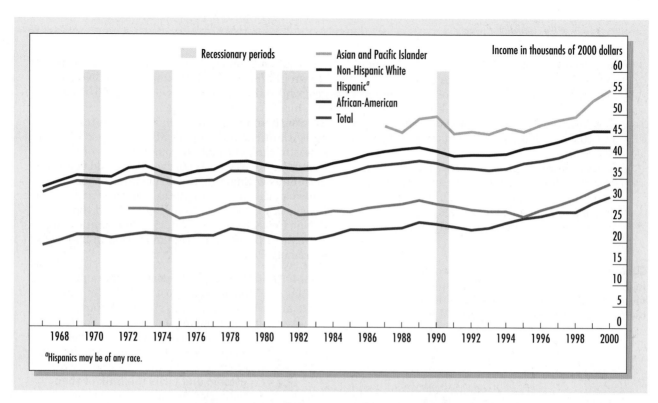

FIGURE 4.5 Trends in U.S. Median Household Income

Median household income (controlled for inflation) for all major population groups remained relatively flat from 1973 until the mid-1990s. Household income then began to rise in response to the strong performance of the U.S. economy. It fell, however, in 2001 as the economy sputtered.

Source: U.S. Bureau of the Census.

In 2001, however, median household income fell by 2.2 percent, a reflection of the poor overall performance of the American economy during the year. Because economic troubles continued in 2002 and 2003, household income is certain to fall even further.

Trends in household income vary by group (see Figure 4.5), as one might expect. African-American and Hispanic households have the lowest household incomes, while Asian-Americans and non-Hispanic whites have the highest. Note as well that median household incomes for all groups declined in the late 1980s and early 1990s, then began to recover at different times for each group. Note that all groups benefited from the long economic boom, with steady rates of household income growth in the late 1990s.

The long stagnation in median household incomes had important political effects in the United States, including the appearance of "the angry middle class." From the mid-1970s to the start of the 1990s economic expansion, in a nation grown accustomed to rising incomes and improvements in the standard of living for each generation, incomes for most American households stayed flat even while more household members were working than in the past, and more people were working longer hours or at more than one job. By the 1980s and early 1990s, political anger had led to frequent outbursts against taxes, immigrants, and welfare recipients and a decline in trust for government and elected leaders. Middle-class anger also had electoral consequences, playing an important role, for example, in the defeat of incumbent president George H. W. Bush in the 1992 election and in the Republican capture of Congress in 1994.[9]

Surveys showed that by the end of the 1990s, Americans were again confident about the country's future as well as their own financial prospects.[10] Talk of middle-class anger had largely disappeared, and the usefulness of resentment as a political mobilizing tool seemed to have declined. But such contentment proved rather short-lived; when it became evident to many Americans that the slumping economy and stock market meltdown of 2001 and 2002 were undermining their standard of living and their retirement plans, middle-class anger began to simmer once again.

Poverty In 1955, almost 25 percent of Americans fell below the federal government's official **poverty line.** The percentage dropped steadily until it reached 11.6 in 1973. Beginning in the late 1970s, however, the percentage of Americans classified as poor began to inch upward, reaching 14.5 percent in 1994. From then until 2000, the percentage of Americans living in poverty declined to 11.3 percent, the lowest number since 1973. The recession in 2001 kicked the poverty rate back up to 11.7 percent, however, leaving 32.9 million people below the poverty line.

poverty line
The federal government's calculation of the amount of income families of various sizes need to stay out of poverty.

The problem of poverty in the United States continues to concern many Americans. Here is why:

- A distressingly large number of Americans still live in poverty.
- The poverty rate here remains substantially higher than in the other rich democracies.
- The official poverty rate is bound to climb because economic difficulties continued to plague the United States in 2002 and 2003.

The distribution of poverty is not random. It is concentrated among racial minorities and single-parent, female-headed households and their children.[11] Roughly 22 percent of African-Americans and 21 percent of Hispanic-Americans live in poverty, for example (although a sizable middle class has emerged in both

Poverty and homelessness have persisted in the face of strong economic growth. The contrast between rich and poor is evident on the streets of most large American cities.

USING THE FRAMEWORK: The Persistence of Poverty

I keep hearing about how well the economy did during the 1990s. How come we couldn't seem to do much about poverty?

Background: Although the strong economy in the 1990s caused poverty rates to fall, there is still a surprisingly high number of poor people in the United States. Surveys show that Americans would like to do something to help the poor, although not through the traditional welfare system. But the federal government, with a few exceptions such as the Low Income Tax Credit, has not made the elimination of poverty a major priority. Former Housing and Urban Development Secretary Andrew Cuomo attempted to draw public attention to the plight of the poor in poverty pockets such as Benton Harbor, Michigan, and East St. Louis, Illinois, but this attempt failed to spark a reaction. Taking a look at how structural, political linkage, and governmental factors interact on this issue will help explain the situation.

Governmental Action

The national government provides small safety nets for the poor but does not institute programs to eliminate poverty.

Governmental Level

- Proposals to eliminate poverty do not improve the electoral prospects of public officials at the present time. →
- Elected leaders in both parties tend to support the position that balanced budgets, deregulation, a friendly environment for investors, and encouragement of private enterprise is the best public policy.

Political Linkages Level

- The poor are politically invisible; they represent a small minority of the electorate, have few organized groups to push their interests, and have not been able to build a social movement. →
- Wealthier Americans and large corporations make large contributions to candidates who promise to keep taxes low and government small. →
- Public opinion opposes big federal government programs to redistribute income. →
- The Democratic Party, historically the party championing the interests of the poor and near-poor, is often afraid of being tagged with the "liberal" and "tax-and-spend" labels.

Structural Level

- American core beliefs about individualism, initiative, and opportunity make it difficult for proposals to assist the poor to gain recognition. →
- The economic boom of the 1990s, with its record levels of employment, reinforced the belief that anyone who wants to work, can.

communities), compared to only 7.5 percent among non-Hispanic whites. About one in six children under the age of 18 live in poverty and more than one in three poor people live in single-parent, female-headed households.[12]

Obviously, the extent of poverty is politically consequential. Most importantly, poverty is associated with a range of socially undesirable outcomes, including crime, drug use, and family disintegration,[13] all of which eventually draw the attention of other citizens who want government to do something about it.

Inequality Income and wealth are distributed in a highly unequal fashion in the United States, and the economic boom of the 1990s did nothing to make it less pronounced. In fact, income inequality increased dramatically during the 1980s and 1990s. By 2000, the top quintile (20 percent) of households took home 49.7 percent of national income (see Figure 4.6), the highest proportion ever recorded. Most of the income and wealth gains from economic growth between 1980 and 2000 went mainly to upper-income groups, rather than being evenly distributed across the entire population. In fact, 47 percent of all real income gains in the United States between 1983 and 1998 went to the top 1 percent of income recipients.[14] It is also worth noting that income inequality is greater in the United States than in any other Western democratic nation.[15]

Wealth (assets such as real estate, stocks and bonds, art, bank accounts, cash-value insurance policies, and so on) in the United States is even more unequally distributed than income. According to a study by economist Edward Wolff, the top 1 percent of households—with a net worth of at least $2.3 million—owned more than 42 percent of the nation's wealth by the mid-1990s, up from only 21 percent in 1975.[16] Inequality of wealth today seems similar to that of the 1920s and is more unequally distributed here than in any other

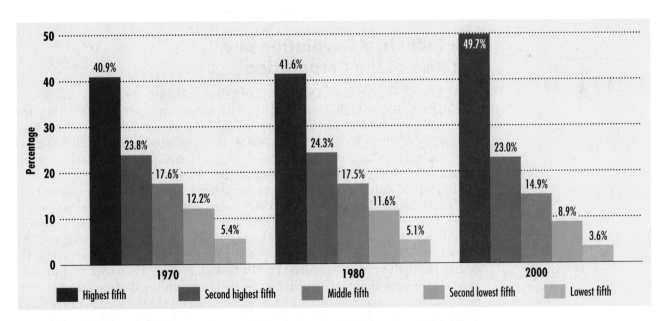

FIGURE 4.6 Household Income Distribution in the United States, by Quintiles, 1970–2000

Income inequality has been increasing in the United States, reaching levels not seen since the 1920s. A standard way to measure income inequality is to compare the proportion of national income going to each 20 percent (*quintile*) of households in the population. Especially striking is the shrinking share of the bottom 40 percent and the increasing share of the top 20 percent.
Source: U.S. Bureau of the Census.

Western democratic nation.[17] With the recent repeal of the estate tax, more-over, wealth inequality will surely increase in the years ahead.

Why worry about income and wealth inequality? Inequality is particularly important in determining how well democracy works. Extensive *material inequality,* as we suggested in Chapter 1, may undermine the possibilities for *political equality,* one of the foundations of democracy. People with access to financial resources can use their resources to enhance their political voice and their ease of access to public officials. Poorer Americans are less likely to exercise their right to vote or to participate in other ways in politics. People with little money are unlikely to make contributions to political campaigns or to groups that will fight for their interests. Those with more income are more likely than others to have computers and Internet access in their homes and are more likely, as a result, to be informed, linked with others into political groups, and in touch with government decision makers. That is why, as we pointed out in Chapter 1, Thomas Jefferson feared that democracy would be at risk in a highly unequal society.

The American Economy

Virtually everything we have discussed so far in this chapter is shaped by the American economy. The growth, diversification, and geographic dispersion of the American population, for example, can be traced directly to changes in the economy. Occupations, standards of living, and the distribution of income and wealth are closely connected to the operations of our economic institutions. Even important elements of the American political culture, as we shall soon see, are associated with our economy and how it works.

The Industrial Revolution and the Rise of the Corporation

Longman
Participate.com
2.0
Timeline
Major Technological Innovations that Have Changed the Political Landscape

Until the Civil War, the American capitalist economy (except in the slave-holding South) was highly competitive, with many small enterprises, first tied to agriculture and then increasingly to manufacturing. After the Civil War, and partly as a result of it, the economy became increasingly industrialized and concentrated in giant enterprises.[18] By the turn of the twentieth century, the United States was the world's leading industrial power.

Industrial enterprises grew to unprecedented size in the late nineteenth and early twentieth centuries. Workers were gathered into enormous work-places that required coordination by an army of managers. Partly, this change in scale was related to technology: The steam engine, electrical power, and the assembly line provided the means of bringing thousands of working people together for industrial production. Partly, this change in scale was tied to cost: Most of the new industrial technologies required unheard-of levels of investment capital. Large enterprises were also encouraged by changes in the laws of incorporation, which allowed competing corporations to merge into single, giant enterprises. A wave of mergers between 1896 and 1904 fashioned the corporate-dominated economy familiar to us today.[19]

The Post–World War II Boom

The American economy and American corporations grew impressively during the first two-thirds of the twentieth century. Although thrown seriously off track for at least a decade by the Great Depression, the economy was pushed

The principles of assembly-line, mass-production manufacturing were honed to near perfection by Henry Ford in the early twentieth century at his Highland Park complex in Michigan. Here workers assemble a portion of a Model T, the first car to reach the mass public in the United States.

forward again by World War II and the Cold War that followed; both triggered rapid and substantial increases in government spending, research and development, and technological innovation. The enormous growth in the wealth of the American economy after World War II, fueled by the activities of the major corporations, was the foundation of the rapid improvements in the American standard of living and the growth of the middle class.

After World War II, the largest American corporations increasingly looked abroad for sources of raw materials and markets for their finished products. American corporations dominated world markets during this time. In 1975, 11 of the largest 15 corporations in the world were American; in 1981, 40 percent of the world's total foreign direct investment was still accounted for by the United States.[20] The global reach of corporate activities inevitably affected U.S. foreign policy. With worldwide economic interests at stake, American political leaders came under great pressure to pay attention to developments and events in the far corners of the world.

The Temporary Fall from Grace

Although the U.S. economy continued to grow in the 1970s and 1980s, its rate of growth began to fall behind that of Western Europe and Japan, even as American corporations began to feel the pinch of intense competition from foreign corporations. Between the early 1970s and the late 1980s, the U.S. share of world manufacturing declined. The United States lost ground in steel, autos, machine tools, electronics, computer chips, and finance.

The relative decline in America's manufacturing position had a devastating impact on the wages of blue-collar workers, raised protectionist sentiments, and spurred proposals to shield American industry from foreign competition. The intensity of the fight over the North American Free Trade Agreement (NAFTA) and the General Agreement on Tariffs and Trade (GATT) shows how America's changing economic position in the world generated a set of important issues in American politics.

Globalization and the American Economy

In the 1990s, however, the American economy rebounded with a vengeance, with its corporations once again becoming the key players in crucial industries. The economies once seen as the principal threats to America's position—the European Union, Japan, and the so-called Asian tigers—began to lose ground. The reason for the turnaround has been the subject of much debate and disagreement among economists and business leaders. Some point to the lighter hand of government and labor unions in the United States, some point to stronger entrepreneurial traditions here, and still others credit the existence of freer markets, but all seem to agree that American corporations were better positioned to succeed in the new global economy that blossomed in the 1990s.

The most important characteristic of this new global economy is the integration of much of the world into a single market and production system. Today the largest corporations design, manufacture, market, sell, and finance their products and services across a wide range of countries and are not constrained much by national boundaries. General Motors, for example, produces and sells more cars abroad than it does in the United States. Boeing designs and assembles the 777 near Seattle, but many parts of the plane are manufactured by subcontractors in Japan, China, England, Germany, and Australia.

U.S. corporations are proving to be the most important actors in the new global economy. Behind the apparent decline in the competitiveness of the American economy in the 1970s and 1980s, something startling seems to have been going on. Leaving older industries such as mining, steel, and shipbuilding to others, American companies proved to be particularly adept in areas such as computer software, biotechnology, business services (insurance, law, accounting, advertising, and so on), computer chips, Internet services, telecommunications, military and commercial aircraft, and popular entertainment. In the emergent global economy, Microsoft, Intel, Boeing, Disney, Amazon.com, Sun, eBay, and Cisco are the companies that draw increasing attention.

The largest American corporations are also global corporations in the sense that they produce and sell their products all over the world. This McDonald's is in Xiamen, China.

U.S. corporations—and foreign ones, as well—have been growing larger through mergers and acquisitions. Even the largest companies have learned that size matters in the battle for global market share, whether in banking (note the merger of NationsBank Corp and BankAmerica Corp), media and entertainment (note AOL's purchase of Time-Warner), telecommunications (note Bell Atlantic's purchase of GTE), pharmaceuticals (note Pfizer's purchase of Warner-Lambert), and software and the Internet (AOL again). The failure of the government's effort to dismantle Microsoft was also a landmark event on the road toward ever-larger corporations.

The dynamism of the American economy in the 1990s had several effects that were politically consequential. On the one hand, the steady economic growth, low inflation, and heady stock market performance of that period (since reversed) helped fuel an impressive rate of job creation, low levels of unemployment, and heightened consumer confidence. On the other hand, the new global economy is one in which certain skills are highly sought after and rewarded— software engineers, portfolio managers, Website creators, filmmakers, and business strategists, for example—while others are not—low-skill manual and service workers, for example. For the former, work tends to be both exciting and lucrative. For the latter, work is routine, not very well paid, and characterized by frequent layoffs and part-time status. This may be why a booming economy in the 1990s did not diminish income inequality in the United States.

Will Globalization Slow?

The heady 1990s were followed in 2001 and 2002 by three developments that threatened the pace of globalization: economic recession in the United States (and in most of the other rich democracies); declining trust in the honesty and accuracy of corporate financial reports in the United States; and terrorism. Recessions are part of the business cycle, of course, so no one should have been surprised that one eventually happened in 2001–2002 after the longest economic expansion in American history. Especially troubling about this particular recession, however, was the poor performance of the former stars of economic expansion: dot-com, high-tech, and telecommunications companies. In such an environment, many of the activities that are central to globalization— investment in overseas facilities, expanding information technology and telecommunications networks, buying securities in diverse markets, building transportation infrastructure, and the like—naturally slow to a crawl. Though no one is entirely confident about predicting the future, it is probably safe to say that the business cycle will reverse at some point and that companies and investors will be looking for financial opportunities again wherever they might find them. With global production, distribution, and sales infrastructures already in place, and with the rich nations still committed to free trade, there is no reason to suppose that globalization will not take off again, though perhaps not at the same frenzied pace.

It is probably also safe to say that the embarrassing disclosures of corporate financial chicanery on the part of companies such as Enron, Arthur Andersen, and WorldCom will eventually lead to a range of regulatory reforms that will restore some measure of confidence in the American investment climate. At some point, this may restore investor confidence and enhance the overall performance of the American economy, which is, after all, the engine of economic globalization.

However, there is no predicting yet what the effects of terrorism and the response to terrorism will have on globalization. In one scenario, fear that radical Islamic terrorism will target western companies and their employees, suppliers, and outlets might convince some companies to draw back from the world and confine themselves to business in the United States. In another scenario, American companies will continue to operate and even expand their activities abroad, either because the war on terrorism proves successful—thus lessening the probability of terrorist attacks—or because companies calculate that business necessity requires that they think in global terms, no matter the risk. It is hard to imagine, for example, how companies such as McDonald's, Microsoft, Pepsi, and AOL/Time-Warner might remain profitable without worldwide operations. Only time will tell which scenario wins out.

The United States in the International System

Longman
Participate.com
2.0
Comparative
**Comparing
Political
Landscapes**

isolationism

The policy of avoiding involvement in foreign affairs.

It is often said that the United States is the world's last remaining superpower. If this is true, then it took awhile to reach this status. For most of the nineteenth century, the attention of most Americans and their leaders was focused on the North American continent. Their energies were devoted primarily to filling in a vast, continental-scale nation-state—which required, of course, moving Native Americans aside, buying territories from France and Spain, and seizing our present Southwest from Mexico—and to building an industrial economy. The great expanse of the Atlantic Ocean allowed our domestic growth and development to move forward, unhindered by the European powers. Our foreign policy was **isolationist:** American policy leaders believed in attending to our own affairs and staying out of world affairs, unless directly threatened. Starting toward the end of the nineteenth century, however, our attentions began to turn abroad, and our growing economic power inevitably provided a seat at the table of the world's most important nations. It was World War II, however, that propelled the United States into its position as the world's most important power.

The United States as a Superpower I

World War II thrust the United States into the leadership position that its economic position in the world had portended since 1900. The war stimulated a massive expansion of the entire industrial economy. At the same time, the financial and manufacturing infrastructures of our prewar economic rivals—Britain, France, Japan, and Germany—were devastated by the war.

The United States emerged from the war with a large military establishment and military superiority in most important areas. There was also a new belief among both the population and the nation's leaders that isolationism was dangerous and contrary to our long-term national interests.

Within a decade of the end of World War II, the United States stood as the unchallenged economic, political, and military power among the Western nations. For the first time in its history, the United States was willing and able to exercise leadership on the world level. It was the United States that pulled together the major capitalist nations for the first time in their history into a political and economic partnership. It provided funds for rebuilding Western Europe and for development projects in the Third World. It successfully pushed for free international trade and provided a stable dollar to serve as the basis of the international monetary system. And it organized and largely paid for the joint military defenses of them all. Is it any wonder, then, that *Life* magazine editor Henry Luce was moved to label the period the "American century"?

During the Cold War, the United States and the Soviet Union avoided direct military conflict because their respective leaders feared mutual annihilation from a nuclear exchange if the disagreements between them ever turned from "cold" to "hot." Here nuclear missiles are on display at the annual parade celebrating the 1917 Bolshevik Revolution.

The fly in the ointment, of course, was the Soviet Union. Although badly crippled by the war (it is said that 20 million of its citizens died in the conflict), the Soviet Union entered the postwar era with the world's largest land army, superpower ambitions of its own, and a strong desire to keep the nations on its periphery in eastern and southern Europe in hands it considered friendly. In the ensuing **Cold War,** which began in the late 1940s and lasted for four decades, the two superpowers faced each other as leaders of conflicting political,

Cold War

The period of tense relations between the United States and the Soviet Union from the late 1940s to the late 1980s.

Web Exploration
Post-Cold War Foreign Policy

Issue: In the post–Cold War period, neither American leaders nor the American people are entirely clear about how the United States ought to relate to the rest of the world.

Site: See what the public thinks about specific issues regarding our role in the international community at Public Agenda On-Line. Access our Website at **www.ablongman.com/greenberg**. In the "Web Explorations" section for Chapter 4, open "world role." Select "America's Global Role," then select "major proposals."

What You've Learned: What do Americans believe to be the most appropriate role for the United States in the world? Should we approach foreign political, military, and economic problems unilaterally, going it alone, as it were? Or should we mainly engage the world through international organizations and in cooperation with our allies? Do you agree or disagree with most Americans on these issues? If you disagree, what would you say to other Americans to change their minds?

HINT: Your answer will probably depend greatly on your own ideas concerning our obligations, the usefulness and risks of U.S. interventions, and how much attention we need to pay to problems at home. There is no wrong answer here.

economic, and ideological alliances; became engaged in a nuclear arms race; and fought surrogate wars with each other in various locations in the Third World, from the Belgian Congo to Central America to Afghanistan.

America's superpower status had many implications for U.S. politics and government policies. For one thing, superpower status required a large military establishment and tilted government spending priorities toward national defense. For another thing, as we will see in later chapters, it enhanced the role of the president in policymaking and diminished that of Congress.

The United States as a Superpower II

The 1990s saw startling changes in the world's military, political, and economic systems, all of which, at least nominally, heightened U.S. power in the world. Communism collapsed in Eastern Europe. The Soviet Union ceased to exist. China switched to a market economy. Most developing countries rejected the socialist development model, embraced "privatization," and welcomed foreign investment. Moreover, the United States took the lead in the global economy. We use the heading "Superpower II" to capture the notion, widely bandied about, of the United States's emergence as the world's single "superpower," without any real challengers to its preeminence.

Oddly, however, although the last "superpower" in a military sense, the United States has not necessarily had its way on all important matters, either with allies or enemies, nor is it likely to do so in the future. With the threat of the Soviet Union no longer supplying the glue to hold them together, U.S. allies feel freer to go their own way on a wide range of international issues. The United States could not agree with the Europeans for a very long time on what to do about the ethnic conflicts in Bosnia and Kosovo, for example, and was often at odds with them over aspects of the conduct of the war in Afghanistan and the relief effort that followed. It also has differences with the European Union over

The United States, though widely acknowledged as the world's only superpower, is not immune from attacks on its interests or citizens, as the events of September 11, 2001, amply demonstrated. Soon after these events, President Bush declared that his administration was prepared to wage a "war on terrorism" and dispatched American troops to Afghanistan to root out the Taliban regime and the al Qaeda network. Here, troops from the Tenth Mountain Division set out on a mission.

trade issues and on what to do about Iraq. Disagreements about nuclear proliferation have strained U.S. relations with Russia, while security issues, human rights violations, and protection of intellectual property have been an irritant in our relations with China. Nor is the United States able single-handedly to bring the Palestinians and Israelis together and force a solution to their conflict.

The Foundational Beliefs of American Political Culture

The kinds of choices Americans make in meeting the challenges posed by a changing economy, society, and post–Cold War world depend a great deal on the kinds of values and beliefs Americans have regarding human nature, society, economic relations, and the role of government. Government policies tend to reflect our ideas and beliefs as a people. The fundamental values and beliefs that have political consequences make up the American *political culture.*

Evidence strongly suggests that Americans share a political culture.[21] To be sure, we are a vast, polyglot mixture of races, religions, ethnicities, occupations, and lifestyles. Nevertheless, one of the things that has always struck observers of the American scene is the degree to which a broad consensus seems to exist on many of the fundamental beliefs that shape our political life. We focus here not on transitory ideas about particular issues that are in the headlines at the moment but on what might be called *foundation beliefs,* beliefs that shape how people classify, think about, and resolve particular issues that arise in the headlines or in their local communities.

Competitive Individualism

Compared to people in other countries, Americans tend to believe that an individual's fate is (and ought to be) tied to his or her own efforts. Those with talent, grit, and the willingness to work hard are more likely than not to end up on top, it is believed; those without at least some of these qualities are more likely to wind up on the bottom of the heap. Americans tend to assume that people generally get what they deserve.

Compared to people in other countries, Americans are also more likely to believe that people are naturally competitive, always striving to better themselves in relation to others. Popular literature in America has always conveyed this theme, ranging from the Horatio Alger books of the late nineteenth century to the many contemporary self-help books with keys to "getting ahead," "making it," and "getting rich."

The belief in competitive individualism affects how Americans think about many issues, including inequality. Americans overwhelmingly endorse the idea of "equality of opportunity" (the idea that people ought to have an equal shot in the competitive game of life), for instance, yet they also overwhelmingly reject the idea that people should have equal rewards. Not surprisingly, Americans tend to look favorably on government programs that try to equalize opportunity—Head Start, education programs of various kinds, school lunch programs, and the like—but are generally against programs such as welfare, which seem to redistribute income from the hardworking middle class to individuals who are considered "undeserving."

Because it is assumed that people get different rewards based on their own efforts, a belief in equality of opportunity is consistent with highly unequal

In Japan, commitment to the work team and the company are more important cultural values than they are in the United States.

outcomes; that is, Americans seem to find inequality of income and wealth acceptable, as long as it is the outcome of a process in which individuals compete fairly with one other.[22] In Sweden, by contrast, citizens generally believe that equality of condition is an important value and support government policies that redistribute income.[23]

Limited Government

Closely associated with the idea of individualism is the belief that government must be limited in its power and responsibilities, for taken too far, a powerful government is likely to threaten individual rights and economic efficiency. This idea—drawn from Adam Smith and John Locke, our early history, and the words of the Declaration of Independence—remains attractive to most Americans even today, when we expect government to do far more than the framers ever imagined. This belief is not universally shared. In countries such as Japan, Sweden, Germany, and France, where governments have always been powerful and have played an important role in directing society and the economy, limited government has little attraction for either the political leaders or the public.

Free Enterprise

Americans tend to support the basic precepts of free enterprise capitalism: the primacy of private property and the efficiencies of the free market. Private property notions, best articulated by the philosopher John Locke, have been reinforced by the experience of fairly widespread property ownership in the United States compared with that in many other countries.[24] Locke argued that God gave the earth and its resources in common to human beings and also gave human beings abilities that they have a right and an obligation to use. When they use these abilities, people turn common property into private property. By mixing their labor with the naturally occurring abundance of the earth, Locke argued, people are justified in taking the product of that effort for their own as private property. Because people are different in their abilities and their willingness to work, this process will always result in inequality. Inevitably, some will end up with more property than others.

The basic theory of the free market was worked out by Adam Smith in his classic work, *The Wealth of Nations*. Smith taught that if the market were left alone to operate naturally, following the laws of supply and demand, it would coordinate economic life in a nearly perfect fashion. Because the market is efficient and effective if left alone, government should not interfere with its operations. Although few Americans now accept this "pure" free market ideal, most Americans today, as in the past, believe that the private sector is usually more effective and efficient than the public sector. Given the esteem in which competitive individualism, private property, and the market are held, as well as the historical success of the American economy, it is entirely understandable that Americans tend to hold the business system (though not large corporations) in very high regard.

This set of ideas about individualism, limited government, and the free market (what some people call *classical liberalism*)[25] influences many aspects of public policy in the United States. Eminent economist John Kenneth Galbraith once decried the fact that ours is a society in which great private wealth exists side by side with public squalor. By that, he meant that Americans favor private consumption over public services and amenities and private over public initiatives.[26] In other rich democracies, citizens and political leaders tend to believe that extensive and high-quality public services in mass transit, health care, housing, and education are part and parcel of the good society.

Citizenship and the Nature of the Political Order

Certain beliefs about what kind of political order is most appropriate and what role citizens should play shape the actual daily behavior of citizens and political decision makers alike.

Democracy At the time of the nation's founding, democracy was not highly regarded in the United States. During our history, however, the practice of democracy has been enriched and expanded, and the term *democracy* has become an honored one.[27] While regard for democracy is one of the bedrocks of the American belief system today, Americans have not necessarily always behaved democratically. After all, African-Americans were denied the vote and other citizenship rights in many parts of the nation until the 1960s. It is fair to say, nevertheless, that most Americans believe in democracy as a general principle and take seriously any claim that their behavior is not consistent with it. For example, public opinion surveys done during the past 25 years consistently show that about 60 to 70 percent of Americans want to abolish the Electoral College.

Freedom and Liberty Foreign visitors have always been fascinated by the American obsession with individual "rights," the belief that in the good society, government leaves people alone in their private pursuits. Studies show that freedom (also called *liberty*) is at the very top of the list of American beliefs and that it is more strongly honored here than elsewhere.[28] From the very beginning, what attracted most people to the United States was the promise of freedom in the New World. Many came for other reasons, to be sure: A great many came for strictly economic reasons, some came as convict labor, and some came in chains as slaves. But many who came to these shores seem to have done so to taste the freedom to speak and think as they chose, to worship as they pleased, to read what they might, and to assemble and petition the government if they had a mind to.

As in many cases, however, to believe in something is not necessarily to act consistently with that belief. There have been many intrusions on basic rights during our history. Later chapters address this issue in more detail.

Populism

The term *populism* refers to the hostility of the common person to concentrated power and the powerful. While public policy is not often driven by populist sentiments (for the powerful, by definition, exercise considerable political influence), populism has always been part of the American belief system and has sometimes been expressed in visible ways in American politics.

One of the most common targets of populist sentiment has been concentrated economic power and the people who exercise it. Andrew Jackson mobilized this sentiment in his fight against the Bank of the United States in the 1830s. The Populist movement of the 1890s aimed at taming the new corporations of the day, especially the banks and the railroads. Corporations were the target of popular hostility during the dark days of the Great Depression and also in the 1970s, when agitation by consumer and environmental groups made the lives of some corporate executives extremely uncomfortable.

Populism is also hostile to the concentration of power in government. Alabama's segregationist governor, George Wallace, successfully tapped into this sentiment in his run for the Democratic presidential nomination in 1968, when he complained about the "pointy-headed intellectuals in Washington." The populist sentiment is evident today in efforts to impose term limits on public officials and in the popularity of anti-establishment figures such as Ross Perot and Governor Jesse Ventura of Minnesota.

Structural Influences on American Politics

We have now examined a number of structural factors that influence American politics. In Chapters 2 and 3, we examined the constitutional rules; in this chapter, we considered the main features of American society, economy, political culture, and the international system and how each influences important aspects of politics and government in the United States. These structural factors are interrelated. The kind of constitutional rules we have are, to a substantial degree, shaped by our beliefs about the nature of the individual, society, and government that make up our political culture. The political culture, in turn, with its ideas celebrating the market, competitive individualism, and private property, is perfectly attuned to a free enterprise economy. How the economy operates and develops has a lot to do with the life of the American people (where people live, what kind of work they do, and so on), as does the nation's place in the world. The characteristics of the American population trigger their own effects; the populace's level of education and skill has a lot to do with American economic performance, for instance.

HOW DEMOCRATIC ARE WE?

Is Real Democracy Possible in the United States?

PROPOSITION: The kind of economy, society, and culture we have in the United States makes it difficult to have a real democracy because the key components of a working democracy—popular sovereignty, political equality, and political liberty—cannot flourish.

AGREE: The free enterprise capitalist system in the United States results in large inequalities in income and wealth that inevitably spill over into political life, making political equality hard to achieve. Moreover, the system's rapid economic and technological changes often contribute to anxiety, fear, and anger among the public, interfering with the compromise and deliberation central to democratic life. Finally, economic and technical change is further fragmenting our highly individualistic culture, making a sense of community and public responsibility even less likely than before.

DISAGREE: American society is open, diverse, and filled with opportunity for those who are ambitious. Economic growth is raising the living standards of the population across the board, which bodes well for democracy; note the evidence that high living standards and democracy are strongly related. Also, economic, technological, and social changes are allowing more and more people to develop their abilities and capacities, to become informed, to link together with others who share their public concerns, to get involved in community and political affairs, and to have their voices heard by public officials.

THE AUTHORS: There is something to be said for each argument. There are some developments and conditions in American society, economy, culture, and world position that are most certainly democracy-enhancing, as the "disagree" position argues. There are other developments and conditions that are worth worrying about, however. First, substantial income and wealth inequality cannot help but undermine political equality. Second, even if popular control over the government in Washington exists (which remains an open question), it may well be the case that this government is not the center of the most important decisions affecting our lives; the rapid globalization of our economy puts important decision-making power into the hands of private investors, currency traders, and the executives of global manufacturing, banking, telecommunications, and transportation corporations.

Summary

How politics and government work is shaped by such structural factors as the nature of society, the economy, the nation's place in the world, and the political culture.

The most important changes in the American population are its growth; its diversification along ethnic, religious, and racial lines; its relocation from rural to urban and suburban areas and to the Sun Belt; and its gradual aging. Americans enjoy a very high standard of living, but inequality is substantial and poverty is surprisingly persistent. These factors affect the agenda of American politics and the distribution of political power.

The American economy is a market economy that has changed over the years from a highly competitive, small-enterprise form to a corporate-dominated one with a global reach. Economic change has had important reverberations in American politics.

The emergence of the United States as a superpower in the twentieth century changed the content of foreign policy, the balance of power between the president and Congress, the size of the federal government, and the priorities of the government's budget. The collapse of socialism in Eastern Europe affirmed the position of the United States as the world's most important military power.

Americans believe strongly in individualism, limited government, and free enterprise. Beliefs about democracy, liberty, and the primacy of the common people also help define the political culture. The political culture shapes American ideas about what the good society should look like, the appropriate role for government, and the possibilities for self-government.

Suggestions for Further Reading

Bellah, Robert N., Richard Madsen, William M. Sullivan, Ann Swidler, and Steven M. Tipton. *Habits of the Heart.* Berkeley, CA: University of California Press, 1985.
  A convincing description of competitive individualism and its effects.

Chafe, William H. *The Unfinished Journey: America Since World War II,* 2nd ed. New York: Oxford University Press, 1995.
  A history of postwar America, with special attention to how structural transformations have shaped American political life.

Dicken, Peter. *Global Shift: The Internationalization of Economic Activity,* 3rd ed. New York: Guilford Press, 1998.
  A comprehensive look at the scope, causes, and consequences of economic globalization.

Friedman, Thomas L. *The Lexus and the Olive Tree.* New York: Farrar, Straus & Giroux, 1999.
  A somewhat breathless yet informative account of globalization and how it is transforming societies around the world, including the United States.

Hochschild, Jennifer L. *Facing Up to the American Dream.* Princeton, NJ: Princeton University Press, 1995.
  A brilliant examination of the ideology of the American dream and how race and social class affect its interpretation and possibilities.

Hughes, James W., and Joseph J. Seneca, eds. *America's Demographic Tapestry.* New Brunswick, NJ: Rutgers University Press, 1999.
  A collection of research essays on the underlying demographic changes that are transforming the United States.

Page, Benjamin I., and James R. Simmons. *What Government Can Do: Dealing With Poverty and Inequality.* Chicago: University of Chicago Press, 2000.
  An extensive overview of poverty and inequality in the United States, their causes, and what government can do about it.

Phillips, Kevin. *Wealth and Democracy: How Great Fortunes and Government Created America's Aristocracy.* New York: Broadway Books, 2002.
  A hard-hitting analysis of wealth inequality and how it shapes American life and public policies.

Wilson, William Julius. *When Work Disappears: The World of the New Urban Poor.* New York: Knopf, 1996.
  A powerful analysis of how globalization and technological change have adversely affected inner-city poor neighborhoods.

Internet Sources

The Economist **http://www.economist.com/**
The home page of one of the world's leading publications on the U.S. and international economies.

Fedstats **http://www.fedstats.gov/**
Statistical information on the U.S. economy and society from more than 70 government agencies.

Globalization and Democracy Homepage
http://www.colorado.edu/IBS/GAD/gad.html
Information on a National Science Foundation–funded graduate training and research program, directed by one of the authors of this textbook.

Statistical Abstract of the United States **http://www.census.gov/statab/www**
A vast compendium of statistical information on the government, the economy, and society.

Statistical Resources on the Web **www.lib.umich.edu/govdocs/statuniv.html**
A vast compendium of statistical information on society, economy, and culture for the United States and other countries, organized by the University of Michigan library in a very user-friendly format.

Yahoo/Business and Economy **http://www.yahoo.com/Business_and_Economy/**
A gateway to a wealth of information about business and the economy.

Yahoo/Society and Culture **http://www.yahoo.com/Society_and_Culture/**
A gateway to a wealth of information about social and cultural issues.

Notes

1. Material for this opening story is from the following sources: "Profile: Loretta Sanchez," *Congressional Quarterly Weekly Report* (January 4, 1997), Vol. 51, no. 1, p. 52; Don Terry, "Bitter Rematch Reflects Changes in Orange County," *The New York Times*, National Edition (October 28, 1998), p. A24; Francis X. Clines, "An Underdog Savors the Limelight," *The New York Times*, National Edition (December 18, 1996), p. B12.

2. Bureau of the Census, *Statistical Abstract of the United States, 2001*, table 5.

3. National Public Radio/the Kaiser Family Foundation/the Kennedy School of Government, "Security and Civil Liberties Poll Results," (November 30, 2001).

4. Michael Reich, "The Proletarianization of the Workforce," in Richard Edwards, Michael Reich, and Thomas A. Weisskopf, eds., *The Capitalist System* (Englewood Cliffs, NJ: Prentice Hall, 1966), p. 125.

5. Stanley Lebergott, "The American Labor Force," in Lance E. Davis, ed., *American Economic Growth* (New York: Harper & Row, 1972), p. 187; ibid., p. 124.

6. U.S. Bureau of Labor Statistics, 2001.

7. *Human Development Report, 2000* (New York: The United Nations, 2000).

8. U.S. Bureau of the Census, 2001.

9. Stanley B. Greenberg, *Middle-Class Dreams* (New York: Times Books, 1995); Susan J. Tolchin, *The Angry American* (Boulder, CO: Westview Press, 1999).

10. "Economic Optimism Abounds," *The Public Perspective* (June–July 1999), pp. 38–39.

11. Peter Gottschalk, "Inequality, Income Growth and Mobility," *Journal of Economic Perspectives*, 11, no. 2 (Spring 1997): 13–19.

12. U.S. Bureau of the Census, 2001.

13. William Julius Wilson, *When Work Disappears: The World of the New Urban Poor* (New York: Knopf, 1996).

14. From Edward Wolff's new book *Top Heavy*, reported in Alexander Stille, "Grounded by Income Gap," *The New York Times* (December 15, 2001), p. A15.

15. Gottschalk, "Inequality, Income Growth and Mobility."

16. Edward Wolff, "International Comparisons of Wealth Inequality," *Review of Income and Wealth,* 42, no. 4 (December 1996).

17. Ibid.

18. See Edward S. Greenberg, *Capitalism and the American Political Ideal* (Armonk, NY: Sharpe, 1985), ch. 4.

19. On this history, see Thomas C. Cochran and William Miller, *The Age of Enterprise* (New York: Harper & Row, 1961); ibid.; Louis M. Hacker, *American Economic Growth and Development* (New York: Wiley, 1970); Robert Wiebe, *The Search for Order* (New York: Hill & Wang, 1967).

20. U.S. Department of Commerce, *International Direct Investment* (Washington, D.C.: U.S. Government Printing Office, 1984), p. 1.

21. Jennifer L. Hochschild, *Facing Up to the American Dream* (Princeton, NJ: Princeton University Press, 1995), ch. 1.

22. See Jennifer L. Hochschild, *What's Fair? American Beliefs about Distributive Justice* (Cambridge, MA: Harvard University Press, 1981); Herbert McClosky and John R. Zaller, *The American Ethos: Public Attitudes Toward Capitalism and Democracy* (Cambridge, MA: Harvard University Press, 1984); Sidney Verba and Gary R. Orren, *Equality in America* (Cambridge, MA: Harvard University Press, 1985).

23. Verba and Orren, *Equality in America,* p. 255.

24. Alexis de Tocqueville, *Democracy in America* (1845).

25. On the domination of classical liberalism in America, see Louis Hartz, *The Liberal Tradition in America* (New York: Harcourt, Brace, 1955). But also see Rogers M. Smith, "Beyond Tocqueville, Myrdal, and Hartz: The Multiple Traditions of America," *American Political Science Review,* 87, no. 3 (September 1993), pp. 549–566.

26. John Kenneth Galbraith, *American Capitalism* (Boston: Houghton Mifflin, 1956); see also McClosky and Zaller, *The American Ethos,* pp. 270–271.

27. Russell Hanson, *The Democratic Imagination in America* (Princeton, NJ: Princeton University Press, 1985).

28. McClosky and Zaller, *The American Ethos,* p. 18.

Part Three
Political Linkage

In Part Two, we discussed a number of fundamental structural factors that affect how American politics works: the Constitution, our federal system, the nature of the American society and economy, the political culture, and the international system.

In Part Three, we turn to what we call political linkage factors: public opinion, the mass media, organized interest groups, political parties, elections, and social movements. These people and institutions are affected in many ways by the structural factors already discussed. They, in turn, strongly affect the governmental institutions that are the subject of the next portion of the book. They are not a formal part of government, but they directly influence what sorts of people are chosen to be government officials—who is elected president and who goes to Congress, for example. They also affect what these officials do when they are in office and what sorts of public policies result.

Chapter 5
Public Opinion

In This Chapter

- What public opinion is and how it is related to democracy
- How much people know about politics
- What sorts of government policies Americans favor or oppose
- How opinions differ according to race, gender, age, income, and other factors
- How much effect public opinion has on what government does

The Vietnam War and the Public

On August 2, 1964, the Pentagon announced that the U.S. destroyer *Maddox,* while on "routine patrol" in international waters in the Gulf of Tonkin near Vietnam, had undergone an "unprovoked attack" by three communist North Vietnamese PT boats. Two days later, the Pentagon reported a "second deliberate attack" on the *Maddox* and its companion destroyer, the *C. Turner Joy.* In a nationwide television broadcast, President Lyndon Johnson referred to "open aggression on the high seas" and declared that these hostile actions required that he retaliate with military force. Air attacks were launched against four North Vietnamese PT boat bases and an oil storage depot.[1]

Years later, the *Pentagon Papers,* a secret Defense Department study leaked to the news media by defense analyst Daniel Ellsberg, revealed that the American people had been deceived. The *Maddox* had not been on an innocent cruise; it had, in fact, been assisting South Vietnamese gunboats make raids on the North Vietnamese coast. The second "attack" apparently never occurred; it was imagined by an inexperienced sonar operator in dark and stormy seas. At the time, however, few skeptics raised questions. On August 7, 1964, by a vote of 88–2, the Senate passed the Tonkin Resolution, which approved the president's taking "all necessary measures," including the use of armed force, to repel any armed attack and to assist any ally in the region. A legal basis for full U.S. involvement in the Vietnam War had been established.

For more than a decade, the United States had been giving large-scale military aid to the French colonialists, and then to the American-installed but authoritarian South Vietnamese government, to fight nationalists and communists in Vietnam. More than 23,000 U.S. military advisers were there by the end of 1964, occasionally engaging in combat. On the other side of the world, the American public knew and cared little about the guerrilla war. In fact, few knew exactly where Vietnam was. Nevertheless, people were willing to go along when their leaders told them that action was essential to resist communist aggression.

After the Tonkin incident, people paid more attention. Public support for the war increased. When asked in August what should be done next in Vietnam, 48 percent said to keep troops there, get tougher, or take definite military action while only 14 percent said negotiate or get out.[2] Through the fall of 1964, more people wanted to step up the war than wanted to pull out, and many endorsed the current policy. In 1965, after the United States had begun the heavy "Rolling Thunder" bombing of North Vietnam, and after large numbers of U.S. troops had gradually engaged in combat in South Vietnam, public support of the war continued. Month after month, pollsters found that only

a small minority wanted to withdraw from Vietnam; as many or more wanted to escalate the war further, and the majority favored continuing the current policy.

But the number of U.S. troops in Vietnam rose rapidly, from 184,300 at the end of 1965 to 536,100 at the end of 1968, and casualties increased correspondingly. A total of 1,369 Americans were killed in 1965; 5,008 in 1966; 9,377 in 1967; and 14,589 in 1968. Many thousands more were wounded, and others were captured or missing.[3] Television news began to display weekly casualty counts in the hundreds, with pictures of dead American soldiers going home in body bags. The war became expensive, as politicians put it, in "American blood and treasure." Senate hearings aired antiwar testimony. Peace marches and demonstrations, though resented by much of the public, nonetheless increased pressure to end the war.

By December 1967, about as many people (45 percent) agreed as disagreed with the proposition that it had been a "mistake" to send troops to fight in Vietnam. A large majority said they favored "Vietnamization," bringing U.S. troops home as South Vietnamese replaced them.

Then catastrophe struck. In January 1968, during Vietnam's Tet holidays, the North Vietnamese army launched what became known as the *Tet Offensive:* massive attacks throughout South Vietnam, including an assault on the U.S. embassy in Saigon. The American public was shocked by televised scenes of urban destruction and bloody corpses, of U.S. soldiers destroying Ben Tre village "in order to save it," of marines bogged down in the rubble of the ancient city of Hue, and of a 77-day siege of Khe Sanh. The chief lesson seemed to be that a U.S. victory in Vietnam, if feasible at all, was going to be very costly in terms of lives and dollars.

After Tet, criticism of the war—by politicians, newspaper editorials, and television commentators such as Walter Cronkite and others—mushroomed, and public support for the war diminished. President Johnson, staggered by a surprisingly strong vote for antiwar candidate Eugene McCarthy in the New Hampshire primary, announced that he would limit the bombing of North Vietnam, seek a negotiated settlement, and withdraw as a candidate for reelection. In March 1968, only 41 percent of Americans described themselves as hawks (supporters of the war), a sharp drop from the 61 percent of early February. Anger over Vietnam contributed to the election defeat of the Democrats the following November.

By January 1969, when the Nixon administration took office, a substantial majority of the public favored monthly reductions in the number of U.S. soldiers in Vietnam: 57 percent approved the idea, while only 28 percent disapproved. In June, Nixon announced the withdrawal of 25,000 troops, followed by announcements of 35,000 more in September, another 50,000 in December, and 150,000 during the following year. Large majorities of the public approved of the withdrawals. Most said they wanted to continue them even if the South Vietnamese government collapsed. There can be little doubt that public opinion influenced U.S. disengagement from the war.

This did not mean that a majority of Americans wanted to get out of Vietnam immediately; most disliked the idea of a communist victory. But antiwar marches and demonstrations continued during 1970 and 1971, and many people wanted a faster pace of withdrawal. Gradually, U.S. troops came out of Vietnam; in January 1973, after the intensive Christmas bombing of North Vietnam, a peace agreement was finally signed. Two years later, the North Vietnamese army took control of Saigon and reunified Vietnam, a nation that had been divided since the end of World War II.

The Vietnam story shows how government officials can sometimes lead or manipulate opinion, especially when it concerns obscure matters in faraway lands, and how opinion is affected by events and their presentation in the mass media. The story also shows that public opinion, even on foreign policy matters, can sometimes have a strong effect on policymaking. ∎

Thinking Critically About This Chapter

This chapter is about the content of public opinion, how it is formed, and what effect it has on American politics and government.

Using the Framework   You will learn in this chapter how public opinion is shaped by a wide range of structural-level factors, including historical events, the political culture, family and community socialization, and economic and social change. You will also learn how public opinion influences the behavior of political leaders and shapes many of the policies of the federal government.

Using the Democracy Standard   Based on the standard of democracy described in Chapter 1, public opinion should be one of the decisive factors in determining what government does. You will see in this chapter, however, that while the influence of public opinion is important, public officials must pay attention to other political forces as well. They sometimes pay close attention to public opinion; at other times, they pay only slight attention to it. ◀

Democracy and Public Opinion

The political attitudes expressed by ordinary citizens are known collectively as **public opinion.** If democracy is, as Abraham Lincoln put it, "government of the people, by the people, and for the people," public opinion—especially the collective policy preferences of ordinary citizens—plays a crucial part in democratic government. In a perfect democracy, based on popular sovereignty and majority rule, the government would do exactly what its citizens wanted, at least in the long run.

public opinion

Political attitudes expressed by ordinary citizens.

An important test of how well democracy is working, then, is how closely government policy corresponds to the expressed wishes of its citizens. To what extent does the government respond to public opinion, as opposed, say, to the demands of organized interest groups?

Curiously, however, many leading political theorists, including some who say they believe in democracy, have expressed grave doubts about the wisdom of the public. James Madison, Alexander Hamilton, and other Founders of our national government worried that the public's "passions" would infringe on liberty and that public opinion would be susceptible to radical and frequent shifts.[4] Journalist and statesman Walter Lippmann declared that most people do not know what goes on in the world; they have only vague, media-provided pictures in their heads. Lippmann approvingly quoted Sir Robert Peel's reference to "that great compound of folly, weakness, prejudice, wrong feeling, right feeling, obstinacy and newspaper paragraphs which is called public opinion."[5]

Modern survey researchers have not been much kinder. The first voting studies, carried out during the 1940s and 1950s, turned up what scholars considered appalling evidence of public ignorance, lack of interest in politics, and reliance on group or party loyalties rather than judgments about the issues of the day. Repeated surveys of the same individuals found that their responses seemed to change randomly from one interview to another. Philip Converse, a leading student of political behavior, coined the term *nonattitudes:* On many issues of public policy, many or most Americans seemed to have no real views at all but simply offered "doorstep opinions" to satisfy interviewers.[6]

Perhaps even more disturbing, it appears that a substantial majority of federal government officials do not hold the abilities of the public in high regard. One major survey on this issue conducted in 2000 showed that 77 percent of presidential appointees, 80 percent of senior civil servants, and 47 percent of members of Congress did not agree with the statement that "Americans know enough about issues to form wise opinions about what should be done."[7] A study of a broader sample of officials concluded that ". . . two-thirds or more of government officials doubted that the public was sufficiently informed, long-sighted, and emotionally detached to provide sound guidance for government decisions."[8]

What should we make of this? If ordinary citizens are poorly informed and their views are based on whim, or if they have no real opinions at all, it hardly seems desirable—or even possible—that public opinion should determine what governments do. Both the feasibility and the attractiveness of democracy seem to be thrown into doubt. When we examine exactly what sorts of opinions ordinary Americans have, however, and how those opinions are formed and changed, we will see that such fears about public opinion have been greatly exaggerated.

Measuring What People Think

Years ago, people who wanted to find out anything about public opinion had to guess, based on what their barbers or taxi drivers said, on what appeared in letters to newspaper editors, or on what sorts of one-liners won cheers at political rallies. But the views of personal acquaintances, letter writers, or rally audiences are often quite different from those of the public as a whole. Similarly, the angry people who called in to radio talk shows at the beginning of the Clinton administration tended to be more conservative and anti-Clinton than most Americans.[9] Listeners could easily get a mistaken impression of what was on their fellow citizens' minds. To figure out what the average American thinks, we cannot rely on unrepresentative groups or noisy minorities.

A clever invention, the opinion poll, or **sample survey,** now eliminates most of the guesswork in measuring public opinion. A survey consists of systematic interviews conducted by trained professional interviewers who ask a standardized set of questions of a rather small number of randomly chosen Americans—usually about 1,000 or 1,500 of them. Such a survey can reveal with remarkable accuracy what all 260 million or so of us are thinking.

The secret of success is to make sure that the sample of people interviewed is representative of the whole population, that is, that the proportions of people in the sample who are young, old, female, college-educated, black, rural, Catholic, southern, western, and so forth are all about the same as in the U.S. population as a whole. This representativeness is achieved best when the people being interviewed are chosen through **random sampling,** which ensures that each member of the population has an equal chance of being chosen. Then survey researchers can add up all the responses to a given question and compute the percentages of people answering one way or another. Statisticians can use probability theory to tell how close the survey's results are likely to be to what the whole population would say if asked the same questions. Findings from a random sample of 1,500 people have a 95 percent chance of accurately reflecting the views of the whole population within about 3 or 4 percentage points.[10]

Perfectly random sampling is not feasible. Personal interviews have to be clustered geographically so that interviewers can easily get from one respon-

sample survey

An interview study asking questions of a set of people who are chosen as representative of the whole population.

random sampling

The selection of survey respondents by chance, with equal probability, to ensure their representativeness of the whole population.

Exit polls, which survey the opinions of people as they leave the polling place after voting, are a major source of information on who votes and how people make their voting decisions. They are also the basis for network television election-night reports on "who won" announcements, made well before all the ballots have been counted.

Harry Truman mocks an edition of the *Chicago Daily Tribune* proclaiming his Republican challenger, Thomas Dewey, president. Opinion polls stopped asking questions too early in the 1948 election campaign, missing Truman's last-minute surge.

Longman
Participate.com
2.0
Simulation
**You Are a
Polling
Consultant**

dent to another. Telephone interviews—the cheapest and most common kind— are clustered within particular telephone exchanges. Still, the samples that survey organizations use are sufficiently representative so that survey results closely reflect how the whole population would have responded if everyone in the United States had been asked the same questions at the moment the survey was carried out.

When you are interpreting surveys, you need to pay close attention to the precise wording of the questions. It often makes a big difference exactly how questions are asked. In one survey, for example, support for a constitutional amendment requiring a balanced budget dropped from 70 percent to 31 percent when the question specified that Medicare would be cut.[11] Moreover, "closed-ended" or "forced-choice" questions, which ask the respondents to choose among preformulated answers, do not always reveal what people are thinking on their own or what they would come up with after a few minutes of thought or discussion. For that reason, "open-ended" questions are sometimes asked in order to yield more spontaneous answers, and small discussion groups or "focus groups" are brought together to show what emerges when people talk among themselves about the topics a moderator introduces. (See "By the Numbers: Do Americans support stem cell research? How do we know which survey to believe?" for more insight into issues in public opinion research.)

Individuals' Ignorance

Several decades of polling have shown that most ordinary Americans do not know or care a lot about politics. Nearly everyone knows some basic facts, such as the name of the capital of the United States and the length of the president's term of office. But only about two-thirds of adults know which party has the most members in the House of Representatives. Only about one-half know that there are two U.S. senators from their state, and fewer can name their representative in the House. Only about 30 percent know that the term of a U.S. House member is two years.[12] And barely one in four Americans can explain what is in the First Amendment.[13]

By the Numbers

Do Americans support stem cell research? How do we know which survey to believe?

One of the emerging controversies in American politics concerns whether the federal government should encourage or discourage medical research that uses embryonic stem cells. Proponents say the use of such cells, today harvested primarily from unused embryos from fertility clinics, is almost certain to lead to new medical treatments for a wide range of genetically linked diseases, such as Parkinson's and juvenile diabetes. Opponents say the expanded use of stem cells for research will encourage more abortions—aborted embryos being a potentially important source of stem cells—as well as the creation of cloned embryos, both of which, in their view, are morally unacceptable.

Why It Matters: In the long run, government policies tend to follow public opinion on major issues. Whether the federal government will allow research in this emerging bio-medical field, and whether it will help pay for basic research, will depend a great deal on how strong the public stance is on the issue.

Behind the Number: At first blush, it certainly looks as if the public strongly supports stem cell research. In early 2001, several leading survey organizations reported the public in favor of moving along this path: An NBC News/*Wall Street Journal* poll showed 69 percent in favor; Gallup reported 54 percent in favor; ABC News weighed in with 58 percent in favor; and the Juvenile Diabetes Foundation reported 70 percent in favor. On the other hand, a poll sponsored by the Conference of Catholic Bishops showed only 24 percent in favor of stem cell research.

Calculating the Number: In the surveys reported above, the various polling organizations did not simply ask respondents whether they were in favor of stem cell research or against it, but offered alternative positions for respondents to consider, briefly spelling out the arguments being made for both sides in the debate. So it would seem, given the care with which questions were written and the opinion numbers reported above, that proponents of stem cell research have won the public opinion battle.

Criticisms of the Number: But not so fast! Consider a number of problems raised by academic critics, all of which are related to a concern about whether

---

People have particular trouble with technical terms, geography, and abbreviations. In the 1980s, very few could identify the important SALT negotiations (the Strategic Arms Limitation Talks) between the United States and the Soviet Union. Today, many are fuzzy about the location of such places as Bosnia, Iraq, and Kosovo.

The things that most Americans don't know may not be vital to their role as citizens, however. If citizens are aware that arms control talks went on between the United States and the Soviet Union, is it crucial that they recognize the acronym *SALT*? How important is it for people to know about the two-year term of office for the U.S. House of Representatives, as long as they are aware of the opportunity to vote each time it comes along? Perhaps most people know as much as they need to know in order to be good citizens, particularly if they can form opinions with the help of better-informed cue givers (experts, political leaders, media sources, informed friends, interest groups, and so on) whom they trust or by means of simple rules of thumb.[14]

In any case, the lack of knowledge does not represent just stupidity or laziness. There are good reasons for it. Most people are busy with their jobs and

Americans really have opinions at all about stem cell research:

- High levels of "don't know" responses are a clue that the public has not formed well-grounded opinions about the survey issue. Unfortunately, among the surveys cited above, only the Gallup organization offered such an option to respondents. The Gallup finding of high numbers of "don't know" responses suggests Americans may be more uncertain about stem cell research than appears on the surface.
- When wide variations in opinion are reported—in this case, between those in the Catholic Bishops' survey and the others—the culprit may be the question wording. Well-established and strongly held opinions are not easily shaken or changed by question wording. Consequently, when question wording leads to wide variations in expressed opinions, public opinion specialists suspect that the public has not yet formed opinions about the issues being addressed in the survey. There is some evidence of this in the Bishops' survey; examination of the survey shows that some fairly loaded language was used, including wording such as "the live embryos would be destroyed in their first week of development." Their questionnaire, moreover, states that the embryos would be used "in experiments," leaving unmentioned possible medical advances arising from research.

What to Watch For: Though respondents in a survey are generally willing to help out survey researchers by saying whether they are "for" or "against" one thing or another, they may not really have solid, well-formed opinions about the issue being addressed. Three very useful clues are:

- a high number of "don't know" responses. Check the original source of the survey results reported in the newspaper or on television to find out the number of these responses.
- wide variations in the results of opinion surveys on a particular issue. Do not depend on the results of one survey but look at several on the same subject.
- the presence of highly detailed questions that explain the issue to the respondent. Go to the original source and see how the question or questions are worded.

What Do You Think? Have you formed an opinion about the benefits and drawbacks of stem cell research? If you have an opinion, do you believe it is based on information you have encountered and thought about carefully? If you have formed a solid point of view on stem cell research, you may want to contact various elected officials and let them know where you stand.

Source: Adam Clymer, "The Unbearable Lightness of Public Opinion Polls," *The New York Times* (August 12, 2001), "Week in Review," p. 1"; and Richard Morin, "Who Knows?" *The Washington Post National Edition* (September 10–16, 2001), p. 34.

families; they don't have much time or energy left for politics. Unless following politics happens to give them pleasure, there is little reason for them to invest much effort in it. Scholars remind us that a single citizen has only a minuscule chance of determining the outcome of an election in which thousands or millions vote; from a purely selfish point of view, it is not worth a lot of trouble to decide how to vote. The real surprise may be that people know as much as they do.[15]

We do not mean to minimize the consequences of people's lack of political knowledge. It has some extremely important implications. As we will see in Chapter 7, for example, when policy decisions are made in the dark, out of public view, interest groups may influence policies that an informed public would oppose. Nor do we mean to encourage complacency, fatalism, or ignorance. Individuals should take the personal responsibility to be good citizens, and organized efforts to alert and to educate the public are valuable. But low levels of information are a reality that must be taken into account. It is unrealistic to expect everyone to have a detailed knowledge of a wide range of political matters.

By the same token, we should not expect the average American to have an elaborately worked out **ideology,** or system of interlocking attitudes and

ideology

A system of interrelated attitudes and beliefs.

beliefs. You yourself may be a consistent liberal or conservative (or populist, socialist, libertarian, or something else), with many opinions that hang together in a coherent pattern. But surveys show that most people's attitudes are only loosely connected to each other. Most people have opinions that vary from one issue to another: conservative on some issues, liberal on others. Surveys and in-depth interviews indicate that these are often linked by underlying themes and values, but not necessarily in the neat ways that the ideologies of leading political thinkers would dictate.[16]

For the same reasons, we should not be surprised that most individuals' expressed opinions on issues tend to be unstable. Many people give different answers when the same survey question is repeated four years or two years or even a few weeks after their first response. Scholars have disagreed about what these unstable responses mean, but uncertainty and lack of information very likely play a part.

Collective Knowledge and Stability

None of this, however, means that the opinions of the public, taken as a whole, are unreal, unstable, or irrelevant. The collective whole is greater than its individual parts. Even if there is some randomness in the average individual's expressions of political opinions—even if people often say things off the top of their heads to survey interviewers—the responses of thousands or millions of people tend to average out this randomness and reveal a stable **collective public**

collective public opinion

The political attitudes of the public as a whole, expressed as averages, percentages, or other summaries of many individuals' opinions.

opinion. Americans' collective policy preferences are actually very stable over time. That is, the percentage of Americans who favor a particular policy usually stays about the same, unless circumstances change in important ways.

Moreover, even if most people form many of their specific opinions by deferring to others whom they trust (party leaders, television commentators, and the like) rather than by compiling their own mass of political information, the resulting public opinion need not be ignorant or unwise because the trusted leaders may themselves take account of the best available information. Some

Web Exploration
Survey Validity

Issue: Seeing the flood of polls about elections and government policies in the news media, many people ask, "How come I've never been asked about my opinions?"

Site: You can take part in a political survey by accessing "Doonesbury On-Line" on our Website at **www.ablongman.com/greenberg**. In the "Web Explorations" section for Chapter 5, open "survey validity," then "poll," and answer the questions posed there. Also, look at "Previous Questions and Results."

What You've Learned: How do your views on the issues compare with others who have taken part? Given what you have learned about surveys and random sampling in this textbook, what would you conclude about the validity of this poll?

HINT: Remember that survey validity depends on the "randomness" of the sample.

recent research, moreover, indicates that Americans' collective policy preferences react rather sensibly to events, to changing circumstances, and to new information, so that we can speak of a "rational public."[17]

How People Feel About Politics

Americans have opinions about many different political matters, including specific policies, basic values, the Republican and Democratic parties, and government itself.

The System in General

At the most general level, Americans are quite proud of their country and its political institutions. In 1998, for example, only 4.8 percent of Americans agreed with the statement that "there are some countries better than the United States." Well over three-quarters of Americans agreed with the statement that the "American system of government is the best in the world."[18] At the more specific level, however, the picture has not looked so rosy. For the past three decades, pollsters, scholars, and journalists have all noted a steady decline in Americans' trust in government and in their regard for public officials.[19] (See Figure 5.1.) The erosion of confidence and trust has had important political consequences. In 1992, for example, fully 70 percent of Americans said they were "dissatisfied" with the overall performance of the national government, a feeling

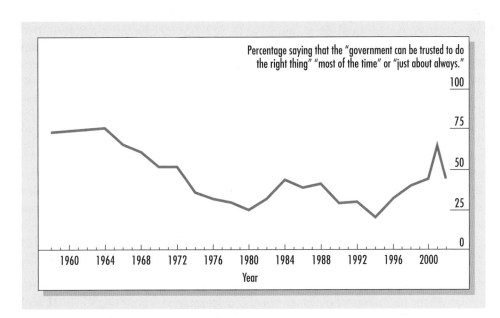

FIGURE 5.1 The Decline (and Rebound?) of Trust in Government

The graph shows the percentage of Americans who say they can "trust the government to do what is right," "most of the time" or "almost always." The steady decline from the 1950s and 1960s is noteworthy, as is the dramatic rebound after Nine-Eleven. But note the drop in 2002.

Source: The American National Election Studies, 1956–1998 and the *Washington Post*/ABC News Poll, October 2001 and August 2002.

Americans report very high levels of patriotism compared with people in other rich democracies, as well as higher levels of confidence in their fundamental government and economic institutions (although not necessarily confidence in their present leaders).

that almost certainly contributed to the independent candidacy of Ross Perot and the defeat of President George H. W. Bush in that year.

The events of September 11, 2001, and the very popular military effort to punish Osama bin Laden and Al Qaeda, and to topple the Taliban regime in Afghanistan, contributed to a remarkable and unprecedented turnaround in Americans' overall sense of trust in government. Though government and government officials almost always gain popular support during war, at least in its earlier stages and as long as things are going well on the battlefield, confidence and trust has never before (at least since the introduction of systematic polling) rebounded to this degree. According to a *Washington Post*/ABC News poll published in December 2001, roughly two-thirds of Americans said they trusted the government to "do what is right just about always or most of the time," the first time that a clear majority had felt this way in more than three decades. In fact, the level of trust at the end of 2001 was roughly three times the figure for 1994, when the public's expressed trust in government reached its lowest point ever. Almost identical results were reported by the *New York Times*/CBS News poll, Gallup, and other journalistic and academic opinion surveys.[20]

It seems that this dramatic turnaround in confidence in the federal government was simply a temporary phenomenon, part of a patriotic response triggered by the attacks on the United States and the war on terrorism. By mid-2002, trust in government was again tracking downward, a response, no doubt, to an avalanche of bad news about government performance: revelations of FBI and CIA intelligence failures surrounding the Nine-Eleven attacks, the return of federal government budget deficits, the reappearance of bitter partisanship in Washington during the run-up to congressional elections, and the seeming inability of government leaders to do much about the slumping economy and the corporate accounting mess.

political efficacy

The sense that one can affect what government does.

Consistent with the long-term decline in trust in government has been the steady decline in Americans' sense of **political efficacy,** their feeling that they can make a difference in what government does and that government will respond to their concerns. In 2000, 56 percent said that "the federal government doesn't care what people like me think"; 61 percent believe that government "is run for a few big interests." By way of comparison, only 36 percent of Americans in 1964 agreed with the "government doesn't care" statement, while only 29 percent agreed in the same year that government "is run for a few big interests."[21] These measures suggest a serious erosion in the level of political efficacy in the United States.

Government Performance

One important aspect of happiness or unhappiness with government is a judgment about how well the president has been doing his job. For many decades, pollsters have been asking people whether they approve or disapprove of the president's handling of his job. The percentage of people saying that they approve—the **presidential approval rating**—is taken as a crucial indicator of a president's popularity. Approval tends to fluctuate up and down with particular events—Lyndon Johnson's approval fluctuated with events in Vietnam, and he decided not to run for reelection when his ratings fell to historic lows after the Tet Offensive—but in the current era, most presidents have come on hard times. Richard Nixon, Gerald Ford, and Jimmy Carter all had low approval ratings by the end of their terms. George H.W. Bush reached a then-record 89 percent approval in March 1991 in the aftermath of the Gulf War, but fell below 30 percent by the summer, an unprecedented collapse. Oddly, Bill Clinton enjoyed the highest job approval ratings of any recent president for the final two years of the presidential term, in spite of the fact that he was impeached by the House of Representatives. George W. Bush's 90 percent job approval in late 2001 broke his father's record. This seems to have been a product not only of a "rally 'round the flag" effect common in wartime, but also

presidential approval rating
A president's standing with the public, indicated by the percentage of Americans who tell survey interviewers that they approve a president's "handling of his job."

The American public's approval of President Bush's job performance soared to historic highs after 9/11. Here he prepares to thank firefighters and other rescue workers at the devastating site of the World Trade Center.

of the widespread admiration for the way he responded to the attacks, coming from virtually every sector of political opinion. By fall 2002, however, Bush's approval had declined, hovering between 65 and 70 percent (which was still very high by historical standards).

We will see in later chapters that a president's popularity has very important consequences. It is a good predictor of whether he will win reelection (if he is running) and whether his party will win or lose congressional seats. Presidential popularity may also affect how much influence the president has in Congress.

The public's evaluations of presidents' handling of their jobs depend on how well things are actually going. The state of the economy is especially important: When the country is prosperous and ordinary Americans are doing well and feeling confident about the future, the president tends to be popular; when there is high inflation or unemployment or when general living standards remain stagnant, the president's popularity falls. International crises may lead the public to "rally 'round the flag" and support the president (providing that leaders in both parties are doing so), but that solidarity lasts only a little while unless the crisis works out well. If bad news keeps coming, people begin to disapprove of the president's performance.[22] In 1980, for example, the long drawn-out Iran hostage crisis undermined President Carter's popularity and political influence and cost him the election against Ronald Reagan.

Party Identification

party identification

The sense of belonging to one or another political party.

Historically, one of the most important political attitudes in the United States has been identification with a political party. Many Americans still feel such an identification. When survey researchers ask people whether, generally speaking, they consider themselves Republicans, Democrats, independents, or something else, about 60 percent pick one of the two major parties (see Figure 5.2). That sense of belonging to a party is called **party identification.** Among the remainder, many say they "lean" toward one party or the other and are sometimes included by political scientists among those who identify with that party.

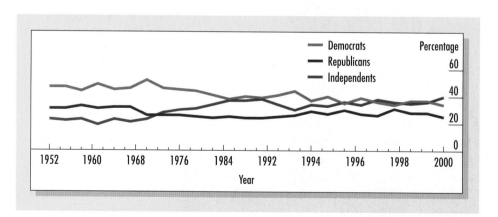

FIGURE 5.2 Trends in Party Identification

Over the years, the split in the population between those who call themselves Democrats and those who call themselves Republicans has been getting closer. This is happening because fewer Americans today identify as Democrats, and more identify as Independents. The Republican share of the population has dropped only a little since 1952.

Source: American National Election Studies, 2001.

People use the party label to help organize their thinking about politics: to guide them in voting, in judging new policy proposals, and so on. For example, people who consider themselves Republicans are much more likely than Democrats to vote for Republican candidates and to approve of Republican presidents; they tend to belong to different social and economic groups; and they are somewhat more likely to favor policies associated with the Republican party.

Beginning at the time of Roosevelt's highly popular New Deal in the 1930s and continuing almost to the present, more Americans have identified themselves as Democrats than as Republicans, making the Democrats the majority party. However, the margin of the Democrats' advantage began to shrink after the 1960s, from a margin of 15–20 percentage points before then, to around 8–9 points by 2000. The shrinking Democratic lead has been caused mainly by defections from the Democrats and an increase in the number of self-identified independents; the proportion of Americans who self-identify as Republicans changed only a little during this period (see Figure 5.2). Note, moreover, that independents make up the largest group today. A number of polling organizations reported a modest swing to the Republicans post 9/11, probably because of the great popularity of Republican President Bush, leaving Democrats with only a small lead over Republicans in early 2002.[23]

The party balance among voters has important effects on who rules in Washington, D.C., especially on which party controls Congress. Democrats controlled Congress for most of the time from the New Deal until the end of the 1970s because of their big lead in party identification. As the gap between the parties narrowed, Republicans began to achieve more success, winning majorities in the Senate from 1981 to 1986, and gaining control of both houses of Congress from 1994 through 2000. In 2002, Republicans again won control of both the House of Representatives and the Senate.

In recent decades, along with a decline in the proportion of people who identify with one of the two parties, there has been a rise in the proportion of broadly defined independents (including those who say they are independents but who say they tend to lean towards one party or another, so-called "leaners"), from the low-20s in the 1960s to around 40 percent today. Although some scholars maintain that these figures exaggerate the rise of independents because many "leaners" behave the same way as people who say they consider themselves Republicans or Democrats,[24] there has clearly been a decline in the proportion of Americans who identify strongly with either of the two major parties. Scholars do not agree about why this decline has occurred.[25]

Government's Role

While most Americans believe in both capitalism and democracy (and their respective core values, freedom and equality),[26] they divide on the relative priority they give to each. Some Americans—those we usually label **economic conservatives**—tend to put more emphasis on economic liberty and freedom from government interference; they believe that a free market offers the best road to economic efficiency and a decent society. Others—whom we usually label **economic liberals**—stress the necessary role of government in ensuring equality of opportunity, regulating potentially damaging business practices, and providing safety nets for individuals unable to compete in the job market. Government regulation of the economy and spending to help the disadvantaged are two of the main sources of political disputes in America; they make up a big part of the difference between the ideologies of liberalism and of conservatism. It is also useful to distinguish between **social liberals** and **social conservatives,** who differ on such social issues as abortion, prayer in the

economic conservatives

People who favor private enterprise and oppose government regulations on spending.

economic liberals

People who favor government regulation of business and government spending for social programs.

social liberals

People who favor civil liberties, abortion rights, and alternative lifestyles.

social conservatives

People who favor traditional social values; they tend to support strong law-and-order measures and to oppose abortion and gay rights.

schools, homosexuality, pornography, crime, and political dissent. Those who favor free choices and the rights of the accused are often said to be liberals, while those preferring government enforcement of order and traditional values are called conservatives. It should be apparent that opinions on economic and social issues do not necessarily go together, however. Many people are liberal in some ways but conservative in others. Followers of Ross Perot and Jesse Ventura, for example, tended to be economic conservatives (in favor of less government, balanced budgets, and so on) but social liberals.

Policy Preferences

policy preferences

Citizens' preferences concerning what policies they want government to pursue.

According to democratic theory, one of the chief determinants of what governments do should be what the citizens *want* them to do, that is, citizens' **policy preferences.**

Spending Programs   As Figure 5.3 indicates, large and rather stable majorities of Americans (around 70 percent in recent years) think we are spending "too little" on education and fighting crime. The public also gives high and stable support to Social Security, Medicare, and environmental programs. Substantial majorities, moreover, want the federal government to help people pay medical bills and for more research on diseases such as cancer and AIDS. About half of all Americans would increase spending on national defense.[27]

By contrast, few people—only about 1 percent—think too little is being spent on foreign aid; many more think too much is being spent. Except for disaster relief, foreign aid is generally unpopular. (The reason may be, in part, that few realize how little is spent on foreign aid—only about 1 percent of the budget. When this is made clear, support for economic aid rises sharply.)[28] Large majorities of the public oppose military aid or arms sales abroad. The space program wins only slightly greater support.

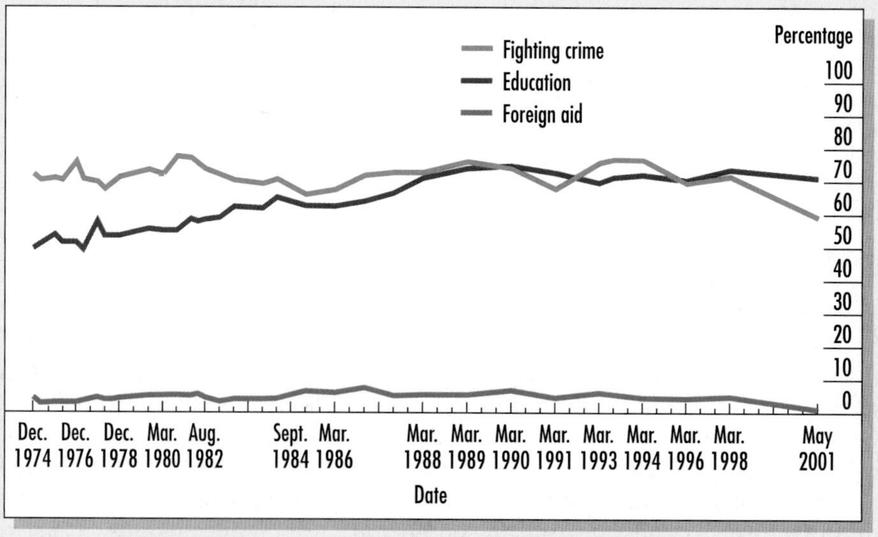

FIGURE 5.3 Public Support for Spending Programs

Large, fairly stable majorities of Americans have favored increased spending for fighting crime and aiding education, but very few have favored increased foreign aid.
Source: General Social Survey, 1973–2001.

Social Issues As Figure 5.4 shows, Americans make sharp distinctions among different circumstances when deciding whether they favor permitting abortions. For much of the past 25 years, about 90 percent of Americans have favored allowing legal abortion if a woman's health is endangered. About 80 percent would permit abortion in cases of serious birth defects. But only about 40 or 50 percent approve of abortion if a woman is poor or simply wants no more children. This same graph indicates that approval of abortion under each of the different circumstances rose markedly between 1965 and the early 1970s.

Other surveys have revealed strong liberalizing trends, over many years, concerning civil rights and civil liberties. Beginning in the 1940s or 1950s, more and more Americans have favored having black and white children go to the same schools and integrating work, housing, and public accommodations. (At the same time, however, there is considerable opposition to busing and affirmative action.) These issues are explored in depth in Chapter 16. More and more members of the public have also favored letting various dissenting groups (communists, socialists, atheists, and others) teach school, speak in public, and have their books in libraries. These trends are discussed further in Chapter 15.

Attitudes about the rights of gays and lesbians are more complicated. Although a slight majority of Americans agree with the statements that "people living in a homosexual relationship is not acceptable" and that "homosexual behavior is morally wrong,"[29] the opinion climate for gays and lesbians may be improving. For one thing, the percentages agreeing with these statements declined by almost 20 percentage points between 1986 and 1998; for another, strong majorities agree that gays and lesbians should not be discriminated against in jobs, education, and housing.[30] About four in ten Americans would bar gays and lesbians from jobs as schoolteachers or clergy, for example, down from six in ten in the late 1970s.[31] And, 76 percent say they favor federal "hate

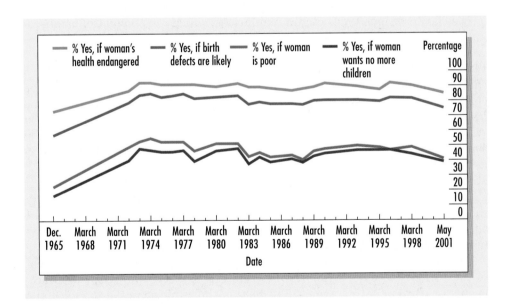

FIGURE 5.4 Public Approval for Allowing Abortions

Public opinion about abortion varies greatly with the circumstances. Large majorities favor allowing abortions if the woman's health is endangered or in the case of serious birth defects, but less than half the public would allow abortions in cases of poverty or simply wanting no more children.

Source: General Social Survey, 1965–2001.

Public opinion polls show that Americans strongly support the idea of integrated public schools. They do not support every method that courts and reformers have proposed for achieving integration, however. Integration-related busing schemes, for example, find little support among the public.

crime" legislation to protect gays and lesbians.[32] Some scholars speculate that gay and lesbian social movements have been primarily responsible for changing the opinion climate.[33]

On a number of issues, Americans are socially conservative. Large majorities, for example, favor allowing organized prayer in the public schools, banning pornography, preventing flag burning, penalizing drug use, punishing crimes severely, and imposing capital punishment for murder. Yet large majorities favor various types of gun regulations, which are thought of as liberal measures.

Foreign Policy In the realm of foreign policy, public opinion sometimes changes rapidly. Major international events affect opinions, as we saw in the chapter opening vignette on public reactions to the Tet Offensive during the Vietnam War. But often foreign policy opinions are quite stable. Since World War II, for example, two-thirds or more of those giving an opinion have usually said that the United States should take an "active part" in world affairs. The exact percentage favoring an active role has varied somewhat, rising to a peak of about 83 percent in 1965, near the onset of the Vietnam War; dropping to about 62 percent after the failure of that war; and recovering in later years. Today, those believing that the United States should play an active role in world affairs again hovers near 80 percent.[34] The percentage supporting a U.S. role has remained consistently high, not fluctuating much with alleged public moods.[35]

Longman
Participate.com 2.0
Timeline
War, Peace, and Public Opinion

The public has been quite hesitant to use troops abroad, unless the threat to the United States is tangible. Just before U.S. troops were sent as peacekeepers to Bosnia, for example, 78 percent of the public opposed the idea, and only 17 percent were in favor.[36] Opposition faded as the operation began to look less risky, but any substantial casualties abroad arouse large-scale public disapproval. This is probably why President Clinton ruled out the use of ground troops in Kosovo to stop ethnic cleansing by Serb militias and the Yugoslav army. However, the public strongly supported the use of the military to destroy Al Qaeda and the Taliban regime in Afghanistan,[37] and to fight Saddam Hussein in Iraq, even if it entailed heavy American casualties.

USING THE FRAMEWORK: Why No Gun Control?

If a majority of Americans want gun control, why hasn't government done much about it?

Background: Public opinion surveys have consistently indicated high public support for stricter federal gun control laws. At a general level, around two-thirds of Americans say they want stricter laws. Several specific proposals receive even higher levels of support. For example, 80 percent want a nationwide ban on assault weapons, while 70 percent want the government to ban gun sales by mail-order and over the Internet. Although some laws, such as the Brady Bill–which requires background checks of gun buyers and a waiting period–have passed Congress, proposals for stricter control over the sale and distribution of weapons almost never get very far. Taking a broad look at how structural, political linkage, and governmental factors affect gun control legislation will help explain the situation.

Governmental Action

Most major gun control bills fail to become law.

Governmental Level

- The reelection calculations of members of Congress favor doing nothing: voting for stricter laws invites the opposition of intense minorities, such as the NRA; voting against such laws does not alienate many voters. →
- Republican presidents have generally opposed stricter gun control laws. →
- Democratic presidents have either had other legislative priorities or have faced daunting GOP opposition in Congress when they have introduced gun control proposals.

Political Linkages Level

- A majority of Americans supports gun control, but don't rank it very high among their priorities for government action. →
- Voters rarely take gun control into account when deciding who they will vote for. →
- The National Rifle Association funnels substantial amounts of money into congressional, presidential, referenda, and issue campaigns. →
- Many candidates are reluctant to attract the negative attention of the National Rifle Association; many others want NRA campaign contributions.

Structural Level

- The Second Amendment to the Constitution guarantees that "the right of the people to keep and bear arms shall not be infringed." →
- The gun has long been an important icon of American popular culture.

isolationism

The policy of avoiding involvement in foreign affairs.

unilateralist

The stance toward foreign policy that suggests that the United States should "go it alone," pursuing its national interests without seeking the cooperation of other nations or multilateral institutions.

multilateralist

The stance toward foreign policy that suggests that the United States should seek the cooperation of other nations and multilateral institutions in pursuing its goals.

Although not many Americans embrace pure **isolationism**—the view that the United States should not be involved abroad and should only pay attention to its own affairs—the public (and political and economic leaders, as well) is divided over whether its involvement in the world should take a **unilateralist** or a **multilateralist** form. Unilateralists want to go it alone, taking action when it suits our purposes, and not necessarily seeking the approval or help of international organizations such as the United Nations or regional organizations such as NATO. Unilateralists are also uncomfortable with entering into too many international treaties. Multilateralists believe that the protection of American interests requires continuous engagement in the world, but do not think that the United States has the resources or ability to accomplish its ends without cooperating with other nations and with international and regional organizations. According to most surveys, roughly two out of three Americans are in the multilateralist camp, telling pollsters they oppose unilateral U.S. military intervention in most cases and support cooperation with the U.N. and NATO and international treaties on human rights, the environment, and arms control.[38]

How People Differ

In talking about American public opinion as a collective whole, we should not ignore important distinctions among different sorts of people in different circumstances. Black people and white people; Catholics, Jews, and Protestants; southerners and northeasterners; poor people and rich people; women and men—all tend to differ from one another in their political attitudes.

Race and Ethnicity

Among the biggest differences are those between white and black Americans. Hispanics and Asian-Americans also have some distinctive political opinions. Many white ethnic groups, however, are no longer much different from other members of the population.

African-Americans On many core beliefs about the American system, few differences are discernible between black and white Americans. Similar percentages of each group believe, for example, that people can get ahead by working hard, that providing for equal opportunity is more important than ensuring equal outcomes, and that the federal government should balance its budget. On a range of other political issues, however, the racial divide looms large.[39]

Blacks, who stayed loyal to the Republican party (the party of Lincoln and of Reconstruction) long after the Civil War, became Democrats in large proportions with the New Deal of the 1930s. Most black Americans have remained Democrats, especially since the civil rights struggles of the 1960s. Today African-Americans are the most solidly Democratic of any group in the population: Some 71 percent call themselves Democrats, while only about 10 percent call themselves Republicans (see Figure 5.5). In 2000, 90 percent of African-Americans voted for Al Gore; only 9 percent supported George W. Bush.[40]

Black Americans also tend to be much more liberal than whites on economic issues, especially those involving aid to minorities or help with jobs, housing, medical care, education, and so on. This liberalism reflects African-Americans' economically disadvantaged position in American society and the still-real effects of slavery and discrimination. On some social issues, however, blacks tend to hold strong religious values and to be rather conservative: More

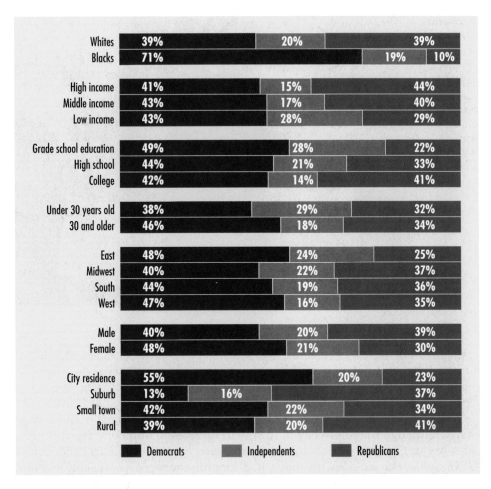

FIGURE 5.5 Party Loyalties Among Various Social Groups

Blacks, city dwellers, women, and people of lower income and educational levels tend to be Democrats, while whites, suburbanites, men, the college-educated, and people with high incomes tend to be Republicans.
Source: General Social Survey, 2001.

are opposed to abortion, for example, than are whites. Overall, more blacks consider themselves "liberal" (37 percent in 1998) than consider themselves "conservative" (31 percent; the rest being "moderate"), while the proportions among white voters are almost exactly reversed.[41] Black and white divisions are most apparent on issues related to affirmative action, the criminal justice system, and whether racism still exists. While 80 percent of African-Americans say they think affirmative action programs should be continued, only 35 percent of whites agree.[42] Similarly, 72 percent of black Americans believe that the criminal justice system is biased against blacks, a position held by only 45 percent of whites.[43]

Hispanics Hispanics—people of Spanish-speaking background—are the fastest-growing ethnic group in America, now making up about 12.3 percent of the population. However, the Hispanic population itself is quite diverse. Cuban-Americans, many of them refugees from the Castro regime, tend to be conservative, Republican, strongly anticommunist (recall the emotional case of the Cuban boat child, Elian Gonzales), and skeptical of government

Cuban-Americans are strongly anticommunist, with special levels of hostility directed at the Cuban regime and its leader, Fidel Castro. Here Cuban-Americans demonstrate in Miami at the home of the relatives of Elian Gonzales, demanding that the young boy be granted political asylum and not be sent back to Cuba. After a series of victories in the courts, the U.S. Immigration and Naturalization Service prevailed, and Elian Gonzales was allowed to leave with his father for Cuba.

programs. The much more numerous Americans of Mexican or Puerto Rican ancestry, by contrast, are mostly Democrats and quite liberal on economic matters, although rather traditional on social questions—reflecting their predominant Roman Catholicism.

Hispanics have been one of the least politically active groups in the United States, although they have begun to vote in increasing numbers (see the opening story in Chapter 4). Low incomes, suspicion of the authorities, and lack of facility with the English language had long discouraged participation. Now, mobilized by social movement groups and worried about anti-immigration and anti-immigrant state and national legislation, this sleeping giant of American politics seems to be awakening.

Asian-Americans Asian-Americans, a small but growing part of the U.S. population, come from quite diverse backgrounds in Japan, Korea, Vietnam, Thailand, China, and elsewhere. As a group, Asian-Americans have tended to be successful educationally and economically, to participate fairly actively in politics, and to be conservative and Republican.

White Ethnics Other ethnic groups are not so distinctive in their political opinions. Irish-Americans and people of Italian, Polish, and other southern or eastern European ancestry, for example, became strong Democrats as part of the New Deal coalition. But as they achieved success economically, their economic liberalism faded, and their social conservatism prevailed. By the 1980s, these groups were not much different from the majority of other white Americans.

Religion

Ethnic differences are often interwoven with differences in religious faith and values.

Catholics Roman Catholics, who constitute 28 percent of the U.S. population, were heavily Democratic after the New Deal but now resemble the majority of Americans in their party affiliations. Catholics' economic liberalism has

First communion at a Roman Catholic church in Tarzana, California. Practicing Catholics tend to be economically liberal and socially conservative.

faded somewhat with rises in their income, although this liberalism remains substantial. Catholics have tended to be especially concerned with family issues and to espouse measures to promote morality (e.g., antipornography laws) and law and order. But most American Catholics disagree with many church teachings: They support birth control and the right to have abortions in about the same proportions as do other Americans.

Jews   American Jews (only about 2 percent of the U.S. population) began to join the Democratic party in the 1920s and did so overwhelmingly in the 1930s, in response to Franklin D. Roosevelt's New Deal social policies and his foreign policy of resisting Hitler. Most Jews have stayed with the party. Next to African-Americans, they remain the most Democratic group in the United States: About 44 percent identify themselves as Democrats and only 20 percent as Republicans. In the 2000 presidential election, Jews cast 79 percent of their votes for Gore and only 19 percent for Bush.

Jews are exceptionally liberal on such social issues as civil liberties and abortion. They also tend to be staunch supporters of civil rights, despite tensions with African-Americans over such matters as U.S. policy toward Israel and the Palestinians and anti-Semitic remarks over the years by some black leaders. Rising incomes have somewhat undercut Jews' economic liberalism, but they remain substantially more supportive of social welfare policies than other groups.

Protestants   Protestants, who constitute a large majority of Americans, do not differ much from the U.S. average in most respects. But Protestants come in many varieties: relatively high-income (socially liberal, economically conservative) Episcopalians and Presbyterians; generally liberal Unitarian-Universalists and middle-class northern Baptists; and lower-income and quite conservative Southern Baptists and evangelicals of various denominations.

In the early 1980s, evangelical Christians played an important part in the "new right" segment of Ronald Reagan's conservative movement, working hard against abortion, against pornography, for law and order, and for their version of family values. Disappointed by failures to achieve their national goals at that time, some turned toward local and state politics and had considerable success in picketing and disrupting abortion clinics, changing public school curricula, and pushing anti-gay-rights referenda. The Christian Coalition provided much energy and activism for the Republicans' 1994 congressional election victory. Fully 76 percent of white born-again Christians voted for Republican House candidates in that year, while only 24 percent voted for Democrats.[44] In 2000, they voted for Bush over Gore by an 80–18 margin.[45]

Region

It is still true that "the South is different." Regional differences have been reduced because of years of migration by southern blacks to northern cities, the movement of industrial plants and northern whites to the Sun Belt, and economic growth catching up with that of the North. But the legacy of slavery and segregation, a large black population, and late industrialization have made the South a unique region in American politics.

Even now, white southerners tend to be somewhat less enthusiastic about civil rights than northerners; only people from the Mountain West are as conservative on racial issues.[46] Southerners also tend to be conservative on social issues, such as school prayer, crime, women's rights, and abortion, and supportive of military spending and a strong foreign policy (although fairly liberal on economic issues, such as job guarantees and health insurance).

These distinctive policy preferences have undercut southern whites' traditionally strong identification with the Democratic party, especially since the 1960s and 1970s, when the national Democrats became identified with liberal social policies and antiwar foreign policy. The white South's switch to the Republican party in the 1994 elections, in fact, is one of the major reasons Republicans were able to win control of Congress. Figure 5.5 shows differences in party loyalties among regional and other social groups.

On many issues, northeasterners tend to be the most different from southerners, with midwesterners, appropriately, in the middle. Pacific Coast residents resemble northeasterners in many respects, but people from the Rocky Mountain states tend to be quite conservative, with strong majorities opposed to government job guarantees and health insurance assistance, for example.[47] The mountain states' traditions of game hunting in wide-open spaces have led them, like southerners, to cherish the right to bear firearms and to resist gun controls.

Social Class

Compared with much of the world, the United States has had rather little political conflict among people of different income or occupational groupings; in fact, rather few Americans think of themselves as members of a social "class" at all. When forced to choose, about half say they are "working class" and about half say they are "middle class."[48] In Great Britain, on the other hand, where the occupational structure is similar to that of the United States, 72 percent of the population calls itself "working class."[49]

Still, since the time of the New Deal, substantially more low-income people—poor people, as well as blue-collar workers and union members—have identified themselves as Democrats rather than as Republicans. The opposite is true at the top of the income and occupational scales. More business executives, doctors, lawyers, and other highly paid people identify themselves as Republicans. In 2000, 62 percent of Americans in the lowest 15 percent of income earners thought of themselves as Democrats, for example, but

The Republican party has been making inroads among blue-collar, unionized workers. Here union members show their support for GOP candidate George W. Bush during the 2000 presidential contest.

only 36 percent of those in the top 5 percent did so. Fifty-five percent of blue collar workers said they were Democrats; 46 percent of professionals said they were also.[50]

Though income and occupation have always differentiated Democratic supporters from Republican supporters, the differences seem to be narrowing. In the middle of the 1960s, for example, 70 percent of blue-collar workers supported the Democrats (now down to 55 percent). Support of the Democrats from union members fell from 77 percent to 61 percent during the same time span. In the 2000 election, only 53 percent of those making more than $50,000 a year voted for the Republican candidate, George W. Bush; in 1988 62 percent of this group had voted for the Republican candidate, George H. W. Bush. A variety of commentators believe that what is happening is that class issues are becoming less salient to voters, and that lifestyle and social issues—abortion, law and order, religion, civil rights, education, gay rights, and more—are becoming more salient. This may help explain why more high-income, high-education congressional districts in places such as California and Connecticut are electing Democrats, and why more white, low-income districts in Kentucky, Tennessee, and West Virginia are sending Republicans to Congress.[51]

Lower-income people have some distinctive policy preferences. Not surprisingly, they tend to favor much more government help with jobs, education, housing, medical care, and the like, whereas the highest-income people, who would presumably pay more and benefit less from such programs, tend to oppose them. To complicate matters, however, some groups of high-income people—especially highly educated professionals—tend to be very liberal on social issues involving sexual behavior, abortion rights, free speech, and civil rights. They also tend to be especially eager for government action to protect the environment. Once again, no simple "liberal" versus "conservative" distinction can accurately sum up all differences in opinions.

Education

The level of formal education that people reach is closely related to their income level because education helps people earn more and also because the wealthy can pay for more and better schooling for their children. But education has some distinct political effects of its own.

As we will see in Chapter 10, education is generally considered the strongest single predictor of participation in politics. College-educated people are much more likely to say that they vote, talk about politics, go to meetings, sign petitions, and write letters to officials than people who have attained only an elementary or a high school education. The highly educated know more about politics. They know what they want and how to go about getting it, joining groups and writing letters, faxes, and e-mail messages to public officials.

People with more schooling also have some distinctive policy preferences. As we have indicated, they are especially protective of the civil rights, civil liberties, and individual freedom of atheists, homosexuals, protesters, and dissenters. Education may contribute to tolerance by exposing people to diverse ideas or by training them in elite-backed norms of tolerance.

Gender

Women were prevented from participating in politics for a large part of our history; they got the vote, by constitutional amendment, only in 1920. Not all women immediately took advantage of this new opportunity. For many years, women voted and participated in politics at lower rates than men—about 10 or 15 percent lower in the elections of the 1950s, for example. Only after the women's movement gained force during the 1970s did substantial numbers of female candidates begin to run for high office. Although an office-holding gap remains, the participation gap has virtually disappeared.[52] We will explore this in more depth in Chapter 10.

Web Exploration
The Gender Gap

Issue: There has been much talk of a "gender gap" in the United States.

Site: Examine male and female political attitudes and behaviors by accessing the American National Election Study on our Website at **www.ablongman.com/greenberg**. In the "Web Explorations" section for Chapter 5, open "gender gap." Look at a few survey questions about public policies in Section 4. For each question you examine, select "percent among demographic groups who responded," and you will see how men and women have responded over the years to the same questions.

What You've Learned: Is there a "gender gap"? If there is one, does the gap exist in all areas of politics and policy, or is the gap more pronounced on some issues compared with others?

HINT: As a measuring rod to determine the seriousness of the "gender gap," look at the differences between whites and blacks on the same survey questions.

A partisan "gender gap" first appeared in the 1980s and persists today, with the percentage of women who identify themselves as Democrats about 8 percentage points higher than men (see Figure 5.5). The difference between men and women is primarily a product of declining Democratic Party identification among men, particularly white southerners.[53]

Women also differ somewhat from men in certain policy preferences. Women tend to be somewhat more supportive of protective policies for the poor, the elderly, and the disabled. Women tend to be more opposed to violence, whether by criminals or by the state. More women over the years have opposed capital punishment and the use of military force abroad and favored arms control and peace agreements.[54] Interestingly, the gender gap on issues like defense spending, the use of military force abroad, and a missile-defense shield disappeared in the wake of terrorist attacks on the United States, as women shifted to a more defense-supportive position similar to that of men.[55]

Age

The young and the old differ on certain matters that touch their particular interests: the draft in wartime, the drinking age, and, to some extent, Social Security and Medicare. Also, people over the age of 60 tend to be more critical of government, perhaps because their expectations about what government can and should deliver are higher.[56] But the chief difference is that young people are more attuned to the particular times in which they are growing up. Those who were young during the 1960s were especially quick to favor civil rights for blacks, for example. In recent years, young people have been especially concerned about environmental issues. Often social change occurs by generational replacement. Old ideas, like the Depression-era notion that women should stay at home and "not take jobs away from men," die off with old people.

Longman
Participate.com
2.0
Visual Literacy
Who Are Liberals and Conservatives? What's the Difference?

Longman
Participate.com
2.0
Participation
Are You a Liberal or a Conservative?

Does Public Opinion Strongly Influence What Government Does?

We have argued that one crucial test of how well democracy is working is how closely a government's policies correspond to the expressed wishes of its citizens. How close, then, is the relationship between what American citizens want—that is, collective public opinion in the whole nation—and what the U.S. government actually does?

"Yes, It Does"

Our opening vignette about the Vietnam War suggests that at least under some circumstances, public opinion does affect policymaking. We have encountered other examples that tell the same "government responsiveness" story in this book. We saw in Chapter 1, for example, that Congress passed the historic Civil Rights Act of 1964 after a period of time when public support for racial segregation was declining.

These stories about government responsiveness to public opinion have been buttressed by important statistical assessments. Looking at many different policy issues—foreign and domestic—one scholar found, for example, that about two-thirds of the time, U.S. government policy coincides with what opinion surveys say the public wants. The same two-thirds correspondence has appeared when other scholars investigated how *changes* in public opinion relate to changes in federal, state, and local policies. Moreover, when public opinion changes by a substantial and enduring amount and the issue is prominent, government policy has moved in the same direction as the public 87 percent of the time within a year or so afterward.[57]

Another study shows that substantial swings in the national political mood have occurred over the past half century or so and that public policy follows accordingly. As the American people have moved first in a liberal direction, then a conservative direction, and back again over the years, elected leaders in Washington have shaped their policies to fit the public mood, being more activist in liberal periods and less activist in conservative periods.[58] Another highly regarded study shows that policies enacted in particular *states* correspond rather closely to the opinions of the states' citizens; that is, the states with mostly liberal citizens tend to have mostly liberal policies, and the states with mostly conservative citizens have mostly conservative policies.[59]

"No, It Doesn't"

While these studies seem to lend substantial support for the idea that public opinion is a powerful determinant of what government does in the United States, this research has no shortage of critics. Showing a high correlation (e.g., a strong statistical relationship) between public opinion and government policy does not prove that public opinion causes government policies. There are any number of plausible reasons why a "causal relationship" may not really exist. Here is what the critics say:[60]

- It may be the case that public opinion and government policies move in the same direction because some third factor causes both of them to change. In this example, the true cause of government action is this third factor, not public opinion. There are many instances in the real world where this has happened. For example, the news media often play up a particular incident or situation and persuade both public opinion and government policy makers that action is needed. This is clearly what happened when the Hearst newspaper chain whipped up fervor among both the public and elected leaders for war against Spain in the wake of the sinking of the battleship *Maine* in Havana harbor. Or an interest group or set of interest groups might sway public opinion and government officials in the same direction, as medical, insurance, and hospital associations did when they launched a successful campaign to sink Bill Clinton's health care initiative in 1994.

- Even if public opinion and government actions are highly correlated, it may be the case that it is government that shapes public opinion. In statistical language, we might say that the causal arrow is reversed, going not from the public to government, but the other way around: that officials act to gain popular support for policies and actions these officials want.[61] Such efforts can range from outright manipulation of the public—the Tonkin Gulf incident described in the opening story in this chapter is such a case—to the conventional public relations efforts carried out every day by government officials and agencies. This is why both the legislative and executive branches of the federal government are so well equipped with communications offices, press secretaries, and public liaison personnel.

So where does all of this leave us on the question of public opinion's influence on government? It is probably reasonable to say that public opinion plays an important role in shaping what government does, but so do a range of other political actors and institutions, including parties, interest groups, the news media, and social movements. It is probably reasonable to say, moreover, that the influence of public opinion on government is significantly less than the statistical studies above suggest (e.g., the "two-thirds" rule) for the reasons given: the impact of "third" factors on both opinion and government, and the significant amount of influence government officials have over popular opinion. And, it is hard to avoid noticing the many times government acts almost exactly contrary to public opinion—Congress's decision to go ahead with the impeachment and trial of Bill Clinton in the face of public opposition being the most recent notable example.

There is one more reason why a simple, straightforward answer cannot be given to the question "How much influence does public opinion have on government policy?" Scholars have reported that opinion plays an important role in shaping government policy under certain conditions, but much less so under others. Public opinion seems to matter the most when issues are highly visible to the public (usually because there has been lots of political conflict surrounding the issue), are about matters that affect the lives of Americans most directly, and concern issues for which people have access to reliable and understandable information. When economic times are tough— during a recession, for example—no amount of rhetoric from political leaders, the news media, or interest groups is likely to convince people "that they never had it so good." People have a reality check in such circumstances. By the same token, many foreign policy questions are distant from people's lives, and involve issues where information is scarce or incomplete. In this circumstance, government officials act with wide latitude and play an important role shaping what the public believes. Additionally, some issues, such as the details of tax legislation or the deregulation of the telecommunications industry, are so obscure and complex that they become the province of interest groups and experts, with the public having but ill-formed and not very intense opinions.

When the House of Representatives impeached President Bill Clinton, it acted against strong preferences of the American people, according to every major polling organization. Here the House Judiciary Committee listens to Clinton's deposition in the Paula Jones case.

HOW DEMOCRATIC ARE WE?

The Influence of Public Opinion on American Government

PROPOSITION: Public opinion is not very important in determining what the federal government does in the United States.

AGREE: Although the news media publish polls and talk a great deal about their meaning and effect on politics, public opinion is far less important than interest groups, business firms, large contributors, and periodic elections in determining what policies are enacted. There are simply too many examples of government acting contrary to the views of the public—including the disconnect between the expressed views of the public and government action on gun control, the impeachment of Bill Clinton, and health care—to plausibly argue for public opinion as a decisive tool of democracy.

DISAGREE: Political leaders pay very close attention to public opinion when they are in the midst of deciding on alternative courses of action. (Some would argue that they do entirely too much of this, in fact.) It is why congressional incumbents, presidents, and government agencies spend so much time and money polling their relevant constituencies. And it is no mystery why elected officials do this, as do their challengers: Public opinion is eventually translated into votes at election time. So, staying on the right side of public opinion—giving people what they want in terms of policies, as it were—is how people gain and keep elected offices. Thus, public opinion strongly influences what government does.

THE AUTHORS: It is tempting to think that public opinion drives government policy, and that democracy is alive and well in the United States, given that the correlation between public preferences and policy outcomes is pretty high. We have seen, however, that the strong statistical relationship is not what it seems at first. For one thing, the federal government takes action in a wide range of areas where the public has no opinion at all. Regulation of financial services and telecommunications comes to mind. It is here that interest groups and large contributors may play particularly important roles. Moreover, we have seen that even when the public has well-formed opinions, these opinions may themselves be the product of incomplete or biased information from the media, interest groups, and political leaders and even of outright manipulation. Political scientist E. E. Schattschneider probably had it right when he said that the American people were "semi-sovereign," meaning that public opinion can strongly influence government policy, but only when the public is engaged and mobilized by political competition and conflict.

Summary

Public opinion consists of the political attitudes and beliefs expressed by ordinary citizens; it can be measured rather accurately through polls and surveys. The democratic ideals of popular sovereignty and majority rule imply that government policy should respond to the wishes of the citizens. An important test of how well democracy is working, therefore, is how closely government policy corresponds to public opinion.

Most people do not know a lot of facts about politics and do not have well-worked-out ideologies or highly stable policy preferences. Contrary to the fears of the Founders and others, however, the *collective* public opinion of Americans is real and stable, and it takes account of the available information.

For the past four decades, Americans' trust in government and approval of the performance of political leaders have been declining. The public's regard for government and political officials rebounded dramatically in the aftermath of the terrorist attacks on the United States and the war on terrorism. Party loyalty, although still widespread, has declined in strength. Most Americans strongly believe in freedom, economic liberty, capitalism, equality of opportunity, and democracy. Liberals and conservatives disagree about economic regulation and safety nets for the unfortunate. Majorities of the public favor government action on crime, education, medical care, and the environment. Support is lower for defense and the space program and lower still for foreign aid. Support for civil rights, civil liberties, and the right to have an abortion has increased, but the public is conservative about patriotism, crime, prayer, and obscenity.

People learn their political attitudes and beliefs from their families, peers, schools, and workplaces; they also respond to political events and the mass media. Structural factors in the society, the economy, and the international system strongly affect public opinion. Opinions and party loyalties differ according to race, religion, region, urban or rural residence, social class, education level, gender, and age. Blacks, Jews, city dwellers, women, and low-income people tend to be particularly liberal and Democratic; white Protestants, suburbanites, males, and the wealthy tend to be conservative and Republican.

Longman
Participate.com
2.0
Comparative
**Comparing
Public
Opinion**

Public opinion has important effects on what federal, state, and local governments do, but so do other political actors and events. And government officials often shape public opinion. When all is said and done, the responsiveness of government to public opinion falls considerably short of the hopes of advocates of strong democracy.

Suggestions for Further Reading

Glynn, Carroll K., Susan Herbst, Garrett J. O'Keefe, and Robert Y. Shapiro, *Public Opinion.* Boulder, CO: Westview Press, 1999.
> *The most comprehensive overview of what scholars have learned about the formation and effects of public opinion in American politics.*

Hochschild, Jennifer L. *What's Fair? American Beliefs about Distributive Justice.* Cambridge, MA: Harvard University Press, 1986.
> *Public opinion explored through in-depth interviews with a small number of people.*

Jacobs, Lawrence C., and Robert Y. Shapiro. *Politicians Don't Pander: Political Manipulation and the Loss of Democratic Responsiveness.* Chicago: University of Chicago Press, 2000.
> *A complex but rewarding argument that carefully describes how government officials manage to deflect and avoid the pressures of public opinion.*

Manza, Jeff, Fay Lomax Cook, and Benjamin I. Page, eds., *Navigating Public Opinion: Polls, Policy, and the Future of American Democracy.* New York: Oxford University Press, 2002.
> *Leading public opinion scholars examine the question of whether and to what extent public opinion determines the shape of government policies in the United States.*

McClosky, Herbert, and John R. Zaller. *The American Ethos: Public Attitudes Toward Capitalism and Democracy.* Cambridge, MA: Harvard University Press, 1984.
> *A major study of some of Americans' most important beliefs and values.*

Page, Benjamin I., and Robert Y. Shapiro. *The Rational Public: Fifty Years of Trends in Americans' Policy Preferences.* Chicago: University of Chicago Press, 1992.
    Extensive description of opinion trends, arguing that the public is rational.

Internet Sources

Doonesbury   **www.doonesbury.com/arcade/strawpoll/index.cfm**
    A daily online poll on current issues.

Gallup Organization   **www.gallup.com/**
    Access to recent Gallup polls as well as to the Gallup archives.

General Social Survey   **www.icpsr.umich.edu/GSS/index.html**
    Online access to the National Opinion Research Center's biennial survey of American attitudes.

National Election Studies   **www.umich.edu/~nes/nesguide/nesguide.htm**
    Biennial survey of voters, focusing on electoral issues.

Polling Report   **www.pollingreport.com**
    A compilation of surveys from a variety of sources on politics and public affairs.

Roper Center   **www.lib.uconn.edu/RoperCenter/**
    Access to the main repository in the United States of public opinion polls on government and politics.

Notes

1. Joseph C. Goulden, *Truth Is the First Casualty: The Gulf of Tonkin Affair—Illusion and Reality* (Chicago: Rand McNally, 1969).

2. All public opinion polls cited in this chapter-opening vignette are from John E. Mueller, *War, Presidents and Public Opinion* (New York: Wiley, 1973).

3. U.S. Department of Defense, OASD (Comptroller), *Selected Manpower Statistics* (Washington, D.C.: Government Publications, June 1976), pp. 59–60.

4. Alexander Hamilton, James Madison, and John Jay, *The Federalist Papers*, ed. Clinton Rossiter (New York: New American Library, 1961; originally published 1787–1788). See Benjamin I. Page and Robert Y. Shapiro, *The Rational Public: Fifty Years of Trends in Americans' Policy Preferences* (Chicago: University of Chicago Press, 1992), chs. 1 and 2.

5. Walter Lippmann, *Public Opinion* (New York: Macmillan, 1922), p. 127.

6. Philip E. Converse, "The Nature of Belief Systems in Mass Publics," in David Apter, ed., *Ideology and Discontent* (New York: Free Press, 1964), pp. 206–261; Philip E. Converse, "Attitudes and Non-Attitudes: Continuation of a Dialogue," in Edward R. Tufte, ed., *The Quantitative Analysis of Social Problems* (Reading, MA: Addison-Wesley, 1970), pp. 168–189.

7. Pew Research Center for the People and the Press, *That Year: A Look Back at 1998* (1999), p. 8.

8. Lawrence R. Jacobs and Robert Y. Shapiro, *Politicians Don't Pander: Political Manipulation and the Loss of Democratic Responsiveness* (Chicago: University of Chicago Press, 2000), p. 301.

9. Times Mirror Center for the People and the Press, "The Vocal Minority in American Politics," press release, July 16, 1993.

10. Robert S. Erikson, *American Public Opinion: Its Origins, Content, and Impact*, 5th ed. (New York: Macmillan, 1995), tells much more about the techniques and the results of polling. Also see Carroll J. Glynn, Susan Herbst, Garrett J. O'Keefe, and Robert Y. Shapiro, *Public Opinion* (Boulder, CO: Westview Press, 1999), ch. 3.

11. Elizabeth Kolber, "Public Opinion Polls Swerve with the Turns of a Phrase," *The New York Times* (June 5, 1995), pp. A1, C11.

12. Erikson, *American Public Opinion*; Page and Shapiro, *The Rational Public*, pp. 9–14. We also calculated some percentages from the National Opinion Research Center's General Social Survey.

13. Glynn et. al., *Public Opinion*, Table 8.1, p. 252.

14. Paul M. Sniderman, Richard A. Brody, and Philip E. Tetlock, *Reasoning and Choice: Explorations in Political Psychology* (New York: Cambridge University Press, 1991); see also Michael X. Delli Carpini and Scott Keeter, *Information and Empowerment: What Americans Know about Politics and Why It Matters* (New Haven, CT: Yale University Press, 1996); Samuel Popkin, *The Reasoning Voter* (Chicago: University of Chicago Press, 1991).

15. See Anthony Downs, *An Economic Theory of Democracy* (New York: Harper, 1957), chs. 11–13.

16. Robert E. Lane, *Political Ideology: Why the American Common Man Believes What He Does* (New York: Free Press, 1962); Jennifer L. Hochschild, *What's Fair? American Beliefs about Distributive Justice* (Cambridge, MA: Harvard University Press, 1986); and Glynn et al., *Public Opinion*, ch. 8.

17. Page and Shapiro, *The Rational Public*.

18. General Social Survey, 1998.

19. Derek Bok, *The Trouble With Government* (Cambridge: Harvard University Press, 2001); Joseph S. Nye Jr., Philip D. Zelikow, and David C. King, eds., *Why People Don't Trust Government* (Cambridge, MA: Harvard University Press, 1997).

20. Robert Putnam, "Bowling Together: The United State of America," *The American Prospect* (February 11, 2002), pp. 20–22.

21. *American National Election Studies, 1948–2000* (Ann Arbor: University of Michigan, 2001).

22. Samuel Kernell, "Explaining Presidential Popularity," *American Political Science Review*, 72 (June 1978), pp. 506–522; Richard A. Brody, *Assessing the President: The Media, Elite Opinion, and Public Support* (Stanford, CA: Stanford University Press, 1991).

23. Michael Barone, "A Turn in the Polls?" *U.S. News.com* (January 11, 2002), **www.usnews.com/usnews/opinion/baroneweb/**.

24. Bruce E. Keith, David B. Magleby, Candice J. Nelson, Elizabeth Orr, Mark C. Westlye, and Raymond E. Wolfinger, *The Myth of the Independent Voter* (Berkeley, CA: University of California Press, 1992).

25. Walter Dean Burnham, "The Appearance and Disappearance of the American Voter," in Richard Rose, ed., *Electoral Participation: A Comparative Analysis* (Beverly Hills, CA: Sage, 1980), pp. 35–73; Jeffrey E. Cohen, *American Political Parties: Decline or Resurgence?* Washington, D.C.: CQ Press, 2001; and Michael B. MacKuen, Robert S. Erikson, and James A. Stimson, "Macropartisanship," *American Political Science Review*, 83 (1989), pp. 1125–1143.

26. Herbert McClosky and John R. Zaller, *The American Ethos: Public Attitudes Toward Capitalism and Democracy* (Cambridge, MA: Harvard University Press, 1984); and Glynn et. al., *Public Opinion*, ch. 8.

27. Princeton Survey Research Associates/PEW Research Center, April, 2001.

28. Steven Kull, *Americans and Foreign Aid: A Study of American Public Attitudes* (Washington, D.C.: Program on International Policy Attitudes, 1995).

29. Survey by Roper Starch Worldwide, July, 1998, reported in Kenneth Sherrill and Alan Yang, "From Outlaws to In-Laws," *Public Perspective* (January/February, 2000), pp. 20–31.

30. *Los Angeles Times* Poll, June 10, 2000.

31. Gallup Poll, February 8–9, 1999.

32. *Time*/CNN Survey, October 14–15, 1998.

33. Sherrill and Yang, "From Outlaws to In-Laws."

34. Gallup Poll, conducted for CNN and *USA Today*, February, 2001.

35. William Caspary, "'The Mood Theory': A Study of Public Opinion and Foreign Policy," *American Political Science Review*, 64 (1970), pp. 536–547; John E. Rielly, ed., *American Public Opinion and U.S. Foreign Policy, 1995* (Chicago: Chicago Council on Foreign Relations, 1995), p. 13; and Princeton Survey Associates/PEW Research Center, October 1999.

36. *Time*/CNN Survey, December 7, 1994.

37. Gallup Poll, conducted for CNN and *USA Today*, September, 2001.

38. Summary of polls on American foreign policy reported at *The Public Agenda On-Line* at **www.publicagenda.org/**.

39. Robert C. Smith and Richard Seltzer, *Contemporary Controversies and the American Racial Divide* (Lanham, MD: Rowman and Littlefield, 2000).

40. *Voter News Service*, November 9, 2000.

41. General Social Survey, 1999.

42. CBS News/*New York Times* Poll, December 1997.

43. Gallup Poll, February, 1997.

44. "Portrait of the Electorate," *The New York Times* (November 13, 1994), p. 15.

45. *Voter News Service*, November 9, 2000.

46. General Social Survey, 1999.

47. General Social Survey, 1999.

48. National Election Studies, 2000.

49. Bernadette C. Hayes, "The Impact of Class on Political Attitudes," *European Journal of Political Research* 27 (1995), p. 76.

50. American National Election Studies, 2001.

51. Thomas B. Edsall, "The Shifting Sands of America's Political Parties," *The Washington Post, National Edition* (April 9–15, 2001), p. 11. For a contrary view see Jeffrey M. Stonecash, *Class and Party in American Politics* (Boulder, CO: Westview, 2000).

52. M. Margaret Conway, Gertrude A. Steuernagel, and John R. Terocik, *Women and Political Participation* (Washington, D.C.: Congressional Quarterly Press, 1997).

53. Karen M. Kaufmann and John R. Petrocik, "The Changing Politics of American Men," *The American Journal of Political Science* 43 (July 1999), pp. 864–887.

54. Mark Schlesinger and Caroline Heldman, "Gender Gap or Gender Gaps?" *The Journal of Politics* (February, 2001), Vol. 63, no. 1, pp. 59–92; Robert Y. Shapiro and Harpreet Mahajan, "Gender Differences in Policy Preferences: A Summary of

Trends from the 1960s to the 1980s," *Public Opinion Quarterly*, 50 (1986), pp. 42–61; Glynn et al., *Public Opinion*, pp. 235–238; and the American National Election Studies, 2001.

55. Richard Morin, "Defense Tops the List," *The Washington Post National Edition* (November 26–December 2, 2001), p. 34.

56. Cantril and Cantril, *Reading Mixed Signals*, Table 2.4, p. 22.

57. Alan D. Monroe, "Consistency Between Public Preferences and National Policy Decisions," *American Politics Quarterly*, 7 (January 1979), pp. 3–19; Benjamin I. Page and Robert Y. Shapiro, "Effects of Public Opinion on Policy," *American Political Science Review*, 77 (1983), pp. 175–190.

58. James A. Stimson, *Public Opinion in America: Moods, Cycles and Swings* (Boulder, CO: Westview Press, 1991).

59. Gerald C. Wright Jr., Robert S. Erikson, and John P. McIver, "Public Opinion and Policy Liberalism in the American States," *American Journal of Political Science*, 31 (1987), pp. 980–1001. See also Robert S. Erikson, Gerald C. Wright Jr., and John P. McIver, *Statehouse Democracy: Public Opinion and Democracy in the American States* (New York: Cambridge University Press, 1994).

60. Summarized in Benjamin I. Page, "The Semi-Sovereign Public," in Jeff Manza, Fay Lomax Cook, and Benjamin I. Page, eds., *Navigating Public Opinion: Polls, Policy, and the Future of American Democracy* (New York: Oxford University Press, 2002).

61. Jacobs and Shapiro, *Politicians Don't Pander*; and John Zaller, *The Nature and Origins of Mass Opinion* (New York: Cambridge University Press, 1992).

Chapter 6
The News Media

In This Chapter

- The role of the news media in a democracy
- How the news is gathered and disseminated
- Why government officials are key news sources
- Whether the news media have a liberal or a conservative bias
- Why some media are more regulated than others
- How the news media affect public opinion and policymaking

Vernon Jordan Meets the Press

The "buzz" inside the Beltway was that Vernon Jordan, advisor, close confidant, and golfing partner of President Bill Clinton, was being investigated by Special Prosecutor Kenneth Starr for obstruction of justice. Word had it that Vernon Jordan, a prominent Washington attorney and former civil rights leader, had instructed Monica Lewinsky to lie about her sexual relationship with the president before Starr's grand jury. The evidence, it was said, was in one of the taped conversations Lewinsky had been having with disgruntled federal employee Linda Tripp.[1]

As is now widely known, Tripp was taping her conversations with Lewinsky at the suggestion of New York book agent Lucianne Goldberg in an effort to help Tripp put together a book exposing the president. Goldberg and Tripp had carefully scripted the telephone conversations with Lewinsky, leading her into areas they wanted her to talk about, encouraging Lewinsky to elaborate the most telling and titillating details, and cajoling her to continue when her interest flagged. Their plan, it seems, was to use the tapes to tweak the interest of one or more of the major newspapers or newsmagazines as a way to hype interest in a book that had yet to be written. After *Newsweek* turned down the opportunity to run a story based on Goldberg and Tripp's characterizations of what was on the tapes, the story of the "story that did not happen" appeared on gossip-webster Matt Drudge's Web site. From there, the story was picked up by ABC's *This Week with Sam Donaldson and Cokie Roberts,* then by other political talk shows, and then (with the apparent help of Kenneth Starr's staff) the *Washington Post.* The rest, as they say, is history.

The *Washington Post* headlined on January 21, 1998, that "Clinton and Jordan directed her [Lewinsky] to testify falsely." *Good Morning America* said the same day that Lewinsky had claimed on the tape that Jordan had "instructed her to lie." Over the next weeks and months, similar reports kept circulating. Although the various media outlets carried Jordan's denials, reporters implied that he was being less than truthful, equivocating, evading, and, as *Time* magazine put it on February 2, "wrapping himself in a protective layer of syntax." Other media outlets carried stories, none corroborated, about Jordan's womanizing and rich lifestyle. *Meet the Press* passed on the rumor that Starr was granting "limited immunity" for Jordan's testimony before the grand jury, implying that Jordan was about to be charged with a crime. All the major TV networks picked up the story, as did all the major newsmagazines. Television, magazine, and newspaper pundits commented on and argued endlessly about Jordan's misbehavior, what it meant for his future, and what it meant for the Clinton presidency. In all of this media frenzy, not a single reporter or commentator had ever listened to the tape or read the tape transcript.

When Special Prosecutor Kenneth Starr finally submitted his report to Congress urging the impeachment and removal from office of Bill Clinton, there was nothing in its pages about Vernon Jordan telling Monica Lewinsky to lie. Nor was there any such evidence in Linda Tripp's tape transcripts, which were also submitted to the House of Representatives and subsequently released to the public. Starr reported that Lewinsky had testified to his grand jury that neither the president nor Vernon Jordan had ever told her to lie. She repeated this testimony in the Senate trial of the president. The Vernon Jordan story, in the end, was baseless—a frenzy in which media outlets fed on the material supplied by other media outlets in the effort to fill space and time in the unending news cycle. Unfortunately, the way the story played in the media—rumor treated as fact, reporting taking a back seat to argument and punditry, "infotainment" pushing aside serious analysis, speed bumping aside accuracy—has become all too familiar to Americans. ∎

Thinking Critically About This Chapter

In this chapter, we turn our attention to the diverse news media in the United States to learn how they are organized, how they work, and what effects they have on the quality of our political life.

Using the Framework In this chapter you will learn about the role the news media play in influencing significant actors in the political system, including citizens and elected leaders. You also will learn how the media can shape what government does. And you will learn how the media are influenced by changes in technology and business organization, and by government regulation and constitutional rules regarding freedom of the press.

Using the Democracy Standard Using the tools presented in Chapter 1, you will be able to evaluate the degree to which the news media advance democracy in the United States or retard it. You will be able to judge whether the media promote popular sovereignty, political equality, and liberty. Finally, you will see how certain changes in the media are cause for concern in terms of the health of democracy.   ◀

Roles of the News Media in Democracy

The central idea of democracy is that ordinary citizens should control what their government does. However, citizens cannot hope to control officials, to choose candidates, to speak intelligently with others about public affairs, or even to make up their minds about what policies they favor unless they have good information about politics and policies. Most of that information must come through the news media, whether newspapers, radio, television, or, increasingly, the Internet. How well democracy works, then, depends partly on how good a job the news media are doing.

Watchdog Over Government

watchdog

The role of the media in scrutinizing the actions of government officials.

One role of the media in a democracy is that of **watchdog** over government. The idea is that the press should dig up facts and warn the public when officials are doing something wrong. Citizens can hold officials accountable for setting things right only if they know about errors and wrongdoing.

The First Amendment to the Constitution ("Congress shall make no law . . . abridging the freedom . . . of the press") helps ensure that the news media will be able to expose officials' misbehavior without fear of censorship or prosecution. This is a treasured American right that is not available in many other countries. Under dictatorships and other authoritarian regimes, the media are usually tightly controlled. Even in a democratic country such as Great Britain, strict secrecy laws limit what the press can say about certain government activities. In many countries, including France, Israel, and Sweden, the government owns and operates major television channels and makes sure that the programs are not too critical.[2] Although freedom of the press is far from perfect in the United States, the news media enjoy greater freedom than their counterparts in other countries.

PUBLIC WATCHDOG

But how often do the media in the United States fulfill their watchdog role? Even without formal censorship or government ownership of the media, various factors, including the way in which the news media are organized and their routines of news gathering, may limit how willing or able they are to be critical of government policies. In addition, the media may be too quick to blow scandals out of proportion and to destroy political leaders' careers.[3]

Clarifying Electoral Choices

A second role of the news media in a democracy is to make clear what electoral choices the public has: what the political parties stand for and how the candidates shape up in terms of personal character, knowledge, experience, and positions on the issues. Without such information, it is difficult for voters to make intelligent choices.

How much or how little attention do the media pay to candidates' stands on public policies? Do they devote too much coverage to the "horse race" (who is winning? who is losing?) aspect of campaigns instead? In scrutinizing the character and personality of candidates, do the media go overboard in digging up dirt and reporting negative material even when it is very minor?

Providing Policy Information

A third role of the news media is to present a diverse, full, and enlightening set of facts and ideas about public policy. Citizens need to know how well current policies are working, as well as the pros and cons of the alternative policies that might be tried, to formulate sensible preferences. In a democracy, government should respond to public opinion, but that opinion should be reasonably well informed.

How much policy information do the U.S. media actually convey, and how accessible is it? How diverse and how accurate is that information? Is it biased—toward liberalism, for example, or toward conservatism? Are some voices heard and others ignored? We will address such questions in this chapter.

The Media Landscape

The media have changed greatly over our history and continue to change ever more rapidly. Taken together, they represent, at least potentially, a multitude of ways for the public to gain access to political news, analysis, and commentary.

Newspapers

The first newspapers in the early Republic were not meant for the mass public. Newspapers were expensive and directed at an elite audience. Technological changes and the gradual democratization of American life made newspapers into a "mass" phenomenon. By the mid-1830s, "penny papers" such as the *New York Herald* reached mass audiences of ordinary working people by means of low prices and human interest stories, written in a breezy and often sensational style. The invention of the telegraph allowed news to be gathered and distributed quickly, eventually to millions of people. In the 1840s, several New York newspapers formed the Associated Press (AP) to cooperate in gathering news and distributing it by telegraph. In the late nineteenth century, Joseph Pulitzer of the *New York World* (1883) and William Randolph Hearst of the *New York Journal* invented **yellow journalism,** a new sort of newspaper that combined sensationalism and political crusades with oversized headlines and full-color illustrations and comics. One Hearst crusade in 1898 helped provoke war against Spain over Spanish control of Cuba, a key step in the emergence of the United States as a world power. Today's tabloids, like the *New York Post,* are less likely to start wars, but their journalistic techniques still resemble Hearst's yellow journalism.

yellow journalism

Sensational newspaper stories with large headlines and, in some cases, color cartoons.

The development of wire services such as the AP, the United Press International, and the Scripps-Howard Service (the last two are now defunct) meant that more political news could be spread much more quickly, to much bigger audiences, and, inevitably, in a much more nationally uniform way than ever before. Homogenization was accentuated by the development of large "chains" of newspapers, owned by the same company and pursuing uniform editorial policies. Most major metropolitan newspapers today are parts of such chains (which are themselves often parts of larger multimedia companies). They depend mainly on the AP for national and international news, syndicated columnists for their editorial page, and their own reporters to cover local affairs.

In addition to the chain-associated metropolitan dailies, newspapers come in three rough categories. First, there are newspapers that give serious, in-depth attention to domestic and international political affairs. Most notable is the *New York Times,* which claims to publish "all the news that's fit to print" and aspires to be America's "newspaper of record." It remains the preeminent U.S. newspaper for reporting on international affairs. It is rivaled only by the *Washington Post* for the extent of its domestic political reporting and by the *Wall Street Journal* for business and financial news. The *Los Angeles Times,* the *Miami Herald,* the *Boston Globe,* and the *Chicago Tribune* also fall on the serious side of the news spectrum. Second, there are newspapers in urban areas that address minority communities of one kind or another and the issues that directly concern them, including gays and lesbians, African-Americans, Hispanics, and Asian-Americans. Finally, there are the sensation-driven supermarket tabloids, such as the *National Enquirer,* the *Globe,* and the *Star,* which also include political stories, many of which eventually end up in the more mainstream press.

Today, despite all of the innovations making newspapers accessible and entertaining, Americans are relying less and less on them for their information

William Randolph Hearst's *New York Journal* stirred war fever in 1898 with unsubstantiated charges that the Spanish had destroyed the U.S. battleship *Maine* in Cuba.

about the world in favor of television and radio.[4] This may be a problem for democracy because television and radio have traditionally been less comprehensive and more shallow in their news coverage than the nation's top newspapers.

Magazines

Several journals of political opinion and analysis were founded in the nineteenth century. Some of these, such as *The Nation* and the *Atlantic Monthly,* are still published, and a wide range of other journals—liberal, conservative, radical, and reactionary—have entered the political debate.

Beginning in the 1920s, Henry Luce's *Time,* the weekly newsmagazine, brought analysis and interpretation of the week's news, written in a brisk and colorful style, to hundreds of thousands and then millions of readers; it later drew competition from *Newsweek* and *U.S. News & World Report.* Large-circulation magazines such as the *Saturday Evening Post, Life,* and especially *Reader's Digest* gained circulations in the millions. Countless specialized journals appeared, providing information and entertainment of diverse sorts.

Radio

Radio significantly changed the face of the media. Commercial radio stations with broad audiences were established during the 1920s and were soon organized into networks that shared news and other programs. In the depths of the Great Depression of the 1930s, millions of Americans could hear the reassuring voice of President Franklin Roosevelt giving "fireside chats." Later, millions could hear the latest news about the battles with Japan and Nazi Germany during World War II.

Radio, once thought vanquished by the television juggernaut, has been reborn, especially for commuters, joggers, and people who work at home. Besides music, AM and FM stations offer frequent news bulletins and call-in talk shows, on which all manner of political opinions, including the cranky and the outrageous, are voiced. Disproportionately middle-aged, male, and politically conservative (both callers and listeners),[5] syndicated talk shows, hosted by

Talk radio has become a very influential—and decidedly conservative—voice in American politics. Right-wing personality Rush Limbaugh, who often criticizes the mass media as being too liberal, draws a large and loyal audience.

people such as Rush Limbaugh (with an estimated audience of 15 million),[6] have become a political force, able to generate a flood of mail to Congress or the White House and even to force decisions on Washington policymakers.

Radio is not all sound and populist fury, however. Public Broadcasting System (PBS) stations provide extended news analysis and commentary, often thoughtful and occasionally unorthodox, on programs such as *Morning Edition* and *All Things Considered.*

Television

The television revolution transformed American media yet again. Television was invented before World War II; it was developed commercially in the late 1940s and entered American households on a large scale in the 1950s. Scores and then hundreds of television stations were established around the country, most eventually affiliating with one of the three major networks—ABC, CBS, and NBC—which provided the bulk of prime-time programming. The networks also produced and distributed national news programs, which in 1963 were expanded from 15 minutes to 30 minutes of early evening time, and became the main source of national news for most Americans. Today, cable all-news networks such as CNN, Fox News, and MSNBC have eaten into the network television news monopoly, while political junkies can turn to C-SPAN for live coverage of Congress and other inside-the-beltway activities. The BET offers news on public affairs that are of particular interest to African-Americans. According to a multitude of polls, Americans name television as their most important source of news, and most say they trust television a great deal.[7] (See "By the Numbers: How much serious crime is there in the United States?" on pages 166–167 to gain a sense of how accurate television news is in informing people about crime.)

The Internet

Longman
Participate.com
2.0
Participation
Democracy
and the
Internet

Personal computers with modems or broadband connections, appearing in a rapidly increasing number of homes, schools, and offices, create opportunities to gather political and public policy information from a host of sources on the Internet, including libraries, government agencies, online newspapers and magazines, special interest groups, scholars, and public interest organizations. This

The Vietnam War was the first American war fully covered by television. Footage of American deaths and casualties, as well as visual reminders of the terrible consequences of the conflict on the Vietnamese civilian population, helped turn public opinion in the United States against the war. This still from television footage of children napalmed by an accidental American attack on a village of Trang Bang is a particularly powerful example of the war coming home to American living rooms.

medium has a ways to go to catch up to traditional mass media, however; during the 1996 election season only 5 percent of the public reported visiting a politically oriented Website.[8] During the 2000 election cycle, only 11 percent of Americans reported visiting a candidate's or political party's Website, though 18 percent went to the Internet to gather political news.[9] However, candidates and parties have recently made huge investments in campaign Websites, so the pace of politically oriented Internet use will probably grow.

The true promise of the Internet, however, is in its capacity to serve as an interactive, two-way communications medium[10] in which citizens can talk back to political leaders and deliberate with one another. Already scores of

Web Exploration
Online Political Participation

Issue: Get involved! There are a number of virtual political communities on the Internet where you can gain information and interact with other people who share your political views.

Site: Visit the conservative "Town Hall" site and the liberal "Turn Left" site. Go to our Website at **www.ablongman.com/greenberg**, open the "Web Explorations" section for Chapter 6, and select "online political participation." Open the site for each. Each site has a bulletin board where you can join others in a discussion of the main issues on today's political agenda. Better yet, open yourself to other viewpoints; if you are liberal, visit the conservative site; if you are conservative, visit the liberal site.

What You've Learned: Do you see any merit in the views being expressed at these sites? Have you learned anything from them?

HINT: Crossing ideological lines with an open mind is hard to do. Keep trying. It's worth the effort.

political chat rooms exist, members of Congress register public opinion coming via e-mail, citizens communicate and share documents with others in their interest groups, and many online magazines and newspapers encourage reader online feedback and commentary. Information technology keeps advancing, opening up possibilities such as two-way video communication and instant electronic referendum voting.

We are also discovering—whether for better or worse is not yet clear—that almost anyone with an Internet connection can become a combination reporter, editor, and publisher. The most famous of these instant media moguls, if you will, is Matt Drudge, whose "Drudge Report" played such a large role in the news cycle leading to the Clinton impeachment. The distinction between rumor and fact is very fine indeed in this "report." His Website is not the only one of its kind, and many more, from diverse political perspectives, are certain to follow.

Commentators disagree about the democratic potential of the Internet. To many, the scarcity of editorial gatekeepers with a strong sense of journalistic integrity on the Internet means that citizens cannot be certain about the reliability of information found at most sites.[11] Also, the Internet makes it easier for fringe groups such as the "militia movement" and hate groups such as the "skinheads" and neo-Nazis to spread their messages and recruit new members. On the other hand, say other commentators, the Internet gives citizens fuller and easier access to information and opinions about government performance, electoral choices, and policy options. And it allows geographically diverse individuals and groups to organize politically and convey their views to policymakers. Some even suggest that the Internet ought to be thought of as a new space for participation in the political process, equal in stature to other participatory spaces in American politics.[12]

How the Media Work

The precise ways in which the news media are organized and function affect whether citizens get the kinds of information they need for democracy to work properly.

Organization of the News Media

Nearly all media in the United States are privately owned businesses. Most are either very large businesses in their own right or, more typically, part of very large corporate empires.

Corporate Ownership   Some television stations and newspapers—especially the smaller ones—are still owned locally, by families or by groups of investors, although they account for a rapidly declining share of the total. Most of the biggest stations and newspapers, however, as well as the television and cable networks, are owned by large media corporations, some of which, in turn, are subsidiaries of enormous conglomerates.

Each media sector is dominated by a few firms. Gannett (*USA Today* and 106 other dailies), Knight-Ridder, and Newhouse dominate the newspaper business. AOL/Time-Warner dominates both magazine publishing and consumer Internet services. General Electric, Westinghouse, Disney, News Corp., and AOL/Time-Warner dominate television. Six corporations receive more than half of all book-publishing revenues. And four firms (Warner Communications, Gulf+Western, Universal-MCA, and Columbia Pictures) get most of the gross box office revenues from movies.[13]

Michael Eisner, here speaking at a media event at Disney World in Florida, is largely responsible for transforming the Walt Disney Company into a global media and entertainment giant.

There has been a strong tendency for newspapers to merge. The vast majority of towns and cities that have any newspaper at all have only one. About two dozen cities, including San Francisco, Seattle, Detroit, and Cincinnati, still have two newspapers, but they are often owned by the same people and share printing and other facilities.

Mergers across media lines have accelerated in recent years. In the late 1990s, Disney bought ABC/Cap Cities, Time-Warner acquired Turner Broadcasting (and was later bought by AOL), and Westinghouse Electric bought CBS. Then Viacom and CBS merged, bringing together many familiar media and entertainment names: MTV, Nickelodeon, Showtime, Paramount Pictures, Simon and Schuster Publishers, Blockbuster Video, and CBS TV and radio. In a stunning deal in early 2000, AOL acquired Time-Warner, merging news, publishing, entertainment, and Internet resources into a single giant company. Familiar companies in this group include AOL, Netscape, Warner Books, Time Life Books, HBO, CNN, Warner Bros. Films and Television, *Time, Fortune, Sports Illustrated, People,* and *Money* magazines, Warner Music Group, Turner Network Television, Turner Sports, the Atlanta Braves, and the Atlanta Hawks. In 2001, Comcast announced that it would acquire AT&T Broadband and bring cable to 20 percent of all American households.

Scholars disagree about the effect of corporate ownership and increased media concentration. A few see efficiency gains and an increase in the output and availability of information. But some critics maintain that the concentrated corporate control of our media adds dangerously to the already strong business presence in American politics. Others worry that increased concentration of ownership may lead to less diversity of news and opinion. Still others worry that news organizations may pull their punches when reporting about the activities of their corporate parents or partners. Will MSNBC—a joint news venture of Microsoft and NBC—report fairly and accurately about Microsoft activities, for example? Will ABC News go easy on Disney, which owns ABC?[14]

Uniformity and Diversity Whoever owns them, most newspapers and television stations depend largely on the same sources for news. Political scientist Lance Bennett points out that while there is a growing diversity of news outlets in the United States—more specialized magazines, television channels, and newspaper home pages on the Web—news sources are contracting. That is to say, much of what comes to us over a multitude of media avenues originates in fewer and fewer centralized sources.[15] Almost all major newspapers in the country now subscribe to the AP wire service. The AP supplies most of the main national and international news stories, even those that are rewritten to carry a local reporter's byline. Most of what appears on network and cable television news, too, is inspired by the AP wire. National and local television news organizations depend on centralized news and video suppliers, with fewer of them using their own reporters. This is why viewers are likely to see the same news (and sports) footage on different stations as they switch channels, although each station adds its own "voice-over" from a reporter or news anchor. In most cases, the person doing the voice-over has no direct relationship to the story.

Along with the centralization and homogenization of the mass media, however, there is also quite a lot of diversity, for anyone who makes the effort to seek it out. People who are especially interested in politics can find special publications that look at the world in a way that they find compatible or interesting, whether it is the *Weekly Standard* or *National Review* (conservative), *The Nation* and *The American Prospect* (liberal), *Commentary* (neoconservative), *Mother Jones* (irreverent), the *New York Review of Books* (intellectual and critical), the *New Yorker, Rolling Stone,* or dozens of others with small circulations. The World Wide Web also provides a wealth of information uncontrolled by government or corporations. And new Internet political magazines such as *Slate* and *Salon* are beginning to appear. African-American, Spanish-language, and gay and lesbian newspapers, magazines, and Websites are also increasingly available. The audiences for these news sources, however, represent but a small fraction of the number of people who depend on the mainstream media for its news.

Profit Motives Media corporations, like other corporations, are in business primarily to make a profit. This fact has important consequences. It means, for example, that the major news media must appeal to large audiences and get many people to buy their publications or the products they advertise. If most people are mainly interested in entertainment and want their news short, snappy, and sensational—what has come to be called **infotainment**—that is what they will get on network and cable television news and in *USA Today*. The process is especially well developed in evening local news broadcasts where coverage of politics and government have been "crowded out by coverage of crime, sports, weather, lifestyles and other audience-grabbing topics. . . ."[16]

infotainment

The merging of hard news and entertainment in news presentations.

Political Newsmaking

The kind of news that the media present is affected by the organization and technology of news gathering and news production. Much depends on where reporters are, what sources they talk to, and what sorts of video pictures are available.

The Limited Geography of Political News For national news, most reporters are located in two main locations: first, inside the beltway in Washington, D.C., site of the federal government and most of the nation's most

Local news is increasingly dominated by stories about crime, both petty and not so petty, crowding out a great deal of more important, substantive information about government policies and social and economic conditions.

influential think tanks and interest group organizations; and second, in New York City, the center of most media operations and the location of key national and global financial institutions. Thus, the national news has a strong Washington–New York orientation.

The major television networks and most newspapers cannot afford to station many reporters outside Washington or New York. The networks usually add just Chicago, Los Angeles, Miami, and Houston or Dallas. When stories break in San Francisco or Seattle, news organizations can rush reporters to the area, or turn to part-time "stringers" to do the reporting. Some significant stories from outside the main media centers simply do not make it into the national news. News-only channels, such as CNN, CNBC, and Fox News, have a big advantage on fast-breaking news, which they are ready to cover (through their own reporters or the purchase of local footage) and to use immediately on their continuous newscasts.

While some newspapers have strong regional bureaus, the majority print mostly wire service reports of news from elsewhere around the country. The television networks' assignment editors also rely on the wire services to decide what stories to cover; during one month that was studied, NBC got the idea for 70 percent of its domestic film stories from the wire services.[17]

Because so much expensive, high technology equipment is involved, and because a considerable amount of editing is required to turn raw video into coherent stories, most television news coverage is assigned to predictable events—news conferences and the like—long before they happen, usually in one of the cities with a permanent television crew. For such spontaneous news as riots, accidents, and natural disasters, special video camera crews can be rushed to the location, but they usually arrive after the main events occur and have to rely on "reaction" interviews or aftermath stories. This is not always true; occasionally television news organizations find themselves in the middle of an unfolding set of events and can convey its texture, explore its human meaning, and speculate about its political implications in particularly meaningful ways. This was certainly true of television coverage of the September 11 terrorist attacks on the United States and the public and government response to them.

Dependence on Official Sources

Most political news is based on what public officials say. This fact has important consequences for how well the media serve democracy.

beat

The assigned location where a reporter regularly gathers news stories.

Beats and Routines A newspaper or television reporter's work is usually organized around a particular **beat,** which he or she checks every day for news stories. Most political beats center on some official government institution that regularly produces news, such as a local police station or city council, the White House, Congress, the Pentagon, an American embassy abroad, or a country's foreign ministry.

In fact, many news reports are created or originated by officials, not by reporters. Investigative reporting of the sort that Carl Bernstein and Robert Woodward did to uncover the Watergate scandal in the early 1970s is rare because it is so time consuming and expensive. Most reporters get most of their stories quickly and efficiently from press conferences and the press releases that officials write, along with comments solicited from other officials.

One pioneering study found that government officials, domestic or foreign, were the sources of nearly three-quarters of all news in the *New York Times* and the *Washington Post.* Moreover, the vast majority, 70 to 90 percent of all news stories, were drawn from situations over which the newsmakers had substantial control: press conferences (24.5 percent), interviews (24.7 percent), press releases (17.5 percent), and official proceedings (13 percent).[18] The same is true of wire service reports and local newspapers.

Military Actions Dependence on official sources is especially evident in military actions abroad. Because it is wary of the release of information that might help an adversary or undermine public support for U.S. actions—as happened during the Vietnam conflict—the Defense Department carefully restricts the access of reporters to military personnel and the battlefield and provides carefully screened information for use by the news media. The Pentagon carefully managed the flow of information in the invasion of Grenada in 1983, the Gulf War in 1991, peacekeeping missions in Bosnia and Kosovo, and the campaign in Afghanistan against the Taliban regime and Osama bin Laden. Information management was especially evident during the Gulf War with its televised news briefings featuring video of "smart" weapons, Defense Department organization of press pools, and tight restrictions on reporters' access to the battlefields in Kuwait and Iraq. Press management was even more highly developed during the conflict in Afghanistan, when reporters found it almost impossible to develop independent information. During phases of the Afghan operation, reporters had little access to military personnel, many of whom were located in scattered and inaccessible locations—often in countries where officials wanted to keep the nature of U.S. involvement out of the public limelight—and involved in special operations that required strict secrecy. They also had only restricted access to events on the ground inside Afghanistan among the population.

Mutual Needs Reporters and officials work with each other every day. They need each other. Reporters want stories; they have to cultivate access to people who can provide stories with quotes or anonymous leaks. Officials want favorable publicity and want to avoid or counteract unfavorable publicity. Thus, a comfortable relationship tends to develop. Even when reporters put on a show of aggressive questioning at White House press conferences, they usually work hard to stay on good terms with officials and to avoid fundamental challenges of the officials' positions.

Journalists and government officials often socialize together, raising questions about the media's ability to serve as honest watchdog. Here reporter Sam Donaldson chats with the Clinton administration's Secretary of Health and Human Services Donna Shalala at a Washington gala.

The media's heavy reliance on official sources means that government officials are sometimes able to control what journalists report and how they report it. The Reagan administration was particularly successful at picking a "story of the day" and having many officials feed that story to reporters, with a unified interpretation.[19] Reliance on officials also means that when officials of both parties agree, debate tends to be constricted. This was true for the momentous Telecommunications Act of 1996, which helped usher in the current dramatic changes in the business of mass media and telecommunications, but which occasioned little public debate.

Newsworthiness   Decisions about what kinds of news to print or to televise depend largely on professional judgments about what is **newsworthy.** Exactly what makes a story newsworthy is difficult to spell out, but experienced editors make quick and confident judgments of what their audiences (and their employers) want. If they were consistently wrong, they would probably not remain in their jobs very long.

newsworthy
Worth printing or broadcasting as news, according to editors' judgments.

In practice, newsworthiness seems to depend on such factors as novelty (man bites dog, not dog bites man), drama and human interest, relevance to the lives of Americans, high stakes (e.g., physical violence or conflict), and celebrity (e.g., the arrest of President George W. Bush's daughter for underage drinking). Some trivial topics are judged newsworthy, such as the hairstyles of O.J. Simpson trial stars Marcia Clark and Kato Kaelin. As the term *news story* implies, news works best when it can be framed as a familiar kind of narrative: an exposé of greed, sex, or corruption; conflict between politicians; or a foreign affairs crisis. On television, of course, dramatic or startling film footage helps make a story gripping. Important stories without visuals are often pushed aside for less important stories for which visuals exist.

Templates   On many important stories, a subtle "governing template" may prevail, a sense among both reporters and editors that news stories must take a generally agreed-upon slant to be taken seriously and to make it into the news broadcast or the newspaper. This is not because of censorship, but because of the development of a general agreement among news reporters and editors that we already know what the big story looks like on a range of issues, and filling in the details is what is important. Take reporting from China as an example. For many years, editors only wanted to hear about economic prosperity, emerging democratic freedoms, and happy peasants liberated from the economic and personal straightjacket of the Maoist collective farm system. After the pro-democracy demonstrations in Tiannanmen Square were brutally repressed by the People's Liberation Army, however, reporters say that it became almost impossible to write anything positive about China, because the prevailing template about China had changed.[20]

Templates help explain why unsubstantiated stories about vandalism in the White House and the Executive Office Building by Clinton staffers after the election of George W. Bush made it so readily into the news media, although several later investigations, including one by the non-partisan investigative arm of Congress, the General Accounting Office, demonstrated conclusively that claims of vandalism were unfounded. (The GAO report says: "The condition of the real property was consistent with what we would expect to encounter when tenants vacate office space after an extended occupancy.") So how did rumors floated by political opponents become a prominent news story? Primarily because of the prevailing template among reporters and news editors that Bill Clinton was a man of flawed character and moral shortcomings who was surely capable of directing and participating in such tasteless pranks.

Episodic Foreign Coverage Very few newspapers other than the *New York Times* can afford to station reporters abroad. Even the *Times* and the networks and wire services cannot regularly cover most nations of the world. They keep reporters in the countries of greatest interest to Americans—those that have big effects on American interests or enjoy close economic or cultural ties with the United States, such as Great Britain, Germany, Japan, Israel, Russia, and China—and they have regional bureaus in Africa and Latin America. In many countries, however, they depend on "stringers" (local journalists who file occasional reports). During major crises or big events, the media send in temporary news teams, such as the armies of reporters that swarmed to Bosnia and Kosovo during the conflicts with the Serbs, and to the countries surrounding Afghanistan during the war to unseat the Taliban and find Osama bin Laden. The result is that most media devote the majority of their attention to limited areas of the world, dropping in only occasionally on others.

Foreign news, therefore, tends to be episodic. An unfamiliar country, such as Rwanda or Haiti, suddenly jumps into the headlines with a spectacular story of a coup, an invasion, or a famine, which comes as a surprise to most Americans because they have not been prepared by background reports. For a few days or weeks, the story dominates the news, with intensive coverage through pictures, interviews, and commentaries. Then, if nothing new and exciting happens, the story grows stale and disappears from the media. Most viewers are left with little more understanding of the country than they began with. Thus, they find it difficult to form judgments about U.S. foreign policy.

Interpreting

objective journalism

News reported with no evaluative language and with any opinions quoted or attributed to a specific source.

Political news does not make much sense without an interpretation of what it means. Under the informal rules of **objective journalism,** however, explicit interpretations by journalists are avoided, except for commentary or editorials that are labeled as such. Thus, even if a reporter knows that an official is lying, he or she cannot say so directly, but must find someone else who will say so for the record. Staged events—such as a news conference held in a national park to announce a bill to protect the environment—cannot be identified by reporters as staged events. In news stories, most interpretations are left implicit (so that they are hard to detect and argue with) or are given by so-called experts who are interviewed for comments. Often, particular experts are selected by print, broadcast, and telecast journalists because the position the experts will take is entirely predictable.

Experts are selected partly for reasons of convenience and audience appeal: Scholars and commentators who live close to New York City or Washington, D.C., who like to speak in public, who look good on camera, and who are skillful in coming up with colorful quotations on a variety of subjects are contacted again and again. They often show up on television to comment on the news of the day, even on issues that are far from the area of their special expertise. In many cases, these pundits are simply well known for being on television often, and are not experts on any subject at all.

The experts and commentators featured in the media are often ex-officials. Their views are usually in harmony with the political currents of the day; that is, they tend to reflect a fairly narrow spectrum of opinion close to that of the party in power in Washington, D.C., or to the prevailing "conventional wisdom" inside the beltway. During the 1980s and early 1990s, for example, the experts most frequently quoted on television were a handful of former Reagan or Bush administration officials and others associated with conservative **think tanks,** such as the American Enterprise Institute and the Center for Strategic and International Studies. The commentator "punditocracy" was also quite conservative.[21]

At other times, with different politicians in power, different kinds of experts have been favored. Antipoverty advocates got a lot of media attention during Lyndon Johnson's administration, for example, and some liberal and centrist voices began to reappear in the media when Bill Clinton replaced George H. W. Bush. Even during the Clinton years, however, the tilt towards liberal experts was quite muted. One scholar reports that a Lexis-Nexis search of political and governmental news stories between January, 1999, and October, 2000, uncovered 753 references to experts from the Brookings Institution (a centrist think tank), 949 references to experts from the Heritage Foundation and the American Enterprise Institute (conservative think tanks), but only 161 references to the liberal Economic Policy Institute.[22] Independent radical thinkers such as I. F. Stone, whose *Weekly* became influential for a time during the Vietnam War, or Noam Chomsky, a fierce critic of media reporting on U.S. foreign policy today, have rarely penetrated the mainstream media at all. There are also strikingly few racial minorities among commentators in the mainstream news media.

think tanks

Nonprofit organizations that do research on public policy issues and distribute their findings through a variety of outlets. Although formally nonpartisan, most have an identifiable ideological stance.

Is the News Biased?

Few topics arouse more disagreement than the question of whether the mass media in the United States have a liberal or conservative **bias**—or any bias at all. For years, a number of journalists and scholars have maintained that the media tend to be a pro-establishment, conservative force, reflecting their corporate ownership and their dependence on official sources for news. Conservative critics have counterattacked, arguing that liberal media elites regularly publish and broadcast anti-establishment, anti-authority news with a liberal bias.

bias

Deviation from some ideal standard, such as representativeness or objectivity.

Liberal Reporters Surveys of reporters' and journalists' opinions suggest that these individuals tend to be somewhat more liberal than the average American—although by no means radical—on certain matters, including the

Longman
Participate.com 2.0
Participation
Are the Media Biased?

By the Numbers

How much serious crime is there in the United States?

"If it bleeds, it leads" seems to be the mantra of television news. Indeed, we are in danger in this country of being overwhelmed by news stories about crime, and the problem seems to be getting worse. While coverage of public affairs and foreign affairs fell throughout the 1990s, news coverage of crime flourished. Local news coverage is even more slanted towards crime.

Why It Matters: If television news broadcasts are accurately portraying real trends in crime, then they are doing a public service. If portrayals are inaccurate, then the public is being misled. This is problematic because public and official perceptions about the scale of particular social problems affect politics and government deeply. For instance:

- When pressed by the public to address a perceived problem, government officials respond by redirecting resources at the problem, and make budget and personnel decisions in light of it. If the problem is a false one, then government attention and resources get used ineffectively.
- Candidates campaign on issues that are most salient to the public. When the public misperceives the scale of a problem, it makes electoral choices based on irrelevant grounds.
- The more threatening the public finds a particular problem, the more it pushes aside other public priorities, such as education and health care.

The Story Behind the Crime Numbers: How accurately are the news media portraying the true state of affairs? To put it bluntly, not very well. Crime in general, and violent crime in particular, declined substantially during the 1990s, at precisely the same time that concerns about crime were at the forefront of media, popular attention, and political saliency. How do we know this to be the case?

The two most widely used measures of the incidence of crime in the United States are the Uniform Crime Report (UCR) of the FBI and the National Crime Victimization Survey (NCVS) of the Department of Justice. Each counts the incidence of crime in a different way. The UCR is based on reports from law enforcement agencies and is meant to help state and local police departments track their own performance and to plan their budgets. The NCVS is based on a survey of victims of crime and is used to assess how crime is experienced by Americans and how it affects them and their families.

Calculating the Crime Rate: The FBI's UCR, based on reports submitted voluntarily by state and local law enforcement agencies, counts the annual incidence of "violent crimes" (murder, forcible rape, robbery, and aggravated assault), "property crimes" (burglary, larceny-theft, motor vehicle theft, and arson), and "serious crimes" (all of the above). However, here is what is most important about the FBI's methodology: *it only counts crimes that come to the attention of police.*

The Justice Department's NCVS is based on an annual survey of roughly 50,000 randomly selected

environment and such social issues as civil rights and liberties, abortion, and women's rights.[23] This is especially true of those employed by certain elite media organizations, including the *New York Times,* the *Washington Post,* and PBS. It is likely that reporters' liberalism has been reflected in the treatment of issues such as nuclear energy, global warming, and toxic waste. In 1990, for example, an exhaustive three-volume government report that found that damage from acid rain had been greatly overestimated was ignored by virtually all the major media, except *60 Minutes* and *The Wall Street Journal.*[24]

But there is little or no systematic evidence that reporters' personal values regularly affect what appears in the media. Journalists' commitment to the idea of objectivity helps them resist temptation, as do critical scrutiny and

U. S. households. One person over the age of 18 in each household is interviewed about any crimes that may have been committed against any member of the household during the previous year. The result is annual crime *victimization* information for more than 100,000 people, a very large number for a national survey. Because the NCVS includes crimes experienced by people that are never reported to the authorities, it tends to show higher rates of serious crime than the UCR.

Criticisms of Crime Rate Calculations: The experts generally prefer the NCVS numbers to those of the UCR for understanding the dimensions of the crime problem. The principal problems with the UCR concern the accuracy of recording and reporting crime. For example:

- Many serious crimes, especially rape, go unreported to police.
- Ideas about what constitutes a serious crime may change as social mores change. Domestic violence was treated in the past by police as a family matter; now it tends to get recorded and reported by police.
- A small number of law enforcement agencies do not participate in the UCR reporting system or do not treat it with the seriousness that the FBI hopes for.

What to Watch For: Each way of measuring crime is valid and has its purposes. Though the UCR measure has some problems, it does a fairly good job of telling us what is going on year to year with respect to police encounters with crime. This, in turn, is useful to national, state, and local governments in deciding on budget and staffing issues for law enforcement. The NCVS does a very good job of telling us what is going on year to year with

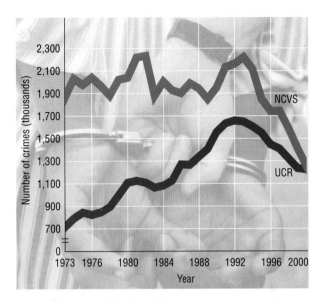

Serious Violent Crimes

Source: Bureau of Justice Statistics, United States Department of Justice, 2001.

respect to overall victimization trends, and gives us a handle on the size of the underlying crime problem. The lesson here is to use the statistic that conforms most closely to the purposes of your inquiry.

What Do You Think? Do you believe that television news programs underplay or overplay the incidence of violent crime? Monitor local and national news for the next week or so and try to keep a running count of stories about crime. How does your count match what the UCR and NCVS numbers are telling us about crime?

rewriting by editors. And in any case, the liberalism of journalists may be offset by their need to rely on official sources, by their reliance on experts who are either former officials or associated with centrist or conservative think tanks, and by conservatism among media owners and publishers. It is also difficult to sustain the position that reporters slant their stories in a liberal direction after witnessing the pummeling Bill Clinton received in the media throughout his presidency.

Conservative Owners

The owners and top managers of most media corporations tend to be very conservative. The shareholders and executives of multibillion-dollar corporations are not very interested in undermining capitalism or, for that matter, in increasing their own taxes, raising labor costs, or losing income from offended advertisers. These owners and managers ultimately decide which reporters, newscasters, and editors to hire or fire, promote or discourage. Journalists who want to get ahead, therefore, may have to come to terms with the policies of the people who own and run media businesses.

One sign of conservatism in the media is newspapers' endorsements of presidential candidates, which are decided mostly by owners and publishers. In all six presidential elections from 1968 through 1988, more newspapers—usually many more—backed the Republican than the Democratic candidate. In 1988, for example, one week before the election, 195 dailies had endorsed George H. W. Bush, whereas just 51 had endorsed Michael Dukakis.[25] Only in 1992 was the picture different: The "new," friendly-to-business Democrat, Bill Clinton, won a majority of endorsements, as he did in 1996.[26]

Prevailing Themes in Political News

Even if we cannot be sure whether or how the media are biased, it is easy to identify certain tendencies in media coverage, certain beliefs that are assumed, and certain values and points of view that are emphasized.

Nationalism   Though perhaps not too terribly surprising, most news about foreign affairs takes a definitely pro-American, patriotic point of view, usually putting the United States in a good light and its opponents in a bad light. While this is especially marked in news concerning military conflicts in which U.S. troops are involved, it can be found as well in a wide range of foreign affairs news reports, including those concerning conflicts with other governments on trade, arms control, immigration, and intellectual property rights (patents and copyrights).

The news media also focus on things that interest and concern ordinary Americans, no matter how important or unimportant they might be in the larger picture. For example, U.S. newspapers and television in 1980 devoted intensive, yearlong coverage to the fate of 49 Americans held hostage in the U.S. embassy in Tehran, Iran; in the early 1990s, they exhaustively covered a U.S. pilot, Scott O'Grady, who had been shot down over Bosnia. But much less attention has been paid to the slaughter of millions of people during the same time in Indonesia, Nigeria, East Timor, Cambodia, and Rwanda.

This nationalistic perspective, together with heavy reliance on U.S. government news sources, means that coverage of foreign news generally harmonizes well with official U.S. foreign policy. Thus, the media tend to go along with the U.S. government in assuming the best about our close allies and the worst about official "enemies." When the U.S. was assisting Iraq in its war against Iran, for example, Saddam Hussein was depicted in a positive light; with the coming of the Gulf War, media characterizations of him changed dramatically.

Approval of the American Economic System   Another tendency of the media is to run stories generally approving of free markets, free international trade, and minimal regulation. Our economic system wins approval, while variant or alternative systems, such as European social democracies with comprehensive social welfare programs, are generally portrayed more negatively. Countries whose economic policies mirror those of the U.S. economy, such as Poland, are praised, while countries trying to preserve a vibrant welfare state, such as France, are criticized. Individual U.S. corporations are criticized for errors and misdeeds—for example, polluters are likely to be hauled before the court of public opinion, as are large firms like Enron and WorldCom who lie about their profits in order to keep their stock prices high— but the economic system itself is rarely challenged. This stance is hardly surprising, since most Americans like the U.S. economic system (see Chapter 4), but it may sometimes discourage the consideration of alternative approaches to enduring problems.

Negativity and Scandal Increasingly, political candidates and officials are being subjected to a relentless barrage of negative coverage. Some of this coverage starts with negative advertisements by opponents, which are then sometimes echoed in media reporting. Research has shown that negative ads increase citizens' anger and alienation and discourage them from voting.[27] News stories often picked up and amplified these negative themes.

Incumbent officials also get plenty of negative publicity, especially when even the appearance of wrong-doing in their personal lives creates dramatic human interest stories. "Whitewater" allegations against President Clinton and First Lady Hillary Rodham Clinton—that they had dealt improperly with a real estate investment and a bank's campaign contributions while Clinton was governor of Arkansas and had obstructed justice while in the White House—were doggedly pursued by the *American Spectator,* the *New York Times,* and other media for most of Clinton's first term. Sex scandals dogged Bill Clinton for most of his presidency and contributed to his eventual impeachment hearings. Sex and financial scandals also claimed, among others, Senator Gary Hart, former House Speakers Jim Wright and Newt Gingrich, and House Speaker–elect Bob Livingston. And, until the September 11 terrorist attacks on the United States shifted the focus of the media, great attention was given to speculations about the affair between Congressman Gary Condit and intern Chandra Levy and her disappearance.

Infotainment One of the most dramatic changes that has occurred in the news is the insertion of entertainment values into political reporting and news presentation. As little as 15 to 20 years ago, news was monopolized by the three major television networks and the big-city daily newspapers, and the audiences

In the view of many observers, the mass media in the United States have become increasingly mired in scandal and sensationalism. During the Pope's historic visit to communist Cuba, for example, the breaking Monica Lewinsky "White House intern" sex scandal dominated television news, talk radio, and newspapers. Dan Rather even left Havana in the middle of the Pope's visit in order to be on top of what CBS News producers considered to be the more important story.

for the news were fairly stable. In the intervening years, we have seen, the media have been revolutionized by the growth of cable television and the Internet and the multiplication of news outlets. In this new world, the networks and the big-city dailies have lost audience, leaving each of the fragments of the old and new media to fight for audience share. The best way to do this, media executives have discovered, is to make the news more entertaining, for the worst sin of this brave new media world is to be boring.[28] All too often, "more entertaining" means that sensation and scandal replace serious public policy issues; short and snappy coverage displaces longer, more analytical coverage; dramatic visuals push aside stories that cannot be easily visualized; and stories that feature angry conflict displace stories in which political leaders are trying to make workable compromises.[29]

The current "culture wars" between liberals and conservatives over the various legacies of the 1960s—involving issues such as abortion, affirmative action, religious values, gay and lesbian rights, and more—is perfect grist for the infotainment mill. Thus, a current staple of cable and broadcast television public affairs programming is the gathering of **pundits** from both sides of the cultural and political divide angrily shouting at one other for 30 or 60 minutes: *The Washington Gang* and *Hard Ball* are examples. And, because bringing together shouting pundits is far cheaper than sending reporters into the field to gather hard news, this form of news coverage is becoming more and more common, especially in the world of cable TV. It is highly unlikely that this emergent journalism of assertion and attack improves public understanding of the candidates, political leaders, and public policies.

Conflict and contestation are also evident in coverage of campaigns, where the media concentrate on who is winning and who is losing the electoral race and what strategies candidates are using to gain ground or to maintain their lead. When candidates sometimes make a stab at talking seriously about issues, the media almost always treat such talk as a mere stratagem of the long campaign. The perpetual struggle between Congress and the president, built into our constitutional system, is also perfect for the infotainment news industry, especially if the struggle can be personalized, as it was in the years when House Speaker Newt Gingrich was doing battle with President Bill Clinton.

Limited, Fragmented, and Incoherent Political Information

Most communications scholars agree that the media coverage of political news has certain distinctive features that result from characteristics of the mass media themselves, including the prevailing technology and organization of news gathering, corporate ownership, and the profit-making drive to appeal to mass audiences. These characteristics of the media mean that news, especially on television, tends to be episodic and fragmented rather than sustained, analytical, or dispassionate.[30] Information comes in bits and pieces, out of context, and without historical background. Its effect is to entertain more than to inform.

Effects of the News Media on Politics

The old idea that the mass media have only "minimal effects" on politics is now discredited. The contents of the media do make a difference; they affect public opinion and policymaking in a number of ways, including setting the agenda for public debate and framing how issues are understood.[31]

---

pundits

Somewhat derisive term for print, broadcast, and radio commentators on the political news.

USING THE FRAMEWORK: Monica All the Time

Why was the Monica Lewinsky story on the TV news for almost a year? It seemed like overkill to me.

Background: President Clinton's sexual liaison with White House intern Monica Lewinsky dominated the nation's political news from the early summer of 1998 through the end of the Senate impeachment trial of the president in early 1999. It was almost as if nothing else of importance was happening in the nation or around the world. Why is that? Taking a look at how structural, political linkage, and governmental factors affected news coverage will help explain the situation.

Governmental Action

Impeachment hearings and vote in the House provided dramatic news material.

Senate deliberations and vote to remove the president from office provided dramatic news material.

Governmental Level

- President Clinton engaged in behavior that was offensive to most Americans. →
- Many members of Congress believed that President Clinton had obstructed justice in the Paula Jones and Monica Lewinsky affairs. →
- A bitter partisan atmosphere permeated the 105th Congress. →
- The Republican Congress and Democratic President Bill Clinton were bitterly deadlocked on a wide range of issues; severe tensions existed between the two branches of government.

Political Linkages Level

- Media television executives used "attack journalism," "infotainment," and scandal as a way to attract viewers from a highly fragmented set of media consumers. →
- The media fell into their "one big story at a time" syndrome, also evident in the O. J. Simpson and JonBenet Ramsey cases. →
- Web-based and scandal-sheet papers fed leads to major mainstream media. →
- The Republican Party used the Lewinsky scandal in advertising for the 1998 congressional elections. →
- Conservative interest groups also saw advantages in a weakened President Clinton and ran ad campaigns highlighting the Lewinsky matter.

Structural Level

- Technological innovations multiplied the number of television channels, all of which require content to fill the hours. →
- As the Internet developed, it became (among other things) a medium for the distribution of information, opinion, and rumors.

Agenda Setting

agenda setting

Influencing what people consider important.

Several studies have demonstrated the effect known as **agenda setting.** The topics that get the most coverage in the media are the same ones that most people tell pollsters are the most important problems facing the country. This correlation does not result just from the media's printing what people are most interested in; it is a real effect of what appears in the media. In controlled experiments, people who are shown doctored television news broadcasts emphasizing a particular problem (e.g., national defense) mention that problem as being important more often than people who have seen broadcasts that have not been tampered with.[32]

Of course, media managers do not arbitrarily decide what news to emphasize; their decisions reflect what is happening in the world and what American audiences care about. If there is a war or an economic depression, the media report it. But some research has indicated that what the media cover sometimes diverges from actual trends in problems. Publicity about crime, for example, may reflect editors' fears or a few dramatic incidents rather than a rising crime rate. When the two diverge, it seems to be the media's emphasis rather than real trends that affects public opinion.[33]

When the media decide to highlight a human rights tragedy in "real time," such as "ethnic cleansing" in Kosovo, public officials often feel compelled to act. When the media ignore equally troubling human tragedies, such as the genocide in Rwanda, public officials can attend to other matters. One scholarly study shows that in the foreign policy area, media choices about coverage shape what presidents pay attention to.[34]

Framing and Effects on Policy Preferences

framing

Providing a context for interpretation.

Experiments also indicate that the media's **framing,** or interpretation of stories, affects how people think about political problems and how they assign blame. Whether citizens ascribe poverty to the laziness of the poor or to the

Web Exploration
Agenda Setting

Issue: Scholarly research shows that the news media help set the political agenda for both political leaders and ordinary citizens.

Site: Access the Center for Media and Public Affairs on our Website at **www.ablongman.com/greenberg**. Go to the "Web Explorations" section for Chapter 6, open "agenda setting," then "factoids" so that you can see what kinds of stories have received the most media attention in different years. Look at the most recent survey and compare it with a survey from the early 1990s.

What You've Learned: Has the emphasis in the news changed over time? Are the same kinds of stories carried year after year or not? Is there more or less substantive news about government and politics? Is there more or less news about scandals and government wrongdoing?

nature of the economy, for example, depends partly on whether the media run stories about poor individuals (implying that they are responsible for their own plight) or stories about overall economic trends such as wage stagnation and unemployment.[35]

What appears in the media affects people's policy preferences as well. One study found that changes in the percentages of the public that favored various policies could be predicted rather accurately by what sorts of stories appeared on network television news shows between one opinion survey and the next. News from experts, commentators, and popular presidents had especially strong effects.[36]

Impact on Policymaking

Longman
Participate.com 2.0
Visual Literacy
The Media and the American Public

By affecting what ordinary Americans think is important, how they understand problems, and what policies they want, the media indirectly affect what government does, because the government tends to respond to public opinion. Heavy support for the North American Free Trade Agreement (NAFTA) by the *New York Times* and other media, for example, probably helped counteract initial public opposition due to fears of job losses. In addition, the media affect who is elected to office. As we will see in Chapter 10, media stories about the character of presidential and other candidates have enormous effects on fundraising and on citizens' judgments of who would make a good leader. Thus, early press portrayal of George W. Bush as a "fresh face" in the Republican Party capable of winning the presidential election helped him raise record-setting amounts of money for his campaign.

Moreover, what appears in the media has a direct effect on policymaking. Policymakers learn about the world and about each other's activities from the media. Investigative journalism that exposes problems, for example, often leads local, state, or federal officials to act. Sometimes, journalists and politicians actively work together: The journalists expose problems that the politicians want to solve, and then the politicians' statements, hearings, and bills prolong the story for journalists to continue reporting.[37]

Cynicism

Americans are quite cynical about the political parties, politicians, and most incumbent political leaders. To some extent, this has been true since the founding of the nation. Nevertheless, scholars and political commentators have noted a considerable increase in negative feelings about the political system over the past two decades or so. Many commentators believe that news media coverage of American politics has a great deal to do with this attitude change.[38] As the adversarial attack journalism style and infotainment have taken over political reporting, serious consideration of the issues, careful examination of policy alternatives, and dispassionate examination of the actions of government institutions have taken a back seat to a steady diet of charges about personal misbehavior. When President George H. W. Bush, for example, joined a world leader to describe the nature of the agreement they had reached, reporters asked him instead about rumors of an extramarital affair a few years earlier. With the message being delivered by the mass media that political issues are really about special-interest maneuvering, that political leaders and aspiring political leaders never say what they mean or mean what they say, that all of them have something in their personal lives they want to hide, and that even the most admired of the lot have feet of clay, is it any wonder that the American people are becoming increasingly disenchanted with the whole business?

Government Regulation of the Media

Our Constitution protects freedom of the press, and the U.S. government has less legal control over the media than the governments of most other countries do. But our government has the authority to make various technical and substantive regulations on the electronic media, if it wishes.

Print Media

Early in American history, government sometimes interfered with the press in a heavy-handed way. Under the Alien and Sedition Acts of 1798, for example, several Anti-Federalist newspaper editors were jailed for criticizing John Adams's administration. In recent years, however, the Constitution has been interpreted as forbidding government from preventing the publication of most kinds of political information or from punishing its publication afterward. The main exceptions involve national security, especially during wartime.

prior restraint

The government's power to prevent publication, as opposed to punishment afterward.

Prior Restraint Several U.S. Supreme Court decisions, beginning in the 1920s and 1930s, have ensured the press a great deal of constitutional protection. The First Amendment provision that Congress shall make no law "abridging freedom of speech, or of the press" has been held by the Supreme Court to prevent the federal censorship of newspapers or magazines. Only under the most pressing circumstances of danger to national security can the government engage in **prior restraint** and prevent the publication of material to which it objects (see Chapter 15).

On June 30, 1971, for example, the Supreme Court denied a request by the Nixon administration to restrain the *New York Times* and the *Washington Post* from publishing excerpts from the *Pentagon Papers,* a secret Defense Department history of the United States's involvement in Vietnam. The Court declared that "the Government 'thus carries a heavy burden of showing justification for the enforcement of such a restraint.' . . . The Government had not met that burden." Justice Hugo Black's concurring opinion has become an important statement on freedom of the press.

Coverage of the Persian Gulf War, even more than that of previous wars, was carefully controlled and censored by the U.S. military.

Wartime Controls In a sense, however, the *Pentagon Papers* case was an easy one because it concerned the right to publish a two-year-old history and analysis of past government policy, not information about current military or foreign policy actions that could jeopardize American lives. During wartime, the government has almost always asserted broad powers to control what reporters can see and what they can print. During World War II, for example, the Office of Censorship monitored all news entering and leaving the country, but it focused mainly on news about casualties and troop and ship movements rather than on political matters.

Relatively free media access to the Vietnam War eventually brought a flood of negative stories.[39] U.S. officials, having learned their lesson, restricted access to the 1991 war with Iraq. During that war, the military imposed an elaborate system of control and censorship, requiring reporters to work only in escorted pools, limiting their access to U.S. troops, and censoring their stories. The media went along with these restrictions at the time, and large majorities of the public approved of it, but the result was incomplete and misleading coverage.[40]

Strict controls were also imposed by the Defense Department on press coverage of the war in Afghanistan. To be sure, many restrictions on reporting were a natural by-product of the type of war being fought; reporters could not easily or safely accompany special forces engaged in lightening raids. Also, many restrictions on reporting were imposed by the Taliban regime, who did not want reporters roaming through areas under their control. Having said that, other barriers to reporting were imposed by the Defense Department in the interest of maintaining control of information about the waging of the war and its effects: disseminating information in tightly controlled press briefings; denying access to officers and enlisted personnel engaged in the conflict; strictly limiting access to the battlefield; and successfully requesting that news organizations not print or show bin Laden speeches.

The Electronic Media

The electronic media are more directly regulated by government than the print media, although such regulation has been diminishing.

Government Licensing of the Airwaves The federal government has broad powers to regulate the use of the airwaves, which are considered public property. Ever since the passage of the Radio Act of 1927 and the

Communications Act of 1934, which established the Federal Communications Commission (FCC), the government has licensed radio and television stations and has required them to observe certain rules as a condition for obtaining licenses.

FCC rules specify the frequencies on which stations can broadcast and the amount of power that they can use, in order to prevent interference among broadcasters of the sort that had brought chaos to radio during the 1920s. Government regulations divide the VHF television band into 12 channels and allocate them in such a way that most major cities have three VHF stations—the main reason for the early emergence of just three major networks. The development of cable television greatly expanded variety and competition.

For a long time, to prevent monopolies of scarce channels, federal rules prohibited networks or anyone else from owning more than five VHF stations around the country. Deregulation during the 1990s loosened these rules. Now, one company's stations can cover up to 35 percent of U.S. households. A federal appeals court decision in 2002 revoked the 35 percent rule, so it is likely that media companies will grow even larger.

The Telecommunications Act of 1996, which revolutionized the industry by allowing telephone companies, cable companies, and broadcasters all to compete with one another, also provided that new frequencies to be used for high-definition TV should be given to broadcasters free of charge. Critics called this a give-away of public airwaves worth as much as $70 billion; they wanted government to require new public services or to auction off the frequencies to generate public revenue. The 1996 act also removed most restrictions on the number of radio and television stations that a company could own nationally and locally, encouraging a wave of mergers in the late 1990s and into the new century.

Public Service Broadcasting The FCC was mandated by Congress to regulate the airwaves for the "public interest, convenience, or necessity." This vague phrase has been interpreted as including "the development of an informed public opinion through the public dissemination of news and ideas concerning the vital public issues of the day," with ideas coming from "diverse and antagonistic sources," and with an emphasis on service to the local community.

In practice, this requirement has mainly meant FCC pressure (backed up by the threat of not renewing stations' licenses) to provide a certain number of hours of news and "public service" broadcasting. Thus, government regulation created an artificial demand for news programming, before it became profitable, and contributed to the rise and expansion of network news and to the development of documentaries and news specials. In that way, government regulation presumably contributed to informed public opinion and to democracy. Recently, however, this public service requirement has been eroded and the amount of this kind of programming has declined.

fairness doctrine

The former requirement that television stations present contrasting points of view.

Fairness For many years, the **fairness doctrine** of 1949 required that licensees present contrasting viewpoints on any controversial issue of public importance that was discussed. This requirement led to efforts at balance—presenting two sides on any issue that was mentioned—and sometimes to the avoidance of controversial issues altogether. It was left mostly up to broadcasters, however, to decide what was important or controversial and what constituted a fair reply and a fair amount of time to give it.

Fairness is not easy to define: Which of the unlimited number of possible opinions deserves a hearing? The FCC itself long ago made clear that it did not intend to make time available to "communist viewpoints," and both of the "two sides" that the media air are usually quite mainstream.

Election year debates, such as this 2000 debate between presidential candidates George W. Bush and Al Gore, have become a regular television feature and may have a profound effect on elections.

Equal Time Similarly, the **equal time provision** of the 1934 Communications Act required that except for news programs, stations that granted (or sold) air time to any one candidate for public office had to grant (or sell) other candidates equal time. This requirement threatened to cause the media great expense when minor party candidates insisted on their share of air time or when opponents wanted to reply to political speeches by incumbent presidents in election years. Contrary to its intent, therefore, this requirement led to some curtailment of political programming.

equal time provision
The former requirement that television stations give or sell the same amount of time to all competing candidates.

The equal time provision was suspended in 1960 to allow televised debates between candidates John F. Kennedy and Richard M. Nixon, and in 1976 and 1980, the FCC permitted the staging of the Ford–Carter and Carter–Reagan debates as "public meetings," sponsored by the League of Women Voters, to get around the provision. In 1983, the FCC declared that radio and television broadcasters were free to stage debates at all political levels among candidates of their own choosing.[41] Broadcasters and the Commission on Presidential Debates (a non-partisan corporation created to sponsor presidential debates) decided to allow Independent candidate Ross Perot to join the debates in 1992 (Bush v. Clinton) and 1996 (Clinton v. Dole), but chose not to include Green Party candidate Ralph Nader in 2000 (W. Bush v. Gore), much to the chagrin of Nader and his supporters.

Rate Regulation Federal and local regulation of the rates charged by cable TV firms (many of them monopoly providers in local areas) has been imposed, removed, and imposed once again. Most recently, the Telecommunications Act of 1996 ended the regulation of cable rates by the FCC in 1999. Congress's thinking was that competition from the telephone companies would keep cable rates down. This remains to be seen.

The Internet

When television and radio were introduced, the industries were regulated by the federal government almost immediately. This has not been the case for the Internet, despite its extraordinary growth and social impact. Although initially a product of government encouragement and financial support—it was first created to link together university and government defense researchers[42]—the Internet has been relatively free from regulation, although there have been calls for government to prevent certain content from appearing on it. The few attempts that have been made have not been successful. Congress, for example, tried to ban obscenity on the Net, but the Supreme Court in 1997 declared the statute an unconstitutional restriction of free

HOW DEMOCRATIC ARE WE?
The Media and Democratic Citizenship

PROPOSITION: The news media are an important ingredient in making American politics democratic.

AGREE: Without the information provided by the news media, ordinary citizens would have little hope of learning what is happening abroad; they could not begin to think about what sorts of policies the United States should pursue in foreign affairs. Nor, without the news media, could most Americans learn what their government is doing domestically, what sorts of candidates are running for office, or what kinds of public policies are being considered.

In these respects, the spread of the news media in the United States, and the penetration of millions of homes by newspapers, radio, television, and computers, has undoubtedly helped democracy. It has made it much easier for ordinary citizens to form policy preferences, to judge the actions of government, and to figure out whom they want to govern them. News media thus tend to broaden the scope of conflict and contribute to political equality. When citizens, rather than just political leaders or special-interest groups, know what is going on, they can have a voice in politics. Moreover, interactive media and media-published polls help politicians hear that voice.

DISAGREE: Scholars and media critics who want the news media to be highly informative, analytical, and issue-oriented are appalled by the personalized, episodic, dramatic, and fragmented character of most news stories, which do not provide sustained and coherent explanations of what is going on. Others worry about ideological biases they think arise from a leftist media elite or from a corporate-owned media industry. Some criticize the media's patriotic and ethnocentric tendencies to support official U.S. foreign policy and even to pass along deliberate untruths stated by government officials. If the news media regularly present one-sided or false pictures of politics, people may form mistaken policy preferences. Government responsiveness to manipulated preferences would not be truly democratic.

Still other critics worry that constant media exposés of alleged official wrongdoing or government inefficiency, and the mocking tone aimed at virtually all political leaders by journalists and talk radio hosts, have fueled the growing political cynicism of the public. If this is true, the media are not serving democracy as well as they might.

THE AUTHORS: It is undeniably the case that the news media have not performed their civic responsibilities very well. They do tend to trivialize, focus on scandal and entertainment, and offer fragmented and out-of-context political and governmental information. However, things may not be quite as bad as they first appear. For one thing, for those who are truly interested in public affairs, there is now more readily accessible information than at any time in our history. For those willing to search for it, there is now little information that is relevant to public affairs that can be kept hidden, ranging from official government statistics to academic and other expert studies. Additionally, the American people have demonstrated an admirable ability on many occasions to sift the wheat from the chaff; to glean the information they need from the background noise, as it were.[44]

As Internet usage has expanded in the United States, various and sundry individuals and groups have called for tighter federal regulation of the new medium, primarily to protect children from material with sexual content and to prevent dissemination of hate material. So far, none of the bills passed by Congress to achieve these regulatory goals has passed constitutional muster with the Supreme Court.

speech. When the Clinton administration tried to prevent people from posting encryption codes, a federal court declared the effort as unconstitutional on the same grounds. In the view of the federal courts, at this writing, the Internet is an open medium where people are free to express their views, no different from dissemination of ideas by voice from atop a soap-box or by a pamphlet. Statute and case law in this area is sure to grow, however, as the Internet comes to play an ever larger role in our lives. The story of Internet regulation is not yet finished.[43]

Taken as a whole, then, government regulation of the media does not now amount to much. The trend has been toward a free market system with little government interference. Though the 2001 USA Patriot Act allows the federal government to more easily conduct surveillances of Internet and e-mail use by suspected terrorists, the overall conclusion about the light regulatory hand of the government still holds.

Summary

The shape of the news media in the United States has been determined largely by structural factors: technological developments, the growth of the American population and economy, and the development of a privately owned, corporation-dominated media industry.

The profit motive leads the major media to appeal to large audiences by limiting the quantity and depth of political news, by appealing to patriotism and other mainstream political values, and by emphasizing dramatic stories with visual impact and human interest.

News gathering is organized around New York City, Washington, D.C., and a handful of major cities in the United States and abroad. Most foreign countries are ignored unless there are crises or other big stories to communicate. Most news comes from government officials, who cultivate friendly relations with the press and provide accessible press conferences and information handouts.

Observers disagree about whether the media are biased in a liberal or a conservative direction. Reporters tend to be liberal, especially on social issues,

Longman
Participate.com
2.0
**Comparative
Comparing
News Media**

but this tendency may be balanced or reversed by conservative owners and editors. The U.S. media tend to reflect ethnocentrism, support U.S. foreign policy, and celebrate American-style capitalism. They also broadcast negative campaign ads, publicize personal scandals, and sharply criticize officials who have lost popularity.

Media stories have substantial effects on the public's perceptions of problems, its interpretations of events, its evaluations of political candidates, and its policy preferences.

The media, especially the print media, are protected from many kinds of government interference by the First Amendment to the Constitution. But censorship occurs during wars and crises, and officials have indirect ways of influencing the news. The electronic media are legally open to direct regulation, but such regulation, including the fairness doctrine and the equal time provision, has mostly lapsed. The Internet remains relatively free from government regulation.

Suggestions for Further Reading

Bagdikian, Ben H. *The Media Monopoly,* 6th ed. Boston: Beacon Press, 2000.
  An analysis of the corporate structure of the media and its consequences.

Bennett, W. Lance. *News: Politics of Illusion,* 3rd ed. New York: Longman, 1996.
  A critique of the news as trivial and uninformative.

Graber, Doris, Denis McQuail, and Pippa Norris, eds. *The Politics of News; the News of Politics.* Washington, D.C.: Congressional Quarterly Press, 1998.
  A collection that reports state-of-the-art scholarship on the subject of the mass media and American politics.

Kovach, Bill, and Tom Rosenstiel. *Warp Speed: America in the Age of Mixed Media.* New York: The Century Foundation Press, 1999.
  A sober and sometimes somber description of the effect of the rapidly changing mass media industry on American politics and government.

Page, Benjamin I. *Who Deliberates? Mass Media in Modern Democracy.* Chicago: University of Chicago Press, 1996.
  A discussion of how the media do or do not serve democracy well, with illustrative case studies.

Internet Sources

Almost every television news organization has a Website on the Internet:

ABC News   **http://www.abcnews.com**

CBS News   **http://www.cbsnews.com**

CNN Interactive   **http://www.cnn.com/**

NBC News   **http://www.nbcnews.com**

The same is true of the major national newspapers:

Chicago Tribune   **http://www.chicagotribune.com**

Los Angeles Times   **http://www.latimes.com**

New York Times   **http://www.nytimes.com**

USA Today   **http://www.usatoday.com**

Washington Post   **http://www.washingtonpost.com**

Other sources for studies on media trends and effects on society include:

The Center for Media and Public Affairs   **www.cmpa.com**
> *Studies, commentaries, and forums on media and public affairs.*

The Columbia Journalism Review   **www.cjr.org**
> *The Website of the leading scholarly monitor of journalism and journalists; loaded with useful information about all aspects of news making and dissemination.*

The Pew Research Center for the People and the Press   **www.people-press.org/**
> *The most complete public opinion surveys on citizen evaluations of the quality of media coverage of public affairs.*

Notes

1. The source for this vignette is Bill Dovach and Tom Rosenthal, *Warp Speed: America in the Age of Mass Media* (New York: The Century Fund Press, 1999).

2. Doris Graber, *Mass Media and American Politics,* 4th ed. (Washington, D.C.: Congressional Quarterly Press, 1993), p. 35.

3. See Suzanne Garment, *Scandal: The Crisis of Mistrust in American Politics* (New York: Random House, 1991); and Larry J. Sabato, Mark Stencel, and S. Robert Lichter, *Peepshow: Media and Politics in an Age of Scandal* (Boulder, CO: Rowman & Littlefield Publishers, 2000).

4. Dovach and Rosenthal, *Warp Speed.*

5. Diana Owen, "Talk Radio and Evaluations of President Clinton," *Political Communications,* 14 (1997), pp. 333–353.

6. *Talkers Magazine Online,* **www.talkers.com**, Fall 2001.

7. Kenneth Dautrich and Thomas H. Hartley, *How the News Media Fail American Voters* (New York: Columbia University Press, 1999).

8. Ibid., p. 33.

9. Mark Gillespie, "Cyber-Politics May Be More Hype Than Reality," *Gallup Poll Release*, February 25, 2000; "Internet Election News Audience," Pew Research Center of the People and the Press (October/November, 2000).

10. Regis McKenna, *Real Time* (Cambridge: Harvard University Press, 1997).

11. Dovach and Rosenthal, *Warp Speed,* pp. 52–57.

12. Erik P. Bucy et al., "The Engaged Electorate: New Media Use as Political Participation," in Lynda Lee Kaid and Dianne G. Bystrom, eds., *The Electronic Election* (Mahwah, NJ: Lawrence Erlbaum and Associates, Publishers, 1997).

13. Ben H. Bagdikian, *The Media Monopoly,* 5th ed. (Boston: Beacon Press, 1997); and "Who Owns What?", *Columbia Journalism Review Online,* **www.cjr.org**, 2001.

14. Symposium, "The Real Dangers of Conglomerate Control," *Columbia Journalism Review* (March–April 1997), pp. 47–51.

15. W. Lance Bennett, *News: The Politics of Illusion,* 3rd ed. (New York: Longman, 1996), p. 15.

16. Doug Underwood, "Market Research and the Audience for Political News," in Graber, McQuail, and Norris, *The Politics of News* (Washington, D.C.: CQ Press, 1998), p. 171.

17. Edward Jay Epstein, *News from Nowhere: Television and the News* (New York: Vantage, 1973), p. 142.

18. Leon V. Sigal, *Reporters and Officials: The Organization and Politics of News Reporting* (Lexington, MA: Heath, 1973), p. 124.

19. Mark Hertsgaard, *On Bended Knee* (New York: Farrar, Straus & Giroux, 1988), p. 5.

20. David Murray, Joel Schwartz, and S. Robert Lichter, *It Ain't Necessarily So: How Media Make and Unmake the Scientific Picture of Reality* (Lanham, MD: Rowan and Littlefield Publishers, 2001), pp. 29–30.

21. Lawrence C. Soley, *The News Shapers: The Sources Who Explain the News* (New York: Praeger, 1992); Eric Alterman, *Sound and Fury: The Washington Punditocracy and the Collapse of American Politics* (New York: HarperCollins, 1992).

22. G. William Domhoff, *Who Rules America: Power and Politics,* 4th ed. (Boston: Mayfield Publishing Company, 2001), p. 115.

23. William Schneider and I. A. Lewis, "Views on the News," *Public Opinion,* 8 (August–September 1985), p. 7; Karlyn Keene et al., "Monitoring Media Attitudes," *American Enterprise* (July–August 1990), p. 95; S. Robert Lichter, Stanley Rothman, and L. S. Lichter, *The Media Elite* (Bethesda, MD: Adler & Adler, 1986).

24. Howard Kurtz, "Acid Rain on the Media Parade: A Big Report Pooh-Poohing the Danger Gets Scant Press," *Washington Post Weekly Edition* (January 21–27, 1991), p. 38.

25. *Editorials on File,* 19 (November 1–15, 1988), p. 1272.

26. *Editor and Publisher* (October 24, 1992), pp. 9–10, 44; *Editor and Publisher* (November 7, 1992), pp. 8–11.

27. Thomas E. Patterson, *Out of Order* (New York: Knopf, 1993); Steven Ansolabehere and Shanto Iyengar, *Going Negative: How Attack Ads Shrink and Polarize the Electorate* (New York: Free Press, 1996).

28. Dovach and Rosenthal, *Warp Speed,* p. 66.

29. W. Lance Bennett, *News: The Politics of Illusion,* 3rd ed. (New York: Longman, 1996), p. 15; and Dovach and Rosenthal, *Warp Speed.*

30. Bennett, *News.*

31. David L. Paletz, "The Media and Public Policy," in Graber et al., *The Politics of News.*

32. Shanto Iyengar and Donald R. Kinder, *News That Matters* (Chicago: University of Chicago Press, 1987).

33. G. Ray Funkhauser, "The Issues of the Sixties: An Exploratory Study in the Dynamics of Public Opinion," *Public Opinion Quarterly,* 37 (Spring 1973), pp. 62–75.

34. George C. Edwards, "Who Influences Whom? The President, Congress and the Media," *The American Political Science Review* 93 (June, 1999), pp. 327–344.

35. Shanto Iyengar, *Is Anyone Responsible? How Television News Frames Political Issues* (Chicago: University of Chicago Press, 1991).

36. Benjamin I. Page, Robert Y. Shapiro, and Glenn R. Dempsey, "What Moves Public Opinion?" *American Political Science Review,* 81 (1987), pp. 23–43.

37. David L. Protess, Fay Lomax Cook, Jack C. Doppelt, James S. Ettema, Margaret T. Gordon, Donna R. Leff, and Peter Miller, *The Journalism of Outrage: Investigative Reporting and Agenda Building in America* (New York: Guilford Press, 1991).

38. Stephen C. Craig, ed., *Broken Contract: Changing Relations Between Americans and Their Government* (Boulder, CO: Westview Press, 1996); Bennett, *News;* Thomas E. Patterson, "Bad News, Period," *PS* (March 1996), pp. 17–20.

39. Daniel C. Hallin, *The "Uncensored War": The Media and Vietnam* (Berkeley, CA: University of California Press, 1989).

40. W. Lance Bennett and David L. Paletz, eds., *Taken by Storm: The Media, Public Opinion, and U.S. Foreign Policy in the Gulf War* (Chicago: University of Chicago Press, 1994).

41. Doris Graber, *Mass Media and American Politics,* 4th ed. (Washington, D.C.: Congressional Quarterly Press, 1993), pp. 67–68.

42. Dan Schiller, *Digital Capitalism: Networking in the New Global Market System* (Cambridge, MA: MIT Press, 1999).

43. Lawrence Lessig, *Code and Other Laws of Cyberspace* (New York: Basic Books, 1999).

44. John A. Ferejohn and James H. Kuklinski, eds., *Information and Democratic Processes* (Urbana: University of Illinois Press, 1990); Benjamin I. Page, *Who Deliberates? Mass Media in Modern Democracy* (Chicago: University of Chicago Press, 1996).

Chapter 7
Interest Groups and Business Corporations

In This Chapter

- Interest groups in democratic theory
- Why interest groups have proliferated
- How interest groups lobby the government
- How interest groups try to mobilize the grass roots
- Biases in the interest group system
- Why large corporations hold a privileged position

Lobbying for China

In 1997, the annual congressional debate on renewal of China's "most favored nation" (MFN) status reached fever pitch. The requirement that certain countries seek "most favored nation" status to avoid extremely high tariffs and other restrictions on their exports to the United States is reserved under American law for communist countries (China, Cuba, North Korea) and a handful of so-called rogue states (Iran, Iraq, Libya) that are not members of the World Trade Organization. Each year, the president makes a determination about these nations, which Congress can override by a two-thirds vote. Presidential decisions to grant China "most favored nation" trade status had easily prevailed since 1981.

The political coalition that formed in 1997 to oppose granting MFN to China was made up of a surprising assortment of private and public interest groups and human rights organizations. Many human rights groups, such as Amnesty International, joined the battle because of the Chinese government's brutal repression of the pro-democracy movement in Beijing's Tiananmen Square in 1989, its abysmal human rights record in general, and its occupation of Tibet. Christian fundamentalists, through organizations such as the Family Research Council, used the MFN legislation to voice their concerns about the treatment of Christians in China and Chinese government family planning practices. MFN was also opposed by groups and individuals, such as the AFL-CIO union federation and anti–free trade politicians such as Dick Gephardt (D–MO), who believe that free trade with low-wage countries depresses the wages of American workers. Finally, a number of software and entertainment companies, including Microsoft, opposed MFN for China because of the Chinese government's toleration of software pirating.

Despite this impressive array of opponents, there were not enough votes in Congress in 1997 to override President Clinton's granting of MFN to China for another year. There are many reasons for this, including the fact that many reasonable people believe that a policy of free trade with China not only benefits both parties economically but also will, in the long run, undermine that country's autocratic government and improve human rights and the chances for democracy. Equally important, perhaps, was the impressive array of American corporations that wanted open trade with China and were willing to lobby intensively for a favorable decision on MFN. The Boeing Corporation was especially involved in this campaign, primarily because its growth and profitability in the near future depend heavily on the sale of commercial aircraft to China.[1] Locked in an intense global competition with the European Airbus consortium for sales in China and elsewhere and knowing that the Chinese government was

happy to play off Boeing and Airbus for favorable policy decisions by their governments, Boeing became a strong advocate for MFN and other policies favorable to China. Boeing lobbied members of Congress directly, contributed to the campaign war chests of candidates from both parties, asked its nearly 200,000 employees to get involved in the political process, and encouraged local political and business leaders in communities where Boeing has major plants (the Puget Sound region; Long Beach, California; St. Louis; and Wichita, Kansas) to talk to members of Congress.

Boeing was not alone; an impressive collection of companies doing business there lobbied Congress to approve MFN status for China. These included some of America's most important companies: the Big Three auto companies, defense high-technology firms such as TRW and United Technologies, Cargill (food products), Coca-Cola, General Electric, Caterpillar, and Aetna Insurance.[2] Many large and medium-sized export-oriented firms and associations lobbied through the 1,000-member Business Coalition for U.S.–China Trade (members include the National Association of Manufacturers, the National Retail Federation, the Business Roundtable, and the U.S. Chamber of Commerce). This impressive coalition greatly strengthened the hands of President Clinton and the congressional Republican leadership, both of whom were favorably disposed to free trade and renewal of China's MFN status.

The annual struggle over China's trade status has now ended—in 2000, Congress granted China permanent status as a trading partner; in 2001, China joined the World Trade Organization—but the issue of free trade still remains an important part of the American political agenda and will remain so for many years to come. More importantly for the purposes of this chapter, the extent of private and public interest group mobilization for and against China's trade status, as well as the wide range of lobbying strategies used by these diverse groups, are fairly typical of what interest groups do with regard to most other important government policy initiatives. ■

Thinking Critically About This Chapter

This story about the 1997 battle over MFN certification for China tells us a lot about how many important government policies are made in the United States and the central role that interest groups and business corporations play in shaping them.

Using the Framework You will see in this chapter how interest groups, in combination with other political linkage institutions, help convey the wishes and interests of people and groups to government decision makers. You will also learn how the kind of interest group system we have in the United States is, in large part, a product of structural factors, including our constitutional rules, political culture, social organization, and economy.

Using the Democracy Standard Interest groups have long held an ambiguous place in American politics. To some, interest groups are "special" interests that act without regard to the public interest and are the instruments of the most privileged parts of American society. To others, interest groups are simply another way by which people and groups in a democratic society get their voices heard by government leaders. Using the democracy standard described in Chapter 1, you will be able to choose between these two positions. ◀

Interest Groups in a Democratic Society: Contrasting Views

interest group

Any private organization or association that seeks to influence public policy as a way to protect or advance some interest.

pressure group

An interest group or lobby; a group that brings pressure to bear on government decision makers.

lobby

An interest or pressure group that seeks to convey the group's interest to government decision makers.

Interest groups are private organizations that try to shape public policy. They are made up of people who share an interest or cause that they are trying to protect or advance with the help of government. To do this, interest groups try to influence the behavior of public officials, such as presidents, members of Congress, bureaucrats, or judges. These efforts are often perceived by officials as pressuring them, so interest groups are often called **pressure groups.** The term **lobby** is also commonly used—because of the practice of interest group representatives' talking to representatives and senators in the lobbies outside committee rooms—as in references to the "dairy lobby" or the "gun lobby."

In the late nineteenth century, most Americans thought of the Senate as the captive of large corporate trusts and other special-interest groups, as depicted in this popular cartoon, "Bosses of the Senate."

The Evils of Factions

The danger to good government and the public interest from interest groups is a familiar theme in American politics. They are usually regarded as narrowly self-interested, out for themselves, and without regard for the public good.

This theme is prominent in *The Federalist,* No. 10, in which James Madison defined **factions** (his term for interest groups and narrow political parties) in the following manner: "A number of citizens, whether amounting to a majority or a minority of the whole, who are united and actuated by some

faction

Madison's term for groups or parties that try to advance their own interests at the expense of the public good.

Web Exploration
What Are Interest Groups?

Issue: Interest groups are different in important ways from political parties.

Site: Access the Republican National Committee and one of its most closely allied interest groups, the National Right to Life Committee, on our Website at **www.ablongman.com/greenberg**. Go to the "Web Explorations" section for Chapter 7 and open "What are interest groups." There you will find links to the Republican National Committee and the National Right to Life Committee. At each of these sites, examine the public policy issues that are addressed. Select "RNC Newsroom" and "Talking Points" for the GOP, and "issue information" for the NRLC.

What You've Learned: What differences are there between the two on the range of issues each pays attention to? How would you explain differences (if there are any) in the issue agendas of the political party and the interest group?

HINT: Only one of these two types of institutions is in the business of trying to elect its people to office and gain control of the government.

common impulse of passion, or of interest, adverse to the rights of other citizens or to the permanent and aggregate interests of the community."[3] The "evils of factions" theme recurs throughout our history, from the writings of the "muckrakers" at the turn of the twentieth century to the Republican presidential primary campaign of John McCain in 2000.

Interest Group Democracy: The Pluralist Argument

pluralist

A political scientist who views American politics as best understood in terms of the interaction, conflict, and bargaining of groups.

According to many political scientists, however, interest groups do not hurt democracy and the public interest but are an important instrument in attaining both. The argument of these **pluralist** political scientists is shown in Figure 7.1 and goes as follows:[4]

- Free elections, while essential to a democracy, do not adequately communicate the specific wants and interests of the people to political leaders on a continuous basis. These are more accurately, consistently, and frequently conveyed to political leaders by the many groups and organizations to which people belong.

- Interest groups are easy to create; people in the United States are free to join or to organize groups that reflect their interests.

- Because of federalism, checks and balances, and the separation of powers, government power in the United States is broadly dispersed, leaving governmental institutions remarkably porous and open to the entreaties of the many and diverse groups that exist in society.

- Because of the ease of group formation and the accessibility of government, all legitimate interests in society can have their views taken into account by some public official. Because of this, the system is highly democratic.

Pluralists see interest groups, then, not as a problem but as an additional tool of democratic representation, similar to other democratic instruments such as public opinion and elections. We shall explore the degree to which this position is valid in this and other chapters.

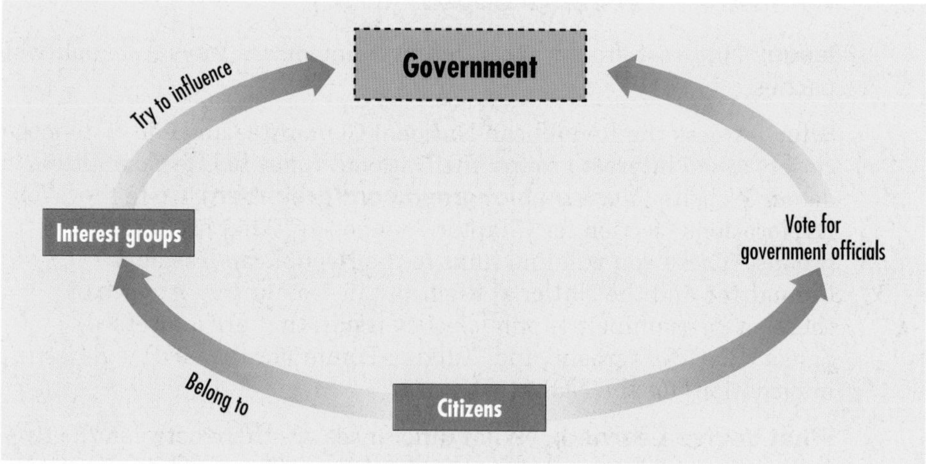

FIGURE 7.1 The Pluralist View of American Politics

In the pluralist understanding of the way American democracy works, citizens have more than one way to influence government leaders. In addition to voting, citizens also have the opportunity to participate in organizations that convey member views to public officials. Because of weak political parties, federalism, checks and balances, and the separation of powers, access to public officials is relatively easy.

Interest Group Formation: Structural, Political Linkage, and Governmental Factors

Nobody knows exactly how many interest groups exist in the United States, but there is wide agreement that the number began to mushroom in the late 1960s and has grown steadily ever since. We have a more precise count, however, of the number of paid lobbyists who work for interest groups in Washington and try to affect government policies. In 1996, more than 17,500 lobbyists worked there, up from 4,000 in 1977.[5]

Much of the increase in the number of interest groups can be explained by the growing number of public interest or citizen groups organized around some cause or idea, rather than an economic or occupational interest, the traditional basis for forming interest groups. These include environmental, consumer protection, anti-abortion, family values, good government, civil rights, pro-life, and women's organizations. Nevertheless, corporations, business trade associations, and the professions still dominate the scene: One study done during the Reagan years showed that corporations made up 52 percent of all organizations with Washington representatives, that trade and other business associations accounted for another 20 percent, and that professional associations accounted for an additional 8 percent, for a total of 80 percent of the organizations.[6] And, there is no evidence to suggest that the proportion of the total made up by citizen groups has grown much since then.[7]

There are a number of reasons so many interest groups exist in the United States.

Diverse Interests

Being a very diverse society, there are simply lots of interests in the United States. Racial, religious, ethnic, and occupational diversity is pronounced. Our economy is also strikingly complex and multifaceted, and becoming more so. In a free society, these diverse interests usually take organizational forms. Thus, the computer revolution has spawned computer chip manufacturers, software companies, software engineers, computer magazines, Internet services, technical information providers, computer component jobbers, Web designers, and countless others. Each has particular interests to defend or advance before government, and each has formed an association to try to do so. Thus, software engineers have an association to look after their interests. So do software and hardware companies, Internet access providers, digital content providers, industry writers, and so on.

Rules of the Game

The rules of the political game in the United States encourage the formation of interest groups. The First Amendment to the Constitution, for instance, guarantees citizens the right to speak freely, to assemble, and to petition the government, all of which are essential to citizens' ability to form organizations to advance their interests before government. Moreover, the government is organized in such a way that officials are relatively accessible to interest groups. Because of federalism, checks and balances, and the separation of powers, there is no dominant center of decision making, as there is in unitary states such as Great Britain and France. In unitary states (see Chapter 3), most important policy decisions are made in parliamentary bodies. In the United States, important decisions are made by many officials, on many matters, in many jurisdictions. Consequently, there are many more places where interest group pressure can be effective. Finally, there are no strong, centralized political parties in the United States, as there are in the European democracies, that might serve to overcome the decentralized, fragmented quality of the policymaking process in the United States. The result is relatively easy access to public officials in the United States.

The Growth in Government

Government does far more today than it did during the early years of the Republic. As government takes on more responsibilities, it quite naturally comes to have a greater effect on virtually all aspects of economic, social, and personal life. People, groups, and organizations are increasingly affected by the actions of government, so the decisions made by presidents, members of Congress, bureaucrats, and judges are increasingly important. It would be surprising indeed if in response, people, groups, and organizations did not try harder to influence the public officials' decisions that affect them.

Government often encourages the formation of groups and associations to help carry out and monitor its policies or to achieve other ends. According to political scientist Anne Costain, a commissioner of the Equal Employment Opportunity Commission (EEOC) played an important role in the formation of the National Organization for Women (NOW) because he wanted a counterweight to the overwhelming influence of African-American civil rights groups over the EEOC.[8]

Disturbances

disturbance theory

A theory that locates the origins of interest groups in changes in the economic, social, or political environment that threaten the well-being of some segment of the population.

The existence of diverse interests, the rules of the game, and the importance of government decisions and policies enable and encourage the formation of interest groups, but formation seems to happen only when interests are threatened, usually by some change in the social and economic environment or in government policy. This is known as the **disturbance theory** of interest group formation.[9] To take one example, the Christian Coalition was formed when many evangelical Christians began to feel threatened by family breakdown, an increase in the number of abortions, the sexual revolution, and the growing voice of gays and lesbians.

Incentives

free rider

One who gains a benefit without contributing; explains why it is so difficult to form social movements and noneconomic interest groups.

Some social scientists argue, however, that people are not inclined to form groups, even when their common interests are threatened, unless the group can offer a selective, material benefit to them.[10] A selective, material benefit is something tangible that is available to the members of an interest group but not to nonmembers. If someone can get the benefit without joining the group, then joining makes no sense as he or she can obtain the same benefit without contributing. This is known as the **free rider** problem, and it generally comes into play when a group is interested in a collective good, such as a government program or action that will be good for all the members of some category whether they belong to a formal organization or not. All women with young children gain when the National Organization for Women helps influence Congress to pass the Family Leave Act and are not required to join the organization to enjoy the benefit. People join, it is argued, when an association has benefits that are available only to its members—for example, discounted life and health insurance programs for the members of the Wheat Growers Association.

Discontent among American farmers in the late nineteenth century led to the formation of protest organizations and, eventually, the Populist party. One predecessor of the Populist party was the Grange, which fought for social and cultural benefits for isolated rural communities.

This theory emphasizes how difficult and unlikely it is that interest groups will form at all. It cannot account very well, therefore, for the upsurge in group formation during the 1960s and 1970s, especially of the public interest and ideological variety.[11] The proliferation of such groups suggests that groups form not only around selective, material incentives but also around "purposive" (ideological, issue-oriented) incentives and around "solidaristic" (in the sense of being part of something that one values) ones. People often join groups, for instance, because they believe in a particular cause (e.g., nuclear disarmament, civil rights, prayer in the public schools, or an end to legal abortion) or because they enjoy the companionship afforded by belonging to a group.

What Interests Are Represented

What kinds of interests find a voice in American politics? A useful place to start is with political scientist E. E. Schattschneider's distinction between "private" and "public" interests. Although the boundaries between the two are sometimes fuzzy, the distinction remains important: Public interests are connected in one way or another to the general welfare of the community; private interests, by contrast, are associated with benefits for some fraction of the community.[12] The latter are mainly economic interests, groups with some tangible stake they wish to protect or to advance by means of government action. The former are mainly noneconomic groups motivated by some ideology, by the desire to advance a general cause—civil rights or environmental protection—or by the commitment to some public policy—gun control or an end to abortion.

Private Interest Groups

Many different kinds of private interest groups are active in American politics.

Business   Because of the vast resources at the disposal of business and because of their strategic role in the health of local, state, and national economies, groups and associations representing business wield enormous power in Washington. Large corporations such as Enron are able to mount their own lobbying efforts and join with others in influential associations such as the Business Roundtable. Medium-sized businesses are well represented by organizations such as the National Association of Manufacturers and the U.S. Chamber of Commerce. Even small businesses have proved to be quite influential when joined in associations such as the National Federation of Independent Business, which helped stop the Clinton health plan in 1994. Agriculture and agribusinesses (fertilizer, seed, machinery, biotechnology, and food processing companies) have more than held their own over the years through such organizations as the American Farm Bureau Federation and the Farm Machinery Manufacturer's Association, and scores of commodity groups, including the American Dairy Association and the American Wheat Growers Association. Business has always been a powerful player in national politics and seems to have become stronger in recent years, especially as large corporations such as Microsoft, Intel, Caterpillar, Archer Daniels Midland, and Chase Bank become more important in the global economy.

The Professions Several associations represent the interests of professionals, such as doctors, lawyers, dentists, and accountants. Because of the prominent social position of professionals in local communities and their ability to make substantial campaign contributions, such associations are very influential in the policymaking process on matters related to their professional expertise and concerns. The American Medical Association (AMA) and the American Dental Association (ADA), for instance, lobbied strongly against the Clinton health care proposal and helped kill it in the 103rd Congress. The Trial Lawyers Association has long been a major financial contributor to the Democratic Party and active in blocking legislation to limit the size of personal injury jury awards.

Labor Although labor unions are sometimes involved in what might be called public interest activities (such as supporting civil rights legislation), their main role in the United States has been to protect the jobs of their members and to secure maximum wages and benefits for them. Unlike labor unions in many parts of the world, which are as much political and ideological organizations as economic ones, American labor unions have traditionally focused on so-called bread-and-butter issues. Union lobbying activities

John Sweeney, the president of the AFL-CIO labor federation, has attempted to reinvigorate the organizing efforts and political presence of the labor movement. Here he addresses a crowd on the need to raise the minimum wage.

are directed at issues that affect the ability of unions to protect the jobs, wages, and benefits of their members and to maintain or increase the size of the union membership rolls. As an important part of the New Deal coalition that dominated American politics well into the late 1960s, labor unions were influential at the federal level during the years when the Democratic party controlled Congress and often won the presidency.

Although organized labor is still a force to be reckoned with in electoral politics, most observers believe that the political power of labor unions has eroded in dramatic ways over the past several decades.[13] Organized labor's well-funded effort during the 1996 congressional elections to unseat conservative House Republicans fizzled. Union opposition also failed to stop the China trade bill in 2000.

Organized labor's main long-range problem in American politics and its declining power relative to business in the workplace is its small membership base; in 2000, only 13.5 percent of American workers were members of labor unions compared to 35 percent in 1954.[14] The long but steady decline in union membership is strongly associated with the decline in the proportion of American workers in manufacturing—the economic sector in which unions have traditionally been the strongest—and has proved resistant to vigorous organizing drives recently mounted by AFL-CIO president John Sweeney.

Public Interest Groups

Public interest groups, sometimes called *citizens' groups,* try to get government to act in ways that will serve the general public and the public interest—as they define the public interest, of course—rather than the direct economic or occupational interests of their members.[15] People active in such groups tend to be motivated by ideological concerns or a belief in some cause.

Public interest groups of one kind or another have always been around, but a great upsurge in their number and influence has taken place since the late 1960s.[16] Many were spawned by social movements. The environmental movement created organizations such as the Environmental Defense Fund, the Nature Conservancy, Clean Water Action, and the Natural Resources Defense

Christian conservatives have created several important and influential interest group organizations. Here Gary Bauer, the president of the Family Research Council, addresses a rally in Washington, D.C., protesting the persecution of Christians in China.

Council, for example. The evangelical Christian upsurge led to the creation of such organizations as the Moral Majority, the Christian Coalition, the National Right-to-Life Committee, and the Family Research Council.

Most citizen groups retain a professional, paid administrative staff and are supported by generous donors (often foundations), membership dues, and/or donations generated by direct-mail campaigns. While some depend upon and encourage grassroots volunteers, and some hold annual membership meetings where members play some role in making association policies, most public interest groups and citizens associations are organizations without active membership involvement (other than check writing), and are run by lobbying and public education professionals.[17]

What Interest Groups Do

Interest groups are in the business of conveying the views and defending the interests of individuals and groups to public officials. There are two basic types of interest group activity: the inside game and the outside game.[18] The inside game—the older and more familiar of the two—involves direct, personal contact between interest group representatives and government officials. The outside game involves interest group mobilization of public opinion, voters, and important contributors in order to bring pressure to bear on elected officials.

The Inside Game

Longman
Participate.com
2.0
Simulation
**You Are a
Lobbyist**

The term *lobbying* conjures up visions of a cigar-chomping interest group representative, his arm around the shoulder of an important senator or representative, advising him on how he ought to vote on some obscure provision of the Tax Code, slipping an envelope, fat with currency, into the politician's jacket pocket. Or it conjures up images of favors given in return for future legislative considerations: paid vacations to exotic locations, honorarium payments for brief speeches at association meetings, and other exchanges verging on bribery.

The images both reveal and confuse. These things surely happened in the past, some continue to happen today, and some will surely happen in the future. In general, however, the images do not help us understand the intricacies of the inside game. This game does not involve bribes. Rather, it is more the politics of insiders and the "old boy" network (although, increasingly, women are also part of the network). It is the politics of one-on-one persuasion, in which the skilled lobbyist tries to get a decision maker to understand and sympathize with the interest group's point of view or to see that what the interest group wants is good for the politician's constituents. Access is critical if one is to be successful at this game.

Many of the most successful lobbyists are recruited from the ranks of retired members of the House, the Senate, and high levels of the bureaucracy. Over half of the powerful drug industry's registered lobbyists, for example, are former members of Congress, former congressional staffers, or former employees of the executive branch.[19] The promise of lucrative employment based on their skills—and especially on their many contacts—is what keeps so many of them around Washington after they leave office or quit federal employment. The very best of them have been in and out of one office or another in one administration or another for many years, know the D.C. scene as a wine connoisseur knows wine, and are compensated very well for their services.

The inside game seems to work best when the issues are narrow and technical, do not command much media attention or public passion, and do not stir up counter-activity by other interest groups.[20] This is not to say that interest groups play a role only on unimportant matters. Great benefit can come to an interest group or a large corporation from a small change in a single provision of the Tax Code or in a slight change in the wording of a regulation. Enron, for example, was very successful at getting Congress to remove federal oversight on many of its energy-trading and acquisitions activities. These stayed well out of public view until they came to light after Enron's spectacular collapse in 2001.

Lobbyists from citizens groups also play the inside game, often with great skill and effect. Many environmental regulations have been strengthened because of the efforts of skilled lobbyists from the Sierra Club, for example.

E. E. Schattschneider has pointed out that the inside game—traditional lobbying—is pretty much outside the view of the public. That is to say, the day-to-day details of this form of lobbying are not the stuff of the evening news, nor the fodder of open political campaigns or conflict; such lobbying takes place behind closed doors. As such, it does not do much to advance democracy. A good example of the effectiveness of the inside game is the story of the airline passengers' bill of rights we examine in the "Using the Framework" feature.

Lobbying Congress The essence of the inside game in Congress is the cultivation of personal relationships with people who matter—Senate and House leaders, other influential and well-placed legislators, chairpersons of important committees or subcommittees, and key staff members. Because much of the action in Congress takes place in the committees and because senators and

An important part of the job of the lobbyist is to convey the views and concerns of interest group members to representatives and senators. The ability to hire and deploy lobbyists, however, is not randomly distributed among Americans. Those with the greatest economic resources tend to dominate the "inside game" of interest group politics.

USING THE FRAMEWORK: Airline Passenger Bill of Rights

Whatever happened to the Airline Passenger Fairness Act?

Background: Senate Bill 383, the Airline Passengers Fairness Act, was introduced in February 1999. Senator John McCain, a long-time critic of the existing campaign financing system and its dependence on corporate and trade association contributions, and an early candidate for the Republican presidential nomination, was one of the Act's most prominent sponsors. Yet, after days of spirited testimony before the Senate Commerce Committee, and within days of a vote on the bill in committee, McCain backed away from the original Act and offered a softer version, which included accepting the proposal of the airlines that they voluntarily improve customer service. Taking a broad look at how structural, political linkage, and governmental factors contributed to the softening of the Airline Passenger Fairness Act will help explain the situation.

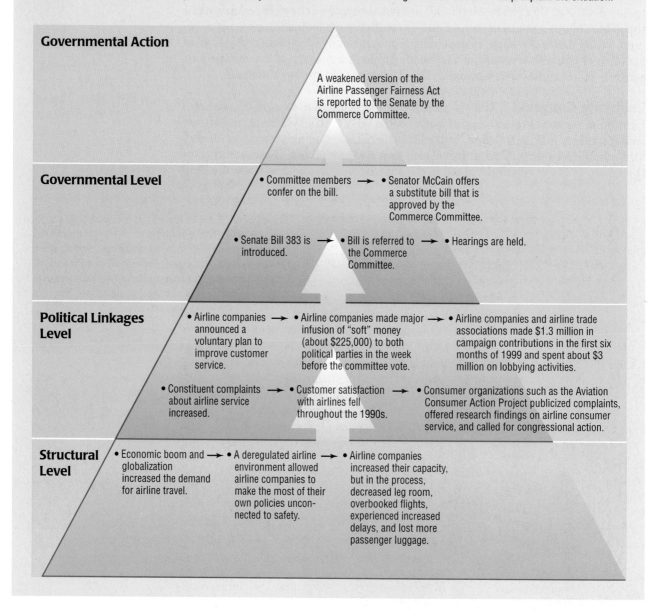

Governmental Action

A weakened version of the Airline Passenger Fairness Act is reported to the Senate by the Commerce Committee.

Governmental Level

- Committee members confer on the bill. → • Senator McCain offers a substitute bill that is approved by the Commerce Committee.

- Senate Bill 383 is introduced. → • Bill is referred to the Commerce Committee. → • Hearings are held.

Political Linkages Level

- Airline companies announced a voluntary plan to improve customer service. → • Airline companies made major infusion of "soft" money (about $225,000) to both political parties in the week before the committee vote. → • Airline companies and airline trade associations made $1.3 million in campaign contributions in the first six months of 1999 and spent about $3 million on lobbying activities.

- Constituent complaints about airline service increased. → • Customer satisfaction with airlines fell throughout the 1990s. → • Consumer organizations such as the Aviation Consumer Action Project publicized complaints, offered research findings on airline consumer service, and called for congressional action.

Structural Level

- Economic boom and globalization increased the demand for airline travel. → • A deregulated airline environment allowed airline companies to make the most of their own policies unconnected to safety. → • Airline companies increased their capacity, but in the process, decreased leg room, overbooked flights, experienced increased delays, and lost more passenger luggage.

representatives are busy with a wide range of responsibilities, cultivating relationships with important legislative and committee staff members is especially important for successful lobbyists. As one lobbyist put it, "If you have a staff member on your side, it might be a hell of a lot better than talking to the member [of Congress]."[21]

Lobbyists are also expected to attend and make contributions at various congressional fundraisers. The *Washington Post* counted 23 such events on a single day, June 24, 1999, a nonelection year.[22]

Lobbying the Executive Branch   Career civil servants and political appointees in the executive branch have a great deal of discretionary authority because Congress often legislates broad policies, leaving it to bureaucratic agencies to fill in the details. Because of this, interest groups try to establish stable and friendly relationships with the agencies of the executive branch that are most relevant to their interests. Pharmaceutical companies, for example, stay in touch with the relevant people at the Food and Drug Administration (FDA).

The key to success in lobbying the executive branch is similar to that in lobbying Congress: personal contact and cooperative long-term relationships. Interest group representatives can convey technical information, present the results of their research, help a public official deflect criticism, and show that what the group wants is compatible with good public policy and the political needs of the official.

Lobbying the Courts   Interest groups sometimes lobby the courts, although not in the same way as they lobby the other two branches. A group may find that neither Congress nor the White House is favorably disposed to its interests and will bring a test case to the courts. Realizing that the improvement of the lot of African-Americans was very low on the agenda of presidents and members of Congress during the 1940s and 1950s, for example, the NAACP turned to the courts for satisfaction. The effort eventually paid off in 1954 in the landmark *Brown* v. *Board of Education* decision.

Interest groups sometimes lobby the courts by filing *amicus curiae* ("friends of the court") briefs in cases involving other parties. In this kind of brief, a person or an organization that is not a party in the suit may file an argument in support of one side or the other in the hope of swaying the views of the judge or judges. Major controversies before the Supreme Court on such issues as abortion, free speech, or civil rights attract scores of *amicus curiae* briefs.

Interest groups also get involved in the appointment of federal judges. Particularly controversial appointments, such as the Supreme Court nominations of Robert Bork (whom many women's and civil rights interests considered too conservative) in 1987 and Clarence Thomas (who was opposed by liberal and women's groups) in 1992, drew interest group attention and strenuous efforts for and against the nominee.

The Outside Game

The outside game is being played when interest groups try to mobilize **grass roots,** constituency, and public opinion support for their goals and bring them to bear on elected officials. By all indications, the outside game has been growing steadily in importance in recent years compared to more traditional forms of lobbying.[23] This may be a good development for democracy, and here is why. Although groups involved in the outside game often try to

grass roots

The constituents, voters, or rank-and-file of a party.

hide their true identities—Americans for Fair Drug Prices, for example, may well be funded by the drug industry—and while some groups involved in the outside game have more resources than others, it is still the case that this form of politics has the effect of expanding and heightening political conflict, bringing issues out into the open and subjecting them to public scrutiny—what Schattschneider has called the "socialization of conflict."[24]

Longman
Participate.com
2.0
Participation
**Gun Rights
and Gun
Control**

Mobilizing Membership
Those interest groups with a large membership base try to persuade their members to send letters and to make telephone calls to senators and representatives when an important issue is before Congress. They sound the alarm, using direct mail and, increasingly, e-mail. They define the threat to members, suggest a way to respond to the threat, and supply the addresses, phone numbers, and e-mail addresses of the people to contact in Washington. Members are grouped by congressional district and state and are given the addresses of their own representatives or senators. The National Rifle Association (NRA) is particularly effective in mobilizing its considerable membership whenever the threat of federal gun control rears its head. (It is said by the NRA and others that the organization can mobilize roughly 175,000 members to stump for candidates or contact a member of Congress.) Environmental organizations such as the Sierra Club and Friends of the Earth sound the alarm to its members whenever Congress threatens to loosen environmental protections.

Organizing the District
Members of Congress are especially attuned to the individuals and groups in their states or districts who can affect their re-election prospects. The smart interest group, therefore, not only will convince its own members in the state and district to put pressure on the senator or congressional representative but will also make every effort to be in touch with the most important campaign contributors and opinion leaders there.

Shaping Public Opinion
"Educating" the public on issues that are important to the interest group is one of the central features of new-style lobbying. The idea is to shape opinion in such a way that government officials will

Mass demonstrations, designed to attract public attention through media coverage, are important tools in the arsenals of many interest groups. Here anti-gun groups show their displeasure with the National Rifle Association's opposition to gun control at the NRA's annual meeting in Denver in 1999, only weeks after the massacre at Columbine High School.

be favorably disposed to the views of the interest group. These attempts to shape public and elite opinion come in many forms. One strategy is to produce and distribute research reports that bolster the group's position. Citizen groups such as the Environmental Defense Fund and the Food Research and Action Center have been very adept and effective in this area.[25]

Another strategy is media advertising. Sometimes this takes the form of pressing a position on a particular issue, such as the Teamsters Union raising the alarm about open borders with Mexico, focusing on the purported unsafe nature of Mexican trucks roaming American highways. Sometimes it is "image" advertising, in which some company or industry portrays its positive contribution to American life.[26]

In the effort to shape public opinion, the well-heeled interest group will also prepare materials that will be of use to radio and television broadcasters and to newspaper and magazine editors. Many produce opinion pieces, magazine articles, television spots and radio "sound bites," and even television documentaries. Others stage events to be covered as news. The environmentalist group Greenpeace puts the news media on full alert, for example, when it tries to disrupt a whaling operation or a nuclear weapons test.

Getting Involved in Campaigns and Elections Interest groups try to increase their influence by getting involved in political campaigns. Many interest groups, for example, rate members of Congress on their support for the interest group's position on a selection of key votes. The ratings are distributed to the members of the interest group and other interested parties in the hope that the ratings will influence their voting behavior. We show how groups do this in the "By the Numbers" feature in this section.

Interest groups also encourage their members to get involved in the electoral campaigns of candidates who are favorable to their interests. Groups often assist campaigns in more tangible ways—allowing the use of their telephone banks, mailing lists, fax and photocopy machines, computers, and the like. Some interest groups help with fund-raising events or ask members to make financial contributions to candidates.

Interest groups also endorse particular candidates for public office. The strategy may backfire and is somewhat risky, for to endorse a losing candidate is to risk losing access to the winner. Nevertheless, it is fairly common now for labor unions, environmental organizations, religious groups, and liberal and conservative ideological groups to make such endorsements.

Interest groups are also an increasingly important part of campaign fund-raising. Many of them channel money directly to candidates, give soft money to political parties (confined to state and local parties after the 2002 elections) to be used in electoral campaigns, and run independent issue campaigns.

Possible Flaws in the Pluralist Heaven

Political scientist E. E. Schattschneider once observed that the flaw in the pluralist (or interest group) heaven is "that the heavenly chorus sings with a strong upper class accent." If his observation is accurate, then political equality is undermined by the interest group system, and democracy is less fully developed than it might be even taking into account the new importance of the outside game (which, as we have said, tends to "socialize conflict"). In this section, we look at inequalities in the interest group system and evaluate their effects.

By the Numbers

How can we evaluate our congressional representatives?

Imagine you are at the end of the semester and four different teachers give you a grade in your introductory political science course. One looks at your performance and gives you a grade of 100 percent. Your day is made! Teacher number 2 gives you an 83. OK, you might say, "I can live with that." Teachers 3 and 4 slam you with a 20 and a 10. Ouch! How to make sense of all of this? How come two teachers love you and two hate you? Surely they must be biased in some way.

This is exactly what happens to members of Congress when they are graded on their performance by interest groups. Unlike you, the confused student in the example above, Congressional representatives expect the wide disparity in the grades they receive, understand what is going on, and are even proud of most of their grades, whether high or low. Note the wildly contrasting grades for Republican Senator Richard Selby of Alabama and Democratic Senator Paul Wellstone of Minnesota (who died in a plane crash in October 2002) given by four organizations in 2000: the Americans for

Democratic Action (ADA), the American Conservative Union (ACU), the League of Conservation Voters (LCV), and the National Taxpayers Union (NTU).

Why It Matters: Having a consistent and reliable way to grade each member of Congress can help voters make more rational electoral choices. Without such grades, each citizen would have to investigate the record of his or her member of Congress, rely on news reports, or depend on information provided by the member.

Behind the Numbers: How are members of Congress graded? The answer is pretty straightforward. Each interest group in this example is strongly ideological or committed to a certain set of concerns, and each grades members of Congress in terms of these standards. The ADA is very strongly liberal—interested in civil liberties, civil rights, and economic and social justice—while the ACU is strongly conservative—in favor of capitalism, traditional moral values, and a strong national defense. The LCV supports legislation to protect the environment while the NTU wants lower taxes, less wasteful government spending, and a balanced budget. So, members of Congress who vote to increase spending on child welfare programs, let us say, are likely to get high grades from the ADA, but low grades from the ACU and the NTU. Members who vote to open the Alaska National Wildlife Reserve for oil exploration would surely receive a low grade from the folks at LCV.

Representational Inequalities

Not all segments of society are equally represented in the interest group system. The interest group game in Washington, D.C., is dominated, in sheer numbers and weight of activity, by business corporations, industry trade associations, and associations of the professions, although liberal and conservative citizen groups play an important role as well. In addition, among citizen or public interest groups, those whose members are among the better educated and more affluent tend to be more visible and more effective in Washington.[27]

Resource Inequalities

Business corporations and professionals are the most economically well-off parts of American society. It is hardly surprising that interest groups representing them can afford to spend far more than other groups to hire profes-

Calculating Interest Group Scores:

Though each group uses a slightly different method to do its grading, at base, each approaches grading in pretty much the same way. For each interest group, its professional staff, sometimes in conjunction with outside experts, selects a set of key votes on which to assess members of Congress. The particular votes selected by each group will differ—a group interested solely in civil rights issues will not, for example, use a vote on the defense budget for its scorecard—but each identifies a set of votes it considers to be a good indicator of ideological or policy loyalty. On each vote, members of Congress are scored "with the group" or "against the group." The numbers are added up, then transformed to percentage terms, with 100 being the highest score and 0 the lowest.

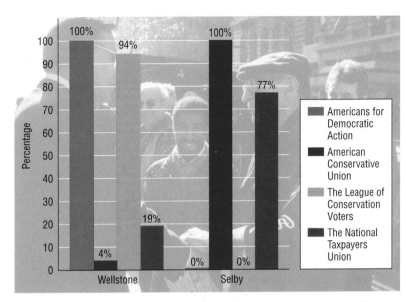

Interest Group Ratings of Senators Wellstone and Selby

Source: Project Vote Smart (www.vote-smart.org) for the year 2000.

What to Watch For: Oddly enough, though not terribly sophisticated in either conceptual or computational terms, these are numbers you can trust. You can, as they say, "take them to the bank." Why? Because each interest group is clear about what it stands for, and each makes it clear that it is judging members of Congress from a particular perspective. When you are considering whether to vote for or against an incumbent member of Congress, a good method would be to check member scores from organizations whose ideology and/or policy views you support.

What Do You Think? How does your representative in Congress score with those groups whose values, policy position, and values come closest to your own? You can investigate this at the Project Vote Smart Website at **www.vote-smart.org** where you can find how your representative is evaluated by different interest groups.

sional lobbying firms, form their own Washington liaison office, place advertising in the media, conduct targeted mailings on issues, mobilize their members to contact government officials, and pursue all of the other activities of old- and new-style lobbying. For example, about 80 percent of all monies spent on lobbying in 1999 was accounted for by business (corporations and trade associations).[28] In 2001, there were 625 registered lobbyists representing the drug industry, more than the total membership of the House and Senate.[29]

Corporate, trade, and professional associations also dominate the world of political action committees, both in sheer numbers (see Figure 7.2) and levels of spending, although labor unions and large and committed citizenship organizations such as the NRA and the Sierra Club are also important. During the 1999–2000 election cycle, for example, **political action committees (PACs)** representing business and the professions accounted for 53 percent of the $579 million spent by all PACs on candidates for federal office, while labor unions accounted for only 22 percent.[30] PACs representing the least-privileged

political action committee (PAC)

A private organization whose purpose is to raise and distribute funds to candidates in political campaigns.

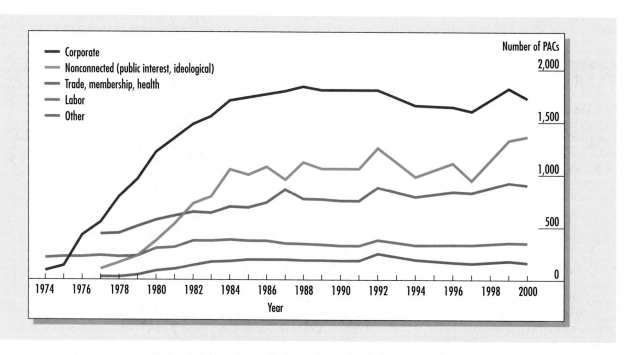

FIGURE 7.2 PACs in the United States, 1974–2000

Political action committees play an important role in financing congressional elections. The growth in the share provided by corporate, nonconnected (ideological), and trade groups is particularly striking, as is the relatively small share accounted for by organized labor.

Source: Federal Election Commission.

soft money

Expenditures by political parties on general public education, voter registration, and voter mobilization.

independent expenditures

Money spent on behalf of candidates by interest groups and individuals who are not connected to a candidate's campaign organization.

Longman
Participate.com 2.0
Visual Literacy
PACs and the Money Trail

Longman
Participate.com 2.0
Timeline
Interest Groups and Campaign Finance

sectors of American society are notable for their absence. As former Senator (R–KS) and presidential candidate Bob Dole once put it, "There aren't any poor PACs or food stamp PACs or nutrition PACs or Medicaid PACs."[31]

During the 1990s, PACs became proportionally less important in campaign financing than **soft money** and **independent expenditures**. Soft money—which has since been banned for national but not state and local party organizations by the 2002 campaign finance reform bill—is money given by interest groups and individuals to the political parties for "party-building" activities, but which is mostly funneled into parallel campaigns supporting candidates for federal office. Soft money expenditures grew rapidly, more than doubling between each election cycle from 1995–1996 to 2001–2002. Of this total, about 63 percent came from corporations, trade associations, and professional organizations.[32] AT&T alone gave $1.3 million in 1999, split between the Republican and Democratic parties. Independent expenditures—money spent by interest groups on issue campaigns that are highly beneficial to candidates—also grew rapidly. The bulk of such independent expenditures are also accounted for by business, trade, and professional organizations. (The 2002 campaign finance reform bans interest group issue campaigns that mention a candidate's name and appear right before an election, but this is already being challenged in the courts.)

Interest groups don't contribute money to campaigns and to candidates without some expectation of a return on their investment. It has been argued that there are so many interest groups around that they tend to neutralize one another, hence contributions don't really matter.[33] This may sometimes be true, in fact, on high-visibility issues in which the public and an array of interest groups are engaged. Where interest groups seem to matter the most is in the small details of legislation, forged mainly in the committees and subcommittees of Congress: a small subsidy in a defense spending bill or a waiver of a regulation for a particular industry or company. Enron's successful push for the deregulation of many of its activities followed this well-worn path.

Access Inequality

Inequalities of representation and resources are further exaggerated by the ability of some groups, especially those representing large business corporations, to gain a permanent foothold within the government. Although scholars have not reached a consensus on its exact form and extent, they have identified several basic forms of this phenomenon, which they call *subgovernments*.

What some scholars call **capture** is a form of government–business relationship in which an independent regulatory agency acts in partnership with the industry it is supposed to regulate.[34] **Interest group liberalism** is an arrangement in which aspects of federal government policymaking are turned over to interest groups.[35] Many (though not all) of the most important of these arrangements involve business and the professions. Thus the private medical community is involved in deciding local payment guidelines in the Medicare program. An **iron triangle** is an alliance of a private interest group (usually, but not always, a corporation or business trade association), an agency in the executive branch, and committees or subcommittees in Congress. The goal of the iron triangle is to advance and protect government programs that work to the mutual benefit of its members. An example is shown in Figure 7.3.

Many political scientists argue that the capture and iron triangle arrangements are no longer very common.[36] Policy, they suggest, is no longer formed in the dark, out of public sight. Many political scientists today are more apt to talk about "issue networks," in which each major policy arena attracts its own broad and diverse set of actors.[37] A set of corporations, bureaucratic agencies, and con-

capture
A situation in which a regulated industry exercises substantial influence on the government agency regulating it.

interest group liberalism
A political regime in which interest groups help formulate and carry out government policies.

iron triangle
An enduring alliance of common interest among an interest group, a congressional committee, and a bureaucratic agency.

Web Exploration
Corporations and Political Money

Issue: It has been suggested that corporations and business and professional associations dominate the campaign finance system, adding to their political influence.

Site: See who contributed what during the 2000 elections by accessing the Center for Responsive Politics on our Website at **www.ablongman.com/greenberg**. Go to the "Web Explorations" section for Chapter 7, select "Corporations and Political Money," then "corporate money." Select "Who's Getting," then "election overview." Look at "Top Overall Donors." Categorize the contributors in this list and the amounts spent.

What You've Learned: Is the claim of corporate and business dominance supported by the evidence?

HINT: Pay attention to the flow of dollars to each party; while there is some overlap, each has distinct sets of contributors.

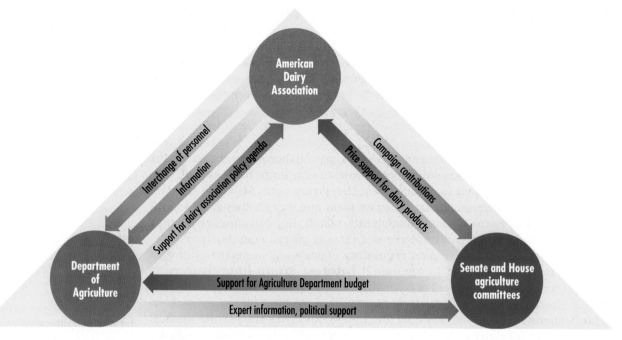

FIGURE 7.3 Iron Triangle

In an iron triangle, an alliance based on common interests is formed among a powerful corporation or interest group, an agency of the executive branch, and congressional committees or subcommittees. In this example from the dairy industry, an alliance is formed among parties that share an interest in the existence and expansion of dairy subsidies. Most scholars think iron triangles are less common today than in the past.

gressional committees is still involved, to be sure, but so are a broad range of interest groups (including public interest groups) and policy experts. On narrower and less public issues, however, a good many political scientists and Washington observers still believe that subgovernments are alive and well.[38]

The Special Place of Business Corporations

In 1977, economist and political scientist Charles Lindblom argued that corporations wield such disproportionate power in American politics that they undermine democracy. He closed his book *Politics and Markets* with this observation: "The large private corporation fits oddly into democratic theory. Indeed, it does not fit."[39] Twenty years later, political scientist Neil Mitchell concluded his book *The Conspicuous Corporation,* which reported the results of careful empirical testing of Lindblom's ideas, with the conclusion that "business interests [in the United States] are not routinely countervailed in the policy process. Their political resources and incentives to participate are usually greater than other interests."[40] Let's see why these scholars reached their somber conclusion about business corporations in American politics.

We have already learned about many of the advantages that corporations and business trade associations representing groups of corporations enjoy over others in the political process. The largest corporations are far ahead of their competitors in the number of interest organizations that represent them, the number of lobbyists they employ, the level of resources they can and do use for political purposes, their ability to shape public perceptions and opinions through such instruments as issue advertising and subsidization of business-oriented think tanks, and the ease of access they have to government officials. Note that after President George W. Bush assigned Vice President Dick Cheney the task of fashioning a new national energy policy, for example, Cheney met almost exclusively with representatives from large energy companies and energy trade associations, including Enron and the Edison Electric Institute, as well as with members of the Business Round Table, the association comprised of the CEOs of the nation's most important business corporations. Lower-level aides were assigned to meetings with representatives of environmental, labor, and consumer groups, and this happened only after news media stories broke about their exclusion.

An additional source of corporate power is the general regard in which business is held in American society and the central and honored place of business values in our culture. Faith in free enterprise gives special advantages to the central institution of free enterprise, the corporation. Any political leader contemplating hostile action against corporations must contend with business's special place of honor in the United States.

Business corporations are also unusually influential because the health of the American economy—and thus the standard of living of the people—is tied closely to the economic well-being of large corporations. It is widely and not entirely unreasonably believed that what is good for business is good for America. Because of their vital role in the economy, government officials tend to interpret business corporations not as "special interests" but as the voice of the national interest and to listen more attentively to their demands than they do to those of other sectors of American society. In this sense, corporations enjoy a privileged position in American politics.

Because the well-being of many Americans depends on the well-being of American corporations, political leaders often equate the interests of business with the interests of the nation. Here former President George H. W. Bush celebrates the opening of a Toys "Я" Us store during a trip to Japan to promote U.S. exports.

Corporations are also powerful because their mobility is an important counterweight to any government effort (local, state, or national) to raise taxes or impose regulations that business deems especially onerous. Increasingly, large corporations are able to design, produce, and market their goods and services all over the world; they are not irrevocably tied to a single location. If government threatens their interests, large corporations can credibly counter with a threat to move all or part of their operations elsewhere. In this new global economic environment, political leaders are increasingly of a mind to maintain a friendly and supportive business climate.

Large corporations do not, of course, run the show entirely. Although they have the most resources, for instance, these resources do not translate automatically into real political influence. One interest group may have enormous resource advantages over other interest groups, for instance, but may use its resources ineffectively. Or an interest group with great resources may find itself opposed by other interest groups that together are able to mobilize impressive resources of their own. A powerful interest group may also find that an elected politician is not cooperative because the voters in the district are of a different mind from the interest group. Politicians may also run from the corporate embrace in times of highly publicized business scandals, like those in 2001 and 2002 involving Enron, Arthur Andersen, WorldCom, and others. So even with this immense set of resources, business power is not automatically and inevitably translated into political power.[41]

Nor does business always get its way in Washington. There are many issues of great importance on which business in general, or one corporation in particular, loses in the give-and-take of politics. There are times when business finds itself squared off against powerful coalitions of other interest groups (labor, consumer, and environmentalist groups, let us say). On occasion, corporations also find themselves at odds with one another on public policy issues. Thus, Microsoft and Sun Microsystems want very different policies regarding federal anti-trust policy.

Most important, corporate political power is not a constant in American politics; it waxes and wanes over time.[42] Corporate political power was most impressive during the 1920s, the Reagan 1980s, and in the 104th Congress after the 1994 elections, for instance. Corporations were less able to get their way during other periods, such as the early 1970s, when the power of corporations was almost matched by that of the consumer and environmental movements.

Corporate power seems to reach its apex under certain conditions.[43] During bad economic times, for instance, Americans are more interested in getting the economy going again than in undertaking reforms that might cut into corporate profits. Politicians in bad times are more solicitous of corporate interests. In good economic times (the late 1960s and the late 1990s, for example), politicians are less worried about corporate profits drying up if tax money is used for social purposes.

Corporations are most powerful when they can build alliances among themselves. Most of the time, corporations are in competition with one another; they do not form a unified political bloc capable of moving government to action on their behalf. On those few occasions when corporations feel that their collective interests are at stake, however, they are capable of coming together to form powerful political coalitions. As political scientist David Vogel put it, "When business is both mobilized and unified, its political power can be formidable."[44] During the mid-1970s, corporations felt that they were under assault, and they responded by building broad political coalitions that proved quite effective. These became the foundation of the movement for deregulation, tax cuts, and curtailment of domestic programs, an important part of the conservative trend in American politics that led to the election of Ronald Reagan in 1980 and the Republican capture of Congress in 1994.

In our view, the best way to think about corporations in American politics is to see their power waxing and waning within their overall privileged position. Corporate power may be greater at certain times and weaker at other times, but always in a game in which corporations enjoy advantages over other groups. If corporations feel that their collective interests are at stake—as when labor unions are particularly aggressive or when government's regulatory burden is perceived to be too heavy—and they are able to present a united front, they are simply unbeatable. This cannot be said about any other sector of American society.[45]

Curing the Mischief of Factions

Americans have worried about the "mischief of factions" ever since James Madison wrote about them in *The Federalist,* No. 10 (see the Appendix). Over the years, various things have been tried to control the purported negative effects of these special interests. Disclosure has been the principal tool of regulation. In 1946, Congress imposed a requirement (in the Federal Regulation of Lobbying Act) that all lobbyists working in Congress be registered. The Lobby Disclosure Act of 1995 requires a wider range of political actors to register as lobbyists and makes them report every six months on which policies they are trying to influence and how much they are spending to do it. So far, the new law has not been strongly enforced.[46]

Reformers have also tried to regulate some of the most troublesome abuses of the politics of factions. Sections of the Ethics in Government Act (1978) aim at the so-called revolving door in which former government officials become lobbyists for interests with whom they formerly dealt in their official capacity. The act forbids ex-officials from lobbying their former agency for a year or lobbying at all on any issue in which the official was substantially involved. Finally, the 1995 Act says that former U.S. Trade Representatives and their deputies are banned for life from lobbying for foreign interests.

Reformers have also tried to control the effects of interest group money in politics. The McCain-Feingold bill, passed in 2002 and designed to put limits on the use of soft money, is the latest attempt. It is too soon to tell how effective this reform will be.

While such steps are to be applauded, many observers worry that these reforms have not gone to the heart of the problem. Some political scientists have suggested that we focus our efforts instead on strengthening the institutions of majoritarian democracy. The key institution of majoritarian democracy, at least in theory (as you will see in Chapter 9), is the political party. Parties can, as political scientist Walter Dean Burnham put it, "generate countervailing collective power on behalf of the many individually powerless against the relatively few who are individually—or organizationally—powerful."[47] Others believe that the narrowness of interest group politics might be tempered by strengthening the presidency, our only nationally elected office.[48]

HOW DEMOCRATIC ARE WE?

Interest Groups and American Politics

PROPOSITION: Because they represent narrow and special interests, the proliferation of interest groups has made American politics less and less democratic.

AGREE: The interest group system is by and for the privileged. The democratic principle of "political equality" is violated because powerful interest groups that play a major role in shaping public policies in the United States represent, by and large, wealthier and better-educated Americans, corporations, and other business interests and professionals such as doctors and lawyers.

DISAGREE: The interest group system enhances democracy because it gives individuals and groups another tool to keep elected and appointed officials responsive and responsible to their needs, wants, and interests. Political parties are important for making popular sovereignty work, to be sure, but being broad and inclusive umbrella organizations, they often ignore the interests of particular groups. And, although elections are essential for keeping public officials on their toes, they happen only every two to four years. The day-to-day work of popular sovereignty is done by interest groups. Additionally, the rise of citizen groups has made the interest group system less unequal; a wider range of groups is now in the game.

THE AUTHORS: The interest group system plays a potentially valuable role in democracy by keeping officials responsive to a wide range of groups and interests among the public, especially in the periods between elections. It is also the case that the rise of citizen groups, including those devoted to civil rights, consumers, the environment, family values, and abortion (both for and against), means that more people participate in the political process than is apparent from election turnout. However, the issue of political inequality remains and cannot be easily ignored by those who would like American politics to be more democratic. Despite the rise of citizen groups, corporations, industry trade associations, and professional associations still have a disproportionate share of political resources and influence. And among citizen groups, representation tends to tilt toward the interests of the more affluent and educated.

Summary

Longman
Participate.com
2.0
Comparative
**Comparing
Interest
Groups**

Americans have long denigrated special interests as contrary to the public good. Some political scientists, however, see interest groups as an important addition to the representative process in a democracy.

The United States provides a rich environment for interest groups because of our constitutional system, our political culture, and the broad responsibilities of our government.

A number of interests are accommodated in our interest group system. The most important private interests include business, agriculture, labor, and the professions. Public interest or citizens' groups try to advance some issue or ideological interest that is not connected to the direct material benefit of their own members. There has been a significant expansion in the number of such groups since 1968.

Interest groups attempt to influence the shape of public policy in a number of ways. In the inside game, interest group representatives are in direct contact with government officials and try to build influence on the basis of personal relationships. In the outside game, interest groups attempt to apply indirect pressure to officials by mobilizing other groups, the members of their own group, public opinion, elite opinion, and the electorate to support their positions on policy matters.

Business, trade, and professional associations dominate the interest group system, although citizens groups are also influential. They enjoy clear advantages over other groups in terms of resources and access to public officials. The business corporation holds an especially privileged place in the interest group system because of the support of business values in our culture and the perceived importance of the corporation to the economic well-being of Americans.

Efforts to control the "mischief of factions" have mainly been regulatory in nature. Some reformers believe that interest groups will only cease to be a problem if the parties and presidency are strengthened.

Suggestions for Further Reading

Berry, Jeffrey M. *The New Liberalism: The Rising Power of Citizen Groups.* Washington, D.C.: Brookings, 1999.
> *A controversial book that argues that liberal citizen groups representing consumer, civil rights, and environmental interests are more influential in the halls of Congress than either business or conservative citizens groups.*

Clawson, Dan, Alan Neustadt, and Mark Weller. *Dollars and Votes: How Business Campaign Contributions Subvert Democracy.* Philadelphia: Temple University Press, 1998.
> *The best book ever written about the campaign finance system, based on interviews with corporate personnel responsible for making PAC and soft money contributions to candidates and parties.*

Dahl, Robert A. *A Preface to Democratic Theory.* Chicago: University of Chicago Press, 1956.
> *The leading theoretical statement of the pluralist position and the democratic role of the interest group.*

Keck, Margaret, and Kathryn Sikkink. *Activists Beyond Borders.* Ithaca, NY: Cornell University Press, 1998.
> *An examination of how public interest groups are increasingly operating at the global level.*

Kollman, Ken. *Outside Lobbying: Public Opinion and Interest Group Strategies.* Princeton, NJ: Princeton University Press, 1998.
> *The first systematic study of how interest groups try to influence government policies by focusing their efforts on shaping public opinion.*

Lindblom, Charles. *Politics and Markets.* New York: Basic Books, 1977.
> *A controversial and widely commented-on book in which one of the leading pluralist theorists concludes that the modern corporation is incompatible with democracy.*

Olson, Mancur. *The Logic of Collective Action.* Cambridge, MA: Harvard University Press, 1965.
> *A "rational choice" argument on the place of material and selective benefits in the formation and maintenance of groups and on the difficulty of forming groups based on values and ideology.*

Vogel, David. *Fluctuating Fortunes: The Political Power of Business in America.* New York: Basic Books, 1989.
  A look at the political power of large corporations during the 1970s and 1980s; useful for its wealth of information, even though the author sometimes underestimates the extent of the political power of business.

Washington Representatives, 2002. Washington, D.C.: Columbia Books, 2002.
  The most complete listing of Washington lobbyists and lobbying firms.

Internet Sources

Center for Responsive Politics   **www.opensecrets.org/**
  Follow the money trail—who gets it? who contributes?—in American politics.

Justice on Campus   **www.mit.edu:8001/activities/safe/resources.html**
  An organization committed to the preservation of free expression and the due process rights of students on college campuses.

Labor Net   **www.labornet.org**
  Access to labor unions and information on labor issues.

National Organization for Women   **www.now.org**
  The women's organization that has long been a "player" in Washington politics.

National Rifle Association   **http://www.nra.org/**
  Home page of one of America's most politically successful interest groups.

Project VoteSmart   **www.vote-smart.org/**
  Information on interest group campaign contributions to and ratings for all members of Congress.

Rightgrrl   **www.rightgrrl.com/**
  Conservative women's issues and organizations.

Student Environmental Action Committee   **http://www.seac.org/**
  A grassroots coalition of student environmental groups.

Townhall   **www.townhall.com/citizens**
  A portal to scores of conservative organizations and citizen groups.

Yahoo/Organizations and Interest Groups
http://www.yahoo.com/Government/Politics/
  Direct links to the home pages of scores of public and private interest groups as well as to Washington lobbying firms.

Notes

1. "China: The Great Brawl," *Business Week* (June 16, 1997), p. 34.

2. Ibid.

3. Alexander Hamilton, James Madison, and John Jay, *The Federalist Papers,* ed. Clinton Rossiter (New York: New American Library, 1961), No. 10. (Originally published 1787–1788.)

4. Arthur F. Bentley, *The Process of Government* (Chicago: University of Chicago Press, 1908); David Truman, *The Governmental Process* (New York: Knopf, 1951); V. O. Key Jr., *Politics, Parties, and Pressure Groups* (New York: A. Crowell, 1952); Robert A. Dahl, *A Preface to Democratic Theory* (Chicago: University of Chicago

Press, 1956); Robert A. Dahl, *Who Governs?* (New Haven, CT: Yale University Press, 1961). See also Jeffrey M. Berry, *The New Liberalism: The Rising Power of Citizen Groups* (Washington, D.C.: Brookings, 1999).

5. Arthur C. Close, ed., *Washington Representatives, 1977–1996* (Washington, D.C.: Columbia Books, 1996).

6. Kay Lehman Schlozman and John T. Tierney, *Organized Interests and American Democracy* (New York: Harper & Row, 1986), pp. 77–78.

7. Berry, *The New Liberalism,* pp. 20–21.

8. Anne Costain, *Inviting Women's Rebellion* (Baltimore: Johns Hopkins University Press, 1992).

9. Truman, *The Governmental Process.*

10. Mancur Olson, *The Logic of Collective Action* (Cambridge, MA: Harvard University Press, 1965).

11. On Olson's theory, see Brian Barry and Russell Hardin, eds., *Rational Man and Irrational Society?* (Newbury Park, CA: Sage, 1982); Dennis Chong, *Collective Action and the Civil Rights Movement* (Chicago: University of Chicago Press, 1991); Russell Hardin, *Collective Action* (Baltimore: Johns Hopkins University Press); Terry Moe, *The Organization of Interests* (Chicago: University of Chicago Press, 1980).

12. E. E. Schattschneider, *The Semi-Sovereign People* (New York: Holt, Rinehart & Winston, 1960).

13. Berry, *The New Liberalism;* Thomas Byrne Edsall, *The New Politics of Inequality* (New York: Norton, 1984); Michael Goldfield, *The Decline of Organized Labor in the United States* (Chicago: University of Chicago Press, 1987); Edward S. Greenberg, *Capitalism and the American Political Ideal* (Armonk, NY: Sharpe, 1985); David Vogel, *Fluctuating Fortunes: The Political Power of Business in America* (New York: Basic Books, 1989), ch. 8.

14. U.S. Bureau of Labor Statistics, 2001.

15. Jeffrey M. Berry, *Lobbying for the People* (Princeton, NJ: Princeton University Press, 1977), p. 7; Berry, *The New Liberalism,* p. 2.

16. Berry, *Lobbying for the People;* David Broder, *Changing the Guard* (New York: Simon & Schuster, 1980); Hugh Heclo, "Issue Networks and the Executive Establishment," in Anthony King, ed., *The New American Political System* (Washington, D.C.: American Enterprise Institute, 1978); Schlozman and Tierney, *Organized Interests;* Jack L. Walker Jr., "The Origins and Maintenance of Interest Groups in America," *American Political Science Review,* 77 (1983), pp. 390–406.

17. Theda Skocpol, "Associations Without Members," *The American Prospect,* (July/August, 1999), Vol. 10, no. 44, pp. 66–73.

18. Jack L. Walker Jr., *Mobilizing Interest Groups in America* (Ann Arbor: University of Michigan Press, 1991).

19. Leslie Wayne and Melody Petersen, "A Muscular Lobby Rolls Up Its Sleeves," *The New York Times,* November 4, 2001, Section 3, p. 1.

20. Mark A. Smith, *Business and Political Power: Public Opinion, Elections and Democracy* (Chicago: University of Chicago Press, 2000).

21. Jeffrey M. Berry, *The Interest Group Society* (Glenview, IL: Scott, Foresman, 1989), p. 141.

22. Susan Glasser and Ben White, "The Dashing Life of Washington Lobbyists," *The Washington Post National Edition* (July 12, 1999), p. A13.

23. Kenneth M. Goldstein, *Interest Groups, Lobbying and Participation in America* (New York: Cambridge University Press, 1999), ch. 2; and Kenneth Kollman, *Outside Lobbying* (Princeton, NJ: Princeton University Press, 1998).

24. E. E. Schattschneider, *The Semi-Sovereign People.*

25. Berry, *The New Liberalism.*

26. Schlozman and Tierney, *Organized Interests,* p. 175.

27. Berry, *The New Liberalism.*

28. Wendy L. Hansen and Neil J. Mitchell, "Money and Power," (unpublished manuscript, 2001), p. 9.

29. Leslie Wayne and Melody Petersen, "A Muscular Lobby Rolls Up Its Sleeves," *The New York Times* (November 4, 2001), Section 3, p. 1.

30. Federal Election Commission.

31. "Money Talks, Congress Listens," *The Boston Globe* (December 12, 1982), p. A24.

32. Federal Election Commission, *Soft Money Expenditures* (Washington, D.C.: U.S. Government Printing Office, 2000).

33. Derek Bok, *The Trouble With Government* (Cambridge, MA: Harvard University Press, 2001), pp. 81–94.

34. Marver Bernstein, *Regulating Business by Independent Commission* (Princeton, NJ: Princeton University Press, 1955).

35. Theodore J. Lowi, *The End of Liberalism* (New York: Norton, 1969).

36. Berry, *The New Liberalism;* Allan J. Cigler, "Interest Groups," in William Crotty, ed., *Political Science: Looking to the Future,* Vol. 4 (Evanston, IL: Northwestern University Press, 1991); Robert H. Salisbury et al., "Who Works with Whom? Interest Group Alliances and Opposition," *American Political Science Review,* 81 (1987), pp. 1217–1234.

37. Jeffrey M. Berry, "Citizen Groups and the Changing Nature of Interest Group Politics in America," *The Annals,* 528 (1993), pp. 16–23; Heclo, "Issue Networks"; Robert H. Salisbury, John P. Heinz, Edward O. Laumann, and Robert L. Nelson, "Triangles, Networks, and Hollow Cores," and Mark P. Petracca, ed., "The Rediscovery of Interest Group Politics," in Mark P. Petracca, ed., *The Politics of Interests: Interest Groups Transform* (Boulder, CO: Westview Press, 1992).

38. Richard Smith, "Interest Group Influence in Congress," *Legislative Studies Quarterly,* 20 (1995), pp. 89–139.

39. Charles Lindblom, *Politics and Markets* (New York: Basic Books, 1977), p. 356. For criticisms from the left, see John Manley, "Neo-Pluralism: A Class Analysis of Pluralism I and Pluralism II," *American Political Science Review,* 77 (1983), pp. 368–383. For criticisms from the right, see Irving Kristol, *Two Cheers for Capitalism* (New York: Basic Books, 1977); James Q. Wilson, "Democracy and the Corporation," in Robert Sessen, ed., *Does Big Business Rule America?* (Washington, D.C.: Ethics and Public Policy Center, 1987). For a recent dissent, see Mark Smith, "Public Opinion, Elections, and Representation Within a Market Economy," *American Journal of Political Science,* 43, no. 3 (1999), p. 842.

40. Neil J. Mitchell, *The Conspicuous Corporation: Business, Public Policy and Representative Democracy* (Ann Arbor: University of Michigan Press, 1997), p. 167.

41. Dan Clawson, Alan Neustadt, and Mark Weller, *Dollars and Votes* (Philadelphia: Temple University Press, 1998), pp. 26–28, 64–71, 97–99.

42. Vogel, *Fluctuating Fortunes.*

43. Ibid.

44. Ibid, p. 291.

45. Jeffrey Berry disagrees in *The New Liberalism*.

46. Roger H. Davidson and Walter J. Oleszek, *Congress and Its Members* (Washington, D.C.: CQ Press, 2002), p. 366.

47. Walter Dean Burnham, *Critical Elections and the Mainsprings of American Politics* (New York: Norton, 1970), p. 133.

48. John E. Chubb and Paul E. Peterson, "American Political Institutions and the Problem of Governance," in John E. Chubb and Paul E. Peterson, eds., *Can the Government Govern?* (Washington, D.C.: Brookings Institution, 1989).

Chapter 8
Social Movements

In This Chapter

- Why social movements develop
- Where social movements fit in a democratic society
- What social movements do in politics
- How social movements influence what government does

Women Win the Right to Vote

The struggle for women's suffrage (e.g., the right to vote) was long and difficult. The main instrument for winning the struggle to amend the Constitution to admit women to full citizenship was a powerful social movement that dared to challenge the status quo, used unconventional tactics to gain attention and sympathy, and demanded bravery and commitment from many women.[1] One of these women was Angelina Grimké.

Abolitionist Angelina Grimké addressed the Massachusetts legislature in February 1838, presenting a petition against slavery from an estimated 20,000 women of the state. In doing so, she became the first woman to speak before an American legislative body. Because women at this time were legally subordinate to men and shut out of civic life—the life of home and church were considered their proper domains—Grimké felt it necessary to defend women's involvement in the abolitionist movement to end slavery. She said the following to the legislators:

> *Are we aliens because we are women? Are we bereft of citizenship because we are mothers, wives and daughters of a mighty people? Have women no country—no interests staked in public weal—no partnership in a nation's guilt and shame?. . . I hold, Mr. Chairman, that American women have to do this subject [the abolition of slavery], not only because it is moral and religious, but because it is political, inasmuch as we are citizens of the Republic and as such our honor, happiness and well-being are bound up in its politics, government and laws.*

Although this bold claim of citizenship for women did not fall on receptive ears—Grimké was derided as ridiculous and blasphemous by press and pulpit—it helped inspire other women who had entered political life by way of the abolitionist movement to press for women's rights as well. Meeting at Seneca Falls, New York, in 1848, a group of women issued a declaration written by Elizabeth Cady Stanton stating that "all men and women are created equal, endowed with the same inalienable rights." The declaration, much like the Declaration of Independence on which it was modeled, then presented a long list of violations of rights.

The Seneca Falls Declaration remains one of the most eloquent statements of women's equality ever written, but it failed to have an immediate effect because most politically active women (and men) in the abolitionist movement believed that their first order of business was to end slavery. Women's rights would have to wait.

After the Civil War destroyed the slave system, women's rights leaders such as Stanton, Susan B. Anthony, and Lucy Stone pressed for equal citizenship rights for all, white or black, male or female. They were bitterly disappointed when the Fourteenth Amendment, ratified after the war, declared full citizenship rights for all males born or naturalized in the United States, including those who had been slaves, but failed to include women. Women's rights activists realized that they would have to fight for rights on their own, with their own organizations.

Women's rights organizations were formed soon after the Civil War. For more than two decades, though, the National Woman Suffrage Association (NWSA) and the American Woman Suffrage Association (AWSA) feuded over how to pressure male politicians. Susan B. Anthony (with the NWSA) and Lucy Stone (with the AWSA) were divided by temperament and ideology. Anthony favored pressing for a broad range of rights and organized dramatic actions to expose men's hypocrisy. At an 1876 centennial celebration of the United States in Philadelphia, Anthony and several other women marched onto the platform, where the emperor of Brazil and other dignitaries sat, and handed over a declaration of women's rights. They then marched off the platform and read the declaration aloud. Stone favored gaining the vote as the primary objective of the rights movement and used quieter methods of persuasion, such as petitions.

In 1890, the two main organizations joined together to form the National American Woman Suffrage Association (NAWSA). They dropped such controversial NWSA demands as divorce reform and legalized prostitution in favor of one order of business: women's suffrage. The movement was now focused, united, and growing more powerful every year.

In 1912, the NAWSA organized a march to support a constitutional amendment for suffrage. More than 5,000 women dressed in white, some on horseback, paraded through the streets of Washington before Woodrow Wilson's inauguration. The police offered the marchers no protection from antagonistic spectators who pelted the marchers with rotten fruit and vegetables and an occasional rock, despite the legal parade permit they had obtained. This lack of protection outraged the public and attracted media attention to the suffrage movement. The NAWSA took advantage of the favorable publicity, launching a petition drive and sending regular delegations to press President Wilson for a national solution.

Almost immediately after the United States entered World War I in April 1916, with the express purpose of "making the world safe for democracy," women began to picket the White House, demanding that full democracy be instituted in America. One demonstrator's sign quoted directly from President Wilson's war message—"we shall fight . . . for the right of those who submit to authority to have a voice in their own government"—and asked why women were excluded from American democracy. As the picketing at the White House picked up in numbers and in intensity, the police began arresting large groups of women. Other women took their place. The cycle continued until local jails were filled to capacity. When suffragists began a hunger strike in jail, authorities responded with forced feedings and isolation cells. By November, public outrage forced local authorities to relent and free the women. By this time, public opinion had shifted in favor of women's right to vote.

In the years surrounding U.S. entry into the war, other women's groups worked state by state, senator by senator, pressuring male politicians to support women's suffrage. After two prominent senators from New England were defeated in 1918 primarily because of the efforts of suffragists and prohibitionists, the political clout of the women's groups became apparent to most elected officials. In June 1919, Congress passed the Nineteenth Amendment, and the necessary 36 states ratified it the following year. By uniting around a common cause, women's organizations gained the right to vote for all women.

Although few social movements have been as effective as the women's suffrage movement in reaching their primary goal, other social movements have also played an important role in American political life. This chapter is about what social movements are, how and why they form, what tactics they use, and how they affect American political life and what government does. ■

Thinking Critically About This Chapter

This chapter is about the important role of social movements in American government and politics.

Using the Framework You will see in this chapter how social movements are a response to structural changes in the economy, culture, and society and how they affect other political linkage actors and institutions—parties, interest groups, and public opinion, for example—and government. You will learn, most importantly, under what conditions social movements most effectively shape the behavior of elected leaders and the content of government policies.

Using the Democracy Standard At first glance, because social movements are most often the political instrument of minorities, it may seem that they have little to do with democracy. You will see in this chapter, however, that social movements play an especially important role in our democracy, principally by broadening public debate on important issues and bringing outsiders and nonparticipants into the political arena. ◀

What Are Social Movements?

Social movements are loosely organized collections of people and groups who act over time, outside established institutions, to promote or resist social change. Today's Christian conservative movement, for example, is a broad collection of people, churches, and other organizations that have come together to resist the **secularization** of American society and to promote religious values in American life.

secularization

The spread of nonreligious values and outlooks.

Although they share some similarities, social movements are different from political parties and interest groups. Unlike political parties, for example, the sole aim of social movements is not to elect their own members to public office, although they may sometimes try to do so. Unlike interest groups, the sole aim of social movements is not to lobby political decision makers about legislative matters, although they may sometimes try to do this as well. What sets social movements apart from parties and interest groups is their focus on broad, societywide issues and their tendency to act outside the normal channels of government and politics, using unconventional and often disruptive tactics.[2] Some scholars call social movement politics "contentious politics."[3] When suffragists disrupted meetings, went on hunger strikes, and marched to demand the right to vote, they were engaged in contentious politics.

This general definition of social movements requires further elaboration if we are to understand their role in American politics. Here we highlight some important things to know about them.

- *Social movements are generally the political instruments of political outsiders.* Social movements often help people who are outside the mainstream gain a hearing from the public and from political decision makers. The women's suffrage movement forced the issue of votes for women onto the public agenda. The civil rights movement did the same for the issue of equal citizenship for African-Americans. Gays and lesbians forced the country to pay attention to issues that had long been left "in the closet." Insiders don't need social movements; they can rely instead on interest groups, political action committees (PACs), lobbyists, campaign contributions, and the like to make their voices heard.

- *Social movements are generally mass grassroots phenomena.* Because outsiders and excluded groups often lack the financial and political resources of insiders, they must take advantage of what they have: numbers, energy, and commitment.

- *Social movements often use unconventional and disruptive tactics.* Officials and citizens almost always complain that social movements are ill-mannered and disruptive. For social movements, that is precisely the point. Unconventional and disruptive tactics help gain attention for movement grievances.

- *Social movements are populated by individuals with a shared sense of grievance.* People would not take on the considerable risks involved in joining others in a social movement unless they felt a strong, shared sense of grievance against the status quo and a desire to bring about social change. Social movements tend to form when a significant number of people come to define their own troubles and problems not in personal terms but in more general social terms (the belief that there is a common cause for all of their troubles) and when they believe that the government can be moved to take action on their behalf. Because this is a rare combination, social movements are very difficult to organize and sustain.

Major Social Movements in the United States

Many social movements have left their mark on American political life and have shaped what government does in the United States. Here we describe some of the most important.

The *abolitionists* aimed to end slavery in the United States. They were active in the northern states in the three decades before the outbreak of the Civil War. Their harsh condemnation of the slave system helped bring on the war that ended slavery.

The *Populist* movement was made up of disaffected farmers of the American South and West in the 1880s and 1890s who were angry with business practices and developments in the American economy that were adversely affecting them. Their aim was to force public ownership or regulation of banks, grain storage companies, and the railroads. For a short time, they were quite successful, winning control of several state legislatures, sending members to Congress, helping to nominate William Jennings Bryan as the Democratic candidate for president in 1896, and forcing the federal regulation of corporations (e.g., in the Interstate Commerce Commission Act).

The *women's suffrage* movement, active in the late nineteenth and early twentieth centuries, aimed to win the right to vote for women. As we saw in the chapter opening vignette, the movement won its objective when the Nineteenth Amendment to the Constitution was ratified in 1920.

The *labor* movement represents efforts by working people over the years to protect jobs, ensure decent wages and benefits, and guarantee safe workplaces. The periods of greatest militancy—when working people took to the streets and the factory floors to demand recognition of their unions—were in the 1880s, the 1890s, and the 1930s. The labor movement eventually forced the federal government to recognize the right of working people to form labor unions to represent them in negotiations with management.

Longman
Participate.com
2.0
Timeline
**Civil Liberties
and National
Security**

A *peace* movement in one form or another has been around since the time of World War I, when it tried to encourage resistance to the draft. Its strategy of encouraging Americans to refuse service on religious or moral grounds—known as *conscientious objection*—was carried over to World War II, the Korean War, the Vietnam War, the war in Kosovo, and the campaign against the Taliban in Afghanistan. The movement has also focused on the threat of nuclear war, taking shape as "ban the bomb" protests in the 1950s, "nuclear freeze" demonstrations in the 1980s, and attempts in the 1980s to force local governments to declare their localities "nuclear-free zones," where no nuclear weapons could be manufactured or stored.

Social movements activists often use dramatic behavior and symbols to gain media and public attention for their cause. Here an antiwar activist in San Francisco protests U.S. actions during the Vietnam War. This particular protest was part of the multicity "moratorium" movement in 1969 that involved hundreds of thousands of people.

The *civil rights* movement began in the late 1950s, reached the peak of its activity in the mid-1960s, and gradually lost steam after that. The movement is one of the most influential on record, having pressed successfully for the end of formal segregation in the South and discriminatory practices across the nation (see Chapters 1 and 16). The main weapons of the movement were non-violent civil disobedience and mass demonstrations.

The *anti–Vietnam War* movement was active in the United States in the late 1960s and early 1970s. Its aim was to end the war in Vietnam. It used a wide variety of tactics in this effort, from mass demonstrations to voting registration and civil disobedience. Fringe elements even turned to violence, exemplified by the Days of Rage vandalism along Chicago's Gold Coast mounted by a wing of Students for a Democratic Society and the bombing of a research lab at the University of Wisconsin in which a graduate student was killed.

The *women's* movement has been important in American life since the late 1960s. Its aim has been to win civil rights protections for women and to broaden the participation of women in all aspects of American society, economy, and politics. Although it did not win one of its main objectives—passage of the **Equal Rights Amendment (ERA)** to the U.S. Constitution—the broad advance of women on virtually all fronts in the United States attests to its overall effectiveness.

The *environmental* movement has been active in the United States since the early 1970s. Its aim has been to encourage government regulation of damaging environmental practices and to raise the environmental sympathies of the public. While the vitality of the movement has waxed and waned over the years, the public's strong support for environmental regulation suggests that it has been unusually successful. Although disruptive and even violent tactics have sometimes been used, the movement has depended more on legal challenges to business practices and the creation of organizations to lobby in Washington.

Equal Rights Amendment (ERA)
Proposed amendment to the U.S. Constitution stating that equality of rights shall not be abridged or denied on account of a person's gender.

The *gay and lesbian* movement began in earnest in the late 1960s. Its aim was to gain the same civil rights protections under the law enjoyed by African-Americans and other minority groups and to gain respect from the public. Ranging from patient lobbying and voting to mass demonstrations and deliberately shocking actions by groups such as ACT-UP, the movement's efforts have been partially successful—antidiscrimination and domestic partner laws have been passed in many communities, for example—but have also sparked strong counterattacks by groups such as the Christian Coalition and Focus on the Family that are opposed to their objectives.

Religious fundamentalist movements have occurred at several different moments in American history and have been very influential. These movements have brought together strongly religious people trying to infuse American society and public policies with their values. These movements were particularly vital during the decades preceding the American Revolution and the Civil War; in the late nineteenth and early twentieth centuries, when religious revivals swept across the country, and in our own day. The contemporary movement of Christian conservatives falls within this tradition and has become very important in American politics, especially on the issues of abortion, school prayer, educational curriculum, and censorship of the media. The *pro-life (anti-abortion)* movement is part of the current larger religious fundamentalist movement. Its main objective is to end the legal availability of abortion in the United States.

An emergent *antiglobalization* movement announced itself to the public with demonstrations against the World Trade Organization in Seattle in late 1999. This movement is extremely diverse and includes people who are worried about the effects of globalization on the environment, income inequality in the United States and Third World countries, food safety, labor rights, sweat shops, unfair trade, and national sovereignty.

In recent years, many religious Americans have become politically active because of their objection to the general secularization of American life and social trends such as gay rights and abortion, which they consider contrary to traditional family values. Here a group of fundamentalist Christians demonstrates against the legal protection of abortion.

Social Movements in a Majoritarian Democracy

At first glance, social movements do not seem to fit very well in a democracy. First, social movements usually start out with only a small minority of people, whereas democracy requires majority rule. Second, social movements often use disruptive tactics, when it seems that many channels already exist (e.g., voting, petitioning and writing to policymakers, and writing letters to newspapers) for people to express their grievances. In this section, we talk about how social movements can (and often do) help make American politics more democratic.

Encouraging Participation

Social movements may increase the level of popular involvement and interest in politics. In one sense, this is true simply by definition: Social movements are the instruments of outsiders. Thus, the women's suffrage movement showed many middle-class women that their activities need not be confined exclusively to home, family, church, and charity work and encouraged them to venture into political life by gathering petitions or joining demonstrations demanding the vote for women. The civil rights movement in the 1960s encouraged southern African-Americans, who had long been barred from the political life of their communities, to become active in their own emancipation. The Christian conservative movement spurred the involvement of previously politically apathetic evangelicals.

Social movements also encourage popular participation by dramatizing and bringing to public attention a range of issues that have been ignored or have been dealt with behind closed doors. The reason is that their contentious actions make these movements' members highly visible. They offer irresistible fare for the television camera. This ability to make politics more visible—called broadening the **scope of conflict** by political scientist E. E. Schattschneider[4]—makes politics the province of the many rather than the few.

scope of conflict

The number of groups involved in a political conflict; few groups mean a narrow scope of conflict, and many groups mean a wide scope of conflict.

Overcoming Political Inequality

Social movements also sometimes allow individuals and groups without substantial resources to enter the game of politics. Many social movements are made up of people who do not have access to the money, time, contacts, or organizational resources that fuel normal politics.[5] The ability of those without resources to disrupt the status quo by mobilizing thousands to take to the streets to voice their demands—what sociologists call **mass mobilization**—is a powerful political tool for people on the outside looking in. In the right circumstances, the disruptive politics of social groups can become as politically useful as other resources such as money and votes. Seemingly politically powerless women were able to mobilize to win the vote in the early part of the twentieth century; seemingly politically powerless blacks in the Deep South were able to secure full citizenship rights in the 1960s.

mass mobilization

The process of involving large numbers of people in a social movement.

Creating New Majorities

Over time, social movements may also help create new majorities in society. Social movements are the province of minorities, of course, and in a majoritarian democracy, minorities should have their way only if they can convince

Great Depression

The period of economic crisis in the United States that lasted from the stock market crash of 1929 to America's entry into World War II.

enough of their fellow citizens that what they want is reasonable. Before the 1930s, for instance, only a minority of Americans may have been convinced that labor unions were a good idea. The **Great Depression** and a vigorous, militant labor movement changed the opinion climate in the nation and created the basis for federal laws protecting the right of working people to form labor unions. Such issues as gender-based job discrimination and pay inequity, to take another example, were not important to the general public until they were brought center stage by the women's movement.

Overcoming Gridlock

Sometimes it takes the energy of a social movement to overcome the anti-majoritarian aspects of our constitutional system (see Chapter 2) and get anything done at all. As political scientist Theodore Lowi describes the issue:

> Our political system is almost perfectly designed to maintain an existing state of affairs. . . . Our system is so designed that only a determined and undoubted majority could make it move. This is why our history is replete with social movements. It takes that kind of energy to get anything like a majority. . . . Change comes neither from the genius of the system nor from the liberality or wisdom of its supporters and of the organized groups. It comes from new groups or nascent groups—social movements—when the situation is most dramatic.[6]

It is important to note that many of the social reforms of which most Americans are most proud—women's right to vote, equal citizenship rights for African-Americans, Social Security, collective bargaining, and environmental protection—have been less the result of "normal" politics than of social movements started by determined and often disruptive minorities.

Web Exploration
Movements and Political Participation

Issue: A common claim for social movements as a democratic instrument is that they increase political participation by outsiders.

Site: Access the American National Election Study on our Website at **www.ablongman.com/greenberg**. Go to the "Web Explorations" section for Chapter 8, select "movements and political participation," then "participation." Select "Political Involvement and Participation in Politics." Choose various questions related to political participation, including voting. At the bottom of the page where you find general results for each question, the results are broken down by racial groups and gender.

What You've Learned: Did the Civil Rights movement and the women's movement increase political participation among African-Americans and women? Did participation increase in the period during and immediately after the social movements were at their height?

HINT: For African-Americans, the relevant dates are the early 1960s to the present; for women, the relevant dates are the early 1970s to the present.

Social movements are a response to a real, immediate social distress or injustice. When women began to enter the job market in increasing numbers during the 1960s and 1970s, discriminatory hiring, barriers to career advancement, and unequal pay were unspoken realities of the business world. As more and more women refused to accept these injustices, the women's movement emerged.

Factors That Encourage the Creation of Social Movements

A certain combination of factors, mainly structural, is apparently necessary for a social movement to develop.[7] We review the most important ones here.

The Existence of Social Distress

People who are safe, prosperous, and respected generally have no need of social movements. By contrast, those whose lives are difficult and unsafe or whose way of life or values are threatened, or whose way of life is disrespected, often find social movements an attractive means of calling attention to their plight and of pressing for changes in the status quo.[8]

Social distress caused by economic, social, and technological change helped create the conditions for the rise of most of the major social movements in American history. For example, the Populist movement occurred after western and southern farmers suffered great economic reverses during the latter part of the nineteenth century. The labor movement during the 1930s was spurred by the Great Depression—the virtual collapse of the industrial sector of the American economy, historically unprecedented levels of unemployment, and widespread destitution. The rise of the Christian conservative movement seems to be associated with the perceived threat of the apparent decline in religious and family values in American life. For many women, distress caused by discriminatory hiring, blocked career advancement—in the form of the "glass ceiling" and the "mommy track"—and unequal pay at a time when they were entering the job market in increasing numbers during the 1960s and 1970s made participation in the women's movement attractive.[9] Discrimination, police harassment, and violence directed against them spurred gays and lesbians to turn to "contentious politics."[10] The AIDS epidemic added to their sense of distress and stimulated further political participation.

Availability of Resources for Mobilization

Social strain and distress are almost always present in society. But social movements occur, it seems, only when the aggrieved group has the resources (including skilled leaders) sufficient to organize those who are suffering strain and distress.[11] The grievances expressed by the labor movement had existed for a long time in the United States, but it was not until a few unions developed—generating talented leaders, a very active labor press, and widespread media attention—that the movement began to take off. The women's movement's assets included a sizable population of educated and skilled women, a lively women's press, and a broad network of meetings to talk about common problems[12] (generally called *consciousness-raising groups*). The Christian conservative movement could build on a base of skilled clergy (for instance, Jerry Falwell and Pat Robertson), an expanding evangelical church membership, religious television and radio networks, and highly developed fund-raising technologies. Gay and lesbian activists could depend on a rich assortment of organizations, an active press, and the financial support of gay- and lesbian-owned businesses. The antiglobalization movement skillfully used the Internet to organize its protest in Seattle against the WTO.

For its part, the 1960s civil rights movement could count on organizationally skilled clergy and close-knit congregations, black-owned newspapers and radio stations, an expanding pool of college-educated African-American youth, and blocs of African-American voters located in electorally important states. The existence of such experienced, tested, and effective organizations as the Congress of Racial Equality (CORE), the Urban League, and the National Association for the Advancement of Colored People (NAACP) was especially valuable.

The anti-globalization movement first gained widespread public attention in the United States when demonstrators converged on Seattle in late 1999 to protest at a meeting of the World Trade Organization.

A Supportive Environment

The rise of social movements requires more than the existence of resources for mobilization among aggrieved groups. The times must also be right, in the sense that a degree of support and tolerance must exist for the movement among the public and society's leaders.[13] The civil rights movement took place when overt racism among the public was declining (even in the South; see Table 8.1), and national leaders were worried about the bad effects of segregation in the South on American foreign policy. Christian conservatives mobilized in an environment in which many other Americans were also worried about changes in social values and practices and when the Republican party was looking for a way to detach traditional Democratic voters from their party. The labor movement's upsurge during the 1930s coincided with the electoral needs of the Democratic party.[14] The women's movement surged at a time when public opinion was becoming much more favorable toward women's equality.[15] In 1972, for example, two out of three Americans reported to pollsters that they supported the ERA; the same proportion said they believed that the issues raised by the women's movement were important.[16] Gays and lesbians benefited from the more tolerant attitudes toward minorities generated by other social movements.

TABLE 8.1 White Support for Integration, 1942–1963

	Total	South	North
"Negroes should have as good a chance as white people to get any kind of job."			
1944	42%	—	—
1963	83	—	—
"White students and Negro students should go to the same schools."			
1942	30%	2%	40%
1956	49	15	61
1963	62	31	73
There should not be "separate sections for Negroes on streetcars and buses."			
1942	44%	4%	57%
1956	60	27	73
1963	79	52	89
Would not make any difference to them if "a Negro with the same income and education as you moved into your block."			
1942	35%	12%	42%
1956	51	38	58
1963	64	51	70

Source: Stephen Thernstrom and Abigail Thernstrom, *America in Black and White* (New York: Simon & Schuster, 1997), p. 141. Data from William G. Mayer, *The Changing American Mind: How and Why American Public Opinion Changed Between 1960 and 1988* (Ann Arbor: University of Michigan Press, 1993), p. 366; Paul B. Sheatsley, "White Attitudes Toward the Negro," *Daedalus,* 95 (1966), pp. 219, 222.

Gays and lesbians have become much more politically visible and assertive since the "Stonewall" incident and riots in 1969. Here, a gay pride parade in San Francisco calls attention to the gay and lesbian communities and to the issues the members of these communities want placed on the political agenda.

A Sense of Efficacy Among Participants

Some scholars believe that to develop an effective social movement, people who are on the outside looking in must come to believe that their actions can make a difference, that other citizens and political leaders will listen and respond to their grievances. A *sense of efficacy* is what political scientists call this "I can make a difference" attitude. Without a sense of **political efficacy,** grievances might explode into brief demonstrations or riots, but they would not support a long-term effort requiring time, commitment, and risk.

political efficacy

The sense that one can affect what government does.

It may well be that the highly decentralized and fragmented nature of our political system helps sustain a sense of efficacy, since movements often find places in the system where they will be heard by officials. Christian conservative social movements have had little effect on school curricula in unitary political systems like that of Great Britain, for instance, where educational policy is made centrally, so few try to do anything about it. In the United States, Christian conservatives know they can gain the ear of local school boards and state officials in regions where religious belief is strong. Gays and lesbians have been able to convince public officials and local voters to pass antidiscrimination ordinances in accepting communities, such as San Francisco, California, and Boulder, Colorado.

A Spark to Set Off the Flames

Social movements require, as we have seen, a set of grievances among a group of people, the resources to form and sustain organization, a supportive environment, and a sense of political efficacy among the potential participants in the movement. But they also seem to require something to set off the mix, some dramatic precipitating event (or series of events), sometimes called a *catalyst,* to set them in motion. Passage of the Fourteenth Amendment, protecting the citizenship rights of males, galvanized the early women's suffrage movement, as we saw in the opening vignette. The gay and lesbian movement

President Clinton awards Rosa Parks a presidential medal to honor her courage 41 years after her simple action on a Montgomery, Alabama, bus—refusing to give up her seat to a white person as required by city ordinance—helped spark the rise of the Civil Rights movement.

seems to have been sparked by the 1969 "Stonewall rebellion," three days of rioting set off by police harassment of the patrons of a popular gay bar in Greenwich Village in New York. The most important catalyst for the civil rights movement was Rosa Parks's simple refusal to give up her seat on a Montgomery, Alabama, bus in 1957.

A number of catalytic events also galvanized the women's movement. There was the 1963 publication of Betty Friedan's *Feminine Mystique,* in which she spoke to women's discontent ("a problem that has no name," as she put it) as no one had done before. The example set by the civil rights movement showed many women that outsiders could gain a hearing in American politics if they were willing to use collective-action tactics. There was also resentment over the failure of the federal government to enforce Title VII of the 1964 Civil Rights Act, which guaranteed women protections in the area of equal employment. Finally, younger women active in the civil rights and anti–Vietnam War movements discovered that they were not well treated within these movements, despite the movements' rhetoric of equality, and concluded that women's problems could be addressed only if women took their own political initiative.

Tactics of Social Movements

Social movements tend to use unconventional tactics to make themselves heard. Such tactics depend on the dramatic gesture and are often disruptive. As you saw in the opening vignette, the women's suffrage movement used mass demonstrations and hunger strikes to great effect. The labor movement invented **sit-down strikes** and plant takeovers as its most effective weapons in the 1930s. Pro-life activists added to the protest repertoire clinic blockades and the harassment of clinic patients, doctors, employees, and their families. More extreme elements within these groups have even added violence against clinics and doctors, including murder.

sit-down strike

A form of labor action in which workers stop production but do not leave their job site.

The sit-down strike was invented by labor movement activists in the American auto industry in the 1930s. Here union members strike but stay put on the job site, daring management to use violence to end the work stoppage.

civil disobedience

Intentionally breaking a law and accepting the consequences as a way to publicize the unjustness of the law.

integration

Policies encouraging the interaction of different races, as in schools or public facilities.

The most effective tool of the civil rights movement was nonviolent **civil disobedience,** a conscious refusal to obey a law that a group considers unfair, unjust, or unconstitutional. A particularly dramatic and effective use of this tactic took place in Greensboro, North Carolina. Four black students from North Carolina Agricultural and Technical State University sat down at a "whites only" lunch counter in a Woolworth's store on February 1, 1960, and politely asked to be served. When requested to leave, they refused. They stayed put and remained calm even as a mob of young white men screamed at them, squirted them with ketchup and mustard, and threatened to lynch them. Each day, more students from the college joined them. By the end of the week, more than 1,000 black students had joined the sit-in to demand an end to segregation. These actions ignited the South. Within two months, similar sit-ins had taken place in nearly 60 cities across nine states; almost 4,000 young people had tasted a night in jail for their actions. Their bravery galvanized other blacks across the nation and generated sympathy among many whites. The student sit-in movement also spawned a new and more impatient civil rights organization, the Student Non-Violent Coordinating Committee (SNCC). (See the story of SNCC in Chapter 1.)

Another particularly effective use of nonviolent civil disobedience was organized in Birmingham, Alabama, by the spiritual leader of the civil rights movement, Dr. Martin Luther King Jr., who led a series of massive nonviolent demonstrations to demand the **integration** of schools and public transportation. Nonviolent demonstrators, most of them schoolchildren, were assaulted by snarling police dogs, electric cattle prods, and high-pressure fire hoses that sent demonstrators sprawling. Police Commissioner Eugene "Bull" Connor filled his jails to overflowing with hundreds of young marchers, who resisted only passively, alternately praying and singing civil rights songs, including "We Shall Overcome." The quiet bravery of the demonstrators and the palpable sense among public officials and private-sector leaders in the nation that matters were quickly spinning out of control convinced President John Kennedy on June 11, 1963, to introduce his historic civil rights bill for congressional consideration.

Nonviolent civil disobedience proved the most effective tool of the civil rights movement. By violating unjust laws quietly and nonviolently, protesters alerted outsiders to the injustice of their situation. The sit-in at a "whites only" lunch counter in Greensboro, North Carolina—shown here—sparked similar protests all over the country, and the arrests of the protesters generated sympathetic interest among previously apathetic whites.

Why Some Social Movements Succeed and Others Do Not

Social movements have had a significant effect on American politics and on what government does. Not all social movements are equally successful, however. What makes some more successful than others seems to be:

- the proximity of the movement's goals to American values;
- the movement's capacity to win public attention and support; and
- the movement's ability to affect the political fortunes of elected leaders.

Low-Impact Social Movements

A social movement will have little effect if it has few followers or activists, has little support among the general public, and is unable to disrupt everyday life significantly or to affect the electoral prospects of politicians. The poor people's movement, which tried to convince Americans to enact policies that would end poverty in the United States, failed to make much of a mark in the late 1960s.

A social movement is particularly unlikely to have an effect on policy when it stimulates the formation of a powerful countermovement. The rational politician may find it prudent to take no action at all when he or she has difficulty calculating the relative weight of the two sides in a dispute between movements. This is one of several things that happened to the proposed Equal Rights Amendment banning discrimination on the grounds of gender. The ERA failed to receive the approval of the necessary three-fourths of the states after anti-ERA forces (mainly Christian conservatives) rallied to block action during the 1970s.[17]

Repressed Social Movements

Social movements committed to a radical change in the society and the economy tend to threaten widely shared values and the interests of powerful individuals, groups, and institutions. As a result, they rarely gain widespread popular support and almost always arouse the hostility of political leaders. Such movements very often face repression of one kind or another.[18] In the late nineteenth and early twentieth centuries, for instance, the labor movement was hindered by court injunctions, laws against the formation of labor unions, violence by employer-hired armed gangs, and strikebreaking by the National Guard and the U.S. armed forces. In 1877, 60,000 National Guardsmen were mobilized in ten states to break the first national railroad strike. The strike against Carnegie Steel in 1892 in Homestead, Pennsylvania, brought the mobilization of 10,000 militiamen, the arrest of 16 strike leaders on conspiracy charges, and the indictment of 27 labor leaders for treason. The Pullman strike of 1894 was abruptly ended by the use of federal troops and by the arrest and indictment of union leaders.

Partially Successful Social Movements

Some social movements have enough power and public support to generate a favorable response from public officials but not enough to force them to go very far. In these situations, government may respond in a partial or half-hearted way. President Franklin D. Roosevelt responded to the social movements pressing for strong antipoverty measures during the Great Depression by proposing the passage of the Social Security Act, which fell far short of movement expectations.[19] The pro-life movement discovered that President Reagan was willing to use movement rhetoric to appoint sympathetic judges but was

Web Exploration
Movements and Public Support

Issue: The federal government and state and local governments have all passed laws banning racial discrimination. Comparatively few governments, however, have passed laws banning discrimination based on sexual orientation.

Site: Access the Public Agenda On-Line on our Website at **www.ablongman.com/greenberg**. Go to the "Web Explorations" section for Chapter 8. Select "Movements and Public Support." Select "Gallup Poll News Service," then "Poll Topics and Trends." From the list of topics, select "homosexual relations" and "race." For each, look at the section titled "major proposals."

What You've Learned: Are Americans more receptive to the claims of racial minorities than they are to the claims of gays and lesbians? How has the pattern changed over the years? Would you say there is evidence in the polls that the public is more likely to support antigay and antilesbian discrimination in the future?

HINT: Americans seem very conflicted about homosexuality and how governments ought to respond to the claims of gays and lesbians for full civil rights, although the climate for such claims has been improving.

USING THE FRAMEWORK: "Don't Ask, Don't Tell"

Why didn't Bill Clinton deliver on his promise to drop all restrictions on gays and lesbians in the military?

Background: Almost immediately after he was elected to office in 1992, Bill Clinton announced that, in his constitutional capacity as Commander-in-Chief, he intended to lift restrictions on gays and lesbians in the armed forces of the United States. In doing so, he was delivering on a campaign promise he had made to gay and lesbian organizations. After only a few weeks, however, he backed off from his promise and instituted a policy that came to be called "don't ask, don't tell, don't pursue." This policy of "turning a blind eye," as it were, satisfied no one. Taking a broad view at how structural, political linkage, and governmental factors affected Clinton's ultimate policy on gays and lesbians in the military will shed light on this situation.

Governmental Action

Bill Clinton announces that he will institute a "don't ask, don't tell" policy for gays and lesbians in the military.

Governmental Level

- Members of Congress from both parties strongly oppose lifting restrictions on gays and lesbians in the military. →
- The Chiefs of each of the branches of the military vehemently and publicly oppose lifting restrictions. →
- The president, though committed to lifting restrictions on gays and lesbians, realizes that pushing the policy will lead to tension with Congress and the military services, and get his new administration off to a shaky start, so he retreats.

Political Linkages Level

- The gay and lesbian movement creates a backlash, particularly among religious conservatives in all denominations. →
- The Republican Party makes rolling back the so-called gay agenda a major part of its platform. →
- Public opinion is conflicted; Americans support nondiscrimination against gays and lesbians in principle, but oppose gays and lesbians on a wide range of specific proposals.

- Gays and lesbians form and effectively use social protest groups. →
- Gays and lesbians play an increasingly open role in political campaigns, as candidates, financial contributors, and party activists. →
- The Democratic Party welcomes gay and lesbian support and participation. →
- The mass media and entertainment industries become more sympathetic to gays and lesbians.

Structural Level

- Higher levels of education among the population increases toleration of alternative lifestyles. →
- Urbanization creates enclaves where gays and lesbians build communities, create social networks, and develop economic and political resources. →
- The individualistic component of American culture and the Fourteenth Amendment to the Constitution favor a nondiscriminatory environment. →
- However, the strongly religious component of American culture is also the foundation for anti-homosexual attitudes.

Though many gay and lesbian activists have called for the legalization of same-sex marriage, American public opinion remains strongly opposed to the idea.

unwilling to submit anti-abortion legislation to Congress. Christian conservatives enjoyed some legislative successes during the height of their power in the 1990s, but failed to achieve their primary objectives: enactment of a law to ban late-term (in their words, "partial birth") abortions and the removal of Bill Clinton from office through the impeachment process.

Gays and lesbians enjoyed some successes, but encountered setbacks as well. The AIDS epidemic helped focus public attention on a range of other issues related to gay and lesbian rights, and several local communities across the nation legislated bans on housing and job discrimination, while still other communities passed same-sex domestic partner ordinances. Same-sex marriage was being considered in a number of states by the mid-1990s. However, the "backlash" created by these successes mobilized opposition groups who were successful winning local and statewide initiatives aimed at ending what its advocates called "special rights" for gays and lesbians, and a number of state legislatures passed bills to prevent same-sex marriages. This mixed picture of success and failure of the gay and lesbian movement may be explained, perhaps, by the overall shape of public opinion in the United States, which is itself mixed. A substantial majority of Americans report, for example, that while they support the general principle of nondiscrimination against gays and lesbians in the areas of jobs and housing, as well as in the provision of education and government benefits,[20] they do not approve of homosexuality and strongly oppose same-sex marriage.

Successful Social Movements

Longman
Participate.com
2.0
Timeline
**The Struggle
for Equal
Protection**

Social movements that have many supporters, win wide public sympathy, do not challenge the basics of the economic and social orders, and wield some clout in the electoral arena are likely to achieve a substantial number of their

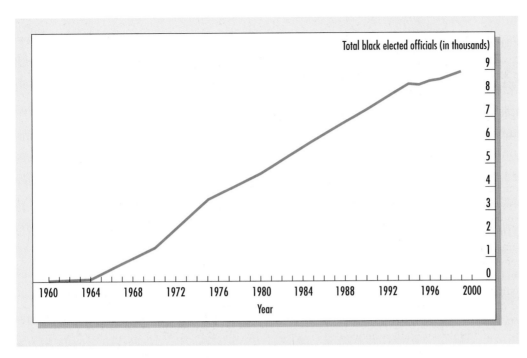

FIGURE 8.1 Black Elected Officials in the United States, 1960–1999
(all levels of government)

One of the success stories of the civil rights movement is the growing number of black officials being elected in the United States.

Source: U.S. Bureau of the Census and the Joint Center for Political and Economic Studies.

goals. The women's suffrage movement, described in the opening vignette, is one of the best examples. The civil rights movement is another, yielding, after years of struggle, the Civil Rights Act of 1964 and the Voting Rights Act of 1965. These enactments helped sound the death knell of the "separate but equal" doctrine enunciated in the infamous *Plessy* decision (1896), engineered the collapse of legal segregation in the South, and made the guarantee of full citizenship rights for African-Americans a reality. The Voting Rights Act was particularly important in transforming the politics of the South. Black registration and voting turnout increased dramatically all over the region during the late 1960s and the 1970s. Elected black officials filled legislative seats, city council seats, the mayors' offices in large and small cities, and sheriffs' offices. Between 1960 and 1997, the number of elected black officials in the United States increased from a mere 40 to more than 8,600 (see Figure 8.1).

Elected white officials, tacking with the new winds of change, soon began to court the black vote. George Wallace, who first became famous by "standing in the schoolhouse door" to prevent the integration of the University of Alabama and who once kicked off a political campaign with the slogan "Segregation Today, Segregation Tomorrow, Segregation Forever," actively pursued the black vote in his last run for public office.

Movements can be successful even if no new laws are passed. Other measures of success include increased respect for members of the movement, changes in fundamental underlying values in society, and increased representation of the group in decision-making bodies. The women's movement has had this kind of success. Although the Equal Rights Amendment (the movement's main goal) failed, women's issues came to the forefront during these years,

HOW DEMOCRATIC ARE WE?
Social Movements and American Politics

PROPOSITION: Social movements make American politics more democratic.

AGREE: Our constitutional system favors the *status quo*. The system of federalism, separation of powers, and checks and balances makes it extremely difficult to institute fundamentally new policies or to change existing social and economic conditions. The primacy of the status quo is further enhanced by the political power of economically and socially privileged groups and individuals. Social movements represent a way—a difficult way, to be sure—by which political outsiders and the politically powerless can become players in the political game. Movements are a way such groups and individuals can gain a hearing for their grievances, work to win over a majority of their fellow citizens, and force elected leaders to take action.

DISAGREE: Social movements are the tool of small minorities who force elected officials to respond to their demands because of the tangible threat of social disruption. Based on the age-old notion that "the squeaky wheel gets the grease," troublesome and disruptive groups can often get their way, even though the majority does not favor such action. In addition, because social movements often defy the law and social conventions, they tend to tear at the foundations of a stable democracy.

THE AUTHORS: Although social movements can sometimes get their way on public policies without or against the majority of Americans, in the long run, social movements only succeed when they are able to convince a majority of their fellow citizens that what the social movement seeks is legitimate. Strong social movements generate attention to a range of specific issues, widespread public debate, and (sometimes) countersocial movements. The government policies that eventually come out of this complex process sometimes favor the demands of the social movement, sometimes contradict them, and sometimes incorporate them into a broader compromise. Whatever the policy outcome, the social movement element of the American political system adds to the strength of our democracy.

and to a very substantial degree, the demands of the movement for equal treatment and respect made great headway in many areas of American life.[21] Issues such as pay equity, family leave, sexual harassment, and attention to women's health problems in medical research are now a part of the American political agenda. Women have made important gains economically and are becoming more numerous in the professions, corporate managerial offices (although there is some evidence that a glass ceiling remains in place), and political office.

Summary

Social movements emphasize rather dramatically the point that the struggle for democracy is a recurring feature of our political life. They are mainly the instruments of political outsiders who want to gain a hearing in American politics. Social movements often contribute to democracy by increasing the visibility of important issues, by encouraging wider participation in public affairs, and sometimes by providing the energy to overcome the many antimajoritarian features of our constitutional system.

Social movements try to bring about social change through collective action. Their rise is tied to the availability of organizational and leadership resources to a group of people who have a strong sense of grievance. Successful social movements happen, moreover, only if the political environment is supportive, in the sense that at least portions of the general population and some public officials are sympathetic to the movements' goals. The decline of particular social movements is associated with a number of things, including goal attainment, factional splits, the exhaustion of movement activists, and the replacement of grassroots activity by formal organization.

Social movements have had an important effect on our political life and in determining what our government does. Some of our most important legislative landmarks can be attributed to them. However, social movements do not always get what they want. They seem to be most successful when their goals are consistent with the central values of the society, have wide popular support, and fit the needs of political leaders.

Suggestions for Further Reading

Branch, Taylor. *Parting the Waters: America in the King Years, 1954–1963.* New York: Simon & Schuster, 1988.
   A detailed and compelling description of the civil rights movement, with a particular focus on Martin Luther King Jr.; winner of the National Book Award and the Pulitzer Prize.

Chafe, William H. *The Unfinished Journey: America Since World War II,* 2nd ed. New York: Oxford University Press, 1995.
   A justly celebrated history of America since 1945, with a particular focus on the civil rights and women's movements.

Dudziak, Mary L. *Cold War Civil Rights.* Princeton, NJ: Princeton University Press, 2002.
   A compelling history of how the Cold War struggle with the Soviet Union provided a supportive environment for the civil rights movement.

Evans, Sarah M. *Born for Liberty: A History of Women in America.* New York: Free Press, 1997.
   A compelling and widely used history of women in America, both substantively rich and a joy to read.

Martin, Mart. *The Almanac of Women and Minorities in American Politics.* Boulder, CO: Westview Press, 2002.
   A detailed, in-depth compendium about every aspect of women's and minorities' places in American political life.

Miller, James. *Democracy Is in the Streets.* New York: Simon & Schuster, 1987.
   A sophisticated account of the student antiwar movement and its roots in a particular strand of participatory democratic theory.

Piven, Frances Fox, and Richard A. Cloward. *Poor People's Movements.* New York: Vintage, 1979.
   A controversial treatment of poor people's movements that argues that they are successful only as long as and to the extent that they remain grassroots, disruptive insurgencies.

Rimmerman, Craig A., and Clyde Wilcox, eds. *The Politics of Gay Rights*. Chicago: University of Chicago Press, 2000.
> *A collection of essays representing the best in recent scholarship on gays and lesbians in American politics and on public policies that affect them.*

Tarrow, Sidney. *Power in Movement: Social Movements and Contentious Politics*. Cambridge: Cambridge University Press, 1998.
> *The leading academic treatment of social movements; analytically sophisticated and loaded with useful information about a broad range of movements.*

Internet Sources

Afronet **www.afronet.com/**
> *A Website devoted to materials on African-American political, social, economic, and cultural life.*

Christian Coalition **www.cc.org/**
> *Information and links from the nation's most influential Christian conservative organization.*

Yahoo!Society and Culture **www.yahoo.com/Society_and_Culture/**
> *A gateway with links to a multitude of social movements, issues, and groups.*

Notes

1. James MacGregor Burns and Stewart Burns, *A People's Charter: The Pursuit of Rights in America* (New York: Knopf, 1991), ch. 5; E. McGlen and Karen O'Connor, *Women's Rights* (New York: Praeger, 1983), ch. 3.

2. Joyce Gelb, *Feminism and Politics: A Comparative Perspective* (Berkeley, CA: University of California Press, 1989), pp. 14, 30. See also Doug McAdams, *Political Process and the Development of Black Insurgency* (Chicago: University of Chicago Press, 1982); David Plotke, "Citizenship and Social Movements," paper delivered at the annual meetings of the American Political Science Association, Washington, D.C., September 2–5, 1993.

3. Sidney Tarrow, "Social Movements as Contentious Politics," *American Political Science Review,* 90 (1996), pp. 853–866.

4. E. E. Schattschneider, *The Semi-Sovereign People* (New York: Holt, Rinehart & Winston, 1960), p. 142.

5. Richard Polenberg, *One Nation Divisible* (New York: Penguin, 1980), p. 268.

6. Theodore J. Lowi, *The Politics of Disorder* (New York: Basic Books, 1971), p. 54.

7. Doug McAdams, John D. McCarthy, and Mayer N. Zald, "Social Movements," in Neil J. Smelser, ed., *Handbook of Sociology* (Newbury Park, CA: Sage, 1994); Sidney Tarrow, *Social Movements, Collective Action, and Politics* (New York: Cambridge University Press, 1994).

8. Neil J. Smelser, *Theory of Collective Behavior* (New York: Free Press, 1962).

9. Barbara Sinclair Deckard, *The Women's Movement* (New York: Harper & Row, 1983); Ethel Klein, *Gender Politics: From Consciousness to Mass Politics* (Cambridge, MA: Harvard University Press, 1984), ch. 2.

10. Donald P. Haider-Markel, "Creating Change—Holding the Line," in Ellen D. B. Riggle and Barry L. Tadlock, eds., *Gays and Lesbians in the Political Process* (New York: Columbia University Press, 1999).

CHAPTER 8 Social Movements 237

11. William Gamson, *The Strategy of Social Protest* (Homewood, IL: Dorsey, 1975); John D. McCarthy and Mayer N. Zald, "Resource Mobilization and Social Movements: A Partial Theory," *American Journal of Sociology,* 82 (1977), pp. 1212–1241.

12. Jo Freeman, *The Politics of Women's Liberation* (New York: McKay, 1975).

13. McAdams, *Political Process;* Peter K. Eisenger, "The Conditions of Protest Behavior in American Cities," *American Political Science Review,* 67 (1973), pp. 11–28.

14. Frances Fox Piven and Richard A. Cloward, *Poor People's Movements* (New York: Vintage, 1979), ch. 3.

15. Klein, *Gender Politics,* pp. 90–91.

16. National Opinion Research Center, General Social Survey, 1972.

17. Jane Mansbridge, *Why We Lost the ERA* (Chicago: University of Chicago Press, 1986).

18. See David Caute, *The Great Fear* (New York: Simon & Schuster, 1978); Robert Justin Goldstein, *Political Repression in Modern America* (Cambridge, MA: Schenkman, 1978); Alan Wolfe, *The Seamy Side of Democracy* (New York: McKay, 1978).

19. Edward S. Greenberg, *Capitalism and the American Political Ideal* (Armonk, NY: Sharpe, 1985).

20. Gregory B. Lewis and Marc A. Rogers, "Does the Public Support Equal Employment Rights for Gays and Lesbians?" in Riggle and Tadlock, eds., *Gays and Lesbians in the Democratic Process.*

21. William H. Chafe, *The Unfinished Journey: America Since World War II* (New York: Oxford University Press, 1986); Deckard, *The Women's Movement;* Klein, *Gender Politics,* ch. 2; Freeman, *Politics of Women's Liberation.*

Chapter 9
Political Parties

In This Chapter

- Why political parties are important in a democracy

- How American political parties differ from parties elsewhere

- Why we have a two-party system

- How our party system has changed over the years

- What role third parties play

- How the Republican and Democratic parties differ

The Rise of the Campaign Party Machine

If the status of their national committees is any indicator, the Republican and Democratic parties are healthy, vital, and growing organizations. Each of the national committees has a shiny new office building in Washington, D.C. Out of these buildings come a range of services for party candidates. In-house TV and radio studios provide attack ads aimed against the other party and its candidates, tailored for the particular district or state in which the ads will be used, while other ads extol its own party and achievements. Direct mail campaigns are mounted to disseminate information and party positions on the issues and to make appeals for campaign contributions. News releases are prepared for the media, as are campaign-oriented sound and video bites to be used as news clips on local radio and television. Each of the parties also produces training courses for potential candidates, complete with "how-to" manuals and videos. Each of the two parties has a Website where one can access information about the party, get news about the nefarious behavior of the opposition, and make monetary contributions to the party (soft money) and to party candidates (hard money).

To carry out these activities, both the Republican and Democratic National Committees have steadily increased the number of employees in their national offices, especially in the areas of finance, advertising, information technology, campaign planning, and video specialists and support personnel, and have expanded their budgets to carry out an ever broader range of campaign activities for party candidates. Each of the national committees, that is to say, has become a highly professionalized campaign organization, filled with highly skilled people who can provide party candidates with what they need to wage first-rate electoral campaigns.

In spite of all of this activity, the public's attachment to and involvement with the parties is becoming weaker and weaker, leading some scholars to talk about the "baseless parties."[1] The evidence is everywhere: Scholarly and media polls show that the number of independents compared with party identifiers has increased, as has "split ticket" voting; turnout for elections is at an all-time low; vital grassroots party organizations have withered and disappeared in many areas; fewer people volunteer to work in candidate campaigns; and regard for both parties has declined, as has confidence in the ability of either one to solve pressing national problems.

What seems to be happening, according to several scholars, is that parties have changed from community-based organizations with close links to voters to campaign service organizations whose main customers are party candidates. It is almost as if the parties do not require the involvement of the public at all, except as voters. Parties are apparently happy if their efforts manage to get people to the polls who will vote for their candidates and discourage people who might be inclined to vote for candidates of the other parties. If this description of "baseless" parties is accurate, it would mark an important change in the traditional role of our political parties and have important implications for how well democracy works in the United States. We will examine these issues in this chapter, as well as in the next chapter on elections and political participation. ■

Thinking Critically About This Chapter

This chapter is about American political parties, how they evolved, what they do, and how their actions affect the quality of democracy in the United States.

Using the Framework You will see in this chapter how parties work as political linkage institutions connecting the public with government leaders and institutions. You will see, as well, how structural changes in the American economy and society have affected how our political parties function.

Using the Democracy Standard You will see in this chapter that political parties, at least in theory, are one of the most important instruments for making popular sovereignty and majority rule a reality in a representative democracy, particularly in a system of checks-and-balances and separated powers such as our own. Evaluating how well our parties carry out these democratic responsibilities is one of the main themes of this chapter. ◀

The Role of Political Parties in a Democracy

Political parties are organizations that try to win control of government by electing people to public office who carry the party label. In representative democracies, parties are the principal organizations that recruit candidates for public office, run their candidates against the candidates of other political parties in competitive elections, and try to organize and coordinate the activities of government officials under party banners and programs.

Many political scientists believe that political parties are essential to democracy.[2] They agree with E. E. Schattschneider that "political parties created democracy and . . . modern democracy is unthinkable save in terms of the parties."[3] What Schattschneider and others see in the political party is the main instrument of popular sovereignty and, especially, majority rule: "The parties are the special form of political organization adapted to the mobilization of majorities. How else can the majority get organized? If democracy means anything at all it means that the majority has the right to organize for the purpose of taking over the government."[4]

In theory, political parties can do a number of things to make popular sovereignty and political equality possible:[5]

- *Keeping elected officials responsive.* Political parties can provide a way for the people to keep elected officials responsive through competitive elections. Competitive party elections help voters choose between alternative policy directions for the future. They also allow voters to make a judgment about the past performance of a governing party and decide whether to allow that party to continue in office. And, a party can adjust its **party platform**—the party's statement of its position on the issues—to reflect the preferences of the public as a way to win elections. (These three ways in which elections relate to democracy are discussed in Chapter 10.)

- *Including a broad range of groups.* Political parties can enhance political equality in a democracy because they tend to include as many groups as they possibly can. Parties are by nature inclusive, as they must be if they are to create a winning majority coalition in elections. It

party platform

A party's statement of its positions on the issues of the day.

Political parties generally try to broaden their appeal by running candidates from a wide range of ethnic, racial, and religious groups.

is customary for parties in the United States to recruit candidates for public office from many ethnic and racial groups and to include language in their platforms to attract a diversity of groups.

- *Stimulating political interest.* When they are working properly, moreover, political parties stimulate interest in politics and public affairs and increase participation.[6] They do this as a natural by-product of their effort to win or retain power in government; they mobilize voters, bring issues to public attention, and educate on the issues that are of interest to the party. Party competition, by "expanding the scope of conflict," attracts attention and gets people involved.[7]

- *Ensuring accountability.* Parties can help make officeholders more accountable. When things go wrong or promises are not kept, it is important in a democracy for citizens to know who is responsible. Where there are many offices and branches of government, however, it is hard to pinpoint responsibility. Political parties can simplify this difficult task by allowing for collective responsibility. Citizens can pass judgment on the governing ability of a party as a whole and decide whether to retain the incumbent party or to throw it out of office in favor of the other party.

- *Making government work.* In a system like ours of separation of powers and checks and balances, designed to make it difficult for government to act decisively, political parties can encourage cooperation across the branches of government among public officials who are members of the same party. Parties can help overcome gridlock, an all too common feature of our constitutional system.

Political parties, then, can be tools of popular sovereignty. Whether our own political parties fulfill these responsibilities to democracy is the question we explore in the remainder of this chapter as well as in Chapter 10.

FIGURE 9.1 Party Systems in the United States

American politics has been characterized by a series of stable-political-party eras punctuated by brief periods of transition from one party era to another.

History of the Two-Party System

The United States comes closer to having a "pure" two-party system than any other nation in the world. Most Western democracies have multiparty systems. In the United States, however, two parties have dominated the political scene since 1836, and the Democrats and the Republicans have controlled the presidency and Congress since 1860. Minor or third parties have rarely polled a significant percentage of the popular vote in either presidential or congressional elections (more will be said later about third parties and independent candidates), although they are sometimes successful at the state and local levels. Jesse Ventura, for example, was elected governor of Minnesota in 1998 as the nominee of the Reform Party.

Although the United States has had a two-party system for most of its history, it has not been static. The party system has, in fact, changed a great

Web Exploration
Multiparty Systems

Issue: Unlike the United States, most democratic countries have a multiparty system.

Site: Access political sources on the Web on our Website at **www.ablongman.com/greenberg** so you can examine the multiparty systems in other democracies. Go to the "Web Explorations" section for Chapter 9, select "Multiparty Systems," then "multiparty." On the left, select "elections," then look at the results in four major democratic countries.

What You've Learned: What is the average number of major parties represented in the parliament? How would you characterize the major parties in an ideological or public policy sense? Is the range of political issues covered by their parties greater or less than what is covered in our political system?

HINT: Multiparty systems usually encourage the representation of a broader range of ideological positions than do two-party systems.

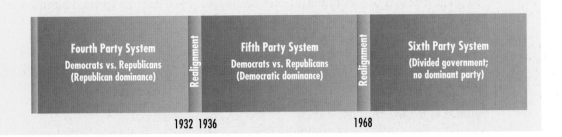

| Fourth Party System | | Fifth Party System | | Sixth Party System |
| Democrats vs. Republicans (Republican dominance) | Realignment | Democrats vs. Republicans (Democratic dominance) | Realignment | (Divided government; no dominant party) |

1932 1936   1968

deal, both mirroring and playing a central role in the dynamic and some-times chaotic story of the development of the United States, as described in Chapter 4. There have been six relatively stable periods in the history of the two-party system in the United States, each stretching over 30 or 40 years, interspersed with much shorter periods of transformation or **realignment.** Realignment is a transition period, most notable in our history in 1896 and 1932, when a party system dominated by one of the two major parties is re-placed by another system dominated by the other party.[8] Figure 9.1 shows this history in graphic form.

realignment

The process by which one party supplants another as the dominant party in a political system.

The First Party System: Federalists Versus Democratic Republicans

Although the Founders were hostile to parties in theory, they created them al-most immediately. The first was formed in the 1790s by George Washington's energetic secretary of the treasury, Alexander Hamilton. In a successful effort

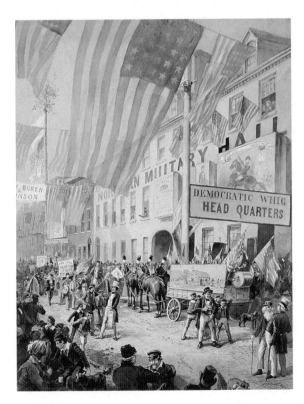

The second party system was characterized by well-organized parties, skilled in the use of methods (such as this parade) to mobilize the "common man" to participate in electoral politics.

to push through the administration's ambitious legislative program, Hamilton persuaded sympathetic members of Congress to form a loosely organized party that eventually took the name Federalist.

Thomas Jefferson, James Madison, and others formed a party in Congress to oppose the Hamilton domestic program and Federalist foreign policy. They used the label Republican, although the Federalists tried to discredit them by calling them Democratic Republicans (the term *democratic* was a term of derision, not praise, in those days).

The Federalist party gradually disappeared, tainted by its pro-British sympathies during the War of 1812 and its image as a party of the wealthy and the aristocratic in an increasingly democratic America. By 1816, the first two-party system had evolved into a one-party or no-party system, generally known (because of the absence of party competition) as the Era of Good Feelings.

The Second Party System: Democrats Versus Whigs

The Era of Good Feelings gave way in the late 1820s to a strong two-party system that grew out of the disputed presidential election of 1824. In that election, Andrew Jackson won a plurality of the popular and electoral votes but failed to win a majority of either. The House of Representatives chose John Quincy Adams as president. Supporters of Jackson formed an opposition that soon became the Democratic party, while supporters of Adams and his ally in the House, Speaker Henry Clay, organized as the Whig party. Starting in 1828, when Jackson defeated Adams for the presidency, the Democrats won six of the next eight presidential elections.

Each of the parties split apart as the nation drifted toward civil war. The Whig party simply disintegrated and disappeared. Several of its fragments came together with *Free-Soilers* (who opposed the expansion of slavery into the western territories) and antislavery Democrats to form a new Republican party—the ancestor of the present-day Republicans—which ran its first presidential candidate, John Frémont, in the election of 1856. The Democrats survived but could not agree on a single candidate to run against Republican Abraham Lincoln in 1860, so each wing of the party nominated its own candidate.

From the Civil War to 1896: Republicans and Democrats in Balance

Once the southern states had reentered the Union after Reconstruction, the Republicans and the Democrats found themselves roughly balanced in national politics. Between 1876 and 1896, the Democrats managed to control the presidency for 8 of 20 years, the Senate for 6 years, and the House of Representatives for 14 years. Each party had a strong regional flavor. The Democratic party was primarily a white southern party, although Catholics and many workers in northern urban areas also supported it. The Republicans (also known as the "Grand Old Party," or GOP) became a party of business, the middle class, and newly enfranchised African-Americans.

The Party System of 1896: Republican Dominance

Beneath the apparent calm of a balanced two-party system, however, a storm was brewing. The late nineteenth century was a time of rapid economic and social change and disruption, one effect of which was to spawn a host of protest movements and third parties. The Populist party, the most important of them, garnered 8.5 percent of the total vote in the 1892 election and won four states in the electoral college, running on the slogan, "Wealth belongs to him who creates it." During the 1890s, Populist party candidates also won governorships in eight states and control of at least as many state legislatures.

In 1896, the Populist party joined with the Democratic party to nominate a single candidate for the presidency, the charismatic orator William Jennings Bryan, who urged "free coinage of silver" to help debtors with cheaper currency. The threat of a radical agrarian party, joining blacks and whites, farmers and labor unionists, proved too much for many Americans and contributed to one of the most bitter electoral campaigns in U.S. history. Conservative Democrats deserted their party to join the Republicans. Businesses warned each other and their workers in no uncertain terms about the dangers of a Populist-Democratic victory. Newly formed business organizations, such as the National Association of Manufacturers, spread the alarm about a possible Democratic victory. In the South, efforts to intimidate potential black voters increased dramatically.[9]

The Republicans won handily and dominated American politics until the Great Depression and the election of 1932. Between 1896 and 1932, the Republicans won control of both houses of Congress in 15 out of 18 elections and of the presidency in 7 out of 9.

The New Deal Party System: Democratic Party Dominance

The Great Depression, the **New Deal,** and the leadership of President Franklin D. Roosevelt ushered in a long period of Democratic party dominance. From 1932 through 1964, the Democrats won seven of nine presidential elections, controlled the Senate and the House of Representatives for all but four years, and prevailed in a substantial majority of governorships and state

New Deal

The programs of the administration of President Franklin D. Roosevelt.

Franklin D. Roosevelt, here campaigning for the presidency in 1932, fashioned an electoral coalition based on the urban working class, racial and ethnic minorities, Catholics and Jews, big cities, and the South that allowed the Democratic party to dominate American politics for almost four decades.

legislatures across the nation. Democratic dominance was built on an alliance of workers, Catholics, Jews, unionists, small- and medium-sized farmers, urban dwellers, white ethnics, southerners, and blacks that came to be known as the **New Deal coalition.** The New Deal coalition supported an expansion of federal government powers and responsibilities, particularly in the areas of old age assistance, aid for the poor, encouragement of unionization, subsidies for agriculture, and regulation of business.

The Sixth Party System: Dealignment and Divided Government

The New Deal coalition began to disintegrate in the 1968 election (won by Republican Richard Nixon) and finally collapsed in 1994,[10] a process triggered in significant part by the Civil Rights revolution (see Chapters 8 and 16) and the subsequent departure of many white southerners and blue collar workers from the Democratic party.[11] Although Democrats continued to control Congress for much of the period, they lost the Senate to the Republicans from 1981 to 1986, the presidency for all but six years during this period (Carter, 1977–1980; Clinton, 1993–1994), and both houses of Congress between 1995 and 2001. A period of divided government began in 1968 in which one party controlled the executive and the other party controlled all or part of the legislative branch. During this period, the two parties became more closely competitive in elections at all levels across the nation as the Democrats gradually lost their big lead over the Republicans in party identification among Americans.

In the transition from the fifth party system to the sixth, a classic party realignment—the replacement of a system dominated by one party by a system dominated by the other party—did not take place as in the elections of 1896 and 1932. Scholars, journalists, and politicians have come to call the process of transition to the sixth party system **dealignment.** Dealignment may be thought of as a transformation in the party system in which a previously dominant party loses preeminence (the Democrats in this case) but no new party takes its place as the dominant party on a long-term basis. This new party system is characterized by the relative parity of the major parties in a context where the population not only identifies less with either party but also becomes increasingly alienated from both parties and less confident that either one can solve the nation's problems.[12]

Why a Two-Party System?

Most Western democracies have multiparty systems, with more than two major parties. Why are we so different from other countries? There are several possible answers.

Electoral Rules

The kinds of rules that organize elections help determine what kind of party system exists.[13] Which rules are chosen, then, has important consequences for a nation's politics.

Proportional Representation
Most other democratic nations use some form of **proportional representation** (PR) to elect their representatives. In PR systems, each party is represented in the legislature in rough proportion to

---

New Deal coalition

The informal electoral alliance of working-class ethnic groups, Catholics, Jews, urban dwellers, racial minorities, and the South that was the basis of the Democratic party dominance of American politics from the New Deal to the early 1970s.

dealignment

A gradual reduction in the dominance of one political party without another party supplanting it.

Longman
Participate.com
2.0
Comparative
**Comparing
Political
Parties**

proportional representation

The awarding of legislative seats to political parties to reflect the proportion of the popular vote each party receives.

the percentage of the popular vote it receives in an election. In a perfect PR system, a party winning 40 percent of the vote would get 40 seats in a 100-seat legislative body, a party winning 22 percent of the vote would get 22 seats, and so on. In such a system, even very small parties would have a reason to maintain their separate identities, for no matter how narrow their appeal, they would win seats as long as they could win a proportion of the popular vote. Voters with strong views on an issue or with strong ideological outlooks could vote for a party that closely represented their views. A vote for a small party would not be wasted, for it would ultimately be translated into legislative seats and, perhaps, a place in the governing coalition.

Israel and the Netherlands come closest to having a pure PR system, organized on a national basis; most Western European nations depart in various ways from the pure form. Most, for instance, vote for slates of party candidates within multimember electoral districts, apportioning seats in each district according to each party's percentage of the vote. Most also have a minimum threshold (often 5 percent) below which no seats are awarded.

Winner-Take-All, Plurality Election, Single-Member Districts

Elections in the United States are organized on a winner-take-all, single-member-district basis. Each electoral district in the United States—whether it is an urban ward, a county, a congressional district, or a state—elects only one person to a given office and does so on the basis of whoever wins the *most* votes (not necessarily a majority). This is why our way of electing leaders is sometimes called a "first past the post" system, analogous to a horse race. This arrangement creates a powerful incentive for parties to coalesce and for voters to concentrate their attention on big parties. Let's see why.

From the vantage point of party organizations, this type of election discourages minor-party efforts because failure to come in first in the voting leaves a party with no representation at all. Leaders of such parties are tempted to merge with a major party. By the same token, a disaffected faction within a party is unlikely to strike out on its own because the probability of gaining political office is very low.

A presidential election is decided by which candidate has won a majority in the electoral college, *not* a majority of the total votes cast. That is why every four years on election night the television networks focus on state-by-state victories and defeats.

From the voter's point of view, a single-member, winner-take-all election means that a vote for a minor party is wasted. People who vote for a minor party may feel good, but most voters have few illusions that such votes will translate into representation and so are not inclined to cast them.

Note that the most important office in American government, the presidency, is elected in what is, in effect, a single-district (the nation), winner-take-all election. The candidate who wins a majority of the nation's votes in the electoral college wins the presidency (see Chapter 10). A party cannot win a share of the presidency; it is all or none. In parliamentary systems, the executive power is lodged in a cabinet, however, where several parties may be represented.

Restrictions on Minor Parties

Longman
Participate.com
2.0
Timeline
**Third Parties
in American
History**

Once a party system is in place, the dominant parties often establish rules that make it difficult for other parties to get on the ballot. A number of formidable legal obstacles stand in the way of third parties and independent candidates in the United States. While many of these restrictions have been eased because of successful court challenges by recent minor-party and independent presidential candidates such as Ross Perot, the path to the ballot remains tortuous in many states, where a considerable number of signatures is required to get on the ballot.

The federal government's partial funding of presidential campaigns has made the situation of third parties even more difficult. Major-party candidates automatically qualify for federal funding once they are nominated. Minor-party candidates must attract a minimum of 5 percent of the votes cast in the general election to be eligible for public funding, and they are not reimbursed until after the election. In recent decades, only the Reform Party among the legion of minor parties has managed to cross the threshold to qualify for federal funding. Because the Green Party's candidate, Ralph Nader, won only 2.7 percent of the national vote in the 2000 election, it is not eligible for federal funding for the 2004 election.

Absence of a Strong Labor Movement

The relative weakness of the American labor movement has already been noted in several places in this book. In the Western European countries, the organized labor movement was instrumental in the creation of Socialist and Labor political parties that challenged classical Liberal (free enterprise, small government) and traditional Conservative (monarchist, Catholic, and aristocratic) parties. The British Labour party, for instance, was created by trade union officials and Socialists in 1906. Strong Socialist and Labor parties in Europe did not replace traditional Liberal and Conservative parties (except in Great Britain) but spurred them on to more spirited organizing and electioneering of their own. The result has been the creation of a basic three-party system in many European countries—Conservative, Liberal, and Labor or Socialist—with a number of small satellite parties (encouraged by PR electoral systems) clustered about them.

The Role of Minor Parties in the Two-Party System

Minor parties have played a less important role in the United States than in virtually any other democratic nation.[14] In our entire history, only a single minor party (the Republicans) has managed to replace one of the major parties. Only six (not including the Republicans) have been able to win even 10 per-

Candidates such as Ralph Nader and third parties such as the Green Party often bring up issues the main parties are unable or unwilling to address.

cent of the popular vote in a presidential election, and only seven have managed to win a single state in a presidential election. Ross Perot won only 8 percent in 1996 as the candidate of the Reform Party, which he founded.

Minor parties have come in a number of forms.

- *Protest parties* sometimes arise as part of a protest movement. The Populist party, for instance, grew out of the western and southern farm protest movements in the late nineteenth century. The Green Party was an off-shoot of the environmental and antiglobalization movements.

Web Exploration
Third Parties in the United States

Issue: We have a two-party system, but many minor parties exist here.

Site: Learn more about these minor, or third, parties at Politics1 on our Website at **www.ablongman.com/greenberg**. Go to the "Web Explorations" section for Chapter 9, select "Third Parties in the United States," then "third parties." Examine the platforms and activities of several minor parties.

What You've Learned: Do any of the parties you examined address issues that neither of the major parties has tackled? Do you find any of them appealing? If you like one of the parties, and that party appears on the ballot, will you vote for that party or not? What are your reasons?

HINT: People with very strong views on a handful of issues are often unhappy with the two main parties.

- *Ideological parties* are organized around coherent sets of ideas. The several Socialist parties have been of this sort, as has the Libertarian party. The Green Party ran in the 2000 elections on an anticorporate, antiglobalization platform.

- *Single-issue parties* are barely distinguishable from interest groups. What makes them different is their decision to run candidates for office. The Prohibition party and the Free-Soil party fall into this category as did Perot's "balanced budget" Reform Party in 1996.

- *Splinter parties* form when a faction in one of the two major parties bolts to run its own candidate or candidates. An example is the Bull Moose Progressive party of Teddy Roosevelt, formed after Roosevelt split with Republican party regulars in 1912.

Minor parties do a number of things in American politics. Sometimes they articulate new ideas that are eventually taken over by one or both major parties. The Socialist party under Norman Thomas, for example, advocated public works projects as a way to battle unemployment during the Great Depression, an idea that became part of the Democrats' New Deal legislative package. Ross Perot's popular crusade for a balanced budget during his 1992 campaign helped nudge the major parties towards a budget agreement that, for awhile, eliminated annual deficits in the federal budget.

The Parties as Organizations

I don't belong to an organized political party. I'm a Democrat.

—WILL ROGERS

American parties don't look much like the parties in other democratic countries. In most of them, the political parties are fairly well-structured organizations led by party professionals and committed to a set of policies and principles. They also tend to have clearly defined membership requirements, centralized control over party nominations and electoral financing, and disciplinary authority over party members holding political office.

The Ambiguous Nature of American Political Parties

The classic boss-led political machines of American folklore—long identified with such names as Tammany Hall, "Boss Tweed" of New York, Richard J. Daley of Chicago, and Huey Long of Louisiana—have disappeared from the cities and states where they once existed, mainly because of reforms that ended party control over government contracts and jobs. Political machines run by a "boss" have never existed at the national level. There have been leaders with clout, reputation, and vision, to be sure, but never a boss who could issue commands. Even popular, charismatic, and skillful presidents, including George Washington, Abraham Lincoln, Woodrow Wilson, Franklin Roosevelt, Harry Truman, John Kennedy, and Ronald Reagan, have had nearly as much trouble controlling the many diverse and independent groups and individuals within their own parties as they have had dealing with the opposition.

The vagueness of party membership is a good indicator of the ambiguous nature of our parties. Think about what it means to be a Republican or a Democrat in the United States. Americans do not join parties in the sense of paying dues and receiving a membership card. To Americans, being a member

Richard Daley, mayor of Chicago for more than 20 years, and head of the Cook County Democratic Party for even longer, was the last in a long line of big-city party bosses in America.

of a party may mean voting most of the time for the candidate of a party or choosing to become a candidate of one of them. Or it may mean voting in a party primary. Or it may mean contributing money to, or otherwise helping in, a local, state, or national campaign of one of the party candidates. Or it may just mean that one generally prefers one party to another most of the time. These are loose criteria for membership, to say the least—looser than for virtually any other organization that one might imagine.

The Organization of American Political Parties

The Republican and Democratic parties are not organizations in the usual sense of the term but rather loose collections of local and state parties, campaign committees, candidates and officeholders, and associated interest groups that get together every four years to nominate a presidential candidate. Unlike a corporation, a bureaucratic agency, a military organization, or even a political party in most other countries, the official leaders of the major American parties cannot issue orders that get passed down a chain of command. The various elements of the party are relatively independent from one another and act in concert not on the basis of orders but on the basis of shared interests, sentiment, and the desire to win elections. Most important, the national party is unable to control its most vital activity—the nomination of candidates running under its party label—or the flow of money that funds electoral campaigns or the behavior of its officeholders. (See Figure 9.2 for a graphical representation of these ideas.)

Party Conventions This is not to suggest that the parties are entirely devoid of tools to encourage coordination and cooperation among their various levels. The national party conventions are the governing bodies of the parties (see Chapter 10). Convention delegates meet every four years not only to nominate presidential and vice-presidential candidates but also to write a party platform and to revise party rules.

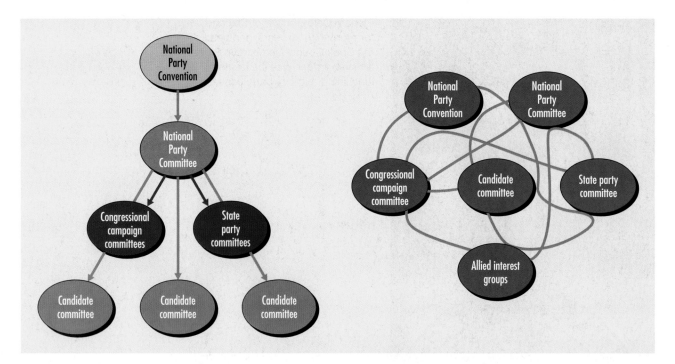

FIGURE 9.2 Political Party Organization in the United States

The graphic on the left shows a hypothetical organizational chart of the Republican and Democratic parties as if they were structured hierarchically like many other organizations you are familiar with. It would be a mistake, however, to think of our national parties this way. The drawing on the right, which depicts our national parties as networks of web-like organizations where there is neither central authority nor a chain of command, is closer to reality. The ties between elements of the parties include money, ideology, sentiment, and common interests.

Although the national convention is the formal governing body of each of the parties, it cannot dictate to party candidates or party organizations at other levels of jurisdiction. The presidential nominee need not adhere to either the letter or the spirit of the party platform, for instance, although most nominees stay fairly close to the platform most of the time (usually because the winning candidate's supporters control the platform-writing committee). State and local party organizations may nominate whomever they choose to run for public office and may or may not support key planks in the national party's platform.

National Party Committees The Democrats and Republicans each have a national committee whose responsibility is to conduct the business of the party during the four years between national conventions. Although the national committees have little direct power, they provide valuable services for local and state parties and for party candidates at all levels (a subject detailed in the story that opens this chapter). These include production of campaign training materials, issue and policy research, design and maintenance of Web sites, assistance in creating radio and TV spots and other campaign materials, and research on the opposition. They also make significant financial contributions to the campaigns of party candidates.

The national committees are made up of elected committeemen and committeewomen from each of the states, a sizable staff, and a chairperson. The

National party conventions serve several purposes for American political parties. Every four years, delegates choose presidential and vice-presidential candidates, settle party rules, write the party platform, repair or build political coalitions, and, as shown here, attempt to whip up enthusiasm for their nominees.

national committees rarely meet. The real business of the committee is run by the party chair, assisted by the committee staff. The chair exercises little power when a president from the party is in office because the party chair is compelled to take direction from the White House. When the opposition controls the presidency, the party chair exercises more influence in party affairs, although the extent of that power is still not very great.

Congressional Campaign Committees Almost as old as the national party committees, but entirely independent of them, are the congressional campaign committees that aid members of Congress in their campaigns for re-election. They help raise money, provide media services (making short videotapes of the members of Congress for local television news shows, for instance), conduct research, and do whatever else the party members in Congress deem appropriate. These committees are controlled by the party members in Congress, not the party chair, the national committees, or even the president. Much as with the national committees, the congressional campaign committees have become highly professionalized and well funded.[15]

State Party Organizations As one would expect in a federal system, separate political party organizations exist in each of the states. Although tied together by bonds of ideology, sentiment, and campaign money and constrained in what they can do by rules set by the national party committees and conventions—rules on how and when to choose delegates to the national convention, for example—the state party organizations are relatively independent of one another and of the national party.

Longman
Participate.com 2.0
Visual Literacy
State Control
and National
Platforms

Associated Interest Groups Although not technically part of the formal party organizations, some groups are so closely involved in the affairs of the parties that it is hard to draw a line between them and the political parties. The Christian Coalition, for example, is barely distinguishable from the Republican party; it contributes campaign money almost exclusively to GOP candidates, gives soft money only to the Republican party, runs its own candidates in the Republican primaries, and counts many of its members among the delegates to the Republican National Convention. Organized labor has had a similar relationship with the Democratic party since the Great Depression and the New Deal.

In candidate-centered politics, office seekers typically run as individuals without visible reminders of their party affiliation. Parties are not absent, however; they are usually there to help with fund-raising, fashioning attack ads against the opposition, and getting out the party faithful to vote on election day.

The Primacy of Candidates

American politics is candidate-centered, meaning that candidates are primary in our political system and parties are secondary.[16] In the United States, not only are candidates relatively immune from party pressure, but their electoral needs also shape what parties are and what they do.[17] Candidates have independent sources of campaign financing, their own campaign organizations, and their own campaign themes and priorities. And party organizations are becoming but another part, an important part to be sure, of candidates' campaign armament.

In the past, party candidates were usually nominated in district, state, and national conventions, where party regulars played a major role. They are now almost exclusively nominated in primaries or grassroots caucuses, where the party organizations are almost invisible. Nomination comes to those who are best able to raise money, gain access to the media, form their own electoral organizations, and win the support of powerful interest groups (such as the National Rifle Association in the GOP and the National Education Association in the Democratic party).

Nominees are so independent they sometimes oppose party leaders and reject traditional party policies. Republicans were embarrassed, for example, when David Duke, former Grand Wizard of the Ku Klux Klan, was elected to the Louisiana state legislature in 1988 under the Republican banner and ran for the governorship as a Republican in 1990, despite the opposition of state and national Republican officials.

In Germany, by way of contrast, individual candidates for the Bundestag (the equivalent of the House of Representatives) are less important than the political parties. Candidates are nominated by local party committees dominated by party regulars. Party lists for the general election are drawn up by state party organizations. Money for conducting electoral campaigns, moreover, is mostly raised and spent by the party organizations, not individual candidates. Finally, the campaign is waged between the parties and their alternative programs, not between individual candidates, and the electorate

In most European countries, people vote for parties rather than individual candidates. These party activists are urging British voters to cast their ballots for the Labour party, for example, rather than for the rival Conservative party.

tends to make its choices based on feelings about the parties rather than about the candidates. Most of the Western European democracies have similar party systems.

Ideology and Program

Because the Republican and Democratic parties are both broad coalitions, seeking to attract as many voters as possible in order to prevail in winner-take-all, single-member-district elections, there are strong pressures on them to be ideologically ambiguous. But each party has a core of loyal supporters and party activists, such as delegates to the party convention and caucus attendees, who are more ideologically oriented than the general public. The result is a party system composed of parties less ideologically focused and identifiable than the parties in other democratic countries, but with significant ideological and policy differences between them nevertheless. In addition, the parties seem to be getting much more ideologically distinct.[18]

Ideology may be understood as an organized set of beliefs about the fundamental nature of the good society and the role government ought to play in achieving it. In other Western democracies, it is common for the major parties to be quite closely connected with an ideology, in the sense that their activists, members, and officeholders identify with it; campaign with themes based on its ideas; and are guided by it in their governmental actions. Socialist and Labor parties often line up in elections against Liberal and Conservative or Catholic parties, with Marxist, Christian Socialist, Monarchist, Neo-Fascist, Nationalist, and other parties entering into the contest as well.

Ideological contests in the European manner are not the norm in U.S. elections because both American parties share many of the same fundamental beliefs: free enterprise, individualism, the Constitution, the Bill of Rights, and so on. Nevertheless, the differences between Democrats and Republicans on many issues—especially on affirmative action, abortion, the environment, taxes, and the role of government in the economy—are real, important, and enduring, and are becoming more distinctive.

Public Perceptions of Party Ideologies

For one thing, the Democratic and Republican parties differ in the electorate's perceptions of them. According to studies by the Center for Political Studies of the University of Michigan, 64 percent of the American people report that they see the parties as different on a whole range of issues.[19] Most accurately see the Democrats as the more **liberal** party (in the sense of favoring an active federal government, helping citizens with jobs, education, medical care, and the like) and the Republicans as the more **conservative** party (opposing such government activism and supporting business).[20] The parties also differ in terms of who supports them. Americans who classify themselves as liberals overwhelmingly support Democratic candidates; self-described conservatives overwhelmingly support Republicans. This alignment is not surprising.

Ideology in Party Platforms

Our parties also tend to write different political platforms at their conventions. Scholars have discovered persistent differences in the platforms of the two parties in terms of rhetoric (Republicans tend to talk more about opportunity and freedom), issues (Democrats worry more about poverty and social welfare), and the public policies advocated.[21]

The Ideologies of Party Activists

The activists of one party are quite different in their views from activists and voters in the other party, as well as the general public. Republican delegates to the 2000 Republican National Convention, for example, as in all recent conventions, were more conservative than Republican voters and much more conservative than the average registered voter. They were also much more hostile to affirmative action, social spending programs, and gun control than Republican voters and regis-

---

liberal

The political position that holds that the federal government has a substantial role to play in economic regulation, social welfare, and overcoming racial inequality.

conservative

The political position that holds that the federal government ought to play a very small role in economic regulation, social welfare, and overcoming racial inequality.

The overwhelming support for Newt Gingrich's Contract with America by Republican candidates for the House of Representatives in 1994 shows how strongly conservative the party became in the mid-1990s.

tered voters in general. Analogously, delegates to the Democratic National Convention in 2000 were more liberal than Democratic voters and registered voters (though not by much) and much more favorable to gun control, affirmative action, and a woman's right to an abortion than the other two groups.[22]

Party Ideologies in Action
Finally, the parties differ in what they do when they win. Republican members of Congress tend to vote differently from Democrats, the former being considerably more conservative on domestic issues. This difference translates into public policy. Republicans and Democrats produce different policies on taxes, corporate regulation, and welfare when they are in power.[23]

Growing Ideological Differences Between the Parties
The Republican party has become much more conservative since the mid-1970s, advocating free markets and less regulation, low taxes, a halt to most abortions, diminished social spending, opposition to affirmative action, and a hard line on "law and order." The party seems to have settled on a programmatic outlook in which government helps create a society where individuals are free to pursue their own happiness and to take the consequences if they fail, without government providing a minimum standard of living below which people cannot fall. This growing conservatism is a product of the increasing influence in the party of the business community, anti-tax and anti-big government groups, the white South and suburbs, and Christian fundamentalists. It is also a product of the declining influence in party affairs of the Northeastern states, the home of GOP moderates (represented in the past by such figures as Nelson Rockefeller of New York and John Chafee of Rhode Island).[24]

It is worth pointing out that not all Republicans support a consistently conservative agenda. Many candidates and party activists (especially from the Northeastern states), support abortion rights, are willing to maintain the current level of immigration, and believe government has a role to play in protecting the environment. Several present and former Republican governors, including John Engler of Michigan and Christine Whitman of New Jersey (who became head of the Environmental Protection Administration under George W. Bush), have diverged from their party's conservative mainstream on social issues, for example.

The Democratic party is split between a very liberal congressional wing—made much more liberal over the past two decades by the declining influence of Southern conservatives in the party (their House and Senate seats became mostly Republican)—and a more "centrist" wing, represented by the Democratic Leadership Council (of which Bill Clinton and Al Gore were prominent members). The former supports traditional Democratic party programs in which government plays a central role in societal improvement, leveling the playing field for all Americans regardless of race or gender, encouraging economic growth, providing substantial social safety nets, and protecting civil liberties. The latter wing of the party opposes racial quotas and set-asides and supports lower taxes, deregulation, and a crackdown on crime. During the Clinton years, the president and congressional Democrats, not surprisingly, often found themselves at loggerheads, especially over the budget, welfare reform, and trade. The trade issue has been particularly divisive for Democrats, with free-traders such as Clinton and Gore faced off against organized labor and environmentalists, important parts of the party base.

The Parties in Government and in the Electorate

Fearful of the tyrannical possibilities of a vigorous government, the framers designed a system of government in which power is so fragmented and competitive that effectiveness is unlikely. One of the roles that political parties can play in a democracy such as ours is to overcome this deadlock by persuading officials of the same party in the different branches of government to cooperate with one another on the basis of party loyalty.[25] The constitutionally designed conflict between the president and Congress can be bridged, it has been argued, when a single party controls both houses of Congress and the presidency.

We will learn in considerable detail what parties do in government in later chapters on Congress (Chapter 11), the president (Chapter 12), the executive branch (Chapter 13), and the courts (Chapter 14). In general, we will see that the parties only partially improve the coherence and responsiveness of our government. The parties seem to be the best institutions we have for making government work in a cohesive and responsive fashion—that is, when the same party controls the legislative and executive branches—but they do not consistently do the job very well. Because they are unable to command the complete loyalty and attention of their adherents or consistently direct the behavior of their officeholders, American parties are tremendously handicapped in playing this important role.

The Problem of Divided Government

For much of the last half century, Republicans controlled the presidency, while Democrats controlled one or both houses of Congress. After the 1994 election, the situation reversed, with Republicans gaining control of Congress and Democrats retaining the presidency (see Figure 9.3). After the 2000 elections, unified government returned for a few months until moderate Vermont Republican Senator James Jeffords quit his party, giving the Democrats control of the Senate. (Republicans retained control of the House and the presidency.) The 2002 congressional elections resulted in a return to unified government when the GOP won both houses of Congress.

Divided party control of the federal government has worried scholars and journalists for many years and has produced a substantial amount of literature that examines its causes and assesses its effects.[26] Many scholars and journalists believe the effects to be unfortunate. At best, they suggest, divided party control adds to the gridlock and paralysis that are built into the constitutional design of our system of government.[27] At worst, they suggest, divided party control gives rise to a state of near civil war between the two branches, in which each tries to damage the other in the interests of advancing the fortunes of its party.[28]

Some scholars have begun to argue, however, that divided party control may not be very important. They point to cases in which unified party control did not produce good results and cases in which divided control did not prevent the fashioning of coherent policy. Unified party control of government under the Democrats after the 1936 election did not guarantee a vigor-

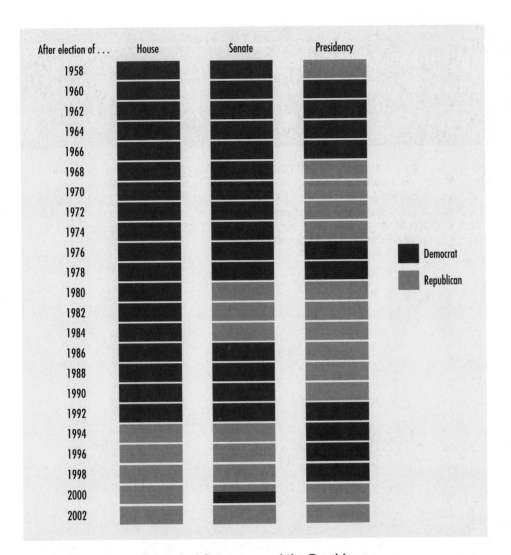

After election of . . .	House	Senate	Presidency
1958			
1960			
1962			
1964			
1966			
1968			
1970			
1972			
1974			
1976			
1978			
1980			
1982			
1984			
1986			
1988			
1990			
1992			
1994			
1996			
1998			
2000			
2002			

Democrat
Republican

FIGURE 9.3 Party Control of Congress and the Presidency

One of the most striking things about our recent political history is the persistence of split party control of the presidency and Congress. Scholars disagree about the effects of this development: Some believe it has crippled the government; others say split party control makes no difference.

ous and effective federal government in the last years of Roosevelt's New Deal. Democratic presidents Carter and Clinton did not produce impressive periods of government performance even when both enjoyed Democratic majorities in Congress. There is some evidence, moreover, that gridlock is no more prominent in periods of divided party control than in periods of unified control.[29] Having completed their studies before the appearance of intense partisan gridlock in the middle and late 1990s, however, these scholars may have seriously underestimated the detrimental effects of divided government. Anyone witnessing the closing of the federal government during the presidential–congressional budget battles during the Clinton years and the intensely partisan impeachment process cannot feel sanguine about divided government.

USING THE FRAMEWORK: Gridlock

Why were things so gridlocked in Washington for most of the 1990s?

Background: In the 1990s, official Washington not only seemed to come to a screeching halt, but there was a dramatic decline in the atmosphere of civility in Congress and in the relations between Congress and the president. Fierce partisan warfare broke out over President Clinton's health care proposal, the federal budget (which led to the closure of the federal government at one point), foreign policy issues (Haiti, Bosnia, Kosovo, and the Test Ban Treaty), abortion and, of course, the impeachment of the president. Taking a look at how structural, political linkage, and governmental factors affect party politics and policymaking in Washington will help explain the situation.

Governmental Action

Government inaction on the nation's agenda in the 1990s.

Governmental Level

• Democratic President Bill Clinton and the Republican-controlled 104th, 105th, and 106th Congresses battled over most important issues, reaching agreement on only a few of them.

Political Linkages Level

• Neither party had a commanding lead in party identification nationally. → • Congressional elections became very close and hotly contested, with control of Congress hanging in the balance every two years. → • The political parties became more ideological, with the virtual disappearance of conservative Democrats in the South and Mountain West and liberal Republicans in New England. → • Partisan warfare and scandals became standard fare in the mass media, making cooperation and civility in public affairs, in general, and between the parties, in particular, less likely.

Structural Level

• The Constitution created a system in which tension always exists between the president and Congress. → • The end of the Cold War ended the semi-crisis atmosphere that encouraged the political parties in Congress, and the Congress and the president, to cooperate with one another on a wide range of issues.

Parties in the Electorate

Parties are not only organizations and officeholders but also images in the minds of voters and potential voters, mental cues that affect the behavior of the electorate. This aspect of the parties was discussed in Chapter 5 and will be considered in greater detail in Chapter 10. We will simply reiterate the points that Americans are less inclined than in the past to identify with or to have confidence in a party and are less willing to vote a straight party ticket. Each of these factors suggests that the two major parties are no longer as central as they once were in tying people's everyday concerns to their choices in the political system. We must also note a growing distaste among the public for the parties as professional campaign organizations, with their stables of consultants and relentless advertising campaigns.

HOW DEMOCRATIC ARE WE?
Political Parties and Responsive Government

PROPOSITION: American political parties don't ensure that government is responsive and responsible to the people.

AGREE: Our parties are so loose and fragmented in an organizational sense, and often so mushy in an ideological sense, that voters do not know what they are getting when they put a party in office and cannot be assured that the majority party will be able to carry out its program, even if it wanted to do so. Matters are made worse by our constitutional system of separation-of-powers and checks-and-balances that undermines coherent government even when the presidency and Congress are held by the same party and that lead to gridlock when the two branches are controlled by different parties.

DISAGREE: Our parties are the only mechanism we have for allowing voters to decide on a program for the government and to hold elected officials responsible in a collective sense. Interest groups and social movements are much too narrow; only parties seek to be inclusive and present broad programs for public approval. Moreover, the parties are becoming better organized and more ideologically distinctive, so voters increasingly know what they are getting when they put a party in office.

THE AUTHORS: It is sad but true that our present parties are the only institution we have for ensuring responsiveness and responsibility. The rise of well-financed, professionally managed state, national, and congressional campaign organizations, which focus on television and direct mail contact with voters, has impoverished the party "grass roots," made the parties seem distant to citizens, and contributed to the decline of party identification and regard among the public. Finally, the rise in the ideological coherence of the parties, potentially a boon to responsiveness and responsibility in government when a single party controls the presidency and Congress, adds to the possibilities of gridlock in periods of divided government.

Summary

The American party system is unique among the Western democracies in several respects. First, ours is a relatively pure two-party system and has been so since the 1830s. Second, our major parties are candidate-centered, having very little power in their national party organizations to affect the behavior of individual candidates, officeholders, or state and local party organizations. American parties are less ideological than parties in other democracies, but the enduring and important differences between Democrats and Republicans are becoming more evident.

Although made up of the same two parties for well over a century, the two-party system has not been stagnant. It has undergone a series of realignments, spurred by structural changes in society and the economy, in which the relative power of the parties has shifted, as have the voting alignments of the public, the dominant political coalitions, and public policy.

The parties play an important role in government, sometimes contributing to governmental effectiveness and policy coherence. In the era of divided government, however, parties often contribute to gridlock.

Suggestions for Further Reading

Aldrich, John. *Why Parties?* Chicago: University of Chicago Press, 1995.
Uses a rational-choice perspective from economics to show that the parties we have are the product of the rational pursuit of the goals of office seekers and officeholders.

Burnham, Walter Dean. *Critical Elections and the Mainsprings of American Politics.* New York: Norton, 1970.
The classic analysis of the realignment process in the American party system.

Cohen, Jeffrey E. *American Political Parties: Decline or Resurgence?.* Washington, D.C.: CQ Press, 2001.
State-of-the-art research by leading political scientists examining whether American political parties are getting weaker and less important or getting stronger and more important.

Mayhew, David R. *Divided We Govern: Party Control, Lawmaking, and Investigations, 1946–1990.* New Haven, CT: Yale University Press, 1991.
A sophisticated attempt to assess the effect of divided government. Argues that the alarm about divided government has been overstated.

Menefee-Libey, David. *The Triumph of Campaign-Centered Politics.* New York: Chatham House, 2000.
A vivid description of how the requirements of modern campaign politics have changed the political parties.

Reichley, A. James. *The Life of the Parties: A History of American Political Parties.* New York: Free Press, 1992.
The leading history of the American party system, with special attention paid to the question of party decline in the modern era and what might be done about it.

Rosenstone, Steven J., Ray L. Behr, and Edward T. Lazarus. *Third Parties in America: Citizen Response to Major Party Failure.* Princeton, NJ: Princeton University Press, 1996.
A rigorous analysis of the conditions under which third parties and independent candidates emerge in American politics.

Internet Sources

Democratic National Committee **www.democrats.org/**
Information about Democratic party candidates, party history, convention and na-
tional committees, state parties, stands on the issues, affiliated groups, upcoming
events, and more.

The Green Party **www.greenpartyus.org**
News about the Green Party and links to state and local Green-affiliated groups.

National Political Index **http://www.politicalindex.com/**
Links to state and local parties and affiliated organizations and interest groups.

Political Resources on the Web **www.politicalresources.net/**
Information about political parties in all democratic countries.

Republican National Committee **http://www.rnc.org/**
Information about Republican party candidates, party history, convention and na-
tional committees, state parties, stands on the issues, affiliated groups, upcoming
events, and more.

The Reform Party **www.reformparty.org/**
Learn about Reform Party candidates, proposals, and issue positions.

Notes

1. David Menefee-Libey, *The Triumph of Campaign-Centered Politics* (New York: Chatham House Publishers, 2000); and Daniel M. Shea, "The Passing of Realignment and the Advent of the 'Baseless' Party System," *American Politics Quarterly* 27 (January 1997), pp. 33–57.

2. Robert A. Dahl, *On Democracy* (New Haven, CT: Yale University Press, 1998).

3. E. E. Schattschneider, *Party Government* (New York: Holt, Rinehart & Winston, 1942), p. 208.

4. Ibid.

5. See A. James Reichley, *The Life of the Parties: A History of American Political Parties* (New York: Free Press, 1992), ch. 1.

6. Steven J. Rosenstone and John Mark Hansen, *Mobilization, Participation, and Democracy in America* (New York: Macmillan, 1993).

7. E. E. Schattschneider, *The Semi-Sovereign People* (New York: Holt, Rinehart & Winston, 1960).

8. On realignment, see Walter Dean Burnham, *Critical Elections and the Mainsprings of American Politics* (New York: Norton, 1970); Walter Dean Burnham, "Critical Realignment Lives: The 1994 Earthquake," in Colin Campbell and Bert A. Rockman, eds., *The Clinton Presidency* (Chatham, NJ: Chatham House, 1996); William Nisbet Chambers and Walter Dean Burnham, eds., *The American Party Systems* (New York: Oxford University Press, 1967); Jerome Clubb, William H. Flanigan, and Nancy H. Zingale, *Partisan Realignment* (Newbury Park, CA: Sage, 1980); V. O. Key Jr., "A Theory of Critical Elections," *Journal of Politics* 17 (1955), pp. 3–18; James L. Sundquist, *Dynamics of the Party System* (Washington, D.C.: Brookings Institution, 1973).

9. C. Vann Woodward, *The Strange Career of Jim Crow* (New York: Oxford University Press, 1966).

10. John Aldrich and Richard Niemi, "The Sixth American Party System," in Stephen C. Craig, *Broken Contract: Changing Relationships Between Americans and Their Government* (Boulder, CO: Westview Press, 1996); and Walter J. Stone and Ronald B. Rapoport, "It's Perot Stupid! The Legacy of the 1992 Perot Movement in the Major-Party System, 1994–2000," *PS: Political Science and Politics* (March 2001), vol. XXXIV, no. 1, pp. 49–56.

11. Thomas Byrne Edsall and Mary D. Edsall, *Chain Reaction: The Impact of Race, Rights and Taxes on American Politics* (New York: Norton, 1991); and Stanley B. Greenberg, *Middle Class Dreams: The Politics and Power of the New American Majority* (New Haven, CT: Yale University Press, 1996).

12. Helmut Norpoth and Jerrold Rusk, "Partisan Dealignment in the American Electorate," *American Political Science Review* 76 (September 1982), pp. 719–736. Also see Larry Sabato, *The Party's Just Begun* (Glenview, IL: Scott, Foresman, 1988); Sundquist, *Dynamics of the Party System;* Martin P. Wattenberg, *The Decline of American Political Parties* (Cambridge, MA: Harvard University Press, 1994); Stanley B. Greenberg, *Middle-Class Dreams* (New York: Times Books, 1995); Everett C. Ladd, "The 1994 Congressional Elections," *Political Science Quarterly* 110, pp. 1–23.

13. The classic statement on electoral rules is Maurice Duverger, *Political Parties* (New York: Wiley, 1954).

14. Much of this discussion is drawn from Steven J. Rosenstone, Roy L. Behr, and Edward H. Lazarus, *Third Parties in America* (Princeton, NJ: Princeton University Press, 1984).

15. Roger H. Davidson and Walter J. Oleszek, *Congress and Its Members* (Washington, D.C.: CQ Press, 2002), chs. 3 and 4; and Shea, "The Passing of Realignment and the Advent of the 'Baseless' Party System."

16. Menefee-Libey, *The Triumph of Candidate-Centered Politics.*

17. J. A. Schlesinger, "The New American Political Party," *American Political Science Review* 79 (1985), pp. 1152–1169; and John Aldrich, *Why Parties?* (Chicago: University of Chicago Press, 1995).

18. Marc J. Hetherington, "Resurgent Mass Partisanship: The Role of Elite Polarization," *The American Political Science Review* (September 2001), Vol. 95, no. 1, pp. 619–632; J. L. Jackson, N. Clayton, and J. C. Green, "Issue Networks and Party Elites in 1996," in J. C. Green and D. M. Shea, eds., *The State of the Parties* (Lanham, MD: Rowman and Littlefield, 1999); and Gerald Pomper, "Parliamentary Government in the United States," in Green and Shea, eds., *The State of the Parties.*

19. *National Election Studies* (Ann Arbor: University of Michigan, 2001).

20. Hetherington, "Resurgent Mass Partisanship," p. 624.

21. Alan D. Monroe, "American Party Platforms and Public Opinion," *American Journal of Political Science* 27 (February 1983), p. 35; Gerald M. Pomper, *Elections in America* (New York: Longman, 1980), p. 169.

22. "Convention Delegates: Who They Are and How They Compare on Issues," *The New York Times* (August 14, 2000), p. A17.

23. Douglas Hibbs, *The American Political Economy* (Cambridge, MA: Harvard University Press, 1987); Dennis P. Quinn and Robert Shapiro, "Business Political Power: The Case of Taxation," *American Political Science Review* 85 (1991), pp. 851–874.

24. Thomas Byrne Edsall, *The New Politics of Inequality* (New York: Norton, 1984); Kevin P. Phillips, *Boiling Point: Democrats, Republicans, and the Decline of Middle-Class Prosperity* (New York: Random House, 1993); David Vogel, *Fluctuating*

Fortunes: The Political Power of Business in America (New York: Basic Books, 1989); Roger Davidson and Walter Oleszek, *Congress and Its Members* (Washington, D.C.: CQ Press, 2000), pp. 190–192.

25. James MacGregor Burns, *Deadlock of Democracy* (Englewood Cliffs, NJ: Prentice Hall, 1967).

26. Morris P. Fiorina, *Divided Government* (New York: Macmillan, 1992); Gary Jacobson, *The Electoral Origins of Divided Government: Competition in U.S. House Elections* (Boulder, CO: Westview Press, 1990); David R. Mayhew, *Divided We Govern: Party Control, Lawmaking, and Investigations, 1946–1990* (New Haven, CT: Yale University Press, 1991).

27. Hedrick Smith, *The Power Game* (New York: Random House, 1988), p. 652.

28. Benjamin Ginsberg and Martin Shefter, *Politics by Other Means: The Declining Significance of Elections in America* (New York: Basic Books, 1990).

29. Mayhew, *Divided We Govern.*

Chapter 10
Participation, Voting, and Elections

In This Chapter

- What the role of elections is in a democracy
- How African-Americans, women, and young people won the right to vote
- Why many Americans don't vote
- How to run for the presidency
- What part money plays in presidential elections
- How voters decide
- Why elections matter

The Contested 2000 Presidential Election

After an extraordinarily long, expensive, and, to many Americans, exhausting campaign that had sparked little interest and enthusiasm among the public, the finale of the 2000 presidential election campaign could not have been more exciting or historically significant: a near dead-heat between Republican George W. Bush and Democrat Al Gore. Excruciatingly close

presidential contests in New Hampshire, New Mexico, Wisconsin, Iowa, and Oregon; and the drama of Florida—where election officials, faced with a legally mandated recount, demands for hand recounts in selected counties, loads of absentee ballots mailed from abroad, multiple charges of ballot confusion and irregularities, and voter lawsuits—could not certify a winner until weeks after election day.

The Florida certification for George W. Bush brought his total electoral vote to 271 (compared to 267 for Al Gore) and decided the outcome of the national election, even though Gore won the national popular vote by a margin of more than half-a-million. The deadlock in Florida was broken only after the controversial intervention by the U.S. Supreme Court. In a 5–4 decision, it overturned a Florida Supreme Court ruling mandating a broad recount across the state and stopped the ballot count then underway in a number of Florida counties. This had the effect of ratifying the earlier certification of Bush's victory by Florida Secretary of State Katherine Harris. George W. Bush took office on January 20, 2001, as the first president since Benjamin Harrison in 1889 to have won the Electoral College vote but to have lost the national popular vote.

The 2000 presidential election nicely highlights the fact that we choose our presidents not by direct popular vote but by the vote of the Electoral College. It is the case, of course, that the winner of the popular vote and the winner of the electoral vote are the same almost all the time, but not always. Three times before, in 1824, 1876, and 1888, the candidate with fewer national popular votes was elected to the presidency by virtue of a majority in the Electoral College.

It is important to know that the electoral vote is what really counts in the final analysis because it shapes the strategy and tactics of the presidential campaigns. It helps explain why the campaign for the presidency is about candidates attempting to put together a package of states whose electoral votes come to a total of 270 or more. In the 2000 election each party started with a solid base of states

with a known number of electoral votes. Bush's electoral vote base was in Texas, most of the South, and the Mountain West; Gore's electoral vote base was in New York, much of New England, and California. The battle for an electoral vote majority was joined in a handful of "battleground" states, namely Florida, Pennsylvania, Ohio, Illinois, Michigan, Wisconsin, Missouri, and Iowa, where the contest could go either way and electoral votes were abundant. It was in these states that the campaigns focused most of the candidate visits and spent most of their television, radio, and print advertising dollars.

The long campaign for the presidency evoked none of the passion, acrimony, and ideological conflict that would eventually surround the tallying of the vote. From the beginning, despite occasional forays to shore up their support on the Left (Gore) and on the Right (Bush), both candidates clung to predominantly centrist and nonideological themes. Debates between the candidates and parties were mostly about alternative approaches to Social Security, education, and prescription drug benefits. Gore tried to link himself to the economic successes of the Clinton years, while also desperately trying to distance himself from the Clinton scandals, stressing that he was his own man, willing to fight every day for ordinary, hard-working Americans. Bush tried to portray himself as a "compassionate conservative," a different and less strident sort of Republican—he even chided congressional Republicans for caring too little about the poor—committed to cutting taxes and reducing the size of the federal government, yet supportive of efforts to help those who genuinely needed help. Although Green Party candidate Ralph Nader tried to push Gore from the Left and Reform Party candidate Pat Buchanan tried to pressure Bush from the Right, neither was successful in changing the main thrust of the campaign.

The presidential contest, more substantive and less heated than recent ones, failed to truly engage the public. No galvanizing issues divided the country; traditional campaign organizing themes such as the Cold War or the New Deal or the Great Society seemed beside the point in a period of American economic boom and prosperity and military and diplomatic preeminence in the world; and many important and potentially divisive issues such as race, income inequality, and American foreign policy in a post–Cold War world were hardly on the radar screen of the candidates. The issue of international terrorism did not come up at all.

The 2000 presidential election falls into the general category of elections that political scientists call the "electoral competition" or "median voter" model in which each party attempts to capture the voters in the middle of the political spectrum, while trying to hold on to as much of its base as possible. Such elections tend to be low-intensity affairs in which the sharp edges of party disagreement are softened in order to attract as many voters from the broad, nonideological, and politically unengaged middle as possible. Although there were some elements of what political scientists call "retrospective" voting in the 2000 election (many voters, for example, chose Al Gore on the grounds that he would continue the economic good times of the Clinton years; many other voters chose Bush because they wished to reject other aspects of the Clinton legacy, particularly the moral aspect), and some elements of what scholars call "prospective" voting (for example, choosing one candidate over another on the basis of the coherent, programmatic, or ideological direction being offered for

the future), both campaigns recognized that the electorate was in a nonideological mood, tired of intense partisanship and government gridlock, and not inclined to favor harsh attacks or elaborate visions of the future, and they responded accordingly. Gore's effort to paint Bush as not quite smart enough for the job, and Bush's effort to remind the public of Gore's exaggerations and questionable fundraising activities, which took up much of the campaign, were hardly the stuff of high political drama.

It is ironic, then, that the vote-tallying process in Florida and the closeness of the presidential and congressional contests in the nation led to such fierce partisan acrimony in the end. Oddly enough, however, the bitter partisanship of party leaders and professionals, and the news media's constant focus on partisan anger, failed to move the American people very much. Though polls showed that many Americans thought the election outcome to be unfair, by the time of the inauguration on January 20 a majority of Americans had come to accept the legitimacy of the Bush presidency and to express a desire to put the election controversy aside and move on. The final nail in the coffin of the 2000 election controversy was driven by the terrorist attacks on the United States on September 11, 2001. The "rally 'round the flag" reaction to these terrible events not only boosted the popularity of President Bush to record levels but turned the public's attention almost entirely to the war on terrorism and homeland security. ■

Thinking Critically About This Chapter

The story of the 2000 presidential election focuses our attention on the issue of democratic control of the national government through the electoral process and on the degree to which the public participates in this key activity of the representative democratic process.

Using the Framework You will see in this chapter that elections are affected by the different rates of participation of groups in American society and how structural factors such as constitutional rules, unequal access to resources, and cultural ideas help determine why some groups participate more than others. You will also learn how elections affect the behavior of public officials.

Using the Democracy Standard We suggest in this chapter that elections are the lynchpin of any discussion about the democratic quality of any system of government because they are, in theory, what makes popular sovereignty possible. You will see in this chapter that while elections in the United States do much to make our system democratic, they fall short of their democratic promise.

Elections and Democracy

Elections are fundamental to democratic politics, the chief means by which citizens control what their government does. Many important struggles for democracy in the United States have involved conflicts over the right to vote. But can elections actually ensure that governments will do what their people want?

Democratic theorists have suggested several ways that elections in a two-party system like that found in the United States can bring about popular control of government. We will briefly discuss three of these ways, indicating how they might work in theory and what might go wrong in practice.[1] The rest of this chapter is concerned with what actually happens in American national elections and with the question of whether these elections really bring about popular control of government.

The Prospective (or Responsible Party) Voting Model

The idea of **responsible party** elections is based on the old commonsense notion that elections should present a "real choice": Political parties should stand for different policies, the voters should choose between them, and the winning party should carry out its mandate. Political scientists call this the **prospective voting model,** meaning that voters are interested in and capable of deciding what government will do in the future.

responsible party

A political party that takes clear, distinct stands on the issues and enacts them as policy.

prospective voting model

A theory of democratic elections in which voters decide what government will do in the near future by choosing one or another responsible party.

Theory   For this system to work perfectly, each of the two parties must be cohesive and unified; each must take clear policy positions that differ significantly from the other party's positions; citizens must accurately perceive these positions and vote on the basis of them; and the winning party, when it takes office, must do exactly what it said it would do. If all these conditions are met, then the party with the more popular policy positions will win and enact its program. In such an electoral system, government will do what the majority of the voters want.[2]

Problems   Even if an election were to work exactly as the responsible party ideal dictates, however, a serious problem arises. There is no actual guarantee that either party would take policy positions that pleased the voters, only that the winning party's stand is less *unpopular* than the loser's. Also, crucial decisions about what the parties stand for and what choices they present to the voters would be made by someone other than ordinary citizens—by party leaders or perhaps by interest groups and big contributors.

Moreover, the conditions under which responsible party government is supposed to work are not fully met—and are not ever likely to be met—in the United States. The Republican and Democratic parties are not always unified on program or ideology; the parties are sometimes deliberately ambiguous on where they stand and are not always distinctly different from one another. Furthermore, the voters do not vote solely on the issues, but take other things into account when casting their ballots. And the parties do not always keep their promises once in office, nor are they often able to win control of the entire government—a precondition of any effort to transform campaign promises into policies.

Clearly, then, the responsible party idea does not correspond exactly to what happens in American elections. But we will see that it comes close enough to the truth to describe at least a part of reality. Also, theories about responsible parties provide some useful standards for judging what may be wrong with U.S. elections and how they might be improved, particularly with respect to the clarity of stands on issues.

The Electoral Competition Voting Model

electoral competition model

A form of election in which parties seeking votes move toward the median voter or the center of the political spectrum.

median voter

Refers to the voter at the exact middle of the political spectrum.

A very different, and less obvious, sort of democratic control can be found in what political scientists call the **electoral competition model** of democratic elections. In this sort of electoral model, unified parties compete for votes by taking the *most popular* positions they can. They do so by trying to take positions that will appeal to the **median voter** at the exact midpoint of the political spectrum. Both parties are therefore likely to end up standing for the *same* policies: those favored by the most voters.

Theory   Scholars have proved mathematically that if citizens' preferences are organized along a single dimension (such as the liberal–conservative continuum shown in Figure 10.1), and if parties purely seek votes, both parties will take positions exactly at the *median* of public opinion, that is, at the point where exactly one-half the voters are more liberal and one-half are more conservative. If either party took a position even a bit away from the median, the other party could easily win more votes by taking a position closer to the median.[3]

If electoral competition drives parties together in this way, and if they keep their promises, then, in theory, it should not matter which party wins; the winner enacts the policies that the most voters want. Democracy is ensured by the hidden hand of competition.

To be sure, electoral competition processes cannot ensure that the parties will educate or mobilize voters, as in a responsible party process. However, they hold out the promise that popular sovereignty and a perfectly democratic outcome—rather than just the lesser of two evils—may result from elections.

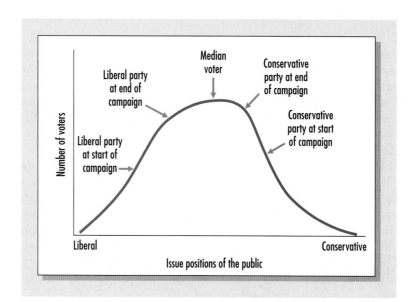

FIGURE 10.1 Electoral Competition Model

This model suggests that in the interest of winning the election, parties will move toward the median voter (where most votes are to be found) as the campaign progresses.

Problems Again, however, the conditions needed for electoral competition to work perfectly are not likely to be met in the real world. Electoral competition ensures democratic control only if the parties are unified and take stands on the issues for pure and direct vote-seeking reasons; it can break down if the parties are fragmented or ambiguous, if they care about policies for ideological reasons, or if they seek contributors' dollars rather than citizens' votes. In order for democratic control to be complete, everyone has to vote. Moreover, the voters must consider nothing but the issues (e.g., not being distracted by candidates' personalities or images) and must know exactly where the parties stand. And the parties have to keep their promises. There are reasons to doubt that any of these things will happen flawlessly.

Still, we will see that these conditions are close enough to the truth so that electoral competition does work, to a significant extent, in real elections. Indeed, electoral competition is probably one of the main reasons that government policy is significantly influenced by public opinion. Also, by looking at how actual elections deviate from the theoretical ideal of electoral competition (e.g., how money and campaign contributions sometimes push parties away from popular policies, or how politicians can sometimes fool the median voter about their real position on the issues[4]), we can see specific ways in which American elections might be improved as instruments of democracy.

The Retrospective (or Reward and Punishment) Voting Model

A third process by which elections might bring about democratic control of government is **electoral reward and punishment,** a form of election in which voters judge how well a group in power has governed and decide if they want this group to continue in office.

Theory Here the idea is that the voters simply make **retrospective,** backward-looking judgments about how well incumbent officials have done in the past, rewarding success with reelection and punishing failure by throwing the

electoral reward and punishment
The tendency to vote for the incumbents when times are good and against them when times are bad.

retrospective voting
A form of election in which voters look back at the performance of a party in power and cast ballots on the basis of how well it did in office.

According to exit polls, voters cast their ballots in the 1980 election to remove President Jimmy Carter from office, rather than to choose the conservative future offered by GOP candidate Ronald Reagan. Their vote of "no confidence" for Carter is an excellent example of "retrospective" voting.

incumbents out. The result, in theory, is that politicians who want to stay in office have strong incentives to bring about peace and prosperity and to solve problems that the American people want solved. Politicians' ambitions force them to anticipate what the public wants and to accomplish it.[5]

The reward-and-punishment process of democratic control has the advantage of simplicity. It requires very little of voters: no elaborate policy preferences, no study of campaign platforms, just judgments of how well or how badly things have been going. Also, like electoral competition, it relies on politicians' selfishness rather than their altruism. It allows time for deliberation, and it lets leaders try out experimental or temporarily unpopular policies, as long as the results work out well and please the public in time for the next election.

Problems   However, reward and punishment may be a rather blunt instrument. It gets rid of bad political leaders only after (not before) disasters happen, without guaranteeing that the next leaders will be any better. It relies on politicians *anticipating* the effects of future policies, which they cannot always do successfully. Moreover, the reward-and-punishment process focuses only on the most prominent issues and may leave room for unpopular policies on matters that are less visible. It may also encourage politicians to produce deceptively happy but temporary results that arrive just in time for Election Day and then fade away.

Web Exploration
Party Platforms and Electoral Theory

Issue: According to democratic theorists, elections can ensure popular accountability in representative democracies in three ways: by allowing the public to choose between future courses of action (responsible party government), by allowing voters to render judgments about a party's performance in office (electoral reward and punishment), and by forcing parties and candidates to offer platforms that conform to what the public wants (electoral competition).

Longman
Participate.com
2.0
Visual Literacy
State Control
and National
Platforms

Site: Access the Democratic and Republican National Committees on our Website at **www.ablongman.com/greenberg**. Go to the "Web Explorations" section for Chapter 10, open "Party Platforms and Electoral Theory," then the national committee sites for each party. At each party site, look at the official platforms passed at their respective conventions aimed at the 2000 elections.

What You've Learned: How did each party present itself during the 2000 national election cycle in terms of the models of electoral democracy described in this chapter? Did Republicans and Democrats ask voters to choose a future direction for government or ask them to simply make a judgment about the party's past performance? Or did the parties simply try to position themselves in terms of where they judged the voters to be?

HINT: You will probably discover that each of the parties shows signs of trying to do all three, although the emphasis will probably be on one.

Imperfect Electoral Democracy

We will see that each of the three processes of democratic control we have discussed works, to some extent, in American elections. On occasion, even, the three processes converge and help produce an election that is enormously consequential for the direction of the nation. The 1932 election was one of these occasions, and is described in the "Using the Framework" feature.

But none of the three processes works well enough to guarantee perfectly democratic outcomes most of the time. In certain respects, they conflict: Responsible parties and electoral competition, for example, tend to push in opposite directions. In other respects, all three processes require similar conditions that are not met in reality.

To pin down politicians' responsibility, all three require more unified political parties than we actually have. Similarly, they cannot ensure government responsiveness to all citizens unless *all* citizens have the right to vote, exercise that right, and have their votes counted. Unfortunately, millions of Americans cannot or do not go to the polls, and many have their ballots invalidated. Their voices are not heard; political equality is not achieved.

Another problem for all three processes is that money, organizational resources, and active campaigning—not just citizens' policy preferences and votes—may influence the stands that parties take and the outcomes of elections. Thus, money givers, activists, and the leaders of organized groups have more influence than ordinary citizens do; again, political equality is not realized.

The Nature of American Elections

American elections differ quite dramatically from those of most other democratic countries. The differences are the result of rules—mainly found in the Constitution but also in federal statutes and judicial decisions—that define offices and tell how elections are to be conducted. Here are the distinguishing features of elections in the United States:

Longman
Participate.com 2.0
Comparative
**Comparing
Voting and
Elections**

The United States Has More Elections Than Any Other Democratic Country
In some sense, we are "election happy" in the United States. We not only elect the president and members of Congress (senators and representatives), but also, being a federal system, we elect governors, state legislators, and (in most states) judges. In addition, state constitutions allow autonomy for counties, cities, and towns, and all of their top officials are elected by the people. We also elect school boards in most places, and the top positions in special districts (water or conservation districts, for example). And then there are the many state and local ballot initiatives that add to the length and complexity of the ballot at election time.

Elections in the United States Are Separate and Independent from One Another
Not only do we have a multitude of elections, but the election to fill each particular office is separate and independent from the others. In parliamentary systems, one votes for a party, and the party that wins a majority gets to appoint a whole range of other officials. The majority party in the British parliament (the legislative branch), for example, chooses the Prime Minister and cabinet ministers (the executive branch) who run the government. The government, in turn, appoints officials to many posts that are filled by elections here. In the United States, the president and members of Congress are

USING THE FRAMEWORK: Elections Bring the New Deal

Have elections ever changed the course of American government?

Background: Occasionally in American history, a national election is so consequential that it alters the overall direction of government policy and the role of government in the United States. The election of Franklin Delano Roosevelt and an overwhelmingly Democratic Congress in the 1932 elections was just such a moment. In the first 100 days of his administration, Roosevelt launched his New Deal, convincing Congress to pass bills to regulate the banking and securities industries, to bail out failing banks and protect the deposits of the public, to launch public works and relief efforts, and to provide price supports for farmers. This revolution in the role of the federal government was made possible by the 1932 elections, but to fully understand what happened, structural, political linkage, and governmental factors have to be taken into account.

Governmental Action

The New Deal is launched.

Governmental Level

• Franklin Roosevelt → interpreted the 1932 election as a mandate for immediate and far-reaching actions by the federal government to meet the crisis of the Great Depression.

• Roosevelt mobilized → business and labor leaders, as well as the public, behind his emergency program.

• The Democratic-controlled Congress, aware of Roosevelt's enormous popularity, and concerned about the national crisis, pass all of the president's emergency measures.

Political Linkages Level

• Public opinion → strongly supported a greater role for the federal government in fighting the depression.

• Social disorder → was widespread, leading to concerns that the country was near the point of collapse.

• Social movements → that demanded government action were growing and making their presence felt.

• Democrats → won big majorities in the House (313 out of 435 total seats) and the Senate (59 of 96 seats).

• Roosevelt won an overwhelming victory in the 1932 presidential election, tallying 472 electoral votes to Hoover's 59.

Structural Level

• The 1932 election was → held in the midst of the Great Depression, with unemployment reaching 33 percent, bank failures at an all-time high, and industrial and farm production at 50 percent of their levels in the mid-1920s.

• The preamble to the Constitution says that the Constitution was intended to create a government that would "…insure Domestic tranquility…[and]…promote the general Welfare."

The United States depends more on direct elections to fill its public offices than other democratic countries, contributing to more frequent elections and longer ballots than elsewhere.

elected independently from one another, as are governors, state legislators, mayors of cities, city councils, and school boards.

Elections Fill Government Positions That Have Fixed Terms of Office
The office of president of the United States is fixed at four years, representatives serve for two years, and Senators for six. At the state level, terms of office for all important elected positions are fixed, whether governors or legislators. The same holds true for county, city, and town elected offices. In parliamentary systems, the government can call an election at any time within a certain number of years (in Britain, it is 5 years), timing the election to maximize chances for reelection. One implication of fixed elections in the United States is that presidents cannot call for new elections in hopes of changing the party mix in Congress to their advantage. It also means that an unpopular president can stay in office until the next election, since there is no method to remove him other than by impeachment.

National (and State-Wide) Elections Are Held on a Fixed Date
The Constitution sets elections for president and members of Congress for the first Tuesday in November. States have generally followed suit for election of governors and members of the legislature. One implication, related to the fixed terms of offices described above, is that neither presidents nor governors can time elections to their political advantage. Another implication is that Tuesday elections may cut down on participation. In other democracies, elections are held either on the weekend or on days that are declared a national holiday.

Elections in the United States Are Almost Always of the "First Past the Post" Type, in Which Only a Single Person Is Elected
Winners in most elections in the United States are those who win the most votes—not necessarily a majority—in a particular electoral district. This type of election is often called "first past the post," as in a horse race where the winner is the first past the finish line. This includes Congressional elections and presidential contests for electoral votes in each of the states. We do not have

proportional representation in national level races, nor do we have "run-off" elections between the top two vote getters in presidential or congressional elections to ensure a majority victor.

Political Participation

In this section, we turn our attention to political participation. For elections to be democratic—whether in the prospective, electoral competition, or retrospective voting models—participation in elections and campaign activities must not only be at high levels, but also must not vary substantially across social groups in the population (that is, by race, gender, income, occupation, religion, ethnicity, region, and so on), or else the principle of political equality would be violated.

Political **participation** is political activity by individual citizens. It includes **unconventional participation,** such as demonstrating, boycotting, and the like (discussed in Chapter 8), and also **conventional participation,** such as writing letters to the editor on political issues, contacting officials, going to public meetings, working in campaigns, and giving money, which we focus on here. The most basic form of conventional political participation, the one that plays the most central part in theories of democratic control through elections, is the act of voting.

Expansion of the Franchise

Until passage of the Fourteenth and Fifteenth Amendments after the Civil War, it was up to each state to determine who within its borders was eligible to vote. In the early years of the United States, many of the states limited the legal right to vote—called the **franchise**—quite severely. In fact, a majority of people could not vote at all. Slaves, Native Americans, and women were excluded altogether. In most states, white men without a substantial amount of property were not allowed to vote. In some states, white men with certain religious beliefs were excluded.

One of the most important developments in the political history of the United States, an essential part of the struggle for democracy, has been the expansion of the right to vote. The extension of the franchise has been a lengthy and uneven process, spanning 200 years.

White Male Suffrage   The first barriers to fall were those concerning property and religion. So strong were the democratic currents during Thomas Jefferson's presidency (1801–1809) and in the years leading up to the election of Andrew Jackson in 1828 that by 1829, property and religious requirements had been dropped in all states except North Carolina and Virginia. That left universal **suffrage,** or the ability to vote, firmly in place for most adult white males in the United States.[6] Most of Europe, including Britain, did not achieve this degree of democracy until after World War I.

Blacks, Women, and Young People   Despite this head start for the United States compared with the rest of the world, the struggle to expand the suffrage to include African-Americans, women, and young people proved difficult and painful. Ironically, universal white male suffrage was often accompanied by the withdrawal of voting rights from black freedmen, even in states that did not permit slavery.[7] It took the bloody Civil War to free the slaves and the Fifteenth Amendment to the U.S. Constitution (1870) to extend the right

participation
Political activity, including voting, campaign activity, contacting officials, and demonstrating.

unconventional participation
Political activity in the form of demonstrations or protests.

conventional participation
Political activity related to elections (voting, persuading, and campaigning) or to contacting public officials.

franchise
The right to vote.

suffrage
The right to vote.

to vote to all black males, in both North and South. Even so, most blacks were effectively disfranchised in the South by the end of the nineteenth century and remained so until the 1960s civil rights movement and the Voting Rights Act of 1965 (see Chapter 1).

Women won the right to vote in 1920 with the Nineteenth Amendment to the Constitution, after a long political battle. (See the opening vignette in Chapter 8 for details of this struggle.) Residents of the District of Columbia were allowed to vote in presidential—but not congressional—elections after 1961, and 18- to 20-year-olds gained the franchise only in 1971.

The result of these changes at the state and national levels was an enormous increase in the proportion of Americans who were legally eligible to vote: from about 23 percent of the adult population in 1788–1789 to nearly 98 percent—practically all citizens except convicted felons and those in mental institutions—by the beginning of the 1970s.

Direct Partisan Elections   A related trend has involved the more direct election of government officials, replacing the old indirect methods that insulated officials from the public. By the time of the Jefferson–Adams presidential campaign of 1800, which pitted the new Republican and Federalist parties against each other, most state legislatures had stopped picking the presidential electors themselves (as the Constitution permits). Instead, the legislatures allowed a popular vote for electors, most of whom were pledged to support the presidential candidate of one party or the other.

This is the same system we use today: In practically every state, there is a winner-take-all popular vote for a slate of electors, who are pledged ahead of time to a particular candidate. In fact, only the name of the candidate and the party to whom the electors are pledged, not the names of the electors we are actually voting for, appear on the ballot. Thus, when the winning electors meet as the **electoral college** in their respective states and cast ballots to elect the president, their actions are generally controlled by the popular vote that chose

electoral college

Representatives of the states who formally elect the president; the number of electors in each state is equal to the total number of its senators and congressional representatives.

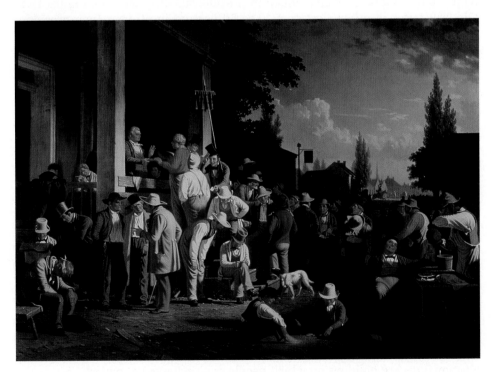

Early U.S. elections were poorly organized and hard to get to. In addition, only a small proportion of the population was eligible to vote.

them. This system, odd and cumbersome as it is, almost always ensures that American citizens choose their president more or less directly (though not in the 2000 Bush–Gore election).

By 1840, the parties had started nominating presidential candidates in national conventions instead of congressional caucuses. Later still, the parties began letting voters elect many convention delegates directly, in primaries, instead of having party activists choose them through state caucuses or state conventions. These innovations have probably increased the democratic control of government, although we will see that each of them has antidemocratic features, too.

The direct popular election of U.S. senators did not replace their being chosen by state legislatures until 1913, with the Seventeenth Amendment to the Constitution. Since 1913, all members of the Senate have been subject to direct choice by the voters.

Taken together, the expansion of the franchise and the development of direct, two-party elections have represented major successes in the struggle for democracy. But victory is not yet complete.

Low Voting Turnout

During the first 100 years or so of the United States' existence, not only did more and more people gain the right to vote but higher and higher proportions of eligible voters actually turned out on election day and voted. It is not easy to be sure of the exact **turnout** percentages because of data inaccuracies and voting fraud, but in presidential elections, the figure of roughly 11 percent of eligible voters who turned out in 1788–1789 jumped to about 31 percent in 1800 (when Thomas Jefferson was first elected) and to about 57 percent in 1828 (Andrew Jackson's first victory). By 1840, the figure had reached 80 percent, and it stayed at about that level until 1896.[8]

The disturbing fact is that today, a much smaller proportion of people vote than did during most of the nineteenth century. Since 1912, only about 50 to 65 percent of Americans have voted in presidential elections (see Figure 10.2) and still fewer in other elections: 40 to 50 percent in off-year (non-presidential-year) congressional elections and as few as 10 to 20 percent in primaries and minor local elections. In recent years, the turnout rate as a percentage of the voting age population has dropped to the lower end of those ranges, though it is higher if we calculate turnout in terms of eligible voters.

Most observers consider low turnout to be a serious problem for democracy in America, particularly because (as we will see) people who vote tend to be different from those who do not. Nonvoters do not get an equal voice in political choices. Political equality, one of the key elements of democracy, is violated.

Causes of Low Turnout
Why do so few Americans participate in elections? Scholars have identified several possible factors.

Barriers to Voting In the United States, only citizens who take the initiative to register before an election are permitted to vote. People who move from one community to another, for example, must register to vote in their new location. In one presidential election, about 35 percent of the nonvoters, but only 16 percent of voters, said that they had moved in the past two years.[9]

In most European countries with high turnout rates, the government, rather than individual citizens, is responsible for deciding who is listed as eligible to vote. In some countries, such as Belgium and Italy, moreover, citizens are *required* to vote and may be fined if they don't. Also, in most countries, election days are holidays on which people don't have to go to work.

turnout

The proportion of eligible voters who actually vote in a given election.

Longman
Participate.com
2.0
Participation
**The Prepared
Voter Kit**

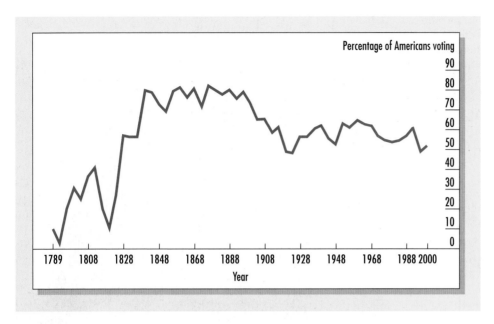

FIGURE 10.2 The Rise and Fall of Turnout in Presidential Elections, 1789–2000

Turnout in presidential elections rose sharply during the nineteenth century but declined in the twentieth century.

Source: U.S. Bureau of the Census; and "Election Summary," *The New York Times* (November 9, 2000), p. A1. From 1920, the Census Bureau has calculated voting turnout as the percentage of the voting age population voting.

The United States might increase political equality and popular sovereignty by making voting easier. One way to do so would be to ease registration requirements,[10] perhaps allowing registration by postcard or same-day registration at polling places. It is worth noting that voting turnout in the United States among those who have registered to vote hovers at about 85 percent—about as high as most Western European countries—and that voting participation in states that allow same-day registration is significantly higher than in other states.[11] These findings suggest that the registration requirement for voting is probably a significant barrier to participation, because participation rates go up when such barriers are lowered. The federal "motor voter" law passed in 1993, providing for registration in motor vehicle bureaus and other government offices, represents an important attempt to lower the registration barrier in the United States.

Another way to increase participation would be to ease the voting act itself. Suggestions include making every election day a holiday, as is done in most Western European countries; allowing an extended voting period, such as the two-and-a-half weeks tried in Texas; broadening the right of absentee voting, as in California; or allowing voting by mail over an extended period, as in Oregon.

Lack of Attractive Choices   Some scholars believe that the nature of the political parties and the choices that they offer also affect turnout. Countries with proportional representation and multiparty systems—that is, with diverse and competitive parties from which to choose—have averaged an 83 percent turnout rate, whereas single-district, plurality-vote countries (which usually have just two parties) have had a voter turnout rate that is closer to 70 percent. Many American citizens may not like the candidates of either of the major parties well enough to bother voting for them and see no reason to vote for a third-party or independent candidate who has no chance of winning.

In Oregon, voting entirely by mail (or by dropping off ballots in convenient collection boxes) has saved the state money and increased turnout.

Alienation That many Americans felt apathetic toward or alienated from politics and government undoubtedly contributed to the declines in turnout that began in the late 1960s.[12] Such unsettling events as the assassination of popular leaders (John F. Kennedy, Robert Kennedy, Martin Luther King Jr.), the Vietnam War, urban unrest, and the Watergate and Iran-Contra scandals surely played a role in the decline in voting.[13] More recently, the turn of the mass media to "infotainment" and scandals as staples of what they do, has probably discouraged potential voters. Some scholars blame the increase in negative campaign advertising as a leading culprit, although other scholars disagree, saying that such ads sometimes even spur people to vote.[14]

Lack of Voter Mobilization by the Parties Another reason why voting turnout is low may be tied to the failure of the political parties to rouse low-income citizens, especially African-Americans and Latinos. In recent years, neither the Republican nor the Democratic party has seemed very eager to increase the number of voters among the poor.[15] Republicans have traditionally avoided mobilizing low-income Americans in favor of more privileged ones. Democrats have made occasional forays but have probably been worried that low-income people might support candidates such as Jesse Jackson or Al Sharpton, who are more liberal than most party officials. Increasingly, as suggested in Chapter 9, the parties also seem less interested in involving the grass roots and more interested in raising soft money from big donors to run highly professionalized but distant campaigns.[16]

Increase in the Number of People Who Are Ineligible to Vote Recall from the "By the Numbers" feature in Chapter 1 that the number of people living in the United States who are not eligible to vote—mainly, recent immigrants and convicted felons—has increased substantially over the past 25 years or so. The apparent decline in voting turnout (where turnout is measured in terms of the total population over the age of 18) may be an artifact of the measure we have been using. A more accurate measure (in which turnout is measured in terms of the total population eligible to vote) shows that voter turnout has held steady for the past several decades, though it still remains lower than turnout in other wealthy democratic countries.

Campaigning Involvement and Contacting Public Officials   Despite the relatively low voter turnout levels in the United States, however, Americans are actually more likely than people in other countries to participate actively in campaigns.[17] During the 1996 presidential campaign, some 7 percent of adults said they gave money to a party or candidate, 9 percent said they had attended political meetings, 10 percent had attended a political rally, and 4 percent had worked actively in a campaign organization.[18] Much the same thing is true of contacting public officials; about one-third (34 percent) of Americans say they have done so during the past year, most often with local elected officials.[19] Americans are also far more likely than citizens in other democracies to be involved in organizations, of both the private and public variety (see Chapter 7), that play such an important role in our electoral politics.[20]

Who Participates?

Not all Americans participate equally in politics; the evidence shows that political participation varies a great deal according to people's income, education, age, and ethnicity. This means that some kinds of people have more representation and influence with elected officials than others and, other things being equal, they are more likely to have their preferences and interests reflected in what government does.

Longman
Participate.com
2.0
Visual Literacy
Voter Turnout:
Who Votes?
Do Americans
Vote as Much
as Other
Citizens?

Income and Education

For the most part, politically active people tend to be those with higher-than-average incomes and more formal education.[21] These people are also more likely to vote. In 2000, 75 percent of those with incomes of $75,000 or above said they had voted, but only 49 percent of those with incomes under $35,000 said they had done so. In 2000, 75 percent of college graduates reported that they had voted, but only 53 percent of high school graduates and 38 percent of those who had not graduated from high school had done so (see Figure 10.3).

Some statistical analyses have indicated that the crucial factor in voter turnout is level of formal education. When other factors are controlled, college-educated people are much more likely to tell interviewers that they have voted than are the less educated. There are several possible reasons: People with more education learn more about politics, are less troubled by registration requirements, and are more confident in their ability to affect political life.

At the same time, citizens with lower incomes are also less likely to work in campaigns, give money, contact officials, and the like. Wealthier Americans, who have more time, more money, and more knowledge of how to get things done, tend to be much more active politically. As a result, they may have more political clout than their fellow citizens.

Race and Ethnicity

In the past, fewer black people than whites voted, but now the proportions are more nearly equal: 62 percent of whites and 57 percent of blacks voted in 2000 (see Figure 10.3). The remaining differences result from blacks' lower average

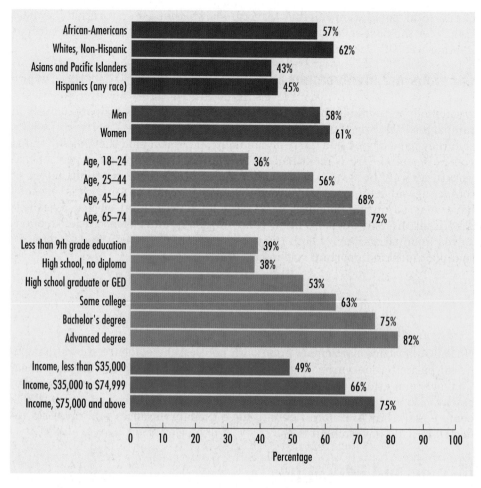

FIGURE 10.3 2000 Presidential Election Turnout by Social Group

Age, education, race, ethnicity, income, and gender all affect voting habits. Members of certain social groups are more likely to vote in elections than others.
Source: U.S. Bureau of the Census.

Hispanics have the potential to be an important force in American politics, but low registration and voting rates have limited their influence until quite recently.

levels of income and education. Blacks are at least equally likely to vote, and sometimes more likely, than whites of similar educational and income backgrounds.

Hispanics, however, have historically had very low participation rates, but things may be changing; though only 45 percent voted in 2000, this was a significant jump from 1996 when only 27 reported voting. Many Hispanics are discouraged from participating by low incomes, language problems, or suspicion of government authorities. This recent jump in the turnout rate for Hispanics has made a difference in states where Hispanic voters are concentrated: California, Texas, and Florida.

Voting has also been relatively low among Asian-Americans; only 43 percent reported voting in 2000. However, Asian-American individuals and organizations have become more active in local politics and have increased campaign contributions to candidates and parties.

Age

The very young are less likely than their elders to vote: Only 36 percent of 18- to 24-year-olds did so in 2000, compared with 72 percent of 65- to 74-year-olds. Young people tend to be less rooted in communities, less familiar with registration and voting procedures, and less clear about what stake they have in elections.[22]

Gender

The gender gap in voting and other forms of political participation disappeared in the United States by the end of the 1980s.[23] Indeed, in the 2000 presidential election, women voted at slightly higher rates than men (again, see Figure 10.3). This marks a dramatic change over the past two decades and may be traced to the improvement in the educational attainments of women; the entrance of more women than ever into the paid workforce; and the increased importance of issues such as pay equity and abortion on the American political agenda.

Does It Matter Who Votes?

Some observers have argued that it doesn't matter if many people don't vote because their preferences aren't much different from those who do; the results would be about the same if everyone voted. In some elections, nonvoters have shown support for the same candidate who won, so their votes would apparently have changed nothing,[24] and some surveys have indicated that nonvoters' policy preferences differ little from those of voters.

However, we should not be too quick to accept these arguments, just as few now accept the nineteenth-century view that there was no need for women to vote because their husbands could protect their interests. Even when the expressed preferences of nonvoters or non-participators do not look very distinctive, their objective circumstances, and therefore their needs for government services, may differ markedly.[25] Latinos, the young, and those with low incomes might benefit from government programs that are of less interest to other citizens. A political system that included and mobilized these people vigorously might produce quite different government policies. Of course, we cannot be sure, but one sign of what a difference participation can make is that when black Americans won effective voting rights, the number of elected black officials rose sharply and non-black politicians and officials paid more attention to black constituents (see Chapters 1 and 8).

In any case, broader participation in U.S. elections would increase popular sovereignty and political equality and would thus contribute to democracy. The limited number of Americans who vote is one major respect in which the struggle for democracy has not fully succeeded.

Campaigning for Office

The ideas we discussed about how elections might ensure democratic policy-making all depend in various ways on what sorts of choices are presented to the voters. It makes a difference what kind of people run for office, whether they take clear policy stands, whether those stands differ from each other, and whether they stand for what the average voter wants. In evaluating how democratic our elections are, therefore, we need to examine what kinds of alternatives are put before the voters in campaigns. In this chapter, we focus on presidential campaigns. Congressional campaigns are addressed in Chapter 11.

Contending for the Party Presidential Nomination

The major party candidates for president of the United States are formally chosen well before the November election, and are effectively chosen even before the parties hold nominating conventions. Candidates are drawn from a rather small pool. Despite what some parents tell their children, not every American has a significant chance of becoming president or of being nominated for president by a major party.

Longman
Participate.com
2.0
Comparative
Comparing
Political
Campaigns

Who Has a Chance   In any given presidential election, only a handful of candidates are serious possibilities. So far in American history, these have virtually always been middle-aged or elderly white Protestant men with extensive formal educations, fairly high incomes, and substantial experience as public figures—usually as government officials (especially governors or senators) or military heroes. Movie stars, media commentators, business executives, and others who would be president almost always have to perform lesser government service before they are seriously considered for the presidency. Ronald Reagan, for example, most of whose career was spent acting in motion pictures and on television, served as governor of California before being elected president.

In recent years, the presidency has been practically monopolized by former governors such as Bill Clinton and George W. Bush (who have demonstrated executive ability) and vice-presidents (who have had a close look at how the job is done). The single best stepping-stone to becoming president is clearly the vice-presidency, which is usually filled by former senators or governors. Since 1900, 5 of the 18 presidents have succeeded from the vice-presidency after the president's death or resignation, and two others, Nixon and Bush (the elder), were former vice-presidents elected in their own right.

Serious candidates for president almost invariably represent mainstream American values and policy preferences. Seldom does an "extreme" candidate get very far. Serious candidates are also generally acceptable to the business community and have enthusiastic support from at least some sectors of industry or finance. And they must be considered "presidential" by the news media.

Getting Started   A person who wants to run for the presidency usually begins at least two or three years before the election by testing the waters, asking friends and financial backers if they will support a run, and observing how

Elizabeth Dole's bid to become the first woman presidential nominee of one of the two major parties ended early when she was unable to attract much financial support or support among Republican voters. In 2002, however, she won a tight contest for the Senate seat from North Carolina.

people react to the mythical "Great Mentioner." A friendly journalist may write that Senator Blathers "has been mentioned" as a smart, attractive, strong candidate; Blathers waits to see whether anyone agrees. The would-be candidate may commission a national survey to check for name recognition and a positive image. He or she may put together an exploratory committee to round up private endorsements, commitments, and financial contributions, perhaps setting up private political action committees to gather money.

If all goes well in the early stages, the presidential aspirant becomes more serious, assembling a group of close advisers, formulating strategy, officially announcing his or her candidacy, forming a fund-raising operation, and putting together organizations ("Draft Blathers" or "Citizens for Blathers" committees) in key states. Early money is crucial to finance organization and advertising and to qualify for federal matching funds later.[26] And it is a clear sign that party big whigs and associated interest groups take the candidacy seriously. For all of these reasons, those who fail to raise early money almost always fail in the first primaries and eventually drop out. By October 1999, months before the first primary, George W. Bush had already gathered $57 million, discouraging several potential rivals; Steve Forbes had set aside almost as much from his personal fortune.

One important early decision involves which state primaries, caucuses, and straw votes to enter. Each entry takes a lot of money, energy, and organization, and any loss is damaging; many candidates drop out after just a few early defeats, as Steve Forbes and Gary Bauer did in 2000. To win the nomination, it is generally necessary to put together a string of primary victories.

Deciding on the theme of the campaign and the strategy to deliver the message is increasingly in the hands of hired pollsters and campaign consultants.[27] Alternative approaches to themes, messages, and issues are proposed; tested with the public in focus groups and surveys; and then crafted into stump speeches, television and radio spots, and Web pages.

Primaries and Caucuses
Party nominees for president are officially selected every four years at national party **conventions,** made up of state party delegations from around the country. Since the 1970s, most of the delegates to

Longman
Participate.com
2.0
Simulation
You Are a Professional Campaign Manager

convention

A gathering of delegates who nominate a party's presidential candidate.

Senator John McCain acknowledges his supporters after his upset of front-runner George W. Bush in the 2000 GOP New Hampshire primary. Although McCain won a handful of additional primaries, he was unable to hold off the Bush onslaught and lost his nomination bid.

primary elections

State elections in which delegates to national presidential nominating conventions are chosen.

caucus

A meeting of party activists to choose delegates to a national presidential nominating convention.

the conventions have been chosen in state **primary elections,** with direct voting by citizens. (Some primaries are open to all voters, as in the 2000 GOP primaries in South Carolina and Michigan; others are closed, reserved for those who register with the party whose primary election it is.) The Democrats' popularly elected delegates are supplemented by "superdelegates," usually members of Congress or local officials. A few states use **caucuses,** where active party members and officials choose delegates to state conventions, which in turn select the delegates to the national convention.

Because the states and the parties—not the federal government—control this nominating process, the system is a disorganized, even chaotic one, and it changes from one election to the next. Some states have primaries for both parties on the same day (including the all-important New Hampshire primaries); others hold primaries for the parties on separate dates. States are particularly anxious that they are not ignored, so an increasing number of them have moved their primary dates forward in the calendar. States with late primaries, even very large ones such as California, have discovered in recent elections that the winners of early primaries had, for all intents and purposes, sewed up the party nominations, discounting the importance of their own primaries. As a result, the primary season was "front-loaded" in 2000, with the bulk of delegates selected for both parties between the New Hampshire primaries on February 1 and the Illinois primaries on March 21.

It is especially important for a candidate to establish momentum by winning early primaries and caucuses. Early winners get press attention, financial contributions, and better standings in the polls as voters and contributors decide they are viable candidates and must have some merit if people in other states have supported them. All these factors—attention from the media, money, and increased popular support—help the candidates who win early contests go on to win more and more contests.[28]

Since 1952, no national party convention has taken more than one ballot to nominate its candidate for the presidency, and the pre-convention front-runner has always been the nominee. Now the trick is to win delegates in primaries and caucuses, which, in reality, decide the nomination before the convention ever takes place.[29]

The Convention Because the front-runner now comes to the national convention with enough delegates to win on the first ballot, the gathering has become a coronation ceremony in which pre-pledged delegates ratify the selection of the leading candidate, accept that candidate's choice for the vice-presidency, and put on a colorful show for the media and the country. Enthusiasm and unity are staged for the national television audience; it is a disaster if serious conflicts break out or the timing goes wrong.

The evidence from polls indicates that at virtually all recent national conventions, the party nominee has been the surviving candidate who has had the most support from rank-and-file party identifiers in the nation as a whole. The candidates who have survived the hurdles of raising money, mobilizing activists, and winning primary votes do not, of course, necessarily include the most popular potential presidents in the country; if they did, Colin Powell would probably have won the Republican presidential nomination in 1996. And the big differences between the delegates of the two parties tend to push the two parties' nominees and issue positions away from each other, in a

The impression conveyed by political conventions can have an important impact on elections. The apparent unhappiness of many anti-Vietnam War delegates with their party's selection at the 1968 Democratic convention in Chicago severely damaged the campaign of nominee Hubert Humphrey. In contrast, the 1980 Republican convention that selected Ronald Reagan as its nominee more nearly resembled a coronation and gave Reagan and the GOP a fast start in the fall campaign.

responsible party rather than a purely electoral competition process. Still, the parties do try to appeal to the voters.

Nomination Politics and Democracy

What does all this have to do with democratic control of government? Several things. On the one hand, as we have indicated, the nomination process has some success in coming up with candidates who take stands with wide popular appeal, much as electoral competition theories dictate. On the other hand, as the sharp differences between Republican and Democratic convention delegates suggest (see Table 10.1), Republican and Democratic nominees tend to differ in certain systematic ways, in responsible party fashion. Party platforms—the parties' official statements of their stand on issues—tend to include appeals to average voters but also distinctive appeals to each party's constituencies.

Both these tendencies might be considered good for democracy. However, the crucial role of party activists and money givers in selecting candidates means that nominees and their policy stands are chosen partly to appeal to party elites and financial contributors, rather than to ordinary voters. Thus, neither party's nominee may stand for what ordinary citizens want, the result being voter dissatisfaction and no ideal democratic outcome.

Longman
Participate.com
2.0
Visual Literacy
Why Is It So
Hard to Defeat
an Incumbent?

Incumbents

We have been focusing on how outsiders and political challengers try to win party nominations. Things are very different for incumbent presidents seeking reelection, like Bill Clinton in 1996 or George H. W. Bush

---

TABLE 10.1 Comparing Major Party Convention Delegates to Other Americans

	Delegates to Democratic National Convention	Democratic Voters	All Voters	Republican Voters	Delegates to Republican National Convention
Very liberal or somewhat liberal	34	34	23	11	1
Very conservative or somewhat conservative	4	16	31	49	57
Favor programs which make efforts to help minorities get ahead to make up for past discrimination	83	59	51	44	29
Believe the penalty for murder should be the death penalty rather than prison	20	46	51	55	60
Believe government should do more to solve national problems	73	44	33	21	4
Believe abortion should be generally available to those who want it	71	48	36	25	14
Favor tax-financed school vouchers to help parents pay for private or religious schooling	10	41	47	53	71

Source: *New York Times*/CBS News poll, *The New York Times*, August 14, 2000, p. A1.

in 1992. These candidates must also enter and win primaries, but they have the machinery of government working for them and, if times are reasonably good, a unified party behind them. They campaign on the job, taking credit for policy successes while discounting or blaming others, such as Congress, for failures. Winning renomination as president is usually easy, except in cases of disaster such as the 1968 Vietnam War debacle for Lyndon Johnson.

The Autumn Campaign

Incumbents and challengers alike, having won a party nomination, must face the autumn campaign, which traditionally began in early September (on Labor Day) but now tends to start right after the conventions or even earlier. In 2000, for example, George W. Bush and Al Gore were aiming fire at each other by March and April.

For the general election, if not before, the candidates set up a campaign organization in each state, sending aides to coordinate backers and local party leaders. Intense money raising continues, and a new round of public financing kicks in. Candidates plan itineraries to make three or four speeches in different media markets each day, concentrating on big states with large blocs of electoral votes but also touching the whole country. In all of this, hired pollsters and campaign consultants are deeply involved, playing a role in virtually all tactical and strategic decision making.[30]

A new media blitz begins, with many brief spot commercials on television, including "attack" ads such as Clinton's in 1992 mocking George Bush's "read my lips, no new taxes" pledge (which he did not keep) and Dole's in 1996

Longman
Participate.com 2.0
Simulation
You Are a Presidential Campaign Consultant

Longman
Participate.com 2.0
Timeline
Television and Presidential Campaigns

In 1988, a Republican group used the case of Willie Horton, a convicted murderer who raped a woman while on furlough from a Massachusetts prison, to imply that Democratic presidential candidate Michael Dukakis, the governor of Massachusetts at the time, was soft on crime.

pointing to Clinton's flawed character. Political consultants use voter focus groups to identify hot-button emotional appeals. Negative advertising has been heavily criticized as simplistic and misleading, but it has often proved effective and is difficult to control or counteract.

Another element of strategy is to get potential supporters registered and to the polls. Organized labor often energizes turnout campaigns for the Democrats, and conservative Christian groups do so for the Republicans. As we have noted, low-income and minority citizens have sometimes been ignored by both major parties.

Informing Voters
What kinds of information do voters get in presidential campaigns? Among other things, voters get information on the candidates' stands on the issues, their past performances, and their personal characteristics.

Issues   Some of the information voters get concerns issues. In accord with electoral competition theories, both the Republican and the Democratic candidates usually try to appeal to the average voter by taking similar, popular stands on policy, especially foreign policy. Gore and Bush both stayed close to the center in 2000, as did Clinton and Dole in 1996. But as responsible party theories suggest, Republican and Democratic candidates usually do differ somewhat on a number of issues, such as medical care, federal aid to education, prescription drug programs, tax cuts, social welfare, civil rights, the environment, and abortion. On these issues, the Democratic candidate tends to take a more liberal stand than the Republican, just as Democratic party identifiers, activists, money givers, and convention delegates tend to be more liberal than their Republican counterparts.

Past Performance   Often candidates talk about past performance and future goals. The "outs" blame the "ins" for wars, recessions, and other calamities. The "ins" brag about how they have brought peace and prosperity and paint a warm picture of a glorious future, without saying exactly how it will come about.

Incumbent presidents, of course, can do things that accurately or inaccurately suggest successful performance. They can try to schedule recessions for off years, pumping up the economy in time for reelection. Or they can make dramatic foreign policy moves just before election day, like Nixon's 1972 trips to the Soviet Union and China.

Personal Characteristics   Most of all, however, voters get a chance to learn about the real or alleged personal characteristics of the candidates. Even when the candidates are talking about something else, they give an impression of either competence or incompetence. Jimmy Carter, for example, emphasized his expertise as a "nuclear engineer," whereas Gerald Ford was haunted by films of him stumbling on airplane ramps.

Candidates also come across as warm or cold. Dwight D. Eisenhower's radiant grin appeared everywhere in 1952 and 1956, as Reagan's did in 1984, but Richard Nixon was perceived as cold and aloof in 1968, despite clever efforts at selling his personality.

Still another dimension of candidates' personalities is strength or weakness. George H. W. Bush overcame the so-called wimp factor in 1988 with his tough talk about crime and the flag. Merely by surviving many personal attacks in 1992 and 1996, Clinton appeared strong and resilient.

The sparse and ambiguous treatment of policy issues in campaigns, as well as the emphasis on past performance and personal competence, fits better with ideas about electoral reward and punishment than with responsible parties or issue-oriented electoral competition. Candidate personalities are not irrelevant to the democratic control of government. Obviously, it is useful for voters to pick presidents who possess competence, warmth, and strength. And citizens may be more skillful in judging people than in figuring out complicated policy issues.

Voters can be fooled, however, by dirty tricks or slick advertising that sells presidential candidates' personalities and tears down the opponent. Moreover, the focus on personal imagery may distract attention from policy stands. If candidates who favor unpopular policies are elected on the basis of attractive personal images, democratic control of policymaking is weakened. By the purchase of advertising and the hiring of smart consultants, money may, in effect, overcome the popular will.

Money and Elections

Most observers agree that money creates problems in U.S. presidential elections. The main problem is probably not that too much money is spent but that the money comes from private sources that may influence government policymaking after the election is over.

The Cost of Presidential Campaigns Presidential campaigns cost a great deal of money. In 2000, for example, *pre-nomination* spending by all candidates totaled $343 million.[31] George W. Bush alone raised about $100 million in private donations to finance his run for the GOP nomination. The Bush and Gore autumn campaigns spent at record levels; taking into account Democratic and Republican National Committee expenditures on their behalf, the candidates together spent about $350 million.[32] In addition, the political parties spent roughly $500 million in unregulated **soft money** (now banned, beginning in 2003, by the campaign finance reform bill passed in 2002), most of which was designed to help presidential candidates, as well as candidates for the House and the Senate. Interest groups also run parallel campaigns on the issues, which are often thinly veiled additions to the campaigns of the candidates and the parties, as we reported in Chapter 7. Thus, ads from the American Federation of Teachers attacking Bush in 2000, and from the National Rifle Association attacking Gore, were clearly designed to generate votes for each association's favorite candidate.

soft money

Expenditures by political parties on general public education, voter registration, and voter mobilization.

Where Does the Money Come From? Since 1971, part of the money for presidential election campaigns has come from the federal treasury, paid by the taxpayers. Taxpayers can check off a box on their tax returns to authorize a $3 contribution from public funds. The government matches small contributions to candidates during the primaries and finances those party nominees who agree to spending limits. In 2000, the Gore and Bush campaigns each received $68 million. Public financing, although not popular with all citizens, has the advantage of eliminating any question of bribery or buying of favors from private interests. In 2000, however, public money accounted for less than 20 percent of Bush and Gore's total expenditures. The remainder came from contributions by individuals, businesses, labor unions, and special-interest groups. The same "reforms" of 1974 and later that required candidates to report the sources of their funds and that prohibited any individual from contributing more than

Longman
Participate.com
2.0
Visual Literacy
**PACs and the
Money Trail**

Longman
Participate.com
2.0
Participation
**The Debate
Over
Campaign
Finance
Reform**

$1,000 directly to a candidate also left large loopholes. For example, political action committees (PACs) were legalized, even for businesses and unions, that had previously been prohibited from making political contributions. PACs are now allowed to contribute up to $5,000 per candidate per election; furthermore, people are permitted to contribute $5,000 to each of as many PACs as they like, so that big interests (e.g., major corporations and large membership organizations) simply create multiple PACs or bundle contributions from individual members and employees.

Most important, people and organizations were able to contribute unlimited amounts of soft money to national, state, and local political parties up through the 2002 elections; after the 2002 campaign reform bill was passed, soft money could only go to state and local parties beginning in 2003. People and organizations have also been able to spend unlimited amounts of money on ad campaigns for or against candidates or in support of or in opposition to an issue. The campaign reform bill bans any such ads that mention a candidate's name for 60 days prior to an election. It remains to be seen if this portion of the reform legislation survives legal challenge.

Does Money Talk?

Money matters a great deal in the presidential nomination process—aspirants for party nominations who cannot raise sizeable funds always drop out of the race—but not so much during the post-convention run for the White House.[33] Once a presidential campaign is under way, each of the major party candidates has at his disposal all of the organizational resources of the party organization and money from traditional party contributors and allied interest groups as well as matching funds from the government; each candidate generally has enough money to run a credible campaign. In the general election, one cannot safely predict the outcome based on who has spent the most money. If that were true, Republicans would almost always win the election.

Money may talk at a later stage, however. It is widely believed, although difficult to prove, that contributors of money often get something back. The point is not that presidential candidates take outright bribes in exchange for policy favors. Indeed, exchanges between politicians and money givers are complex and varied, sometimes yielding little benefit to contributors. Undeniably, however, cozy relationships do tend to develop between politicians and major money givers. Contributors gain access to, and a friendly hearing from, those whom they help to win office.

It is clear that money givers are different from average citizens. They have special interests of their own. As we have indicated, a large amount of campaign money comes from large corporations, investment banking firms, wealthy families, labor unions, professional associations (e.g., doctors, lawyers, or realtors), and issue-oriented groups such as the National Rifle Association, the Christian Coalition, and the National Abortion Rights League. The big contributors generally do not represent ordinary workers, consumers, or taxpayers, let alone minorities or the poor. Surveys show that the individuals who give money tend to have much higher incomes and more conservative views on economic issues than the average American.[34]

The result is political inequality. Those who are well organized or have a lot of money to spend on politics have a better chance of influencing policy than ordinary citizens do, and they tend to influence it in directions different from those the general public would want. The role of money in presidential nomination and election campaigns (and in congressional campaigns, as we show in Chapter 11) is a major problem for the working of democracy in the United States.

Election Outcomes

After the parties and candidates have presented their campaigns, the voters decide. Exactly how people make their voting decisions affects how well or how poorly elections contribute to the democratic control of government.

How Voters Decide

Years of scholarly research have made it clear that feelings about the parties, the candidates, and the issues have substantial effects on how people vote.[35]

Longman
Participate.com
2.0
Participation
**Deciding on a
Political Party**

Social Characteristics   People's socioeconomic status, religion, and ethnic background are significantly related to how they vote. Since the 1930s, for example, African-Americans, Jews, and lower-income citizens have tended to vote heavily for Democrats, while white Protestants and upper-income Americans have voted mostly for Republicans: In 2000, 90 percent of blacks, but only 42 percent of whites, voted for Al Gore against George W. Bush; 57 percent of people with family incomes under $15,000, but only 44 percent of those with incomes over $75,000, voted for Gore; and 79 percent of Jews, but only 18 percent of white born-again Christians, voted for Gore. Recently, women have voted for Democrats in greater number than have men; they cast 54 percent of their vote for Gore in 2000. Older people have traditionally supported Democratic candidates more often, and at higher rates than other age groups, although this has begun to change. In 2000, they gave almost 50 percent of their vote to Bush (see Figure 10.4).

Party Loyalties   To some extent, these social patterns work through long-term attachments to, or identification with, political parties. As indicated earlier, a majority of Americans still say they consider themselves Republicans or Democrats. Party loyalties vary among different groups of the population, often because of past or present differences between the parties on policy issues, especially economic and social issues.[36] For this reason, party cues help many people vote for candidates who are close to them on the issues.

Party loyalties are very good predictors of how people will vote.[37] Those who say they consider themselves Republicans tend to vote for Republican candidates in one election after another, and those who consider themselves Democrats vote for Democratic candidates. This is especially true in congressional elections and in state and local races, where most voters know little more about the candidates than their party labels, but the party loyalty factor is extremely important in presidential elections as well. Thus, in 2000, 86 percent of Democratic identifiers voted for Gore, and 91 percent of Republican identifiers voted for Bush.

Candidates   Another reason presidential election outcomes have not simply reflected the party balance and the Democrats have lost so often is that voters pay a lot of attention to their perceptions of the personal characteristics of candidates. They vote heavily for candidates who have experience, appear strong and decisive, and convey personal warmth. The Republican candidate in 1952 and 1956, Dwight D. Eisenhower, had a tremendous advantage in these respects over his Democratic opponent, Adlai Stevenson;[38] so did Republicans Richard Nixon over George McGovern in 1972, Ronald Reagan over Walter Mondale in 1984, and George Bush over Michael Dukakis in 1988.

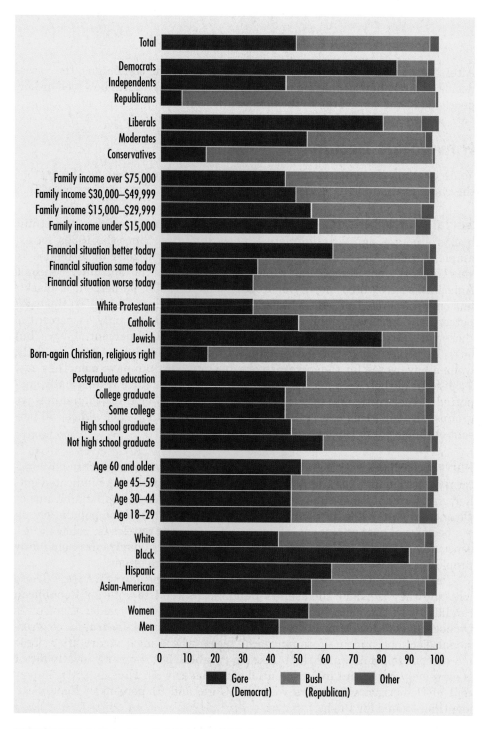

FIGURE 10.4 Presidential Vote in 2000, by Social Group

Minorities, lower-income voters, and women tended to vote for Al Gore in the 2000 election, while white Protestants, higher-income people, and men tended to favor George W. Bush.
Source: *Voter News Service,* November 8, 2000.

Only in 1964 did the Democratic candidate (Lyndon Johnson) appeal to voters substantially more than the Republican candidate (Barry Goldwater). In elections between 1952 and 1972, the contrast between Republican and

News photos and video of Democratic presidential candidate Michael Dukakis taking a ride in a new M1-A-1 battle tank during the 1988 campaign did not convince very many people that he was strong on national defense, which was his apparent objective. Much to the chagrin of his campaign team, the ride became the butt of jokes by late-night comedians and editorial cartoonists.

Democratic candidates typically gained the Republicans 4 or 5 percentage points—just enough to overcome the Democrats' advantage in what political scientists call the **normal vote:** how votes would be cast if only party identification determined voters' choices for president.

normal vote

The proportion of the votes that each party would win if party identification alone affected voting decisions.

Issues Voters also pay attention to issues. Sometimes this means choosing between different policy proposals for the future (as in the responsible party voting model), such as Reagan's 1980 promises to cut back federal government activity or Clinton's 1992 pledges of jobs and a middle-class tax cut. More often, however, issue voting has meant retrospective voting (the electoral reward and punishment model), making judgments about the past, especially on major questions about war or peace and the state of the economy. The voters tend to reward the incumbent party for what they see as good times and to punish it for what they see as bad times, though this did not occur in 2000 for reasons that are still being debated by political observers.[39] Several scholars and pollsters believe that cultural issues—such as gay and lesbian rights, abortion, civil rights and affirmative action, law and order, and the like—may have become more important than economic issues in determining voter choices. This may help explain why increasing numbers of affluent and educated Americans are voting Democratic, while lower income, less educated, and church-going whites are increasingly casting their ballots for Republicans.[40]

The Economy The state of the economy and how Americans feel about their economic well-being and prospects are especially important. After severe economic downturns, Americans tend to vote the incumbent party out of office, as they did the Republicans during the Great Depression in 1932. In 1992, the electorate punished Republican George H. W. Bush for the poor state of the economy and, in 1996, it rewarded Bill Clinton for being president during good economic times.

Foreign Policy Foreign policy can be important. Bitter disillusionment over the Korean War hurt the Democrats in 1952, just as the Vietnam War cost them in 1968, and unhappiness about American hostages in Iran and the Soviet intervention in Afghanistan hurt Jimmy Carter in 1980. During nearly all of the past half-century, in fact, Republican candidates have been seen as better at providing foreign policy strength and at keeping us out of war. In most elections, however, foreign policy concerns take a back seat to domestic ones for most voters.

New Issues In recent years, new issues have also become important to voters. These include deficit cutting, law and order, the environment, affirmative action, and abortion. Becoming increasingly important are issues related to globalization, including free trade. Certain to be important in future elections is the public's assessment of progress in the war against terrorism, especially if a protracted war brings with it a wide range of problems.

The Electoral College

Longman
Participate.com
2.0
Participation
The Electoral
College

As many Americans may have learned for the first time in 2000, the outcome of presidential elections is determined not by the number of popular votes cast for each candidate; it depends on the votes in the Electoral College. (See "By the Numbers: Did George W. Bush really win the 2000 presidential vote in Florida?" for more information on the 2000 election.)

When Americans vote for a presidential candidate whose name appears on the ballot, they are actually voting for a slate of **electors**—equal to the number of U.S. senators and representatives from their state—who have promised to support the candidate. (Very rarely have electors reneged on their promises and cast ballots for someone else; there was one so-called "faithless elector" in 2000.) Nearly all states now have winner-take-all systems which select the entire slate of electors for the candidate who wins the most popular votes; Maine and Nebraska, in slight variations, choose electors by congressional district rather than statewide.

The "college" of electors from the different states never actually meets; instead, the electors meet in their respective states and send lists of how they have voted to Washington, D.C. (see the Twelfth Amendment to the Constitution). The candidate who receives a majority of all the electoral votes in

electors

Representatives who are elected in the states to formally choose the U.S. president.

Web Exploration
The Electoral College

Issue: Although until 2000 it had been a very long time since a presidential candidate had won the popular vote but lost the electoral college vote (which determines who will be president), it remains the case that the margin of the electoral vote victory of a candidate always looks very different from the popular vote victory.

Site: Compare the popular vote and the electoral college vote on our Website at **www.ablongman.com/greenberg**. Go to the "Web Explorations" section for Chapter 10. Select "the electoral college, " then "college." Select "Electoral College Boxscores," then look at the period 1944–1996.

What You've Learned: Calculate the winner's percentage of the popular vote and the electoral vote for each election. What is the main effect of the Electoral College? Is the effect you found good or bad for American democracy? Would you support a proposal to change our present system into a direct popular voting system? Why?

HINT: Some scholars believe that the magnification of the winning candidate's margin of victory adds to the winner's mandate and legitimacy among the people, making for more effective government.

HOW DEMOCRATIC ARE WE?

Do Elections Matter?

PROPOSITION: Elections don't matter much in determining what government leaders do. It's probably the reason so many Americans don't bother to vote.

AGREE: The people are not able to control the government by means of elections. For one thing, our political parties are such that they undermine the ability of elections to play the democratic role reserved for them in responsible party government, electoral competition, and electoral reward-and-punishment theories of democratic elections. The kinds of parties we have do not allow voters to choose future policy directions or hold elected officials responsible for their actions, or allow parties to conform to the wishes of the median voter. For another thing, the political equality norm of democracy is violated by the role of interest groups and money in elections. Fully aware of this, and unhappy about it, potential voters stay away from the polls.

DISAGREE: Scholars have shown that government officials, in the long run, do what the American people want them to do about two-thirds of the time. Although a variety of instruments help convey what the people want to officials—public opinion polls, interest groups, and social movements—it is ultimately the fact that officials must face the voters that keeps them in line. Although nonvoting is a problem, it is not entirely clear why so many people stay away from the polls.

THE AUTHORS: In terms of the responsible party idea, the fact that Republicans tend to be more conservative than Democrats on a number of economic and social issues provides voters with a measure of democratic control by enabling them to detect differences and make choices about the future. Alternatively, through electoral punishment, voters can exercise control by reelecting successful incumbents and throwing failures out of office, thus making incumbents think ahead. Finally, electoral competition forces the parties to compete by nominating centrist candidates and by taking similar issue stands close to what most Americans want. This, in fact, may be the chief way in which citizens' policy preferences affect what their government does.

Clearly, then, U.S. elections help make the public's voice heard, but they do not bring about perfect democracy. Two key reasons are the limited and biased participation of citizens and the effects of money and activists on election outcomes. Both uneven participation and the role of money and activists impair political equality by giving some people more political influence than others.

Although elections provide a strong measure of democratic control, low voter turnout remains a problem. The causes of low turnout are varied and not strictly related to the inability of elections to provide perfect popular control of government. Low voter turnout is also explained by registration requirements, inequality of resources among citizens, tepid mobilization actions by the parties, and the "infotainment" orientation of the mass media.

the country is elected president. Not since 1824 has it been necessary to resort to the odd constitutional provisions that apply when no one gets a majority of electoral votes: The House of Representatives chooses among the top three candidates, by majority vote of state delegations.

By the Numbers

Did George W. Bush really win the 2000 presidential vote in Florida?

George W. Bush was officially certified the winner of the presidential contest in Florida on December 12, 2000, thirty-five days after the November election. Florida's 25 electoral votes brought his national total to 271, just barely enough to win the White House.

Interestingly, however, a comprehensive review of Florida ballots has come up with several other possible outcomes to the Florida vote, depending on different ways the ballots could have been counted. In fact, the outcomes vary from Bush winning by 537 votes, to Gore winning by 200!

Why It Matters: Elections must be fair if they are to play the role assigned to them in democratic theory. Part of a fair election is an accurate count of votes cast. Without an accurate count, voter wishes will not be conveyed to public officials, and the legitimacy of elected officials is at risk, making governance more difficult.

Behind the Vote Count Numbers: A consortium of eight leading news organizations—including the *Wall Street Journal,* the *New York Times, The Washington Post,* the Associated Press, and CNN— recently sponsored a 10-month study by the widely respected National Opinion Research Center at the University of Chicago. Center researchers examined every uncounted "under-vote" ballot (where no vote for president was recorded by the voting machine), with an eye towards determining each voter's intent. Only ballots that showed evidence of clear voter intention were included in the consortium's recount. These included ballots with "hanging" and "pregnant" chads which the machines failed to record, and optical scan ballots where voters indicated their vote with a check mark or an "x" rather than filling in the bubble as instructed.

Calculating the Winner's Margin of Victory: The official tally concluded that Bush won by 537 votes. However, Center investigators found that different counting methods would have yielded the results shown on page 299.

There are some incredible ironies in these numbers.

- Had the Gore team gotten everything it asked for from election officials and the courts, Gore still would have lost to George W. Bush.
- The U.S. Supreme Court did not steal the election, as many Gore supporters claimed, for had it allowed the Florida Supreme Court's solution to stand, Bush would have won anyway.
- A majority of Florida voters went to the polls on November 8 to cast a vote for Al Gore for president. The method proposed by the U.S. Supreme Court shows this; recounting all "under-count" disputed ballots on a state-wide basis using consistent standards yields a Gore victory. The upshot: Gore was badly advised by his team of lawyers, who insisted on recounts in only certain counties.
- Because of the enormous boost in George W. Bush's popularity following the terrorist attack on the United States and the subsequent "war on terrorism," most Americans ignored the consortium's findings. Most seemed perfectly content to have Bush as president, no matter what had happened in Florida.

Most of the time, this peculiar Electoral College system works about the same way as if Americans chose their presidents by direct popular vote, though this was not true in 2000 when Bush won the electoral vote while losing the popular vote. The old idea that electors would exercise their independent judgments is long gone. But the system does have certain consequences:

- *It magnifies the popular support of winners.* A candidate who wins in many states, by a narrow margin in each, can win a "landslide" in the

Criticisms of the Florida "Recount":
Some have argued that the consortium's recount was flawed in two major ways:

- First, it did not include "over-votes" in its estimates—those ballots where more than one name for president was indicated or where the same name was entered more than once—which were also ruled invalid by election officials in Florida. For the most part, these involved ballots where voters made two punches on very confusing ballots (the infamous "butterfly ballots") or where voters wrote in the same name as the candidate they had punched or marked, presumably to make clear to election officials who they had voted for. A substantial majority of over-vote ballots had Gore as one of the choices.
- Second, there is the issue of absentee ballots from overseas armed forces personnel. Had they been counted in the same way other ballots were counted—that is, not counting ballots kicked out because of "under-vote" or "over-vote" problems—Bush would have lost hundreds of votes to Gore and probably lost Florida and the White House.

What to Watch For: When counting votes, as in all other counts, the rules for doing so matter. This is why the lawyers from the Gore and Bush teams fought so ferociously following the Florida election about how to do the recount. Whenever you run across a statistic that involves counting, in one

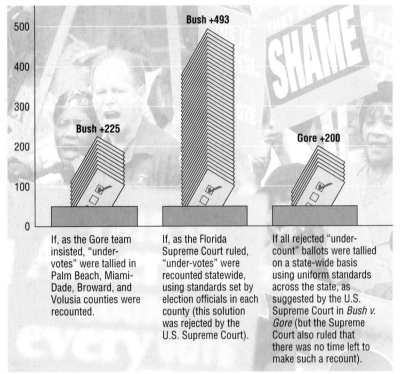

Alternative Florida Presidential Election Outcomes

If, as the Gore team insisted, "under-votes" were tallied in Palm Beach, Miami-Dade, Broward, and Volusia counties were recounted.

If, as the Florida Supreme Court ruled, "under-votes" were recounted statewide, using standards set by election officials in each county (this solution was rejected by the U.S. Supreme Court).

If all rejected "under-count" ballots were tallied on a state-wide basis using uniform standards across the state, as suggested by the U.S. Supreme Court in *Bush v. Gore* (but the Supreme Court also ruled that there was no time left to make such a recount).

form or another, you might want to look further into what counting rules were used.

What Do You Think? Can you think of any other way to decide the winner of an election when, for all intents and purposes, the race ends up in a dead heat? Some countries use a "run-off" system in which the two top people run against each other to determine who has won a majority of popular votes before a winner is declared. In the 2000 presidential elections, this would have meant a run-off election between Gore and Bush, without Ralph Nader or Pat Buchanan on the ballot.

electoral college. In 1996, for example, Bill Clinton's 49 percent of the popular vote translated into 379 electoral votes, or 70 percent of the total. Ordinarily, this magnification just adds legitimacy to the democratic choice, especially when the winner has only a **plurality** of the popular vote, that is, more than anybody else but less than a majority of all votes. Many of our presidents have been elected with less than 50 percent of the popular vote—most recently, Clinton (1992 and 1996), Richard Nixon (1968), John Kennedy (1960), and Harry Truman (1948).

plurality

More votes than any other candidate but less than a majority of all votes cast.

- *It may let the less popular candidate win.* A president can be elected who had *fewer* votes than an opponent, if those votes happened to produce narrow margins in many states. Such a result has occurred three times: in 1876, when Rutherford Hayes defeated Samuel Tilden; in 1888, when Benjamin Harrison beat the more popular Grover Cleveland; and in 2000, when George W. Bush defeated Al Gore. (Gore beat Bush by over one-half a million votes nationally.) Several early-nineteenth-century presidents were probably chosen with only small fractions of the popular vote, although we cannot be sure because some of the statistics are unreliable. Most notably, in 1824, John Quincy Adams defeated the very popular Andrew Jackson in the House of Representatives.

- *It discourages third parties.* Our constitutional arrangements for a single president and single-member congressional districts (rather than proportional representation) already discourage third parties; if candidates cannot win a plurality, they get nothing. The Electoral College adds symbolically to this discouragement: A third party with substantial support may get no electoral votes at all, if its support is scattered among many states. In 1992, for example, Ross Perot's impressive 19 percent of the popular vote translated into zero electoral votes because he failed to win a plurality in any single state.

People who would like to abolish the Electoral College point to its narrowing of choices and the possibility of undemocratic outcomes. Those who like it claim that it discourages fraud by limiting the votes that any one state can cast, that the two-party system it encourages is good, and that the added legitimacy of electoral college "landslides" is helpful—or at least harmless.

Summary

Elections are the most important means by which citizens can exert democratic control over their government. Voters can choose *responsible parties* to carry out their distinctive programs. *Electoral competition* forces vote-seeking parties and candidates to appeal to the center of public opinion. *Electoral reward and punishment* gives officials incentives to carry out policies that will win public approval. However, none of these processes guarantees a perfectly democratic outcome.

Political participation can be conventional (voting, helping in campaigns, and contacting officials) or unconventional (protesting or demonstrating). The right to vote, originally quite limited, was expanded in various historical surges to include nearly all adults and to apply to most major offices. Turnout has declined, however, and in recent years only about half the eligible voters have cast ballots for the presidency.

Candidates for president start by testing the waters, raising money, and forming campaign organizations; in a series of state primaries and caucuses, they seek delegates to the national nominating conventions, which generally choose a clear front-runner or the incumbent president. During the campaign, the candidates are generally vague about issues; they concentrate on building personal images and emphasizing past performance.

About one-third of the cost of presidential campaigns is paid from public funds; the rest of the money comes from individuals and organizations, many of which seek self-benefiting policies. Contributions probably hurt democracy by leading to a degree of political inequality.

Voters' decisions depend heavily on party loyalties, the personal characteristics of the candidates, and the issues, especially the state of the economy and of U.S. foreign policy. After recessions and unsuccessful wars, the incumbent party generally loses. The Electoral College does not always accurately reflect popular votes. Elections matter not only when there is a clear choice but also when electoral reward or punishment occurs or when electoral competition forces both parties to take similar popular stands.

Suggestions for Further Reading

"Anonymous." *Primary Colors: A Novel of Politics.* New York: Random House, 1996.
Journalist Joe Klein's lively and sometimes ribald account of Bill Clinton's campaign for the 1992 Democratic presidential nomination, thinly disguised as fiction.

Burns, Nancy, Kay Lehman Schlozman, and Sidney Verba. *The Private Roots of Public Action: Gender, Equality and Political Participation* (Cambridge, MA: Harvard University Press, 2001).
A comprehensive examination of the differences in the political activity of men and women and the reasons why differences exist.

Ferguson, Thomas. *Golden Rule.* Chicago: University of Chicago Press, 1995.
A highly critical account of the role of money in recent elections.

Keyssar, Alexander. *The Right to Vote: The Contested History of Democracy in the United States.* New York: Basic Books, 2001.
A fresh look at the history of the vote as a struggle between those who believe common people are not fully qualified to vote and those who believe that American democracy is enriched by their full participation.

Polsby, Nelson W., and Aaron Wildavsky. *Presidential Elections,* 10th ed. New York: Free Press, 2000.
A comprehensive textbook on the presidential nominating process, campaigning, and voting.

Verba, Sidney, Kay Lehman Schlozman, and Henry E. Brady. *Voice and Equality: Civic Volunteerism in American Politics.* Cambridge, MA: Harvard University Press, 1995.
A comprehensive analysis of inequalities in political participation and their meaning for the quality of democracy in the United States.

Internet Sources

The Center for Public Integrity **www.publicintegrity.org/**
An especially good site for following the money trail—how campaign money is gathered and spent.

Democratic National Committee **www.democrats.org/**
Official site of the Democratic party with information on party positions and candidates, how to work as a volunteer or contribute money, and more.

E-Vote **www.evote.com/**
Up-to-the-minute news, commentary, and polls on national campaigns.

The National Archives Electoral College Site
www.archives.gov/federal_register/electoral_college/electoral_college.html
   Everything there is to know about the law and practices of the Electoral College and the process by which it elects the president.

Project Votesmart   **www.vote-smart.org/**
   A political portal loaded with links to information about candidates, parties, election rules, and issues.

Republican National Committee   **www.rnc.org/**
   Official site of the Republican party with information on party positions and candidates, how to work as a volunteer or contribute money, and more.

Notes

1. For further discussion, see Benjamin I. Page, *Choices and Echoes in Presidential Elections: Rational Man and Electoral Democracy* (Chicago: University of Chicago Press, 1978), ch. 2; Robert A. Dahl, *Democracy and Its Critics* (New Haven, CT: Yale University Press, 1989).

2. See Austin Ranney, *The Doctrine of Responsible Party Government: Its Origins and Present State* (Urbana: University of Illinois Press, 1962); E. E. Schattschneider, *Party Government* (New York: Holt, Rinehart & Winston, 1942).

3. Anthony Downs, *An Economic Theory of Democracy* (New York: Harper & Row, 1957); Otto Davis, Melvin Hinich, and Peter Ordeshook, "An Expository Development of a Mathematical Model of the Electoral Process," *American Political Science Review* 64 (1970), pp. 426–448.

4. Lawrence R. Jacobs and Robert Y. Shapiro, *Politicians Don't Pander: Political Manipulation and the Loss of Democratic Responsiveness* (Chicago: University of Chicago Press, 2000).

5. See V. O. Key Jr., *Public Opinion and American Democracy* (New York: Knopf, 1961); Morris P. Fiorina, *Retrospective Voting in American National Elections* (Cambridge, MA: Harvard University Press, 1981).

6. Chilton Williamson, *American Suffrage* (Princeton, NJ: Princeton University Press, 1960), pp. 223, 241, 260. More precisely, there was universal suffrage for white male taxpayers.

7. See John Hope Franklin, *From Slavery to Freedom* (New York: Knopf, 1967); Leon Litwack, *North of Slavery* (Chicago: University of Chicago Press, 1961); and Alexander Keyssar, *The Right to Vote: The Contested History of Democracy in the United States* (New York: Basic Books, 2001).

8. Walter Dean Burnham, "The Turnout Problem," in A. James Reichley, ed., *Elections, American Style* (Washington, D.C.: Brookings Institution, 1987), pp. 113–114.

9. *The New York Times* (November 21, 1988), p. B16.

10. Nelson W. Polsby and Aaron Wildavsky, *Presidential Elections,* 10th ed. (New York: Chatham House/Seven Bridges Press, 2000), p. 6.

11. Polsby and Wildavsky, *Presidential Elections*, pp. 23-24.

12. Polsby and Wildavsky believe that barriers to registration are more important than alienation in explaining nonvoting. See Ibid., pp. 5–7.

13. Joseph S. Nye Jr., Philip D. Zelikow, and David C. King, eds., *Why People Don't Trust Government* (Cambridge, MA: Harvard University Press, 1997).

14. "Forum" in *The American Political Science Review* 93 (December 1999), pp. 851–910; and Richard R. Lau and Gerald M. Pomper, "Effects of Negative Campaigning on Turnout in U.S. Senate Elections, 1988–1998, *The Journal of Politics* (August 2001), Vol 63, no. 3, pp. 804–819.

15. Walter Dean Burnham, "The Class Gap," *New Republic* (May 9, 1988), pp. 30–34; Steven J. Rosenstone and John Mark Hansen, *Mobilization, Participation, and Democracy in America* (New York: Macmillan, 1993); Jacobs and Shapiro, *Politicians Don't Pander,* pp. 318–320; and Michael Martinez and David Hill, "Did Motor Voter Work?" *American Politics Quarterly* 27 (1999), pp. 308–309.

16. David Menefee-Libey, *The Triumph of Campaign-Centered Politics* (New York: Chatham House/Seven Bridges Press, 2000).

17. Russell Dalton, *Citizen Politics in Western Democracies* (Chatham, NJ: Chatham House, 1988), p. 42.

18. National Opinion Research Center, *The General Social Survey,* 1999.

19. Sidney Verba, Kay Lehman Schlozman, and Henry E. Brady, *Voice and Equality: Civic Volunteerism in American Politics* (Cambridge, MA: Harvard University Press, 1995), pp. 51, 56.

20. Jack C. Doppelt and Ellen Shearer, *Non-Voters: America's No-Shows* (New York: Sage, 1999); Jeffrey Berry, *The New Liberalism* (Washington, D.C.: Brookings, 1999), pp. 39–40.

21. Verba, Schlozman, and Brady, *Voice and Equality,* ch. 7; Sidney Verba and Norman H. Nie, *Participation in America* (New York: Harper & Row, 1972).

22. Susan A. MacManus, *Young v. Old* (Boulder, CO: Westview Press, 1996), ch. 2.

23. Margaret M. Conway, *Political Participation in the United States* (Washington, D.C.: CQ Press, 3rd ed., 2000), p. 37.

24. E. J. Dionne, "If Nonvoters Had Voted: Same Winner, but Bigger," *The New York Times* (November 21, 1988), p. B16.

25. Sidney Verba, Kay Lehman Schlozman, Henry E. Brady, and Norman H. Nie, "Citizen Activity: Who Participates? What Do They Say?" *American Political Science Review* 87 (1993), pp. 303–318.

26. Polsby and Wildavsky, *Presidential Elections,* pp. 56, 67, 99–101.

27. Ibid., pp. 65–66.

28. Larry Bartels, *Presidential Primaries and the Dynamics of Public Choice* (Princeton, NJ: Princeton University Press, 1988); John H. Aldrich, *Before the Convention* (Chicago: University of Chicago Press, 1980).

29. Stephen J. Wayne, *The Road to the White House, 1992* (New York: Worth, 2000).

30. Polsby and Wildavsky, *Presidential Elections,* pp. 157, 173, 182.

31. Federal Election Commission, 2001.

32. Opensecrets.org, *The 1999–2000 election cycle.*

33. Polsby and Wildavsky, *Presidential Elections,* p. 151.

34. See Verba, Schlozman, and Brady, *Voice and Equality.*

35. Efforts to sort out their relative contributions include Benjamin I. Page and Calvin Jones, "Reciprocal Effects of Policy Preferences, Party Loyalties, and the Vote," *American Political Science Review* 73 (1979), pp. 1071–1089; Gregory B. Markus and Philip E. Converse, "A Dynamic Simultaneous Equation Model of Public Choice," *American Political Science Review* 73 (1979), pp. 1066–1070.

36. Carlos Elordi, "Ideology: Assessing Its Impact on Political Choices," *Public Perspective* (March/April 2000), pp. 34–35.

37. Larry M. Bartels, "Partisanship and Voting Behavior, 1952–1996," *American Journal of Political Science* 44 (January 2000), pp. 35–50.

38. Donald E. Stokes, "Some Dynamic Elements of Contests for the Presidency," *American Political Science Review* 60 (1966), pp. 19–28.

39. Fiorina, *Retrospective Voting*.

40. Thomas B. Edsall, "The Shifting Sands of America's Political Parties," *The Washington Post National Edition* (April 9–15, 2001), p. 11.

Part Four

Government and Governing

The chapters in Part Four examine how federal government institutions operate and how and why public officials, both elected and appointed, behave as they do in office. Part Four includes chapters on Congress, the presidency, the executive branch, and the Supreme Court.

The chapters in this part assume that government institutions and public officials can be understood only in their structural and political contexts. What government does is influenced strongly by structural factors such as the constitutional rules, the economy, the political culture, society, and the nation's place in the world. What government does is also shaped by political linkage institutions such as elections, parties, interest groups, public opinion, and social movements that transmit the preferences of individuals and groups to public officials.

Democracy is the evaluative thread that runs through each chapter. We ask about the degree to which federal government institutions and public officials advance or retard the practice of democracy in the United States.

Chapter 11
Congress

In This Chapter

- How the Constitution shapes Congress
- How Congress has changed over the years
- How the members of Congress represent their constituents
- What role money and interest groups play in congressional elections
- What leaders, political parties, and committees do in Congress
- How a bill becomes a law

The 2002 Elections and the Return of Unified Government

Sometimes very small changes can generate very large outcomes. Scientists often speak, for example, of the climate effects in one part of the world that are generated by a single butterfly flapping its wings in another part of the world. Something similar sometimes happens in American politics. In the 2002 elections, the switch of a very small handful of House and Senate seats from one party to the other fundamentally changed the balance of political power in Washington.

Going into the 2002 mid-term election, few commentators saw the changes coming. Most thought the election would look pretty much like past mid-term elections, with the president's party losing a few seats in the House and a few in the Senate. Because the margin between the parties in Congress was so close going into the election, the playing out of the normal historical tendencies would have enhanced the Democratic Party's slim majority in the Senate and put it within striking distance of a majority in the House of Representatives. This was not to be, however. For only the third time in a hundred years, the party of the president gained seats in the House of Representatives in a mid-term election. While Republicans didn't gain very many seats, they gained just enough to solidify their existing majority, ensuring their continuing control over the business of the House. For the first time since the Civil War, moreover, the president's party grabbed control of the Senate from the opposition party in a mid-term election. Again, Republicans didn't take many seats from Democrats, but they took just enough to give them a bare majority, and with it, control of the Senate.

With Republican George W. Bush in the Oval Office, the 2002 elections returned unified government to Washington, a condition in which one party controls Congress and the presidency. Unified government is something that has not been much in evidence since the 1960s. In fact, unified government has existed for only a little more than six years since 1968 (see Figure. 9.3 in Chapter 9). Unified government under Democratic control was last in evidence in 1994 when Bill Clinton was president. Unified government under

Republican direction existed for less than three months in early 2001 (until Senator Jeffords of Vermont left the GOP, giving the Democrats a majority), and for two years during the second Reagan administration in the mid-1980s. With Congress and the presidency in Republican hands after the 2002 mid-term elections, and a solid conservative majority on the Supreme Court, George W. Bush and the Republican Party can potentially reshape federal government policies in a number of important areas, including taxes, business regulation, foreign policy, and affirmative action.

So how did the Republicans defy history by picking up seats in the House and Senate in a mid-term election with one of their own in the White House? There are three likely possibilities.[1] Perhaps most importantly, George W. Bush threw himself into the campaign, using his enormous popularity—his job approval rating from the public was the highest for any president at the end of his first two years in office in the history of public opinion polling—to help Republican House and Senate candidates who were in tight election races. In the final two weeks, at the urging of his political advisor, Karl Rove, he campaigned relentlessly, supporting GOP candidates, rallying party workers, and mobilizing Republican and independent voters. It seems to have worked. The Gallup Poll reported a Republican surge in the final two weeks of the campaign, changing a 3-percentage-point deficit to the

Democrats to a 6-point lead in the projected vote for Congress. Gallup also reported that the projected turnout rate for Republicans was significantly higher than for Democrats and that Republicans were considerably more enthusiastic and involved in the election campaign than Democrats. Gallup's report of the late surge to a 6-point GOP lead was right on the money: the nationwide vote in Senate elections came in at 52 percent Republican and 48 percent Democratic; for the House, it was 53 percent to 47 percent in favor of Republicans.

Also important in the Democratic Party's loss of the Senate was the death in a plane crash of Senator Paul Wellstone of Minnesota just ten days before the election. Though in a tight race against Republican Norm Coleman, the polls had Wellstone ahead going into the final stages of the campaign. The last-minute substitution of venerable party leader Walter Mondale, a former vice president, candidate for the presidency, and senator from Minnesota, did not work as Democratic leaders had hoped. Mondale lost. Commentators suggested that Mondale was hurt badly by the televised memorial service for Wellstone, which turned into a highly partisan political rally in which Gov. Jesse Ventura and Republican senate leader Trent Lott were booed lustily.

Finally, many experienced political observers and Democratic activists blamed party leaders for failing to articulate a clear, alternative vision to that of the Republicans that would motivate the Democratic party base and attract independent voters. In a time of economic troubles, they charged, Democrats offered no coherent alternative to Bush's tax cuts. In a time of mounting pressure to go to war with Iraq and growing unease about it among many Americans, Democratic leaders, afraid to take on an extremely popular president, fell in line with President Bush's tough foreign policy line. In a time when many Americans were beginning to worry about how the war on terrorism might affect civil liberties and domestic social programs, the Democrats failed to present a coherent defense of traditional party positions. Unable to act as a vigorous opposition party, these party activists charged, party supporters and others had no reason to go to the polls. Scattered evidence supports this position. Gallup reported that Democratic identifiers were less enthused than Republican identifiers and less likely to vote. And, it appears that turnout among African-Americans, a key part of the Democratic Party base, was lower than usual, which especially hurt party candidates in the South.

Despite departing from historical norms in many respects, the 2002 mid-term elections were similar to recent elections in three key ways.[2] First, incumbents continued to be reelected at very high rates—roughly 98 percent in the House and 85 percent in the Senate. Second, campaign spending continued its ever-upward trajectory, reaching almost $900 million, with hard-money candidate expenditures and party soft-money expenditures almost double what they were in the 1998 mid-term elections. Candidates, parties, and special-interest groups also doubled what they had spent four years earlier on television advertising. Third, Republicans collected more hard and soft money and outspent Democrats by a substantial margin, something that has become quite common in American politics. ∎

Thinking Critically About This Chapter

In this chapter, we turn our attention to the Congress of the United States, examining how Congress works as both a representative and governing institution.

Using the Framework In this chapter you will learn how the way in which Congress works is affected by other government actors and institutions; political linkage level factors such as interest groups, public opinion, the media, and elections; and structural factors, such as constitutional rules and economic and social change.

Using the Democracy Standard Using the concept of democracy developed in Chapter 1, you will be able to evaluate how well Congress acts as a democratic institution. You will see that the story of Congress and democracy is a mixed one: Congress is, at times and under certain circumstances, highly responsive to the American public; at other times and under other circumstances, it is most responsive to special interest groups and large contributors. ◄

Constitutional Foundations of the Modern Congress

As we saw in Chapter 2, the framers of the Constitution were concerned about the possibility of government tyranny. Yet they also wanted an energetic government capable of accomplishing its assigned tasks. These multiple objectives and concerns are reflected in the constitutional design of Congress.

Empowering Congress

The framers began by empowering Congress, making the legislative branch the center of lawmaking in the federal government. In Article I, Section 1, of the Constitution, they gave Congress the power to make the laws: "All legislative power herein granted shall be vested in a Congress of the United States." For the framers, Congress was the main bearer of federal governmental powers. In listing its powers and responsibilities in Article I, Section 8—the **enumerated powers**—they were largely defining the powers and responsibilities of the national government itself.[3] The framers enhanced the enumerated powers by adding the **elastic clause,** granting broad power to Congress to pass whatever legislation was necessary to carry out its enumerated powers.

Constraining Congress

Worried that too strong a legislative branch would lead to tyranny, the framers also limited congressional power. As we learned in Chapter 2, they made Congress a **bicameral** body—divided into two chambers—so that legislation could occur only after patient deliberation. Single-house legislative bodies, they believed, would be prone to rash action. They then added provisions—Article I, Section 9—specifically to prohibit certain kinds of actions: **bills of attainder, ex post facto laws,** the granting of titles of nobility, and the suspension of the right of **habeas corpus.** In the 1st Congress, additional constraints on congressional action were added in the form of the Bill of Rights. Note that the First Amendment, perhaps the most important constitutional provision protecting political liberty, begins with the words "Congress shall make no law. . . ."

We also learned in Chapter 2 that the national government was organized on the basis of a "separation of powers" and "checks and balances" so that "ambition might check ambition" and protect the country from tyranny. This means that although the framers envisioned the legislative branch as the vital center of a vigorous national government, they wanted to make sure that Congress would be surrounded by competing centers of government power. We will see that this fragmentation of governmental power in the United States affects how Congress works and often makes it difficult for it to fashion coherent and effective public policies.

Bicameralism and Representation

Congress is organized into two legislative chambers with different principles of representation as well as different constitutional responsibilities. While we often use the word "Congress" and think of it as a single institution, it is worth remembering that the House and Senate are very different from one another and are "virtually autonomous chambers."[4] In what came to be known as the Great

---

enumerated powers

Powers of the federal government specifically mentioned in the Constitution.

elastic clause

Article I, Section 8, of the Constitution, also called *the necessary and proper clause;* gives Congress the authority to make whatever laws are necessary and proper to carry out its enumerated responsibilities.

bicameral

As applied to a legislative body, consisting of two houses or chambers.

bill of attainder

A governmental decree that a person is guilty of a crime that carries the death penalty, rendered without benefit of a trial.

ex post facto law

A law that retroactively declares some action illegal.

habeas corpus

The legal doctrine that a person who is arrested must have a timely hearing before a judge.

Longman
Participate.com 2.0
Comparative
Comparing
Legislatures

Today, candidates for the Senate like Tim Hutchinson (R–AR) must hit the campaign trail if they want to be elected or reelected. Prior to passage of the Seventeenth Amendment in 1913, which mandated that members of the Senate be elected directly by the people, candidates were mainly attuned to members of state legislatures who elected them to office, rather than to the public.

Compromise, the framers decided to apportion the House of Representatives on the basis of population and the Senate on the basis of equal representation of the states (see Chapter 2 for details). The terms of office of the members of the House of Representatives were set at two years. The terms of the members of the Senate were set at six years, with only one-third of the seats up for election in each two-year election cycle. We learn in this chapter how these differences affect the legislative process.

The Constitution called for the election of senators by state legislatures, not by the people. The objective was to insulate one house of Congress from popular pressures and to make it a seat of deliberation and reflection. As James Madison put it, "The use of the Senate is to consist in its proceeding with more coolness . . . and with more wisdom than the popular branch."[5] The election of senators by the state legislatures could not survive the democratizing tendencies in the country, however. The Seventeenth Amendment, passed in 1913 after years of agitation for reform pressed by labor and farm groups and progressive reformers, gave the people the power to elect senators directly.

In addition to its general grants of power to Congress, the Constitution assigns particular responsibilities to each of the legislative chambers (see Table 11.1). For example, the House of Representatives has the power to impeach the president for "high crimes and misdemeanors," which it did in the case of Bill Clinton; the Senate has the power to conduct the trial of the president and remove him from office, if the impeachment charges are proved to its satisfaction (which they were not for Clinton).

Federalism

Congress is also greatly affected by the federal design of the Constitution. As we learned in Chapter 3, in our federal system, some powers and responsibilities are granted to the national government, some are shared between the national government and the states, and some are reserved for the states. It is inevitable in such a system that conflicts will occur between state governments and the national government and its legislative branch. Such conflicts sometimes reach the Supreme Court for resolution. In *United States* v. *Lopez* (1995), for instance, the Court ruled that Congress had gone too far in the use of its commerce clause

TABLE 11.1 Constitutional Differences Between the House and the Senate

	Senate	House of Representatives
Term	6 years	2 years
Elections	One-third elected in November of even-numbered years	Entire membership elected in November of even-numbered years
Number per State	2	Varies by size of state's population (minimum of 1 per state)
Total Membership	100	435 (determined by Congress; at present size since 1910)
Minimum Age for Membership	30 years	25 years
Powers	Advice and consent for judicial and upper-level executive branch appointments	Origination of revenue bills
	Trial of impeachment cases	Bringing of impeachment charges
	Advice and consent for treaties	

powers when it passed a law banning firearms in and around public schools. Although the goal of the law might be worthy, such a matter, in the opinion of the Court, was the business of the states, not Congress.

Federalism also infuses "localism" into congressional affairs.[6] Although Congress is charged with making national policies, we should remember that the members of the Senate and the House come to Washington as the representatives of states and districts. They are elected by and are beholden to the voters at home and have voters' interests and opinions in mind even as they struggle with weighty issues of national importance.

Representation and Democracy

Members of Congress serve as our legislative representatives. But do they carry out this representative responsibility in a way that can be considered democratic?

Styles of Representation

In a letter to his constituents written in 1774, English politician and philosopher Edmund Burke described two principal styles of representation. As a **delegate,** the representative tries to mirror perfectly the views of his or her constituents. As a **trustee,** the representative acts independently, trusting to

delegate

According to the doctrine articulated by Edmund Burke, an elected representative who acts in perfect accord with the wishes of his or her constituents.

trustee

According to the doctrine articulated by Edmund Burke, an elected representative who believes that his or her own best judgment, rather than instructions from constituents, should be used in making legislative decisions.

his or her own judgment of how to best serve the public interest. Burke preferred the trustee approach: "Your representative owes you, not his industry only, but his judgment; and he betrays you, instead of serving you, if he sacrifices it to your opinion."[7]

Campaigning for Congress in Illinois several decades later, Abraham Lincoln argued otherwise: "While acting as [your] representative, I shall be governed by [your] will, on all subjects upon which I have the means of knowing what [your] will is."[8] (If only he had access to public opinion polls!)

Every member of the House and Senate chooses between these two styles of representation. Their choice usually has less to do with their personal tastes than it has to do with the relative safety of their seats and how often they must face the electorate. Senators with six-year terms face the electorate less often than members of the House, so they are generally freer than representatives to assume the trustee style. As they get closer to the end of their term and the prospect of facing the voters, however, senators edge towards the delegate style. Because members of the House must run for reelection every two years, and tend to be in campaign mode at all times, they are pushed almost inexorably toward the delegate style.

Race, Gender, and Occupation in Congress

Representation also implies that elected officials are like us in important ways—that they represent us because they are similar to us. Which raises the question: Is the make-up of Congress in a demographic sense similar to that of the nation? If we want a political system in which the views of women are taken into account, for example, we might want a significant number of women in Congress. From this perspective, a perfectly representative legislative body would be similar to the general population in terms of race, sex, ethnicity, occupation, religion, age, and the like. In this sense, the U.S. Congress is highly *unrepresentative*.

Gender and Race Both women and racial minorities are significantly under-represented in Congress, particularly in the Senate, despite important recent gains. We can see this in Figure 11.1, which compares the distribution of women and minorities in the 107th Congress (2001–2002) with their distribution in the country as a whole.

Black representation reached its peak during the post–Civil War Reconstruction period, when blacks played an important political role in several southern states. African-Americans disappeared from Congress for many years after the reimposition of white supremacy in the South at the end of the nineteenth century. Although a handful of black representatives from northern cities served during the first half of the twentieth century—Oscar De Priest from Chicago's predominantly black South Side and Adam Clayton Powell from New York City's Harlem, for example—very few African-Americans were elected to Congress until the late 1960s. While there has been some improvement in representation of African-Americans in the House of Representatives—from 26 to 39 between the 102nd (1991–1992) and 107th Congresses (2000–2001)—their numbers are still well below what one might expect, given the proportion of African-Americans in the population. All but four twentieth-century African-American representatives were Democrats. In the 107th Congress, there was only one black Republican representative, J. C. Watts of Oklahoma.

Hispanics are even more poorly represented than African-Americans relative to their proportion of the population, but the increase in their number in recent years has given the Hispanic caucus a greater voice in legislative af-

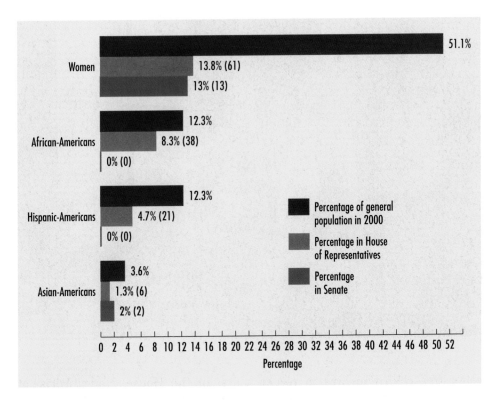

FIGURE 11.1 Women and Minorities in Congress

Although their numbers in Congress have increased in recent years, women and racial minorities are still substantially underrepresented compared with their proportion in the American population. This graph compares the percentage of women and racial minorities in each house of the 107th Congress with their percentages in the population in 2000.

Source: U.S. Bureau of the Census, 2001.

fairs than in the past. Interestingly, while Hispanics reached parity with African-Americans in the population, they are less well represented than African-Americans in Congress. Twenty-one served in the House (there were no Hispanics in the Senate) in the 107th Congress.

Other minority groups are represented among members of the House. There were seven Arab-Americans in the 107th Congress and one Native American. Another Native American, Ben Nighthorse Campbell (R–CO), holds a seat in the U.S. Senate.

The first woman to sit in Congress was Jeannette Rankin of Montana, a suffragist and pacifist, elected in 1916. The number of women in Congress increased during the 1990s, with the big gain coming in the 1992 elections (often called the "year of the woman"), which sent 48 women to the House and 7 to the Senate in the 103rd Congress (compared with 29 and 2 in the 102nd). Proportionally, however, female representation in Congress is quite low, given that slightly more than half of all Americans are female; however, the proportion of women in the House of Representatives is about average for national legislative bodies around the world (with the exception of the Scandinavian countries, where it is higher).[9] Four women were elected to the Senate in 2000, however, bringing their total to 13, the highest ever. Though leadership posts in Congress are overwhelmingly held by men, a few women have gained

Ben Nighthorse Campbell of Colorado is the first and only Native American to be elected to the U.S. Senate. He surprised both his constituents and colleagues when he switched his party affiliation from Democratic to Republican just a few years after he was first elected to office.

committee chairmanships in recent years. In the House, Nancy Pelosi of California serves as the Democratic Whip, second only to Dick Gephardt among Democratic party leaders.

Occupation Members of Congress are far better educated than the rest of the population. They tend to come from high-income families, have personal incomes that are substantially above average, and lean heavily towards legal or business occupations. There were 209 lawyers in Congress in 2001, or 39 percent (compare this to the late nineteenth century, however, when 60 to 70

Web Exploration
Demographic Representation

Issue: Some people believe that groups are best represented in Congress when members of the group hold office in the House and Senate.

Site: Access the U.S. Senate on our Website at **www.ablongman.com/greenberg**. Go to the "Web Explorations" section for Chapter 11. Select "demographic representation," then "demographics." Select "Senate History," then "Statistics," then examine "women in the Senate" and "minorities" in the Senate. Calculate the numbers of women and minorities that have served in the Senate.

What You've Learned: Has the number increased over the years, stayed the same, or decreased? How would you go about explaining the patterns you have uncovered?

HINT: Because senators, unlike representatives, are elected from a statewide constituency, rather than from relatively homogeneous and smaller House districts, minorities have had a hard time getting elected.

percent were lawyers). The next most numerous occupational groups in Congress are business and banking (together, about 30 percent). Educators made up another 18 percent.[10] Notably absent are lawmakers from blue-collar families or from traditional blue-collar jobs.

Does it matter that Congress is demographically unrepresentative of the American people? Some political scientists and close observers of Congress think not. They suggest that the need to face the electorate forces lawmakers to be attentive to all significant groups in their **constituencies.** A representative from a farm district tends to listen to farm **constituents,** for example, even if that representative is not a farmer.

Nevertheless, many who feel they are not well represented—women, African-Americans, Asian-Americans, Hispanics, blue-collar workers, gays and lesbians, those with disabilities, and the poor—often believe that their interests would get a much better hearing if their numbers were substantially increased in Congress. There is some tentative evidence to support this view: Women members of the House introduce more bills related to women's and children's issues than do their colleagues.[11] The demographic disparity between the American population and the makeup of Congress, then, suggests a violation of the norm of political equality, an important element of democracy.

The Electoral Connection

The election is the principal instrument in a democracy for keeping representatives responsive and responsible to citizens. Let's see how congressional elections affect the quality of representation in the United States.

Electoral Districts   Each state is entitled to two senators. Equal representation gives extraordinary power in the Senate to states with small populations. Alaska, for instance, has exactly the same number of senators as California, but it has only one-fiftieth of California's population. This arrangement can substantially distort popular sentiment and thus diminish democracy.

Representation in the House of Representatives is determined by a state's population, with the proviso that each state must have a least one congressional district. The House of Representatives decided that, beginning in 1910, its upper limit would be 435 members (the House can change this number at any time, though it is highly unlikely). Because the American population is constantly changing with respect to both size and location, the 435 House districts must be periodically redistributed among the states. **Reapportionment,** the technical name for this redistribution, occurs every ten years, after the national census (see Figure 11.2 for the most recent changes). Based on the official census, some states keep the same number of seats; others gain or lose them depending on their relative population gains or losses.

States gaining or losing seats must redraw the boundary lines of their congressional districts. Redrawing district lines within a state is known as **redistricting.** In the past, redistricting was left entirely to state legislatures. Very often, the result was congressional districts of vastly different population size—in New York in the 1930s, some congressional districts were ten times larger than others—and a significantly overrepresented rural population. The Supreme Court ruled in *Wesberry* v. *Sanders* (1964), however, that the principle of one person, one vote applies to congressional districts. Today, all congressional districts within a state must be of roughly equal population size. Because the distribution of the population changes in many states over the course of ten years—some people moving from the cities to the suburbs; some people moving from rural areas to cities—many

constituency

The district of a legislator.

constituent

A citizen who lives in the district of an elected official.

reapportionment

The reallocation of House seats among the states, done after each national census, to ensure that seats are held by the states in proportion to the size of their populations.

redistricting

The redrawing of congressional district lines within a state to ensure roughly equal populations within each district.

Longman
Participate.com
2.0
Simulation
You Are Redrawing the Districts in Your State

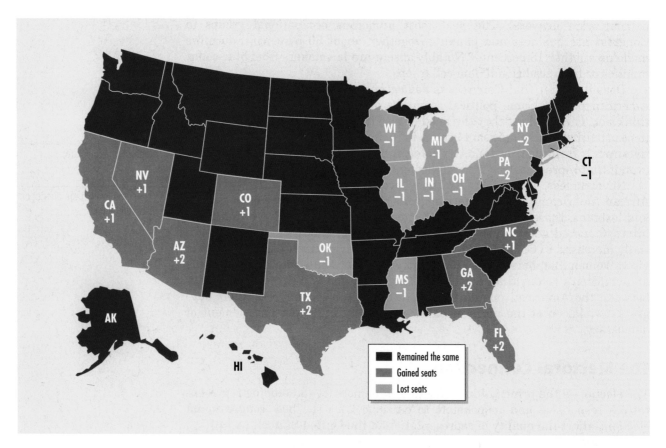

FIGURE 11.2 States Gaining and Losing Congressional Seats Following the 2000 Census

The number of representatives for each state in the House of Representatives is based on the size of its population. Because the relative sizes of the states' populations change over time, the number of representatives from each state is recalculated after each census. This map shows which states gained and lost representatives after the 2000 census. **Source:** U.S. Bureau of the Census, 2001.

district boundaries must be redrawn even in those states that have neither gained nor lost congressional seats.

Although congressional districts must hold approximately equal numbers of citizens, state legislatures are relatively free to draw district lines where they choose. The party that controls the state legislature usually tries to draw the lines in a way that will help its candidates win elections.[12] The results are often strange indeed. Rather than creating compact and coherent districts, neighborhoods, towns, and counties can be strung together in odd-looking ways in order to take full partisan advantage of the redistricting process. Taken to an extreme, the process is known as **gerrymandering,** after Governor Elbridge Gerry of Massachusetts, who signed a bill in 1811 that created a district that looked like a salamander. It made wonderful raw material for editorial cartoonists.

The Supreme Court has tried to prevent the most flagrant abuses, especially when some identifiable group of voters—for example, a racial or ethnic group—is disadvantaged, but it has turned a blind eye to partisan redistricting in which parties in power try to draw district lines to their own advantage. (The Court, along with most politicians, seems to accept the notion that "to the victor

gerrymandering

Redrawing electoral district lines to give an advantage to a particular party or candidate.

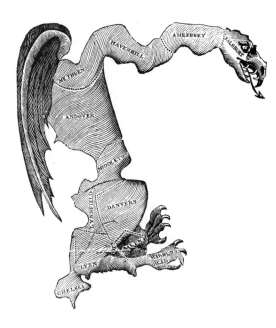

The term *gerrymander* is derived from this 1812 Elkanah Tinsdale cartoon, which lampoons a Massachusetts district drawn to ensure the election of a Republican candidate. The "Gerrymander" was named after Massachusetts Governor Elbridge Gerry, who signed the bill that created the salamander-shaped district.

belongs the spoils.") This redistricting tends to be easily achieved when the same party controls both houses of the state legislature and the governor's office, though even here there are sometimes conflicts if one or another of the party's incumbent House members feels that he or she has been hurt by the redrawn district lines. But this situation of unified party control existed in only 15 states in 2001. So divided party control of the redistricting process was the rule in 30 states in the period leading up to the 2002 congressional elections. (Five additional states used bipartisan commissions to redraw boundaries.) Needless to say, intense partisan conflict and deadlock were often the result, with resolution coming only after the matter was turned over to the courts.

Amendments passed in 1982 to the 1965 Voting Rights Act encouraged the states to create House districts in which racial minorities would be in the majority. Sponsors of the legislation hoped that this would lead to an increase in the number of members of racial minority groups elected to the House. The result was the formation of 24 new **majority-minority districts,** 15 with African-American majorities and 9 with Hispanic-American majorities.[13] Each of these districts did, in fact, elect a member of a racial minority group to office, accounting for most of the increase in minority representation after the 1992 congressional elections. Ironically, however, the creation of such districts tended to undermine Democratic party strength in other districts by taking traditionally Democratic-oriented minority group voters from them. Naturally, Republicans were happy to support minority group efforts to form their own districts. Concentrating black voters in homogeneous districts has tipped the balance to Republicans in many congressional districts, especially in the South. One result is that policies favored by a majority of African-American citizens are less likely to be enacted because of the decreased strength of Democrats in the House, this despite an increase in the number of African-American representatives.[14]

The creation of some of these districts has taken great imagination. North Carolina's Twelfth District, for instance, created after the 1990 census, linked a narrow strip of predominantly African-American communities along 160 miles of Interstate 85 connecting Durham and Charlotte. After first encouraging the creation of majority-minority districts, the Supreme Court had second thoughts about districts that are highly irregular in form, noncontiguous (not compact),

majority-minority districts
Districts drawn to ensure that a racial minority makes up the majority of voters.

unconnected to traditional political jurisdictions (*Shaw* v. *Reno*, 1993), or drawn with race as the sole criterion (*Miller* v. *Johnson*, 1995). In *Hunt* v. *Cromartie* (2001), and much to the surprise of legal and political observers, the Court approved a slightly redrawn North Carolina Twelfth District map, ruling that race can be a significant factor in drawing district lines "so long as it is not the dominant and controlling one." This ruling suggests that most of the other majority-minority districts will probably survive legal challenges, even if their lines are slightly redrawn in the end. (For more insight into how district lines are drawn, see "By the Numbers: How are congressional districts drawn to include equal numbers of voters?")

Money and Congressional Elections Running for the House or the Senate is a very expensive proposition, and it keeps getting more expensive. The average Senate race now costs more than $5.6 million, while the price tag for a House race in a competitive district has gone past $1.5 million.[15] This spending by the candidate's campaign—called hard money—is but the tip of the iceberg. To the grand total, we must add the dollars raised and spent by the political parties on soft-money party-building activities—including get-out-the-vote efforts and issue advertising that supports a party candidate—and money raised and spent by private groups on issue advertising to get the full picture. Such interest group parallel campaigns, many of which involve attack ads on candidates the groups do not want to see elected, were essentially unregulated through the 2002 congressional elections, with no limits on spending. Both soft-money and independent expenditures are now greatly restricted under the new

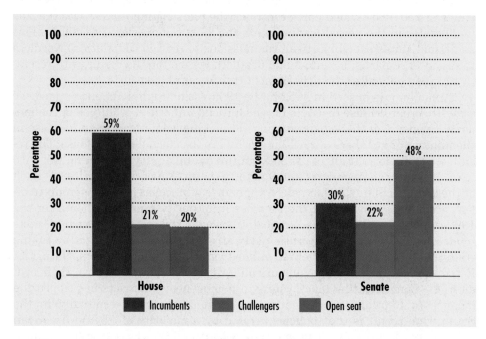

FIGURE 11.3 Campaign Money Spent by Incumbents, Challengers, and Open-Seat Candidates, 1999–2000

Because campaign contributors want access to important decision makers in the House, and because incumbents almost always win there, they tend to give a disproportionate share to House incumbents rather than to challengers. In the Senate, where seats are much more competitive, contributors give the most in open-seat elections, though they do not ignore incumbents.

Source: Federal Election Commission.

campaign finance reform legislation that became effective in 2003—only state and local party organizations can now accept soft-money contributions, and independent campaigns can no longer mention candidates in their ads in the days leading up to an election—but many worry that contributors and candidates will eventually find ways to raise and spend whatever is needed.

Incumbents, especially in the House, have an easier time raising money than their challengers and spend more. **Open-seat election** races in which no incumbent is involved also attract and use lots of money (see Figure 11.3). Being a member of the majority party in Congress also serves as a magnet for money because contributors generally want to be able to have access to those in power.[16]

There is nothing particularly surprising about the high cost of political campaigns, given the ever-greater reliance on expensive campaign technologies such as mass and targeted mailings; polling; focus groups; television, radio, and print advertising; Websites; and phone banks. Also important is the decline of party loyalty in the electorate, which compels candidates to try to reach potential voters on their own—an effort that requires money.

Congressional campaign hard-money comes from four main sources: individuals, political action committees (PACs), political parties, and the candidates themselves (see Figure 11.4). In elections for the House, the largest share comes from individual contributors—53 percent in 2000. Individuals were able to give $1,000 per election to a candidate prior to 2003; the limit was increased to $2,000 after 2003. PACs are the next largest, contributing 30 percent of all campaign money in that election cycle. In Senate races, candidates spend a significant amount of their own money, reaching 25 percent of the total in the 1999–2000 election cycle (compared to only 7 percent in the House).[17]

Participation
The Debate
Over
Campaign
Finance
Reform

open-seat election

An election in which there is no incumbent officeholder.

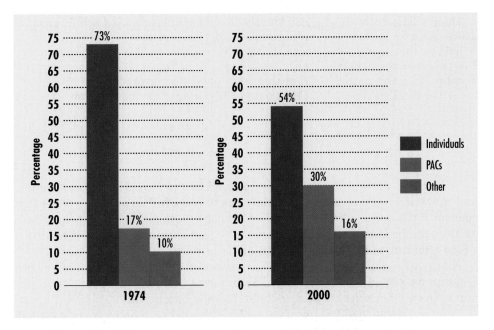

FIGURE 11.4 Sources of Congressional Hard Money, 1974 and 2000

Although the largest share of hard-money campaign contributions still comes from individuals, the share contributed by political action committees (PACs) has grown significantly, as shown by a comparison of the sources of campaign giving in 1974 and 2000.
Source: Federal Election Commission.

By the Numbers

How are congressional districts drawn to include equal numbers of voters?

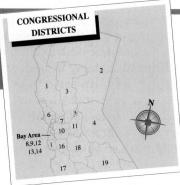

CONGRESSIONAL DISTRICTS

Here is a headline that might have appeared in any city newspaper in late 2001 or early 2002: "Legislature fails to reach agreement on congressional district lines; Issue to be decided by the state courts." What's going on? How difficult can it be to count people and draw congressional district lines? Actually, it is difficult and the issues are important.

Here is what is going on. Every ten years, immediately after the census is conducted, a complicated process of redrawing congressional district lines goes on in the states. In five of them (Arizona, Hawaii, Idaho, New Jersey, and Washington), redistricting is done by a special commission; in the remainder, legislatures and governors must do the job. Agreement becomes especially difficult in states with divided government—those with a legislature controlled by one party and the governorship held by the other party, or those where the two houses of the legislature are controlled by different parties. Often, the courts are called upon to break the deadlock.

Why It Matters: How congressional district lines are drawn has a lot to do with which political party will control the House of Representatives, at least until the next census.

Behind Redistricting: In the House of Representatives, seats are apportioned to each state based on the state's population. Thus, after a new census is taken, a state may gain or lose seats based on the current count of people residing there. To gain a seat means that a new congressional district must be carved out of the state; to lose a seat means that lines must be redrawn to fill in the gap. Even in states where the size of its congressional delegation has not changed, lines must always be redrawn because of population shifts within state boundaries (for example, more people moving to the suburbs). They must make such adjustments because the Supreme Court ruled in *Wesberry* v. *Sanders* (1964) that each congressional district within a state must be of roughly the same population size.

How District Lines Are Drawn: In theory, as long as district lines create congressional districts of roughly equal size, and as long as district lines do not unduly disadvantage racial and ethnic groups, congressional district lines can be drawn in any way that politicians choose. The politicians can be very imaginative in doing so, as they try to ensure that their own party and favored members of Congress are advantaged by the outcome.

PACs are allowed to contribute up to $5,000 per candidate per election, and they can give to as many candidates as they wish. The private groups that sponsor PACs are also free to spend without limit when publicizing their positions on public issues, as you have seen. Such issue campaigns are often thinly veiled efforts to help a particular candidate or party.

Many especially wealthy candidates support their election campaigns out of their own pockets. In the record to date, John Corzine (D–NJ) spent $62 million in his bid for a Senate seat in 2000. He only barely won.

Congressional candidates also receive campaign money from national, congressional, and state party committees. Party committees are allowed to make a $5,000 contribution per campaign to each House candidate. National and senatorial party committees are allowed to give $17,000 to each candidate for each stage of the electoral process. And as you learned in Chapter 9,

Where the district lines are drawn is extremely important in determining the composition of the congressional delegation from each state. Note the following hypothetical example, which shows how easily district lines can be used to effect different outcomes. Let "D" stand for 100,000 Democratic voters; let "R" stand for 100,000 Republican voters; and let "A" stand for 100,000 African-Americans, most of whom vote for Democrats. Taking the same number and locations of voters, district lines can be drawn to yield three Democratic seats and no Republican seats, and to yield two Republican seats and one Democratic seat.

Comment on the Process for Drawing District Lines:

This example is somewhat exaggerated in order to make a point about how politicians strive for maximum flexibility in the redistricting process. In real life, the Court has also demanded that district lines not deviate too much from their historical patterns and that they be relatively compact, putting people who live near each other in the same district. The second example above also shows what happened when African-American organizations and leaders, seeking to increase their representation in Congress, and Republicans, seeking to gain an advantage over Democrats, formed an alliance of convenience during the 1990s to create majority-minority districts across a swath of southern states. These majority-minority districts increased the number of African-Americans in Congress, but the process of concentrating black voters in these districts made the other districts in these states more homogeneously white and Republican, increasing the GOP advantage.

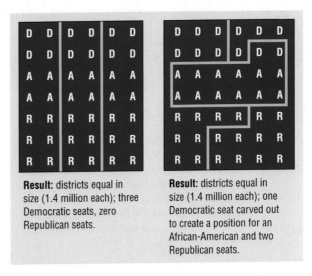

Result: districts equal in size (1.4 million each); three Democratic seats, zero Republican seats.

Result: districts equal in size (1.4 million each); one Democratic seat carved out to create a position for an African-American and two Republican seats.

Different Congressional District Lines, Different Party Outcomes

What to Watch For: Redistricting is one of the most important things that goes on in our political system, yet it is virtually invisible to the general public. Pay attention to the debates over redistricting in your state and determine what political alliances appear and what political bargains are being struck.

What Do You Think? Do you think there might be some non-partisan, scientific method to draw district lines that would avoid the sometimes unseemly process of reshaping congressional districts to suit political parties and interested groups? If there was such a method, do you think it would be better than our current system? Why or why not?

through the 2002 elections, there were no limits to soft-money party expenditures that indirectly helped party candidates.

A majority of Americans have been saying for a long time that they wanted to change the system of funding campaigns. Why did it take so long to reform the system? We examine this question in the "Using the Framework" feature.

The Incumbency Factor Incumbents—current officeholders—win at much higher rates in the House today than ever before. The ability of House incumbents to get reelected improved especially from the late 1940s into the early 1990s (see Figure 11.5), allowing the Democratic party to maintain control over the House of Representatives for four decades (from 1955 to 1994), even as Republicans such as Dwight Eisenhower, Richard Nixon, Ronald

USING THE FRAMEWORK: Campaign Finance Reform

Why did it take so long to get campaign finance reform when so many Americans wanted it?

Background: Campaign finance reform finally happened in 2002 when President George W. Bush signed the Shays-Meehan bill (similar to the earlier McCain-Feingold bill passed in the Senate in 2001). Becoming effective in 2003, the new legislation bans soft-money contributions to the national parties, and limits the ability of independent groups to run campaign ads during the 60 days before an election. The public had long been bothered by the existing campaign finance system, but politicians had not paid much attention.

Things began to change only after John McCain made reform the keystone of his campaign to win the Republican nomination for president in 2000. Further impetus to reform came from the Enron collapse in 2001, and revelations of how free it had been with its money in funding parties and candidates. But why did it take so long for reform to happen? Here we take a broad view of the question, considering how structural, political linkage, and governmental factors affected the fortunes of reform.

Governmental Action

Campaign finance reform bills died in the House and Senate.

Governmental Level

- The Supreme Court has → • Incumbent representatives, ruled that government senators, and presidents cannot limit the amount of were very successful money spent during under the existing system campaigns by candidates, of campaign finance; it is individuals, and organiza- not necessarily in their tions (although it can limit interest to reform the hard-money contributions system. to candidates).

Political Linkages Level

- Private groups of all → • Voters had not → • Public opinion surveys → • Political party political persuasions shown much interest show that Americans committees at all worked in Congress in demanding that wanted campaign finance levels found the and in the states to local, state, or reform but cared more existing system to be block campaign finance national candidates about other things, compatible with their reform in order to support campaign including the state interests. preserve their influence finance reform. of the economy, crime, in electoral campaigns. terrorism, and education.

Structural Level

- The Bill of Rights protects → • Income and wealth free expression by all inequality give some citizens, as well as Americans, but not freedom of association; others, the means to individuals can support contribute to candidate whomever they want in and issue campaigns. the political arena and can form groups to advance their political causes.

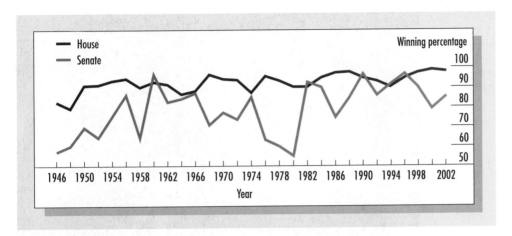

FIGURE 11.5 Rates of Incumbent Reelection in Congress

The probability that incumbents will be reelected remains at historic highs. This does not mean, however, that the membership of Congress is stagnant. Turnover in membership is substantial because of retirements and the defeat of incumbents in primary elections.

Source: Calculations by the authors from various issues of the *Congressional Quarterly Weekly Report.*

Reagan, and George H. W. Bush were winning presidential elections. In spite of mounting discontent with Congress and the anti-incumbent talk of recent years, members of the House of Representatives who choose to run for reelection are still almost always successful. Recently, incumbent senators have been doing almost as well (though not in 2000). In 2002, 98 percent of incumbents returned to the House and 85 percent returned to the Senate.

One important outcome of high incumbency reelection rates in the House is that an overwhelming majority of electoral contests for the House are not really competitive; almost all seats are considered "safe," with the party candidate certain of winning at least 55 percent of the vote. It is common to talk of Democratic districts and Republican districts because such districts, given their histories and the makeup of their populations, almost always elect the candidate of one party to Congress. In the 2000 elections, for example, party pros on both sides estimated that only about 25 to 35 out of 435 districts nationwide were really "in play" in November. Not surprisingly, given that control of the House of Representatives depended on the outcome in these swing districts, party and interest group contributions, as well as issue and parallel campaign activities, were heavily concentrated in them.

Why Incumbents Have the Advantage   Incumbency continues to be a valuable resource. For one thing, as you have seen, incumbents attract and spend more money than their rivals. Many contributors look at campaign contributions as an "investment" in access to key members of Congress.[18] To contribute to a challenger is to jeopardize access if the challenger loses, which is most often the case.

Longman
Participate.com 2.0
Visual Literacy
Why Is It So Hard to Defeat an Incumbent?

Federal projects awarded to districts are part of what is commonly called the legislative *pork barrel.* Pork has long been an important reelection resource for congressional incumbents because they can claim credit for having obtained it for their constituents.

It may seem odd, at first glance, that incumbents, who almost always get reelected, still feel the need to raise and spend so much money on their nomination and election campaigns. They do so, according to most observers, to preempt challenges from within their own party to their renominations, and to convince candidates of the other party that they stand little chance in the fall elections. As one congressional staffer put it, "if you look like a 900 pound gorilla, no one will want to take you on."[19]

Incumbents also use the congressional machinery to help their reelection chances.[20] Already well known to voters because they garner so much free media coverage, members of Congress have many ways to advertise their accomplishments and keep their names before the public. For example, the **franking privilege** allows them to mail newsletters, legislative updates, surveys, and other self-promoting literature free of charge. The House and the Senate also provide travel budgets for lawmakers to make periodic visits to their states or districts. Because members believe that time spent in their districts helps their electoral chances—a belief supported by a great deal of research[21]—they spend lots of time back home.[22] Some manage to spend three or four days a week in their districts or states, meeting constituents, giving speeches, raising money, and keeping in the public eye. The congressional leadership helps by scheduling important legislative business for the Tuesday-to-Thursday period and cutting down the number of hours Congress is in session. (Between 1995 and 2001, the number of hours the House was in session during the year dropped from 1000 hours to 551).[23]

Incumbents also use their offices to "service the district." One way is through **casework,** helping constituents cut through the red tape of the federal bureaucracy, whether it be by speeding up the arrival of a late Social Security check or expediting the issuance of a permit for grazing on public land.[24] Generous budgets for establishing and staffing offices in the constituency help representatives and senators do casework. Another way to service the district is to provide **pork**—federal dollars for various projects in the district or state. In 1998, with the federal budget in surplus, members of Congress heightened their prospects in the coming congressional elections by passing a massive highway spending bill that included more than 1,400 "demonstration projects" targeted for specific roads and bridges in 400 congressional districts.

franking privilege

Public subsidization of mail from the members of Congress to their constituents.

casework

Services performed by members of Congress for constituents.

pork

Also called *pork barrel;* projects designed to bring to the constituency jobs and public money for which the members of Congress can claim credit.

Members of Congress must spend a considerable amount of their time staying in touch with their constituents. Here Representative Rosa DeLauro (D–CT) visits a school in her district.

How Representative?   Representatives and senators pay a great deal of attention to the interests and the preferences of the people in their districts and states. Because they are worried about being reelected, they try to see as many people as they can during their frequent visits home, and they pay attention to their mail and the public opinion polls. Moreover, they vote on and pass laws in rough approximation to public opinion. Members of Congress vote in a manner that is consistent with public opinion in their districts about two-thirds of the time[25] (but members also are pretty skilled at influencing public opinion in their districts) and Congress produces laws that are consistent with national public opinion at about the same rate.[26]

In a substantial number of cases, however, Congress does *not* follow public opinion, even on highly visible issues. If members of Congress follow public opinion two-thirds of the time on important bills, that still leaves one-third of the time that they go their own way. The determination of House Republicans to impeach Bill Clinton in 1998 in the face of strong public opinion opposition is the most obvious recent example. Moreover, on many issues of high complexity or low visibility, such as securities and telecommunications regulation, the public may have no well-formed opinions at all. It is in these areas that one can most fully see the influence of money and interest groups at work. The lobbying community, as we have learned, overwhelmingly represents business and the professions. Moreover, legislators, who are almost entirely on their own in organizing and financing their reelection campaigns, are tempting targets for interest groups. To the degree that these influences distort popular sovereignty and undermine political equality, democracy is impaired.

One of the reasons members of Congress have some latitude in representing public opinion in their districts—indeed, in the nation—is that most come to Congress from relatively "safe" districts where being turned out by the voters is not common. Consequently, House elections do not entirely fulfill the role assigned to elections in democratic theory: as the principle instrument for keeping elected leaders responsive and responsible.

How Congress Works

Congress is a vital center of decision making and policymaking in our national government. It is not a place where the executive's bills are simply rubber-stamped, as it is in legislative bodies in many parliamentary systems. By all accounts, Congress is the most influential and independent legislative body among the Western democratic nations. In this section, we turn our attention to how Congress is organized and how it functions as a working legislative body.

There are a number of very important things to keep in mind as we examine how Congress is organized and operates. First, while they are alike in many ways, the House and Senate are very different institutions. The bodies differ in size, the kinds of constituencies House members and senators represent, the terms of office of their members, and their constitutional responsibilities; together, these differences give each chamber a distinctive character.

Second, both the House and Senate are plagued by what could almost be called centrifugal forces in the sense that things are always on the verge of flying apart, with each representative and senator tempted to go his or her own way. The task of running each body has been likened to "herding cats." The reasons are fairly obvious: Representatives and senators are like independent contractors. Congressional leaders lack the normal tools of organizational leadership to force compliance with their wishes; they cannot order members about, they cannot hire or fire them (this is the role of voters), nor can they control the size of their paychecks or benefits. Moreover, in our candidate-centered form of politics, congressional leaders have little control over the reelection of representatives and senators who run their own campaigns, from fundraising to deciding how to pitch their messages to the voters. Because of this, members of Congress come to Washington as relative equals, and are not easily pushed about. In this section, we examine ways that Congress tries to pull itself together and work effectively as a legislative body.

Political Parties in Congress

Political parties have a very strong presence in Congress. Its members come to Washington, D.C., as elected candidates of a political party. At the start of each session, they organize their legislative business along political party lines. At the start of each new Congress, each **party caucus** meets to select party committees and leaders. The majority party in the House selects the Speaker of the House, while the majority party in the Senate selects the president pro tempore (usually its most senior member) and the majority leader. The majority party in each house also selects the chairs of the committees and subcommittees and determines the party ratios for each.

party caucus
An organization of the members of a political party in the House or Senate.

The Party Composition of Congress
From the 1932 elections in the midst of the Great Depression until the 1994 elections, with brief interludes of Republican control along the way, Congress was dominated by the Democratic party (see Figure 11.6). The Democratic domination of House elections during this period is especially notable, even surviving GOP landslide wins in the presidential elections of 1980 (Reagan), 1984 (Reagan), and 1988 (Bush). In the Senate, Republicans were in the majority for only ten years during this same period. Democratic party domination ended with the 1994 elections, however, when Republicans won control of both houses of Congress for the

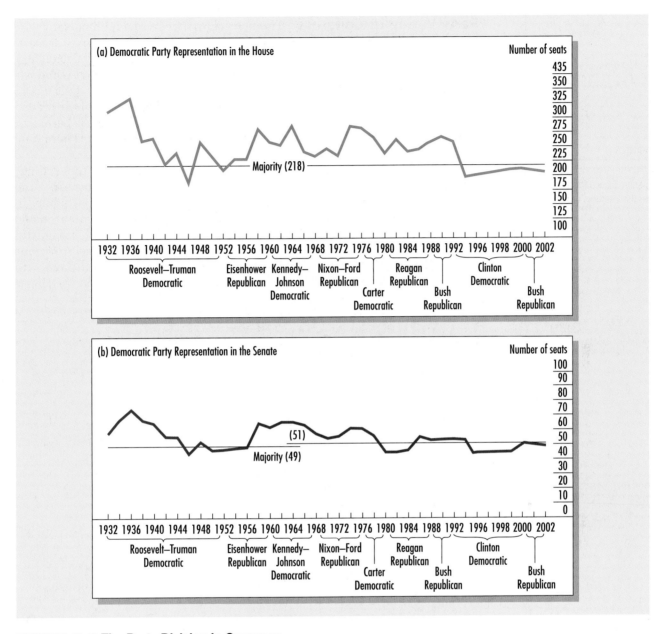

FIGURE 11.6 The Party Division in Congress

Democrats were in the majority in both houses of Congress for most of the years between the early 1930s and 1994. Democratic dominance ended with the 1994 elections, when the Republicans won majority control of both houses for the first time in 40 years. They repeated their victories in 1996 and 1998 but narrowly lost the Senate in 2000. In 2002, the Democrats are once again in the minority position in both houses.

Sources: Harold W. Stanley and Richard G. Niemi, *Vital Statistics on American Politics,* 1999–2000 (Washington, D.C.: Congressional Quarterly Press, 2000); and additional calculations by the authors.

first time in 40 years. The Republicans retained control of Congress until 2001, when Democrats regained control of the evenly divided Senate after moderate Vermont Republican James Jeffords quit his party, uncomfortable with its conservative drift.

Party Voting in Congress   The political parties provide important glue for the decentralized fragments of Congress and the legislative process. Party labels are important cues for members of Congress as they decide how to vote on issues before the committees and on the floor of the House and the Senate. We know this from a long tradition of research on party divisions in roll call voting. This research tells us that party affiliation is the best predictor of the voting behavior of members of the Congress and that it is becoming ever more important.[27] That is to say, both houses of Congress are becoming more **partisan.**

Figure 11.7 shows how often the average Democrat and the average Republican voted with his or her party in partisan votes in Congress.[28] You can see that partisanship is very high—now members vote along party lines in four out of every five votes—and has been steadily increasing. Partisanship was particularly high among Republicans in the 104th Congress, especially in the House, where Newt Gingrich led a party effort to legislate the provisions of the House GOP's congressional campaign platform, the Contract with America. Extraordinary levels of partisanship were also evident in the House

partisan

A committed member of a party; seeing issues from the point of view of the interests of a single party.

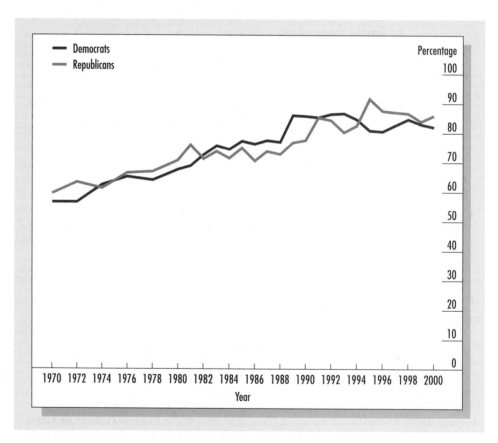

FIGURE 11.7 Partisan Roll Call Votes in Congress

Partisanship has been growing in Congress. One indicator is the increase in the percentage of times the average Democrat and Republican in the House and Senate sided with his or her party on partisan votes—those votes when a majority of Democrats voted against a majority of Republicans.

Source: Calculations by the authors from various issues of the *Congressional Quarterly Weekly Report.*

on votes to impeach President Clinton in December 1999; in the votes associated with his trial in the Senate in early 1999; and in the House vote in 2001 on President George W. Bush's proposed $1.6 trillion tax cut, when hardly any representative or senator broke ranks with his or her party. In the aftermath of the September 11 attacks on the United States, bipartisanship was the rule in both houses for a few months as Congress tackled legislation connected to the war on terrorism. The honeymoon did not last; Congress adjourned at the end of 2001 torn again by intense party conflict.

There are a number of reasons within-party unity is increasing. For one thing, southern conservative Democrats—frequent allies of Republicans in Congress in the past—are fast disappearing, as many politicians and voters have switched over to the Republican party in the rapidly realigning South. The few that remain, such as Zell Miller of Georgia, very often vote with Republicans on major bills. There are also fewer liberal or moderate Republicans in Congress, especially since the tidal wave of conservative Republicans that were elected in 1994 entered Congress.

It's not entirely clear whether party voting differences are caused directly by party affiliation, or indirectly by the character of constituencies by ideology. Some scholars have found strong independent party effects regardless of constituency or ideology. Others argue that the tendency of people in the same party to vote together is simply a reflection of the fact that Democratic lawmakers tend to come from districts and states that are similar to one another and that Republican lawmakers come from places that are different from the constituencies of Democrats. Republicans generally come from higher-income districts than Democrats. Democratic districts, in turn, tend to contain more union members and racial minorities. The strongest tie, in this line of argument, is between the member of Congress and the constituency, not between the member and the party.[29]

Increasingly, internal party unity and conflict between the parties seem attributable to ideology. Both in the electorate and among the members of Congress and other political elites, Democrats are becoming more consistently liberal, while Republicans are becoming more consistently conservative.[30] People who see the world in liberal terms tend to drift toward the Democratic party, while those who see the world in conservative terms find their way to the Republican party. Ideology thus strengthens the glue of party unity and increases partisanship.[31]

Congressional Leadership

The political parties work through the leadership structure of Congress because the leaders of the majority political party are, at the same time, the leaders of the House and the Senate.[32] As Congress becomes more partisan, party becomes ever more important in shaping the actions of House and Senate leaders.[33]

Longman
Participate.com 2.0
Timeline
The Power of the Speaker of the House

Leadership in the House   The leader in the House of Representatives is the Speaker of the House. This position is recognized in the Constitution and stands in the line of succession to the presidency, immediately after the vice-presidency.

Until 1910, the Speaker exercised great power over the House legislative process. The bases of his power were his right to appoint committees and their chairs and his position as chair of the powerful Rules Committee. The revolt of the rank and file against Speaker "Uncle Joe" Cannon in 1910 resulted in the Speaker's removal from the Rules Committee and the elimination of the Speaker's power to appoint committees and their chairs.

The majority party organizes the House at the beginning of each session of Congress and generally has its way if its members remain disciplined. Here the leadership of the minority Democrats in the 104th Congress protest their exclusion from House deliberations by holding mock sessions outside on the Capitol lawn.

From 1910 until the early 1970s, the weakened Speaker competed with a handful of powerful committee chairs for leadership of the House. A few Speakers, such as Sam Rayburn of Texas, were able to lead by sheer dint of their personalities and legislative skills, but power tilted toward the committee chairs most of the time.

The Democratic Caucus staged a revolt against the committee system after 1974 and restored some of the powers of the Speaker, especially in making committee assignments. The Democratic Caucus also gave the Speaker more power to refer bills to committee, control the House agenda, appoint members to select committees, and direct floor debate. This change gave Speakers Tip O'Neill, Jim Wright, and Tom Foley considerable leadership resources.

In 1995, the Republican Caucus gave even more power to control the House legislative process to their first Speaker since 1954, Newt Gingrich. Some scholars suggest that Gingrich's speakership was the most powerful one since Cannon's.[34] Unexpected losses of Republican House seats in the 1998 elections, after a campaign featuring a Gingrich-designed advertising blitz to impeach the president, led to his resignation of the Speakership and from the House. He was succeeded as Speaker by Dennis Hastert of Illinois, a person much less charismatic than Gingrich and one more tied to the traditional way of doing things in the House.

The majority party in the House also selects a majority leader and **whip** to help the Speaker plan strategy and manage the legislative business of the House. Neither House nor party rules spell out the responsibilities of this office. The nature of these jobs depends very much on what the Speaker wants and on the majority leader's and whip's talents and energy. In the 106th and 107th Congresses (1999–2002), partly because of Hastert's understated style and his apparent aversion to the media spotlight, and majority leader Dick Armey's mixed success, it appeared to many observers that Republican Whip Tom DeLay of Texas was the real leader of the House of Representatives.[35] His hard-nosed, "take-no-prisoner" partisanship and his ability to keep his party's

whip

A political party member in Congress charged with keeping members informed of the plans of the party leadership, counting votes before action on important issues, and rounding up party members for votes on bills.

Though only the party Whip, Tom DeLay of Texas was considered by most close observers to be the real leader of the Republican Party in the House of Representatives in the 107th Congress, rather than the Speaker, Denny Hastert, or the Majority Leader, Dick Armey.

representatives in line earned him the nickname "the hammer." DeLay became the majority leader in the 108th Congress.

The minority party elects a minority floor leader, who acts as the chief spokesperson and legislative strategist for the opposition. The minority leader not only tries to keep the forces together but also seeks out members of the majority party who might be won over against the House leadership on key issues. Like the majority party, the minority party elects a whip to assist the minority

Democratic leader Nancy Pelosi of California is the highest-ranking woman in the U.S. House of Representatives. Here she talks to the party faithful about the need to recapture the House from the Republicans in the 2002 elections. The Democrats, however, were unable to accomplish this goal.

leader count and mobilize votes. In 2001, Democrats elected to the post Nancy Pelosi of California, who became the highest-ranking woman in the House.

Leadership in the Senate   Leadership in the Senate is less visible. Senators with formal leadership titles exercise little influence. The presiding officer of the Senate is the vice-president of the United States, but he is rarely in evidence and has no power other than the right to break tie votes. On rare occasions, however, this becomes an important power. Because the 2000 elections left the Senate split 50–50, Vice President Cheney's tie-breaking vote allowed the Republicans to control that body. The majority party also elects a president pro tempore (always the member with the most seniority) to preside in the absence of the vice-president.

The Senate majority leader is as close as one comes to a leader in this body, but the powers of the office pale before those of the Speaker of the House. The Senate majority leader has some influence in committee assignments, office space designation, and control of access to the floor of the Senate. The majority leader is also important in the scheduling of the business of the Senate. The degree of actual influence is based less on formal powers, however, than on skills of personal persuasion, the respect of colleagues, visibility in the media as majority party spokesperson, and a role at the center of many of the various communication networks.

The power of the position is thus personal and not institutional; it cannot be passed on to the next leader. The Senate remains a body of independent, relatively equal members loosely tied together by threads of party loyalty, ideology, and mutual concern about the next election. It is not an environment conducive to decisive leadership, though a few, such as Lyndon Johnson, managed to transcend the limited powers of the office.

Web Exploration
Parties and Leaders in Congress

Issue: Much of what Congress does is determined by the parties and the leadership in the House and Senate.

Site: Access the home pages of the Speaker of the House and of the Senate Majority Leader on our Website at **www.ablongman.com/greenberg**. Go to the "Web Explorations" section for Chapter 11. Select "Parties and leaders in Congress," then "leaders" for each house of Congress. For the House, select "leadership offices," then "Office of the Speaker." For the Senate, select "Senators," then "Senate Leadership." At these sites, you will be able to examine not only the biographies of the present leaders, but also the party legislative programs each has fashioned for his institution.

What You've Learned: What do you think of these programs? Where are the major areas of agreement and disagreement between the parties?

HINT: Your answer will probably depend a great deal on whether you identify with one of the parties and its agenda.

Later president of the United States, Lyndon B. Johnson of Texas was one of the most effective majority leaders in the history of the Senate. Here he urges Senators Kennedy, Symington, Humphrey, and Proxmire to vote for an important civil rights bill.

Congressional Committees

Most of the work of Congress takes place in its many committees and subcommittees. Committees are where many of the details of legislation are hammered out and where much of the oversight of executive branch agencies takes place.

Why Congress Has Committees   Committees serve several useful purposes. For one thing, they allow Congress to process the huge flow of business that comes before it. The committees serve as screening devices, allowing only a small percentage of the bills put forward to take up the time of the House and the Senate.

Committees are also islands of specialization, where members and staff develop the expertise to handle complex issues and to meet executive branch experts on equal terms. The Ways and Means Committee of the House can go toe-to-toe with the Treasury Department, for instance, on issues related to taxation. Committee expertise is one of the reasons Congress remains a vital lawmaking body.

Members of Congress also use their committee positions to enhance their chances for reelection. Rational lawmakers usually try to secure committee assignments that will allow them to channel benefits to their constituents or to advance an ideological agenda popular in their district or state.

Types of Committees in Congress   There are several kinds of committees, each of which serves a special function in the legislative process.

Standing committees are set up permanently, as specified in the House and Senate rules. These committees are the first stop for potential new laws. The ratio of Democrats to Republicans on each committee is set for each house through a process of negotiation between the majority and minority party leaders. The majority party naturally enjoys a majority on each of the committees and controls the chair, as well as a substantial majority on the most

standing committees

Relatively permanent congressional committees that address specific areas of legislation.

important committees, such as the Budget and Finance Committee in the Senate and the Rules Committee and the Ways and Means Committee in the House. The ratio of Democrats and Republicans on committees is a point of considerable contention between the two parties, especially when they are evenly divided, as in the 107th Congress. Senate Democrats threatened to hold up the business of the chamber unless given equal membership (though not the chairmanship) on committees in recognition of the 50–50 split in the Senate at the start of the 107th Congress; then-Majority Leader Trent Lott eventually, though reluctantly, agreed to these terms.

The avalanche of legislative business cannot be managed and given the necessary specialized attention in the full House and Senate standing committees. For most bills, **hearings,** negotiations, and **markup** take place in subcommittees. It is in the subcommittees, moreover, that most oversight of the executive branch takes place.

Select committees are temporary committees created to conduct studies or investigations. They have no power to send bills to the House or Senate floor. They exist to resolve matters that standing committees cannot or do not wish to handle. Often the issues before select committees are highly visible and gain a great deal of public attention for their members. Select committees investigated the Watergate scandal, the Iran-Contra affair, and the purported Chinese nuclear spying effort at the Los Alamos federal laboratories.

Joint committees, with members from both houses, are organized to facilitate the flow of legislation. The Joint Budget Committee, for instance, helps speed up the normally slow legislative process of considering the annual federal budget.

Before a bill can go to the president for signature, it must pass in identical form in each chamber. The committee that irons out the differences between House and Senate versions is called a **conference committee,** and one is created anew for each piece of major legislation. While it is probably an exaggeration to call conference committees the "third house of Congress," as some political observers do, there is no denying their central role in the march of bills through the legislative labyrinth. Although they are supposed to reconcile versions of bills coming out of the House and the Senate, conference committees sometimes add, subtract, or amend provisions that are of great consequence. Much of the power of conference committees comes from the fact that bills reported by them to the House and Senate must be voted up or down; no new amendments are allowed.

How Members of Congress Get on Committees

Because committees are so central to the legislative process, getting on the right one is important for reelection and for achieving policy and ideological goals. Committee assignments are determined by the political parties, guided (but not determined) by the members' **seniority** and preferences. Each party in each chamber goes about the assignment process in a slightly different way. House Democrats use their Steering Committee, chaired by their floor leader, to make assignments. House Republicans have their own Steering Committee on which the Speaker (when Republicans are in the majority) has direct control of one-fourth of the votes. The Speaker also appoints Republican members to the powerful Rules and Ways and Means Committees. In the Senate, both parties use small steering committees made up of party veterans and leaders to make assignments.

Lawmakers have traditionally tried to land positions on committees that will help them serve their constituents and better their prospects for reelection. Thus, they will try to join a committee that directly serves their con-

hearings

The taking of testimony by a congressional committee or subcommittee.

markup

The process of revising a bill in committee.

select committees

Temporary committees in Congress created to conduct studies or investigations. They have no power to report bills.

joint committees

Congressional committees with members from both the House and the Senate.

conference committees

Ad hoc committees, made up of members of both the Senate and the House of Representatives, set up to reconcile differences in the provisions of bills.

seniority

Length of service.

stituency—Agriculture if the member is from a farm district or state, or Interior if the member is from a mining or oil district—or one of the elite committees, such as Rules, Ways and Means, Finance, or Appropriations. Appointment to an elite committee gives a lawmaker not only high visibility and a central role in policymaking, but also a strategic vantage point from which to help the constituency, advance personal and party policy and ideological goals, and attract campaign contributions—all of which help his or her reelection prospects. There is a long waiting list for assignments to the most powerful committees, so new members are unlikely to be appointed to them. For assignments to non-elite standing committees, congressional leaders try to accommodate the wishes of their members, within the constraints of the seniority system.[36]

The Role of Committee Chairs   Not long ago, chairs of committees were the absolute masters of all they surveyed. From 1910, when substantial power was stripped from the Speaker of the House and distributed to committee chairs, until the early 1970s, when the Democrats reined in the autocratic chairs they had created, the heads of congressional committees went unchallenged. Committee chairs hired and assigned staff, controlled the budget, created or abolished subcommittees at will, controlled the agenda, scheduled meetings, and reported (or refused to report) bills to the floor.

Things are different today. Committee chairs now exercise more power over subcommittees and their resources than they did in the 1970s and 1980s, but they have seen much of their power migrate to the party leadership in each house.[37] Republicans in the House and Senate even imposed term limits of six years on committee chairs. The upshot is that decisions that were entirely the province of the chair in the past are now shared with others.

Still, committee chairs remain the most influential and active members of their committees. They cannot command obedience, but they are at the center of all of the lines of communication, retain the power to schedule

The undisputed king of "pork" in recent years was Congressman Bud Schuster from Pennsylvania's Ninth District. As chair of the House Committee on Transportation and Infrastructure, he was in the ideal position to deliver hundreds of federally funded highway, bridge, harbor, and airport projects to congressional districts across the United States.

meetings and control the agenda, control the committee staff, manage committee funds, appoint members to conference committees, and are usually the most senior and experienced members of their committees, to whom some deference is owed. A few, such as Bud Schuster (R–PA), the chair of the House Transportation and Infrastructure Committee (responsible for financing highways, bridges, and airports), continue to exercise power in the traditional mold. Not even Newt Gingrich was able to block his massive $218 billion, budget-busting highway bill in 1997, and Tom DeLay and Dennis Hastert were helpless to stop Schuster's airport construction bill in 1999. His power is based on the loyalty and size of his committee (at 75 members, the largest in the House) and the campaign money he attracts from private groups interested in federally financed projects, most of which he uses to assist other members of the House in their reelection efforts.

Rules and Norms in the House and Senate

Like all organizations, Congress is guided by both formal rules and informal norms of behavior.[38] Rules specify precisely how things should be done and what is not allowed. Norms are generally accepted expectations about how people ought to behave and how business ought to proceed.

Traditionally, members of the House have been expected to become specialists in some area or areas of policy and to defer to the judgment of other specialists on most bills. This mutual deference is known as **reciprocity.** While reciprocity is still common, deference to specialists—usually chairs or ranking members of committees—is declining in favor of deference to the wishes of party leaders. In the Senate, the norm of reciprocity was always less prevalent than it was in the House. Because there are fewer members in the Senate, because senators are elected on a statewide basis, and because the Senate has been the breeding ground for many presidential candidacies, a senator has more prestige, visibility, and power than a member of the House. As a result, senators are generally unwilling to sit quietly for a term or two, waiting their turn. It is not unusual for a first-term senator to introduce major bills and make important speeches. In the House, such a thing was very unusual in the past. There, the old rule held sway: "To get along, go along."

It is expected in both chambers that lawmakers will respect, or at least tolerate, the reelection motivations of their colleagues. They are expected, for instance, to support a legislative schedule that allows for abundant visits back to the constituency and to vote for funding for campaign-related activities such as the right to send mail to constituents free of charge and for budgets for district offices. They must learn, moreover, to put up with activities that have no specific legislative purpose but allow their fellow lawmakers to advertise, take credit, and take positions—good examples are the insertion of materials into the *Congressional Record* and speeches on the floor tailored to the evening news back home.

At one time, senators and representatives were expected to act with courtesy and civility toward one another, even if they detested one another—hence the informal prohibition against the use of names and the elaborate references to the "honorable gentleman from Wisconsin" or the "senior senator from California." This expectation of civility has largely disappeared in recent years, especially in the House, as Congress has become a more partisan and ideological place.[39]

Legislative life is much more rule-bound in the House of Representatives, because of its large size, than in the Senate; it tends to be more organized and hierarchical (see Table 11.2). Leaders in the House have more power, the majority party exercises more control over legislative affairs, the procedures are

reciprocity

Deferral by members of Congress to the judgment of subject-matter specialists, mainly on minor technical bills.

TABLE 11.2 Differences Between House and Senate Rules and Norms

Senate	House
Informal, open, nonhierarchical	Rule-bound, hierarchical
Leaders have few formal powers	Leaders have many formal powers
Members may serve on two or more major committees	Members restricted to one major committee
Less specialized	More specialized
Unrestricted floor debate	Restricted floor debate
Unlimited amendments possible	Limited amendments possible
Amendments need not be germane	Amendments must be germane
Unlimited time for debate unless shortened by unanimous consent or halted by invocation of cloture	Limited time for debate
More prestige	Less prestige
More reliance on staff	Less reliance on staff
Minority party plays a larger role	Minority party plays a smaller role
Less partisan	More partisan

more structured, and the individual members have a harder time making their mark. It is geared toward majority rule, with the minority playing a lesser role. The Senate tends to be a more open and fluid place, and it lodges less power in its leaders than the House does. Each senator is more of an independent operator than his or her House colleagues. The Senate is a much more

Congressional staff help members of Congress carry out their many legislative responsibilities. Here Representative Dick Gephardt (D–MO) meets with a member of his staff to plan the day's activities.

relaxed place, one that accommodates mavericks, tolerates the foibles of its members, and pays more attention to members of the minority party. It is a place where the minority and individual senators play important roles in the legislative process.

Differences between the House and the Senate are especially apparent in floor debate. Bills are scheduled for floor debate in the Senate, for instance, not by a powerful committee but by **unanimous consent,** meaning that business can be blocked by a single dissenter. In the Senate, in a growing practice that is beginning to draw criticism, each senator has the power to place a hold on a bill or nomination to delay consideration by the whole body. Unlike the House, where debate on a bill is strictly regulated as to amendments and time limits (determined by the Rules Committee with the agreement of the Speaker), the Senate's tradition allows for unlimited numbers of amendments and unlimited debate. Senators in the minority have periodically used this tolerance of unlimited amendments and debate to good effect. Because limiting debate is so difficult in the Senate, the opponents of a bill can tie up legislative business by refusing to stop debating its merits. This practice is known as the **filibuster.** During a filibuster, senators opposing a bill have been known to talk for hour upon hour, often working in shifts. The only requirement is that they say something; they cannot hold the floor without speaking. During a filibuster, senators need not even talk about the bill itself; Senate rules do not require remarks to be germane. Senators have read from novels or quoted verse, have told stories about their children, and have quoted long lists of sports statistics. The purpose is to force the majority to give up the fight and move on to other business.

When a very strong majority favors a bill or when a bill that has great national import and visibility is before the body, the Senate can close debate by invoking **cloture.** Cloture requires support by three-fifths of those present and voting. It is very rarely tried; it very rarely succeeds. Cloture is so difficult to invoke that the mere threat of a filibuster by a determined minority party, a growing trend in the Senate, often forces the majority to comply with the wishes of the minority. Many observers believe that the increasing use of the filibuster threat circumvents majority rule and therefore undermines democracy.

Legislative Responsibilities: How a Bill Becomes a Law

We can put much of what we have learned to work by seeing how a bill moves through the legislative labyrinth to become a law. The path by which a bill becomes a law is so strewn with obstacles that few bills survive; in fact, only about 6 percent of all bills that are introduced are enacted. To make law is exceedingly difficult; to block bills from becoming laws is relatively easy. At each step along the way (see Figure 11.8), a "no" decision can stop the passage of a bill in its tracks. As one account points out, members of the House or the Senate have "two principal functions: to make laws and to keep laws from being made. The first of these [they] perform only with sweat, patience, and a remarkable skill in the handling of creaking machinery; but the second they perform daily, with ease and infinite variety."[40]

What follows describes how a bill becomes a law most of the time. Minor bills are often considered in each house under special rules that allow shortcuts. Thus, in the House, the "suspension calendar" and the "corrections calendar" set aside certain times for consideration of minor matters. It is also worth noting that bills involving the federal budget—authorization and appropriations bills—have several unique aspects to them, which need not concern us here.

unanimous consent

Legislative action taken "without objection" as a way to expedite business; used to conduct much of the business of the Senate.

filibuster

A parliamentary device used in the Senate to prevent a bill from coming to a vote by "talking it to death," made possible by the norm of unlimited debate.

cloture

A vote to end a filibuster or a debate; requires the votes of three-fifths of the membership of the Senate.

Longman
Participate.com 2.0
Simulation
You Are a Member of Congress

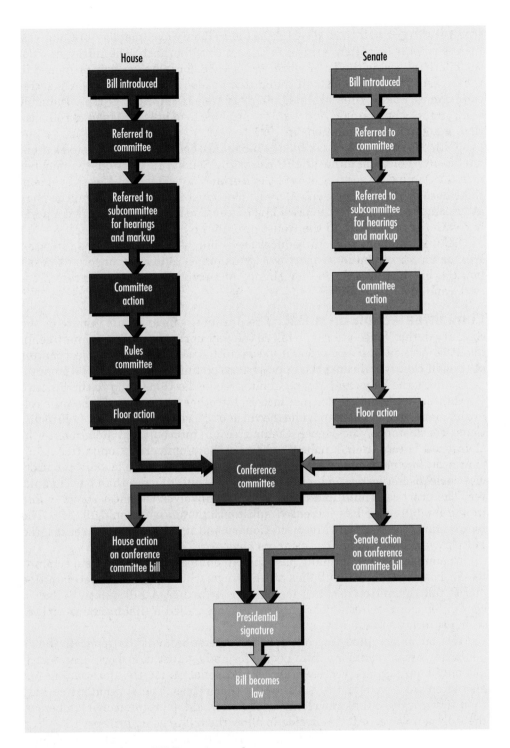

FIGURE 11.8 How a Bill Becomes a Law

This diagram shows the path by which most bills introduced in Congress become law. As explained in the text, the road that bills must travel is complex and difficult, and few bills survive it. A bill can be derailed at any stop in its passage. A subcommittee can refuse to report a bill; a bill may be defeated on the floor of each chamber; a conference committee may fail to reach an agreement on a compromise; the conference bill may be defeated in either chamber; or the president may veto the bill.

Introducing a Bill A bill can be introduced only by a member of Congress. In reality, bills are often written in the executive branch. The initial draft of the bill that became the Tax Reform Act of 1986, for instance, was fashioned in the Treasury Department by a committee headed by the department's secretary, James Baker. Bills are also often written by interest groups. Industry trade groups, for example, wrote substantial parts of bills designed to roll back timber and mining regulations in 1995.

With the exception of tax bills (which must originate in the House), a bill may be introduced in either the House or the Senate. In the House, a member introduces a bill by putting it into the **hopper** (a box watched over by one of the House clerks). In the Senate, a member must announce a bill to the body after being recognized by the presiding officer. The bill is then assigned a number, with the prefix *H.R.* in the House or *S.* in the Senate.

The lawmaker who introduces the bill is known as its *sponsor.* Lawmakers try to build support by signing on as many cosponsors as possible; the bill has an even better chance of surviving if its cosponsors cross party and ideological lines.

Committee Action on a Bill The presiding officer in the Senate or the Speaker in the House refers the bill to the appropriate standing committee. In about 80 percent of cases, referral to committee is routine; the subject matter of the bill clearly indicates the appropriate committee. Revenue bills go automatically to the Ways and Means Committee in the House and to the Finance Committee in the Senate, for instance. In the other 20 percent of cases, the relevant committee is not so obvious because of overlapping committee jurisdictions. For instance, the House Committee on International Relations is in charge of "international policy," whereas the Commerce Committee is in charge of "foreign commerce generally." In such cases, House leaders can exercise some discretion or send a bill (or parts of a bill) to more than one committee. The practice of multiple referral usually involves the most complex and important bills and has increased substantially since the mid-1970s.[41] The more committee referrals are discretionary and not automatic, of course, the more power House and Senate leaders have.

Committee chairs normally pass the bill on to the appropriate subcommittee for hearings. Many a bill dies at this stage, when either the subcommittee or the full committee declines to consider it further. A bill quietly killed in committee can reach the floor only by a device called a **discharge petition,** which is rarely successful.

If a bill is accepted for consideration, the subcommittee generally holds hearings, taking testimony from people for and against it. Subcommittee staff not only help prepare representatives and senators for the questioning but also often take part in the questioning themselves. The subcommittee may then forward the bill as rewritten by the staff and subcommittee members to the full committee, or it can decide to allow the bill to go no further.

Rewriting the bill in committee is called the *markup* (discussed earlier), which usually occurs amid very intense bargaining and deal making, with an eye toward fashioning a bill that will muster majority support in the full committee and on the floors of the House and the Senate and that will gain the support of the president. The staff plays a central role in the markup.

The subcommittee reports its action to the full committee. The committee chair, in consultation with other important members of his or her committee, may opt for the committee to hold its own hearings and markup sessions, may decide to kill the bill outright, or may simply accept the action of the subcommittee. If the subcommittee has done its job well and has consulted with the most important players on the full committee (especially the

hopper

The box in the House of Representatives in which proposed bills are placed.

discharge petition

A petition signed by 218 House members to force a bill that has been before a committee for at least 30 days while the House is in session out of the committee and onto the floor for consideration.

chair), the committee will simply rubber-stamp the bill and move it along for floor action.

Floor Action on a Bill

If a bill is favorably reported from committee, congressional leaders schedule it for floor debate. In the House, a bill must first go to the Rules Committee, which must issue a rule under whose terms the bill will be considered. A rule specifies such things as the amount of time for debate and the number (if any) and nature of amendments allowed. The Rules Committee may choose not to issue a rule at all or to drag its feet, as it did with civil rights bills until the mid-1960s. This has happened less often in recent years because both Democratic and Republican Speakers have had more power over Rules Committee appointments. The committee can also grant a "closed rule," allowing only a yes or no vote without amendments, as it generally does with tax bills.

Floor debate in the Senate, where rules do not limit debate as in the House, is much more freewheeling. Floor debate is also more important in the Senate in determining the final form a bill will take because Senate committees are less influential than House committees. Senators are also less likely to defer to committee judgments.

After floor debate, the entire membership of the chamber votes on the bill, either as reported by the committee or (more often) after amendments have been added. If the bill receives a favorable vote, it then goes through the same obstacle course in the other chamber or awaits action by the other house if the bill was introduced there at the same time.

Conference Committee

Even if the bill makes it through both houses, its journey is not yet over. Bills passed by the House and the Senate almost always differ from one another, sometimes in minor ways and sometimes in quite substantial ways. Before the bill goes to the president, its conflicting versions must be rewritten so that a single bill gains the approval of both chambers of Congress. This compromise bill is fashioned in a conference committee made up of members from both the House and the Senate, customarily from the relevant committees.

A bill from a conference committee must be voted up or down on the floors of the House and the Senate; no amendments or further changes are allowed. If, and only if, both houses approve it, the bill is forwarded to the president for consideration.

Presidential Action

Because the president plays an important constitutional role in turning a bill into a law, he or his assistants and advisers are usually consulted throughout the legislative process. If the president approves the bill, he signs it and it becomes law. If he is not particularly favorable but does not want to block the bill, it becomes law after ten days if he takes no action. He can also **veto** the bill and return it to Congress. A bill can still become law by a two-thirds vote of each house, which will override the president's veto. A president can also kill a bill at the end of a congressional session if he takes no action and Congress adjourns before ten days pass. This is known as a **pocket veto.**

veto

Presidential disapproval of a bill that has been passed by both houses of Congress. The president's veto can be overridden by a two-thirds vote in each house.

pocket veto

Rejection of a bill if the president takes no action on it for ten days and Congress has adjourned during that period.

Legislative Oversight of the Executive Branch

Oversight is another important responsibility of Congress. Oversight involves keeping an eye on how the executive branch carries out the provisions of the laws that Congress has passed and on possible abuses of power by executive branch officials, including the president.

Holding hearings to determine if new laws are needed and if executive branch agencies are properly carrying out their responsibilities under existing laws is one of Congress's most important functions. Here the Senate Energy Committee hears testimony from Enron Chairman Kenneth Lay about the collapse of his company.

Oversight is primarily the province of the committees and subcommittees of Congress, and it is among Congress's most visible and dramatic roles. High-profile examples of legislative probes of alleged administrative misconduct include Watergate, the Iran-Contra affair, Whitewater, the savings-and-loan collapse and bailout, purported Chinese nuclear spying, and the Branch Davidian tragedy at Waco.

Hearings are an important part of the oversight process. Testimony is taken from agency officials, outside experts, and such congressional investigatory institutions as the Government Accounting Office and the Office of Technology Assessment. The hearings are not simply information-gathering exercises, however. As often as not, they are designed to send signals from committee members to the relevant part of the bureaucracy. Hearings that focus on the overly aggressive efforts of Internal Revenue Service agents to collect taxes, for example, are a clear signal to IRS officials that they had better rein in their agents before the next round of hearings on the budget. Tough questioning of Attorney General John Ashcroft in 2001 by Senator Patrick Leahy's Judiciary Committee concerning the use of military tribunals, the practice of listening in on conversations between terror suspects and their attorneys, and the detention of suspects and material witnesses for an indeterminant time period, was meant as a signal to both Ashcroft and the Bush administration that Congress would be vigilant on how the "war on terrorism" was being waged at home.

Congress's most powerful instrument of oversight of the Executive Branch is impeachment (responsibility of the House) and removal from office (responsibility of the Senate) of high executive officials, including the president. This is a blunt tool, rarely used, except in the most partisan atmosphere or in cases involving truly egregious executive behavior. Over the course of American history, only seven executives have been removed from office by the Senate. No president has ever been convicted and removed from office, but the impeachment processes in the House of presidents Andrew Johnson, Nixon, and Clinton were so divisive that Congress treads very cautiously in this area.

Congress, Public Policy, and the American People

The way Congress is organized and operates greatly influences the kinds of public policies we have, how people feel about government, and the quality of democracy in the United States.

Congress as Policymaker

A frequently heard criticism of Congress is that it is so parochial and fragmented that it cannot fashion coherent national policy.[42] The argument goes like this. First, Congress is filled with members who are judged by the voters on the basis of their individual attributes and service to the district and to interest groups, not on the basis of the performance of Congress as a whole. One result is that lawmakers worry more about themselves than about the standing and effectiveness of their institution or its collective national policymaking responsibilities.[43]

Second, because lawmakers are responsive to organized interests, serve the constituency as their first order of business, and try to avoid difficult decisions that might put their reelection at risk (or so it is claimed), Congress cannot easily tackle the nation's most difficult problems or think about solutions in general terms. Congress would rather practice "distributive" politics, in which benefits are parceled out to a wide range of constituency and interest group claimants. While this pattern conforms to the self-interested electoral calculations of the individual member, it is, according to many observers, the basis for the overall ineffectiveness and decline of Congress as a national policymaking institution.

It is hard to assess the validity of these criticisms. The evidence is mixed. Congress has, at times, fashioned broad and coherent national policies in response to tangible problems and strong majority opinions. We have also seen that Congress retains a far greater policymaking role than legislative bodies in parliamentary systems and that on domestic issues, it is becoming ever more forceful. Nevertheless, historically, Congress has functioned best as a policymaker when the president, supported by the existence of a national majority in favor of a particular course of action, is able to provide strong leadership. Franklin Roosevelt's New Deal legislative program, Lyndon Johnson's Great Society, and Ronald Reagan's conservative triumphs in 1981 come to mind. For a time, during Newt Gingrich's leadership of the conservative revolution in the House of Representatives in the 104th Congress, it appeared that a major legislative program could be passed without (or against) presidential leadership. Once most bills from the Contract with America failed to become law, however, it became apparent again that the creation of broad and coherent national policies requires presidential leadership.

Congress and the American People

Although Americans tend to approve of their own representatives and senators, they have low regard for Congress as an institution. Except in rare instances, fewer Americans say they believe Congress is "doing a good job" than believe that the president is doing a good job. Fewer report having "a great deal of confidence" in Congress as an institution than for the Supreme Court or the president. This pattern has endured for a long time and shows no sign of abating.[44] Approval and confidence ratings, much as those for the

344 PART FOUR Government and Governing

HOW DEMOCRATIC ARE WE?

Is Congress Out of Touch?

PROPOSITION: Congress is out of touch with the American people and doesn't do what the people want it to do.

AGREE: Although representatives and senators must ultimately face the voters, their reelection prospects are strongly related to how much money they can raise for their campaigns. With a healthy campaign war chest, as well as the advantages they have as incumbents, representatives and senators can get their message to voters and make the case that they should remain in office. Building a healthy campaign war chest also depends heavily on money from special interests and wealthy individuals. It is not surprising, then, that they pay particular attention to what these contributors want. Finally, the way Congress is organized and works makes it very difficult to turn the wishes of the majority into concrete laws, even if members of Congress are inclined to be responsive.

DISAGREE: Although they have to attend to the interests of big contributors, representatives and senators are ultimately accountable to the voters. It is for this reason that they pay a great deal of attention to their constituent mail, spend substantial time in their home districts and states talking to the voters, and invest heavily in polling to stay in touch. And, in the end, on most major issues, Congress legislates in ways that match what the American people want.

THE AUTHORS: If you believe, as the framers did, that Congress ought to be a deliberative body, free from popular pressures, acting in the public interest as representatives and senators define it, then the failure to legislate exactly as the public would want will cause you no great anxiety. If you believe that Congress ought to be democratically responsive, then you might take solace in the evidence that shows that Congress follows public opinion to a substantial degree in the long run. However, whatever you believe about the nature of the relationship between the public and Congress, you ought to be discomforted by the disproportionate role of special interests and large contributors on a wide range of important issues, particularly those that are out of public view.

president, tend to track the economy and confidence about the future among Americans, being higher in good times and lower in bad times. But it is inescapable that when it comes to national institutions, Congress does not fare well.

Scholars and journalists have advanced a number of reasons for this state of affairs, including rising partisanship, gridlock within Congress and between Congress and the president, and the apparent influence in Congress of special interests. Two scholars have a unique and intriguing alternative explanation: The American people, they suggest, often do not really like the messiness of the democratic process itself, so evident in the give-and-take of the legislative process. As they put it,

People do not wish to see uncertainty, conflicting opinions, long debate, competing interests, confusion, bargaining, and compromised, imperfect solutions. They want government to do its job quietly and efficiently, sans conflict and sans fuss. In short . . . they often seek a patently unrealistic form of democracy.[45]

Summary

The framers of the Constitution wanted to fashion a legislative branch that was both energetic and limited. They granted Congress legislative power, gave it an existence independent of the executive branch, and enumerated an impressive range of powers. They also gave the other branches powers to check legislative excesses, created a bicameral body, and strictly denied certain powers to Congress.

Structural change in the nation has shaped Congress, influencing it to increase in size, expand the volume and complexity of its business, and become more institutionalized and professional.

Congress is a representative institution. Its members are constantly balancing the preferences of the people in their constituencies and important interest groups and contributors. Because elections are the most important mechanism for representation, and because they are the way in which members attain office, elections dominate the time and energy of lawmakers and shape how Congress organizes itself and goes about its business.

To conduct its business, Congress depends on an elaborate set of norms and rules and a web of committees and subcommittees, political parties, legislative leaders, and an extensive staff. Several of these elements encourage fragmentation, decentralization, and occasional gridlock but also allow the development of the specialized expertise that enables Congress to meet the executive branch on equal terms. Other tools help the members coordinate and expedite legislative business.

Suggestions for Further Reading

Caro, Robert. *The Years of Lyndon Johnson*. New York: Knopf, 1982.
  This classic and award-winning biography of Lyndon Baines Johnson of Texas reveals more about how Congress worked in the "old days" than virtually any academic treatise.

Davidson, Roger H., and Walter J. Oleszek. *Congress and Its Members,* 8th ed. Washington, D.C.: Congressional Quarterly Press, 2002.
  The classic textbook on Congress, now in its eighth edition.

Oleszek, Walter J. *Congressional Procedures and the Policy Process.* Washington, D.C.: Congressional Quarterly Press, 1996.
  The most comprehensive compilation yet published of the rules and operations of the legislative process in Congress, written by a scholar who served as the policy director of the Joint Committee on the Organization of Congress.

Sinclair, Barbara. *Unorthodox Lawmaking: New Legislative Processes in the U.S. Congress.* Washington, D.C.: Congressional Quarterly Press, 1997.
  Argues that the traditional textbook rendition of "how a bill becomes a law" has dramatically changed over the past two decades.

Specialized newspapers and journals: *The Hill, Roll Call, Congressional Quarterly, National Journal.*
  Valuable sources for up-to-the-minute, in-depth coverage of what is happening in Congress.

Internet Sources

Capweb   **www.capweb.net**
  An extremely rich site for information on Congress. Features include commentary on the issues before Congress, access to information on pending legislation, legislative schedules and ways to contact members of Congress, caucuses, committees, rules, histories of the House and Senate, and much more. Links, as well, to Congressional Quarterly (journal) and The Hill *(weekly newspaper), the House and Senate, and the other two federal branches.*

Federal Election Commission   **www.fec.gov**
  Information on campaign finance for presidential and congressional elections.

Thomas   **http://thomas.loc.gov/**
  Expansive repository of information on the House of Representatives, including the full text and progress of bills, the Congressional Record, legislative procedures and rules, committee actions, and more.

U.S. House of Representatives Home Page   **www.house.gov**
  House schedule, House organization and procedures, links to House committees, information on contacting representatives, and historical documents on the House of Representatives.

U.S. Senate Home Page   **www.senate.gov**
  Similar to the House of Representatives Home Page, focused on the Senate. One exciting new feature is a virtual tour of the Capitol.

Notes

1. This section is based on a number of sources: Allen G. Breed, "Low Black Turnout Helped South GOP," *Salon* (**www.salon.com**), November 6, 2002; Elisabeth Bumiller and David E. Sanger, "Republicans Say Rove Was Mastermind of Big Victory," *The New York Times,* November 7, 2002, p. B1; Jeanne Cummings and Tom Hamburger, "White House Efforts Fueled GOP Gains in House and Senate," *The Wall Street Journal Online* (**www.wsj.com**), November 7, 2002; "Higher Turnout Among Republicans Key to Victory," The CNN/USA Today/Gallup Poll (**www.gallup.com/poll/releases/pr021107.asp**), November 7, 2002.

2. Information in this paragraph is based on a number of sources: calculations from official election returns by the authors; Yochi J. Dreazen, "TV Election Ads Cost a Record $900 Million," *The Wall Street Journal Online* (**www.wsj.com**), November 5, 2002; and Thomas B. Edsall, "Republicans: Big Cash Edge," *Washington Post Online* (**www.washingtonpost.com**), November 7, 2002.

3. Roger H. Davidson and Walter J. Oleszek, *Congress and Its Members,* 8th ed. (Washington, D.C.: Congressional Quarterly Press, 2002), pp. 17–18.

4. Davidson and Oleszek, *Congress and Its Members,* p. 24.

5. Quoted in Charles Warren, *The Supreme Court in U.S. History* (Boston: Little, Brown, 1919), p. 195.

6. Walter J. Oleszek, *Congressional Procedures and the Policy Process,* 4th ed. (Washington, D.C.: Congressional Quarterly Press, 1996), p. 4.

7. Quoted in Charles Henning, *The Wit and Wisdom of Politics* (Golden, CO: Fulcrum, 1989), p. 235.

8. Abraham Lincoln, announcement in the *Sagamo Journal,* New Salem, Illinois (June 13, 1836).

9. Paul Lewis, "In the World's Parliaments, Women Are Still a Small Minority," *The New York Times* (March 16, 1997), p. 7.

10. Davidson and Oleszek, *Congress and Its Members,* pp. 124–125.

11. Arturo Vega and Juanita Firestone, "The Effects of Gender on Congressional Behavior and the Substantive Representation of Women," *Legislative Studies Quarterly* (May 1995), Vol. 20, pp. 213–222. Also see the collection of research on women's impact on the legislative process in Cindy Simon Rosenthal (ed.), *Women Transforming Congress* (Norman: University of Oklahoma Press, 2002).

12. Gary W. Cox and Jonathan Katz, "The Reapportionment Revolution and Bias in U.S. Congressional Elections," *American Journal of Political Science* 43 (1999), pp. 812–840.

13. Davidson and Oleszek, *Congress and Its Members,* pp. 51–58.

14. Charles Cameron, David Epstein, and Sharon O'Halloran, "Do Majority-Minority Districts Maximize Black Representation in Congress?" *American Political Science Review* 90 (1996), pp. 794–812; David Epstein and Sharon O'Halloran, "A Social Science Approach to Race, Districting and Representation," *American Political Science Review* 93 (1999), pp. 187–191; and David Lublin, *The Paradox of Representation: Racial Gerrymandering and Minority Interests* (Princeton, NJ: Princeton University Press, 1997).

15. Davidson and Oleszek, *Congress and Its Members,* pp. 70–71.

16. Gary W. Cox and Eric Magar, "How Much Is Majority Status in the U.S. Congress Worth?" *American Political Science Review* 93 (1999), pp. 299–309.

17. Federal Election Commission, news release, January 9, 2001.

18. Richard Hall and Frank W. Wayman, "Buying Time: Moneyed Interests and the Mobilization of Bias in Congressional Committees," *American Political Science Review* 84 (1990), pp. 797–820.

19. Sara Fritz and Dwight Morris, *Gold-Plated Politics: Running for Congress in the 1990s* (Washington, D.C.: CQ Press, 1992), p. 28.

20. David R. Mayhew, *Congress: The Electoral Connection* (New Haven, CT: Yale University Press, 1974).

21. Malcolm Jewell, "Legislators and Their Districts," *Legislative Studies Quarterly* 13 (1988), pp. 403–412.

22. Richard F. Fenno Jr., *Senators on the Home Trail* (Norman, OK: University of Oklahoma Press, 1996).

23. Juliet Eilperin, "The House Member as Perpetual Commuter," *The Washington Post National Edition* (September 10–16, 2001), p. 29.

24. Bruce Cain, John A. Ferejohn, and Morris P. Fiorina, *The Personal Vote: Constituency Service and Electoral Independence* (Cambridge, MA: Harvard University Press, 1987); Glenn Parker, *Homeward Bound: Explaining Change in Congressional Behavior* (Pittsburgh: University of Pittsburgh Press, 1986).

25. Robert S. Erikson, "Constituency Opinion and Congressional Behavior," *American Journal of Political Science* 22 (1978), pp. 511–535; Robert S. Erikson and Gerald C. Wright, "Voters, Candidates, and Issues in Congressional Elections," in Lawrence C. Dodd and Bruce I. Oppenheimer, eds., *Congress Reconsidered,* 4th ed. (Washington, D.C.: Congressional Quarterly Press, 1989), pp. 91–116.

26. Alan Monroe, "Consistency Between Public Preferences and National Policy Decisions," *American Politics Quarterly* 7 (1979), pp. 3–19; Benjamin I. Page and Robert Y. Shapiro, "Effects of Public Opinion on Policy," *American Political Science Review* 77 (1983), pp. 175–190.

27. Davidson and Oleszek, *Congress and Its Members,* p. 274.

28. Ibid., p. 276.

29. Davidson and Oleszek, *Congress and Its Members,* pp. 279–280.

30. Alan I. Abramowitz and Kyle L. Saunders, "Ideological Realignment in the U.S. Electorate," *Journal of Politics* (1998), Vol. 60, pp. 634–652.

31. Keith T. Poole and Howard Rosenthal, *Congress: A Political-Economic History of Roll-Call Voting* (New York: Oxford University Press, 1997).

32. See John J. Kornacki, ed., *Leading Congress: New Styles, New Strategies* (Washington, D.C.: Congressional Quarterly Press, 1990); David W. Rohde, *Parties and Leaders in the Postreform Congress* (Chicago: University of Chicago Press, 1991).

33. Alan A. Abramowitz, "'Mr. Mayhew, Meet Mr. DeLay,' or the Electoral Connection in the Post-Reform Congress," *PS* (June 2001), Vol. 34, no. 2, pp. 257–258.

34. Oleszek, *Congressional Procedures and the Policy Process,* p. 33.

35. Melinda Henneberger, "DeLay Holds No Gavel, But Firm Grip on Reins," *The New York Times* (June 21, 1999), p. 1.

36. David A. Rohde and Kenneth A. Shepsle, "Democratic Committee Assignments in the House of Representatives: Strategic Aspects of a Social Choice Process," in Matthew D. McCubbins and Terry Sullivan, eds., *Congress: Structure and Policy* (New York: Cambridge University Press, 1987).

37. Lawrence C. Dodd and Bruce I. Oppenheimer, "Revolution in the House: Testing the Limits of Party Government," in Lawrence C. Dodd and Bruce I. Oppenheimer, eds., *Congress Reconsidered,* 4th ed. (Washington, D.C.: Congressional Quarterly Press, 1989).

38. Davidson and Oleszek, *Congress and Its Members,* ch. 8; Donald R. Matthews, *U.S. Senators and Their World* (Chapel Hill, NC: University of North Carolina Press, 1960).

39. Eric M. Uslaner, *The Decline of Comity in Congress* (Ann Arbor, MI: University of Michigan Press, 1996).

40. Robert Bendiner, *Obstacle Course on Capitol Hill* (New York: McGraw-Hill, 1964), p. 15.

41. Garry Young and Joseph Cooper, "Multiple Referral and the Transformation of House Decision Making," in Lawrence C. Dodd and Bruce I. Oppenheimer, eds., *Congress Reconsidered,* 5th ed. (Washington, D.C.: Congressional Quarterly Press, 1993).

42. Morris P. Fiorina, *Congress: Keystone of the Washington Establishment,* 2nd ed. (New Haven, CT: Yale University Press, 1989); Mayhew, *Congress;* Gary C. Jacobson, *Politics of Congressional Elections,* 2nd ed. (Boston: Little, Brown, 1987).

43. Morris P. Fiorina, "The Decline of Collective Responsibility," *Daedalus* (Summer 1980), pp. 24–37; Cain, Ferejohn, and Fiorina, *The Personal Vote.*

44. Davidson and Oleszek, *Congress and Its Members,* pp. 426–428; and John R. Hibbing and Elizabeth Theiss-Morse, *Congress as Public Enemy: Public Attitudes Toward American Political Institutions* (New York: Cambridge University Press, 1995).

45. Hibbing and Theiss-Morse, *Congress as Public Enemy,* p. 147.

Chapter 12
The President

In This Chapter

- Why the presidency grew to be a powerful office
- How presidents play many roles
- Why presidents often disagree with Congress
- How democratic the presidency is—whether presidents listen and respond to the public
- Why different presidents often pursue similar policies

George W. Bush's War Presidency

It was an inauspicious beginning for a presidency. In the November election, George W. Bush had beaten Al Gore by only four electoral votes nationwide—and then only when the U.S. Supreme Court intervened to settle the disputed election result in Florida. Moreover, though he had won the electoral vote contest, Bush had lost the national popular vote to Gore by over one-half million votes, becoming the first president since Benjamin Harrison in 1889 to assume the presidential office under such circumstances. For many Americans, then, George W. Bush assumed the presidential office under a cloud of illegitimacy and without a mandate.

As if that were not enough, administration actions within the first few months of his presidency—overruling Clinton ad-

ministration rules regulating the amount of arsenic in drinking water, and renunciation of the Kyoto Treaty on global warming—brought a cascade of criticism from editorial writers and political leaders both at home and abroad. His well-known troubles as a speaker—mispronouncing words and confusing the names of foreign leaders—became the fodder for late night comedians. By spring, Bush had also seen control of the Senate go to the Democrats after Senator James Jeffords of Vermont bolted from the Republican Party. By the end of the summer 2001, an economic recession was in full flower and the budget surplus was about to disappear. It is no wonder, then, that Bush's job approval ratings among the public hovered in the mid- to upper-50 percent range—quite low in historical terms—for the first seven months of his presidency. About the same percentage of people reported that President Bush "inspired confidence." Questions about his leadership were being whispered virtually everywhere.

All of this changed dramatically after the terrorist attacks on the United States on September 11. With the public solidly behind him, President Bush took the war to the enemy in Afghanistan and elsewhere, initiated measures to protect the nation on the homefront, and constructed an international alliance against terrorism. His actions inspired confidence among the American people—his job approval

ratings reached and stayed at record levels in public opinion polls in the months after the attacks.

What had happened? How was a presidency transformed in so short a time? As with any presidency, the nature of the Bush presidency is the result of the combination of the office the president inherits from his predecessors, the demands of the times, and the personal qualities of the president. George W. Bush had brought to the terrorism crisis a set of skills and qualities of character that had gone unnoticed by many. But we must not overlook how foreign policy crises, war, and the nature of the presidential office create a context for the expansion of presidential power, influence, and stature for a president with the skill to take full advantage of them.

War most clearly creates the potential for presidential leadership. Because the president is the commander in chief under the Constitution, responsible for the disposition and use of U.S. armed forces, and because the people generally look to presidential leadership during war emergencies, waging war increases presidential power relative to other government actors, including Congress and the courts. In wartime, presidents generally have their way with Congress on defense and foreign policy matters, and are tempted to govern by executive order and executive agreement, with only minimal consultation with Congress.

As in previous wars, both the public and other political leaders turned to the president for leadership following 9/11. President Bush responded vigorously and skillfully, using his commander-in-chief powers to organize the military response, his diplomatic powers to forge an anti-terrorism alliance (even incorporating Russia and China, and India and Pakistan), and his police powers to attempt to ferret-out terror networks and their sponsors and financiers at home and abroad. In launching these multidimensional actions, the president not only neglected to consult very much with congressional leaders, but promulgated a series of actions by executive order that seemed intended to bypass both Congress and the courts.[1]

His actions were breathtaking in scope. The following actions were made by executive orders: freezing the financial assets of organizations thought to be tied to terrorism; closing charities in the United States thought to be funneling money to terrorist groups; establishing military tribunals for the trial of foreign nationals accused of terrorism; ordering the interrogation of thousands of people of Middle Eastern descent and Muslims who might conceivably have information about terrorism; detaining hundreds of people as part of a sweep to disrupt possible terrorist cells in the United States; announcing that conversations between terror suspects and their lawyers would be monitored; and imposing strict new visa requirements for people from predominantly Muslim countries. He also created a new Office of Homeland Security and appointed former Pennsylvania governor Tom Ridge to head it, without statutory authority from Congress.

(Bush later proposed the creation of a Department of Homeland Security.)

When the president required congressional action on matters related to Nine-Eleven, the legislative branch responded swiftly in the crisis atmosphere created by the attacks on the United States. The anti-terrorism bill, titled the USA Patriot Act, included virtually everything the president asked for from Congress—including expansion of the government's power to conduct surveillance of terror suspects, to review student records and the records of grand jury proceedings, and to detain people suspected of terrorist links without charges being brought and without opportunity for review by the courts. Congress also responded quickly and favorably to the president's emergency budget requests. Later, after much deliberation, Congress granted the president the authority to go to war against Iraq.

Using this review of the first months of the Bush presidency as a backdrop, this chapter will look at the office of the president, with special attention to how it has evolved over time, and how the nature of the office at any particular time is the result of the interaction of constitutional rules, historical precedent, the nature of the times, and the qualities of the person who sits in the Oval Office. Because of the constitutional rules and historical precedent, every presidency is, in some respects, similar to every other presidency. On the other hand, because of the importance of contemporary events and the personal qualities of particular presidents in determining how the office operates, every presidency is, to a certain extent, unique. ∎

Thinking Critically About This Chapter

This chapter is about the American presidency, how it has evolved, and what role it plays in American politics and government.

Using the Framework You will see in this chapter how the presidential office has changed substantially from how the framers envisioned it, primarily because of changes in America's international situation, the nature of its economy, and popular expectations. You will also see how presidents interact with other governmental institutions, such as Congress and the Court, and with political linkage level actors, such as political parties, public opinion, the mass media, and interest groups, and how these interactions influence what government does.

Using the Democracy Standard You will see in this chapter how the presidential office, although not envisioned by the framers to be a democratic one, has become more directly connected to and responsive to the American people. On the other hand, you will be asked to think about whether presidents' growing ability to influence the thinking of the public and shape their perceptions of public events undermines democracy. ◀

The Expanding Presidency

The American presidency has grown considerably since our nation's beginning. The increase has occurred in presidential responsibilities, burdens, power, and impact.

The Earliest and Latest Presidencies Compared

When George W. Bush was sworn into office in January 2001, he presided over a federal budget with more than $1.8 trillion in annual expenditures and a federal establishment with approximately 2.4 million civilian employees. He was commander in chief of the armed forces, with about 1.4 million men and women in uniform; hundreds of military bases at home and scattered throughout the world; and perhaps 20,000 deliverable nuclear warheads, enough to obliterate every medium-sized or large city in the world many times over. The United States in 2001 had a population of almost 278 million diverse people; a Gross Domestic Product of more than $9.5 trillion; and a land area of some 3.8 million square miles, stretching from Alaska to Florida and from Hawaii to Maine.[2]

By contrast, when George Washington took office as the first president, he had a total budget (for 1789–1791) of just over $4 million. Washington had only a handful of federal employees. Even by 1801, there were only about 300 federal officeholders in the capital. Washington's cabinet consisted of just five officials: the secretaries of state, war, and the treasury; a postmaster general; and an attorney general (who acted as the president's personal attorney, rather than as head of a full-fledged Justice Department). The entire Department of State consisted of just one secretary, one chief clerk, six minor clerks, and one messenger.

In 1790, only about 700 Americans were in uniform, and they had no way to project force around the world. Federal government functions were few. The entire United States consisted of the 13 original eastern and southeastern states, with only 864,746 square miles of land area; the population was only about 4 million persons, most living on small farms.[3]

The Founders' Conception of the Presidency

The Founders certainly had in mind a presidency more like Washington's than Bush's. As discussed in Chapter 2, Article II of the Constitution provided for a single executive who would be strong, compared with his role under the

The presidency has grown in scale and responsibility. As commander in chief of the armed forces, President George Washington commanded an army of just over 700 soldiers and had little to do with affairs outside the United States. Today, the president commands a force of about 1.4 million stationed all over the world.
Source: © Gift of Edgar William, Chrysler & Bernice Garbish/The Metropolitan Museum of Art.

Congress-dominated Articles of Confederation, but the Constitution's sparse language barely hinted at the range of things twenty-first-century presidents would do. The Constitution made the president "commander in chief" of the armed forces, for example, without any suggestion that there would be a vast standing army that presidents could send abroad to fight without a declaration of war. It empowered presidents to appoint and to "require the opinion in writing" of executive department heads without indicating that a huge federal bureaucracy would evolve. The Constitution provided that presidents could from time to time "recommend . . . measures" to Congress without specifying that these proposals would very often (especially in the twentieth century) come to dominate the legislative agenda. Still, the vague language of the Constitution proved flexible enough to encompass the great expansion of the presidency.

The Dormant Presidency

From the time of George Washington's inauguration at Federal Hall in New York City to the end of the nineteenth century, the presidency, for the most part, conformed to the designs of the Founders. The presidency did not, by and large, dominate the political life of the nation. Presidents saw their responsibility as primarily involving the execution of policies decided by Congress. Congress was a fully equal branch of government, or perhaps more than equal. But the office changed after that.

Structural Factors
Why does the early presidency seem so weak in comparison with the contemporary presidency? Surely, it is not because early presidents were less intelligent, vigorous, or ambitious; some were and some were not. A more reasonable answer is that the nation did not often require a very strong presidency before the twentieth century, particularly in the key areas of foreign policy and military leadership. Only in the twentieth century did the United States become a world power, involved in military, diplomatic, and economic activities around the globe. With that *structural* development came a simultaneous increase in the power and responsibility of the president.

It was not until the late nineteenth century, moreover, that the economy of the United States was transformed from a simple free market economy of farmers and small firms to a corporate-dominated economy, with units so large and interconnected that their every action had social consequences. This transformation eventually led to demands for more government supervision of the American economic system. As this role of government grew, so did that of the president.

Although the presidency was largely dormant until the end of the nineteenth century, events and the actions of several presidents during the early period anticipated what was to happen to the office in our own time. Precedents were set; expectations were formed; rules were changed.

Longman
Participate.com **2.0**
Participation
**Rate the
Presidents**

Important Early Presidents
The war hero George Washington solidified the prestige of the presidency at a time when executive leadership was mistrusted. Washington also affirmed the primacy of the president in foreign affairs and set a precedent for fashioning a domestic legislative program. Thomas Jefferson, although initially hostile to the idea of a vigorous central government, boldly concluded the Louisiana Purchase with France, which roughly doubled the size of the United States and opened the continent for American settlement. Rough-hewn frontiersman Andrew Jackson, elected with broader popular participation than ever before, helped transform the presidency into a popular institution, as symbolized by his vigorous opposition to the Bank of the United States (which was seen by many ordinary Americans as a tool of the wealthy).

Andrew Jackson was hailed as a hero for opposing the "monster" Bank of the United States.
Source: © Collection of The New York Historical Society.

James Polk, although often ignored in textbook accounts of "great" presidents, energetically exercised his powers as commander in chief of the armed forces; he provoked a war with Mexico and acquired most of what is now the southwestern United States and California. Abraham Lincoln, in order to win the Civil War, invoked emergency powers based on his broad reading of the Constitution: He raised and spent money and deployed troops on his own initiative, with Congress acquiescing only afterward; he temporarily suspended the right of **habeas corpus** and allowed civilians to be tried in military courts; and he unilaterally freed the slaves in the Confederate states by issuing the Emancipation Proclamation.

habeas corpus

The legal doctrine that a person who is arrested must have a timely hearing before a judge.

The Twentieth-Century Transformation

More enduring changes in the presidency came only in the twentieth century, when new structural conditions made an expanded presidency both possible and necessary.

Theodore Roosevelt Theodore Roosevelt vigorously pushed the prerogatives and enhanced the powers of the office as no president had done since Lincoln. Roosevelt was happiest when he was deploying the troops as commander in chief or serving as the nation's chief diplomat to protect American economic and political interests. On the domestic front, Roosevelt pushed for regulation of the new and frightening business corporations, especially by breaking up **trusts,** and he established many national parks. In Teddy Roosevelt, we see the coming together of an energetic and ambitious political leader and a new set of structural factors in the United States, particularly the nation's emergence as a world power and an industrialized economy.

trusts

Large combinations of business corporations.

Woodrow Wilson Woodrow Wilson's presidency marked further important steps in the expansion of the federal government and the presidency. Wilson's "New Freedom" domestic program built on the Progressive Era measures of Teddy Roosevelt, including further regulation of the economy by establishment of the Federal Reserve Board (1913) and the Federal Trade Commission (1914). Under Wilson, World War I brought an enormous increase in activity: a huge mobilization of military personnel and a large, new civilian bureaucracy to oversee the production and distribution of food, fuel, and armaments by the American "arsenal of democracy."

Franklin Roosevelt

It was Franklin D. Roosevelt, however, who presided over the most significant expansion of presidential functions and activities in American history. In a very real sense, the founding of the modern American presidency occurred during Roosevelt's administration, in response to the Great Depression and World War II.

In response to the Great Depression, Roosevelt and the Democratic majority in Congress pushed into law a series of measures for economic relief that grew into vast programs of conservation and public works, farm credit, business loans, and relief payments to the destitute. Roosevelt's New Deal also established a number of independent commissions to regulate aspects of business (the stock market, telephones, utilities, airlines) and enacted programs such as Social Security, which provided income support for retired Americans, and the Wagner Act, which helped workers join unions and bargain collectively with their employers.

Even bigger changes, however, resulted from World War II when the government mobilized the entire population and the whole economy for the war effort. With the end of World War II, the United States was established as a military superpower. Since the time of Franklin Roosevelt, all U.S. presidents have administered a huge national security state with large standing armed forces, nuclear weapons, and bases all around the world.

Similarly, World War II brought substantial government involvement in the economy, with temporary war agencies regulating prices, rationing necessities, monitoring and stimulating industrial output, and helping develop human resources for domestic production. These agencies were dismantled after the war, but they trained a large cadre of officials in an activist view of what the federal government could and should do, and they set precedents for presidential and governmental actions that continue to the present day. All presidents since Roosevelt have presided over a huge government apparatus that has been active in domestic policy as well as in foreign policy.

By staying in touch with and responding to the people during the crisis of the Great Depression, Franklin Delano Roosevelt helped define the modern presidency.

John F. Kennedy   Although he accomplished little on the legislative front during his brief time in office—he did introduce the 1964 Civil Rights Act, passed after his death—John F. Kennedy was the first president to appreciate the importance of television as both a campaign tool and as an instrument for influencing the public and political actors in Washington, the states, and other countries. His televised speeches and press conferences, where his charm, intelligence, and sense of humor were clearly evident, became one of his most effective governing tools. Presidents after him tried to follow his lead, but only Ronald Reagan and Bill Clinton came close to Kennedy's mastery of the medium.

Ronald Reagan   Only occasionally does the word "revolution" become associated with the name of a president, and rarely does it mean very much, but in the case of Ronald Reagan, the phrase "Reagan revolution" fits like a glove. In policy terms, Ronald Reagan was largely responsible for bringing the main items of the conservative agenda to fruition: a massive tax cut to stimulate the economy, cutbacks in the number of regulations that affect business, cuts in a wide range of domestic social programs, and a substantial build-up of U.S. armed forces. Perhaps more importantly, he showed the American people and others around the world that a vigorous and popular presidency was still possible after the failed presidencies of Richard Nixon, Gerald Ford, and Jimmy Carter. He maintained his impressive public standing until the end of his term, despite foreign missteps, such as the Iran-Contra Affair, and the appearance of large and persistent budget deficits.

How Important Are Individual Presidents?

We cannot be sure to what extent presidents themselves caused this great expansion of the scope of their office. Clearly, they played a part. Lincoln, Wilson, and Franklin Roosevelt, for example, not only reacted vigorously to events but also helped create events; each had something to do with the coming of the wars that were so crucial in adding to their activities and powers. Yet these

Ronald Reagan's warmth, charm, and sincerity contributed to his enormous appeal not only among Republicans but also among many Democrats. His personal attractiveness helped him successfully push several important conservative initiatives through Congress.

great presidents were also the product of great times; they stepped into situations that had deep historical roots and dynamics of their own.

Lincoln found a nation in bitter conflict over the relative economic and political power of North and South and focused on the question of slavery in the western territories; war was a likely, if not inevitable, outcome. Wilson and Franklin Roosevelt each faced a world in which German expansion threatened the perceived economic and cultural interests of the United States and in which U.S. industrial power permitted a strong response. The Great Depression fairly cried out for a new kind of presidential activism. Kennedy faced an international system in which the Soviet Union had become especially strident and menacing. Thus, the great upsurges in presidential power and activity were, at least in part, a result of forces at the *structural* level and the result of developments in the economy, American society, and the international system.

We see, then, that it is this mixture of a president's personal qualities (personality and character) and deeper structural factors (such as the existence of military, foreign policy, or economic crises) that determines which presidents leave a positive historical mark and transform their office.

The Many Roles of the President

Longman
Participate.com
2.0
Simulation
**You Are
Appointing a
Supreme
Court Justice**

Since Franklin Roosevelt's day, the American presidency has assumed powers and duties, unimaginable to the Founders, that touch the daily lives of everyone in the United States and indeed everyone in the world. Political scientist Clinton Rossiter's writings introduced generations of students to the many different hats that presidents wear: chief of state, commander in chief, legislator, manager of the economy, chief diplomat, and party leader.[4]

Chief of State

Longman
Participate.com
2.0
Comparative
**Comparing
Chief
Executives**

The president is a symbol of national authority and unity. In contrast to European parliamentary nations such as Britain or Norway, where a monarch acts as chief of state while a prime minister serves as head of the government, in the United States the two functions are combined. It is the president who performs many ceremonial duties (attending funerals, proclaiming official days, honoring heroes, celebrating anniversaries) that are carried out by members of royal families in other nations. Jimmy Breslin, an irreverent New York newspaper columnist, once wrote, "The office of President is such a bastardized thing, half royalty and half democracy, that nobody knows whether to genuflect or spit."[5]

Commander in Chief

The Constitution explicitly lodges command over the American armed forces in the office of president. The development of so-called war powers has grown enormously over the years, to the point where the elder President Bush, in 1990, was quickly able to put more than 500,000 U.S. troops in the Persian Gulf area, poised to strike against Iraq. Despite substantial congressional opposition, President Clinton claimed the power to send several thousand American troops as peacekeepers to Bosnia in 1995, Haiti in 1996, and Kosovo in 1999, and to wage an air war against Serbia to try to prevent "ethnic cleansing." For his part, George W. Bush, in the months after the September 11 attacks on the

United States, launched a military campaign against the Taliban regime and the al Qaeda terrorist network in Afghanistan. He also massed troops in the Persian Gulf in 2002 as Congress and the United Nations debated military action against Iraq.

Legislator

While constitutional responsibility for the legislative agenda seems to rest with Congress, the initiative for public policy has partly shifted to the president and the executive branch over the years. It has become customary for Congress to wait for and respond to presidential State of the Union addresses, budgets, and legislative proposals. The twentieth century is dotted with presidential labels on legislation: Wilson's New Freedom, Roosevelt's New Deal, Truman's Fair Deal, Kennedy's New Frontier, and Johnson's Great Society. Ronald Reagan pushed through major changes in 1981 and remained an important legislative force during much of the 1980s.

Manager of the Economy

We now expect presidents to "do something" about the economy when things are going badly. The Great Depression taught most Americans that the federal government has a role to play in fighting economic downturns, and the example of Franklin Roosevelt convinced many that the main actor in this drama ought to be the president. The role is now so well established that even conservative presidents, such as Ronald Reagan and George H. W. Bush, felt compelled to involve the federal government in the prevention of bank failures, the stimulation of economic growth, and the promotion of exports abroad.

In the rapidly expanding global economy, moreover, presidents have become increasingly engaged in the effort to open world markets on equitable terms to American goods and services. President Reagan pressured Japan into import quotas on automobiles, and President Bush helped push through an agreement with Japan on semiconductors. President Clinton was especially active as a spokesperson for the benefits of the American way of doing business and pushed hard to expand a global free trade regime, negotiating and

Responding to the September 11 terrorist attacks on the United States, President George W. Bush, using his powers as commander in chief, ordered a military intervention into Afghanistan to topple the Taliban regime and destroy the al Qaeda terrorist organization. Here Special Force Troops prepare for insertion into battle.

Richard Nixon scored a number of foreign policy successes during his presidency, including reestablishing friendly U.S. relations with mainland China after a 23-year break.

gaining congressional approval for the NAFTA treaty and the creation of the World Trade Organization under GATT.

Chief Diplomat

Longman
Participate.com 2.0
Simulation
You Are the President: Policy Toward Iran

The Constitution, by specifying that the president "shall have the power . . . to make Treaties" and to appoint and receive ambassadors, assigns the main diplomatic responsibility of the United States to the presidency. It is in this role, perhaps, that American presidents are most visible: traveling abroad, meeting with foreign leaders, and negotiating and signing treaties. President George H. W. Bush's successful arms control negotiations with Soviet leaders and his extraordinary efforts to assemble and hold together the multinational coalition against Iraq made the diplomatic function especially prominent in his presidency. His son George W. Bush skillfully put together a coalition to fight terrorism, but caused some diplomatic fuss when he rejected the Kyoto global warming treaty and pulled the United States out of the Anti-Ballistic Missile treaty with Russia.

Head of the Political Party

One of the great difficulties all presidents face is the seeming contradiction between their role as president of all the people—as commander in chief and chief diplomat, for example—and their role as leader of their political party, seeking partisan advantage as well as the public good. Much of the apparent contradiction has been eased by the fact that presidents (and other political leaders) generally see the public good and commitment to party principles as one and the same. Thus, Ronald Reagan, as the leader of the Republican party and as president, believed that the public good was served by increasing defense spending, deregulating the economy, and decreasing domestic spending. For his part, Lyndon Johnson, as the leader of the Democratic party and as president, believed that the federal government ought to play a leading role in ending racial discrimination and poverty in American life. Often, however, the public has reacted very negatively when presidents play their party leadership role too vigorously, seeing it as perhaps unpresidential.

The President's Staff and Cabinet

Each of the president's functions is demanding; together, they are overwhelming. "Passive" presidents may well be a vanishing breed. Of course, presidents do not face their burdens alone; they have gradually acquired many advisers and helpers. The number and responsibilities of these advisers and helpers have become so extensive, and the functions they perform so essential, that they have come to form what some call the **institutional presidency.**[6]

The White House Staff

The White House staff, for example, which is specially shaped to fit the particular needs of each president, includes a number of close advisers.

Chief of Staff One top adviser, usually designated **chief of staff,** tends to serve as the president's right hand, supervising other staff members and organizing much of what the president does. Presidents use their chiefs of staff in different ways. Franklin Roosevelt kept a tight rein on things himself, granting equal but limited power and access to several close advisers in a *competitive* system. Dwight Eisenhower, used to the *hierarchical* army staff system, gave overall responsibility to his chief of staff, Sherman Adams. In the early Reagan White House, James Baker shared power *collegially* with Assistant to the President Michael Deaver and Counselor to the President Edwin Meese.

National Security Adviser Another important staff member in most presidencies is the **national security adviser,** who is also head of the president's National Security Council, operating out of the White House. The national security adviser generally meets with the president every day to brief him on the latest events and to offer advice on what to do. Several national security advisers, including Henry Kissinger (under Nixon) and Zbigniew Brzezinski (under Carter), have been strong foreign policy managers and active, world-hopping diplomats who sometimes clashed with the secretaries of state and defense. Most recent presidents, however, have appointed team players who have closely reflected the president's wishes and quietly coordinated policy among the various executive departments. Condoleezza Rice followed this pattern in the George W. Bush administration.

Other Advisers Most presidents also have a top domestic policy adviser who coordinates plans for new domestic laws, regulations, and spending, although this role is often subordinate to that of the chief of staff and is not usually very visible. Close political advisers, often old comrades of the president from past campaigns, may be found in a number of White House or other government posts (James Baker served as George H. W. Bush's secretary of state, for example, while Karen Hughes served as White House Counselor to the younger Bush) or may have no official position at all, such as Republican consultant Dick Morris, who crafted Clinton's 1996 reelection strategy. Prominent in every administration is the press secretary, who holds press conferences, briefs the media, and serves as the voice of the administration.

Nearly all presidents have a legal counsel (a hot seat for Bill Clinton's counsel given the Whitewater, campaign finance, and Monica Lewinsky inquiries and his impeachment and trial in Congress), a special assistant to act as a liaison with Congress, another to deal with interest groups, another for political matters, and still another for intergovernmental relations. However,

institutional presidency

The permanent bureaucracy associated with the presidency, designed to help the incumbent of the office carry out his responsibilities.

chief of staff

A top adviser to the president who also manages the White House staff.

national security adviser

A top foreign policy and defense adviser to the president who heads the National Security Council.

The White House Press Secretary is an increasingly important member of the president's staff, responsible for imparting the president's view on the issues and events of the day to the news media. Ari Fleischer is the Press Secretary for President George W. Bush.

the exact shape of the White House staff changes greatly from one presidency to another, depending on the preferences and style of the president. What is particularly striking about President George W. Bush's management style is his penchant for setting overall goals and policies but giving his staffers a great deal of freedom and latitude in getting the job done.

The Executive Office of the President

Executive Office of the President (EOP)

A group of organizations that advise the president on a wide range of issues; includes the Office of Management and Budget, the National Security Council, and the Council of Economic Advisers.

Office of Management and Budget (OMB)

An organization within the Executive Office of the President that advises on the federal budget, domestic legislation, and regulations.

Council of Economic Advisers (CEA)

An organization in the Executive Office of the President made up of a small group of economists who advise on economic policy.

National Security Council (NSC)

An organization in the Executive Office of the President made up of officials from the State and Defense Departments, the CIA, and the military, who advise on foreign and security affairs.

One step removed from the presidential staff, and mostly housed in the Executive Office Building next door to the White House, is a set of organizations that forms the **Executive Office of the President (EOP).**

Most important of these organizations is the **Office of Management and Budget (OMB).** The OMB advises the president on how much the administration should propose to spend for each government program and where the money will come from. The OMB also exercises legislative clearance; that is, it examines the budgetary implications of any proposed legislation and sometimes kills proposals it deems too expensive or inconsistent with the president's philosophy or goals.

The **Council of Economic Advisers (CEA)** advises the president on economic policy. Occasionally, the head of the council exercises great influence, as Walter Heller did during the Kennedy administration. More often, the head of the CEA is inconspicuous.

The Executive Office of the President also includes the **National Security Council (NSC),** a body of leading officials from the State and Defense Departments, the Central Intelligence Agency (CIA), the military, and elsewhere who advise the president on foreign affairs. The NSC has been particularly active in crisis situations and covert operations. The NSC staff, charged with various analytical and coordinating tasks, is headed by the president's national security adviser. At times, the NSC staff has gone beyond analysis to conduct actual operations, the most famous of which was the Iran-Contra affair, under the direction of Lieutenant Colonel Oliver North, when weapons were secretly sold to Iran in the hope of freeing U.S. hostages and some of the proceeds were illegally diverted to the Nicaraguan Contra rebels.

In recent years, the Executive Office of the President has also included the Office of Science and Technology Policy, the Council on Environmental Quality, and the Office of the U.S. Trade Representative. Again, however, the makeup of the EOP changes from one administration to another, depending on which national problems seem most pressing and on the preferences and operating styles of individual presidents. President George W. Bush, for example, created the Office of Homeland Security directed by Tom Ridge to coordinate governmental efforts to protect against further terrorist attacks.

The Vice-Presidency

Vice-presidents find themselves in an awkward position because their main job is simply to be available in case something happens to the president. This happened several times in the twentieth century; Theodore Roosevelt, Calvin Coolidge, Harry Truman, Lyndon Johnson, and Gerald Ford each stepped up from the vice-presidency after the death or resignation of the president.

A Once-Insignificant Office
The vice-presidency itself, however, has not always been highly regarded. John Nance Garner, Franklin Roosevelt's first vice-president, has been quoted as saying in his earthy Texan way that the office was "not worth a pitcher of warm piss."[7] Within administrations, vice-presidents used to be fifth wheels, not fully trusted (since they could not be fired) and not personally or politically close to the president. Vice-presidents used to spend much of their time running minor errands of state, attending funerals of foreign leaders not important enough to demand presidential attention, or carrying out

Richard Cheney plays a more important role in fashioning administration policy and strategy than any other vice-president in American history. Here Cheney consults with then-Senate majority leader Trent Lott on George W. Bush's 2002 budget proposal.

limited diplomatic missions. Some vice-presidents were virtually frozen out of the policy-making process. Harry Truman was never informed of the existence of the Manhattan Project, which built the atomic bomb, for example. He learned of the bomb only months before he was obligated to make a decision on using it to close out the war against Japan.

Increasing Importance of the Vice-Presidency   Recent presidents, however, have involved their vice-presidents more.[8] Ronald Reagan included the elder George Bush in major policy meetings and put him in charge of anti-drug efforts. Bill Clinton gave Al Gore important responsibilities, including the formulation of environmental policy, coping with Ross Perot's opposition to NAFTA, and the ambitious effort to "reinvent government." More than any vice-president in recent memory, Dick Cheney is at the center of the policy-making process in the George W. Bush White House, serving as one of the president's principal advisors on both domestic and foreign policy.

Presidential Succession   In 1804, the Twelfth Amendment fixed the flaw in the original Constitution under which Aaron Burr, Thomas Jefferson's running mate in 1800, had tied Jefferson in electoral votes and tried, in the House of Representatives, to grab the presidency for himself. Since then, vice-presidents have been elected specifically to that office on a party ticket with their presidents. But now there is also another way to become vice-president. The Twenty-Fifth Amendment (ratified in 1967) provides for the succession in case of the temporary or permanent inability of a president to discharge his office. It also states that if the vice-presidency becomes vacant, the president can nominate a new vice-president, who takes office on confirmation by both houses of Congress. This is how Gerald Ford became vice-president in 1973, when Spiro Agnew was forced to resign because of a scandal, and how Nelson Rockefeller became vice-president in 1974, when Ford replaced Richard Nixon as president.

The Cabinet

The president's cabinet is not mentioned in the Constitution. No legislation designates the composition of the cabinet, its duties, or its rules of operation. Nevertheless, all presidents since George Washington have had one. It was Washington who established the practice of meeting with his top executive officials as a group to discuss policy matters. Later presidents continued the practice, some meeting with the cabinet as often as twice a week, and others paying it less attention or none at all.

Today, the cabinet usually consists of the heads of the major executive departments, plus the vice-president, the director of the CIA, and whichever other officials the president deems appropriate.

Limited Role   Rarely, if ever, though, have presidents actually relied on the cabinet as a decision-making body. Presidents know that they alone will be held responsible for decisions, and they alone keep the power to make them. According to legend, when Abraham Lincoln once disagreed with the entire cabinet, he declared, "Eight votes for and one against; the nays have it!"

Most recent presidents have convened the cabinet infrequently and have done serious business with it only rarely. Ronald Reagan held only a few cabinet meetings each year, and those were so dull and unimportant that Reagan was said to doze off from time to time. Bill Clinton, with his "policy wonk" mastery of details, thoroughly dominated cabinet discussions.

President George H. W. Bush makes a point to members of his cabinet. Although the cabinet occasionally meets as a body, most presidents do not rely on it very much for making important decisions.

Why the Weak Cabinet?   One reason for the weakness of the cabinet, especially in recent years, is simply that government has grown large and specialized. Most department heads are experts in their own areas, with little to contribute elsewhere. It could be a waste of everyone's time to engage the secretary of housing and urban development in discussions of military strategy.

Another reason is that cabinet members occupy an ambiguous position: They are advisers to the president but also represent their own constituencies, including the permanent civil servants in their departments and the organized interests that their departments serve. They may have substantial political stature of their own, somewhat independent of the president's.

Close Confidants   Most presidents also try to include in the cabinet some people with whom they have close personal and political ties. Thus, John Kennedy appointed his brother Robert attorney general. When criticized, Kennedy replied (tongue in cheek): "I can't see that it's wrong to give him a little legal experience before he goes out to practice law."[9] Likewise, President George W. Bush appointed long-time confidant Donald Rumsfeld to be Secretary of Defense.

The President and the Bureaucracy

Many people assume that the president has firm control over the executive branch, that he can simply order departments and agencies to do something and they will do it. But Richard Neustadt, in his important book *Presidential Power and the Modern Presidents,* showed that that is far from the whole truth.[10]

Giving Orders

In the day-to-day operation of government, direct command is seldom feasible. Too much is going on. Presidents cannot keep personal track of each one of the millions of government officials and employees. The president can only

Longman
Participate.com
2.0
Timeline
With the
Stroke of a
Pen:
The Executive
Order

Harry Truman reminded General Douglas MacArthur that the president is the commander in chief of America's armed forces when he fired the general for disobeying presidential orders during the Korean War.

issue general guidelines and pass them down the chain of subordinates, hoping that his wishes will be followed faithfully. But lower-level officials, protected by civil service status from being fired, may have their own interests, their own institutional norms and practices, that lead them to do something different. President Kennedy was painfully reminded of this during the Cuban Missile Crisis of 1962, when Soviet Premier Khrushchev demanded that U.S. missiles be removed from Turkey in return for the removal of Soviet missiles from Cuba: Kennedy was surprised to learn that the missiles had not already been taken out of Turkey, for he had ordered them removed a year earlier. The people responsible for carrying out this directive had not followed through.[11]

Persuasion

To a large extent, a president must *persuade* other executive branch officials to do things. He must bargain, compromise, and convince others that what he wants is in the country's best interest and in their own interest as well. Neustadt put it strongly: "Presidential power is the power to persuade."[12]

Of course, presidents can do many things besides persuade: appoint top officials who share the president's goals; put White House observers in second-level department positions; reshuffle, reorganize, or even—with the consent of Congress—abolish agencies that are not responsive; influence agency budgets and programs through OMB review; and stimulate pressure on departments by Congress and the public.

Still, the president's ability to gain bureaucratic acquiescence is limited. The federal bureaucracy is not merely a creature of the president but is itself a partly independent governmental actor. It is also subject to influences from the political linkage level—especially by public opinion and organized interests, often working through Congress. Congress, after all, appropriates the money. This constrains what presidents can do and helps ensure that the executive branch will respond to broad forces in society rather than simply to the wishes of one leader.

It's never too late for presidential persuasion. Here Ronald Reagan tries to win one more vote for a bill in the Senate before heading off to a White House reception.

The President and Congress: Perpetual Tug-of-War

The president and Congress are often at odds. This is a *structural* fact of American politics, deliberately intended by the authors of the Constitution.[13]

Conflict by Constitutional Design

The Founders created a system of checks and balances between Congress and the president, setting "ambition to counter ambition" in order to prevent tyranny. Because virtually all constitutional powers are shared, there is a potential for conflict over virtually all aspects of government policy.

Shared Powers   Under the Constitution, presidents may propose legislation and can sign or veto bills passed by Congress, but both houses of Congress must pass any laws and can override presidential vetoes. Presidents can appoint ambassadors and high officials and make treaties with foreign countries, but the Senate must approve them. Presidents nominate federal judges, including U.S. Supreme Court justices, but the Senate must approve the nominations. Presidents administer the executive branch, but Congress appropriates funds for it to operate, writes the legislation that defines what it is to do, and oversees its activities.

Presidents cannot always count on the members of Congress—even members of their own political party—to agree with them. The potential conflict written into the Constitution becomes real because the president and Congress often disagree about national goals, especially when there is **divided government,** that is, when the president and the majority in the House and/or the Senate belong to different parties.

divided government

Control of the executive and the legislative branches by different political parties.

Separate Elections   In other countries' parliamentary systems, the national legislatures choose the chief executives so that unified party control is ensured. But in the United States, there are separate elections for the president and the members of Congress. Moreover, our elections do not all come at the same time. In presidential election years, two-thirds of the senators do not have to run and are insulated from new political forces that may affect the choice of a president. In nonpresidential, "off" years, all members of the House and one-third of the senators face the voters, who sometimes elect a Congress with views quite different from those of the president chosen two years earlier. In 1986, for example, halfway through Reagan's second term, the Democrats re-captured control of the Senate and caused Reagan great difficulty with Supreme Court appointments and other matters. The Republicans did the same thing to Clinton in 1994 after they gained control of Congress.

Outcomes   In all these ways, our constitutional structure ensures that what the president can do is limited and influenced by Congress, which in turn reflects various political forces that may differ from those that affect the president. At its most extreme, Congress may even be controlled by the oppos-ing party. This divided government situation always constrains what presi-dents can do and may sometimes lead to a condition called "gridlock"[14] in which a president and Congress are locked in battle, neither able to make much headway.

What Makes a President Successful with Congress?

A number of political scientists have studied presidents' successes and fail-ures in getting measures that they favor enacted into law by Congress and have suggested reasons some presidents on some issues do much better than others.

Party and Ideology   The most important factor is a simple one: the num-ber of people in Congress who agree with the president in ideology and party affiliation. When the same political party controls both the presidency and Congress, presidents are more likely to get their way. When the opposite party controls one or the other house in Congress, or both, presidents tend to be frustrated. The bigger the majority a president's party has, the better the president does (see Figure 12.1).[15]

This success does not necessarily mean that presidents actively whip their fellow partisans into line. As we have seen, the parties are rather weakly orga-

Presidents must cultivate good working relationships with Congress if they are to have any success with their legislative program. Here, President George W. Bush consults with congressional leaders about pending legis-lation.

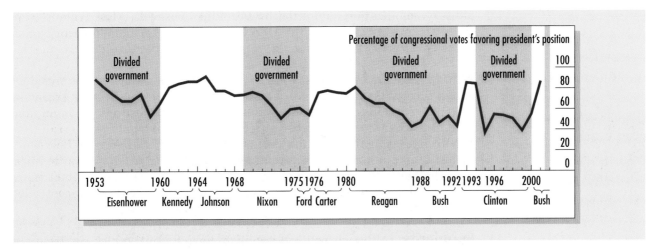

FIGURE 12.1 Presidential Success in Congress

The party in control of Congress can have a strong effect on a president's success. In periods of divided government (see shaded areas), when the opposing party has a majority in Congress, policies favoring the president's position receive fewer votes. Note the anomalies in 2001. For the first half of the year, President Bush enjoyed a Republican-controlled Congress. When Senator Jeffords left the GOP, Democrats gained control of the Senate, and divided government returned. President Bush continued to have success with Congress, however, because the country rallied around the president's leadership in the aftermath of the September 11 terrorist attacks.

Source: Calculated by the authors from various issues of the *Congressional Quarterly Weekly Report.*

nized in Congress and do not often enforce discipline. But party members do tend to be like-minded; they tend to vote together because they share the same values, and for the same reason, they tend to go along with a president of their own party.[16]

Foreign Policy and National Security Issues Presidents tend to do better on foreign policy issues than on domestic ones. Political scientist Aaron Wildavsky went so far as to refer to "two presidencies," domestic and foreign, with the latter president much more dominant. Wildavsky found that during the 1948–1964 period, 59 percent of presidents' proposals on foreign policy were passed, but only 40 percent of their domestic proposals.[17] The reason is that political leaders generally want to show a unified face to a potentially hostile world.

This difference between domestic and foreign policy success by the president has decreased since the Vietnam War, but it remains significant. Although there was significant dissent, Congress voted in January 1991, despite many misgivings, to authorize President George H. W. Bush to use force against Iraq, once again illustrating presidential primacy in foreign affairs. Congress eventually supported Clinton's decision to send U.S. forces to Haiti, Bosnia, and Kosovo as part of multinational peacekeeping operations, despite considerable initial grumbling. The generalization about presidents having an easier time with Congress on foreign policy issues than on domestic ones does not hold, however, when foreign policy concerns trade and other global economic issues that directly affect constituents.

In a national defense crisis, of course, presidents almost always get their way. After the attack on Pearl Harbor, Congress swiftly approved bills on military mobilization submitted by Franklin Roosevelt. After Nine-Eleven, Congress quickly approved the USA Patriot Act on homeland security and passed emergency military budget supplements as the president requested.

Vetoes   When the issue is a presidential veto of legislation, the president is again very likely to prevail. Vetoes have not been used often, except by certain "veto-happy" presidents, such as Franklin Roosevelt, Truman, and Ford. But when vetoes have been used, they have seldom been overridden—only 5 percent of the time for Truman and only 1.5 percent for Roosevelt. Bill Clinton did not use the veto at all during his first two years in office, when he had a Democratic majority in Congress, but then used it 11 times in 1995 alone during his budget battles with the Republican-controlled 104th Congress.

Popularity   Although political scientists have had little luck confirming it statistically,[18] most scholars and observers of Washington politics agree that presidential effectiveness with Congress is significantly affected by how popular a president is with the American people. This is probably because of fear among many members of Congress that opposing a highly visible proposal from a popular president might jeopardize their electoral future.

Legislative Skills   Again, although statistical studies of roll call votes reveal little effect of presidents' legislative skills (this may be the result of poor measures of legislative skills), most longtime observers of Washington politics believe that such skills make a difference. Lyndon Johnson's famous wheeling and dealing surely picked up votes for his favored legislation, as did Ronald Reagan's efforts on the 1981 tax and budget measures that began the so-called Reagan Revolution.

Web Exploration
Impeachment

Issue: Although rarely used, Congress's ultimate weapon in its perpetual struggle with the president is its power to impeach the president and remove him from office.

Site: Access the Jurist Website at the University of Pittsburgh Law School on our Website at **www.ablongman.com/greenberg**. Go to the "Web Explorations" section for Chapter 12 and open "impeachment." Scroll down to "Impeachments in History" and select "Articles of Impeachment Against Richard M. Nixon." Then scroll down to the "Clinton Controversy" and select "Proposed Articles of Impeachment." Compare the articles of impeachment brought against each president.

What You've Learned: How serious do you judge the accusations to be against each president? Did Nixon and/or Clinton, in your view, violate their oaths of office? Had you been a senator at the time, would you have voted for removal of the president from office? Why?

HINT: Pay special attention to the "obstruction of justice" charges against the two presidents, and judge their relative seriousness.

As Senate Majority Leader, Lyndon Johnson was famous for exerting strong personal pressure on legislators, a skill he carried with him to the presidency.

The President and the People: An Evolving Relationship

The complicated relationships among the president, the executive branch as a whole, and Congress have a lot to do with the different political forces that act on them at different times; that is, with the different effects of public opinion, the political parties, and organized interests. Particularly important is the special relationship between the president and the general public, which has evolved over many years.

Getting Closer to the People

The Founders thought of the president as an elite leader, relatively distant from the people, interacting with Congress often but with the people only rarely. Most nineteenth-century presidents and presidential candidates thought the same. They seldom made speeches directly to the public, for example, generally averaging no more than ten such speeches per year.[19]

In the earliest years of the American Republic, presidents were not even chosen directly by the voters but by electors chosen by state legislators or, in case no one got an Electoral College majority, by the House of Representatives. The Constitution thus envisioned very indirect democratic control of the presidency.

More Democratic Elections
As we have also seen, however, this system quickly evolved into one in which the people played a more direct part. The two-party system developed, with parties nominating candidates and running pledged electors and the state legislators allowing ordinary citizens to vote on the electors. Presidential candidates began to win clear-cut victories in the

Electoral College, taking the House of Representatives out of the process. Voting rights were broadened as well. Property and religious qualifications were dropped early in the nineteenth century. Later, slaves were freed and given the right to vote; still later, women, Native Americans, and 18-year-olds won the franchise.

Going Public   By the beginning of the twentieth century, presidents began to speak directly to the public. Theodore Roosevelt embarked on a series of speech-making tours in order to win passage of legislation to regulate the railroads. Woodrow Wilson made appeals to the public a central part of his presidency, articulating a new theory of the office that highlighted the close connections between the president and the public. Wilson saw the desires of the public as the wellspring of democratic government: "As is the majority, so ought the government to be."[20] He argued that presidents are unique because only they are chosen by the entire nation. Presidents, he said, should help educate the citizens about government, interpret their true will, and faithfully respond to it.

Wilson's theory of the presidency has been followed more and more fully in twentieth-century thought and practice. All presidents, especially since Franklin Roosevelt, have attempted to both shape and respond to public opinion; all, to one degree or another, have attempted to speak directly to the people about policy.[21]

Using the Media   More and more frequently, presidents go public, using television to bypass the print media and speak to the public directly about policy. They have held fewer news conferences with White House correspondents (where awkward questions cannot be excluded).[22] Richard Nixon pioneered prime-time television addresses, at which Ronald Reagan later excelled. Bill Clinton was more interactive with citizens, appearing on radio and TV talk shows and holding informal but televised "town hall meetings."

More and more, presidents have traveled outside the White House to make public appearances. Often the settings convey a visual message: George W. Bush used appearances with "typical" American families in their homes to dramatize his tax cut proposals. Most spectacular is travel abroad, which portrays the chief executive as *presidential,* a head of state, and highlights his foreign policy achievements: Kennedy speaking at the Berlin Wall in 1963; Nixon raising his glass in toast at the Great Hall of the People in Beijing in 1972; Reagan strolling through Red Square in Moscow with Mikhail Gorbachev in 1988.

Leading Public Opinion

Especially since the rise of television, modern presidents have enhanced their power to shape public opinion. Some studies have indicated that when a popular president takes a stand in favor of a particular policy, the public's support for that policy tends to rise. A determined president, delivering many speeches and messages over a period of several weeks or months, may be able to gain 5 to 10 percentage points in support of that policy in the polls.[23] This is not an enormous effect, but it tends to confirm Theodore Roosevelt's claim that the presidency is a "bully pulpit."

The power to lead the public also implies a power to *manipulate* public opinion, if a president is so inclined—that is, to deceive or mislead the public so that it will approve policies that it might oppose if it were fully informed.[24] Especially in foreign affairs, presidents can sometimes control what information the public gets, in least in the short run. Lyndon Johnson, for example, purposely misstated the facts about the Gulf of Tonkin incident at the beginning of the Vietnam War (recall the story in Chapter 5).

Champions of energetic presidential leadership must face the possibility that that leadership will go wrong and result in demagoguery or manipulation. The dilemma cannot be resolved. The power to do good is the power to do evil as well. But some safeguards may exist, including the capacity of the public to judge character when it is choosing a president, as well as the ability of other national leaders to counteract a deceitful president. Johnson and Nixon learned this bitter lesson—the former declined to run for a second term; the latter resigned.

Responding to the Public

In any case, the relationship between presidents and the public is very much a two-way street. Besides trying to lead the people, presidents definitely tend to respond to public opinion. Electoral competition produces presidents who tend to share the public's policy preferences. Moreover, most presidents want to be reelected or to win a favorable place in history, and they know that they are unlikely to do so if they defy public opinion on many major issues. Usually, they try to anticipate what the public will want in order to win electoral reward and avoid electoral punishment.

Quiet Influence What presidents *want* to do so often resembles what the public wants—that is one reason they were elected in the first place—that there is no conflict to observe. Only occasionally does a modern president get so badly out of touch with the public that the full power of public opinion is revealed.

More often, in day-to-day politics, it simply turns out that what the president does is largely in harmony with what the general public wants. When public opinion moved toward favoring a buildup of defense during the late

Web Exploration
The President and Public Opinion

Issue: Effective presidents try to stay attuned to public opinion and have created tools to enhance their ability to track what the public wants.

Site: Access Public Agenda Online on our Website at **www.ablongman.com/greenberg**. Go to the "Web Explorations" section for Chapter 12 and open "the president and public opinion," then select "contact the president." Select an issue you care about from the list on the left-hand side of the page. Read background materials on the issue, then examine the competing proposals for addressing the problem you care about in the section "major proposals."

What You've Learned: Decide what you want the federal government to do about the problem you care about. Formulate a policy that you believe would be both achievable and effective. Let the president (or at least one of his staff members) know what action you want taken. Send an e-mail to **President@whitehouse.gov**.

HINT: The more thoughtful your e-mail, the more likely it is to reach the ears of people who matter in the White House.

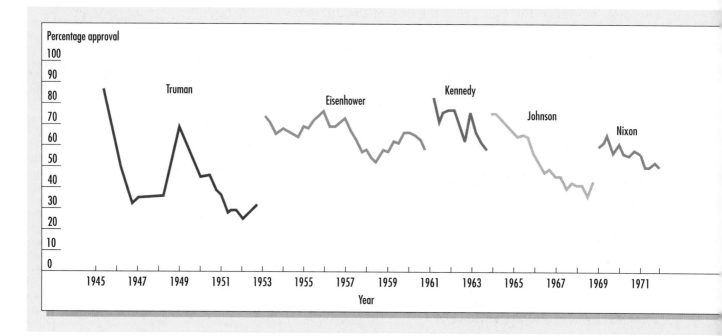

FIGURE 12.2 Trends in Presidential Popularity, 1945–2002

Popularity ratings of presidents rise and fall in response to political, social, and economic events.

Source: Gallup surveys.

1970s, Carter and Reagan followed suit. When the public wanted something done about the welfare problem, Clinton acted in concert with Congress. As a general matter, when polls show that public opinion has changed, presidents have tended to shift policy in the same direction.[25]

Listening to the Public There is plenty of evidence that presidents pay attention to what the public is thinking. At least since the Kennedy administration, presidents and their staffs have carefully read the available public

Modern presidents make concerted efforts to stay in touch with public opinion. Pollster Stanley Greenberg played this role during the first years of the Clinton administration.

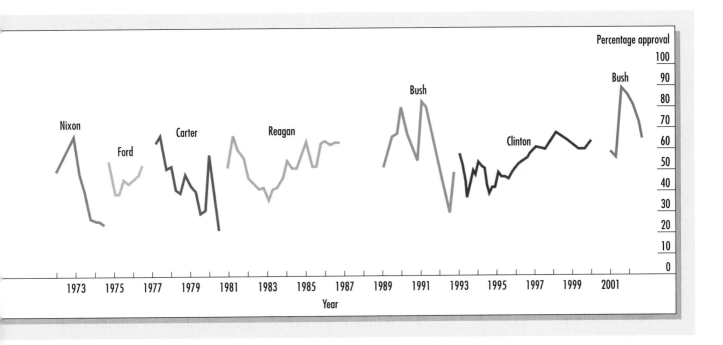

opinion surveys and now have full-blown polling operations of their own.[26] President Clinton employed several of the best pollsters in the business—including Stanley Greenberg (the author's brother)—to chart his electoral campaigns and legislative agenda. Although such polling is often deplored, it helps presidents choose policies that the American public favors and change or discard those that are unpopular.

The Role of Presidential Popularity

The public also influences presidents through its judgments about presidential performance: that is, through **presidential popularity** or unpopularity. Since the 1930s, Gallup and other poll takers have regularly asked Americans whether they approve or disapprove of "the president's handling of the job." The percentage of people who approve varies from month to month and year to year, and as time passes, these varying percentages can be graphed in a sort of fever chart of how the public has thought the president was doing (see Figure 12.2).

A number of factors seem to be especially important in determining presidential popularity, including time, the state of the economy, and foreign policy crises.

Time Historically, most presidents have begun their terms of office with a majority of Americans—usually 60 percent or more—approving of how they are handling their job. Most presidents have tended to lose popularity as time passes. But this loss of popularity does not represent an inexorable working of time; Eisenhower, Reagan, and Clinton actually gained popularity during their second terms. Those who lose popularity do so in response to bad news. Good news generally makes presidents more popular.[27]

The Economy One of the most serious kinds of bad news involves economic recession. When the economy goes sour, fewer Americans approve of the president. This happened to George H. W. Bush in mid-1991, as the economy faltered. On the other hand, the spectacular performance of the American

presidential popularity
The percentage of Americans who approve a president's handling of his job.

economy in the mid- and late 1990s greatly benefited Bill Clinton, whose historically high approval numbers were sustained even as Congress was attempting to remove him from office.

War Successful military actions tend to add to presidential popularity, as Ronald Reagan happily discovered after the U.S. invasion of Grenada in 1982. The senior Bush's approval rating soared on the successful conclusion of the war with Iraq, while the junior Bush's success in Afghanistan sustained his high popularity. Conversely, an unsuccessful war is bad news for a president, especially a limited war that drags on with high casualty rates, such as the Korean War (which detracted from Truman's already low popularity in 1950 and 1951) or the Vietnam War.

Interest Groups, Political Parties, and Social Movements

Presidents are also influenced by organized interest groups, by political parties, and, sometimes, by social movements.

Interest Groups

As we saw in Chapters 7 and 10, interest groups' relationships with presidents, like other aspects of interest group politics, are a sort of unexplored continent. Much of what goes on is probably kept hidden from scholars and observers. But we can be reasonably sure, from various hints and fragments of evidence, that organized groups exert important kinds of influence.[28]

Interest group and other special-interest money helps candidates win presidential nominations and elections, so those who take office do not simply reflect the preferences of ordinary citizens; they tend to share, or at least sympathize with, the goals of their benefactors. At the least, presidents give special access to those who helped get them into office.

Precisely which interest groups have the most influence on policy depends partly on which party controls the presidency, because some groups are much more closely allied with one party than with the other. Since the 1930s, for example, organized labor and certain businesses have been closely tied to the Democratic party; more recently, civil rights, women's, trial lawyers, teachers union, and environmental groups have joined this alliance. The Republican party, for its part, has had much closer ties to most manufacturing and energy corporations, small businesses, agribusiness, and organizations of well-to-do professionals, such as doctors and lawyers.[29] The policies of the parties in office tend to reflect these differences. George W. Bush's energy policy, for example, was apparently fashioned in conjunction with large energy companies, including representatives from Enron—not surprising, perhaps, in light of the president's and vice-president's long association with the oil industry and the oil industry's sizeable contributions to the 2000 Bush campaign.[30]

Political Parties

Republican presidents tend to do different things from Democratic presidents. Changes in party control of the presidency produce significant changes in policy.

Despite the pressure that electoral competition puts on political parties to win votes by moving to the center, the parties also maintain some real differences, as the responsible party model indicates. As we saw in Chapters 9 and 10, the parties consist of activists and contributors with distinctive policy goals and of ordinary voters who differ, although less sharply, in the same sorts of ways.

As a result of party influence, there tend to be partisan cycles of presidential action, with different policies, depending on which party holds office. Democratic presidents tend to fight unemployment,[31] to favor civil rights and environmental measures, and to promote domestic social welfare programs; Republicans tend to worry about inflation, to cut taxes and domestic expenditures, and to take conservative stands on social issues such as abortion.

Social Movements

Social movements occasionally provide yet another political-level influence on presidents. They do so in at least two different ways. Mass demonstrations and protests cause disruptions that are inconvenient or dangerous to ignore, forcing presidents to take action to defuse them. Or mass movements may produce changes in general public opinion that in turn affect presidents. Either way, presidents and other political leaders have to pay attention. The anti–World Trade Organization (WTO) demonstrations in Seattle in late 1999, for example, helped convince Bill Clinton to push the organization to include environmental and labor protections in its rules (see the "Using the Framework" feature).

Structural Influences on the Presidency

Some of the political linkage influences on presidents that we have discussed—especially public opinion—provide substantial continuity from one president to the next. So do a range of governmental factors, including Congress and the courts. Continuity is also provided by the Constitution, which sets the rules of the political game, and the American political culture, which shapes the outlooks of presidents, other political leaders, and the people. Thus, we can speak of an *enduring* presidency, a presidency that does not merely fluctuate with the whims of whoever holds office but that also reflects the goals and preferences of the people, groups, and institutions that make up American society. The enduring presidency is also a product of two structural factors: the international system and the economy.

The International System

From the end of World War II to the end of the Cold War, all presidents, Republicans and Democrats alike, pursued a broadly similar set of foreign policies. Although postwar presidents differed in their means, they fundamentally agreed on the ends: containment of the influence of the Soviet Union, solidification of the Western alliance, encouragement of open economies in which American business might compete, and opposition to leftist or nationalist movements in the developing world. The reason for this continuity is that U.S. foreign policies reflected the basic features of the international system (particularly its bipolarity, with two superpowers), the U.S. position in that system as the dominant superpower, and the nature of U.S. economic interests in markets, raw materials, and investment opportunities.

When the international system changes, presidential policy tends to change, no matter who is president. Thus, when it became painfully evident by the 1970s that the United States had declined in international economic

USING THE FRAMEWORK: Clinton and Free Trade

How could Bill Clinton support free trade, yet also support ideas of anti-free-trade advocates?

Background: In late November 1999, the Seattle meetings of the World Trade Organization were disrupted by large anti-WTO street demonstrations. The labor, human rights, and environmental organization demonstrators were demanding that the WTO be more open to public scrutiny and accountability and that it write into trade rules protections against child and slave labor and standards for work and environmental protections. President Clinton, one of the nation's leading free traders and a strong proponent of the WTO (he believed the world trading system needed a set of agreed-upon rules to make it safe and fair), nevertheless sided with most of the arguments pushed by the demonstrators. How could he be for both sides in this dispute? Taking a broader look at how structural, political linkage, and governmental factors affected President Clinton's views on global trade issues will help explain this situation.

Governmental Action

The president proposes in his speech to WTO delegates that the organization be more accountable and pay attention to demands for labor and environmental protections in its rules.

Governmental Level

- President Clinton was a strong believer in both free trade and labor and environmental protections. →
- The president also felt pressure from interest groups on both sides of the issue; these political pressures accentuated the conflict between his own beliefs. →
- President Clinton wanted Al Gore to follow him as president and did not want to alienate the Democratic Party base (which includes labor and environmentalists).

Political Linkages Level

- Many business firms involved in the global economy have lobbied Congress and the President for a world trade regime that emphasizes free and open trade, protection of intellectual property rights, and access to markets. →
- Labor and environmental organizations are against a free-trade system without protections for labor and environmental protections in less developed nations; these groups were very important parts of President Clinton's Democratic Party. →
- Social movement demonstrators in the streets of Seattle brought the issues of labor and the environment, and the nature of the WTO, to public attention. →
- The mass media, although mainly attending to the conflict in the streets of Seattle, also covered the issues raised by the protesters.

Structural Level

- Since the end of World War II, the United States has been the leading proponent of global free trade. →
- Globalization of the world economy, pushed by technological revolutions in telecommunications, computers, and transportation, was and is advancing at a rapid rate. →
- The United States is the leading nation in the globalizing economy and, overall, has been benefiting from it. →
- However, some groups in the population are hurt by globalization and by rapid technological change. →
- The United States has in place a strong set of environmental, labor, and consumer protection laws that some believe will be threatened if the WTO gains too much authority.

HOW DEMOCRATIC ARE WE?

Presidents and the American People

PROPOSITION: The presidency has evolved into a highly democratic institution that is responsive to the American people.

AGREE: The framers did not conceive of the office in very democratic terms, but it has become the most democratic institution in the American federal system. It is, after all, the only office directly elected by the American people as a whole. Members of the Supreme Court are not elected by the people, and members of the House and Senate, although elected by the people, represent only congressional districts and states. Being elected by the whole people, it is only the president who can claim a national mandate for his programs and actions. Thus, it is only the president who can overcome the inherent stasis of the constitutional system and move the government to action in the interests of and in response to the American people.

DISAGREE: Although presidents often claim mandates from the people, they are more likely to lead and shape public opinion than to respond to it, especially in the area of foreign and military affairs, so the institution cannot be said to be democratic. Presidents can pretty much go their own way, knowing that the people will eventually follow their lead. Because elections happen only every four years, moreover, and assuming that the public has a short memory, presidents have plenty of time to follow their own agendas early in their term without regard to the public. Because presidents can only serve two terms, then, there is no compelling reason they need to pay close attention to the public during their second term.

THE AUTHORS: It is abundantly clear that the presidency is far more democratic than the framers had intended: Presidents are directly elected by the people (although the Electoral College is still in place and it mattered in the 2000 election); their actions are open to intense public scrutiny by the media, interest groups, the courts, and Congress; and they pay close attention to what the public wants, following public opinion polls closely and commissioning their own. They pay close attention to what the people want for a variety of reasons, including their desire to put in place policies that they favor, to leave a legacy, and to attain an honored place in the history books. It is true that presidents can sometimes manipulate the public, especially in foreign and military affairs where presidential constitutional powers are considerable and public scrutiny is lower, but in the end, presidents cannot be successful unless they enjoy strong public support.

competitiveness and relative economic strength, Presidents Carter and Reagan introduced measures to reduce taxes, to lighten the burden of regulation, to subsidize high-technology industries, and to encourage exports. When the Soviet Union began to move in conciliatory directions and then collapsed, Reagan and the elder Bush responded in friendly fashion, despite their history of fierce anticommunism. After Nine-Eleven, George W. Bush enunciated a new military doctrine stressing preemptive strikes against terrorist groups and countries.

The Economy

Similarly, all presidents, Republican or Democrat, must work to help the economy grow and flourish while keeping unemployment and inflation low. A healthy economy is essential to a president's popularity and continuation in office, to tax receipts that fund government programs, and to the maintenance of social peace and stability. A healthy economy in turn requires that investors continue to have confidence in the future. This has tended to create a set of presidential policies that favor such investors no matter whether a Democrat or a Republican is in the White House.

Summary

The American presidency began small; only a few nineteenth-century presidents (among them Jefferson, Jackson, Polk, and Lincoln) made much of a mark. In the twentieth century, however, as a result of industrialization, two world wars and the Cold War, and the Great Depression, presidential powers and resources expanded greatly. The presidency attained much of its modern shape under Franklin Roosevelt.

Presidents have varied in personality and style, with significant consequences. Despite the enormous resources and large staffs available to presidents, they are constrained in what they can do, especially concerning domestic policy. Presidents cannot always control their own executive branch. They engage in tugs-of-war with Congress, pushing their programs with varying success, depending on their party's strength in the legislature and the nature of the issue.

The presidency has become a far more democratic office than the Founders envisioned. Presidents listen to public opinion and respond to it, in addition to leading (and sometimes manipulating) the public. But presidents are also influenced by interest groups, party activists, and financial contributors in ways that may diverge from what the public wants. Further, presidents are affected by such structural factors as the nature of the American economic and social systems and the U.S. position in the world.

Suggestions for Further Reading

Barber, James David. *The Presidential Character: Predicting Performance in the White House,* 4th ed. Englewood Cliffs, NJ: Prentice Hall, 1992.
> *A fascinating, but controversial, analysis of the nature and effect of presidential personalities on the office.*

Cronin, Thomas E., and Michael A. Genovese. *The Paradoxes of the American Presidency.* New York: Oxford University Press, 1998.
> *Examines the implications of our often conflicting and unrealistic expectations about the office of president.*

Kessel, John H. *Presidents, the Presidency and the Political Environment.* Washington, D.C.: CQ Press, 2001.
> *A comprehensive overview of how the nature of a particular presidency is largely determined by the personal qualities of the man in the White House, the constitutional rules and historical precedents, and the political environment of the times.*

Morris, Edmund. *Theodore Rex.* New York: Random House, 2001.
> *A fascinating account of the presidency of Theodore Roosevelt and how the intersection of his personality with a particular moment in American history helped transform the presidential office.*

Neustadt, Richard E. *Presidential Power and the Modern Presidents: The Politics of Leadership from Roosevelt to Reagan.* New York: Free Press, 1991.
> *The classic study of how presidents do or do not get their way, updated to include recent presidencies.*

Skowronek, Stephen. *The Politics Presidents Make.* Cambridge, MA: Harvard University Press, 1993.
An in-depth historical look at the ways in which the political context of the times shapes the nature of the presidency.

Tulis, Jeffrey K. *The Rhetorical Presidency.* Princeton, NJ: Princeton University Press, 1987.
Traces how presidents have moved from the Founders' conception of a distant relationship with the public to the modern closeness.

Internet Sources

Potus **www.potus.com**
Biographies and other information about American presidents.

Presidential Library Consortium **http://metalab.unc.edu/lia/president/**
Links to all existing presidential libraries and their vast repositories of information.

Roper Center **http://www.lib.uconn.edu/RoperCenter/**
Reports on all major presidential performances and popularity polls.

Watergate Site
www.washingtonpost.com/wp-srv/national/longterm/watergate/front.htm
Complete information on the Watergate affair: background, congressional testimony, official statements, press coverage, speeches, court rulings, biographies of the leading players, and more.

White House Home Page **www.whitehouse.gov/**
Information on the first family, recent presidential addresses and orders, text from news conferences, official presidential documents, and ways to contact the White House.

Notes

1. Robin Toner and Neil A. Lewis, "White House Push on Security Steps Bypasses Congress," *The New York Times* (November 14, 2001), p. A1.

2. U.S. Bureau of the Census.

3. U.S. Department of Commerce, *Historical Statistics of the United States, Colonial Times to 1970* (Washington, D.C.: U.S. Government Printing Office, 1971), pp. 8, 1143.

4. Clinton Rossiter, *The American Presidency,* rev. ed. (New York: Harcourt, Brace, 1960).

5. Quoted in Laurence J. Peter, *Peter's Quotations* (New York: Morrow, 1977), p. 405.

6. James P. Pfiffner, *The Modern Presidency* (New York: St. Martin's Press, 1998), ch. 4.

7. Nathan Miller, *FDR: An Intimate History* (Lanham, MD: Madison Books, 1983), p. 276.

8. Thomas E. Cronin and Michael A. Genovese, *The Paradoxes of the American Presidency* (New York: Oxford University Press, 1998), ch. 10; and Joseph A. Pika, "The Vice-Presidency: New Opportunities, Old Constraints," in Michael Nelson, ed., *The Presidency and the Political System,* 4th ed. (Washington, D.C.: Congressional Quarterly Press, 1995), pp. 496–528.

9. Benjamin Bradlee, *Conversations with Kennedy* (New York: Norton, 1975), p. 38.

10. Richard E. Neustadt, *Presidential Power and the Modern Presidents: The Politics of Leadership from Roosevelt to Reagan* (New York: Free Press, 1990).

11. Graham T. Allison, *Essence of Decision: Explaining the Cuban Missile Crisis* (Boston: Little, Brown, 1971), pp. 141–142.

12. Neustadt, *Presidential Power and the Modern Presidents,* ch. 2.

13. Charles O. Jones, *Separate but Equal: Congress and the Presidency* (New York: Chatham House, 1999).

14. For the view that divided government affects the content of public policy, see James L. Sundquist, "Needed: A Political Theory for the New Era of Coalition Government in the U.S.," *Political Science Quarterly* 103 (1988), pp. 613–635; L. Mezey, "The Legislature, the Executive and Public Policy," and N. Pfiffner, "Divided Government and the Problems of Governance," in James Thurber, ed., *Divided Democracy* (Washington, D.C.: Congressional Quarterly Press, 1991). For the view that divided government doesn't matter much, see David R. Mayhew, *Divided We Govern: Party Control, Lawmaking, and Investigations, 1946–1990* (New Haven, CT: Yale University Press, 1991); Charles Jones, *The Presidency in a Separated System* (Washington, D.C.: Brookings Institution, 1994). It may be that divided government matters for some issue areas and not others; for this view, see Martha Gibson, "Issues, Coalitions, and Divided Government," *Congress and the Presidency* 22 (1995), pp. 155–165.

15. George C. Edwards III, *Presidential Influence in Congress* (San Francisco: Freeman, 1980); Jon R. Bond and Richard Fleischer, *The President in the Legislative Arena* (Chicago: University of Chicago Press, 1990); Mark A. Peterson, *Legislating Together* (Cambridge, MA: Harvard University Press, 1990). For a contrary view suggesting that an ideologically cohesive majority is what matters, not the actual size of the majority, see Jon R. Bond and Richard Fleischer (eds.), *Polarized Politics: Congress and the President in a Partisan Era* (Washington, D.C.: CQ Press, 2000).

16. Terry Sullivan, "Headcounts, Expectations and Presidential Coalitions in Congress," *American Journal of Political Science* 32 (1988), pp. 657–689.

17. Aaron Wildavsky, "The Two Presidencies," in Aaron Wildavsky, ed., *Perspectives on the Presidency* (Boston: Little, Brown, 1975), pp. 448–461.

18. Edwards, *Presidential Influence in Congress,* pp. 90–100; Jon R. Bond and Richard Fleischer, *The President in the Legislative Arena* (Chicago: University of Chicago Press, 1990).

19. Jeffrey K. Tulis, *The Rhetorical Presidency* (Princeton, NJ: Princeton University Press, 1987), chs. 2 and 3, esp. p. 64.

20. Woodrow Wilson, *Leaders of Men,* ed. T. H. Vail Motter (Princeton, NJ: Princeton University Press, 1952), p. 39; quoted in Tulis, *The Rhetorical Presidency,* ch. 4, which analyzes Wilson's theory at length and expresses some skepticism about it.

21. Tulis, *The Rhetorical Presidency,* pp. 138, 140.

22. Samuel Kernell, *Going Public: Strategies of Presidential Leadership,* 2nd ed. (Washington, D.C.: Congressional Quarterly Press, 1993), p. 92 and ch. 4.

23. Benjamin I. Page and Robert Y. Shapiro, "Presidents as Opinion Leaders: Some New Evidence," *Policy Studies Journal* 12 (1984), pp. 649–661; Benjamin I. Page, Robert Y. Shapiro, and Glenn R. Dempsey, "What Moves Public Opinion," *American Political Science Review* 81 (1987), pp. 23–43; but see Donald L. Jordan, "Newspaper Effects on Policy Preferences," *Public Opinion Quarterly* 57 (1993), pp. 191–204.

24. Lawrence R. Jacobs and Robert Y. Shapiro, *Politicians Don't Pander: Political Manipulation and the Loss of Democratic Responsiveness* (Chicago: University of Chicago Press, 2000).

25. Benjamin I. Page and Mark P. Petracca, *The American Presidency* (New York: McGraw-Hill, 1983), p. 122. Also see Benjamin I. Page and Robert Y. Shapiro, "Effects of Public Opinion on Policy," *American Political Science Review* 77 (1983), pp. 175–190.

26. Lawrence Jacobs and Robert Y. Shapiro, "The Rise of Presidential Polling: The Nixon White House in Historical Perspective," *Public Opinion Quarterly* 59, (1995), pp. 163–195.

27. Richard A. Brody, *Assessing the President* (Stanford, CA: Stanford University Press, 1991). See also John E. Mueller, "Presidential Popularity from Truman to Johnson," *American Political Science Review* 64 (1970), pp. 18–34; Samuel Kernell, "Explaining Presidential Popularity," *American Political Science Review* 72 (1978), pp. 506–522.

28. See Mark P. Petracca, ed., *The Politics of Interests* (Boulder, CO: Westview Press, 1992).

29. Alexander Heard, *The Costs of Democracy* (Chapel Hill, NC: University of North Carolina Press, 1960); Ferguson and Rogers, *Right Turn;* Thomas Ferguson, *Golden Rule* (Chicago: University of Chicago Press, 1995).

30. Howard Fineman and Michael Isikoff, "Big Energy at the Table," *Newsweek* (May 14, 2001), pp. 19–22.

31. Douglas A. Hibbs Jr., "Partisan Theory After Fifteen Years," *European Journal of Political Economy* 8 (1992), pp. 361–373.

Chapter 13
The Federal Bureaucracy

In This Chapter

- How our bureaucracy compares to those in other countries
- Who bureaucrats are and what they do
- How the executive branch is organized
- What's wrong and what's right with the federal bureaucracy
- Myths about the federal bureaucracy

The Federal Bureaucracy After Nine-Eleven

For much of the 1990s, anger at the federal government and disrespect for federal government workers were rampant in the United States. Complaints about the size, cost, inefficiency, and excessive interference of the "bureaucracy in Washington" were common, as was unhappiness about particular agencies in the executive branch, such as the Internal Revenue Service, the Postal Service, the Bureau of Land Management, and the Bureau of Alcohol, Tobacco, and Firearms. For example, after running on a set of promises to get the federal government off the backs of the American people—part of the so-called "Contract With America"—Republicans captured the House of Representatives in 1994. In that same year, Americans' sense of trust in the federal government fell to an all-time low when only 21 percent of the public said that the "federal government can be trusted to do the right thing most of the time" or "almost always." Talk radio and TV "chatting heads" carried on the same refrain, with attacks on President Clinton and the Clinton-led government accounting for much of the total air time. Sensing the antigovernment tide, Clinton declared in his 1996 State of the Union Address that "the era of big government is over," and carried through by successfully pushing tax and spending bills through Congress that would first balance the federal budget, then put it into surplus. The implication was that the federal government would be smaller and do less.

More extreme expressions of antigovernment and anti-bureaucratic sentiments surfaced, as well. When news of the terrorist bombing of the Frederick P. Murrah Federal Building in Oklahoma City hit the airwaves on April 19, 1995, retired sheriff Howard Stewart of Meadville, Pennsylvania, immediately dismissed the speculation of the experts that it was somehow connected to the troubled politics of the Middle East: "When I realized the date [the anniversary of the FBI raid on the Branch Davidians in Waco, Texas], and I thought about all the anger and fear that's out there," Stewart says, "I said to my wife, 'I don't think it was Arabs that did this.'"[1]

Stewart had reason to suspect a homegrown origin for the attack on a government center; he had been hearing some strange antigovernment rumblings in his quiet, conservative rural community. In the coffee shops on Main Street, talk was of a government conspiracy to enslave Americans to the United Nations. Color-coded highway signs, it was being said, were guideposts for foreign invaders. Meadville citizens were particularly upset by federal gun control laws, the 1993 siege in Waco of the Branch Davidians, and restrictive environmental regulations.

Anti-federal-government anger is a staple of American political history. In the early days of the nation, many Anti-Federalists believed that the Constitution gave undue power to the central government. Buttressed by the theories of John C. Calhoun, the state of South Carolina passed a resolution in

1830 suggesting that the states had the right to nullify federal laws. Several of the New England states thought about seceding from the union in 1812 to remove themselves from federal authority, and the South did so in 1860, bringing on the Civil War. Many conservatives, including a majority on the Supreme Court for a few years, believed that the expansion of federal authority during the Great Depression in the 1930s was unconstitutional. Many whites in the South grew angry with the federal government in the 1960s and 1970s because of federal championing of civil rights. Antiwar activists during the years of the Vietnam War were unhappy with the Defense Department for waging the war and with the CIA and the FBI for interfering with legitimate protest activities. Much of the corporate community turned against the federal government in the 1980s and 1990s for what seemed like undue zeal on the part of government officials for environmental and consumer protection. Western ranchers opposed to extensive government ownership of land sparked what came to be called the "sagebrush rebellion" in the 1990s. The chorus of anti-federal-government complaints has ebbed and flowed throughout our history.

The attacks on the United States on September 11, 2001, and the subsequent war on terrorism, seemed to change everything, at least for awhile. Government came rushing back into fashion. "Trust in government" scores among the public rebounded to a heady level of 64 percent by December 2001. Recruiters for the CIA, FBI, the Foreign Service, and the armed forces reported a rush of people trying to join. ROTC was invited back onto several campuses from where it had been exiled after the Vietnam conflict. The reasons are not hard to fathom. It was, after all, government workers on whom Americans counted during the crisis caused by the attack: local police and fire-fighters who gave their lives to save others at the World Trade Center; members of the armed services who struck back at the Taliban regime and the al Qaeda network; sci-entists at the Center for Disease Control who tracked and tried to contain the Anthrax outbreak; postal workers who continued to deliver the mail despite Anthrax deaths; agents of the FBI and the CIA who tracked terror cells in the United States and abroad; and federally employed per-sonnel who screened airline passengers and baggage.

Despite Americans' long mistrust of government, these de-velopments fit our history. In a national crisis, particularly war, we have always turned to the government in Washington to mobilize and coordinate the vast human and material re-sources that are required. In such times, we grant more power to, ask more of, and give greater respect to the national gov-ernment, particularly the executive branch: the president, the Department of Defense, the National Security Council, the CIA, the uniformed services, and other agencies newly cre-ated for the emergency. Though it is too early to tell if these dramatic changes in how government and government em-ployees are perceived will last, they remain a sharp departure from sentiments that have prevailed in the United States for the past quarter century. ∎

Thinking Critically About This Chapter

This chapter is about the federal bureaucracy, how it is organized, what it does, and what effects its actions have on public policies and American democracy.

Using the Framework   You will see in this chapter how the federal bu-reaucracy has grown over the years, primarily as a result of structural trans-formations in the economy and international position of the United States, but also because of the influence of political linkage level actors and institutions, including voters, public opinion, and interest groups. Primary responsibility for many of the enduring features of the federal bureaucracy will be shown to be associated with our political culture and the Constitution.

Using the Democracy Standard   You will see in this chapter that the federal bureaucracy in general, despite much speculation to the contrary, is fairly responsive to the American people, reacting in the long run to pressures brought to bear on it by the elected branches, the president, and Congress. On the other hand, bureaucrats in specific agencies, in specific circumstances, can be relatively immune from public opinion, at least in the short and medium run. You will be asked to think about what this means in terms of our democ-ratic evaluative standard.   ◀

A Comparative View of the American Bureaucracy

Longman
Participate.com 2.0
Comparative
Comparing
Bureaucracies

The American bureaucracy is different from bureaucracies in other democratic nations. Structural influences such as the American political culture and the constitutional rules of the game have a great deal to do with these differences.

Hostile Political Culture

As we indicated in the story that opens this chapter, Americans generally do not trust their government, nor do they think it can accomplish most of the tasks assigned to it. They believe, on the whole, that the private sector can usually do a better job, and most of the time want responsibilities lodged there rather than with government. As suggested, this traditional outlook towards government and those who work for it may have changed since Nine-Eleven, but for how long, no one knows.

This generally hostile environment influences the American bureaucracy in several important ways. For one thing, our public bureaucracy is surrounded by more legal restrictions and is subject to more intense legislative oversight than bureaucracies in other countries. Because **civil servants** have so little prestige, moreover, many of the most talented people in our society tend to stay away; they do not generally aspire to work in government, though this may be changing, as suggested above. In many other democratic countries, by way of contrast, civil servants are highly respected and attract talented people. In France, Britain, and Germany, for example, the higher **civil service** positions are filled by the top graduates of the countries' elite universities and are accorded enormous prestige. Finally, the highest policymaking positions in the U.S. executive branch are closed to civil servants; they are reserved for presidential political appointees. This is not true in other democracies.

civil servants

Government workers employed under the merit system; not political appointees.

civil service

Federal government jobs held by civilian employees, excluding political appointees.

Incoherent Organization

Our bureaucracy is an organizational hodgepodge. It does not take the standard pyramidal form, as bureaucracies elsewhere do. There are few clear lines of control, responsibility, or accountability. Some executive branch units have

Web Exploration
Comparing Bureaucracies as Information Providers

Issue: The bureaucracies of the United States and other democratic governments around the world have been racing to put information about their activities, policies, and services online. Some do it better than others.

Site: Access the Executive Branch Website at the Library of Congress and the official site of the government of Canada on our Website at **www.ablongman.com/greenberg**. Go to the "Web Explorations" section for Chapter 13. Select "comparing bureaucracies. . . ," then "information for each country." Browse each of the sites; examine four or five of their most important departments, ministries, agencies, and bureaus.

What You've Learned: Which national government does a better job of serving its constituency on the Web? How informative are the sites? How easy or difficult are they to navigate? Which are more graphically interesting?

HINT: To a large extent, your response to this query is strictly a matter of personal preference. However, one thing to be alert to is whether or not the government sites are simply conveying "good news."

no relationship at all to other agencies and departments. As one of the leading students of the federal bureaucracy once put it, other societies have "a more orderly and symmetrical, a more prudent, a more cohesive and more powerful bureaucracy," whereas we have "a more internally competitive, a more experimental, a noisier and less coherent, a less powerful bureaucracy."[2] Our bureaucracy was built piece by piece over the years in a political system without a strong central government. Bureaucracies in other democratic nations were often created at a single point in time, by powerful political leaders, such as Frederick the Great in Prussia and Napoleon in France.[3]

Divided Control

Adding to the organizational incoherence of our federal bureaucracy is the fact that it has two bosses—the president and Congress—who are constantly vying with one another for control. In addition, the federal courts keep an eye on it. This situation is created by the separation of powers and checks and balances in our Constitution, which give each branch a role in the principal activities and responsibilities of the other branches. No other democratic nation has opted for this arrangement. Civil servants in parliamentary democracies are accountable to a single boss, a minister appointed by the prime minister.

Transformation of the Bureaucracy

The Constitution neither specifies the number and kinds of departments to be established nor describes other bureaucratic agencies. The framers apparently wanted to leave these questions to the wisdom of Congress and the president. Over the years, they created a large and complex bureaucracy to meet a wide range of needs.

A Brief Administrative History of the United States

Longman
Participate.com 2.0
Timeline
Evolution of
the Federal
Bureaucracy

The most immediate causes for the transformation of the role of the federal government and the scale of the bureaucracy are political linkage sector pressures—from public opinion, voters, parties, interest groups, and social movements—on government decision makers. The more fundamental causes are changes in such structural level factors as the U.S. economy, the nation's population, and the role of the United States in the world, including involvement in war.

Nineteenth-Century Changes   Until the Civil War, the federal government had few responsibilities, and the administrative apparatus of the executive branch was relatively undeveloped. Rapid population growth, westward expansion, the Industrial Revolution, and economic uncertainty in the last quarter of the nineteenth century gradually changed people's thinking about the appropriate responsibilities of government and the size of the bureaucracy.[4] The Department of the Interior, created in 1849, was given responsibility for Indian affairs, the census, and the regulation of public lands and mining. The Department of Justice was created in 1870 to handle the federal government's growing legal burden in the fields of civil and criminal, antitrust, tax, and natural resources law. The Department of Agriculture became a full-fledged cabinet department in 1889 in response to economic crisis in the farm economy and the demands of farm groups. The Department of Labor was created in 1913 in an effort to ease the rising tensions between workers and

Certain problems that cross state boundaries—such as the production for a national market of unsafe and unwholesome food by companies—are probably best solved by the federal government. Upton Sinclair's description of a meat-packing plant like this one in his novel *The Jungle* helped swing public opinion behind the Pure Food and Drug Act, passed in 1906.

owners. The Department of Commerce was created in the same year to foster technological development, standardization, and business cooperation.

The Corporation and the Progressives   The rise to prominence of the large corporations in the late nineteenth and early twentieth centuries, and the problems they caused, also contributed to a rethinking of the role of the federal government. Monopoly practices in the railroad, manufacturing, oil, and banking industries triggered reform movements that resulted in new federal regulatory laws, of which the most important were the Interstate Commerce Act (1887) and the Sherman Antitrust Act (1890). Progressive reformers and farsighted business leaders, who were worried about the growing public hostility to big business, helped convince Congress to pass such landmark legislation as the Federal Reserve Act (passed in 1914 to stabilize the banking industry), the Pure Food and Drug Act (1906), the Meat Inspection Act (passed in 1906 in response to the horrors reported in Upton Sinclair's "muckraking" book *The Jungle*), and the Federal Trade Commission Act (1914).[5] Each piece of legislation was a response to a set of problems, each expanded the federal government's responsibilities, and each created a new executive branch agency to carry out the law.

The Great Depression   The Great Depression forever changed how Americans thought about their government. Economic collapse, widespread social distress, and serious threats of violence and social unrest impelled President Franklin Roosevelt and Congress to respond with a range of new programs: work programs for the unemployed, relief for the poor, Social Security, regulation of the banking and the securities industries, agricultural subsidy programs, collective bargaining, and programs to encourage business expansion. Each program added new bureaucratic agencies to the executive branch.

During World War II and the Cold War that followed, the increased responsibilities of a superpower were thrust on the U.S. federal government. The executive branch grew so rapidly during World War II that temporary buildings were constructed along the mall in Washington, D.C., to house new bureaucratic entities such as the Atomic Energy Commission.

World War II and Its Aftermath   World War II, America's new role as a superpower, and the long Cold War with the Soviet Union also brought a substantial increase in the federal government's responsibilities and in the size of the executive branch. Some old-line departments, such as the Department of State, grew substantially after World War II. The Department of Defense was created by merging the old Army and Navy departments and adding an Air Force component. New administrative units such as the Central Intelligence Agency, the National Security Agency, the National Security Council, the Agency for International Development, and the U.S. Arms Control and Disarmament Agency were created to fill new needs and missions. The Atomic Energy Commission was created both to regulate and to encourage atomic power and weapons production. The Internal Revenue Service expanded its operations so that it could collect the revenues to pay for these new responsibilities. By 1950, a federal bureaucracy of substantial size and effect was firmly in place.[6]

The Regulatory State   During the 1960s and 1970s, successful social reform movements and important changes in public opinion convinced political leaders to take on new responsibilities in the areas of civil rights, urban affairs, environmental and consumer protection, workplace safety, and education. Important among these initiatives was the formation of the Department of Health, Education, and Welfare (now split into the Department of Health and Human Services and the Department of Education). The Environmental Protection Agency was created to monitor compliance with federal environmental laws and to regulate business activities that might pollute the nation's air and water. The Occupational Safety and Health Administration keeps its regulatory eye on potentially dangerous workplace practices. Each expansion of responsibility, as in the past, brought an expansion in the size of the bureaucracy. Although the Reagan Revolution slowed the growth in the federal government's responsibilities, it was unable to roll back most of the programs and agencies created since the Great Depression.

Devolution and Rollback   On taking control of Congress after their 1994 landslide electoral victory, Republicans began to pare down the size of the federal government, roll back many of its regulatory responsibilities, and shift a number of functions to the states. For instance, Congress made it more diffi-cult to identify and protect wetlands. It also shifted much of the responsibility for providing public assistance to the states (see Chapter 3). Finally, Congress made deep slashes in the federal budget, which forced substantial "downsiz-ing" in a broad range of executive branch agencies. Increasingly, Republicans especially, but many Democrats as well, have been asking what essential ser-vices the federal government should provide.

Devolution and rollback may be related to changes in the global econ-omy, where success seems to go to business enterprises that are "lean and mean," nimble and entrepreneurial, and to countries that allow their major companies to succeed by lowering regulatory and tax burdens. Whether this is cause or excuse is too early to tell. It may well be that globalization forces are not the cause of these changes, as some analysts suggest, but merely a rhetorical device used by the business community to lighten the burden of government regulation on corporations. Whether cause or rhetorical weapon, political leaders in the United States have been paying attention recently to globalization processes and have acted to diminish the role and size of the federal government and its bureaucracy.

The War on Terrorism   Because waging war requires the organization and mobilization of vast material and human resources, it has always led to an expansion in the size and reach of the executive branch of government. This looks to be true for the war on terrorism, as well. Within only a few months of September 11, virtually every federal police and intelligence agency—including the FBI, the CIA and the NSA—was authorized to hire more people, as was the Department of Defense, funded by emergency budget authorizations. Budgets for these agencies and a range of others involved in the war, including the Federal Emergency Management Administration

Tom Ridge headed the new Office of Homeland Security created by President Bush's executive order in the aftermath of the terrorist at-tacks on the United States. Here Ridge speaks with workers at Ground Zero in New York.

Longman
Participate.com
2.0
Visual Literacy
**The Changing
Face of the
Federal
Bureaucracy**

(FEMA), were all beefed up in President Bush's annual budget request to Congress in early 2002. The Airline Security Act, moreover, created a new federal agency that will hire its own people to screen baggage and passengers rather than depend on the private sector to do the job. President Bush issued an executive order creating an Office of Homeland Security to run the war against terrorism at home, appointing former Pennsylvania governor Tom Ridge to be its head. Bush later asked Congress to create a new cabinet-level Department of Homeland Security with enhanced authority to coordinate the counterterrorism effort on the home front. There is every indication, then, that bureaucratic expansion, at least in those areas either directly or indirectly associated with the war on terrorism, is here to stay as long as the threat of terrorism remains a reality.

So, although there have been more than a few fits and starts, the general picture over the course of American history has been toward a growth in the size and responsibilities of the national government. However, determining just how big the government has grown depends on what measures one uses. (See "By the Numbers: How big is the federal government?" on pages 394–395.)

How the Executive Branch Is Organized

The executive branch is made up of several different kinds of administrative units, which make the federal bureaucracy a very complicated entity.

- The most familiar are *departments,* which are headed by cabinet-level secretaries, appointed by the president and approved by the Senate. Departments are meant to carry out the most essential government functions. The first three ever established were War, State, and Treasury. Departments vary greatly in size and internal organization. The Department of Agriculture, for example, has almost 50 offices and bureaus, whereas the Department of Housing and Urban Development has only a few operating agencies.[7] Over the years, departments (and employees) were added as the need arose, as powerful groups demanded them, or as presidents and members of Congress wished to signal a new national need or to cement political alliances with important constituencies. During wartime, the Department of Defense becomes particularly important. To protect the homefront as the war on terrorism is waged, President Bush pushed for a new Department of Homeland Security.

- Subdivisions within cabinet departments are known as *bureaus* and *agencies.* In some departments, such as the Department of Defense, these subdivisions are closely controlled by the department leadership, and the entire department works very much like a textbook hierarchical model. In other cases, where the bureaus or agencies have fashioned their own relationships with interest groups and powerful congressional committees, the departments are little more than holding companies for powerful bureaucratic subunits.[8] During the long reign of J. Edgar Hoover, for example, the FBI did virtually as it pleased, even though it was (and remains) a unit within the Justice Department.

- *Independent executive agencies* report directly to the president rather than to a department- or cabinet-level secretary. They are usually created to give greater control to the president in carrying out some execu-

The Immigration and Naturalization Service, an agency in the Department of Justice, is being called upon to do more about slowing the flow of illegal immigration and screen for possible terrorists, but it must operate within guidelines and budgets determined by Congress.

tive function or to highlight some particular public problem or issue that policymakers wish to address. The Environmental Protection Agency was given independent status to focus government and public attention on environmental issues and to give the federal government more flexibility in solving environmental problems.

- *Government corporations* are agencies that operate very much like private companies. They can sell stock, retain and reinvest earnings, and borrow money, for instance. They are usually created to perform some crucial economic activity that private investors are unwilling or unable to perform. The Tennessee Valley Authority, for example, was created during the Great Depression to bring electricity to most of the upper South; today it provides about 6 percent of all U.S. electrical power. The U.S. Postal Service was transformed from an executive department to a government corporation in 1970 in the hope of increasing efficiency.

- *Quasi-governmental organizations* are hybrids of public and private organizations. They allow the federal government to be involved in a particular area of activity without directly controlling it. They are distinguished from government corporations by the fact that a portion of the boards of directors are appointed by the private sector. The Corporation for Public Broadcasting fits into this category, as does the Federal Reserve Board, responsible for setting the nation's monetary policy (see Chapter 17 for more on the "Fed").

- *Independent regulatory commissions,* such as the Securities and Exchange Commission and the Consumer Product Safety Commission, are responsible for regulating sectors of the economy in which it is judged that the free market does not work properly to protect the public interest. The commissions are "independent" in the sense that they stand outside the departmental structure and are protected against direct presidential or congressional control. A commission is run by commissioners with long, overlapping terms, and many require a balance between Republicans and Democrats.

- *Foundations* are units that are separated from the rest of government to protect them from political interference with science and the arts. Most prominent are the foundations for the Arts and for the Humanities and the National Science Foundation.

By the Numbers

How big is the federal government? Is it really shrinking, as people say?

When Bill Clinton proclaimed in 1996 that "the era of big government is over," he was sharing a vision of government espoused by his two conservative predecessors: Ronald Reagan and George H. W. Bush. The notion that the government in Washington is too big and ought to be cut down to size is a recurring theme in American political discourse. Recently, the call to "downsize" or "right size" government has taken an especially strong turn, with recent presidents committed to this vision of a "leaner" and theoretically more efficient government.

What should we make of all these calls to downsize? Just how big is government?

Why It Matters: A significant number of Americans want a smaller government that does less; a significant number of Americans want a bigger government that does more. Whichever camp you fall into, it makes sense that we have accurate measures of what is actually going on.

Calculating the Size of the Federal Government: In addition to using the size of the federal budget as a measure of the size of government—we do this in

Chapter 17—it is fairly common among academics, journalists, and politicians to use the number of federal government employees as a simple, straightforward measure. Using this metric, the size of the government in Washington is not only relatively small at 1.9 million employees (only one-sixth the size of the manufacturing sector in 1996 in terms of employees, and one-thirty-sixth the size of the service sector), but shrinking.

Criticism of the Measure of Government Size: Critics point out that the number of federal civilian employees measures only a portion of the total number of employees who produce goods and services for the federal government. The following, they say, should be included (all figures are for 1996, based on research by Light):

- Employees who work in government contract-created jobs, such as employees working for defense contractors on federal projects (5.6 million)
- Employees who work in government grant-created jobs, such as employees working on federally funded road construction grants or on federally funded research projects (2.4 million)
- Employees hired by state and local governments to meet federal mandates in areas such as child health and nutrition, safe schools, and pollution control (4.6 million)
- U.S. Postal workers, who are not counted as federal civilian employees (0.8 million)
- Uniformed military personnel (1.5 million)

What Do Bureaucrats Do?

Bureaucrats engage in a wide range of activities that are relevant to the quality of democracy in the United States and affect how laws and regulations work.

Executing the Law

The term *executive branch* suggests the branch of the federal government that executes or carries out the law. The framers of the Constitution assumed that Congress would be the principal national policymaker and stipulated that the president and his appointees to administrative positions in the executive

Adding these categories together, we have a total of direct and indirect federal government employment of almost 17 million people in 1996, almost as many as work in the American manufacturing sector.

How about the question of whether government is shrinking? The following graph shows what is happening. (Unfortunately, there is no information available for "mandate-created jobs" prior to 1996, so it cannot be included.)

The picture is pretty clear: Although the overall size of government is considerably larger than it first appears using only the numbers of federal civilian employees, the size of government shrank during the period 1984 to 1996. One other fact is worth noting: Most of the shrinkage of government in this period was related to decreases in the size of the defense sector, including cuts in the number of uniformed military personnel and decreases in defense contracting to the private sector. Considering only the domestic side of the equation, the total size of the federal government actually increased by about 15 percent between 1984 and 1996.

What to Watch For: Numbers that are reported by government, journalists, and academics about government may often be correct, yet incomplete. Always try to expand your search to include multiple measures of the phenomenon or institution you are trying to understand.

What Do You Think? In formulating an opinion about the appropriate size for government, consider what responsibilities and tasks should be the responsibility of the federal government. Are these responsibilities and tasks being accomplished to your satisfaction? Are there too many people working either directly or indirectly for the federal government in

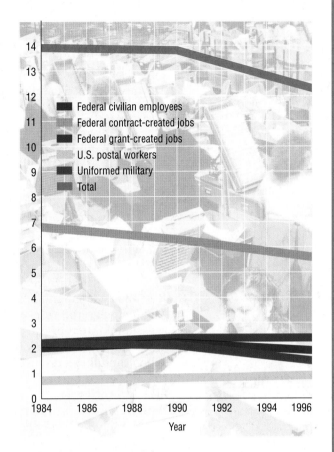

Federal civilian employees
Federal contract-created jobs
Federal grant-created jobs
U.S. postal workers
Uniformed military
Total

Federal Government Jobs

terms of the responsibilities and tasks? Too few? Or just about the right number?

Source: Paul C. Light, *The True Size of Government* (Washington, D.C.: The Brookings Institution, 1999).

branch "shall take care that the laws be faithfully executed" (Article II, Section 2). For the most part, this responsibility is carried out routinely; mail is delivered, troops are trained, and Social Security checks are mailed on time.

Sometimes, executing the law is not so easy, however, because it is not always clear what the law means. Often (all too often, according to some critics[9]), Congress passes laws that are vague about goals and short on procedural guidelines. It may do so because its members believe that something should be done about a particular social problem but are unclear on specifics about how to solve it or disagree among themselves. The Office of Economic Opportunity, for example, was created in 1965 as part of Lyndon Johnson's War on Poverty, with a mandate to "eliminate poverty," but it received virtually no guidance about what time frame was contemplated or what specific things it ought to do. Vaguely written statutes and directives, then, leave a great deal of discretion to bureaucrats.

Regulating (Rule Making)

Congress often gives bureaucratic agencies the power to write specific rules. Because of the complexity of the problems that government must face, Congress tends to create agencies and to specify the job or mission that it wants done and then charges the agency with using its expertise to do the job. Congress created the Environmental Protection Agency (EPA), for instance, and gave it a mission—to help coordinate the cleanup of the nation's air and water—but it left to the EPA the power to set the specific standards that communities and businesses must meet. The standards set by the EPA have the force of law unless they are rescinded by Congress or overruled by the courts. The Food and Drug Administration (FDA) writes rules about the introduction of new drugs that researchers and pharmaceutical companies are obliged to follow. (See the "Using the Framework" feature for more on the FDA.)

Some critics believe that Congress delegates entirely too much lawmaking to the executive branch, but it is difficult to see what alternative Congress has. It cannot micromanage every issue. And in the end, Congress retains control; it can change the rules written by bureaucrats if they drift too far from congressional intent or constituent desires.

Other critics simply believe that there are too many rules and regulations. When candidates promise to "get government off our backs," the reference is to the purported burdens of regulation. Several attempts have been made to roll back executive branch rule making. Under Ronald Reagan, required **cost-benefit analysis** was introduced as a way to slow the rule-making process, for example. And all recent presidents have used the Office of Management and Budget (OMB) to review "excessive" rule making.

cost-benefit analysis

A method of evaluating rules and regulations by weighing their potential costs against their potential benefits to society.

Congress identifies tasks and creates agencies to complete them using their own expertise. For example, the Environmental Protection Agency was created by Congress to clean up and prevent pollution in the nation's air and water; the EPA creates and implements environmental standards without much direct congressional involvement.

USING THE FRAMEWORK: Bureaucratic Rule-Making

How can a bureaucratic agency such as the Food and Drug Administration (FDA) make rules on important things like genetically engineered food? The members of the FDA aren't even elected by the people!

Background: One of the emerging conflicts that will be playing itself out over the next few years, both in the United States and in the global economy, concerns the safety of genetically engineered food and the rules that will apply for protecting the public from its possible harmful effects. In the United States, unless Congress chooses to act in its own right, the rules will be made by the Food and Drug Administration. We can better understand why the FDA can make rules on genetically engineered foods by using a broad perspective that takes into account structural, political linkage, and governmental level factors.

Governmental Action

The FDA issues rules on genetically engineered food products.

Governmental Level

• The FDA scientific staff pressed the FDA's leadership to become active in this area of rulemaking. → • The FDA leadership, attentive to the growing interest in rules to regulate in the area of genetically engineered food, held a series of hearings on the subject in 1999. → • The FDA issued rules in 2000 specifying how genetically engineered food is to be tested for safety and wholesomeness and requiring packaging to carry a warning label for consumers.

• Congress created the Food and Drug Administration, defined its overall mission, but left room for the FDA to make rules in its areas of responsibility. → • The Court has allowed bureaucratic agencies to make rules within the boundaries set by Congress. → • No laws specifically addressing genetically engineered food have been enacted, leaving rulemaking in this area to the FDA.

Political Linkages Level

• Public opinion polls show that some Americans are beginning to worry about genetically engineered food and want some action. → • Interest groups, for and against genetically engineered food, have pressed their positions on public officials, using both "inside" and "outside" forms of lobbying. → • Demonstrators at the WTO protests in Seattle targeted genetically engineered food, putting further pressure on public officials to take action.

Structural Level

• The Constitution says little about the organization and operations of the Executive Branch and leaves the details to be filled in by Congress. → • Scientific researchers have made dramatic breakthroughs in plant and animal genetics, causing some segments of society to call for regulations. → • Global agribusiness corporations are always looking for the most efficient forms of production, and genetically engineered products help them do this.

Adjudicating

Congress has given some executive branch agencies the power to conduct quasi-judicial proceedings in which disputes are resolved. Much as in a court of law, the decisions of an administrative law judge have the force of law, unless appealed to a higher panel. The National Labor Relations Board, for instance, adjudicates disputes between labor and management on matters concerning federal labor laws. Disputes may involve claims of unfair labor practices, for example—firing a labor organizer falls into this category—or disagreements about whether proper procedures were followed in filing for a union certification election.

It is quite clear that bureaucrats exercise a great deal of discretion. They do not simply follow a set of orders from Congress or the president, but find many opportunities to exercise their own judgment. Because bureaucrats make important decisions that have consequences for many other people, groups, and organizations, we can say that they are policymakers. They are *unelected* policymakers, however, and this fact should immediately alert us to some potential problems with regard to the practice of democracy.

Who Are the Bureaucrats?

Longman
Participate.com
2.0
Participation
**Who Wants to
Be a
Bureaucrat?**

Because bureaucrats exercise substantial discretion as policymakers, we want to know who they are. How representative are they of the American people? In a democracy, we would probably want to see a pretty close correspondence between the people and bureaucrats. There are several different personnel systems in the executive branch: career civil service, separate merit services in specific agencies, and political appointees.

The Merit Services

Merit services choose employees on the basis of examinations and educational credentials.

spoils system

The practice of distributing government offices and contracts to the supporters of the winning party; also called patronage.

Career Civil Service From the election of Andrew Jackson in 1828 until the late nineteenth century, the executive branch was staffed through what is commonly called the **spoils system.** It was generally accepted that the "spoils of victory" belonged to the winning party. Winners were expected to clear out people who were loyal to the previous administration and to replace them with their own people. Also known as *patronage,* this system of appointment caused no great alarm in the beginning because of the small and relatively unimportant role of the federal government in American society. The shortcomings of the War Department and other bureaucratic agencies during the Civil War, however, convinced many people that reform of the federal personnel system was required. Rampant corruption and favoritism in the government service during the years after the Civil War gave an additional boost to the reform effort, as did the realization that the growing role of the federal government required more skilled and less partisan personnel. The final catalyst for change was the assassination in 1881 of President James Garfield by a person who, it is said, badly wanted a government job but could not get one.

The Civil Service Act of 1883, also known as the Pendleton Act, created a bipartisan Civil Service Commission to oversee a system of appointments to certain executive branch posts on the basis of merit. Competitive examinations were to be used to determine merit. In the beginning, the competitive civil service system included only about 10 percent of federal positions. Congress has gradually extended the reach of the career civil service; today, it covers about 60 percent of federal employees. In 1978, Congress abolished the Civil Service Commission and replaced it with two separate agencies, the Office of Personnel Management and the Merit Systems Protection Board. The former administers the civil service laws, advertises positions, writes examinations, and acts as a clearinghouse for agencies that are looking for workers. The latter settles disputes concerning employee rights and obligations, hears employee grievances, and orders corrective action when needed.

Agency Merit Services   Many federal agencies require personnel with particular kinds of training and experience appropriate to their special missions. For such agencies, Congress has established separate merit systems administered by each agency itself. The Public Health Service, for instance, recruits its own doctors. The State Department has its own examinations and procedures for recruiting foreign service officers. The National Aeronautics and Space Administration (NASA) recruits scientists and engineers without the help of the Office of Personnel Management. About 35 percent of all federal civilian employees fall under these agency-specific merit systems.

How Different Are Civil Servants?   Civil servants are very much like other Americans.[10] Their educational levels, regional origins, average incomes, and age distribution match almost exactly those of the general population. Civil servants' political beliefs and opinions also match almost exactly those of

Web Explorations
Who Are the Bureaucrats?

Issue: Although women are well represented in the federal bureaucracy, their presence in the upper-most, politically appointed, decision-making positions in the Executive Branch may be less than equitable. Or, they may be well represented in decision-making positions in some agencies and not others.

Site: Access the Plumbook, which lists all federal politically appointed offices, on our Website at **www.ablongman.com/greenberg**. Go to the "Web Explorations" section for Chapter 13. Select "Who are the bureaucrats?" and then open "how representative?" Select three Executive Branch Departments and review the names of the people who hold top offices in the Departments.

What You've Learned: How well are women represented in the Executive Branch departments you selected? If women are better represented in some as compared with others, why do you think that is the case?

HINT: Because women professionals in American society are most heavily represented in education, welfare, the health professions, and in the law, the Departments with their principal missions in these areas are likely to have the most women available for appointment.

the general American public, although they tend to favor the Democrats a bit more than the general public and are slightly more liberal on social issues than the national average.[11] Women and minorities are very well represented (the latter are actually overrepresented), with women holding 43 percent of all nonpostal jobs and African-Americans 17 percent. It is worth noting, however, that women and minorities are overrepresented in the very lowest civil service grades and are underrepresented in the highest. They also are far less evident in the special-agency merit systems (such as the Foreign Service and the FBI) and in the professional categories (scientists at the National Institutes of Health; doctors in the Public Health Service).

In addition, the demographic representativeness of the bureaucracy is far greater in the United States than in virtually any other democratic nation.[12] In Britain and France, for example, people of aristocratic background have long dominated the upper levels of the civil service in the former; graduates of the elite *grandes écoles,* like the École Nationale d'Administration, dominate in the latter.

Political Appointees

The highest policymaking positions in the federal bureaucracy (e.g., department secretaries, assistants to the president, leading officials in the agencies) enter government service not by way of competitive merit examinations but by presidential appointment. About 1,200 of these top appointments require Senate confirmation, and about 2,000 more do not. These patronage positions, in theory at least, allow the president to translate his electoral mandate into public policy by permitting him to put his people in place in key policymaking jobs.

Most presidents use patronage not only to build support for their programs but also to firm up their political coalition by being sensitive to the needs of important party factions and interest groups. Ronald Reagan used his appointments to advance a conservative agenda for America and made conservative beliefs a prerequisite for high bureaucratic appointments.[13]

Secretary of the Interior Gale Norton was one of several prominent women conservatives appointed by President George W. Bush.

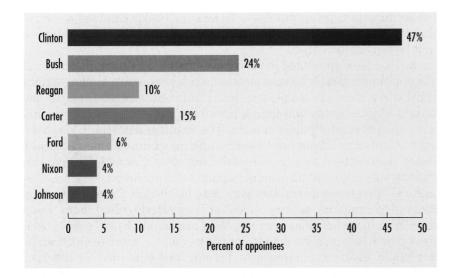

FIGURE 13.1 Percentage of Women and Minorities Appointed by Presidents to the Executive Branch

Presidents have appointed women and minorities to top posts in the federal government with increasing frequency. President Clinton had a particularly notable record in this regard.

Note: Data for the George W. Bush administration not available at this writing, though preliminary reports suggest that George W. Bush's record on women and minority appointments approaches that of Clinton's.

Source: Calculations by the authors from data in the *Congressional Quarterly Weekly Editions* through 2000 and from the Office of Presidential Personnel.

President Clinton, by contrast, promised to make government "look more like America," and did so by appointing many women and minorities to top posts in his administration, (see Figure 13.1). George W. Bush combined the Reagan and Clinton approaches by making quite conservative but racially and ethnically diverse appointments. Particularly notable conservative Bush appointments included: John Ashcroft as Attorney General; Eugene Scalia, son of Supreme Court justice Antonin Scalia and a prominent anti-labor, corporate lawyer, to be the solicitor at the Department of Labor; and long-time critic of the Securities and Exchange Commission Harvey Pitt to be its chairman. Prominent minority and women appointments included Colin Power as Secretary of State, Elaine Chao as Secretary of Labor, Rod Paige as Secretary of Education, Mel Martinez as Secretary of Housing and Urban Development, and Gale Norton as Secretary of the Interior.

Presidents also reserve important appointments for people they trust and who bring expertise and experience. George W. Bush has been particularly eager and successful in filling both cabinet posts and his inner circle with people with much experience in the upper reaches of the federal government, including several who had served in his father's administration; namely Donald Rumsfeld (Secretary of Defense), Colin Powell (Secretary of State), and Condoleezza Rice (National Security Advisor).

Top political appointees are not very representative of the American people. They tend to be much better educated and wealthier than other Americans. They also tend to be professionals, independent businesspeople, or executives from large corporations and financial institutions. Using this narrow and privileged pool of appointees has important ramifications for the practice of democracy, because it is these officials who exercise the most discretion and make the most important policy decisions. To be sure, background is not everything in the determination of the outlook and behavior of political appointees, but it cannot be discounted either.

Despite having been appointed to their posts by the president, political appointees cannot automatically be assumed to do the president's bidding. High-level political appointees are subject to many influences in addition to the president, including Congress, the courts, personnel in their own departments and agencies, the press, and public opinion. The result is sometimes unpleasant. President Clinton could not have been happy, for example, when Attorney General Janet Reno agreed to allow Special Prosecutor Kenneth Starr to investigate allegations of sexual misconduct against the president.

Top political appointees do not last very long on the job. On average, they stay in office only 22 months; political scientist Hugh Heclo called them "birds of passage."[14] They leave for many reasons. Most are accomplished people from the private sector who see government service as only a short-term commitment. Most make financial sacrifices to become top bureaucratic officials. Many don't find the public notoriety appealing. Some find themselves the target of partisan campaigns that later prove groundless but leave them with damaged reputations. Finally, many become frustrated by how difficult it is to change and implement public policy.

Political and Governmental Influences on Bureaucratic Behavior

Rather than there being a single chain of command with clear lines of authority, the bureaucracy in general (and bureaucrats in particular) must heed several important voices, among the most important of them, the public, the president, Congress, and the courts.

The Public

Most Americans pay little attention to bureaucratic agencies as such. The public focuses mainly on the *content* of public policies rather than on the bureaucratic agencies or the bureaucrats who carry them out. Americans have opinions about Social Security—level of benefits, eligibility, taxes, and so on—but do not concern themselves much with the Social Security Administration per se. In general, then, the public does not directly know or think much about bureaucratic agencies.

There are many exceptions to this generalization, however. Some bureaucratic agencies are constantly in the public eye and occasion the development of opinions. So many businesses are affected by environmental regulations, for instance, that the Environmental Protection Agency finds itself under constant scrutiny. Because taxes are a constant irritant for most people, Americans tend to have opinions—not very favorable, to be sure—about the Internal Revenue Service and its agents.

Foul-ups often focus public attention on an agency, as NASA discovered to its discomfort with the *Challenger* explosion and the failed Mars missions in 1999. The Branch Davidian tragedy in Waco, Texas, focused a harsh light on the Bureau of Alcohol, Tobacco, and Firearms, the FBI, and Attorney General Janet Reno. The FBI was further embarrassed in recent years by the shootout at Ruby Ridge, the revelation that one of their top counterintelligence officials (Robert Hanssen) was spying for the Russians, news that it had withheld evidence in the case of Oklahoma City bomber Timothy McVeigh, and revelations of intelli-

The public mainly pays attention to a bureaucratic agency when it has failed in its mission in some dramatic way. Here FBI agent Coleen Rowley testifies before the Senate Judiciary Committee about her letter accusing FBI headquarters of intelligence failures related to the 9/11 terrorist attacks on the United States.

gence failures (shared with the CIA) surrounding the 9/11 attacks on the United States. Lax enforcement at the Securities and Exchange Commission came to public attention in the aftermath of the collapse of Enron, WorldCom, and Arthur Andersen.

The President

The president, as the nation's chief executive, is the formal head of the executive branch. But as we saw in Chapter 12, the president's ability to control the executive branch is limited. Virtually every modern president has been perplexed by the discovery that he cannot assume that bureaucrats will do what he wants them to do.[15]

Richard Nixon was so frustrated by his inability to move the federal bureaucracy that he came to think of it as an alien institution filled with Democratic party enemies. His strategy was to intimidate bureaucrats or bypass them. He created the notorious "plumbers" unit in the White House to act as his personal domestic surveillance and espionage unit. Revelation of its activities was one of the factors leading the House Judiciary Committee to recommend approval of three articles of impeachment in the Watergate scandal.

Why Presidents Are Often Stymied by the Bureaucracy
The sheer size and complexity of the executive branch is one reason why presidents are frustrated by it. There is so much going on, in so many agencies, involving the activity of tens of thousands of people, that simply keeping abreast of it all is no easy task. Moreover, because of civil service regulations, presidents have no say about the tenure or salary of most bureaucrats. When presidents want something to happen, they are unlikely to get instantaneous acquiescence from bureaucrats, who do not fear them as they would fear a private employer. Presidents also find that they are not the only ones

trying to control the actions of bureaucrats; they must always share executive functions with Congress and sometimes with the courts. Finally, bureaucratic agencies are heavily insulated against presidential efforts to control them because of agency alliances with powerful interest groups.

Tools of Presidential Leadership   Presidents are not entirely helpless, of course. They have a number of ways to encourage bureaucratic compliance.[16] Occasionally, because of a crisis or a widely shared national commitment, decisive bureaucratic action is possible, as during Roosevelt's New Deal era, Lyndon Johnson's first years as president, Ronald Reagan's first administration, and George W. Bush's war on terrorism.

Even during ordinary times, however, the president is not helpless. First, although it is difficult to measure precisely, the president's prestige as our only nationally elected political leader makes his wishes hard to ignore. When Teddy Roosevelt called the presidency a "bully pulpit," he meant that only the president can speak for the nation, set the tone for the government, and call the American people to some great national purpose. A popular president, willing and able to play this role, is hard to resist. Bureaucrats are citizens and respond like other Americans to presidential leadership. When a president chooses to become directly involved in some bureaucratic matter—for example, with a phone call to a reluctant agency head or a comment about some bureaucratic shortcoming during a press conference—most bureaucrats respond.

The power of appointment is also an important tool of presidential leadership. If a president is very careful to fill the top administrative posts with people who support him and his programs, he greatly increases his ability to have his way. Although the Senate must advise on and consent to many of his choices, it rarely interferes, recognizing, perhaps, that a coherent administration requires that a president have his own people in place. Thus, George W. Bush was able to fill top executive branch posts with people such as John Ashcroft at Justice and Gale Norton at Interior, who believed firmly in carrying forward his conservative domestic agenda.

Popular presidents can use the office, in Teddy Roosevelt's words, as a "bully pulpit" to move the nation to action on a broad range of fronts, even in noncrisis times. Roosevelt was very effective in using the "bully pulpit" to establish the national park system, build a more powerful navy, and move vigorously against the powerful "trusts" that dominated the American economy in the early years of the twentieth century.

The president's power as chief budget officer of the federal government is also a formidable tool of the administration. No agency of the federal bureaucracy, for instance, can make its own budget request directly to Congress. The president's main budgetary instrument, the Office of Management and Budget, also has the statutory authority to block proposed legislation coming from any executive branch agency if it deems it contrary to the president's budget or program.

Congress

Congress also exercises considerable influence over the federal bureaucracy by legislating agency organization and mission, confirming presidential appointments, controlling the agency budget, and holding oversight hearings.

Legislating Agency Organization and Mission The president and Congress share control over the executive branch. The congressional tools of control, in fact, are at least as formidable as those of the president.[17] Congress legislates the mission of bureaucratic agencies and the details of their organization and can change either one. President George W. Bush's proposed Department of Homeland Security, for example, could only be created by congressional action. Congress can also alter agency policy or behavior. For example, it recently passed a bill requiring the Census Bureau to do the 2000 census by direct count, disallowing the use of statistical sampling.

Confirming Presidential Appointments Although the Senate almost always approves presidential appointments to top positions in the executive branch, it will sometimes use the "advice and consent" process to shape policies in bureaucratic departments and agencies. It occasionally turns down

Attorney General John Ashcroft ponders an answer to a question posed by a member of the Senate Judiciary Committee worried about the impact of Justice Department policies on civil liberties in the United States. This kind of oversight is one of the most important congressional tools for influencing the behavior of executive branch agencies and officials.

presidential nominations, as it did in the case of George H. W. Bush's nominee for the post of defense secretary, John Tower. At other times, it can simply draw out and delay the process in a bid to gain concessions from the president and the nominee on future policies. Former Senate Foreign Relations Committee Chairman Jesse Helms was a master at this, gaining concessions on policies concerning Cuba, foreign aid, and funding for international population control agencies. Defeat of nominees and long delays are most likely to happen during periods of divided government, when the atmosphere in the Senate is highly partisan.[18]

Controlling the Agency Budget Congress can also use its control over agency budgets to influence agency behavior. In theory, Congress uses the budget process to assess the performance of each agency each year, closely scrutinizing its activities before determining its next **appropriation,** the legal authority for the agency to spend money. Congress has neither the time nor the resources actually to do such a thing and usually gives each agency some small increment over what it had in the previous year.[19] Of course, if a particular agency displeases Congress, its budget may be cut; if a new set of responsibilities is given to an agency, its budget is usually increased. Sometimes these agency budget actions are taken with the full concurrence of the president; often they are not. Congress sometimes lends a sympathetic ear and increases the budgets of agencies that are not favored by the president. In the 1980s, Congress consistently gave more money than President Reagan wanted given to the EPA, the National Institutes of Health, and the National Science Foundation.

Holding Oversight Hearings Oversight hearings are an important instrument for conveying the views of the members of Congress to bureaucrats. There is a great deal of evidence that agency heads listen when the message is delivered clearly.[20] The head of the Internal Revenue Service, for example, recently responded to Senate Finance Committee hearings on the agency's harassment of taxpayers by apologizing to taxpayers and promising changes in IRS behavior and policies. The SEC took a tougher line on accounting practices in public corporations after the collapse of Enron and WorldCom in 2002.

Congress does not always speak with a single voice, however. Congress is a highly fragmented and decentralized institution, and its power is dispersed among scores of subcommittees. Often the activities of a particular bureaucratic agency are the province of more than a single committee or subcommittee, and the probability of receiving mixed signals from them is very high. A skilled administrator can often play these competing forces off of each other and gain a degree of autonomy for his or her agency.

Common Criticisms of the Federal Bureaucracy

Bureaucrats are often portrayed in popular culture as lazy paper shufflers or as indifferent, unresponsive, inhumane clerks denying us the benefits or services to which we are entitled. Politicians feed on this popular culture when they "run against Washington," promising to pare the bureaucracy down to size and to get it off the backs of the American people. (Interestingly enough, however, the 2001 "customer satisfaction" survey of federal government

appropriation

Legal authority for a federal agency to spend money from the U.S. Treasury.

services shows that Americans are only slightly less satisfied with government agencies than with private businesses.[21])

Let's look at the four most common criticisms of the federal bureaucracy and see how much merit they have.

"The Federal Bureaucracy Is Always Expanding"

Surprisingly, this complaint has no basis in fact. Although the number of federal civilian employees expanded dramatically in the first half of the twentieth century, it remained relatively stable at about 3 million from the mid-1960s to the early 1990s and has since dropped to less than 2.4 million, although federal regulations and mandates have required states and localities to hire more people. (See the "By the Numbers" feature earlier in this chapter.) Government does more and spends more money today than it did in 1950, but it does so with fewer employees. Nor is it the case that all bureaucratic agencies grow without stopping. Even important ones decrease in size, as the Departments of Defense, Agriculture, and State have done since 1970. It will be interesting to see, of course, if the war on terrorism leads to a significant expansion in the size of the bureaucracy—particularly at Defense, the CIA, the National Security Agency, Homeland Defense, and Justice—and reverses the long-term trends.

"The Federal Bureaucracy Is Ineffective"

The record of the federal bureaucracy with respect to effectiveness—the ability to carry out its missions and reach its goals—is mixed. NASA landed a man on the moon in less than a decade, fulfilling President Kennedy's promise to the American people. But by the same token, NASA has suffered some problems in its shuttle and Mars programs over the years. To take another example, the Defense Department and American armed forces had difficulties in Somalia in the early 1990s, but it managed a brilliant and lightning fast campaign against the Taliban regime in Afghanistan in 2001.

People who worry about government effectiveness must contend with the fact that the framers did not necessarily want government to be effective because they were worried first and foremost about tyranny. They created a system in which power would be fragmented. They were willing to trade some efficiency for inoculation against an overbearing and threatening government. Remember also that the federal bureaucracy was not designed as a rational machine with a clear chain of command, as in most democratic nations.

Finally, one must ask, "Compared to what?" Although most of us feel absolutely certain that the federal bureaucracy cannot be as effective in meeting its goals as private organizations, evidence to support such a belief is not overwhelming. Many studies on productivity, costs, and innovation show no public-private differences.[22] Large organizations, public or private, may be quite similar. It took private American automakers at least two decades to formulate an effective response to the challenge of foreign imports, for example. More research needs to be done on this issue, to be sure, but it is prudent to be skeptical of the conventional wisdom about government bureaucratic ineptitude.

"The Federal Bureaucracy Is Wasteful and Inefficient"

Waste in government is such an enduring theme in American politics that it is hard to imagine a political campaign without it. Once again, however, the matter is more complex than it may seem.

The National Science Foundation funds most basic scientific research in the United States, something that private companies have generally been unwilling or unable to do. Funding of such "public goods" is one of the most important things the federal government does.

entitlements

Government benefits that are distributed automatically to citizens who qualify on the basis of a set of guidelines set by law; for example, Americans over the age of 65 are entitled to Medicare coverage.

In actuality, the opportunity for agencies to waste money is quite limited, because the bureaucracy has discretionary control over only about 5 percent of the total federal budget. Ninety-five percent is earmarked for specific purposes or is distributed to beneficiaries by formula, or **entitlements.** Almost all of the federal budget goes to pay the interest on the national debt, to direct payments to individuals (e.g., military pensions and Social Security benefits), and to grants-in-aid and block grants to states and localities. The small discretionary pot that remains is closely monitored and encumbered with strict rules on its use. None of this suggests that there isn't waste or inefficient use of taxpayers' money in bureaucratic agencies. It is to say, however, that the charges are probably exaggerated. Of course, if what we mean by "waste of taxpayers' money" is spending on programs that we don't like (for some, it may be bilingual education; for others, it may be a new strategic bomber), then our complaint is not with the bureaucracy but with the policymaking branches of the federal government: the president and Congress. Government can seldom please everyone.

public goods

Products and services that citizens want but the private sector does not provide, such as national defense and pollution control.

Perhaps more important, there are certain things we want government to do that the private sector cannot or will not provide because they are hard to assess in terms of economic costs and benefits. Economists call such products and services—things that society needs but the private sector does not provide—**public goods.** Most Americans want things such as pollution control, first-class airports and harbors, national defense, and basic scientific research, even though private companies are unlikely to provide them. Where there is inefficiency and waste, of course, the president and Congress should insist that the bureaucracy do better.

"The Federal Bureaucracy Is Mired in Red Tape"

red tape

Overbearing bureaucratic rules and procedures.

Americans complain incessantly about bureaucratic rules, regulations, formal procedures, and forms—in short, about **red tape.** At one time or another, we have all felt stymied by rules and procedures, irritated by delays, and frustrated by forms. But how valid is the complaint that we are bound up in red tape?

Again, we run into the problem of measurement. Is there more red tape in the federal bureaucracy than in other large institutions such as HMOs, universities, and private corporations? Red tape, moreover, is often in the eye of the beholder. What is a waste of time and an inconvenience to one person may represent good public policy to another. Complaints about red tape are almost always directed at agencies that are carrying out policies we don't like. For example, following federal procedures for the disposal of dangerous chemicals may not be what chemical companies would want to do on their own, but Americans have shown that they want strong environmental protection laws. Monitoring disposal is part of what protects us.

All in all, there is some truth to the stereotypes about the federal bureaucracy: It is large; there are programs that do not work; there is waste and inefficiency; there is a great deal of red tape. We would suggest, however, that the stereotypes greatly exaggerate the extent of the problem because our measuring instruments are very imprecise. Nor do we have reason to believe that the pathologies are unique to the federal bureaucracy. Finally, we must recognize that many of the pathologies, to the extent that they do exist, do not necessarily originate in the bureaucracy but are imposed by the Constitution.

Reforming the Federal Bureaucracy

How should we fix what's wrong with the federal bureaucracy? It depends on what we think is wrong.

Scaling Back the Size of the Bureaucracy

Government activities can be trimmed in two ways: by slimming down and by transferring control.

Cutting the Fat For observers who worry that the federal bureaucracy is simply too big and costly, what might be called the "meat ax" approach is the preferred strategy. Virtually every candidate worth his or her salt promises to "cut the fat" if elected. Bill Clinton made such a promise during the 1992 presidential campaign, and he carried through after his election. In the early weeks of his administration, he ordered that 100,000 federal jobs be eliminated within four years, that freezes be placed on the salaries of government workers, that cost-of-living pay adjustments be reduced, and that the use of government vehicles and planes be sharply restricted.[23]

Privatizing A much talked about strategy for scaling back the federal bureaucracy is to turn over some of its functions and responsibilities to the private sector.[24] The **privatization** approach is based on two beliefs:

privatization
The process of turning over certain government functions to the private sector.

- First, that private business can almost always do things better than government.
- Second, that competitive pressure from the private sector will force government agencies to be more efficient.

Many states and local communities have "contracted out" public services such as trash collecting, the management of jails and prisons, and even the schools, to private companies. For many years, the federal government has contracted out some activities; the defense contracting system by which the Department

One strong argument against the privatization of government agencies is that private corporations might discontinue or increase the price of services that are costly or marginally profitable. For example, the U.S. Postal Service provides mail delivery to remote and less populous areas, such as the Alaskan outback, for the same cost as it does for the rest of the country. A private, profit-motivated company might be less inclined to do so.

of Defense buys fighter planes, submarines, and missiles from private corporations is a good example. Advocates of privatizing simply want the process to go further, turning over to private companies things such as the postal system, the federal prisons, and air traffic control.

Critics worry that privatizing government carries significant costs.[25]

- First, some matters seem so central to the national security and well-being that citizens and officials are unwilling to run the risk that the private sector will necessarily do the job well or at all. A good recent example is the transfer of the responsibility for screening airline passengers and baggage from private companies to a new government agency.

- Second, private business firms might not provide services that do not turn a profit. Delivery of mail to remote locations is something that the Postal Service does, for instance, but that a private company might decide not to do.

- Third, a private business under government contract is several steps removed from political control, and the normal instruments of democratic accountability, however imperfect, might not be as effective as they are in controlling government agencies. The voice of the public, expressed in public opinion polls or elections, might not be heard with much clarity by private companies, particularly if they are the only supplier of some essential service. Cable TV customers have an inkling, perhaps, of the meaning of "nonaccountability."

Reinventing Government

President Clinton turned over the responsibility for "reinventing government" to Vice-President Al Gore at the beginning of his administration. The ideas for these reforms come from advocates of what is called "the new public management,"[26] though the term "reinventing government" comes from a popular and influential book by that name written by David Osborne and

President Clinton and Vice-President Al Gore cut "red tape" as a dramatic way to introduce Gore's plan to reinvent government by introducing business principles into the operations of the executive branch. Congress approved only a few of the plan's provisions.

Ted Gaebler.[27] "Reinventing" advocates propose transforming the federal bureaucracy not only by cutting the fat and privatizing (as discussed in the preceding section) but also by introducing business principles into the executive branch. Their idea is that government agencies will provide better public services if they are run like private businesses. Forcing agencies to compete for customers, for instance, would motivate government employees to be more attentive to their customers (citizens). Paying employees on the basis of their performance rather than by pay grade (the present system) would make them work harder and better. Allowing agency heads more freedom to experiment—allowing them to be more entrepreneurial, if you will—might lead to innovative solutions to pressing social problems.

Gore's report closely followed the proposals made by Osborne and Gaebler and other "reinventing government" advocates.[28] Although Congress was unwilling to cooperate, many changes were made in the agencies by presidential executive order. The most notable change was the dramatic streamlining of the drug approval process at the FDA.[29]

Protecting Against Bureaucratic Abuses of Power

Many people believe that a bureaucracy of the size and shape of our present one, albeit necessary in a modern society, is potentially dangerous. Closer control over the bureaucracy by elected political bodies and by clear legislative constraints has been the preferred solution. There are many legislative enactments that try to keep bureaucratic activity within narrow boundaries. The Freedom of Information Act of 1966 was designed to enhance the ability of the press and private citizens to obtain information about bureaucratic policies and activities. The Ethics in Government Act of 1978 strengthened requirements of financial disclosure by officials and prohibitions against conflicts of interest.

whistle-blowers

People who bring official misconduct in their agencies to public attention.

Some reformers would like to see greater protection provided for **whistle-blowers**—bureaucrats who report corruption, financial mismanagement, abuses of power, or other official malfeasance. All too often, these courageous people, acting in the public interest, are fired or harassed on the job. This happened to Ernest Fitzgerald, a civilian cost accountant at the Pentagon, who lost his job after he revealed $2 billion cost overruns on the C5A military transport plane (he eventually won reinstatement through the courts, but it took 14 years to do so).

HOW DEMOCRATIC ARE WE?
The Bureaucracy and Democracy

PROPOSITION: The federal bureaucracy is inherently undemocratic because it is filled with people, none of whom are elected, who make important government decisions that affect the lives of Americans.

AGREE: The bureaucracy is out of control. Although the number of federal civil servants has stabilized and even declined in the last few years, the federal government and its unelected bureaucrats seem to intrude further and further into our lives. Career civil servants at the Environmental Protection Agency issue rules on how farmers can use wetlands and on which animal species are endangered and protected from hunters. Employees of the Bureau of Land Management make rules for grazing on public lands that ranchers must follow.

DISAGREE: Civil servants are merely carrying out the missions defined for them by elected public officials, namely, Congress and the president. And, because they are especially sensitive to the wishes of the public because of their desire to be effective and to be reelected, the president and members of Congress pay close attention to what civil servants in the bureaucratic agencies are doing and intervene to force changes when civil servants go astray and act contrary to the public interest and the wishes of the public.

THE AUTHORS: While there are very powerful constraints on the actions of civil servants in the federal bureaucracy, they nevertheless enjoy substantial discretion in carrying out their missions. Most of what the bureaucracy does on a day-to-day basis goes unnoticed and unchallenged for a number of reasons. First, there are simply so many decisions being made and rules issued that no one could possibly keep track of them all. Second, many of the rules and decisions are highly technical in nature, with only specialists and experts paying very close attention. Having said that, however, the bureaucratic system in the United States retains important democratic dimensions. For one thing, civil servants are very much like other Americans, both in their demographic makeup and in what they think the government should be doing. For another thing, interest groups concerned with a particular area of bureaucratic activity do pay close attention, even if the public in general does not, and they do not hesitate to bring their concerns to the attention of elected officials. Finally, when bureaucratic misconduct or mismanagement comes to light, elected officials tend to intervene. Knowing this, civil servants try not to stray too far from the mainstream of public and governmental opinion. The elite and big business backgrounds of most high-level presidential appointees, however, must remain the cause for some concern for those who care strongly about democratic responsiveness.

Increasing Popular Participation

Many people worry that federal bureaucrats go about their business without the public's having much say in what they do. Without citizen input, it is argued, bureaucrats lose touch with the people they are supposed to serve—a situation that leads to irrational policies and citizen alienation from the bureaucracy. Citizen participation in agency affairs has been pushed by some reformers as a solution.[30] The antipoverty program of Lyndon Johnson's Great Society required the "maximum feasible participation" of the poor in its design and implementation. President George H. W. Bush's housing secretary, Jack Kemp, introduced tenant councils to help administer federal housing programs at the neighborhood level.

Increasing Presidential Control

Popular sovereignty requires that the elected representatives of the people closely control the bureaucracy. Popular sovereignty implies that administrative discretion should be narrowed as much as possible and that clear directions and unambiguous policies should be communicated by elected officials to bureaucratic agencies. (Note that this is a very different goal from the one envisioned by the advocates of privatization and reinventing government.) Some have argued that the only public official who has an interest in seeing that the bureaucracy *as a whole* is well run and coherently organized is the president. Accordingly, one suggestion for reform is to increase the powers of the president so that he can be the chief executive, in fact and not just in name.[31]

Summary

The executive branch has grown in size and responsibility. This growth is a consequence of a transformation in the conception of the proper role of government because of structural changes in the economy and society. Although *bureaucracy* is not a popular concept in the American political tradition, we have created a sizable one. The reason is partly that bureaucratic organizations have certain strengths that make them attractive for accomplishing large-scale tasks.

Bureaucrats are involved in three major kinds of activities: executing the law, regulating, and adjudicating disputes. In each of these, they exercise a great deal of discretion. Because they are unelected policymakers, democratic theory demands that we be concerned about who the bureaucrats are. In the merit services, they are very much like other Americans in terms of background and attitudes. Political appointees, however, the most important bureaucratic decision makers, are very different from their fellow citizens.

Several political and governmental actors and institutions affect bureaucratic behavior, including the president, Congress, and the courts, as well as public opinion and interest groups. Bureaucratic pathologies, while real, are either exaggerated or the result of forces outside the bureaucracy itself: the constitutional rules and the struggle between the president and Congress. Proposals to reform the executive branch are related to what reformers believe is wrong with the federal bureaucracy. Those who worry most about size and inefficiency propose budget and personnel cuts, privatization, and the introduction of business principles into government. Those who want to make democracy more of a reality propose giving more control over the bureaucracy to the president and diminishing the role of interest groups.

Suggestions for Further Reading

Donahue, John. *Making Washington Work: Tales of Innovation in the Federal Government.* Washington, D.C.: Brookings, 1999.
> *Description of 14 winners of the Ford Foundation's Innovation in Government award; demonstrates that innovation is possible (although difficult) to achieve in the bureaucracy.*

Goodsell, Charles T. *The Case for Bureaucracy,* 3rd ed. Chatham, NJ: Chatham House, 1994.
> *A well-written polemic that gives the other side of the bureaucratic story.*

Osborne, David, and Ted Gaebler. *Reinventing Government.* Reading, MA: Addison-Wesley, 1992.
> *The bible for "reinventing government" advocates.*

Peters, B. Guy. *American Public Policy: Promise and Performance,* 5th ed. New York: Chatham House, 1999.
> *A review of American public policies with a particularly informative discussion of the role of the federal bureaucracy in policy implementation.*

Skowronek, Stephen. *Building a New American State: The Expansion of National Administrative Capacities, 1877–1920.* New York: Cambridge University Press, 1982.
> *A careful historical analysis of the first budding of an expanded federal bureaucracy.*

Washington Monthly.
> *Washington's leading journal of "bureaucracy bashing"; filled with outrageous and (sometimes) illuminating stories.*

Wilson, James Q. *Bureaucracy: What Government Agencies Do and Why They Do It.* New York: Basic Books, 1991.
> *A look at the federal bureaucracy by one of the nation's leading conservative academics.*

Internet Sources

Fedworld   **http://www.fedworld.gov/**
> *The gateway to the federal government's numerous Websites and Gophers; connections to virtually every federal department, bureau, commission, and foundation, as well as access to government statistics and reports.*

Yahoo: Executive Branch
http://dir.yahoo.com/Government/U_S_Government/Executive_Branch/
> *Similar to Fedworld; which one to use depends on personal taste.*

Notes

1. All quotes in this section are from Dale Russakoff, "Panic in Middle America," *Washington Post Weekly Edition* (May 15, 1995), p. 10.

2. Wallace Sayre, "Bureaucracies: Some Contrasts in Systems," *Indian Journal of Public Administration* 10 (1964), p. 223.

3. Richard J. Stillman II, *The American Bureaucracy* (Chicago: Nelson-Hall, 1987), p. 18.

4. Stephen Skowronek, *Building a New American State: The Expansion of National Administrative Capacities, 1877–1920* (New York: Cambridge University Press, 1982), pp. 19–46.

5. See Edward S. Greenberg, *Capitalism and the American Political Ideal* (Armonk, NY: Sharpe, 1985); Samuel P. Hays, *The Response to Industrialization* (Chicago: University of Chicago Press, 1957); Gabriel Kolko, *The Triumph of Conservatism* (Chicago: Quadrangle, 1967); Robert Wiebe, *The Search for Order, 1877–1920* (New York: Hill & Wang, 1967); James Weinstein, *The Corporate Ideal in the Liberal State* (Boston: Beacon Press, 1968).

6. Matthew A. Crenson and Francis E. Rourke, "American Bureaucracy Since World War II," in Louis Galambos, ed., *The New American State* (Baltimore: Johns Hopkins University Press, 1987).

7. B. Guy Peters, *American Public Policy: Policy and Performance,* 5th ed. (New York: Chatham House Publishers, 1999), p. 95.

8. Ibid., p. 97.

9. Theodore J. Lowi, *The End of Liberalism,* 2nd ed. (New York: Norton, 1979).

10. See Samuel Krislov and David H. Rosenbloom, *Representative Bureaucracy and the American Political System* (New York: Praeger, 1981); Goodsell, *The Case for Bureaucracy.*

11. Stanley Rothman and S. Robert Lichter, "How Liberal Are Bureaucrats?" *Regulation* (November–December 1983), pp. 35–47.

12. See Goodsell, *The Case for Bureaucracy,* ch. 5; Kenneth J. Meier, "Representative Bureaucracy: An Empirical Analysis," *American Political Science Review* 69 (June 1975), pp. 537–539.

13. Richard P. Nathan, *The Administrative Presidency* (New York: Wiley, 1983).

14. Hugh Heclo, *A Government of Strangers* (Washington, D.C.: Brookings Institution, 1977), p. 103.

15. Richard E. Neustadt, *Presidential Power* (New York: Wiley, 1960).

16. Terry M. Moe, "Control and Feedback in Economic Regulation," *American Political Science Review* 79 (1985), pp. 1094–1116; Richard W. Waterman, *Presidential Influence and the Administrative State* (Knoxville, TN: University of Tennessee Press, 1989).

17. Roger H. Davidson and Walter J. Oleszek, *Congress and Its Members,* 6th ed. (Washington, D.C.: CQ Press, 2002), p. 322; and Matthew D. McCubbins, "The Legislative Design of Regulatory Structure," *American Journal of Political Science* 29 (1985), pp. 421–438.

18. Nolan McCarty and Rose Razaghian, "Advice and Consent: Senate Responses to Executive Branch Nominations, 1885–1996," *American Journal of Political Science* 43 (October 1999), pp. 1122–1143.

19. Richard Fenno, *The Power of the Purse* (Boston: Little, Brown, 1966); Aaron Wildavsky, *The Politics of the Budgetary Process* (Boston: Little, Brown, 1964).

20. John A. Ferejohn and Charles R. Shipan, "Congressional Influence on Administrative Agencies: A Case Study of Telecommunications Policy," in Lawrence C. Dodd and Bruce I. Oppenheimer, eds., *Congress Reconsidered,* 4th ed. (Washington, D.C.: Congressional Quarterly Press, 1989).

21. "American Customer Satisfaction Index" (Ann Arbor, MI: University of Michigan Business School, 2001).

22. See Goodsell, *The Case for Bureaucracy,* pp. 61–69.

23. Ibid., p. 177.

24. See Derek Bok, *The Trouble With Government* (Cambridge: Harvard University Press, 2001), ch. 9; Emanuel S. Savas, *Privatization: The Key to Better Government* (Chatham, NJ: Chatham House, 1987); Sheila B. Kamerman and Alfred J. Kahn, eds., *Privatization and the Welfare State* (Princeton, NJ: Princeton University Press, 1989).

25. Derek Bok, *The Trouble With Government,* pp. 233–34; Roberta Lynch and Ann Markusen, "Can Markets Govern?" *American Prospect* (Winter 1994), pp. 125–134.

26. Bok, *The Trouble With Government,* pp. 234–239; Joel D. Aberbach and Bert A. Rockman (eds.), *In the Web of Politics: Three Decades of the U.S. Federal Executive* (Washington, D.C.: Brookings Institution Press, 2000).

27. David Osborne and Ted Gaebler, *Reinventing Government* (Reading, MA: Addison-Wesley, 1992).

28. Al Gore Jr., *From Red Tape to Results: Creating a Government That Works Better and Costs Less* (Washington, D.C.: U.S. Government Printing Office, 1993).

29. Jim Collins, "Turning Goals Into Results: The Power of Catalytic Mechanisms," *Harvard Business Review* (July–August 1999), pp. 13–17.

30. Milton Kotler, *Neighborhood Government* (Indianapolis: Bobbs-Merrill, 1969); Marilyn Gittell, *Participants and Participation* (New York: Praeger, 1967).

31. Terry M. Moe, "The Politics of Bureaucratic Structure," in John E. Chubb and Paul E. Peterson, eds., *Can the Government Govern?* (Washington, D.C.: Brookings Institution, 1989), p. 280; John E. Chubb and Paul E. Peterson, "American Political Institutions and the Problem of Governance," in Chubb and Peterson, eds., *Can the Government Govern?* p. 41; James L. Sundquist, *Constitutional Reform and Effective Government* (Washington, D.C.: Brookings Institution, 1986).

Chapter 14
The Courts

In This Chapter

- How the court system is organized and how it operates
- What judicial review is and how it came to be
- How the Supreme Court works
- How and why judicial interpretations of the Constitution have changed
- The role of the Supreme Court in a democratic society

The Supreme Court Stops the Florida Recount

Relatively early in the evening of election night, November 7, 2000, the major television networks proclaimed that Al Gore had won the state of Florida, giving him a major advantage in the race for the presidency against George W. Bush. Later in the evening, the networks pulled Florida from the Gore win column, calling the contest in Florida "too close to call." At 3:00 AM on Wednesday, the networks announced a Bush win in Florida, and declared him the winner of the presidential election. By 7:00 AM, however, they again called the race in Florida "too close to call," and said they could not yet declare a winner of the presidential contest. Meanwhile, first reports of voting irregularities and inaccurate vote counting had begun to surface. Responding to these reports, Democrats demanded—and county election officials agreed to—hand recounts in Miami-Dade, Broward, and Palm

Beach counties, where the voting returns seemed most suspect. Immediately, a state-wide machine recount began as required by the state election code in extremely close elections. On November 13, Florida Secretary of State Katherine Harris announced that her November 14 deadline for certifying election results from each county would not be extended, leaving insufficient time for completion of hand counts. At the end of the day on the 14th, depending entirely on machine recount results from the various counties, Harris declared George W. Bush the winner of Florida's 25 electoral votes. But this hardly settled the affair.

From November 14 until the U.S. Supreme Court ruled on December 12, Americans lived through a period of intense and bitter political and legal combat the likes of which had not been seen here since the disputed Hayes-Tilden presidential election of 1876. Election officials in several counties continued with their hand recounts despite Harris's decision. Lawsuits were filed by candidates and party organizations in various county, state, and federal district courts to have recounts started or stopped. Republican Party activists descended on Florida to mount demonstrations against hand recounts, and local Gore and Bush partisans shouted at each

other across police barricades. Republican and Democratic national committees and congressional committees mounted public relations campaigns to support their respective sides in the dispute, while various liberal and conservative citizen groups joined the fray on the ground and on the airwaves. The Florida legislature went into special session to consider whether it ought to award the state's electoral votes to Bush, whatever the outcome of the hand recounts.

The drama came to a head on December 8, when the Florida Supreme Court, responding to a request from the Gore campaign, ruled that hand recounts could continue in three counties, setting December 12 as the deadline for reporting results to the Florida Secretary of State. On December 9, responding to an appeal by the Bush campaign, the U.S. Supreme Court ordered that the hand recount be temporarily suspended. On December 12, after considering legal briefs and oral arguments from each side, a closely divided U.S. Supreme Court overturned the Florida Supreme Court in *Bush* v. *Gore,* saying the Florida Court's order to recount in only three counties violated "equal protection" of the laws. With no time left to mount a recount in a way that would address the Court's "equal protection" concerns—that very day, December 12, was the absolute deadline for settling the election contest in Florida, according to a majority of the justices—Secretary of State Harris's previous certification of Bush as the winner in Florida prevailed. On December 13, seeing the handwriting on the wall, Al Gore conceded the presidential election to George W. Bush.

The U.S. Supreme Court's decision in *Bush* v. *Gore* was remarkable for many reasons, not least of which was the degree to which its actions contradicted what scholars, jurists, historians, and journalists have taken to be iron-clad rules and traditions of the Court:

- *The Court has generally avoided becoming involved in "political" and "partisan" issues. Bush* v. *Gore* is the first and only decision that decided the outcome of a presidential election.

- *The Court has generally avoided cases that might hurt its reputation or that of the courts in general.* As Justice John Paul Stevens put it in his dissent, "The endorsement of [plaintiff's position] by the majority of this Court can only lend credence to the most cynical appraisal of the work of judges throughout the land. . . . Although we may never know with complete certainty the identity of the winner of this year's presidential election, the identity of the loser is perfectly clear. It is the nation's confidence in the judge as an impartial guardian of the law."

- *The Court generally tries to avoid 5–4 votes on controversial issues.* While this is less true for the Rehnquist Court than earlier ones, the 5–4 vote in *Bush* v. *Gore* undermined the legitimacy of its decision in the eyes of many Americans, especially since the majority was comprised of the same conservative majority that has recently dominated the Court on other controversial decisions.

- *The Court almost always intends that its decisions will serve as precedents for all other courts to follow.* The Court clearly did not want *Bush* v. *Gore* to serve as a legal precedent with broader meaning. Not wishing to bring the possible harsh light of "equal protection" to other aspects of American elections, the Court made the following incredible point in its opinion: "Our consideration is limited to the present circumstances, for the problem of equal protection in election processes generally presents many complexities."

- *The Court usually tries to be consistent with its previous rulings in a particular domain of the law.* On federalism, the Court has moved decisively to limit federal government power in deference to state autonomy. In *Bush* v. *Gore* it reversed direction (but probably for this case only), something that caught Justice Stevens by surprise. As he put it in his dissent: "When questions arise about the meaning of state laws, including election laws, it is our settled practice to accept the opinions of the highest courts of the States as providing the final answers. On rare occasions, however, either federal statutes or the Federal Constitution may require federal judicial intervention in state elections. This is not such an occasion."

Though the *Bush* v. *Gore* story is probably best understood as the "exception that proves the rule" in terms of how the Court normally behaves, it still gives us insight into many things about the Supreme Court that will be elaborated on in this chapter. Like the president and Congress, the Court makes decisions that have important consequences for the American people. Unlike the president and Congress, it does not pass new laws; it merely interprets the meaning of laws and, especially, the Constitution. In doing so, however, the Court cannot help but make law. In this sense, the Court is a national policymaker. ∎

Thinking Critically About This Chapter

Using the Framework   You will see in this chapter that the Court is embedded in a rich governmental, political linkage, and structural environment that shapes its behavior. The other branches of government impinge on its deliberations; political linkage institutions such as elections, interest groups, and social movements matter; and structural factors such as economic and social change influence its agenda and decisions.

Using the Democracy Standard   You will see in this chapter that an unelected Court makes important decisions about public policies, raising fundamental questions about the degree to which popular sovereignty and majority rule prevail in our system. You will also see that the Court often turns its attention to cases that involve issues of political equality and liberty, so essential to the existence of a healthy representative democracy. ◀

The Structural Context of Court Behavior

The judicial Power of the United States shall be vested in one supreme Court, and in such inferior Courts as the Congress may from time to time ordain and establish.
—U.S. CONSTITUTION, ARTICLE III, SECTION 1

We are under a Constitution, but the Constitution is what the judges say it is, and the judiciary is the safeguard of our liberty and our property under the Constitution.
—CHIEF JUSTICE CHARLES EVANS HUGHES (1907)

Constitutional Powers

The Constitution speaks only briefly about the judicial branch and doesn't provide much guidance about what it is supposed to do or how it is supposed to go about its job. The document says little about the powers of the judicial branch in relationship to the other two federal branches or about its responsibilities in the area of constitutional interpretation. Article III is considerably shorter than Articles I and II on Congress and the president. It creates a federal judicial branch; it creates the office of "chief justice of the United States"; it states that judges shall serve life terms; it specifies the categories of cases the Court may or must hear (to be explained later); and it grants Congress the power to create additional federal courts as needed. Article III of the Constitution is virtually devoid of detail.

The Power of Judicial Review

Extremely interesting is the Constitution's silence about **judicial review,** the power of the Supreme Court to declare state and federal laws and actions null and void when they conflict with the Constitution. Debate has raged for many years over the question of whether the framers intended that the Court should have this power.[1]

> **judicial review**
>
> The power of the Supreme Court to declare actions of the other branches and levels of government unconstitutional.

The framers surely believed that the Constitution ought to prevail when other laws were in conflict with it. But did they expect the Supreme Court to make the decisions in this matter? Jefferson and Madison thought that Congress and the president were capable of rendering their own judgments about the constitutionality of their actions. Alexander Hamilton, however, believed that the power of judicial review was inherent in the notion of the separation of powers and was essential to balanced government. As he put it in *The Federalist,* No. 78 (see Appendix), the very purpose of constitutions is to place limitations on the powers of government, and it is only the Court that can ensure such limits in the United States. The legislative branch, in particular, is unlikely to restrain itself without the helping hand of the judiciary.

Hamilton's view was undoubtedly the prevailing one among the framers. They were firm believers, for instance, in the idea that there was a "higher law" to which governments and nations must conform. Their enthusiasm for written constitutions was based on their belief that governments must be limited in what they could do in the service of some higher or more fundamental law, such as that pertaining to individual rights. The attitudes of the time strongly supported the idea that judges, conversant with the legal tradition and free from popular pressures, were best able to decide when statutory and administrative law were in conflict with fundamental law.[2]

Marbury v. *Madison*

Chief Justice John Marshall boldly claimed the power of judicial review for the U.S. Supreme Court in the case of *Marbury* v. *Madison* in 1803.[3] The case began with a flurry of judicial appointments by

Although the Constitution is silent on the issue of judicial review, most of the Founders probably agreed with Alexander Hamilton (left), who argued that the Supreme Court's power to interpret the Constitution and declare state and federal laws and actions unconstitutional is inherent in the notion of the separation of powers. However, it was not until the Supreme Court's 1803 *Marbury v. Madison* decision that Chief Justice John Marshall (right) affirmed the Court's power of judicial review.

 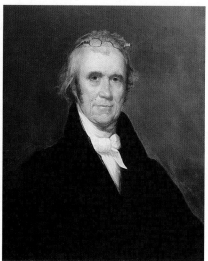

President John Adams in the final days of his presidency, after his Federalist party had suffered a resounding defeat in the election of 1800. The apparent aim of these so-called midnight appointments was to establish the federal courts as an outpost of Federalist party power (federal judges are appointed for life) in the midst of Jeffersonian control of the presidency and the Congress.

William Marbury was one of the midnight appointments, but he was less lucky than most. His commission was signed and sealed, but it had not been delivered to him before the new administration took office. Jefferson, knowing what Adams and the Federalists were up to, ordered Secretary of State James Madison not to deliver the commission. Marbury sued Madison, claiming that the secretary of state was obligated to deliver the commission, and asked the Supreme Court to issue a **writ of mandamus** to force Madison to do so.

writ of mandamus

A court order that forces an official to act.

Marshall faced a quandary. If the Court decided in favor of Marbury, Madison would almost surely refuse to obey, opening the Court to ridicule for its weakness. The fact that Marshall was a prominent Federalist political figure might even provoke the Jeffersonians to take more extreme measures against the Court. But if the Court ruled in favor of Madison, it would suggest that an executive official could defy without penalty the clear provisions of the law.

Marshall's solution was worthy of Solomon. The Court ruled that William Marbury was entitled to his commission and that James Madison had broken the law in failing to deliver it. By this ruling, the Court rebuked Madison. However, the Court said it could not compel Madison to comply with the law because the section of the Judiciary Act of 1789 that granted the Court the power to issue writs of mandamus was unconstitutional. It was unconstitutional because it expanded the **original jurisdiction** of the Supreme Court as defined in Article III, which could not be done except by constitutional amendment.

original jurisdiction

The authority of a court to be the first to hear a particular kind of case.

On the surface, the decision was an act of great modesty. It suggested that the Court could not force the action of an executive branch official. It suggested that Congress had erred in the Judiciary Act of 1789 by trying to give the Supreme Court too much power. Beneath the surface, however, was a less modest act: the claim that judicial review was the province of the judicial branch alone. In Marshall's words in his written opinion, "It is emphatically the province and duty of the judicial department to say what the law is." In making this claim, he was following closely Hamilton's argument in *The Federalist,* No. 78.

Until quite recently, the Supreme Court used the power of judicial review with great restraint, perhaps recognizing that its regular use would invite retaliation by the other branches. Judicial review of a congressional act was not exercised again until 54 years after *Marbury* and was used to declare acts of Congress unconstitutional only about 150 times since then until the late 1990s. (In the last few years, however, it has been less reluctant to review and overturn congressional actions, especially in cases involving the nature of federalism.) The Court has been much less constrained about over-ruling the laws of the states and localities; it has done so more than 1,000 times.

Judicial Review and Democracy Judicial review involves the right of a body shielded from direct accountability to the people—federal judges are appointed, not elected, and serve for life (barring unseemly behavior)—to set aside the actions of government bodies whose members are directly elected. Some observers believe that this is the only way to protect the rights of political and racial minorities, to check the potential excesses of the other two government branches and the states, and to preserve the rules of the democratic process. Others believe that judicial review has no place in a democratic society. We come back to this issue later in this chapter.

Longman
Participate.com
2.0
Comparative
Comparing
Judiciaries

The U.S. Court System: Organization and Jurisdiction

Ours is a federal court system. There is one system for the national government (the federal courts) and another in each of the states. Each state has its own system of courts that adjudicate cases on the basis of its own constitution, statutes, and administrative rules. In total, the great bulk of laws, legal disputes, and court decisions (roughly 99 percent) are located in the states. Most important political and constitutional issues, however, eventually reach the national courts. In this chapter, our focus is on the national courts.

Constitutional Provisions

The only court specifically mentioned in the Constitution's Article III is the U.S. Supreme Court. The framers left to Congress the tasks of designing the details of the Supreme Court and establishing "such inferior courts as the Congress may from time to time ordain and establish." Beginning with the Judiciary Act of 1789, Congress has periodically reorganized the federal court system. The end result is a three-tiered pyramidal system (see Figure 14.1), with a handful of offshoots. At the bottom are 94 U.S. federal district courts, with at least one district in each state. In the middle are 13 courts of appeal. At the top of the pyramid is the Supreme Court. These courts are called **constitutional courts** because they were created by Congress under Article III, which discusses the judicial branch. Congress has also created a number of courts to adjudicate cases in highly specialized areas of concern, such as taxes and maritime law. These were established under Article I, which specifies the duties and powers of Congress, and are called **legislative courts.**

Article III does not offer many guidelines for the federal court system, but the few requirements that are stated are very important. The Constitution requires, for instance, that federal judges serve "during good behavior," which, in practice, means for life. Because impeachment by Congress is the only way to remove federal judges, the decision about who will be a judge is an important

constitutional courts

Federal courts created by Congress under the authority of Article III of the Constitution.

legislative courts

Highly specialized federal courts created by Congress under the authority of Article I of the Constitution.

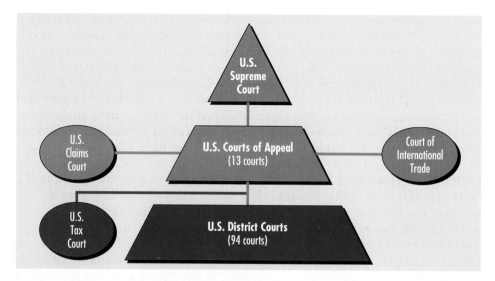

FIGURE 14.1 The U.S. Federal Court System

The federal court system is a three-tiered pyramidal system, with the Supreme Court at the top. Below it are 13 federal courts of appeal and 94 district courts, with at least one district in each state. Additional courts exist to hear cases in highly specialized areas, such as taxes, international trade, and financial claims against the U.S. government.
Source: Administrative Office of the U.S. Courts.

one. Article III also states that Congress cannot reduce the salaries of judges once they are in office. This provision was designed to maintain the independence of the judiciary by protecting it from legislative intimidation.

Article III also specifies the kinds of cases that are solely the province of the federal courts:

- The Constitution (disputes involving the First Amendment or the commerce clause, for example).
- Federal statutes and treaties (including disputes involving ambassadors and other diplomats).
- Admiralty and maritime issues.
- Controversies in which the U.S. government is a party.
- Disputes between the states.
- Disputes between a state and a citizen of another state.
- Disputes between a state (or citizen of a state) and foreign states or citizens.

Federal District Courts

grand juries

Groups of citizens who decide whether there is sufficient evidence to bring an indictment against accused persons.

petit (trial) juries

Juries that hear evidence and sit in judgment on charges brought in civil or criminal cases.

Most cases in the federal court system are first heard in one of the 94 district courts. District courts are courts of original jurisdiction, that is, courts where cases are first heard; they do not hear appeals from other courts. They are also trial courts; some use juries—either **grand juries,** which bring indictments, or **petit (trial) juries,** which decide cases—and in some, cases are heard only by a judge.

Most of the business of the federal courts takes place at this level. Almost 300,000 cases are filed annually; roughly 80 percent of them are civil cases, and 20 percent are criminal cases. Civil cases include everything from antitrust cases brought by the federal government (as in the recent Justice

Department action against Microsoft) to commercial and contract disputes between citizens (or businesses) of two or more states. Criminal cases include violations of federal criminal laws, such as bank robbery, interstate drug trafficking, and kidnapping.

Most civil and criminal cases are concluded at this level. In a relatively small number of disputes, however, one of the parties to the case may feel that a mistake has been made in trial procedure or in the law that was brought to bear in the trial, or one of the parties may feel that a legal or constitutional issue is at stake that was not taken into account at the trial stage or was wrongly interpreted. In such cases, one of the parties may appeal to a higher court.

Longman
Participate.com
2.0
Visual Literacy
Case Overload

U.S. Courts of Appeal

The United States is divided into 12 geographic **circuits** (see the map in Figure 14.2) to hear appeals from the district courts. There is also a thirteenth appeals court, called the U.S. Court of Appeals for the Federal Circuit, located in Washington, D.C., which hears cases on patents and government contracts. More than 50,000 cases are filed annually in the federal appeals courts,

circuits

The 12 geographical jurisdictions and 1 special court that hear appeals from the federal district courts.

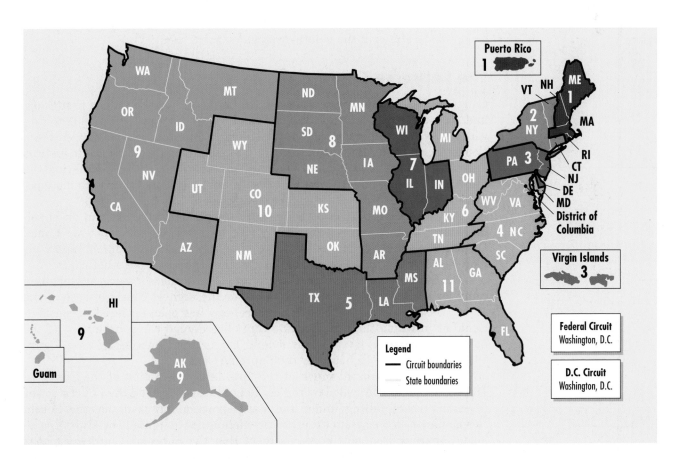

FIGURE 14.2 U.S. Federal Circuit Courts

The United States is divided into 12 geographic regions (including the D.C. Circuit Court), each housing a federal circuit court of appeals; there are also 94 U.S. district courts, where most cases originate. One additional circuit court of appeal, the Federal Circuit Court, is located in Washington, D.C.

Source: Administrative Office of the U.S. Courts.

although only about 5,000 reach the formal hearing stage (most of these end in negotiated settlements without going to trial). Cases cannot originate in these courts but must come to them from other courts. Because they exist only to hear appeals, they are referred to as **appellate courts.** New factual evidence cannot be introduced before such courts; no witnesses are called or cross-examined. Lawyers for each side argue with one another and make their cases for the judges not by the examination of witnesses or documents but by the submission of **briefs** that set out the legal issues at stake. Judges usually convene as panels of three (on important cases, there are more—sometimes seven members) to hear oral arguments from the lawyers on each side of the case and to cross-examine them on points of law. Weeks or even months later, after considerable study, writing, and discussion among the judges, the panel issues a ruling. In important cases, the ruling is usually accompanied by an **opinion** that sets forth the majority side's reasoning for the decision.

Once appellate decisions are published, they become **precedents** that guide the decisions of other judges in the same circuit. Although judges do not slavishly follow precedents, they tend to move away from them only when necessary and only in very small steps. This doctrine of closely following precedents as the basis for legal reasoning is known as **stare decisis.**

Sometimes, particular circuits play a particularly important role in changing constitutional interpretation. Currently, the Fourth Circuit Court, based in Richmond, Virginia, has been a leader in the trend toward reasserting the power of the states in the federal system.[4]

The Supreme Court

Congress decides how many judges sit on the Supreme Court. The first Court had six members. The Federalists reduced the number to five in 1801 to prevent newly elected president Thomas Jefferson from filling a vacancy. In 1869, Congress set the number at its present nine members (eight associate justices and the chief justice). It has remained this way ever since, weathering the failed effort by President Franklin Roosevelt to "pack" the Court with more politically congenial justices by expanding its size to 15.

The Supreme Court is both a court of original jurisdiction and an appellate court. That is, some cases must first be heard in the Supreme Court. Disputes involving ambassadors and other diplomatic personnel, or one or more states, start in the Supreme Court rather than in some other court.

The Supreme Court also, in its most important role, serves as an appellate court for the federal appeals courts and for the highest courts of each of the states. Cases in which a state or a federal law has been declared unconstitutional or in which the highest state court has denied the claim of one of the parties that a state law violates federal law or the Constitution (see Figure 14.3) are eligible to be heard by the Supreme Court.

Congress determines much of the appellate jurisdiction of the Court. In 1869, a Congress controlled by radical Republicans removed the Court's power to review cases falling under the Reconstruction program for the South. Responding to a plea from Chief Justice Rehnquist to lighten the Court's caseload, Congress dropped the requirement that the Supreme Court *must* hear cases in which a state court declares a federal statute unconstitutional. It can choose, but is not obligated, to do so.

Because it is the highest appellate court in the federal court system, the decisions and opinions of the Supreme Court become the main precedents on federal and constitutional questions for courts at all other levels of jurisdiction. It is for this reason that Supreme Court decisions receive so much attention from other political actors, the media, and the public.

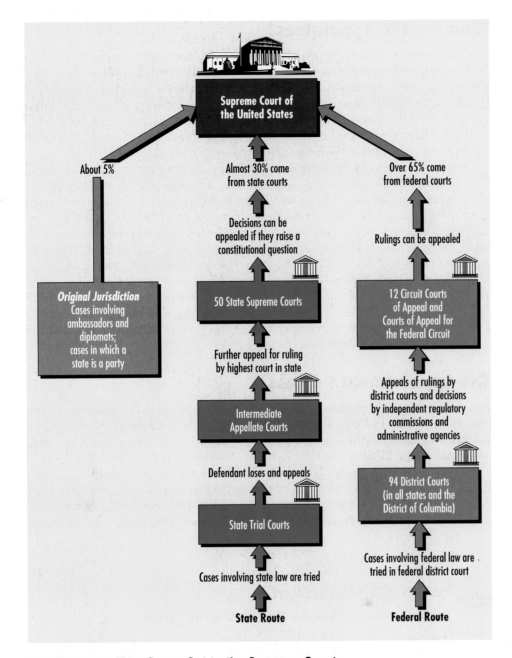

FIGURE 14.3 How Cases Get to the Supreme Court

The vast majority of cases that reach the Supreme Court come to it from the federal court system. Most of the others come on appeal from the highest state courts. A handful originate in the Supreme Court itself.

Source: Adapted from David O'Brien, *Storm Center: The Supreme Court in American Politics,* 5th ed. (New York: Norton, 2000).

Appointment to the Federal Bench

Because federal judges are appointed for life and make important decisions, it matters in a democratic society who they are and how they get to the bench. If they are isolated from popular influence, democracy is at risk. If they are too responsive, they ignore their judicial role.

Who Are the Appointees?

Appointees to the federal bench must (by custom, not law) be lawyers, but they need not have judicial experience. Almost one-half of all Supreme Court justices during this century have had no prior experience as judges. Among the ranks of the "inexperienced" are some of the most prominent and influential justices in our history, including John Marshall, Louis Brandeis, Harlan Stone, Charles Evans Hughes, Felix Frankfurter, and Earl Warren, as well as the present chief justice, William Rehnquist.[5]

Because federal judges are lawyers, they tend to come from privileged backgrounds. Moreover, federal judges, and particularly Supreme Court justices, come from the most elite parts of the legal profession. For the most part, they have been white male Protestants from upper-income or upper-middle-class backgrounds, who attended the most selective and expensive undergraduate and graduate institutions.[6] There have been only two African-American justices (Thurgood Marshall and Clarence Thomas), two women (Sandra Day O'Connor and Ruth Bader Ginsburg), seven Jews, and seven Catholics on the High Court during its history, through 1999. The representativeness of judicial appointees at the circuit and district court levels is better, but is still a long way from reflecting the composition of the legal profession, much less the American people as a whole.

The Appointment Process

Federal judges assume office after they have been nominated by the president and approved by the Senate. Presidents pay special attention to judicial appointments, because they are a way for presidents to affect public policy long after they leave office.

Presidents take many things into consideration besides merit. No president wants a nomination rejected by the Senate, so he and his advisers consult with key senators, especially those on the Judiciary Committee, before nominations are forwarded. Nominations for district court judgeships are subject to

Web Exploration
Who Is Appointed to the Supreme Court?

Issue: Appointees to the Supreme Court come from a very select group of Americans, not at all representative of the general population either in terms of demographic background or achievement and training.

Site: Access the Cornell Law School home page on our Website at **www.ablongman.com/greenberg**. Go to the "Web Explorations" section for Chapter 14 and open "who is appointed. . . ," then open "biographies." Read the short biographies of each of the present members of the Supreme Court.

What You've Learned: What kinds of people become justices? What can you say about their occupational and educational backgrounds and their other experiences?

HINT: While they are all lawyers, not all have served as judges. And politics and public service have been part of the equation as well.

what is called **senatorial courtesy,** the right of the senior senator from the president's party in the state where the district court is located to approve the nominee. Senatorial courtesy does not operate, however, in appointments to the circuit courts, whose jurisdictions span more than a single state, or to the Supreme Court, whose jurisdiction is the entire nation. Nevertheless, presidents must be extremely attentive to the views of key senators.

On occasion, despite presidential efforts to placate it, the Senate has refused to give its "consent." Of the 143 nominees for the Supreme Court since the founding of the Republic, the Senate has refused to approve 28 of them, although only 5 in the twentieth century. Rejection of nominees has usually happened when the president was weak or when the other party was in control of the Senate. The defeat of Ronald Reagan's nominee, Robert Bork, was the product of deep ideological differences between a Republican president and a Democratic-controlled Senate. There have also been several near defeats. Bush's nominee, Clarence Thomas, was confirmed by a margin of only four votes after questions were raised about his legal qualifications and about sexual harassment charges brought by law professor Anita Hill.

Although presidents must be concerned about the merit of their candidates and their acceptability to the Senate, they also try by their appointments to make their mark on the future. Presidents go about this in different ways.

Many presidents have been interested in nominating judges who shared their ideological and program commitments. John Adams nominated John Marshall and a number of other judges to protect Federalist principles during the ascendancy of the Jeffersonians. Franklin Roosevelt tried to fill the courts with judges who favored the New Deal. Ronald Reagan favored conservatives who were committed to rolling back affirmative action and other civil rights claims, abortion rights, protections for criminal defendants, and broad claims of **standing** in environmental cases. Both George H. W. Bush and his son George W. Bush carried on the Reagan tradition of nominating very conservative judges to the federal courts.

Bill Clinton, eager to avoid a bitter ideological fight in the Senate, where he was trying to forge a bipartisan coalition to support the North American Free Trade Agreement and a national crime bill, nominated two moderates for the High Court—Ruth Bader Ginsburg and Stephen Breyer—in the first years of his administration. The Ginsburg nomination was also indicative of

senatorial courtesy

The tradition that judicial nominations for federal district court appointments be cleared by the senior senator of the president's party from the relevant state.

Longman
Participate.com
2.0
Simulation
You Are Appointing a Supreme Court Justice

standing

Authority to bring legal action because one is directly affected by the issues at hand.

Robert Bork, one of Ronald Reagan's nominees for the Supreme Court, was turned down by a historic margin after lengthy committee hearings and a bruising debate on the floor of the Senate. Many Americans and a majority of senators considered his views too extreme.

Clinton's apparent commitment to diversifying the federal court system. More than one-half of federal court nominees during the first six years of his presidency were women and minorities.

Presidents are often disappointed in how their nominees behave once they reach the Court. Dwight Eisenhower was dumbfounded when his friend and nominee, Earl Warren, led the Court to transform constitutional law with regard to civil rights and criminal procedure. Nixon was stunned when Chief Justice Warren Burger voted with a unanimous Court to override the president's claim of **executive privilege** and forced him to give up the documents that would seal his fate in the Watergate affair. The elder George Bush was surprised when his nominee, David Souter, refused to vote for the overturn of *Roe* in *Planned Parenthood* v. *Casey* (1992). Despite these dramatic examples, the past political and ideological positions of federal court nominees are a fairly reliable guide to their later behavior on the bench.[7]

executive privilege

A presidential claim that certain communications with subordinates may be withheld from Congress and the courts.

The Supreme Court in Action

The Supreme Court meets from the first Monday in October until late June or early July, depending on the press of business. Let's see how it goes about deciding cases.

Norms of Operation

A set of unwritten but clearly understood rules of behavior—called *norms*—shapes how the Court does things. One norm is *secrecy,* which keeps the conflicts between justices out of the public eye and elevates the stature of the Court as an institution. Justices do not grant interviews very often. Reporters are not allowed to stalk the corridors for a story. Law clerks are expected to keep all memos, draft opinions, and conversations with the justices they work for confidential. Justices are not commonly seen on the frantic Washington, D.C., cocktail party circuit. When meeting in conference to argue and decide cases, the justices meet alone, without secretaries or clerks. Breaches of secrecy have occurred only occasionally. As a result, we know less about the inner workings of the Court than about any other branch of government.

Seniority is another important norm. Seniority determines the assignment of office space, the seating arrangements in open court (the most junior are at the ends), and the order of speaking in conference (the chief justice, then the most senior, and so on down the line). Speaking first allows the senior members to set the tone for discussion.

Finally, the justices are expected to stick closely to *precedent* when they decide cases. When the Court departs from a precedent, it is essentially overruling its own past actions, exercising judicial review of itself. In most cases, departures from precedent come in only very small steps over many years. For example, several decisions chipped away at the **separate but equal doctrine** of *Plessy* v. *Ferguson* (1896) before it was decisively reversed in *Brown* v. *Board of Education of Topeka* (1954).

separate but equal doctrine

The principle articulated in *Plessy* v. *Ferguson* (1896) that laws prescribing *separate* public facilities and services for nonwhite Americans are permissible if the facilities and services are *equal* to those provided for whites.

Controlling the Agenda

The Court has a number of screening mechanisms to control what cases it will hear so that it can focus on cases that involve important federal or constitutional questions.

Most major policy and political disputes in the United States eventually make their way to the Supreme Court, so demonstrations at the Court are common. Here pro-abortion and anti-abortion demonstrators clash on the steps of the Supreme Court building in Washington, D.C., on the anniversary of *Roe* v. *Wade.*

Several technical rules help keep the numbers down. Cases must be *real* and *adverse;* that is, they must involve a real dispute between two parties. The disputants in a case must have *standing;* that is, they must have a real and direct interest in the issues that are raised. The Court sometimes changes the definition of *standing* to make access for **plaintiffs** easier or more difficult. The Warren Court favored an expansive definition; the Rehnquist Court, a restricted one. Cases must also be *ripe;* that is, all other avenues of appeal must have been exhausted, and the injury must already have taken place (the Court will not accept hypothetical cases). Appeals must also be filed within a specified time limit, the paperwork must be correct and complete, and a filing fee of $200 must be paid. The fee may be waived if a petitioner is poor and files an affidavit **in forma pauperis** ("in the manner of a pauper"). One of the most famous cases in American history, *Gideon* v. *Wainwright* (1963), which established the right of all defendants to have lawyers in criminal cases, was submitted in forma pauperis on a few pieces of lined paper by a Florida State Penitentiary inmate named Clarence Earl Gideon. The Rehnquist Court has been less friendly to indigent petitions than previous Courts and has taken several steps to cut down what the chief justice calls "frivolous" suits by "jailhouse lawyers."

The most powerful tool that the Court has for controlling its own agenda is the power to grant or not to grant a **writ of certiorari.** A grant of "cert" is a decision of the Court that an appellate case raises an important federal or constitutional issue that it is prepared to consider.[8] Under the **rule of four,** petitions are granted cert if at least four justices vote in favor. There are several reasons a petition may not command four votes, even if the case involves important constitutional issues: It may involve a particularly controversial issue that the Court would like to avoid, or the Court may not yet have developed a solid majority and may wish to avoid a split decision. Few petitions survive all of these hurdles. Of the almost 8,000 cases that are filed in each session, the Court grants cert for only about 140 (this number varies a bit year to year). In cases denied cert, the decision of the lower court stands.

plaintiff

One who brings suit in a court.

in forma pauperis

Describing a process by which indigents may file a suit with the Supreme Court free of charge.

writ of certiorari

An announcement that the Supreme Court will hear a case on appeal from a lower court; its issuance requires the vote of four of the nine justices.

rule of four

An *unwritten* practice that requires at least four justices of the Supreme Court to agree that a case warrants review by the Court before it will hear the case.

Deciding how freely to grant cert is a tricky business for the Court. Used too often, it threatens to inundate the Court with cases. Used too sparingly, it leaves in place the decisions of 13 different federal appeals courts on substantial federal and constitutional questions, as well as the decisions of state supreme courts. Because the Court now typically hears oral arguments for only about 95 cases a year—compared to roughly 150 in the seventies and eighties—more influence than ever is being exercised by the 13 federal circuit courts. For many important cases, the federal circuit courts are becoming the forum of last resort.

Deciding Cases

Cases granted cert are scheduled for oral argument. Lawyers on each side are alerted to the key issues that the justices wish to consider, and new briefs are invited. Briefs are also submitted on most important cases by other parties who may be interested in the disputes. These "friend of the court," or **amicus curiae,** briefs may be submitted by individuals, interest groups, or some agency of the federal government, including the Justice Department or even the president.

amicus curiae

Latin for "a friend of the court"; describes a brief in which individuals not party to a suit may have their views heard.

Each case is argued for one hour, with 30 minutes given to each side in the dispute. Oral argument is not so much a presentation of arguments, however, as it is a give-and-take between the lawyers and the justices and among the justices themselves. When the federal government is a party to the case, the solicitor general or one of his or her deputies presents the oral arguments. Some justices—Antonin Scalia, for instance—are famous for their close grilling of lawyers. Ruth Bader Ginsburg often asks that lawyers skip abstract legal fine points and put the issues in terms of their effect on ordinary people.

Longman
Participate.com 2.0
Timeline
The Chief Justice of the United States

After hearing oral arguments and reading the briefs in the case, the justices meet in conference to reach a decision. The custom is for each justice to state his or her position, starting with the chief justice and moving through the ranks in order of seniority. Chief justices of great stature and intellect, such as John Marshall and Charles Evans Hughes, used the opportunity to speak first as a way of structuring the case and of swaying votes. Those who did not command much respect from the other justices (for example, Warren Burger) were less able to shape the decision process.

Political scientists have tried to determine what factors are most important in predicting how the justices will vote. One approach looks at the ideological predilections of the justices and manages to explain a great deal about their voting behavior.[9] Another approach focuses on the diaries and personal papers of retired justices and shows that a great deal of negotiating and "horse trading" goes on, with justices trading votes on different cases and joining opinions they do not like so that they can have a hand in modifying them.[10] Another approach tries to link voting behavior to social background, types of previous judicial experience, and the political environment of family upbringing.[11] None of these approaches has been totally successful because much of what the Court does in conference is secret and can be only imperfectly reconstructed. About all that one can say is that the justices tend to form relatively stable voting blocs over time. Many scholars attribute the change of direction of the Court on civil rights, church-state issues, and state-federal government relations in the 1995 session and after, for example, to the emergence of a strong conservative bloc (Scalia, Thomas, Rehnquist, Kennedy, and O'Connor). This bloc formed the majority in *Gore* v. *Bush* (2000), which effectively determined the outcome of the presidential election, as well as in *Zelman* v. *Simmons-Harris,* (2002), upholding Cleveland's school voucher program.

Supreme Court justices here take turns signing opinions that will be published with the Court's decision on a case. Few cases before the Court result in unanimous decisions, so virtually all decisions are announced with attached majority and minority opinions.

The vote in conference is not final. As Justice John Harlan once explained it, "The books on voting are never closed until the decision finally comes down."[12] The justices have an opportunity to change their votes in response to the opinion supporting the majority decision. An opinion is a statement of the legal reasoning that supports the decision of the Court. There are three kinds of opinions. The **opinion of the Court** is the written opinion of the majority. A **concurring opinion** is the opinion of a justice who supports the majority decision but has different legal reasons for doing so. A **dissenting opinion** presents the reasoning of the minority. Dissenting opinions sometimes become the basis for future Court majorities.

If he or she votes with the majority in conference, the chief justice assigns the opinion. He or she can assign it to any justice in the majority, often to him- or herself. Some jurists and scholars believe that this power to assign is the most important role of the chief justice, and it is guarded jealously. Warren Burger was so eager to play a role in opinion assignments that, much to the distress of his colleagues, he would often delay announcing his vote so that he could place himself with the majority. Justice William Douglas angrily charged that Burger voted with the majority in *Roe* only so that he could assign the case to a justice who was closer to the minority view.[13] If the chief justice's opinion is with the minority, the opinion is assigned by the most senior member of the majority.

The justice assigned to write the opinion does not work in isolation. He or she is assisted not only by law clerks but also by other justices, who helpfully provide memoranda suggesting wording and reasoning. Justices also consider the legal reasoning presented to the Court in amicus curiae briefs.[14] Most opinions go through numerous revisions and are subject to a considerable amount of bargaining among the justices.

Only when an opinion is completed is a final vote taken in conference. The justices are free to change their earlier votes: They may join the majority if they are now persuaded by its reasoning, or a concurring opinion may be so compelling that the majority may decide to replace the original majority opinion with it.

opinion of the Court

The majority opinion that accompanies a Supreme Court decision.

concurring opinion

The opinion of one or more judges who vote with the majority on a case but wish to set out different reasons for their decision.

dissenting opinion

The opinion of the judge or judges who are in the minority on a particular case before the Supreme Court.

The Supreme Court as a National Policymaker

People often say that the Court should settle disputes and not make policy. But because the disputes it settles involve contentious public issues (such as abortion rights and affirmative action) and fundamental questions about the meaning of our constitutional rules, the Court cannot help but make public policy.

It seems likely that the Court recognizes and cultivates its policymaking role. In the main, the Court does not see itself as a court of last resort, simply righting routine errors in the lower courts or settling minor private disputes. It sees itself, instead, as the "highest judicial tribunal for settling policy conflicts" and constitutional issues and chooses its cases accordingly.[15] The fact that decisions are not simply handed down but come with an opinion attached for the purpose of guiding the actions of other courts, litigants, and public officials is another demonstration that the Court recognizes its policymaking role.

Structural Change and Constitutional Interpretation

Scholars generally identify three periods in the history of constitutional interpretation by the Supreme Court in the United States, one stretching from the founding to the Civil War, the next from the end of the Civil War to the Great Depression, and the last from World War II to the present.[16] We would add a fourth, covering the years from the mid-eighties to the present. We will see how changes in constitutional law have been influenced by structural factors, particularly economic change.

Period 1: National Power and Property Rights
We saw in Chapter 4 that the United States experienced significant growth and change during the first 75 years of its existence. This growth was accompanied by changes in constitutional law. Chief Justice John Marshall, who presided over the Supreme Court from 1801 to 1835, was the key judicial figure during this important period in our history.[17] Marshall was a follower of the doctrines of Alexander Hamilton, who believed that American greatness depended on a strong national government, a partnership between government and business in which industry and commerce were encouraged, and a national market economy free of the regulatory restraints of state and local governments. In a string of opinions that have shaped the fundamentals of American constitutional law—especially important are *Fletcher* v. *Peck* (1810), *Dartmouth College* v. *Woodward* (1819), *McCulloch* v. *Maryland* (1819), and *Gibbons* v. *Ogden* (1824), discussed elsewhere in this text—Marshall interpreted the Constitution to mean "maximum protection to property rights and maximum support for the idea of nationalism."[18]

Period 2: Government and the Economy
The Civil War and the Industrial Revolution triggered the development of a mass-production industrial economy dominated by the business corporation. Determining the role to be played by government in such an economy was a central theme of late-nineteenth- and early-twentieth-century American political life. The courts were involved deeply in this rethinking. At the beginning of this period, the Supreme Court took the position that the corporation was to be protected against regulation by both the state and federal governments; by the end, it was more sympathetic to the desire of the people and the political branches for the expansion of government regulation and management of the economy during the crisis of the Great Depression.

Under the leadership of Chief Justice John Marshall, the Supreme Court weakened the power of the states to regulate and interfere with interstate commerce, encouraging the emergence of a vital national economy.

The main protection for the corporation against regulation was the Fourteenth Amendment. This amendment was passed in the wake of the Civil War to guarantee the citizenship rights of freed slaves. In one of the great ironies of American history, this expansion of federal power over the states to protect rights—the operative phrase was from Section 1: "nor shall any state deprive any person of life, liberty, or property without due process of law"—was gradually translated by the Court to mean the protection of corporations (which were considered "persons" under the law) and other forms of business from state regulation.

This reading of **laissez-faire** economic theory into constitutional law made the Supreme Court the principal ally of business in the late nineteenth and early twentieth centuries. The Court overturned efforts by both the state and federal governments to provide welfare for the poor; to regulate manufacturing monopolies; to initiate an income tax; to regulate interstate railroad rates; to provide scholarships to students; to regulate wages, hours, and working conditions; and to protect consumers against unsafe or unhealthy products. The Court also supported the use of judicial injunctions to halt strikes by labor unions.

The business–Supreme Court alliance lasted until the Great Depression. Roosevelt's New Deal reflected a new national consensus on the need for a greatly expanded federal government with a new set of responsibilities: to manage the economy; to provide a safety net for the poor, the unemployed, and the elderly; to protect workers' rights to form labor unions; and to regulate business in the public interest. The Supreme Court, however, filled with justices born in the nineteenth century and committed to the unshakable link between the Constitution and laissez-faire economic doctrine, was opposed to the national consensus and in 1935 and 1936 declared unconstitutional several laws that were part of the foundation of the New Deal. In an extraordinary turn of events, however, the Supreme Court reversed itself in 1937, finding the Social Security Act, the Labor Relations Act, and state min-

laissez-faire

The political-economic doctrine that holds that government ought not interfere with the operations of the free market.

During the crisis of the Great Depression, the federal government took on greater responsibilities for protecting the welfare of the American people. The Supreme Court was slow to endorse the changes but eventually did so under intense political pressure.

imum wage laws acceptable. It is not entirely clear why the so-called switch-in-time-that-saved-nine occurred, but surely Roosevelt's landslide reelection in 1936, the heightening of public hostility toward the Court, and Roosevelt's plan to "pack the Court," all played a role. Whatever the reason, the Court abandoned its effort to prevent the government from playing a central role in the management of the economy and the regulation of business, and it came to defer to the political linkage branches of government on such issues

Web Exploration
FDR and the Court

Issue: Franklin Roosevelt, frustrated by a Court that, in his view, failed to appreciate the importance of New Deal programs for fighting the Great Depression, tried to expand the Court so that he could appoint new and more sympathetic justices.

Site: Access information about FDR's Court-packing scheme on our Website at **www.ablongman.com/greenberg**. Go to the "Web Explorations" section for Chapter 14. Select "FDR and the Court," then "court packing."

What You've Learned: What do you think of his plan? Should a group of unelected judges be allowed to overturn programs that the public clearly wants? Would you have voted for or against the proposal had you been a member of Congress?

HINT: The Constitution says nothing about the size of the Supreme Court; Congress can change the number of justices whenever it wishes, but it has not done so for a very long time. Your view on Court packing will probably depend on what you think about how responsive government should be to the majority.

by the end of the 1930s. In doing so, it brought another constitutional era to a close.

Period 3: Individual Rights and Liberties

Three fundamental issues of American constitutional law—the relationship of the states to the nation, the nature of private property and the national economy, and the role of government in the management of the economy—were essentially settled by the time World War II broke out. From then until the mid-to-late 1980s, the Court turned its main attention to the relationship between the individual and government.[19]

Most of this story is told in Chapters 15 and 16 on civil rights and civil liberties. For now, it is sufficient to point out that the Court, especially during the tenure of Chief Justice Earl Warren, decided cases that expanded protections for free expression and association, religious expression, fair trials, and civil rights for minorities. In another series of cases dealing with the apportionment of electoral districts, the Court declared for political equality, based on the principle of "one person, one vote." In many of its landmark decisions, the Court applied the Bill of Rights to the states. Although the Court's record was not without blemishes during and after World War II—see the "Using the Framework" feature on *Korematsu* v. *United States* (1944)—it made significant strides in expanding the realm of individual freedom.

Period 4: Conservative Retrenchment

Constitutional law and the Court do not stand still, however; both are responsive to changes in the world around them. A new conservative majority emerged on the Supreme Court in the late 1980s, fashioned by the judicial nominations of Presidents Ronald Reagan and George H. W. Bush. This new majority has moved the Court to reconsider many of the Court's established doctrines in the areas of rights and liberties (see Chapters 15 and 16), and on the relationship between the national and state governments. Its reconsideration of federalism in favor of "states rights" has been particularly noteworthy (see Chapter 3). In a string of landmark cases, the Court has curtailed national authority in favor of the states. Its main tool has been to strike down federal statutes that are, in its view, based on an overly expansive reading of the Commerce Clause by Congress. Rather than allowing Congress to act with respect to any issue that might be connected—even loosely and indirectly—to the national economy (which has settled constitutional doctrine since the late 1930s), the present Court is insisting upon a much stricter relationship of congressional action to interstate commerce. In 1995, the Court overturned a federal statute that banned guns from the area immediately around public schools, saying that Congress had exceeded its powers under the Commerce Clause. Using the same reasoning, it overturned legislation requiring background checks for gun buyers. Recently, the Court used such reasoning to strike down parts of the Violence Against Women Act and the federal law barring age discrimination in employment.

The conservative majority on the Court has also become fond of the notion of "state sovereign immunity," an idea drawn by them from the Eleventh Amendment that the states enjoy a broad area of immunity from national government interference. Using this doctrine, the Court ruled in 2001 that states are immune from suits brought by state employees under the Americans with Disabilities Act. Dissenters on the Court expressed concern that this will spell trouble for many federal civil rights laws. The Court ruled in another case in 2002 that states are shielded from rulings by federal agencies acting on complaints from private individuals, a determination that may decrease the powers of agencies such as the Environmental Protection Agency.

USING THE FRAMEWORK: Japanese-American Internment

If the Supreme Court exists to protect individual rights, why did it allow the military to keep Japanese-Americans in internment camps during World War II?

Background: On the advice of the U.S. military, President Franklin Roosevelt signed a series of executive orders in early 1942 authorizing the relocation of 112,000 Japanese-Americans living on the West Coast, 70,000 of whom were citizens, into internment camps. In 1944, the Supreme Court in *Korematsu* v. *United States* upheld the legality of the exclusion and confinement orders.

Constitutional scholar Edward Corwin described the internment and the Court's action as "the most drastic invasion of the rights of citizens of the United States by their own government" in modern American history. Taking a broad overview of structural, political linkage, and governmental factors that influenced the Supreme Court's decision will help explain this situation.

Governmental Action

The Supreme Court announces its decision allowing the internment of Japanese-Americans in *Korematsu* v. *United States* (1944).

Governmental Level

- President Franklin Roosevelt, → troubled by the action, but fully aware of the feelings of the public and the wishes of military leaders in wartime, signed the necessary executive orders.

- The Supreme Court, unwilling to act against opinion of military leaders that Japanese-Americans living on the West Coast posed a national security threat, supported the exclusion order in a case brought by Fred Korematsu.

- Military authorities believed that → Japanese-Americans living on the West Coast posed a national security threat to the United States; asked the President to authorize curfews, relocation, and confinement.

- Congress passed supporting legislation making relocation and internment possible.

Political Linkages Level

- Anti-Japanese attitudes → were widespread among the public, particularly in the West Coast states.

- Public opinion strongly → supported the war against Japan and whatever military policies were necessary to win it.

- The media whipped up hysteria about a possible Japanese invasion.

Structural Level

- Japanese immigrants → to the United States in the late nineteenth and early twentieth centuries settled mainly in the West Coast states.

- The Japanese attack on → Pearl Harbor on December 7, 1941, plunged the United States into World War II and helped trigger negative attitudes toward Americans of Japanese descent.

- The Constitution vests enormous powers in the president as commander-in-chief during wartime.

The Debate Over Judicial Activism

Has the Court become too involved in national policymaking? Many people think so; others think not. Let us examine several of the ways in which what is called **judicial activism** is expressed.

Judicial Review We have already seen how the Court, under John Marshall's leadership, claimed the right of judicial review in the case of *Marbury* v. *Madison* (1803). The power was not exercised by the Court to any great extent until the late nineteenth century. The rate of judicial review picked up during the twentieth century, however, with most of the Court's adverse attention being paid to the states. As described above, however, the present Court has become increasingly aggressive in overturning federal statutes, with an eye towards constraining the power of the national government. Overall, trends in judicial review suggest that the Court has become more willing in modern times to monitor the activities of other governmental entities.

Reversing the Decisions of Past Supreme Courts We have seen that adherence to precedent is one of the traditional norms that guides judicial decision making. The Warren, Burger, and Rehnquist Courts, however, have not been reluctant to overturn previous Court decisions. The most dramatic instance was the reversal of *Plessy* v. *Ferguson* (1896), which endorsed legal segregation in the South, by *Brown* v. *Board of Education* (1954), which knocked out segregation's legal underpinnings. There are many other examples of the Court reversing itself: the gradual whittling back of abortion protections for women, first enunciated in *Roe* v. *Wade* (1973) (see Chapter 16); the reversal of a range of precedents involving the rights of criminal defendants (see Chapter 15); and the reconsideration of the nature of federalism and national government power reviewed above.

Deciding "Political" Issues Critics claim that the Court is taking on too many matters that are best left to the elected branches of government. An often-cited example is the Court's willingness to become increasingly involved in the process of drawing congressional electoral district boundaries in the states. Defenders of the Court argue that when such basic constitutional rights as equality of citizenship are at peril, the Court is obligated to protect these rights, no matter what other government bodies may choose to do. The Court's intervention in the 2000 presidential election generated widespread criticism for its meddling in politics, though its many defenders insist that the Court's decision in *Bush* v. *Gore* saved the nation from a constitutional crisis.

Remedies The most criticized aspect of judicial activism is the tendency for federal judges to impose broad remedies on states and localities. A **remedy** is what a court determines must be done to rectify a wrong. Since the 1960s, the Court has been more willing than in the past to impose remedies that require other governmental bodies to take action. Some of the most controversial of these remedies include court orders requiring states to build more prison space and mandating that school districts bus students to achieve racial balance. Such remedies often require that governments spend public funds for things they do not necessarily want to do. Critics claim that the federal judiciary's legitimate role is to prevent government actions that threaten rights and liberties, not to compel government to take action to meet some policy goal.

Original Intention Much of the debate about the role of the Court centers on the issue of **original intention.** Advocates of original intention and its twin,

judicial activism

Actions by the courts that go beyond the strict role of the judiciary as interpreter of the law and adjudicator of disputes.

Longman
Participate.com 2.0
Participation
The Court and
School
Vouchers

remedy

An action that a court determines must be taken to rectify a wrong.

original intention

The doctrine that the courts must interpret the Constitution in ways consistent with the intentions of the framers rather than in light of contemporary conditions and needs.

Federal courts often require that states "remedy" a situation found to be in violation of federal standards or constitutional protections. A good example is prison overcrowding, shown here in an Alabama prison. For many years, the courts have insisted that the states do something to end the problem, even if it means spending additional state monies.

strict construction

The doctrine that the provisions of the Constitution have a clear meaning and that judges must stick closely to this meaning when rendering decisions.

strict construction, believe that the Court must be guided by the original intentions of the framers and the words found in the Constitution. They believe that the expansion of rights that has occurred since the mid-1960s—such as the new right to privacy that formed the basis of the *Roe* v. *Wade* decision and rights for criminal defendants—is illegitimate, having no foundation in the framers' intentions or the text of the Constitution. Justices Antonin Scalia and Clarence Thomas are the strongest "originalists" on today's Court.

Opponents of original intention believe that the intentions of the Founders are not only impossible to determine but also unduly constricting. In this view, jurists must try to reconcile the fundamental principles of the Constitution with changing conditions in the United States.

When all is said and done, however, it is apparent that the modern Supreme Court is more activist than it was in the past; most justices today hold a more expansive view of the role of the Court in forging national policy than did their predecessors. Because the Court is likely to remain activist—note the present Court's vigorous reinterpretation of the meaning of federalism—the debate about judicial activism is not likely to disappear from American politics.

Outside Influences on the Court

The courts make public policy and will continue to do so, but they do not do so in splendid isolation; many other governmental and political linkage actors and institutions influence what they do. Recall that the influence of structural factors has already been examined at several places in this chapter.

Governmental Factors

The Supreme Court must coexist with other governmental bodies that have their own powers, interests, constituencies, and visions of the public good. Recognizing this, the Court usually tries to stay somewhere near the boundaries of what is acceptable to other political actors. Being without "purse or sword," as Hamilton put it in *The Federalist,* No. 78, the Court cannot force others to obey its decisions. It can only hope that respect for the law and the Court will cause government officials to do what it has mandated in a decision. If the Court fails to gain voluntary compliance, it risks a serious erosion of its influence, for it then appears weak and ineffectual.

Presidential Influence The president, as chief executive, is supposed to carry out the Court's decrees. However, presidents who have opposed or have been lukewarm to particular decisions have been known to drag their feet as President Eisenhower did on school desegregation after the Court's *Brown* decision.

The president has certain constitutional powers that give him some degree of influence over the Court. In addition to the Court's dependence on the president to carry out its decisions (when the parties to a dispute do not do it voluntarily), the president influences the direction of the Court by his power of appointment. He can also file suits through the Justice Department, try to move public opinion against the Court (as Richard Nixon tried to do), and threaten to introduce legislation to alter the Court's organization or jurisdiction (as Franklin Roosevelt did with his Court-packing proposal).

Congressional Influences Congress retains the power to change the size, organization, and appellate jurisdiction of the federal courts. During the Civil War, Congress removed the Court's jurisdiction over habeas corpus cases so that civilians could be tried in military courts. Congress can also bring pressure to bear by being unsympathetic to pleas from the justices for pay increases or for a suitable budget for clerks or office space. The Senate also plays a role in the appointment process, as we have learned, and can convey its views to the Court during the course of confirmation hearings. Finally, Congress can change statutes or pass new laws that specifically challenge Supreme Court decisions, as it did when it legislated the Civil Rights Act of 1991 to make it easier for people to file employment discrimination suits.

Political Linkage Factors

The Supreme Court is influenced not only by other government officials and institutions but also by what we have termed political linkage factors such as social movements, interest groups, and elections.

Groups and Movements Interest groups, social movements, and the public not only influence the Court indirectly through the president and Congress but often do so directly. An important political tactic of interest groups and social movements is the **test case.** A test case is an action brought by a group that is designed to challenge the constitutionality of a law or an action by government. Groups wishing to force a court determination on an issue that is important to them will try to find a plaintiff on whose behalf they can bring a suit. When Thurgood Marshall was chief counsel for the NAACP in the 1950s, he spent a long time searching for the right plaintiff to bring a suit that would drive the last nail into the coffin of the *Plessy* separate-but-equal doctrine that was the legal basis for southern segregation. He settled on a fifth-grade girl named Linda Brown who was attending a segregated school in Topeka, Kansas. Several years later, he won the landmark case *Brown* v. *Board of Education of Topeka.*

Many test cases take the form of **class action suits.** These are suits brought by an individual on behalf of a class of people who are in a similar situation. A suit to prevent the dumping of toxic wastes in public waterways, for

test case

A case brought to force a ruling on the constitutionality of some law or executive action.

class action suit

A suit brought on behalf of a group of people who are in a situation similar to that of the plaintiffs.

Social movements use test cases to challenge the constitutionality of laws and government actions. After a long search, NAACP attorney Thurgood Marshall selected Linda Brown, a fifth-grader from Topeka, Kansas, as the principal plaintiff in *Brown* v. *Board of Education of Topeka,* the historic case that successfully challenged school segregation.

example, may be brought by an individual in the name of all the people living in the area who are adversely affected by the resulting pollution. Class action suits were invited by the Warren Court's expansion of the definition of standing in the 1960s. The Rehnquist Court later narrowed the definition of standing, making it harder to bring class action suits.

Interest groups often get involved in suits brought by others by filing amicus curiae briefs. Pro-abortion and anti-abortion groups submitted 78 such briefs in *Webster* v. *Reproductive Health Services* (1989), a decision which allowed states to regulate and limit abortion availability.[20] These briefs set out the group's position on the constitutional issues or talk about some of the most important consequences of deciding the case one way or the other. In a sense, this activity is a form of lobbying. Some scholars believe that the Court finds such briefs to be a way to keep track of public and group opinion on the issues before it, which is helpful to its work.[21]

Leaders   The Supreme Court does not usually stray very far from the opinions of public and private sector leaders.[22] Social and economic leaders use their influence in a number of ways. As we learned in earlier chapters, their influence is substantial in the media, the interest group system, party politics, and elections at all levels. It follows, then, that elites play a substantial role in the thinking of presidents and the members of Congress as they, in turn, deal with the Court. In addition to this powerful but indirect influence, the Court is also shaped by developments on issues and doctrine within the legal profession as these are expressed by bar associations, law journals, and law schools.

Although the Court has become an important bulwark of rights and liberties, it has occasionally felt it prudent to go along with the political branches when they have tried to silence dissident voices and keep racial minorities from enjoying the full protection of the law. For instance, it went along with local, state, and federal actions to punish dissident voices during the McCarthy era's anti-Communist hysteria of the 1950s. It also approved the forced relocation and internment of Japanese-Americans during World War II, as discussed in the "Using the Framework" feature earlier. Whereas the

Warren Court changed much of this, the Rehnquist Court is more inclined to favor the authorities.[23]

Public Opinion We might think that the Supreme Court is immune from public opinion, since the justices are appointed for life and do not need to face the electorate. There is reason to believe, however, that the Court pays attention to public opinion. A substantial amount of research shows that the Court conforms to public opinion about as much as the president and Congress do.[24] It must be noted, on the other hand, that the Court sometimes takes a very long time to move closer to public and elite opinions. For example, during the Great Depression, the Court's strong commitment to laissez-faire economics in the midst of a national economic emergency almost led to a constitutional crisis.

HOW DEMOCRATIC ARE WE?

Is the Supreme Court a Democratic or Nondemocratic Institution?

PROPOSITION: The Supreme Court was designed to be a nondemocratic institution, and it ought to stay that way. It has served us well throughout our history.

AGREE: For a representative democracy to function at all, there must be a referee who stands above the fray, preserving the rules, overseeing the orderly changing of some rules when the situation demands it, protecting minorities against the potentially tyrannical behavior of the majority, and protecting individuals in the exercise of the constitutionally guaranteed rights. The Supreme Court has done a pretty good job carrying out these responsibilities throughout our history.

DISAGREE: A representative democracy cannot remain democratic if one of its core government institutions, with the power to make binding decisions for the nation as a whole, is neither responsible nor responsive to the people. At some point, it cannot avoid going its own way, sometimes legitimately so (e.g., when it has occasionally protected the constitutional rights of unpopular individuals and minority groups) and sometimes illegitimately (e.g., when it has acted to protect the interests of powerful economic interests).

THE AUTHORS: In the conception of democracy used throughout this book, the appropriate role of the Court is to encourage the play of popular sovereignty, political equality, and liberty in American politics. In the game of American politics, the role of the Court ought to be that of a referee ensuring that the rules of democracy will be followed. The rules of the game of democracy involve assurances that the majority will prevail in the determination of public policy, that all members of the society will be allowed to enter on an equal basis into the public dialogue about the public business, and that each individual will be allowed all of the rights of conscience and expression connected with human dignity. We have learned at various places in this book that the Court does not always live up to these standards, but that it must do so for the health of our democracy goes without saying. We have learned that the Court, although sometimes slow in doing so, acts consistently with public opinion about as often as Congress and the president do. We will see in Chapters 15 and 16 on civil rights and civil liberties, moreover, that the Court, although often inconsistent and slow in doing so, has come to play an important and positive role in the protection of rights and liberties in the United States.

Summary

Article III of the Constitution is vague about the powers and responsibilities of the U.S. Supreme Court. Especially noteworthy is the Constitution's silence on the Court's most important power, judicial review. Nevertheless, the Court has fashioned a powerful position for itself in American politics, coequal with the executive and legislative branches.

The federal court system is made up of three parts. At the bottom are 94 federal district courts, in which most cases originate. In the middle are 13 appeals courts. At the top is the Supreme Court, with both original and appellate jurisdiction.

The Supreme Court operates on the basis of several widely shared norms: secrecy, seniority, and adherence to precedent. The Court controls its agenda by granting or not granting certiorari. Cases before the Court wend their way through the process in the following way: submission of briefs, oral argument, initial consideration in conference, opinion writing, and final conference consideration by the justices. Published opinions serve as precedents for other federal courts and future Supreme Court decisions.

The Supreme Court is a national policymaker of considerable importance. Its unelected, life-tenured justices cannot, however, do anything they please, because the Court is significantly influenced by other political linkage and governmental factors. As a result, Court decisions rarely drift very far from public and elite opinion.

Constitutional interpretation by the Supreme Court, heavily influenced by structural changes in American history, has progressed through three stages. In the first, the Court helped settle the question of the nature of the federal union. In the second, it helped define the role of the government in a free enterprise economy. In the third, the Court focused on issues of civil liberties and civil rights.

The decisions of the Court are influenced by structural, political linkage, and governmental factors. The president and Congress are especially important in this regard, but so too are interest groups and public and elite opinion.

Suggestions for Further Reading

Ackerman, Bruce. *We the People: Foundations.* Cambridge, MA: Harvard University Press, 1991.
> *A compelling interpretation of American constitutional history in which popular pressures are the prime cause for major transformations in the U.S. Supreme Court's approach to major issues.*

Barber, Sotirios A. *The Constitution of Judicial Power.* Baltimore: Johns Hopkins University Press, 1997.
> *A compelling defense of an activist Court.*

Clayton, Cornell W., and Howard Gillman, eds. *Supreme Court Decision Making: New Institutionalist Approaches.* Chicago: University of Chicago Press, 1999.
> *An argument by a collection of leading scholars that the most important factor in Supreme Court decision making is neither ideology nor political pressures, but the nature of the law and judicial institutions.*

Dionne, E. J., and William Kristol, eds. *Bush* v. *Gore: the Court Cases and the Commentaries.* Washington, D.C.: the Brookings Institution, 2001.
> *Read the court cases about the disputed 2000 presidential election and commentaries about them from both liberal and conservative perspectives.*

Garbus, Martin. *Courting Disaster.* New York: Henry Holt and Co., 2002.
A wide-ranging critique of the conservative drift of the Court and how its decisions are undermining long established legal doctrines.

O'Brien, David M. *Storm Center: The Supreme Court in American Politics.* New York: W. W. Norton, 2000.
The leading textbook on the Court and how it operates.

Schwartz, Bernard. *Decision: How the Supreme Court Decides Cases.* New York: Oxford University Press, 1997.
A revealing behind-the-scenes look at how the Supreme Court considers and decides the cases before it.

Sunstein, Cass R. *One Case at a Time.* Cambridge, MA: Harvard University Press, 1999.
A defense of the present Supreme Court's tendency to render narrow decisions and avoid breaking ground for grand new constitutional theories; argues that this leaves room for the play of democracy.

Internet Sources

Federal Courts Home Page   **www.uscourts.gov**
Information and statistics about the activities of U.S. District Courts, Circuit Courts of Appeal, and the Supreme Court.

Find Law.com   **www.findlaw.com**
A treasure trove of links to information about the nation's courts and the legal profession.

Legal Information Institute, Cornell University Law School
http://www.law.cornell.edu
The gateway to a world of information and links to associated law and court sites on the Web. Among its sections you will find the following: the Supreme Court Calendar; Biographies and Opinions of the Justices; Directories of law firms, law schools, and legal associations; Constitutions and Codes, including U.S. statutes, regulations, and judicial rules of procedure; and Court opinions, including those of state supreme courts.

Notes

1. J. M. Sosin, *The Aristocracy of the Long Robe: The Origins of Judicial Review in America* (Westport, CT: Greenwood Press, 1989).

2. Robert G. McCloskey, *The American Supreme Court* (Chicago: University of Chicago Press, 1960), pp. 12–13.

3. On *Marbury,* see Sylvia Snowmiss, *Judicial Review and the Law of the Constitution* (New Haven, CT: Yale University Press, 1990).

4. Neil Lewis, "An Appeals Court That Always Veers to the Right," *The New York Times* (May 24, 1999), p. A.1.

5. David M. O'Brien, *Storm Center: The Supreme Court in American Politics,* 3rd ed. (New York: Norton, 1993), p. 68.

6. Robert A. Carp and Ronald Stidham, *Judicial Process in America,* 3rd ed. (Washington, D.C.: Congressional Quarterly Press, 1996), ch. 8; Sheldon Goldman, "Federal Judicial Recruitment," in John B. Gates and Charles Johnson, eds., *The American Courts: A Critical Assessment* (Washington, D.C.: Congressional Quarterly Press, 1991), pp. 195, 199.

7. Ronald Stidham and Robert A. Carp, "Judges, Presidents, and Policy Choices," *Social Science Quarterly* 68 (1987), pp. 395–404; Carp and Stidham, *Judicial Process in America,* ch. 9.

8. For details, see H. W. Perry Jr., *Deciding to Decide: Agenda Setting in the United States Supreme Court* (Cambridge, MA: Harvard University Press, 1991).

9. David Adamany, "The Supreme Court," in Gates and Johnson, *The American Courts,* pp. 111–112; Glendon Schubert, *The Judicial Mind* (Evanston, IL: Northwestern University Press, 1965); Jeffrey A. Segal and Harold J. Spaeth, *The Supreme Court and the Attitudinal Model* (New York: Cambridge University Press, 1993); John D. Sprague, *Voting Patterns of the United States Supreme Court* (Indianapolis: Bobbs-Merrill, 1968).

10. Walter Murphy, *Elements of Judicial Strategy* (Princeton, NJ: Princeton University Press, 1964).

11. Joel B. Grossman, "Social Backgrounds and Judicial Decision-Making," *Harvard Law Review* 79 (1966), pp. 1551–1564; S. Sidney Ulmer, "Dissent Behavior and the Social Background of Supreme Court Justices," *Journal of Politics* 32 (1970), pp. 580–589.

12. John Harlan, "A Glimpse of the Supreme Court at Work," *University of Chicago Law School Record* 1, no. 7 (1963), pp. 35–52.

13. Bob Woodward and Scott Armstrong, *The Brethren: Inside the Supreme Court* (New York: Simon & Schuster, 1979).

14. Lee Epstein and Jack Knight, "Mapping Out the Strategic Terrain: The Informational Role of Amici Curiae," in Cornell Clayton and Howard Gillman, eds., *Supreme Court Decision-Making* (Chicago: University of Chicago Press, 1999).

15. Herbert Jacob, *Justice in America,* 3rd ed. (Boston: Little, Brown, 1978), p. 245.

16. McCloskey, *The American Supreme Court.*

17. Carp and Stidham, *Judicial Process in America,* p. 28.

18. McCloskey, *The American Supreme Court,* p. 57.

19. Ibid. Also see H. W. Perry Jr., *The Transformation of the Supreme Court's Agenda: From the New Deal to the Reagan Administration* (Boulder, CO: Westview Press, 1991).

20. Edward Lazurus, *Closed Chambers* (New York: Penguin, 1999), pp. 373–374.

21. Epstein and Knight, "Mapping Out the Strategic Terrain."

22. Robert A. Dahl, "Decision Making in a Democracy: The Supreme Court as a National Decision Maker," *Journal of Public Law* 6 (1957), pp. 279–295; Thomas R. Marshall, "Public Opinion, Representation, and the Modern Supreme Court," *American Politics Quarterly* 16 (1988), pp. 296–316; McCloskey, *The American Supreme Court,* p. 22; O'Brien, *Storm Center,* p. 325.

23. Adamany, "The Supreme Court," pp. 15–18; Lincoln Caplan, "The Reagan Challenge to the Rule of Law," in Sidney Blumenthal and Thomas Byrne Edsall, eds., *The Reagan Legacy* (New York: Pantheon Books, 1988); Linda Greenhouse, "The Court's Counterrevolution Comes in Fits and Starts," *The New York Times* (July 4, 1993), sec. 4, p. 1.

24. G. Caldeira, "Courts and Public Opinion," in Gates and Johnson, *The American Courts;* Jay Casper, "The Supreme Court and National Policy Making," *American Political Science Review* 70 (1976), pp. 50–63; Marshall, "Public Opinion, Representation, and the Modern Supreme Court"; William Mishler and Reginald S. Sheehan, "The Supreme Court as a Counter-Majoritarian Institution: The Impact of Public Opinion on Supreme Court Decisions," *American Political Science Review* 87 (1993), pp. 87–101; Benjamin I. Page and Robert Y. Shapiro, "Effects of Public Opinion on Policy," *American Political Science Review* 77 (1983), p. 183.

Part Five

What Government Does

Parts Two and Three of this book examined the structural and political linkage influences on government institutions and public officials. Part Four examined government institutions and public officials. This part examines what government does and how effective it is in tackling the most important problems facing the United States.

As such, this part represents a kind of summing up; it examines how effectively our political and governmental institutions operate to fulfill the needs and expectations of the American people. These chapters also address the democracy theme, asking whether public policies are the outcome of a democratic process and whether policies improve the health and vitality of democracy in the United States.

Chapters 15 and 16 look at the status of civil liberties and civil rights in the United States, with special attention paid to the decisions of the Supreme Court concerning our most cherished rights and liberties. Chapter 17 examines domestic policies, with particular attention given to patterns of government spending, the tax system, regulation of the economy, and social welfare. Chapter 18 looks at American foreign and military policies.

Chapter 15
Freedom: The Struggle for Civil Liberties

In This Chapter

- Why liberty is so important in a democracy
- How liberties were gradually applied to the states by the Supreme Court
- How the Supreme Court's interpretation of the meaning of liberties has changed
- How the struggle for democracy has increased the enjoyment of liberties in the United States
- How the war on terrorism may affect civil liberties

Campus Speech Codes and Free Speech

- During a class at the University of Michigan, a student argues that homosexuality could be treated with psychotherapy. He is accused of violating a campus rule against victimizing people on the basis of their sexual orientation.

- At Southern Methodist University, a student is sentenced to work with minority organizations for 30 hours because, among other things, he sang "We Shall Overcome" in a sarcastic manner.[1]

- At the University of Minnesota, four women students brought sexual harassment charges against faculty members in the Scandinavian Studies Department for disagreeing with students about the role of a female character in a story and for greeting a female student in a "nonsupportive" way.[2]

- The University of Montana's harassment policy says that if a woman "feels" she has been mistreated, that alone proves mistreatment.

- At San Diego State University a student is admonished by school administrators and warned that he might be expelled after getting into a heated argument with four Arab students in the school's library who had been quietly celebrating the September 11 attacks on the World Trade Center.[3]

- Campus newspapers across the nation refuse to accept a paid advertisement opposing reparations for slavery from conservative activist David Horowitz. Many of the handful of newspapers that run the ad "Ten Reasons Why Reparations for Slavery is a Bad Idea—and Racist Too" face angry demonstrations, vandalism of their offices, and theft of the papers containing the offending ads.

- Stanford University enacts a speech code in 1990 that prohibits "personal vilification of students on the basis of their sex, race, color, handicap, religion, sexual orientation, or national and ethnic origin." The code is pressed by, among others, the African-American Law Students Association, the Asian-American Law Students Association, and the Jewish Law Students Association. It

is strongly opposed by Stanford's eminent constitutional scholar Gerald Gunther, who claims that hate speech should not be banned but vigorously rejected "with more speech, with better speech, with repudiation and contempt." The California Supreme Court in 1995 agrees with the Gunther position, saying that the Stanford code unconstitutionally restricts free speech rights under the First Amendment to the Constitution.[4]

The college campus has become one of the most visible battlegrounds in the continuing struggle over the meaning of free speech in the United States. Campus speech codes have been instituted at many colleges and universities across the country in an effort to rid campuses of speech that may offend women and members of minority groups. Many civil libertarians, like Gerald Gunther, though protective of the rights of minority students to have a supportive learning environment, have fought hard against such codes in the service of free speech and a free society. By and large, the courts have sided with the civil libertarians, as in the Stanford case.

This chapter examines civil liberties in the United States. It shows that the meaning of each of our freedoms—whether of speech, of the press, of association, or of religion—is never settled but is the subject of continuing disagreement and even, on occasion, of contentious political struggle. ∎

Thinking Critically About This Chapter

Using the Framework You will see in this chapter how structural, political, linkage, and governmental factors influence the meaning and practice of civic freedoms. Although the decisions of the Supreme Court are particularly important in determining the status of civil liberties at any particular moment in American history, you will learn how they are also the product of influences from a wide range of actors, institutions, and social processes.

Using the Democracy Standard You will see in this chapter how the expansion of the enjoyment of civil liberties in the United States has been a product of the struggle for democracy and how civil liberties are fundamental to the democratic process itself. ◄

Civil Liberties in the Constitution

civil liberties

Freedoms found primarily in the Bill of Rights that are protected from government interference.

We saw in Chapter 2 that the framers were particularly concerned about establishing a society in which liberty might flourish. While government was necessary to protect liberty from the threat of anarchy, the framers believed that government might threaten liberty if it became too powerful. **Civil liberties** are freedoms protected by constitutional provisions, laws, and practices from certain types of government interference. As embodied in the Bill of Rights, civil liberties are protected by prohibitions against government actions that threaten the enjoyment of freedom.

In the Preamble to the Constitution, the framers wrote that they aimed to "secure the Blessings of Liberty to ourselves and our Posterity." But in the original Constitution, they protected few liberties from the national government they were creating and almost none from state governments. The safeguard against tyranny that the framers preferred was to give the national government little power with which to attack individual liberties. Rather than listing specific prohibitions against certain kinds of actions, they believed that liberty was best protected by a constitutional design that fragmented government power, a design that included separation of powers, checks and balances, and federalism. Still, the framers singled out certain freedoms as too crucial to be left unmentioned. The Constitution prohibits Congress and the states from suspending the writ of **habeas corpus,** except when public safety demands it because of rebellion or invasion, and from passing **bills of attainder** or **ex post facto laws** (see Table 15.1 for an enumeration).

habeas corpus

The legal doctrine that a person who is arrested must have a timely hearing before a judge.

bill of attainder

A governmental decree that a person is guilty of a crime that carries the death penalty, rendered without benefit of a trial.

ex post facto law

A law that retroactively declares some action illegal.

As we saw in Chapter 2, many citizens found the proposed Constitution too stingy in its listing of liberties, so that the Federalists were led to promise a "bill of rights" as a condition for passing the Constitution. The Bill of Rights was passed by the 1st Congress in 1789 and was ratified by the required number of states by 1791. Passage of the Bill of Rights made the constitution more democratic by specifying protections of political liberty and by guaranteeing a context of free political expression that makes popular sovereignty possible.

Looking at the liberties specified by the text of the constitution and its amendments, however, emphasizes how few of our most cherished liberties are to be found in a reading of the bare words of the Constitution. Decisions by government officials and changes brought about by political leaders, interest groups, social movements, and individuals remade the Constitution in the long run; hence many of the freedoms we expect today are not specifically

TABLE 15.1 Civil Liberties in the U.S. Constitution

The exact meaning and extent of civil liberties in the Constitution are matters of debate, but here are some freedoms spelled out in the text of the Constitution and its amendments or clarified by early court decisions.

Constitution

Article I, Section 9
Congress may not suspend a writ of habeas corpus.
Congress may not pass bills of attainder or ex post facto laws.

Article I, Section 10
States may not pass bills of attainder or ex post facto laws.
States may not impair obligation of contracts.

Article III, Section 2
Criminal trials in national courts must be jury trials in the state in which the defendant is alleged to have committed the crime.

Article III, Section 3
No one may be convicted of treason unless there is a confession in open court or testimony of two witnesses to the same overt act.

Article IV, Section 2
Citizens of each state are entitled to all privileges and immunities of citizens in the several states.

The Bill of Rights

First Amendment
Congress may not make any law with respect to the establishment of religion.
Congress may not abridge the free exercise of religion.
Congress may not abridge freedom of speech or of the press.
Congress may not abridge the right to assemble or to petition the government.

Second Amendment
Congress may not infringe the right to keep and bear arms.

Third Amendment
Congress may not station soldiers in houses against the owner's will, except in times of war.

Fourth Amendment
Citizens are to be free from unreasonable searches and seizures.
Federal courts may issue search warrants based only on probable cause and specifically describing the objects of search.

Fifth Amendment
Citizens are protected against double jeopardy (being prosecuted more than once for the same crime) and self-incrimination.
Citizens are guaranteed against deprivation of life, liberty, or property without due process of law.
Citizens are guaranteed just compensation for public use of their private property.

Sixth Amendment
Citizens have the right to a speedy and public trial before an impartial jury.
Citizens have the right to face their accuser and to cross-examine witnesses.

Eighth Amendment
Excessive bail and fines are prohibited.
Cruel and unusual punishments are prohibited.

mentioned there. Some extensions of protected liberties were introduced by judges and other officials. Others have evolved as the culture has grown to accept novel and even once-threatening ideas. Still other liberties have secured a place in the Republic through partisan and ideological combat. The key to understanding civil liberties in the United States is to follow their evolution over the course of our history.

Rights and Liberties in the Nineteenth Century

During the nineteenth century, the range of protected civil liberties in the United States was somewhat different from their range today. Especially noteworthy were the special place of **economic liberty** and the understanding that the Bill of Rights did not apply to state governments.

economic liberty

The right to own and use property free from excessive government interference.

Economic Liberty in the Early Republic

Liberty may be understood as protection against government interference in certain kinds of private activities. Among the few such protections mentioned in the original Constitution was one that concerned the use and enjoyment of private property: "No State shall... pass any... Law impairing the Obligation of Contracts" (Article I, Section 10). The importance of property rights as a fundamental liberty in the body of the Constitution was reinforced by more than a century of judicial interpretation.

contract clause

The portion of Article I, Section 10, of the Constitution that prohibits states from passing any law "impairing the obligation of contracts."

The Marshall Court (1801–1835)   Although the Supreme Court ruled (in *Barron* v. *Baltimore,* 1833) that the Bill of Rights did not apply to the states, it ruled on several occasions that the **contract clause** in the Constitution directly applied against unwarranted state action. In the hands of Chief Justice John Marshall, the clause became an important defense of property rights against interference by the states. In *Fletcher* v. *Peck* (1810), for example, the Marshall Court upheld a sale of public land, even though almost all of the legislators who had voted for the land sale had been bribed by the prospective purchasers. Chief Justice Marshall argued that even a fraudulent sale created a contract that the state could not void. In *Dartmouth College* v. *Woodward* (1819), Marshall argued that New Hampshire could not modify the charter of Dartmouth College because the original charter constituted a contract, the terms of which could not be changed without impairing the obligations in the original contract. The Founders' attempt to protect the contractual agreements of private parties ballooned in the hands of the Marshall Court to bar virtually any and all changes by the states of established property relations.[5] This expansion of property rights protections made it very difficult for states to regulate business activities.

The Taney Court (1836–1864)   Under the leadership of Chief Justice Roger Taney, the Court began to make a distinction between private property used in ways that encouraged economic growth and private property used for simple enjoyment. In landmark cases, the Taney Court issued rulings favoring the former when the two concepts of property conflicted.[6] In his opinion in *Charles River Bridge* v. *Warren Bridge* (1837), Chief Justice Taney said that Massachusetts, in chartering the Charles River Bridge, had not agreed to create a monopoly that closed off competitors. He ruled that Massachusetts could charter the rival Warren River Bridge because the states should encourage economic competition and technological advances. It did not matter that as a result the stockholders in the Charles River Bridge would lose money. Taney argued that the "creative destruction" of established but idle property in a dynamic market economy is the price of economic and social progress.

Human Property   The defense of property rights was especially and tragically strong when it came to slavery. Until the Civil War, courts in the North and the South consistently upheld the right of slaveholders to recapture fugitive slaves. In his opinion in *Dred Scott* v. *Sandford* (1857)—a case that helped bring on the Civil War—Chief Justice Taney claimed that slaves were not citizens who possessed rights but simply private property belonging to their owners, no different from land or tools.

Economic Liberty After the Civil War

The Fourteenth Amendment, passed after the Civil War, was designed to guarantee the citizenship rights of the newly freed slaves. It included a clause—the **due process clause**—stating that no state "may deprive a person of life, liberty, or property, without due process of law." Strangely, the Supreme Court in the late nineteenth century interpreted this clause as a protection for businesses against the regulatory efforts of the states.

> **due process clause**
>
> The section of the Fourteenth Amendment that prohibits states from depriving anyone of life, liberty, or property "without due process of law," a guarantee against arbitrary or unfair government action.

The Court's most famous decision in this regard was *Lochner* v. *New York* (1905). Lochner ran a bakery in Utica, New York. He was convicted of requiring an employee to work more than 60 hours per week, contrary to a New York state maximum-hours statute. But Justice Rufus Peckham wrote for a 5–4 Supreme Court majority that the right of employer and employee to negotiate hours of work was part of the "liberty" of which, under the Fourteenth Amendment, no person could be deprived without due process of law. In other words, New York State had no right to regulate the hours of labor.

The nineteenth century was an era in which the rights of property were expanded, refined, and altered to become consistent with an emerging, dynamic industrial economy. The twentieth century would bring new approaches to property rights and to political liberties in general. These new approaches would be triggered by structural transformations in the economy and culture, the efforts of new political groups and movements, and the actions of government officials, all of which we will examine in greater detail.

Nationalization of the Bill of Rights

Americans rightly understand the Bill of Rights to be a foundation of American liberties. Until the twentieth century, however, the Bill of Rights did not apply to the states, only to the national government. The Supreme Court only gradually applied the Bill of Rights to the states through a process known as *selective incorporation*.

Selective Incorporation

The framers were worried more about national government intrusion on freedom than about state government intrusion. Most of the states, after all, had bills of rights in their own constitutions, and being closer to the people, state governments would be less likely to intrude on the people's freedom, or so the framers believed. This reading of the Bill of Rights as a prohibition of certain actions by the national government seems explicit in the language of

Whereas the Second Amendment makes it difficult for Congress to pass laws restricting the sale and use of firearms, states can do so more easily because the Second Amendment has not yet been incorporated by the Supreme Court.

many of the first ten amendments. The first, for instance, starts with the words *"Congress shall make no law. . . ."* This understanding of the Bill of Rights as a set of prohibitions against certain actions by the national government and not the states was confirmed by John Marshall in *Barron* v. *Baltimore* (1833). It is apparent that the majority in Congress wanted to change the reach of the Bill of Rights, extending it to the states, however, when it approved the Fourteenth Amendment after the Civil War. Three clauses in this amendment specify that the states cannot violate the rights and liberties of the people living in them:

- The first specifies that all persons born or naturalized in the United States are citizens of both the United States and the states in which they reside.

- The **privileges and immunities clause** specifies that no *state* "shall make or enforce any law which shall abridge the privileges or immunities of citizens of the United States."

- The due process clause specifies that no *state* shall "deprive any person of life, liberty, or property, without due process of law."

Although Congress wrote the Fourteenth Amendment to guarantee that the states would protect all of U.S. citizens' rights and liberties, including those found in the Bill of Rights, the Supreme Court was very slow in **nationalizing** or **incorporating** the Bill of Rights, making it binding on the state governments. Indeed, the Supreme Court has not yet fully incorporated or nationalized the Bill of Rights. Rather, it has practiced what constitutional scholars term **selective incorporation,** only slowly adding, step-by-step, even traditional civil liberties to the constitutional obligations of the states.

Standards for Incorporation

How does the Supreme Court decide whether to incorporate some portion of the Bill of Rights? That is, what standard does the Court use to protect a liberty specified in the Bill of Rights from violation by a state government? The answer is quite simple and is spelled out, strange as it may seem, in footnote 4 of the opinion of the Court in *United States* v. *Carolene Products Company* (1938), written by Justice Harlan Fiske Stone. Stone suggested that most legislative enactments by states should be considered constitutional and sub-

privileges and immunities clause
The portion of Article IV, Section 2, of the Constitution that states that citizens from out of state have the same legal rights as local citizens in any state.

nationalizing
The process by which provisions of the Bill of Rights become incorporated. See *incorporation*.

incorporation
The gradual use of the Fourteenth Amendment by the Supreme Court to make the Bill of Rights and other constitutional protections binding on the states.

selective incorporation
The U.S. Supreme Court's gradual and piecemeal making of the protections of the Bill of Rights binding on the states.

ject only to **ordinary scrutiny** by the Court. However, the footnote declares, three classes of state actions would automatically be presumed unconstitutional, the burden being on the states to prove otherwise. When state actions are presumed to be unconstitutional, the Court is said to be exercising **strict scrutiny.** The three classes of suspect state actions that bring strict scrutiny are those that seem to

- contradict specific prohibitions in the Constitution, including those of the Bill of Rights;
- restrict the democratic process; and
- discriminate against racial, ethnic, or religious minorities.

The first of these is the subject matter of this chapter. The second has been addressed at several points in the text. The third is the subject of Chapter 16.

In the remainder of this chapter, we focus on specific civil liberties, clarifying their present status in both constitutional law and political practice.

> **ordinary scrutiny**
>
> The assumption that the actions of elected bodies and officials are legal under the Constitution.
>
> **strict scrutiny**
>
> The assumption that actions by elected bodies or officials violate constitutional rights.

Freedom of Speech

Congress shall make no Law . . . abridging the freedom of speech.
—FIRST AMENDMENT TO THE U.S. CONSTITUTION

Speech can take many forms. The Court has had to consider which forms of speech are protected under the Constitution.

Political Speech   For many people, the right to speak one's mind is the first principle of a free and democratic society. Yet the right to free speech was not incorporated (made applicable to state governments) by the Supreme Court until 1925 in *Gitlow* v. *New York* (1925). Benjamin Gitlow had published *The Left*

Web Exploration

Does Your Representative Support First Amendment Freedoms?

Issue: The enjoyment of First Amendment freedoms depends, in part, on how fully they are supported by elected representatives.

Site: Access the ACLU online on our Website at **www.ablongman.com/greenberg**. Go to the "Web Explorations" section for Chapter 15. Select "Does your representative support . . . ," then "ACLU." Select "Freedom Scorecard." Enter your ZIP code to see how the ACLU scored your representative and senators.

What You've Learned: Do your representative and senators score well or badly on the ACLU freedom index? Do your representative and senators reflect your own views on civil liberties issues? How would you score on the ACLU index if you represented your district in the House or your state in the Senate?

HINT: Look at the legislation that the ACLU uses to compose their index. You may or may not agree that these votes are important. Depending on your political point of view, you may not agree that a high score on the ACLU index is the best indicator of support for freedom.

Once "free speech" was incorporated by the Supreme Court, states were no longer at liberty to suppress unpopular speech, as many of them had done with some frequency. This radical political rally in Gary, Indiana, in 1919 was broken up by the police soon after this photo was taken.

Wing Manifesto, which embraced a militant, revolutionary socialism to mobilize the proletariat to destroy the existing order in favor of communism. Gitlow did not advocate specific action to break the law, but he was nonetheless convicted of a felony under the New York Criminal Anarchy Law (1902).

The Supreme Court majority held that New York State was bound by the First Amendment but then argued that even the First Amendment did not prohibit New York from incarcerating Gitlow for his pamphlet. Said Justice Edward Sanford, "A single revolutionary spark may kindle a fire that, smoldering for a time, may burst into a sweeping and destructive conflagration. It cannot be said that the State is acting . . . unreasonably when . . . it seeks to extinguish the spark without waiting until it has enkindled the flame or blazed into the conflagration." In his famous dissent, Justice Oliver Wendell Holmes said, "Every idea is an incitement. . . . Eloquence may set fire to reason. But whatever may be thought of the redundant discourse before us, it had no chance of starting a present conflagration."

Although the *Gitlow* precedent proved to be an important advance for civil liberties in the United States, the Court was still willing to leave Gitlow in jail and allow the states wide latitude in controlling what they considered dangerous speech. For many years, especially during the 1940s and 1950s anti-Communist "Red scare," the Court deferred to political hysteria and allowed the widespread suppression of what we now consider acceptable speech and publication. The Court seldom moved far ahead of the political branches on free speech issues during this period or later.[7]

This early stage of the nationalization of the Bill of Rights by the Court was helped along by a new force, the American Civil Liberties Union (ACLU), which brought the *Gitlow* appeal. Less than ten years old, the ACLU had little to show for its legal challenges to the suppression of free speech until 1925, when *Gitlow* provided a spark of hope for civil libertarians. The Court's application of the First Amendment to the states provided the ACLU with opportunities to resist censorship and the strangulation of dissent by the states as well as by the national government. Victories remained rare, but the Court's willingness to incorporate free speech encouraged and energized the ACLU.[8]

Freedom of speech has grown in the ensuing years so that far more speech is protected than is not. In general, no U.S. government today may regulate or interfere with the content of speech without a compelling reason. For a reason to be compelling, a government must show that the speech poses a "clear and present danger"—the standard formulated by Holmes in *Schenck* v. *United States* (1919)—that it has a duty to prevent. The danger must be very substantial, and the relationship between the speech and the danger must be direct, such as falsely yelling "Fire!" in a crowded theater. The danger must also be so immediate that the people responsible for maintaining order cannot afford to tolerate the speech. Abstract advocacy of ideas, even ideas considered dangerous by police, politicians, or popular majorities, is protected unless it meets both conditions. Freedom of speech has grown, then, and with it, an important part of democracy in the United States.

One disturbing trend for those who support an expansive concept of free expression are surveys showing that Americans are becoming increasingly willing to constrain or suppress political speech when it make some members of the larger community uncomfortable. Almost one-third of Americans, for example, "would not allow a rally for a cause or issue that could offend" some members of the community.[9] Two-thirds would be willing to ban speech that was offensive to racial groups; over one-half would forbid speech that offended religious groups.

Longman
Participate.com
2.0
Visual Literacy
**What Speech
Is Protected by
the
Constitution?**

Actions and Symbolic Speech

Difficult questions about free expression persist, of course. Speech mixed with *conduct* may be restricted if the restrictions are narrowly and carefully tailored to curb the conduct while leaving the speech unmolested. Symbolic expressions (such as wearing armbands or picketing) may also receive less protection from the Court. The use of profanity or words that are likely to cause violence ("fighting words") may be regulated in some cases, as may symbolic actions that prevent others from carrying out legitimate activities. Still, freedom of speech throughout the United States has grown to the point at which contenders wrestle with relatively peripheral issues, leaving a large sphere of expressive freedom. *Texas* v. *Johnson* (1989) shows just how far the protection of free speech has expanded. In this case, Gregory Johnson challenged a Texas state law

Can state legislatures or Congress pass laws prohibiting flag burning? Though many Americans are infuriated by flag burning, the Supreme Court has ruled that such laws violate freedom of expression.

against flag desecration under which he had been convicted for burning an American flag as part of a demonstration at the 1984 Republican convention. Although dominated by a conservative majority, the Rehnquist Court overturned the Texas law, saying that flag burning falls under the free expression protections of the Constitution unless imminent incitement or violence is likely.

Suppression of Free Expression   A major exception to the expansion of freedom of expression has been the periodic concern about "internal security." The past century has witnessed several periods when dissenters and radicals were persecuted for their political speech and writings. Censorship of dissent and protests during World War I proved to be a portent of abuses after the war. At least 32 states enacted laws to suppress dangerous ideas and talk, and the Lusk Committee in New York State raided the offices of "radicals." Hoping to become president, New York State Attorney General A. Mitchell Palmer conducted raids on the headquarters of suspect organizations in 1919 and 1920, sending the young J. Edgar Hoover out to collect information on radicals and nonconformists.

Longman
Participate.com 2.0
Timeline
Civil Liberties and National Security

A similar period of hysteria followed World War II. Its foundations were laid when the Democrat-controlled House of Representatives created the House Committee on Un-American Affairs (generally referred to as the HUAC). When the Republicans won control of the Congress, they professed to see security risks in the Truman administration and Hollywood. HUAC found no spies and contributed little to security, but it managed to ravage lives and reputations. Soon Democrats and Republicans alike were exploiting the "Red scare" for political gain. The greatest gain (and, subsequently, the hardest fall) was for Senator Joseph McCarthy (R–WI). McCarthy brandished lists of purported communists and denounced all who opposed him as traitors. McCarthy and "McCarthyism" eventually fell victims, however, to the newest force in U.S. politics: television. Once ordinary Americans saw McCarthy and his tactics in their living rooms, support for him declined rapidly. McCarthy's downfall led to a slow retreat from this period of utter disregard for liberty.[10]

High emotions in the days immediately following the September 11 terrorist attacks on the United States caused the speech of some dissenters to be

Senator Joseph McCarthy issues a warning about the "Red tide" of communism sweeping the nation. McCarthy discovered few communists but managed to wreck the lives of many innocent people and created an atmosphere that threatened liberty in the United States for many years in the 1950s.

quelled temporarily. One professor at the University of New Mexico faced a disciplinary hearing after remarking in class that "anybody who can blow up the Pentagon gets my vote." A librarian at UCLA was suspended after he sent out an e-mail to people on campus decrying American support for Israeli terrorism as the root cause of the terrorist attacks on the United States. Authorities said the views he expressed created a hostile climate for Jewish students.

Freedom of the Press

Congress shall make no law . . . abridging the freedom . . . of the press.
—First Amendment to the U.S. Constitution

In an aside in the opinion of the Court in *Gitlow* v. *New York* (1925), the Supreme Court included freedom of the press as a freedom guaranteed against state interference by the Fourteenth Amendment. Incorporation of this aspect of the Bill of Rights seems reasonable in light of the importance of the free flow of information in a society that aspires to freedom and democracy. In *Near* v. *Minnesota* (1931), the Court made good on the promise of *Gitlow* by invalidating the Minnesota Public Nuisance Law as a violation of freedom of the press.[11] Jay Near published the *Saturday Press,* a scandal sheet that attacked local crime, public officials, and a few other groups that he disliked: Jews, Catholics, blacks, and unions, for example. Near and his associates were ordered by a state court not to publish, sell, or possess the *Saturday Press.* This sort of state action is called **prior restraint,** because it prevents publication before it has occurred. Freedom of the press is not necessarily infringed if publishers are sued or punished for harming others after they have published, but Minnesota was trying to keep Near and his associates from publishing in the future.

prior restraint
The government's power to prevent publication, as opposed to punishment afterward.

Prior Restraint The prohibition of prior restraint on publication remains the core of freedom of the press. Freedom of the press and freedom of speech tend to be considered together as freedom of expression, so the general principles applicable to free speech apply to freedom of the press as well. Thus, the Court will allow the repression of publication only if the state can show some "clear and present danger" that publication poses, similar to its position on free speech. In *New York Times* v. *United States* (1971), the Court ruled that the U.S. government could not prevent newspapers from publishing portions of the Pentagon Papers, secret government documents revealing the sordid story of how the United States had become involved in the Vietnam War. A major expansion of freedom of the press in *New York Times* v. *Sullivan* (1964) protects newspapers against punishment for trivial or incidental errors when they are reporting on public persons. This limits the use or threat of libel prosecutions by officials because officials can recover damages only by showing that the medium has purposely reported untruths or has made no effort to find out if what is being reported is true.

Offensive Mass Media The limits of freedom of expression are often tested by media publications that offend many Americans. Pornography, for example, has challenged the ability of citizens, legislatures, and courts to distinguish art from trash that degrades human beings. Typically, communities and legislatures have tried to regulate or eliminate pornography, while civil liberties lawyers and courts have tried to leave choices up to consumers and the market.

Pornography is a nonlegal term for sexual materials: the legal term is **obscenity.** Although the courts have held that *obscenity* is unprotected by the First Amendment, the definition of obscenity has provoked constitutional

obscenity
As defined by the Supreme Court, the representation of sexually explicit material in a manner that violates community standards and is without redeeming social importance or value.

struggles for half a century. Early disputes concerned the importation and mailing of works that we regard today as classics: James Joyce's *Ulysses* and D. H. Lawrence's *Lady Chatterley's Lover,* for example.[12] Although the justices admitted that principled distinctions sometimes eluded them (Justice Potter Stewart once said that he did not know how to define hard-core pornography but that he knew it when he saw it), a reasonably clear three-part test emerged from *Miller* v. *California* (1973):

1. The average person, applying contemporary community standards, must find that the work as a whole appeals to the prurient interest (lust).
2. The state law must specifically define what sexual conduct is obscene.
3. The work as a whole must lack serious literary, artistic, political, or scientific value.

If the work survives even one part of this test, it is not legally obscene and is protected by the First Amendment. Community standards, applied by juries, are used to judge whether the work appeals to lust and whether the work is clearly offensive. However, literary, artistic, political, and scientific value (called the *LAPS test,* after the first letter of each of the four values) is *not* judged by community standards but by the jury's assessment of the testimony of expert witnesses. If, and only if, all three standards are met, the Supreme Court will allow local committees to regulate the sale of pornographic materials.

Recently, many Americans have begun to worry about the availability to minors of sexually offensive material on the Internet. Responding to this concern, Congress and President Clinton cooperated in 1996 to pass the Communications Decency Act, which made it a crime to transmit over the Internet or to allow the transmission of indecent materials to which minors might have access. The Supreme Court, in *Reno, Attorney General of the United States* v. *American Civil Liberties Union* (1997), ruled unanimously that the legislation was an unconstitutional violation of the First Amendment, being overly broad and vague and violative of the free speech rights of adults to receive and send information. The strong and unambiguous words of the opinion of the Court make it clear that government efforts to regulate the content of the Internet will not get very far. It may well be the case, however, that Internet-filtering software that allows parents to keep objectionable material from their children will accomplish the same end as government regulation without danger of violating the Constitution.

The distinction between art and obscenity can be very difficult to establish, and battles over the banning of controversial works, such as Robert Mapplethorpe's homoerotic photographs, are quite common in American communities.

Free Exercise of Religion

Congress shall make no law . . . prohibiting the free exercise [of religion].
—First Amendment to the U.S. Constitution

For much of our history, Congress did not impede the exercise of religion because it did not legislate much on the subject. Since the states were not covered by the First Amendment, the free exercise of religion was protected by state constitutions or not at all. The Supreme Court was content to defer to the states on issues of religious freedom.

As late as 1940, in *Minersville School District* v. *Gobitis,* the Supreme Court upheld the expulsion of two schoolchildren who refused to salute the flag because it violated their faith as Jehovah's Witnesses. Justice Harlan Stone wrote a stinging dissent:

> The Constitution expresses more than the conviction of the people that democratic processes must be preserved at all costs. It is also an expression of faith and a command that freedom of mind and spirit must be preserved, which government must obey, if it is to adhere to that justice and moderation without which no free government can exist.

Stone's dissent, as well as a series of decisions deferring to state restrictions on Jehovah's Witnesses in 1941 and 1942, eventually moved other justices to Stone's side. In *West Virginia* v. *Barnette* (1943), the Court reversed *Gobitis* and firmly established free exercise of religion as protected against the states.

The core of the nationalized **free exercise clause** today is that government may not interfere with religious *beliefs.* This is one of the few absolutes in U.S. constitutional law. Religious *actions,* however, are not absolutely protected. The Court has upheld state laws, for instance, outlawing the use of peyote (an illegal hallucinogen) in Native American religious ceremonies (*Employment Division* v. *Smith,* 1990). Congress and President Clinton tried to overturn this decision with the Religious Freedom Restoration Act in 1993, but the Act was declared unconstitutional in *City of Boerne* v. *Flores* (1997) because the Act, in view of the Court majority, unduly extended national government power over the states.

free exercise clause

That portion of the First Amendment to the Constitution that prohibits Congress from impeding religious observance or impinging upon religious beliefs.

Establishment of Religion

Congress shall make no law respecting an establishment of religion.
—First Amendment to the U.S. Constitution

Freedom of conscience requires that government not favor one religion over another by granting it special favors, privileges, or status. It requires, in Jefferson's famous terms, "a wall of separation between church and state." Nevertheless, incorporation of the **establishment clause** proved to be a particularly messy matter. In *Everson* v. *Board of Education* (1947), Justice Hugo Black for the Supreme Court determined that no state could use revenues to support an institution that taught religion, thus incorporating the First Amendment ban into the Fourteenth Amendment. But the majority in that case upheld the New Jersey program that reimbursed parents for bus transportation to parochial schools. A year later, Justice Black wrote another opinion incorporating the establishment clause in *McCollum* v. *Board of Education* (1948). This time, a program for teaching religion in public schools was found unconstitutional. In *Zorach* v. *Clauson* (1952), however, the Court upheld a similar program in New York State that let students leave school premises early for religious instruction. The establishment

establishment clause

The part of the First Amendment to the Constitution that prohibits Congress from establishing an official religion; the basis for the doctrine of the separation of church and state.

clause had been incorporated, but the justices were having a difficult time determining what "separation of church and state" meant in practice.

The *Lemon* Test   The Warren Court (1953–1969) brought together a solid church-state separationist contingent whose decisions the early Burger Court (1969–1973) distilled into the major doctrine of the establishment clause: the "*Lemon* test." In *Lemon* v. *Kurtzman* (1971), Chief Justice Warren Burger specified three conditions that every law must meet to avoid "establishing" religion:

1. The law must have a secular *purpose*. That secular purpose need not be the only or primary purpose behind the law. The Court requires merely some plausible nonreligious reason for the law.
2. The *primary effect* of the law must be neither to advance nor to retard religion. The Court will assess the probable effect of a governmental action for religious neutrality.
3. Government must never foster *excessive entanglements* between the state and religion.

While lawyers and judges frequently disagree about each of the three "prongs" of the *Lemon* test, the test has erected substantial walls that bar mixing church and state. The Rehnquist Court has been taking many of the bricks out of the walls, however. In *Rosenberger* v. *University of Virginia* (1995), it ruled that the university (a state-supported institution) must provide the same financial subsidy to a student religious publication that it provides to other student publications. In 2002, by a 5–4 vote, the Court approved Cleveland's program of school vouchers that provides public money to parents who want to send their children to private schools, whether secular or religious. The Court majority based its ruling on the fact that public monies do not go directly to religious schools in the Cleveland program but rather to parents who are free to choose their children's school(s). It remains too early at this writing to know whether this decision will encourage the spread of vouchers, a goal long cherished by conservatives.

Web Exploration
Disputes About Religious Freedom

Issue: Americans continue to disagree with one another about the meaning of religious freedom.

Site: Access the Christian Coalition and Americans United for the Separation of Church and State on our Website at **www.ablongman.com/greenberg**. Go to the "Web Explorations" section for Chapter 15. Select "Disputes About . . . ," then "religious freedom." Examine the "news releases" section of both organizations.

What You've Learned: Compare which issues each organization focuses upon and how the issues are treated by each. Which site is closer to reflecting your own understanding of religious freedom? Do you believe there is common ground upon which the two groups might meet, or do you believe that the differences in view are irreconcilable?

HINT: Your views on religious freedom probably depend not only on your specific religious views but upon your support for the doctrine of "separation of church and state."

Many school districts still allow religious observations in classrooms, despite a long string of Supreme Court decisions defining such practices as a violation of the doctrine of the separation of church and state.

School Prayer   One of the most controversial aspects of constitutional law regarding the establishment of religion concerns school prayer. Although a majority of Americans support allowing a nondenominational prayer or a period of silent prayer in the schools, the Court has consistently ruled against such practices since the early 1960s. In *Engel* v. *Vitale* (1962), the Court ordered the state of New York to suspend its requirement that all students in public schools recite a nondenominational prayer at the start of each school day. Writing for the majority, Justice Hugo Black found the prayer requirement to be a state-sponsored religious activity "wholly inconsistent with the establishment clause." In *Stone* v. *Graham* (1980), the Court ruled against posting the Ten Commandments in public school classrooms. In *Lee* v. *Weisman* (1992), it ruled against allowing school-sponsored prayer at graduation ceremonies. In *Santa Fe Independent School District* v. *Doe* (2000), the Court ruled that student-led prayers at school-sponsored events such as football games are not constitutionally permissible because they have the "improper effect of coercing those present to participate in an act of religious worship." In these and other cases the Court has consistently ruled against officially sponsored prayer in public schools as a violation of the separation of church and state. The Court has been willing, however, to allow religious groups to meet in public schools and to allow students to pray on their own or in unofficial study groups while on public school premises.

Returning prayer to the public schools and making them less secular are very high on the agenda of Christian conservatives. Bills supporting voluntary classroom prayer (such as a moment of silent contemplation) are constantly being introduced into Congress and state legislatures, with little success so far. Christian conservatives have also tried without success to pass a school prayer constitutional amendment. In several very religious communities, school officials have simply ignored the Supreme Court and continue to allow prayer in public classrooms.

With no sign that the tide of religious feeling is about to recede in the United States, school prayer, and the question of where to draw the line between church and state in general, are likely to be with us for some time to come.

Privacy

The freedoms addressed so far—speech, press, and religion—are explicitly mentioned in the Bill of Rights. The freedom to be left alone in our private lives—what is usually referred to as the *right to privacy*—is nowhere mentioned. Nevertheless, most Americans consider the right to privacy one of our most precious freedoms; most believe we ought to be spared wiretapping, e-mail snooping, and the regulation of consensual sexual activities in our own homes, for instance. Many (though not all) constitutional scholars believe, moreover, that a right to privacy is *inherent* (there, but not explicitly stated) in the Bill of Rights; note the prohibitions against illegal searches and seizures and against quartering of troops in our homes, as well as the right to free expression and conscience. Such scholars also point to the Ninth Amendment as evidence that the framers believed in the existence of liberties not specifically mentioned in the Bill of Rights: "The enumeration in the Constitution of certain rights, shall not be construed to deny or disparage others retained by the people." The Supreme Court agreed with this position in *Griswold* v. *Connecticut* (1965), in which it ruled that a constitutional right to privacy exists when it struck down laws making birth control illegal.

It is relatively unclear yet whether the courts will support a privacy-based "right to die." So far the Supreme Court has refused to endorse the existence of such a right. Indeed, in *Vacco* v. *Quill* (1997), it threw out two federal circuit court decisions that had overturned state laws in Washington and New York banning doctor-assisted suicide as unconstitutional. The Court majority ruled that states were free to ban doctor-assisted suicide because there is no constitutionally protected right to die. Their ruling did not prohibit states from passing laws establishing such a right, however. Indeed, five of the justices suggested in their written opinions that they might support a claim for the existence of such a right in the future.

A case concerning the right to die is likely to reach the high court before too long, given Attorney General Ashcroft's recent effort to nullify Oregon's "Death With Dignity" Act, approved by the state's voters in 1997. Ashcroft announced

The Supreme Court has not yet made up its mind about doctor-assisted suicide. Because several states have passed laws allowing such suicides, and more are considering it, the Court will no doubt revisit the issue in the next few years. Here Dr. Jack Kevorkian helps terminally ill patient Thomas Youk end his life.

that any doctor prescribing drugs that are used by patients to end their lives would be subject to prosecution under the federal "Controlled Substances" Act. Oregon officials filed suit in federal district court in November, 2001, to stop the Justice Department from acting against Oregon doctors.

Rights of the Accused

Five of the ten amendments that make up the Bill of Rights concern protections for individuals suspected or accused of a crime, suggesting that the Founders were deeply concerned about this aspect of freedom. Most Americans today treasure the constitutional rights and liberties that protect innocent individuals from wrongful prosecution and imprisonment. But most Americans also want to control crime as much as possible. Balancing the two sentiments is not easy. Those alarmed by lawlessness—actual or imagined—tend to support "whatever it takes" to reduce that lawlessness, even if the rights or liberties of others must be restricted. Others are more alarmed by the lawlessness—real or imagined—of police and prosecutors. These advocates of due process values see violations of rights and liberties as unnecessary and dangerous in a free society.

During the 1950s and 1960s, the Warren Court favored the due process approach and subjected the states' criminal procedures to rigorous interpretations of constitutional guarantees. Increased protections for criminal defendants, however, gave many political candidates an electorally useful explanation for rising crime: Too much regard for "legal technicalities" was "coddling" the guilty and "handcuffing" the police. Republican presidential candidates Nixon, Ford, Reagan, and Bush all promised to appoint federal

Longman
Participate.com
2.0
Participation
**Privacy and
Rights of the
Accused**

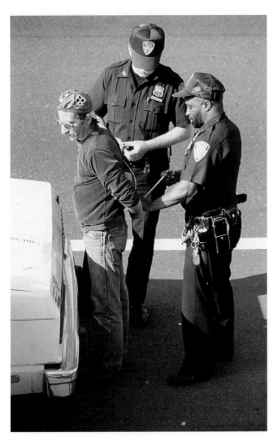

The right to due process was incorporated into the Constitution from the outset, but it was the Supreme Court's *Miranda* decision in 1966 that required law enforcement officials to inform the accused of their rights at the time of arrest.

court judges who would be more sympathetic to crime control and less insistent on protecting the rights of suspects and defendants. One result of Republican domination of the White House between 1968 and 1993 is that a majority of federal judges have been appointed by presidents who "ran against the courts" on the issue of criminal procedure. A gradual but important shift to a higher regard for crime control than for due process has followed from electoral politics and has reshaped constitutional interpretation.

The shift is obvious in the decisions of the Supreme Court. The Warren Court (1953–1969) expanded due process, preferring constitutional guarantees to efficient law enforcement. The Burger Court (1969–1986) preserved most of the basic due process decisions that the Warren Court had crafted but limited the further growth of protections and introduced many exceptions. The Rehnquist Court (1986–present) has reversed many due process protections.

Longman
Participate.com
2.0
Simulation
**You Are a
Police Officer**

exclusionary rule

A standard promulgated by the Supreme Court that prevents police and prosecutors from using evidence against a defendant that was obtained in an illegal search.

Unreasonable Searches and Seizures Consider, for example, the Fourth Amendment, which secures the right of all persons against unreasonable searches and seizures and allows the granting of search warrants only if the police can specify evidence of serious lawbreaking that they reasonably expect to find. Until the Warren Court compelled the states to abide by the Fourth Amendment in 1961, they had frequently used searches and seizures that the federal courts would consider "unreasonable" in an effort to control crime.

In *Mapp* v. *Ohio* (1961), the Supreme Court enunciated the **exclusionary rule** to prevent the police and prosecutors from using evidence that had been gained through warrantless and unreasonable searches to convict people. In this case, the police forcibly entered the apartment of Dollree Mapp looking for a fugitive. They found no fugitive but decided to search Mapp's apartment anyway, even though they had no search warrant. Finding what they considered obscene photos and books, they arrested Mapp under Ohio's law covering the possession of obscene materials. She was convicted, an action later supported by the Ohio Supreme Court. The conviction was overturned by the U.S. Supreme Court. A majority of the justices believed that the threat of perpetrators' being freed in cases like this would force the police to play by the constitutional rules. The justices did not believe that due process threatened crime control because police lawlessness was not the only way to deal with crime.

The Warren Court demanded that the police get warrants whenever the person to be subjected to a search had a "reasonable expectation of privacy."[13] The Burger Court limited the places in which privacy could be reasonably expected, allowing searches of moving cars stopped even for routine traffic infractions and of garbage cans set out for collection. The Burger Court authorized a "good faith" exception to the exclusionary rule, under which prosecutors may introduce evidence obtained illegally if they can show that the police had relied on a warrant that appeared valid but later proved to be invalid.[14] The Court allowed another exception for illegally gathered evidence that would have been discovered eventually without the illegal search.[15] The Rehnquist Court has gone well beyond these exceptions. In *Murray* v. *United States* (1988), it allowed prosecutors to use products of illegal searches if other evidence unrelated to the illegal evidence would have justified a search warrant. The combination of "good faith," "inevitable discovery," and "retroactive probable cause" has considerably narrowed the exclusionary rule.

The Rehnquist Court continued to narrow the exclusionary rule when it held in *Minnesota* v. *Carter* (1998) that an officer acting on a drug tip could peer through the gap in Venetian blinds to observe illegal activity without violating the Fourth Amendment. When the Court announced in *Wyoming* v. *Houghton* (1999) that police who have probable cause to search an automobile for illegal substances may also search personal possessions (in this case, a purse) of passengers in the car, the War on Drugs seemed to be trumping privacy. However, the Court also ruled that police could not search every driver or car involved in petty traffic offenses. Thus, a bag of marijuana discovered in a search incident to a speeding ticket in *Knowles* v. *Iowa* (1998) was excluded as the product of an illegal search. Moreover, the Court ruled in *Kyllo* v. *United States* (2001) that police could not use high-technology thermal devices to search through the walls of a house to check for the presence of high-intensity lights used for growing marijuana. Justice Scalia was especially incensed, saying in his opinion that to allow such searches "would leave the homeowner at the mercy of advancing technology. . . ." These four cases show that the fine-tuning of the "exclusionary rule" continues.

Self-Incrimination

Concerning the Fifth Amendment protection against self-incrimination, the Warren Court similarly waxed, the Burger Court waffled, and the Rehnquist Court waned. The Warren Court determined that the privilege not to be forced to incriminate oneself was useless at trial if the police coerced confessions long before the trial took place. To forestall "third-degree" tactics in the station house, the Court detailed a stringent set of procedural guarantees: the famous rights established in *Miranda* v. *Arizona* (1966). Once detained by authorities, all persons had to be informed of their rights to remain silent and to consult with an attorney. Although the Burger Court upheld *Miranda,* it allowed exceptions: It allowed the use of information obtained without "Mirandizing" suspects if the suspects took the stand in their own defense. It also allowed the use of information obtained without *Miranda* warnings if some immediate threat to public safety had justified immediate questioning and postponing warnings.[16] The Rehnquist Court has gone beyond these exceptions in holding that a coerced confession may be "harmless error" that does not constitute self-incrimination.[17] The main principle of the Miranda decision was upheld by the Rehnquist Court, however, in *Dickerson* v. *United States* (2000).

The Right to Counsel

The Sixth Amendment's right to counsel was nationalized—made binding on the states—in two landmark cases. In *Powell* v. *Alabama* (1932)—the famed Scottsboro Boys prosecution—the Court ruled that legal counsel must be supplied to all indigent defendants accused of a **capital crime** (any crime in which the death penalty can be imposed). Before this decision, many poor people in the southern states, especially African-Americans, had been tried for and convicted of capital crimes without the benefit of an attorney. Thirty-one years later, in *Gideon* v. *Wainwright* (1963), the Court ruled that defendants accused of any felony in state jurisdictions are entitled to a lawyer and that the states must supply a lawyer when a defendant cannot afford to do so. In this case, Clarence Earl Gideon asked for but was denied a lawyer in a Florida court where he was being tried for having broken into a poolhall. He conducted his own defense and lost. After years of study in his Florida prison's law library and the submission of numerous handwritten appeals to the courts to overturn his conviction, the Supreme Court finally agreed to hear his case, assigning the prominent attorney Abe Fortas (later a Supreme Court justice) to argue for Gideon. Justice Black wrote the following for a unanimous Court:

> Not only . . . precedents but also reason and reflection require us to recognize that in our adversary system of criminal justice, any person hauled into court, who is too poor to hire a lawyer, cannot be assured of a fair trial unless counsel is provided for him. This seems to be an obvious truth.

capital crime
Any crime for which death is a possible penalty.

The right to counsel for those accused of a felony crime was not binding on the states until 1963. Here, an attorney vigorously defends her clients in a Los Angeles court room.

The Court ordered a new trial. This time, assisted by a public defender supplied by the state of Florida, Gideon was acquitted. By incorporating the Sixth Amendment's guarantee of legal counsel, the Court has ensured that every criminal defendant in the United States can mount a defense regardless of socioeconomic status.

Capital Punishment   The Burger Court examined capital punishment under the Eighth Amendment's prohibition of "cruel and unusual punishment." In *Furman* v. *Georgia* (1972), a split Court found that the death penalty, as used, constituted "cruel and unusual punishment." Congress and 70 percent of the states passed new authorizations of the death penalty, most of which met the Court's objections with procedures to make the infliction of capital punishment less capricious. The Burger Court held that capital punishment was not inherently cruel or unusual in *Gregg* v. *Georgia* (1976). However, the Court tended to create an "obstacle course" of standards that the states had to meet if they wanted to use the death penalty. Basically, the Court insisted that defendants be given every opportunity to show mitigating circumstances so that as few convicts as possible would be killed.

Longman
Participate.com
2.0
Visual Literacy
**Race and the
Death Penalty**

The Rehnquist Court at first tried to expedite the use of the death penalty. (Some of the reasons are examined in the "Using the Framework" feature.) In *McCleskey* v. *Kemp* (1987), the Court chose to ignore statistical evidence that blacks who kill whites are four times more likely to be sentenced to death than whites who kill blacks. The Court insisted that individual defendants must show that racism played a role in their specific cases. In *Penry* v. *Lynaugh* (1989), the Court allowed the execution of a convicted murderer who had the intelligence of a 7-year-old. In *Stanford* v. *Kentucky* (1989), the Court allowed the execution of a minor who had been convicted of murder.

The Rehnquist Court has also limited avenues of appeal and delay in death penalty cases. In *McCleskey* v. *Zant* (1991), the Court made delays much less likely by eliminating many means of challenging capital convictions. In its 6–3 decision, the majority reached out to eliminate delays even though no party to the case had requested the Court to do so. In *Keeney* v. *Tamayo-Reyes* (1992), the Court limited the right of "death row" inmates convicted in state

courts to appeal to the Supreme Court. The Court is never entirely predictable, however. In *Wright* v. *West* (1992), it rejected Bush administration efforts to sharply restrict appeals by state prisoners to the federal courts.

The environment for the use of the death penalty became steadily more
favorable from the middle of the 1960s to the middle of the 1990s. The Court
removed most of the obstacles to its use, and public opinion swung solidly in
favor (see Figure 15.1). Given this context, it is hardly surprising, then, that
the number of people executed in the United States in 1999 reached its highest level (98) since 1976 when the Court reinstated the death penalty, with
Texas accounting for more than one-third of the total.[18]

Though still in favor of capital punishment in principle, the public and
many elected officials seem to be having second thoughts about how fairly it is
being used in practice (a Columbia University study reports that two of every
three capital convictions have been overturned on appeal since 1976). At least
a dozen state legislatures in 2002 were considering bills to place a moratorium on capital punishment, following action by Governor George Ryan of
Illinois, to test the fairness of trials and sentencing procedures. On January
31, 2000, Ryan stopped all executions in his state system because at least 13
men on death row in Illinois had been shown to have not committed the
crimes for which they were sentenced to death; most of the new evidence was
based on DNA. Governor Ryan claimed that he would maintain his moratorium until he could be certain that everyone on death row was truly guilty.

The early evidence suggests that Ryan and other advocates of reconsider-
ing the death penalty are having an impact; annual executions in 2001
dropped to 66,[19] and support for the death penalty among the public dropped
15 percentage points between 1994 and 2001. Most of the rethinking seems to
be based on rising concerns about executing the mentally retarded, the quality of legal defense for those accused of murder, the fairness of the system toward racial minorities, and the desire to see a wider use of DNA evidence.
Interestingly, several committed conservatives, including columnist George

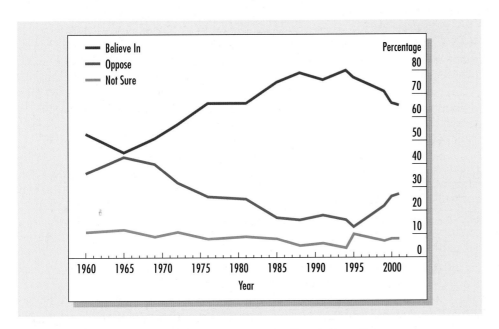

FIGURE 15.1 American Public Opinion on the Death Penalty

Question: Are you in favor of the death penalty for a person convicted of murder?
Source: The Gallup Poll, various years.

USING THE FRAMEWORK: The Death Penalty

Why was there a dramatic increase in executions in the 1990s?

Background: Between the reinstatement of the death penalty by the Supreme Court in 1976 and the end of 2001, 737 inmates were executed in the United States. Of that total, 619 (84 percent) took place in the 1990s. In 1999, 98 executions were carried out, the highest total since 1951, with Texas, Virginia, and Florida leading the way. Although a range of individuals and organizations have been fighting to end the use of the death penalty in the United States, their efforts have been strikingly unsuccessful until quite recently. We can understand better why this is so by looking broadly at how structural, political linkage, and governmental factors have influenced the death penalty issue.

Governmental Action

38 states allow use of the death penalty; of these, 30 have used it since 1976.

The pace of executions increased steadily during the 1990s, though it slowed in 2000 and 2001.

Governmental Level

- Since 1976, the Supreme Court has supported most state efforts to reinstate the death penalty and to limit the time and number of appeals for death-row inmates. →
- The Anti-Terrorism and Effective Death Penalty Act of 1996, passed by a Republican Congress and signed by Democratic president Bill Clinton, placed limits on the appeals process and hastened the execution of many inmates. →
- Elected on "get tough on crime" platforms, few governors responded favorably to requests for clemency in death penalty cases, though Gov. Ryan of Illinois imposed a moratorium in 2000.

Political Linkages Level

- Public opinion has strongly supported the principle of capital punishment. →
- Fear of crime among the public rose throughout the 1980s and 1990s, contributing to the supportive public climate for use of the death penalty; rising fear was a response to both a real increase in violent crime and to news media sensationalism. →
- In response to the public mood during this period, most candidates for elected office took a strong "tough on crime" approach. →
- Opponents of capital punishment were not successful in changing public or leadership attitudes.

Structural Level

- The Constitution leaves most of the responsibility for criminal statute writing, prosecution, and punishment to the states. →
- The Constitution prohibits "cruel and unusual punishment," but there is little evidence that the framers considered the death penalty, as such, "cruel and unusual." →
- The popular culture has long supported the death penalty. →
- Violent crime, much of it drug-related, increased during the 1970s, 1980s, and early part of the 1990s.

The execution by the state of Texas of born-again Christian and convicted murderer Karla Faye Tucker in February 1998 brought the issue of capital punishment to the forefront of network news, news magazines, radio talk shows, and newspapers across America. Tucker was the first woman executed in Texas since the Civil War.

Will and Christian conservative Pat Robertson, have expressed reservations about the death penalty.

Much to the surprise of seasoned observers, the Rehnquist Court began in 2002 to pull back from its unstinting and unqualified support for the death penalty. In *Atkins* v. *Virginia* (2002), the Court followed the lead of 18 states in banning the use of the death penalty for mentally retarded defendants saying, in Justice John Paul Stevens's majority opinion, that "a national consensus now rejects such executions as excessive and inappropriate . . ." and that "society views mentally retarded offenders as categorically less culpable than the average criminal." In *Ring* v. *Arizona* (2002), the Court overruled the death sentences of more than 160 convicted killers, declaring that only juries, and not judges, can decide on the use of the death penalty for those convicted of capital crimes. Taken together, these two Court decisions are likely, over the long term, to decrease the number of people executed each year in the United States.

Civil Liberties and the War on Terrorism

Wars encourage the flowering of patriotic sentiments and feelings of national unity. Wars also raise legitimate concerns about public safety and national security. Because of this, wars have almost always led to some restrictions on civil liberties in the United States, particularly for those who vocally dissent from the war effort and for those who seem to be associated with the enemy in one way or another.

The war on terrorism has also brought some civil liberties restrictions, mostly affecting non-citizens. How long these restrictions will remain in place and how widely they will be used in practice by the authorities will probably depend on the length of the war on terrorism, on whether additional terrorist attacks take place within the United States, and on the degree of public support for anti-terrorist measures. Though we are only in the early stages of the war against terrorism, civil libertarians—who include in their ranks not only the usual liberal suspects such as the ACLU, but also conservative libertarians such as the CATO Institute, former Congressman Bob Barr, and *New York Times* columnist William Safire—are already quite alarmed by developments. Here is what is in place at this writing:

- Under terms of the USA Patriot Act, the federal government has been given expanded powers to use wire-tapping and electronic surveillance; impose stricter penalties for harboring or financing terrorists; monitor the banking accounts and e-mail of suspect individuals and organizations; turn away from our borders anyone who endorses terrorism; and detain any non-citizens living in the United States whom the attorney general deems to be a threat to national security.

- A number of other actions have been taken under executive order. Perhaps most importantly, the president authorized the use of military tribunals to try any non-citizen, whether arrested here or abroad, suspected of being tied directly or indirectly to acts of terrorism against the United States. The president also authorized the detention of more than 600 people for questioning (without releasing their names or specification of crimes purported to have been committed); the questioning of more than 5,000 non-citizens of Middle Eastern and/or Muslim origins about terrorism; the tightening of visa restrictions on people from the Middle East; and surveillance of conversations between some suspected terrorists and their attorneys. The president also authorized the detention of American citizens discovered to have been fighting against U.S. troops in Afghanistan or aiding al Qaeda, calling them "enemy combatants."

The American people support most of the measures taken so far. Strong majorities say they favor the use of military tribunals, detention of terrorism suspects, restrictions on immigration from the Middle East and other Muslim countries, greater use of electronic surveillance, and more. Very large majorities also say that people who have expressed support for the attacks on the United States, or who take the position that terrorism is the fault of the United States, should not be allowed to teach in public schools or work for the government. Strong majorities express the opinion that government should be able to censor

Young male visitors from Arab countries are being scrutinized more intensely by the authorities since the start of war on terrorism. Here a Kuwaiti national is questioned by police after leaving an unattended bag at Miami International Airport.

the press on news related to the war. And, strong majorities say that, although they worry that government officials might go too far in their zeal to combat terrorism, they are willing to trade some civil liberties for greater security.[20]

On the brighter side for civil libertarians, the Bush administration drew back from some of its most extreme measures in the face of strong criticism. The rules for military tribunals, for example, were altered to approximate the protections of the military justice system, and, in many parts of the country, the process for interrogating Middle Eastern and Muslim men was made into a voluntary program. In a sharp rebuke to the administration, moreover, the Sixth Circuit Court ruled in 2002 that the government could not hold deportation hearings for Middle Eastern men behind closed doors. The Fourth Circuit Court ruled that American citizens being held as "enemy combatants" could not be indefinitely detained.

Longman
Participate.com
2.0
Comparative
**Comparing
Civil Liberties**

The direction that civil liberties will take as a result of the war on terrorism is hard to predict. All one can say with assurance at this point is that

HOW DEMOCRATIC ARE WE?

Civil Liberties and Democracy

PROPOSITION: One reason that democracy is alive and well in the United States is that civil liberties are so well developed and protected.

AGREE: Citizens of the United States live in the freest political society in the world. Powerful constraints prevent government from intruding upon people's ability to believe what they want and to exercise their rights of free expression, association, and petition. Although government has violated several of these rights in the past, political practices and Supreme Court decisions have greatly expanded the domain of political freedom in the current era and made violation of basic civil liberties unlikely in the future.

DISAGREE: Although civil liberties today are fairly well protected against intrusions by government, not all people have the capacities and resources to use their liberties effectively. All Americans may enjoy freedom of expression as a formal right, for example, but only a handful can make their voices heard in an effective way. Thus, only a privileged few can make campaign contributions, form political lobbying organizations, and run ads for their favorite candidates, parties, and issues.

THE AUTHORS: It is important to recognize that the freedoms of speech, association, press, conscience, and religion are far more extensively developed and protected in the United States today than they were in the past. There has, in fact, been an enormous expansion of freedom in the United States. However, we must also recognize two "flies in the ointment," as it were. First, the "disagree" position cannot be easily evaded. While formal freedom is available to virtually all Americans, the actual use of several of our civil liberties requires resources that are not available to all. Thus, substantial income and wealth inequality in the United States often creates political inequality. Second, we cannot say with total confidence that freedom cannot and will not be violated by government in the future. Waves of hysteria in the past among political leaders and citizens have led to the violation of civil liberties; given the right conditions— say, war, civil unrest, economic depression—the same might happen again. The war on terrorism may represent just such a setting for the suppression of civil liberties. We can only hope that such a thing will not happen and that people will struggle for democracy if it does.

some restrictions will exist for the duration of the war and that their severity will be directly related to the degree to which the American people continue to support these and other civil liberties restrictions.

Summary

The formal foundation of American liberties is found in the Constitution and its amendments, particularly the Bill of Rights and the Fourteenth Amendment, but their actual enjoyment depends on the actions of courts, the behavior of government officials, and the struggle for democracy. American history has witnessed an expansion of the boundaries of liberties, especially during the twentieth century, although much remains to be done.

During the nineteenth century, the Supreme Court concerned itself mainly with rights to property. Somewhat belatedly, it nationalized the constitutional protection of civil liberties (that is, made them applicable to the states) by using the Fourteenth Amendment as its main instrument. The familiar liberties of expression, association, press, and religion, as well as certain due process protections for the accused, were gradually incorporated and guaranteed throughout the nation. The expansion of the rights of the accused was always a hotly disputed political issue, and the conservative orientation of the present Court has resulted in the reversal of many of the due process innovations of the Warren and Burger Courts.

The war on terrorism has resulted in restrictions on the civil liberties of non-citizens living in the United States. How long these restrictions remain in place will depend on the severity and duration of the war on terrorism.

Suggestions for Further Reading

Abraham, Henry J., and Barbara A. Perry. *Freedom and the Court,* 7th ed. New York: Oxford University Press, 1998.
  A trusted introduction to the study of civil rights and liberties for 25 years.

Hentoff, Nat. *Free Speech for Me . . . but Not for Thee: How the American Left and Right Relentlessly Censor Each Other.* New York: HarperPerennial, 1992.
  A disturbing survey of efforts across the nation by both the right and left to censor speech and publications they do not like.

Irons, Peter. *The Courage of Their Convictions.* New York: Free Press, 1988.
  Brief histories of U.S. Supreme Court cases involved in the struggle for civil rights and civil liberties since 1940.

Lane, Rovet Wheeler. *Beyond the Schoolhouse Gate: Free Speech and the Inculcation of Values.* Philadelphia: Temple University Press, 1995.
  A response, based on educational and constitutional grounds, to those who would censor students in public schools.

Sarat, Austin. *When the State Kills: Capital Punishment and the American Condition.* Princeton, NJ: Princeton University Press, 2001.
  A passionate yet scholarly call for the end of the death penalty; argues that the death penalty undermines democracy.

Walker, Samuel. *In Defense of American Liberties: A History of the ACLU.* New York: Oxford University Press, 1990.
  A comprehensive review of the American Civil Liberties Union, highlighting most major battles for civil liberties in the twentieth century.

Internet Sources

First Amendment Cyber-Tribune   **http://w3.trib.com/FACT/index.html**
This site is so complete and well organized that it is the only one recommended in this chapter. This gateway is concerned with each of the First Amendment freedoms discussed in this chapter and provides links for each freedom to background documents, court cases, breaking news, op-ed pieces, bibliographies, First Amendment Websites, civil liberties organizations, and even an online question-and-answer section.

Notes

1. The first two examples were cited in George F. Will, "Compassion on Campus," *Newsweek* (May 31, 1993), p. 66.

2. Kenneth Lasson, "Political Correctness," *Tennessee Law Review* 63 (Spring, 1996), p. 32.

3. Diana Jean Schemo, "New Battles in Old War Over Freedom of Speech," *The New York Times* (November 21, 2001), p. B6.

4. Nat Hentoff, "Chilling Codes," *The Washington Post,* Nexis: LEGI-SLATE Article No. 225/226.

5. Laurence H. Tribe, *American Constitutional Law,* 2nd ed. (Mineola, NY: Cornell Law Foundation, 1988), ch. 9.

6. Morton J. Horwitz, *The Transformation of American Law, 1780–1860* (Cambridge, MA: Harvard University Press, 1977); J. Willard Hurst, *Law and the Conditions of Freedom in the Nineteenth-Century United States* (Madison, WI: University of Wisconsin Press, 1956).

7. Robert A. Dahl, "Decision-Making in a Democracy: The Supreme Court as National Policy-Maker," *Journal of Public Law* 6 (1967), pp. 279–295.

8. Samuel Walker, *In Defense of American Liberties: A History of the ACLU* (New York: Oxford University Press, 1990).

9. Richard Morin, "The High Price of Free Speech," *The Washington Post Weekly Edition* (January 8–14, 2001), p. 34.

10. See Stanley I. Kutler, *The American Inquisition: Justice and Injustice in the Cold War* (New York: Hill & Wang, 1982).

11. See Fred W. Friendly, *Minnesota Rag* (New York: Vintage, 1981).

12. See Charles Rembar, *The End of Obscenity* (New York: Harper & Row, 1968).

13. *Katz* v. *United States* (1967).

14. *United States* v. *Leon* (1984); *Massachusetts* v. *Sheppard* (1984).

15. *Nix* v. *Williams* (1984).

16. *Harris* v. *New York* (1971); *New York* v. *Quarles* (1984).

17. *Arizona* v. *Fulminate* (1991).

18. Jim Yardley, "A Role Model for Executions," *The New York Times* (January 9, 2000), p. A1, IV–5.

19. Jim Yardley, "Number of Executions Falls for Second Year in a Row," *The New York Times* (December 13, 2001), p. A13.

20. "Security Trumps Civil Liberties," a report of a poll conducted by National Public Radio, the Kennedy School of Government of Harvard University, and the Kaiser Family Fund, November 30, 2001.

Chapter 16
Civil Rights: The Struggle for Political Equality

In This Chapter

- Why civil rights are important in a democracy
- Civil rights in the Constitution
- How civil rights protections expanded
- The present status of civil rights protections for racial minorities, women, and gays and lesbians

From Martin Luther King to Louis Farrakhan

On August 28, 1963, approximately half a million people converged on the Lincoln Memorial in Washington, D.C., to urge passage of the civil rights bill then being considered by Congress. The gathering was predominantly African-American, but a substantial number of whites were there as well to lend support. The crowd was festive and optimistic. Most who were there believed that Congress had no choice but to pass the civil rights bill because Americans were now ready to accept a fully integrated society without significant barriers to black and white cooperation or to black advancement and equality. The mood of the historic "March on Washington"

was perfectly captured by Dr. Martin Luther King Jr. in his memorable "I Have a Dream" speech.

Three decades later, between 800,000 and 900,000 African-American men gathered in front of the U.S. Capitol building on a beautiful October day in 1995 in response to a call from Louis Farrakhan, the leader of the Nation of Islam. His "Million Man March" was designed, he said, to encourage self-reliance and responsibility among African-American men. Although few of the attendees said they supported Farrakhan's overall program of racial separatism, anti-Semitism, and hostility to gays and lesbians, three aspects of the event were striking: that so many people responded to the call of a man long regarded as being on the extreme "black nationalist" fringe of American politics, that traditional civil rights organizations had not displayed for many years an equivalent ability to mobilize the African-American population, and that women and white men were conspicuously absent on the speakers' platform and in the crowd.

The Million Man March, with its sometimes harsh separatist temper, reflected the uncertain climate for civil rights in the nation as a whole in the mid-1990s compared with the headier times of the mid-1960s. Long gone was the biracial political coalition that had achieved passage of the 1964 Civil Rights Act and the 1965 Voting Rights Act. Also gone was the optimism among many people about the future of race relations and the possibilities for an integrated society that had propelled the civil rights movement. In its place stood racial polarization and isolation and competing visions of what civil rights policies might be most appropriate for the future.

That the racial climate had changed was not in question. In 1994, Republicans swept to a stunning victory in congressional elections, running on a "Contract with America" platform that was silent on the need to make further advances in the area of racial justice and filled with promises that most observers believed would adversely affect African-Americans: cuts in a wide range of social programs, punitive anti-crime measures, and termination of federal entitlement programs such as Aid to Families with Dependent Children. In 1995, Governor Pete Wilson convinced the Regents of the University of California to end all affirmative action programs in the statewide university system. In 1996, President Clinton ordered a broad review of federal affirmative action programs after the Supreme Court ruled in *Adarand Construction* v. *Peña* (1995) that it would subject affirmative action to strict scrutiny (i.e., presume such programs to be unconstitutional unless a compelling government interest could be demonstrated). Also in 1996, California voters approved Proposition 209 to end all government affirmative action programs in the state (which the Supreme Court later approved). Voters in the state of Washington followed suit in 1998.

Civil rights are government guarantees of political equality—the promise of equal treatment by government of all citizens and equal citizenship for all Americans. Civil rights became a more prominent part of the American agenda as democracy itself became more widely accepted in the United States. Because most formal barriers to equal participation in political life have been used to exclude particular groups of people (women, various ethnic groups, and racial minorities), civil rights initiatives over the years have been directed at removing group barriers and helping groups overcome the disadvantages created by past discrimination.

The expansion of civil rights protections for African-Americans, as well as for other racial, ethnic, and religious minorities and for women, is one of the great achievements of American history. This expansion did not come easily or quickly; it took the struggle of millions of Americans to force change from political leaders and government institutions. But change happened, and the result has been the enrichment of American democracy. As this opening vignette suggests, however, the expansion of civil rights protection in the United States is neither complete nor free of problems and controversy.   ■

Thinking Critically About This Chapter

Using the Framework   In this chapter, you will see that the meaning of civil rights has changed over the course of American history and you will learn how structural, political linkage, and governmental factors, taken together, explain that change.

Longman
Participate.com
2.0
Comparative
**Comparing
Civil Rights**

Using the Democracy Standard   In this chapter, you will learn how civil rights is at the very center of our understanding of democracy in the United States. You will see, on the one hand, how the struggle for democracy helped expand civil rights protections. You will see, on the other hand, how the expansion of civil rights has enhanced formal political equality in the United States, one of the basic foundations of a democratic political order.   ◄

Civil Rights Before the Twentieth Century

Concern about civil rights protections for women and racial minorities was a comparatively late development in the United States, and most major advances were not evident until well into the twentieth century.

An Initial Absence of Civil Rights

Neither the original Constitution nor the Bill of Rights said anything about political equality beyond insisting that all Americans are equally entitled to due process in the courts. Indeed, the word *equality* does not appear in the Constitution at all. Nor did state constitutions offer much in the way of guaranteeing citizenship equality other than equality before the law. Americans in the late eighteenth and early nineteenth centuries seemed more interested in protecting individuals against government (see Chapter 15) than in guaranteeing certain political rights through government.[1] For most racial or ethnic minorities and women, political equality eluded constitutional protection until the twentieth century, although the groundwork was laid earlier.

The political inequality of African-Americans and women before the Civil War is apparent. In the South, African-Americans lived in slavery, with no rights at all. Outside the South, although a few states allowed African-Americans to vote, the number of states doing so actually declined as the Civil War approached, even as universal white male suffrage was spreading. In many places outside the slave South, African-Americans were denied entry into certain occupations, required to post bonds guaranteeing their good

Many African-Americans took an active role in fighting for their civil rights before emancipation. Free blacks helped organize the Underground Railroad to smuggle slaves out of the South.

behavior, denied the right to sit on juries, and occasionally threatened and harassed by mobs when they tried to vote or to petition the government. Chief Justice Roger Taney, in *Dred Scott* v. *Sandford* (1857), went so far as to claim that the Founders believed that blacks had no rights that whites or government were bound to honor or respect. As for women, no state allowed them to vote, few allowed them to sit on juries, and a handful even denied them the right to own property or enter into contracts.

Many African-Americans and women refused to play a passive political role, however, even though the pre–Civil War period was not conducive to their participation in politics. African-Americans, for instance, voted in elections where they were allowed, helped organize the Underground Railroad to smuggle slaves out of the South, and were prominent in the abolitionist movement against slavery. Both black and white women played an important role in the abolitionist movement—the antislavery speaking tours of Angelina and Sarah Grimké caused something of a scandal in the 1840s when women's participation in public affairs was considered improper—and a few began to write extensively on the need for women's emancipation and legal and political equality. In 1848,

In 1848, Elizabeth Cady Stanton helped organize the Seneca Falls Convention on women's rights. The resulting Declaration of Sentiments and Resolutions was patterned after the Declaration of Independence, stating that "all men and women are created equal," and included a list of the injustice of men against women.

Elizabeth Cady Stanton issued her call for a convention on women's rights to be held at the village of Seneca Falls, New York. The Declaration of Sentiments and Resolutions issued by the delegates to the convention stands as one of the landmarks in women's struggle for political equality in the United States:

> *All men and women are created equal . . . but the history of mankind is a history of repeated injuries and usurpations on the part of man toward woman, having in direct object the establishment of a direct tyranny over her. . . . [We demand] that women have immediate admission to all the rights and privileges which belong to them as citizens of the United States.*

The Civil War Amendments

After the Civil War, the Thirteenth Amendment to the Constitution outlawed slavery throughout the United States, settling the most divisive issue of the nineteenth century. The Fourteenth Amendment reversed *Dred Scott* by making all people who are born or naturalized in the United States, black or white, citizens both of the United States and of the states in which they reside. To secure the rights and liberties of recently freed slaves, Article I of the amendment further provided that "no State shall make or enforce any law which shall abridge the privileges or immunities of citizens of the United States" (the *privileges and immunities clause*); "nor shall any State deprive any person of life, liberty, or property, without due process of law" (the *due process clause*); "nor deny to any person within its jurisdiction the equal protection of the laws" (the *equal protection clause*). The Fifteenth Amendment guaranteed African-American men the right to vote. Imposing as this constitutional language sounds, the Supreme Court would soon transform it into a protection for property rights, but not for African-Americans or women.

Undermining the Civil War Amendments
The privileges and immunities clause was rendered virtually meaningless by the *Slaughterhouse Cases* (1873). Writing for the Court, Justice Samuel Miller found that the clause protected only the rights of citizens of the United States as citizens and not rights that were the responsibility of states. In these cases, the Court denied citizens protection against abuses by state governments, including African-Americans disfranchised by state actions. Within five years of its passage, then, the Fourteenth Amendment had been seriously compromised by the Court, which foiled an attempt by the post–Civil War Radical Republican Congress to amend the Constitution in favor of equality.

The equal protection clause survived the *Slaughterhouse Cases* but soon lost all practical meaning. First, the Court said that the Fourteenth Amendment gave Congress no power to prohibit discrimination unless it was practiced by state government. "Equal protection of the laws" did not, therefore, preclude race discrimination by private owners or managers of restaurants, theaters, hotels, and other public accommodations, the Court said in the *Civil Rights Cases* (1883). Then the Court made even state-sponsored discrimination constitutional in *Plessy* v. *Ferguson* (1896). The Court said that the states could separate the races in intrastate railways if they provided "equal" facilities for the races. This doctrine of "separate but equal" would provide the legal foundation for **Jim Crow** segregation in the South and would remain in force until it was overturned in *Brown* v. *Board of Education of Topeka* more than half a century later.

The Fifteenth Amendment's voting guarantees were rendered ineffectual by a variety of devices invented to prevent African-Americans from voting in the former states of the Confederacy. The **poll tax** was a tax required of all voters in many states, and it kept many African-Americans away from the polls. Even a

Jim Crow

Popular term for the system of legal racial segregation that existed in the American South until the middle of the twentieth century.

poll tax

A tax to be paid as a condition of voting; used in the South to keep African-Americans away from the polls.

small tax was a heavy burden for many to bear, given the desperate economic situation of African-Americans in the South in the late nineteenth and early twentieth centuries. Several states required voters to pass a **literacy test** devised and administered by local officials (see Table 16.1). The evaluation of test results was entirely up to local officials, who rarely passed blacks, even those with a college education or a Ph.D. degree. If white voters failed the literacy test, many states allowed them to vote anyway under the **grandfather clause,** which provided that anyone whose grandfather had been a voter could vote as well. Since the grandfathers of African-Americans in the South had been slaves, the grandfather clause was no help to them at all. Several states instituted **white primaries** that excluded African-Americans from the process of nominating candidates for local, state, and national offices. The states based these primaries on the argument that political parties were private clubs that could define their own membership requirements, including skin color. For those African-Americans who might try to vote anyway in the face of the poll tax, the literacy test, and the white primary, there was always the use of terror as a deterrent: Night riding, bombings, and lynchings were used with regularity, especially during times when blacks showed signs of assertiveness.

The statutory devices for keeping African-Americans away from the polls were consistently supported by state and federal courts until well into the twentieth century. Terror remained a factor until the 1960s, when the civil rights movement and federal intervention finally put an end to it.

literacy test

A device used by the southern states to prevent African-Americans from voting before the passage of the Voting Rights Act of 1965, which banned its use; usually involved interpretation of a section of a state's constitution.

grandfather clause

A device that allowed whites who had failed the literacy test to vote anyway by extending the franchise to anyone whose grandfather had voted.

white primaries

Primary elections open only to whites.

TABLE 16.1 Selected Items from the Alabama Literacy Test

1. A person appointed to the U.S. Supreme Court is appointed for a term of _____ .

2. If a person is indicted for a crime, name two rights which he has.

3. Cases tried before a court of law are of what two types: civil and _____ .

4. If no candidate for president receives a majority of the electoral vote, who decides who will become president?

5. If no person receives a majority of the electoral vote, the vice president is chosen by the Senate. True or False?

6. If an effort to impeach the President of the U.S. is made, who presides at the trial?

7. If the two houses of Congress do not agree to adjournment, who sets the time?

8. A president elected in November takes office the following year on what date?

9. Of the original thirteen states, the one with the largest representation in the first Congress was _____ .

10. The Constitution limits the size of the District of Columbia to _____ .

These 10 questions are part of the 68-question Alabama Literacy Test used to decide on the eligibility of voters in that state. The test and others like it were declared illegal by the 1965 Voting Rights Act. Most white voters who were unable to pass this or similar tests in the states of the Deep South were protected by a "grandfather clause" allowing people to vote whose grandfathers had done so.

ANSWERS: (1) good behavior: life (2) jury trial, protection against self incrimination, right to counsel, speedy trial, protection against excessive bail (3) criminal (4) the House of Representatives (5) true (6) though not stipulated in the Constitution, the House has always turned to its Judiciary Committee to manage the impeachment process (7) no one; XXth Amendment says they would automatically adjourn on January 3 of the following year (8) January 20 (9) Virginia (10) not to exceed ten square miles.

Lynching was used as a tool well into the twentieth century to intimidate African-Americans and keep them from pressing too hard for equal citizenship, mainly in the Deep South, but also at times in other states. This lynching took place in Marion, Indiana, in 1930.

Women and the Fifteenth Amendment   Stung by the exclusion of women from the Fifteenth Amendment's extension of the right to vote to African-Americans—the amendment said only that no state could exclude people on the grounds of "race, color, or previous condition of servitude"—politically active women turned their attention to winning the vote for women. Once the Supreme Court had decided, in *Minor* v. *Happersett* (1874), that women's suffrage was not a right inherent in the national citizenship guarantees of the Fourteenth Amendment, women abandoned legal challenges based on their inferior political position and turned to more direct forms of political agitation: petitions, marches, and protests. After many years of struggle, the efforts of the women's suffrage movement bore fruit in the Nineteenth Amendment, ratified in 1920: "The right of citizens of the United States to vote shall not be denied or abridged by the United States or by any State on account of sex."

The Contemporary Status of Civil Rights

strict scrutiny

The assumption that actions by elected bodies or officials violate constitutional rights.

We saw in Chapter 15 how the Supreme Court, using the guidelines written by Justice Harlan Fiske Stone in *United States* v. *Carolene Products Company* (1938), gradually extended the protections of the Bill of Rights to the states, based on the Fourteenth Amendment. Recall that among the actions by the states that would trigger **strict scrutiny** under the *Carolene* guidelines were those that either "restricted the democratic process" or "discriminated against racial, ethnic, or religious minorities." This reading of the Fourteenth Amendment, particularly the equal protection clause, lent judicial support to the gradual advance of civil rights guarantees for African-Americans and other minorities and eventually (though less so) for women. In the following sections, we look at the extension of the civil rights of racial minorities, women, and other groups. Here we concentrate mainly (although not exclusively) on Supreme Court decisions (see Chapter 8 for more information on the civil rights, women's, and other movements).

Civil Rights for Racial Minorities

Two basic issues have dominated the story of the extension of civil rights since the mid-1960s:

- The ending of legally sanctioned discrimination, separation, and exclusion from citizenship.
- The debate over what actions to take to remedy the past wrongs done to minority groups.

We examine both in this section.

The End of "Separate but Equal" We reviewed earlier how the Constitution was long interpreted to condone slavery and segregation. In the twentieth century, however, the legal and political battles waged by the civil rights movement eventually pushed the Supreme Court, the president, and Congress to take seriously the equal protection clause of the Fourteenth Amendment.

In 1944, amid World War II (a war aimed in great part at bringing down the racist regime of Adolf Hitler) and the NAACP's campaign to rid the nation of segregation, the Supreme Court finally declared that race was a **suspect classification** that demanded strict judicial scrutiny. This meant that any state or national enactment using racial criteria was presumed to be unconstitutional.

Pressed by the legal efforts of the NAACP, the Court gradually chipped away at *Plessy* and the edifice of segregation. In *Smith* v. *Allwright* (1944), the Court declared that the practice of excluding nonwhites from political-party primary elections was unconstitutional. Then the Court ruled that the states' practice of providing separate all-white and all-black law schools was unacceptable. Many of the key cases before the Supreme Court that eroded the official structure of segregation were argued by Thurgood Marshall—later a justice of the Supreme Court—for the NAACP.[2]

Longman
Participate.com
2.0
Timeline
The Struggle for Equal Protection

suspect classification

The invidious, arbitrary, or irrational designation of a group for special treatment by government.

The erosion of official segregation in education came slowly and reluctantly in many parts of the nation. When ordered by a federal court in 1948 to admit a qualified black applicant, the University of Oklahoma law school did so but forced the lone student to sit separated from other students.

Thurgood Marshall was one of the nation's preeminent civil rights lawyers who argued some of the most important civil rights cases of the twentieth century before the Supreme Court. Eventually, he became a justice of the Supreme Court.

The great legal breakthrough for racial equality came in *Brown* v. *Board of Education of Topeka* (1954), also argued by Thurgood Marshall, in which a unanimous Court declared that "separate but equal" was inherently contradictory and that segregation was constitutionally unacceptable in public schools. *Brown* was a constitutional revolution, destined to transform racial relations law and practices in the United States.

The white South did not react violently at first, but it did not desegregate either. Once recognition spread that the Court was going to enforce civil rights, however, massive resistance to racial integration gripped the South. This resistance was what Dr. Martin Luther King Jr. and others had to work (and die) to overcome. The Court—even with many follow-up cases—was able to accomplish little before the president and Congress backed up the justices with the 1964 Civil Rights Act and the 1965 Voting Rights Act. These legislative actions were forced by the civil rights movement and supportive changes in American public opinion.

The drive to protect the rights of racial minorities has occupied the nation ever since. The main legal doctrine on racial discrimination is straightforward: Any use of race in law or government regulations to discriminate will trigger strict scrutiny (a presumption of unconstitutionality) by the courts. Recall from our earlier discussion that a state or the federal government can defend its acts under strict scrutiny only if it can produce a *compelling* government interest for which the act in question is a *necessary* means. Almost no law survives this challenge; laws that discriminate on the basis of race are dead from the moment of passage. Needless to say, other racial minority groups in addition to African-Americans—Hispanics, Asian-Americans, and Native Americans—have benefited from the constitutional revolution that has occurred.

To say that racial discrimination in the law is no longer constitutionally acceptable does not mean that racial discrimination has disappeared from the United States. A recent Washington Post/Kaiser Foundation/Harvard University poll reports, for example, that more than one-third of African-Americans and more than one-in-five Latino and Asian men have experienced job discrimination. Overwhelming majorities of African-Americans, Latinos, and Asians say they have been subject to poor service in stores and restaurants because of their race, and have had disparaging remarks directed at them.[3] All minorities report bad experiences with racial profiling by police. In the same poll reported above, for example, 52 percent of black men and 25 percent of Latino and Asian men claim to have been unfairly stopped by police. Though various police departments have taken steps to stop these practices, the courts have never defined racial profiling as suspect, especially if some important law enforcement need is being met by it. This has become increasingly relevant to Arab Americans who find that they have become objects of suspicion and the targets of law enforcement attention in the wake of the September 11 terrorist attacks on the United States.

Affirmative Action Constitutional interpretation now protects racial minorities against discrimination that is sanctioned or protected by law or government action. The issues are not as clear-cut, however, in the area of government actions that *favor* racial minorities (and women) in **affirmative action** programs designed to rectify past wrongs.[4]

affirmative action

Programs of private and public institutions favoring minorities and women in hiring and in admissions to colleges and universities in an attempt to compensate for past discrimination.

Origins The main goal of the civil rights movement of the 1950s and 1960s was to remove barriers to equal citizenship for black Americans. President Lyndon Johnson, Robert Kennedy, and Martin Luther King Jr., among others, eventually came to believe that the advancement of black Americans would require more; namely, a broad societal effort to eradicate poverty by equipping the poor, black and white, with the tools for success. This led to the founding of the Johnson administration's Great Society and War on Poverty and programs such as Head Start. After King's assassination, however, many people in government, the media, higher education, and the major foundations began to support the notion that racial progress would happen only if government encouraged racial preferences in hiring, contracts, and college admissions.

Somewhat surprisingly, it was Richard Nixon, not generally thought of as a booster of civil rights, who took the most important step, requiring in his 1969 Philadelphia Plan that construction companies with federal contracts and the associated construction trade unions hire enough blacks and other minorities to achieve "racial balance" (a proportion roughly equal to the racial balance in the community). Most civil rights organizations opposed the plan, believing that it violated basic civil rights principles and would drive a wedge between African-Americans and whites in the labor unions (which it eventually did). When the Philadelphia Plan reached the

Web Exploration
The Continuing Struggle for Equality

Issue: The content of the civil rights agenda today has broadened significantly.

Site: Access the Leadership Conference on Civil Rights on our Website at **www.ablongman.com/greenberg**. Go to the "Web Explorations" section for Chapter 16. Select "The Continuing Struggle. . . ," then the "civil rights agenda." On the left side, select "civil rights issues."

What You've Learned: Examine the list of issues that the Leadership Conference, a broad coalition of civil rights organizations, considers to be important. From this list, do an analysis of what the most important remaining issues are on the national civil rights agenda. Which do you consider to be most important?

HINT: One of the most interesting developments in American politics over the past several decades has been the transformation of many conventional political issues into "rights" issues.

Dr. Martin Luther King Jr. waves to the March on Washington crowd at the Lincoln Memorial after delivering his "I Have a Dream" speech. This event, one of the high points of the civil rights movement, helped convince Congress to pass the Civil Rights Act of 1964.

House of Representatives in 1970, Republicans supported it by a margin of 124–41, while Democrats opposed it, 115–84. The two parties soon switched positions on the issue, however. Nixon himself disavowed it in 1972 when he ordered federal agencies to avoid the use of quotas; meanwhile, the Democrats embraced the principle of racial preferences in their platform at the 1972 party convention.

Although initially skeptical of racial preferences, Justices William Brennan, Byron White, Thurgood Marshall, and Harry Blackmun supported temporary programs to remedy the effects of past discrimination. Joined by Justice Lewis Powell, they formed the majority in *Regents* v. *Bakke* (1978), in which the Court authorized a compromise on affirmative action programs. The Constitution and federal law prohibited employers and admissions committees from using strictly racial quotas, the Court said, but it saw no problem with the use of race as one factor among several in hiring or admissions.

Since *Bakke,* government and higher education racial preference programs have become relatively permanent rather than temporary, and their aim has shifted from providing remedies for past discrimination to enhancing diversity. The proliferation of diversity programs, diversity training, and diversity offices has become commonplace in colleges and universities, in government, and in the corporate world.

Why Affirmative Action?   According to proponents, affirmative action programs in government and education that promote diversity are needed for the following reasons:

- The effects of past discrimination disadvantage, to one degree or another, all members of discriminated-against groups, so simply removing barriers to advancement is insufficient. The proper remedy is to prefer members of such groups in hiring, contracts, and education until such time as they reach parity with the majority.

- In a diverse society such as the United States, tolerance and a sense of community can develop only if we work together in educational, workplace, and government institutions that are diverse.

- People from disadvantaged and discriminated-against groups will improve themselves only if they have experience with successful role models in important institutions.

Critics of affirmative action are not convinced by these arguments. They believe the following to be true:

- Affirmative action violates one of the most basic American principles: that people be judged, rewarded, and punished as individuals, not because they are members of one group or another.

- Affirmative action benefits those within each preferred group who are already advantaged and need little help. Thus, the main beneficiaries of affirmative action in higher education have been middle-class African-Americans, not the poor.

- Affirmative action seeks to remedy the effects of past discrimination by discriminating against others today simply because they belong to non-preferred groups.

- Affirmative action increases intergroup and interracial tension by heightening the saliency of group membership. That is, social friction is increased by encouraging people to think of themselves and others as members of groups and to seek group advantages in a zero-sum game in which one group's gain is another group's loss.

Public Opinion   In the court of public opinion, the critics of the "preferential treatment" form of affirmative action seem to have won the day. In survey after survey, a vast majority of Americans approve of the diversity goals of affirmative action—special programs to help those who have been discriminated against get ahead; outreach programs to hire minority workers and find minority students—but disapprove of racial preferences in hiring, awarding of government contracts, and admission to colleges.[5] Most polling organizations show the following pattern: When asked whether they generally support affirmative action, about 60 to 65 percent of Americans say they approve; when the survey asks whether they favor affirmative action programs that involve preferential treatment or "set-asides" for racial minorities and women, support erodes dramatically. It is no wonder, then, that a *New York Times*/CBS News poll in late 1997 reported that 68 percent of Americans wanted these kinds of programs either fundamentally changed or eliminated.[6]

To many proponents of affirmative action, this is simply a reflection of the enduring racism of Americans. People oppose affirmative action, in this view, because they are hostile to racial minorities. Political scientists Paul Sniderman and Edward Carmines suggest otherwise. In a series of ingenious studies reported in their book *Reaching Beyond Race,* they set out to unravel the roots of opposition to affirmative action. Their conclusion is that while some people oppose these programs because of their racist attitudes, most do so because they believe that affirmative action is fundamentally unfair and contrary to American values.[7] Judging, rewarding, and punishing people not as individuals but as members of groups does not seem right to many Americans. We can see this in the fact, as sociologist Seymour Martin Lipset reported after examining a wide range of surveys on the issue, that a majority of women and Hispanic-Americans, not just white males, oppose affirmative action programs as presently constituted.[8]

The position of the public on affirmative action, expressed in surveys and in elections, has obviously affected public policies, with affirmative action in retreat in most states and in Washington, D.C. The role of the Supreme Court has been especially notable in this regard.

Affirmative action programs are increasingly in jeopardy in the United States. Here students protest the decision of the University of California Board of Regents to end affirmative action in admissions to the university.

The Supreme Court's Turnabout on Affirmative Action Recently, the Supreme Court has been taking the position that laws that are not colorblind be subject to strict scrutiny. In *Wygant* v. *Jackson Board of Education* (1986) and *Richmond* v. *Croson Co.* (1989), the Supreme Court said that programs that narrowly redress specific violations will be upheld as constitutional but that broader affirmative action programs that address society's racism will be struck down. In *Adarand Constructors* v. *Peña* (1995), the Court ruled by a 5–4 majority that the federal government must abide by the strict standards for affirmative action programs imposed on the states in the *Richmond* case and could not award contracts using race as the main criterion. In *Miller* v. *Johnson* (1995), the Court ruled, again by a 5–4 majority, that race could not be used as the basis for drawing House district lines in an effort to increase the number of racial minority members in Congress. The Court also refused to overturn a Fifth Circuit Court ruling that race cannot be considered at all in admissions decisions at the University of Texas Law School, putting the *Bakke* principle in jeopardy. In 1997, the Court refused to overturn a ruling of the Ninth Circuit Court that California's anti-affirmative action Proposition 209 was constitutionally permissible. (See the "Using the Framework" feature.) In 2001, the Court let stand a decision by the 11th U.S. Circuit Court of Appeals that disallowed a Fulton County, Georgia, program setting annual goals for awarding county contracts to blacks, Hispanics, Asians, Native Americans, and women.

Here is where affirmative action programs stand at the present time:

- Any program that is based on race is subject to "strict scrutiny"—that is, considered unconstitutional unless some compelling reason for the program is proved.

- With respect to the award of government contracts and government hiring, affirmative action programs are acceptable only if they are narrowly tailored to rectify past discriminatory actions by that particular government agency. In the view of the Court, rectifying past racist

USING THE FRAMEWORK: Affirmative Action

Why have the federal courts been cutting back affirmative action programs?

Background: In 1997, the Supreme Court refused to overturn the ruling of the Ninth Circuit Court of Appeals that upheld the constitutionality of California's Proposition 209 ending affirmative action programs in the state. The behavior of the Court can be better understood by examining how structural, political linkage, and governmental factors interacted to influence this outcome.

Governmental Action

The Supreme Court turns down the appeal of opponents of California Proposition 209.

Governmental Level

- Republican presidents Reagan and Bush nominated conservatives to the Court. → • The Senate approved the nominees. → • A narrow but firm conservative majority under the leadership of Chief Justice William Rehnquist controls the Court on many issues.

Political Linkages Level

- The Christian conservative movement and other conservative organizations—who are against affirmative action—gained political influence in the 1980s. → • Republicans, whose platform rejects affirmative action, reached parity with Democrats in national elections. → • Republicans won control of the Senate from 1981–1986 and from 1995 to 2000.

- The political influence of civil rights organizations declined in the 1980s and 1990s. → • The majority white population reports in polls that it believes the goals of the civil rights movement have been met. → • A substantial majority of Americans report support for nondiscrimination laws but distaste for laws that give minorities and women special advantages in college admissions, jobs, and government contracts.

Structural Level

- The Fourteenth Amendment's promise of "equal protection of the laws" clearly bars government discrimination against groups of citizens but is unclear about the need for remedies for past discrimination. → • The political culture honors individual rather than group rights and responsibilities. → • The white middle and working classes suffered economic reverses during the 1980s and early 1990s, creating a climate that was generally hostile to affirmative action programs.

actions by a particular government agency is a compelling reason. Such programs, however, must be temporary efforts to transcend past practices and not a permanent feature of hiring and contracting. Affirmative action is not valid if it is designed simply to increase diversity or to decrease racism in society.

- With respect to admission to educational institutions—into undergraduate and graduate programs, law school, and medical school—actions to rectify past discriminatory admissions policies by a particular higher education institution are permitted. The issue of whether increasing diversity is a compelling reason for preferential admissions policies has not yet been finally decided by the Court, though the Court majority is leaning very strongly against the proposition that diversity is a sufficiently important educational goal to pass the "compelling reason" bar.

If the Court decides to settle the issue once and for all, it has the opportunity to do so, given the existence of contradictory decisions on affirmative action admissions in higher education by lower federal courts. For example, one federal district judge has allowed affirmative action admissions at the University of Michigan for undergraduates, while another federal district judge has disallowed a similar admissions program at the University of Michigan Law School. Meanwhile, the Fifth Circuit Court has found preferential admissions at the University of Texas Law School unlawful, while the Ninth Circuit Court has ruled a similar program permissible at the University of Washington Law School. The Supreme Court generally does not like to see such inconsistency on an important constitutional matter, so it may eventually choose to take up these cases and make a definitive judgment.

Civil Rights for Women

The expansion of civil rights protections for women has taken a decidedly different path from that of civil rights protections for African-Americans.

Intermediate Scrutiny For all its egalitarian reputation, the Warren Court did not significantly advance the cause of women's rights. Once the Burger Court seriously looked at sex discrimination laws, it had to decide whether to apply ordinary scrutiny (the presumption of constitutionality that almost all laws survive) or strict scrutiny (the presumption of unconstitutionality that dooms almost all laws). The Burger Court opted for a new position, called **intermediate scrutiny,** but not before coming to the very brink of declaring gender a suspect classification demanding strict scrutiny.

By 1976 the proposed **Equal Rights Amendment** to the Constitution to guarantee full legal equality for women had stalled, falling short of the required three-fourths of the states. Moreover, the Supreme Court did not have the necessary votes for a strict scrutiny interpretation of gender classification. There was support, however, for the new doctrine that came to be called intermediate scrutiny. In *Craig* v. *Boren* (1976), six justices supported Justice William Brennan's compromise, which created a more rigorous scrutiny of gender as a *somewhat* suspect classification. This intermediate scrutiny provided a compromise solution to the problem of choosing between strict and ordinary scrutiny. In the view of the justices, the use of strict scrutiny would endanger traditional sex roles, while the use of ordinary scrutiny would allow blatant sex discrimination to survive. The Burger Court defined a test that it believed to be "just right." Under intermediate scrutiny, government enactments that relied on gender would be constitutional if the use of gender were

intermediate scrutiny

A legal test falling between ordinary and strict scrutiny relevant to issues of gender; under this test, the Supreme Court will allow gender classifications in laws if they are *substantially* related to an *important* government objective.

Equal Rights Amendment (ERA)

Proposed amendment to the U.S. Constitution stating that equality of rights shall not be abridged or denied on account of a person's sex.

Title IX had the effect of increasing funding for women's sports in American colleges and universities and encouraging more women to participate in sports. One result was a dramatic improvement in the quality of America's national teams. Here members of the U.S. Women's Soccer Team celebrate their victory in the Women's World Cup in 1999.

substantially related to an *important objective*. Intermediate scrutiny defines a legal test, then, somewhere between strict and lax. Thus, for example, certain laws protecting pregnant women from dangerous chemicals in the workplace have passed this test.

The improvement of women's rights under the doctrine of intermediate scrutiny is less than what many in the women's movement wanted. While the new standard has allowed the courts to throw out some laws based on degrading stereotypes of women, it was used in *Craig* v. *Boren* to justify invalidating an Oklahoma law that discriminated against young *men*. Similarly, the beneficiaries of intermediate scrutiny decisions in *Wengler* v. *Druggists Mutual Insurance Company* (1980) and *Mississippi University for Women* v. *Hogan* (1982) were also men.

Thus, women's rights have not followed the path of other rights and liberties. The nation has not restructured civil rights for women based on an expansive reading of the equal protection clause of the 14th Amendment by the courts. Rather, advances have come by virtue of changing societal attitudes about the role of women in society, increased involvement of women in politics, and new statutes designed to equalize women's opportunities. In the private sector, women have made important advances in the corporate world and in the professions. In the public sector, more and more women hold important elected and appointed positions in all levels of government, and serve in all branches of the armed services. Women also have successfully pushed for laws that compensate for past injustices. One example of such a law is Title IX of the Civil Rights Act of 1964, which prohibits discrimination against women at federally funded institutions, including universities. Title IX is generally credited with enhancing funding for women's sports programs in colleges and dramatically improving the quality of women's athletics in the United States.

Abortion Rights One of the most controversial decisions of the Burger Court was *Roe* v. *Wade* (1973). Two recent graduates of the University of Texas Law School, Linda Coffee and Sarah Weddington, were looking for a client who would challenge a Texas statute that prohibited physicians from performing abortions except to save the life of the pregnant woman.[9] They found a client in Norma "Pixie" McCorvey, a 21-year-old divorcee who had already given birth to a child. McCorvey claimed that she had been gang-raped, but her attorneys doubted her story. They argued instead for a general constitutional right to decide not to complete a pregnancy.

For women's rights activists Coffee and Weddington, the federal courts offered an alternative to the Texas legislature. The case transformed abortion from a legislative issue into a constitutional issue, from a matter of policy into a matter of rights. Eleven states had reformed their statutes to allow women to have abortions when the woman's health, fetal abnormalities, or rape or incest were involved. Four more states (Alaska, Hawaii, Washington, and New York) went further and repealed prohibitions of abortion. In most states, however, progress was slow or nonexistent.

The litigation over abortion reflected changes in public opinion, pressure by interest groups, and persisting inequities against women. Disapproval of abortion decreased and discussion of abortion increased during the 1960s, even among Roman Catholics.[10] Numerous groups worked to reform or to eliminate abortion laws before *Roe* was decided.[11] Norma McCorvey's case relied greatly on the money of supporters of women's rights. The pro-choice team benefited from 42 amicus curiae briefs. The medical profession, which had been instrumental in making abortion a crime in the nineteenth century,[12] supported reform in the 1960s. Justice Harry Blackmun's opinion for the majority prohibited the states from interfering with a woman's decision to have an abortion in the first two trimesters of her pregnancy. He based his opinion on the right to privacy, first given constitutional protection in *Griswold* v. *Connecticut* (1965), even though no such right is mentioned in the Constitution.

The Court's decision hardly resolved matters. Antiabortion groups, energized by the repeal of abortion laws, struck back after *Roe*. Single-issue antiabortion politics surfaced in the 1976 and subsequent elections and became an important pillar of the conservative Reagan movement. The pro-life forces that helped elect Ronald Reagan insisted that he appoint antiabortion judges to the federal courts. He did so with great effectiveness. In the end, the Supreme Court

The women's movement helped raise Americans' awareness of the issue of "equal pay for equal work" and contributed to improvements in pay equity for women in both the public and private sectors. Here, a demonstrator in New York presses for pay equity.

responded to antiabortion politics by deciding two cases, *Webster* v. *Reproductive Health Services* (1989) and *Planned Parenthood* v. *Casey* (1992), that gave considerable latitude to the states in restricting abortions. Many states have acted. In 1996, nine states enacted 14 measures restricting abortion in one way or another: mandating parental notification, waiting periods, counseling against abortion, and/or prohibiting using public money for the procedure. In 1997, 31 states enacted 44 such measures. In 1998, 22 states passed 46 restrictive bills. And, in 1999, pro-choice New Jersey Governor Christine Todd Whitman signed a bill requiring teenage girls to notify their parents before getting an abortion.[13]

To the surprise of many observers, however, the Court majority, despite the appointment of new conservative justices by Presidents Reagan and Bush, affirmed its support of the basic principles of *Roe* in the *Planned Parenthood* opinion. Also surprising was the Court's decision, in *National Organization for Women* v. *Scheidler* (1994), that abortion clinics could sue antiabortion groups for damages under the federal racketeering law. And, during its 2000 session, the Court ruled that states could not ban so-called late-term abortions and said that state laws and local ordinances keeping antiabortion demonstrators away from clinic entrances were constitutional.

Abortion has been an important issue in recent judicial confirmations. Judge Robert Bork ascribed his own defeat to the issue,[14] and hearings on Judge David Souter in 1990 and Clarence Thomas in 1992 raised the issue repeatedly. Ruth Bader Ginsburg took a Solomonic position: Like conservative pro-lifers, she opposed the reasoning of *Roe* v. *Wade,* but like liberal pro-choicers, she insisted that some abortion rights are essential to women's equality.

Sexual Harassment   Another issue of concern to many women (and men) is sexual harassment in the workplace. One poll reports that 21 percent of women say they have experienced sexual harassment at work.[15] The Equal Employment Opportunity Commission (EEOC) reports that 35 percent of female federal employees have been subjected to unwelcome sexual remarks and that 26 percent have experienced unwelcome touching.[16]

People disagree, of course, about what kinds of behavior constitute sexual harassment, although the courts, regulatory agencies, and legislative bodies are gradually defining the law in this area. In 1980, the EEOC ruled that

Professor Anita Hill's dramatic testimony before the Senate Judiciary Committee considering the nomination of Clarence Thomas to the Supreme Court raised the visibility in American politics of the issue of sexual harassment.

making sexual activity a condition of employment or promotion violates the 1964 Civil Rights Act, a ruling upheld by the Supreme Court. The EEOC also ruled that creating "an intimidating, hostile, or offensive working environment" is contrary to the law. State courts have begun to fill in the meaning of "intimidating, hostile, or offensive." The Florida Supreme Court ruled in 1991, for instance, that an open display of nude pinups in a mixed-gender workplace fits the definition. A California court ruled that unwelcome love letters from a supervisor constitute harassment. The U.S. Supreme Court took a major step in defining sexual harassment when it ruled unanimously, in *Harris* v. *Forklift Systems, Inc.* (1993), that workers do not have to prove that offensive actions make them unable to do their jobs or cause them psychological harm, only that the work environment is hostile or abusive. In a pair of rulings in June 1998, the Court broadened the definition of sexual harassment by saying that companies were liable for the behavior of supervisors even if top managers were unaware of harassing behavior. However, companies were offered a measure of protection by the Court when it ruled that companies with solid and well-communicated harassment policies could not be held liable if victims failed to report harassment in a reasonable period of time.

An increase in public awareness about sexual harassment has triggered an increase in lawmaking by state legislatures to erase sexual harassment in the workplace. Many private companies have also begun to specify appropriate behavior on the job for their employees.

Affirmative Action   Affirmative action guidelines and laws passed by national, state, and local governments have been aimed at rectifying past discrimination against women as well as against racial minorities. The precarious legal and political status of these guidelines and laws, reviewed in the section on racial minorities, means that affirmative action programs for women are in jeopardy across the nation. For this reason, many women's organizations have become increasingly engaged in the struggle over affirmative action. The unsuccessful fight in 1996 against California's Proposition 209 ending all affirmative action programs in the state was spearheaded by women's groups.

Enlarging the Civil Rights Umbrella

The expansion of civil rights protections for women and racial minorities encouraged other groups to press for expanded rights protections.

Longman
Participate.com
2.0
Simulation
You Are the Mayor

The Elderly and the Disabled   Interest groups for the elderly have pressed for laws barring age discrimination and have enjoyed some success in recent years. Several federal and state laws, for instance, now bar mandatory retirement. The courts have also begun to strike down hiring practices based on age unless a compelling reason for such age requirements can be demonstrated.

Disabled Americans have also pushed for civil rights and other protections and have won some notable victories, including passage of the Americans with Disabilities Act of 1990. The act prohibits employment discrimination against the disabled and requires that reasonable efforts be made to make places of employment and public facilities (such as concert halls, restaurants, retail shops, schools, and government offices) accessible to them. The proliferation of wheelchair ramps and wheelchair-accessible toilet facilities is a sign that the legislation is having an important effect. Several advocates for the disabled, however, claim that the act depends too much on voluntary compliance.

In 2001, however, the Supreme Court dramatically narrowed the reach of the Disabilities Act, saying that state employees could not sue states for damages arising from violations of the Act, as provided for in the legislation. Advocates for the rights of the disabled have expressed the fear that this judicial ruling expanding the scope of state immunity from congressional actions means that other sections of the Disabilities Act are doomed, including the requirement that state governments make their services and offices accessible to people with disabilities. Others are worried that a wide range of civil rights laws that require non-discriminatory behavior by state agencies—schools and hospitals, for example—may be at risk, as well, because the basis of the Court's decision was that Congress had gone beyond its authority in telling the states what to do under the interstate commerce clause.[17] If the states are immune from the requirements of the Americans With Disabilities Act, the reasoning goes, why should it not be immune from the provisions of other civil rights laws passed by Congress? It remains to be seen how this will eventually play out.

Gays and Lesbians Efforts to secure constitutional rights for gays and lesbians exemplify political exertions in the face of governmental wavering. When the U.S. Supreme Court upheld Georgia's law against sodomy in *Bowers* v. *Hardwick* (1986), the majority opinion declared assertions of a constitutional right to homosexuality to be "facetious." Gay and lesbian activists and their opponents have now shifted the battle to other political arenas, including housing and job discrimination and funding for AIDS research. In the electoral arena, candidate Bill Clinton promised to lift the ban on gay people in the military but was forced to reverse his course in light of the hostile reaction from Congress and the armed services. The resulting "don't ask, don't tell, don't pursue" policy satisfied very few people, and the navy has routinely flouted the policy, as when in 1998 it dismissed a sailor whom it discovered to be gay by tracking down his identity on his America Online profile page. (The sailor eventually won monetary settlements from both the U.S. Navy and AOL.)

The beating death in 1999 of Army Pfc. Barry Winchell, after a long period of harassment by fellow soldiers and noncommissioned officers, again brought the "don't ask, don't tell" policy into the public spotlight. In January 2000, in

Longman
Participate.com **2.0**
Participation
Civil Rights
and Gay
Adoption

Web Exploration
Same-Sex Marriage

Issue: Passions run high on the issue of same-sex marriages.

Site: Access two sites that take contrasting positions on the issue of same-sex marriage: the Family Research Council and TurnOut. Go to our Website at **www.ablongman.com/greenberg**. Go to the "Web Explorations" section for Chapter 16, select and open "same-sex marriage." At the Family Research Council site, select "FRC issues," then look at both "marriage and family" and "sexuality and culture." At the TurnOut site, select "issues," and then "the right to marry."

What You've Learned: Compare the coverage of the issue of same-sex marriage at each site. Is each telling the full story? Are there areas of agreement between the two sides, or is the gap between them a yawning one?

HINT: On issues involving conflicts over fundamental values, agreement and compromise are often very difficult to achieve.

Gay and lesbian Americans have become much more assertive recently in pressing for civil rights protections.

the midst of the New Hampshire presidential primary campaign, Democrats Bill Bradley and Al Gore both stated that they expected military leaders to soon let openly gay persons serve in the armed forces; Republicans George W. Bush and John McCain favored the status quo.

Clinton's efforts in 1993 embroiled the White House, Congress, the Pentagon, and the media in a policy struggle that highlighted the strengths and weaknesses of gay political advocates and their opponents. Although gays and lesbians have recently lost a string of contests in several states and localities to provide protection for gays and lesbians, and while 27 states had passed laws banning same-sex marriages by early 2000, gays and lesbians won some victories as well.

The Supreme Court ruled in *Romer* v. *Evans* (1996), for example, that Colorado's constitutional provision (known as Amendment 2) prohibiting local communities from passing gay antidiscrimination ordinances is unconstitutional. As Justice Anthony Kennedy put it in his opinion, "a state cannot so deem a class of persons a stranger to its laws." Gay rights advocates can also point to some successes in winning protections of privacy and sexual orientation in *state* laws: Eight states and many localities ban discrimination against gay people, and seven other states operate under executive orders that prohibit such discrimination.[18] Vermont has granted same-sex couples the same legal rights, protections, and benefits as heterosexual married couples (regarding matters such as joint tax returns, property ownership, insurance benefits, and medical decisions involving a spouse). Many local governments and private companies have instituted domestic partner benefit programs for same-sex couples. Perhaps most importantly, opinion surveys show that public attitudes about gays and lesbians are growing steadily more tolerant. Fewer Americans today than in the past think that gay and lesbian relationships are wrong. Substantial majorities, moreover, favor ending discrimination against gays and lesbians in jobs, housing, and education and favor passing hate-crime legislation. The portrayals of gays and lesbians in the mass media and culture have also become steadily more positive.[19]

It is evident that the struggle over gay and lesbian rights will remain an important part of the American political agenda for a long time to come, the eventual outcome being very much in doubt.[20] Recently, for example, the Court ruled that the Boy Scouts of America, and, by implication, other private "expressive or advocacy" organizations whose association was protected by the First Amendment, were within their rights to exclude gays from leadership positions. Several other important cases on gay and lesbian civil rights await action by the Supreme Court, including the constitutionality of bans on same-sex marriages.

HOW DEMOCRATIC ARE WE?
Civil Rights in the United States

PROPOSITION: Civil rights were not a prominent feature of the original Constitution nor has the promise of equal citizenship (which goes hand-in-hand with political equality) been realized over the course of our history.

AGREE: There is no provision in the original Constitution ensuring equality of citizenship for women, African-Americans, and Native Americans. Women were denied the vote well into the twentieth century; most African-Americans were slaves until passage of the Thirteenth Amendment and were not admitted into full citizenship across the nation until at least 1965 after passage of the Civil Rights Act and the Voting Rights Act. Even today, women, racial and ethnic minorities, and gays and lesbians continue to be discriminated against in a wide range of institutions and fail to play a role in the political process commensurate with their numbers in the population.

DISAGREE: While it is true that the framers largely ignored the issue of equal citizenship, the story of the United States is the story of the gradual inclusion of all identifiable groups into the political process as equal citizens. Although the levels of political participation and political power are not the same for all groups, this has more to do with inequalities in the distribution of income, wealth, and education than with formal mechanisms of exclusion.

THE AUTHORS: Political equality is one of the three pillars of democracy, equal in importance to popular sovereignty and political liberty. For most of our history, political equality was not a very high priority in the United States, and the quality of democracy was less than it might have been. The advance of civil rights protections since the end of World War II has enriched American democracy because it has helped make political equality a reality in the United States. It is no longer acceptable, for instance, to deny minorities and women the right to vote, to assemble, to petition the government, or to hold public office, practices widely enforced in this country for most of our history. This is not to say that racial minorities and women have attained full social or material equality; many areas of American life, from wealth holding to representation in the professions and in Congress, remain unequal and unrepresentative. Nor is this to say that all civil rights issues are settled; note the continuing disagreements over same-sex marriages and affirmative action. Nevertheless, the attainment of formal political equality is real and something about which Americans might take great pride.

Summary

The Constitution and the Bill of Rights are relatively silent on political equality, other than providing for equality before the law. Important advances for civil rights were the passage of the Thirteenth, Fourteenth, and Fifteenth Amendments after the Civil War. The Fourteenth Amendment, with its specification that all persons born or naturalized in the United States are citizens of both the nation and the states in which they live and that federal and state governments must provide for "equal protection of the laws," was a particularly important civil rights milestone, even though the Supreme Court was slow to act on its promise.

The Court paid little attention during the nineteenth century to the issue of political equality for racial minorities and women. Under the pressure of structural changes in society, the transformation of attitudes about race and gender, and the political efforts of racial and ethnic minority group members and women of all races, the Court slowly began to pay attention by the middle of the twentieth century. Important advances toward equality have been made by both racial minorities and women. Although constitutional law now fully protects both racial minorities and women against discrimination sanctioned by law or government action, the status of affirmative action programs meant to rectify past wrongs and to compensate for institutional barriers to equality remains unsettled. The question of whether lesbians and gay men can be discriminated against in housing, employment, and education has been largely settled, although the issues of gays and lesbians in the military and same-sex marriages remain the subject of considerable political debate.

Suggestions for Further Reading

Barry, Brian. *Culture and Equality.* Cambridge: Harvard University Press, 2001.
An assault on multiculturalism in the name of liberal egalitarianism by a distinguished political philosopher.

Bowen, William G., and Derek C. Bok. *The Shape of the River: Long-term Consequences of Considering Race in College and University Admissions.* Princeton, NJ: Princeton University Press, 1998.
Based on surveys of more than 60,000 white and African-American students at highly selective colleges and universities, Bowen and Bok argue that affirmative action in college and university admissions has had substantial and widespread positive effects on American society.

Burns, James MacGregor, and Stewart Burns. *A People's Charter: The Pursuit of Rights in America.* New York: Knopf, 1991.
A magisterial survey of the history of civil rights and liberties in the United States.

Chavez, Lydia. *The Color Bind: California's Battle to End Affirmative Action.* Berkeley, CA: University of California Press, 1998.
A readable and revealing look at the political and legal forces that fought over California's Proposition 209 ending affirmative action.

Evans, Sarah M. *Born for Liberty: A History of Women in America.* New York: Free Press, 1997.
A compelling history of women's struggle for civil rights.

Kahlenberg, Richard D. *The Remedy: Class, Race, and Affirmative Action.* New York: Basic Books, 1996.
A history of the changing meaning of affirmative action and an examination of its effects.

Sniderman, Paul M., and Edward G. Carmines. *Reaching Beyond Race*. Cambridge, MA: Harvard University Press, 1997.
   A brilliant examination of what Americans really mean when they answer survey questions about race.

Internet Sources

Cornell Law Library/Civil Rights   **http://www.law.cornell.edu**
   Links to the Constitution, landmark and recent Supreme Court civil rights decisions, international treaties on human rights, the Civil Rights Division of the Justice Department, and more.

Martin Luther King Jr. Home Page   **http://www.seattletimes.com/mlk/**
   Created by the Seattle Times, *the site includes study guides on King and the civil rights movement, interactive exercises, audios of King speeches, and links to other King and civil rights Websites.*

Yahoo/Civil Rights
http://www.yahoo.com/Society_and_Culture/Issues_and_Causes/Civil_Rights/
   Linkages to a vast compendium of information on civil rights and to organizations devoted to the protection and expansion of domestic and international rights.

Notes

1. James MacGregor Burns and Stewart Burns, *A People's Charter: The Pursuit of Rights in America* (New York: Knopf, 1991), p. 37.

2. William H. Chafe, *The Unfinished Journey: America Since World War II* (New York: Oxford University Press, 1986), p. 149.

3. Richard Morin and Michael H. Cottman, "The Invisible Slap," *The Washington Post National Edition* (July 2–8, 2001), p. 5.

4. This section is based on Richard D. Kahlenberg, *The Remedy: Class, Race, and Affirmative Action* (New York: Basic Books, 1996).

5. Sam Howe Verhovek, "In Poll, Americans Reject Means But Not the Ends of Racial Diversity," *The New York Times* (December 14, 1997), p. A1; Martin Gilens, Paul M. Sniderman, and James H. Kuklinski, "Affirmative Action and the Politics of Realignment," *British Journal of Political Science* 28 (January 1998), pp. 159–184; Jack Citrin, David O. Sears, Christopher Muste, and Cara Wong, "Multiculturalism in American Public Opinion," *British Journal of Political Science* (2001), Vol. 31, pp. 247–275.

6. Verhovek, "In Poll, Americans Reject Means. . . ."

7. Paul M. Sniderman and Edward G. Carmines, *Reaching Beyond Race* (Cambridge, MA: Harvard University Press, 1997).

8. Seymour Martin Lipset, *American Exceptionalism* (New York: Norton, 1996), ch. 4.

9. See Marian Faux, *Roe v. Wade* (New York: Macmillan, 1988).

10. Ibid., p. 45.

11. Eva R. Rubin, *Abortion, Politics, and the Courts* (Westport, CT: Greenwood Press, 1982), ch. 2.

12. Kristen Luker, *Abortion and the Politics of Motherhood* (Berkeley: University of California Press, 1984), ch. 2.

13. Katharine Q. Seelye, "Advocates of Abortion Rights Report a Rise in Restrictions," *The New York Times* (January 15, 1998), p. A1; and David Kocieniewski, "Abortion Rights Movement Stunned by Whitman," *The New York Times* (June 15, 1999), p. A29.

14. Robert Bork, *The Tempting of America: The Political Seduction of the Law* (New York: Free Press, 1990), p. 281.

15. *Newsweek* (October 21, 1991), p. 34.

16. Ibid., p. 36.

17. Linda Greenhouse, "Justices Give the States Immunity From Suits by Disabled Workers," *The New York Times* (February 22, 2001), p. A1.

18. Lisa Keen, "Referendums and Rights: Across the Country, Battles over Protection for Gays and Lesbians," *The Washington Post* (October 31, 1993), p. C3.

19. Kenneth Sherrill and Alan Yang, "From Outlaws to In-Laws," *Public Perspectives* (January/February 2000), pp. 20–23.

20. See Aart Hendriks, Rob Tielman, and Evert van der Veen, eds., *The Third Pink Book* (Buffalo, NY: Prometheus Books, 1993); Louis Diamant, ed., *Homosexual Issues in the Workplace* (Washington, D.C.: Taylor & Francis, 1993).

Chapter 17
Domestic Policy: The Economy and Social Welfare

In This Chapter

- Why government is involved in the economy and social welfare

- What tools government uses to manage the economy

- The federal budget, the deficit, and the national debt

- Why government subsidizes some business activities and regulates others

- Why the American welfare state is the way it is

- How interest groups, parties, social movements, and public opinion affect economic and social welfare policy

Whatever Happened to the Budget Surplus?

In early 2001, federal officials and private economists were issuing confident predictions that the government's budget would be in the black by more than $230 billion in 2002, and that total cumulative surpluses over a ten-year period would be about $5.6 trillion. For elected officials in Washington, the news could not have been better. As officeholders who must periodically face the voters, elected officials of both parties were delighted with the prospect of an ever-growing budget cornucopia that could be used to safeguard Social Security and Medicare, pay down the national debt, and pay for new educational and drug benefit programs—with ample room left over for tax cuts.

This change in the budgetary picture was long overdue. After all, the federal government's budget had been spilling red ink from 1970 to 1997, the longest stretch of budget shortfalls in American history. The national debt rose accordingly, as did the amount of interest that had to be paid every year to service the debt. As the annual deficits continued year after year and the debt accumulated, politicians in the 1980s and 1990s came under tremendous pressure to balance the budget by cutting programs, raising taxes, or some combination of both. For elected officials, this was not a happy time. Few new benefits could be added to existing programs; few new programs were possible in such an environment. Hard choices had to be made. Much to the surprise of political observers, congressional leaders and presidents George H. W. Bush and Bill Clinton rose to the occasion, and, over a period of years, managed to make tax and spending decisions that first brought the annual budget into balance, then produced budget surpluses. It did not hurt that the booming American economy produced more government revenues (more income and wealth results in more tax revenues) and reduced demands for social safety net programs such as Food Stamps and Unemployment Insurance.

This changed dramatically in 2002. The Bush White House announced that the federal budget was going to be at

least $106 billion in the red for 2002 and would remain in deficit until at least 2005, perhaps longer. The Congressional Budget Office also reported that it had revised its estimates, and now predicted that the budget would be in the red until 2005, then go into positive territory after that, though with much smaller annual surpluses than it had predicted only one year earlier. Thus, rather than an accumulated surplus from 2001 to 2011 of $5.6 trillion, the CBO suggested that $1.6 trillion might be more realistic. This reversal in the fiscal health of the nation was the most dramatic in more than 50 years. Talk in Washington of paying down the debt, a new prescription drug benefit program, and protecting Social Security and Medicare declined markedly.

So, how had things changed so dramatically in so short a time? Some reasons are fairly obvious. First, budget estimates did not accurately predict nor take into proper account the 2001 economic recession or the 2002 stock market collapse. Within a very short period of time, the "go-go" economy of the late 1990s slowed d own sharply: GDP contracted, an overvalued stock market lost almost 20 percent of its value, and previously hot dot-com companies folded by the dozens. Telecommunications and computer companies reported huge losses, as did most of the nation's airlines. Most remarkably, the energy trading company Enron collapsed early in 2002, leaving stockholders and employees in the lurch. WorldCom reported that it had failed to report $5 billion in expenses, and other accounting and reporting failures rocked Wall Street. These developments put a serious dent in government receipts; with individuals and companies earning less, and capital gains falling, fewer taxes were flowing into the federal treasury.

Second, earlier budget estimates seriously overestimated the annual growth rate of the American economy over the ten-year period. By 2002, it had become clear to most economists and budget officials that the impressive economic growth rates typical of the late 1990s could not be sustained. Realizing this, budget officials in the White House and Congress lowered their estimates of the rate of economic growth through 2011, how much revenue would be flowing to the government, and the size of the surpluses that might be expected in the future.

Third, budget officials in early 2001 could not have imagined the terrorist attacks on the United States and the tremendous costs that eventually would be associated with rebuilding and recovery from them. Nor could they have anticipated the occurrence or the cost of the subsequent war on terrorism—including the conflict in Afghanistan—and homeland security.

Finally, there is no gainsaying the impact of President Bush's $1.35 trillion, ten-year tax cut on the shrinking long-term surplus. While the rebates to taxpayers in 2001 and the reductions in certain taxes in 2002 probably kept the recession from becoming more serious than it was (because the returned taxes acted as an economic stimulant), budget officials were eventually forced to take account of substantially reduced federal revenues caused by the massive tax cuts over the next ten years when thinking about the eventual size of long-term surpluses.

The annual decisions about taxes and spending are among the most important things that presidents and members of Congress do. These decisions determine in broad outline what activities and programs will be carried out by the federal government and how the government will go about paying for them. These decisions affect how the national economy works, and who in society will benefit or lose from government activities. Finally, budget policies are not made in a vacuum; these decisions are profoundly affected by what is going on in the nation and in the world outside of Washington.

In this chapter and the next, we turn our attention to an examination of a broad range of these federal government activities and programs and the effect they have on the American people. Obviously, we cannot cover every policy area in the allotted space. We focus, instead, on policy areas we consider most important for protecting the security of American citizens and ensuring their economic and social well-being. In Chapter 18, we look in detail at U.S. foreign and military policy. In this chapter, we look at two broad areas of domestic policy: (1) federal government activities related to the U.S. economy, including the budget, fiscal and monetary policies, subsidies, and regulation; and (2) social welfare programs, including Social Security, Medicare, and public assistance. ■

Thinking Critically About This Chapter

Using the Framework You will see in this chapter how the framework can be used to explain why government does what it does in the areas of economic and social welfare policies. You will use what you learned in previous chapters about structural, political linkage, and government factors to better understand what government does in terms of spending, taxing, regulating, and providing income support and social services.

Using the Democracy Standard In previous chapters, you used the democracy standard to examine the extent to which American political and government institutions enhanced popular sovereignty, political equality, and liberty. You will use the democracy standard in this chapter to ask whether the American people get the sorts of policies and performance they want from government. ◀

Why Government Is Involved in the Economy and Social Welfare

Governments in all modern capitalist societies play a substantial role in managing their national economies and providing social welfare for their citizens. Let's see why they do so.

Economic Management

No government today would dare leave problems such as stagnant economic growth, unemployment, international trade imbalances, or inflation to work themselves out "naturally." Citizens and political leaders in the Western democracies have learned that free market economies, left to themselves, are subject to periodic bouts of **inflation** and unemployment, as well as occasional collapses of employment and economic output (called **depressions**). The worldwide trauma of the Great Depression in the 1930s was the event that etched this lesson into the minds of virtually everyone and forever changed the role of government in economic affairs.

inflation
A condition of rising prices.

depression
A severe and persistent drop in economic activity.

The inclination to use the federal government to manage the national economy has been enhanced by the relative success of this endeavor since the end of World War II. Although many economic troubles are still with us—note the 2001–2002 economic turmoil—government has proved surprisingly effective in easing the swings of the business cycle (see Figure 17.1) and stimulating steady economic growth.[1]

Government responsibility for the state of the national economy is now so widely accepted that national elections are often decided by the voters' judgment of how well the party in power is carrying out this responsibility. When times are good, the party or president in power is very likely to be reelected; when times are bad, those in power have an uphill battle staying in office.

Industrial work is often dangerous to life and limb. To cope with industrial illness, disability, and death, most industrial societies have created government medical and safety net programs to help victims and their families.

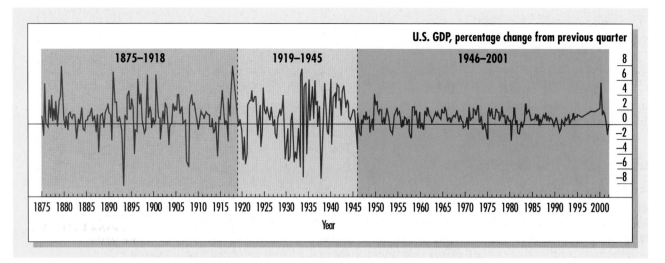

FIGURE 17.1 Gaining Control of the Business Cycle

This graph shows changes in the U.S. gross domestic product (GDP) from the previous quarter. Several things are immediately apparent. First, there were frequent deep plunges in GDP—representing depressions—before the early 1940s but none after that. Particularly noteworthy are the economic collapses in 1893, 1907, 1915, 1920, and 1921 and the Great Depression years of the 1930s; the postwar years have periods of economic slowdown but no crises. Second, the earlier period is characterized by a wild rollercoaster, boom-and-bust pattern; this pattern disappears in the later period. Third, the earlier period shows as many down years as up years; since World War II, there have been more up than down years. These indicators suggest that government management of the economy, which began only after World War II, has had an important stabilizing effect.

Source: "Taking the Business Cycle Pulse," *The Economist* (October 28, 1995), p. 89; and *The Economic Report of the President, 2002* (Washington, D.C.: Council of Economic Advisors, 2002).

Social Welfare

welfare state

The set of government programs that protects the minimum standard of living of families and individuals against loss of income.

All rich democracies have programs that protect the minimum standards of living of families and individuals against loss of income due to economic instability, old age, illness and disability, and family disintegration.[2] Nations that provide such a range of programs are often called **welfare states.** All rich democracies are also social welfare states, and the reason is simple: Their citizens have demanded it. They have apparently recognized that market economies, even when working at peak efficiency, do not guarantee a minimum decency of living for all or offer protection against economic dislocations even for people making their best efforts.[3]

Economic Policy

Government economic policies have a number of objectives; all have consequences for the American people.

The Goals of Economic Policy

What are political leaders trying to accomplish when they fashion economic policies? You will see that economic policy goals sometimes conflict and that important trade-offs are involved whenever economic policies are selected.[4]

Economic Growth Sustained economic growth—defined here as an annual increase in the **gross domestic product (GDP)**—is the "holy grail" of economic policymakers. Although some environmentalists have argued for the long-term benefits of a smaller, less technologically driven economy, Americans generally want an economy in which each year brings more jobs, more products, and higher incomes. Economic growth is also the basis for increased profits, so business tends to support this goal. For political leaders, economic growth, accompanied by rising standards of living, brings public popularity and heightened prospects for reelection, as well as more revenues for government programs.

Low Unemployment Americans want to be working. To a very great extent, their ability to do so depends on a growing economy. Economic **recessions** bring slower job growth and rising unemployment rates. Depressions bring a collapse of the job market (during the Great Depression, the U.S. unemployment rate twice reached 33 percent) and often in its wake social unrest and political instability. It is no wonder, then, that public officials try to keep unemployment levels from rising too high.

Stable Prices Most people want to avoid inflation, a condition in which the purchasing power of money declines. With serious inflation, people's wages, salaries, savings accounts, and retirement pensions are worth less. So, too, are the holdings of banks and the value of their loans. Economists point out that inflation also brings uncertainty and erratic economic behavior as consumers and businesses try to shape their behavior to protect themselves from the effects of future price changes. To nobody's surprise, political leaders seek policies that dampen inflation and provide stable prices. Their problem is that such policies often require slower economic growth, with lower wages and higher levels of unemployment.

A Positive Balance of Payments The **balance of payments** is the difference between the value of a nation's imports and the value of its exports, including both manufactured goods and services, such as insurance and banking.

gross domestic product (GDP)
Monetary value of all goods and services produced in a nation each year, excluding income residents earn abroad.

recession
Two straight quarters of declining economic activity.

balance of payments
The annual difference between payments and receipts between a country and its trading partners.

The government is regularly held accountable for economic hardships such as inflation and unemployment. Here demonstrators protest what they believe to be President George H. W. Bush's unwillingness to take strong fiscal measures to stimulate the economy. Many analysts believe that these economic difficulties cost Bush his reelection bid in 1992.

Before government regulation, industries were allowed to dump hazardous wastes into the environment without threat of financial or legal repercussions. This lake is contaminated with PCBs from the plant in the background.

All nations, including the United States, strive to keep the balance positive; that is, to export more than they import. They do so because sustained negative trade balances lead to a decline in the value of a nation's currency in international markets, as more money leaves the country than is brought in. In this situation, businesses and consumers find that their dollars buy less, and they must either do without or borrow to make up the difference.

Minimizing Negative Externalities   A growing free enterprise economy always produces, in addition to rising living standards, a range of negative side effects, such as air and water pollution, toxic wastes, and workplace injuries and health hazards. These side effects of economic activity—called **negative externalities**—have generated enormous public pressure for compensatory government action. Much of the regulatory activity of the federal government is designed to decrease the incidence of diseconomies.

externalities

The positive and negative effects of economic activities on third parties.

Supporting Key Economic Sectors   Certain economic activities are important for the general health of the national economy but are unlikely to be provided by private firms. Almost without exception, governments in the Western democracies, including the United States, have stepped into the breach and provided support for such vital activities and services, either by direct subsidy and tax incentives or by public ownership (although not in the United States). All European countries and the United States, for example, subsidize farmers. The federal government supports the defense industry by direct purchases of weapons systems and subsidization of research and pays for essential infrastructure such as airports, harbors, and highways.

Longman
Participate.com
2.0
Participation
**Farm
Subsidies and
Domestic
Policy**

The Tools of Macroeconomic Policy

Government actions affect (but do not solely determine) the rate of inflation, the level of unemployment, and the growth of income and output in the national economy. This always has been so. What is new since World War II is that government leaders, economists, and citizens know this to be true and insist that government use whatever means it has available to ensure good economic outcomes.

Government efforts to encourage economic growth, low unemployment, and stable prices fall under the heading of **macroeconomic policy,** or policy that affects the performance of the economy as a whole. The main tools of macroeconomic policy are **fiscal policy** (having to do with government spending and taxes) and **monetary policy** (having to do with the supply and cost of money).

macroeconomic policy
Having to do with the performance of the economy as a whole.

Fiscal Policy   In theory, fiscal policy is a flexible tool for stimulating the economy when it is underperforming and for slowing the economy down when things are getting too hot. Government leaders can increase government spending or decrease taxes when economic stimulation is required (one of the arguments George W. Bush made in favor of his proposed tax cut in 2001); they can cut spending or increase taxes when the economy needs a cooling-off period.

Fiscal tools are not easy to use, however. Decisions about how much government should spend or what level and kinds of taxes ought to be levied are not made simply on the basis of their potential effects on economic stability and growth. The elderly want Social Security and Medicare benefits to keep pace with inflation, for example, regardless of their effect on the overall economy.

fiscal policy
Government's actions affecting spending and taxing levels; affects overall output and income in the economy.

monetary policy
Government's actions affecting the supply of money and the level of interest rates in the economy.

Monetary Policy   Fiscal policy is made by the president and Congress when they determine the annual federal government budget. The Federal Reserve Board (commonly known as the Fed) is responsible for monetary policy, decisions that affect how much money is available to businesses and individuals from banks, savings and loans, and credit unions. The more money that is available and the lower the interest rates at which money can be borrowed, the higher overall consumer and business spending are likely to be. If the Fed wants to increase total spending in the economy (called *aggregate demand*), it increases the money supply (by having its *open market committee* buy back government securities from the private sector) and lowers interest rates (by lowering the **discount rate,** or the cost of money to member banks to borrow from the Fed). If it wants to slow the economy down, it decreases the money supply and increases interest rates. Some observers believe that Fed interest rate policymaking is becoming less effective in stimulating economic growth, as the relative health of the stock market becomes more important than interest rates in determining whether consumers and companies make purchases.[5] Note that the Fed cut interest rates 11 times during the 2001–2002 recession, with very little to show for it in terms of growth.

discount rate
The interest rate the Federal Reserve charges member banks to cover short-term loans.

The Debate About the Proper Role of Government in the Economy

People may agree that government has a role to play in the management of the economy, but they disagree about how it should be done. **Keynesians**—who trace their roots to English economist John Maynard Keynes's classic work, *The General Theory of Employment, Interest, and Money*—believe that in an economy where the tools of production (labor, tools, factories, and the like) are not being used to full capacity, which they believe is the case most of the time, government must stimulate economic activity by increasing government spending or by cutting taxes (or both). Most Keynesians have come down on the spending side of the equation and are associated with an activist conception of the role of government most favored by liberal Democrats.

Monetarists, such as Nobel Prize–winning economist Milton Friedman, believe that government (the Federal Reserve in particular) should confine its activity to managing the growth in the supply of money and credit so that it

Keynesians
Advocates of government programs to stimulate economic activity through tax cuts and government spending.

monetarists
Advocates of a minimal government role in the economy, limited to managing the growth of the money supply.

closely tracks the growth in productivity in the economy as a whole. In the monetarist view, this will allow slow but steady economic growth without inflation powered by private investment. Balanced federal budgets are essential in the monetarist position because unbalanced budgets, in their view, make it difficult for central banks to control the money supply properly. Monetarism is the economic policy, then, of those who believe in a minimal federal government and the virtues of the free market most associated with conservatives and Republicans.

The Federal Budget and Fiscal Policy

Decisions by the president and Congress on spending and taxes in the federal budget constitute America's fiscal policy.

Spending, Taxes, and Debt

Longman
Participate.com
2.0
Visual Literacy
Evaluating
Federal
Spending and
Economic
Policy

Government Spending   The federal government spent a little more than $2.05 trillion in 2002.[6] This represents a more than fourfold increase since 1960 (in constant dollars) and an expansion of federal outlays as a proportion of GDP from about 18 percent to almost 20 percent. (It reached its post–World War II high point of 24 percent of GDP in 1983.) Figure 17.2 shows the change over time in federal outlays as a percentage of GDP. Several things are immediately apparent.

First, the most dramatic increases in federal government spending are associated with involvement in major wars; note the big spikes in the graph for the years associated with World War I, World War II, and the Korean War. Second, the relative spending level of the federal government increased steadily from the early 1930s to the early 1980s. Third, from the early 1980s to 2001, the relative scale of federal spending first leveled off and then declined. This decrease was caused, in large part, by a substantial decrease in the relative size of the national defense budget in the post–Cold War environment, some cuts in domestic programs instituted by presidents Ronald Reagan and George H. W. Bush, and the Clinton–Republican Congress budget agreement in 1995. Fourth and finally, the costs of recovery from the terrorist attacks on the United States and the subsequent war on terrorism pushed up federal spending once more, primarily for national defense (including homeland defense).

In 2002, 16 percent of federal government expenditures was for *national defense*, considerably higher than that of other rich democracies but much lower than it was in 1980, when it accounted for almost 23 percent of federal spending. (In 1960, it accounted for more than half of all federal government spending!) As the opening story points out, President Bush asked Congress to fund national defense at a much higher level in his fiscal year 2003 budget request, so the proportion of the budget going for national defense is certain to increase in the years ahead.

Outlays as a proportion of total federal expenditures for *human resources,* including welfare, health, veterans' benefits, and education and training, have grown considerably since 1980 and now account for around 64 percent of federal spending. Most of the growth is accounted for by just two programs, Social Security and Medicare. Outlays for *physical resources,* including transportation, energy, and the environment, account for about 6 percent of federal dollars, a considerable drop from 1980. Other federal non-defense outlays, which support programs ranging from housing to agriculture, national parks, science and tech-

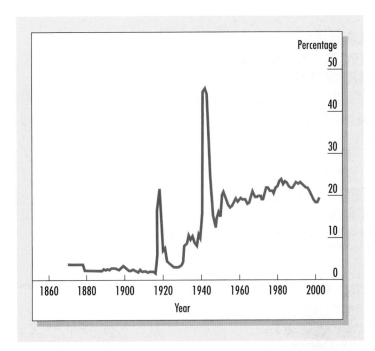

FIGURE 17.2 Federal Government Spending as a Percentage of GDP,
1869–2002

This graph shows the scale of federal government spending relative to the size of the
U.S. economy. We see that the increase in the relative size of the federal government is a
twentieth-century phenomenon. We also see that involvement in major wars has been an
important factor in the growth in federal spending, with the major spikes coming during
World Wars I and II. The permanent change in the role of the federal government in
American society is also seen in the steady rise in spending triggered by the Great
Depression during the 1930s. Also noteworthy is the recent decline of federal spending
as a proportion of total U.S. economic activity.

Source: U.S. Bureau of the Census, *Statistical Abstract of the United States, 2001* and *The Budget
of the United States, Fiscal 2003.*

nology, international affairs, and the administration of justice, now attract five
cents of every federal dollar spent. Interest payments on the national debt are
substantial, accounting for 9 percent of federal expenditures in 2002 (down from
its modern high point in 1996 of 15.9 percent).

Taxes   Government can spend money, of course, only if it has a stream of revenues coming in. Such revenues are raised by various kinds of taxes. Although
the American system of taxation shares some features with those of other
countries, it is unique in a number of ways.

Size of the Tax Bite   Although Americans from all walks of life report feeling
squeezed by taxes, the total of all taxes levied by all government jurisdictions
in the United States as a proportion of GDP is relatively low, at 34 percent,
when compared with the tax bite in the other rich democracies (see Figure
17.3). And, on average, what Americans pay in taxes as a percentage of their
incomes has stayed about the same for the past 25 years.[7]

Forms of Taxation   In our federal system, states and localities levy their own
taxes. The national government depends primarily on income taxes (personal
and corporate) and payroll taxes to fund its activities (see Figure 17.4). Other

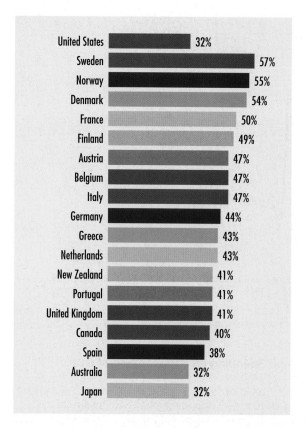

FIGURE 17.3 Tax Receipts as a Percentage of GDP in the United States and the OECD Countries, 2000

The tax burden of the United States is much lighter than that of most other rich democracies.

Source: U.S. Bureau of the Census, *Statistical Abstract of the United States, 2001.*

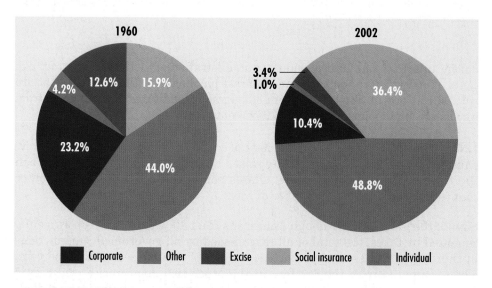

FIGURE 17.4 Sources of Federal Tax Revenues, 1960 and 2002

The source of federal tax receipts has shifted over the years. Most notable have been the increase in the share of taxes accounted for by social insurance payroll taxes and the shrinking share shouldered by corporations.

Source: Office of Management and Budget, *Budget of the United States, Fiscal 2003.*

rich democracies depend more on national sales and consumption taxes. In the United States, the states get most of their revenues from sales taxes, although many have income taxes as well. Local governments depend most heavily on property taxes.

Complexity of Our Tax System   The American tax system is unique in its complexity and particularism. The U.S. Tax Code is a very thick document, filled with endless exceptions to the rules and special treatment for individuals, companies, and communities. These range from the tax deductibility of home mortgage interest to special treatment of capital gains (income from the sale of property). Often called *tax expenditures,* these shortfalls in what government would collect on income in the absence of these devices amount to a great deal of money, about $679 billion in 2002.[8]

Non-redistributive Character of Our Tax System   Though the federal income tax is slightly progressive in its effects—that is, those with the highest incomes pay somewhat higher percentages of their income than others, after all deductions, exclusions and credits are taken into account—other taxes are slightly or seriously regressive (take a higher proportion of income in taxes from those lower in the income scale). The following taxes are regressive: state and local sales taxes; user taxes (such as those on cigarettes and alcohol); and Social Security payroll taxes. Though calculating how these various taxes affect income distribution is very complex and not without controversy, most scholars believe that virtually all Americans pay about the same percentage of their income in taxes, taking all taxes at every level of government into consideration. The rich pay a slightly higher percentage, but so do the poor (because of sales, user, and payroll taxes).[9] The overall impact on the distribution of income in the United States is negligible. Critics of President Bush's ten-year, $1.35 trillion tax passed in 2001 fear that it will reduce the very mild progressivity of the federal income tax system because an estimated 38 percent of its benefits will go to the top 1 percent of income earners in the United States.[10] Especially noteworthy in the new law is the gradual repeal of the Estate Tax, a tax paid mainly by the wealthiest Americans.

The Deficit and the National Debt

Few issues received more attention over the past two decades than the annual federal budget deficit and the national debt. The **budget deficit** is the annual difference between what the government spends and what it receives in revenues. Like any other person, organization, or institution that spends more than it makes, the federal government must borrow from others to cover the shortfall and must pay interest to those from whom it borrows. The total of what government owes in the form of treasury bonds, bills, and notes to American citizens and institutions (financial institutions, insurance companies, corporations, etc.), foreign individuals and institutions (including foreign governments and banks), and even to itself (that is, to units such as the Social Security Trust Fund) is the **national debt**.

The national debt was much in the news in the late 1980s and early 1990s because persistent annual budget deficits had caused the debt to increase significantly over a very short period of time. Before the 1980s, the national debt grew mainly because of deficit spending to wage war. After each war, the debt, relative to GDP, gradually declined.[11] This pattern changed dramatically during the 1980s, however, when the size of annual federal budget deficits escalated, despite the absence of a major war (see Figure 17.5). The national debt as a percentage of GDP began to decline in the 1990s as annual budget deficits turned into annual (and growing) surpluses caused by changes in federal fiscal policies and by the tax windfalls from a booming

budget deficit

The amount by which annual government expenditures exceed revenues.

national debt

The total outstanding debt of the federal government.

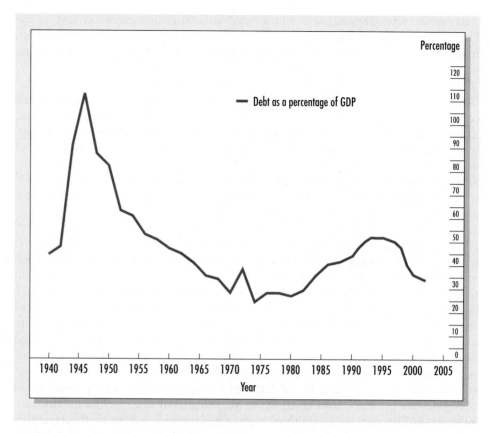

FIGURE 17.5 The National Debt as a Percentage of GDP

In strictly dollar terms, the national debt grew steadily from the early 1970s until 1997, when it began to shrink. The relative national debt—that is, the debt compared with the total size of the American economy (GDP)—also grew from the early 1970s, but it reached its high point in 1993 and has been declining ever since. With annual budgets of the federal government in surplus and the economy growing at a brisk pace in the late 1990s, the debt shrank. It is likely to again grow a little because of the recent return of annual budget deficits. Even at its worst, however, the size of the relative national debt in recent decades was nowhere near the historic high point it reached during World War II.

Source: Office of Management and Budget, *The Budget of the United States, 2003.*

economy. As suggested in the chapter opening story, however, deficits returned in 2002 and are projected to continue until at least 2005, caused by the costs of the war on terrorism and homeland defense, revenue shortfalls caused by a sputtering economy, and the 2001 tax cut.

Regulation

regulations

The issuing of rules by government agencies with the aim of reducing the scale of negative externalities produced by private firms.

Regulation is one of the most visible and important things the federal government does. Federal agencies issue rules that private businesses must follow. These rules may involve how a company treats its toxic wastes, what hiring procedures it practices, or how it reports its profits and losses.

Why Government Regulates The level of government regulation of private business activities has grown substantially. Scholars disagree on why this has happened.

The Democratic Explanation A free market economy, even when it is working optimally, produces a range of negative externalities that cannot be or are unlikely to be solved by private businesses on their own. These problems include, among others, air and water pollution, inadequate information for investors, unsafe products, unsafe and unwholesome workplaces, toxic wastes, and reckless financial practices. The American people have demonstrated on a number of occasions and consistently in public opinion surveys that they want government to do something about these problems. In a democracy, of course, politicians must respond to such popular pressures or risk losing office.

The Business Power Explanation Not all scholars are convinced, however, that regulation is solely the product of democratic politics. The *economic theory of regulation* holds that regulation is caused by the political efforts of powerful businesses that turn to government for protection against competitors. Regulation allows firms, it is argued, to restrict overall output, to deny entry to business competitors, and to maintain above-market prices.[12]

A History of American Regulation

A brief review of the history of regulation illustrates how the interaction of democratic and nondemocratic factors has produced the regulatory agencies and policies that we have today.[13]

Progressive Era Regulation Between 1900 and World War I, laws were passed to regulate some of the activities of powerful new corporations. Reform was pushed by labor unions, the Populists, and middle-class Americans anxious about the conditions reported by muckraking journalists. Landmark regulatory measures included the Federal Trade Commission Act, the Meat Inspection Act, the Pure Food and Drug Act, and the Federal Reserve Act. These measures dealt with such problems as monopolies, unstable financial institutions, unwholesome products, and unsafe working conditions.

Some scholars believe, however, that large corporations were major players in the conception, formulation, and enactment of regulatory legislation.[14] Seen in this light, the Federal Reserve Act was primarily a government

The stock market crash in 1929 convinced many Americans, including the financial community, that the federal government had an important role to play in regulating and protecting the securities industry against some of its worst excesses. The result was creation of the Securities and Exchange Commission.

response to the entreaties of the American Bankers Association, which worried about financial panics.

New Deal Regulation   The next wave of regulatory reform occurred in the 1930s when the New Deal turned its attention to speculative and unsafe practices in the banking and securities industries that had contributed to the onset of the Great Depression. The goal was to restore stability to financial markets and important industries. Legislation included federal bank inspection, federal deposit insurance, the prohibition of speculative investments by banks, and the creation of the Securities and Exchange Commission to regulate stock market operations.

Again, the political sources of New Deal regulation were mixed. Some came from popular pressures,[15] but some also came from the business community seeking stability in its various industries. Large companies, as we saw in Chapter 7, eventually gained considerable control over regulatory commissions.[16]

The 1960s and 1970s   The successes of the consumer, environmental, and civil rights movements from the late 1960s to the late 1970s resulted in a substantial increase in the federal government's regulation of business with the aim of protecting against health and environmental hazards, providing equal opportunity, and allowing more public access to regulatory rule-making. Under the authority of new laws, agencies such as the Environmental Protection Agency, the Equal Opportunity Employment Agency, and the Federal Drug Administration issued numerous rules that affected business operations and decisions. It was one of the only times in our history when business was almost entirely on the defensive, unable to halt the imposition of laws and regulations to which it was strongly opposed.[17]

While strong environmental policies are supported by a majority of Americans, business and industry as well as their employees often exert strong pressure to reduce government action in this area.

Deregulation By the end of the 1970s, the mood of opinion leaders both inside and outside the government had turned against regulation in the name of economic efficiency. Many blamed excessive regulation for forcing inefficient practices on American companies, contributing to sluggish economic growth, slow productivity gains, and disappointing competitiveness in the global economy. Many began to find fault with government imposition on companies of uniform national standards, strict deadlines for compliance with regulations, and detailed instructions.[18] The deregulatory mood was spurred by a business political offensive that took the form of funding for think tanks, journals of opinion, and foundations favorable to the business point of view, as well as funding for the electoral campaigns of sympathetic candidates.[19] From then until today, the watchword has been *deregulation,* loosening the hand of government in a variety of economic sectors including banking and finance, transportation, and telecommunications.

President George W. Bush is an enthusiastic deregulator. He supported rule changes early in his administration, for example, that allow more road-building in national forests, reverse the decision to decrease snowmobile use in national parks, and allow developers more freedom to build in wetlands. He also made several appointments of critics of regulation to important regulatory bodies: Mary Sheila Gall, a long-time critic of consumer safety regulation, for example, was President Bush's choice to head the Consumer Product Safety Administration.[20] The position of administration supporters is that more sensible and economically efficient ways of regulating business are possible, but only after the heavy hand of government is removed.

The Future of Regulation
While deregulation may mean that especially egregious, unfair, and inefficient regulations will be erased from the books, the regulatory state is likely here to stay, mainly because the public supports most existing regulatory programs, especially those aimed at environmental and

When companies such as Enron and WorldCom collapse because of legal but ethically suspect and financially dangerous actions by their executives, lawyers, and accountants, many people are hurt, including employees like these at Enron. Not surprisingly, when this happens, pressure builds on elected officials to protect the public by regulating such corporate practices.

consumer protection. Even at the height of President Reagan's popularity, for example, the Roper Poll reported that only 21 percent of Americans believed that "environmental protection laws and regulations have gone too far," while 69 percent believed that "they are about right or haven't gone far enough."[21]

The regulatory state is here to stay, moreover, because economic activity and technological change bring new problems and demands for government intervention to protect the public. The ready availability of pornography on the Internet, for example, has triggered efforts by Christian conservatives and others to regulate its content. Unraveling the human genome has led to calls for regulating how this new knowledge will be used. When children become ill from E. coli microbes in ground beef, the public demands higher standards of meat inspection. And when companies such as Enron collapse, taking with them the retirement savings of their employees, or when accounting firms such as Arthur Andersen allow large corporations to mislead investors, Americans demand that government protect them against similar behavior by other companies.

Making Economic Policy: The Main Players

Longman
Participate.com
2.0
Comparative
**Comparing
Economic
Policy**

Many influences shape American economic policies. Here we discuss political linkage factors and governmental factors.

Political Linkage Factors

Interest groups, particularly those representing business, but also labor, consumer, and environmental groups, take a keen interest in economic policy, and their permanent representatives in Washington are a constant presence in the halls of Congress and at regulatory agencies. *Voters* and *public opinion* are also important. The public is attuned to overall economic conditions and generally pays attention to what its elected leaders are doing to curb inflation, avoid unemployment, and stimulate growth. We saw in Chapter 10 that the general state of the economy is one of the most important factors in the outcome of national elections. Knowing this, elected leaders do what they can to ensure steady economic growth with low inflation and to prevent economic downturns at election time. *Political parties* also play a role in economic policymaking. Because each has its own electoral and financial constituency made up of groups with identifiable economic interests, the two parties tend to support different economic policies.

Governmental Factors

The president, Congress, and the Federal Reserve Board are particularly important in fashioning economic policies.

The President   When things go wrong in the economy, it is the president to whom we usually turn for action. This role is recognized formally in the Employment Act of 1946, which requires that the president report on the state of the economy and recommend action to ensure maximum employment and economic stability. At the center of every modern president's legislative program are proposals for spending, taxing, and regulation that usually have broad macroeconomic effects. President George W. Bush, for example, favors deregulation, tax cuts, and decreases in the size of the federal budget in virtually all areas not associated with national defense and homeland security.

Congress   Nearly everything that Congress does has macroeconomic consequences, especially when it makes decisions about the annual federal budget. The decisions it makes about the overall balance of government spending and taxes are, as we have seen, a powerful fiscal instrument, either stimulating or

Federal Reserve monetary polices have an important impact on the U.S. and global economies. Here, Fed Chairman Alan Greenspan testifies before the House Banking Committee.

retarding the economy. Taxes levied by Congress shape the incentives for individual and company economic decision making. Laws that regulate, grant subsidies, or supply loan guarantees influence private-sector economic behavior, and trade bills and treaties affect the fortunes of American consumers and many companies.

The Federal Reserve Board The Federal Reserve Board makes monetary policy for the nation. It is made up of seven members (called governors) who serve overlapping 14-year terms and a chair who serves a renewable 4-year term. Each is appointed by the president. The Fed is closely connected with, and very solicitous of, the needs of commercial and investment bankers and generally prefers to control inflation as a first order of business to protect the value of financial assets.

The Fed is relatively independent. Aggressive actions by Congress or the president to pressure the Fed would surely trigger adverse reactions on Wall Street and in the financial community at home and abroad—reactions that neither the president nor Congress is eager to confront.

Social Welfare

Another important domain of domestic policy in the United States is social welfare, a broad range of programs that protects the minimum standards of living of families and individuals against some of life's unavoidable circumstances: unemployment, income loss and poverty, physical and mental illness and disability, family disintegration, and old age. Such programs account for the largest share of the annual federal budget.

Longman
Participate.com 2.0
Timeline
The Evolution of Social Welfare Policy

Outline of the American Welfare State

Social welfare in the United States is provided by a complex mix of programs. Here we discuss the types of programs in existence and the cost of the social welfare state.

social insurance

social insurance

Government programs that provide services or income support in proportion to the amount of mandatory contributions made by individuals to a government trust fund.

means-tested

Meeting the criterion of demonstrable need.

Simulation
You Are a State Legislator

entitlements

Government benefits that are distributed automatically to citizens who qualify on the basis of a set of guidelines set by law; for example, Americans over the age of 65 are entitled to Medicare coverage.

Visual Literacy
Where the Money Goes

Types of Programs

There are two basic kinds of welfare state programs in the United States. The first is **social insurance,** in which individuals contribute to an insurance trust fund by way of a payroll tax on their earnings and receive benefits based on their lifetime contributions. Social Security is an example. The second kind is **means-tested,** meaning that benefits are distributed on the basis of need to those who can prove that their income is low enough to qualify. These programs are funded by general income tax revenues, rather than by payroll taxes. The food stamp program is an example.

Some social welfare programs are administered directly from Washington, while others are jointly administered by federal and state governments. Social Security is an example of a program run from the nation's capital. Taxes for Social Security are levied directly on wages and salaries by the federal government, and benefit checks are issued to the elderly and the disabled by the Social Security Administration. By contrast, Medicaid is jointly funded and administered. One result of such mixed programs is wide variation in benefit levels across the states.

Some welfare state programs are **entitlement** programs; payments are made automatically to people who meet certain eligibility requirements. All Americans over the age of 65 are covered by Medicare, and most citizens whose income is under a certain limit are entitled to food stamps. Because payments are made automatically, much of the federal budget is locked in, and Congress can only tinker around the margins of the budget. In 2001, about 53 percent of the federal budget went to various entitlements.

Cost of the Social Welfare State

The federal government spends a great deal of money supporting the welfare state (state and local governments add to the total); outlays for Social Security, Medicare, Medicaid, and means-tested entitlement programs account for almost one-half of federal spending. Of this total, social insurance programs account for the lion's share, a bit more than one-third of federal government expenditures. As Figure 17.6 shows, these programs have grown dramatically over the past three decades relative to means-tested programs. And in a turnabout from the situation that existed in the 1950s and 1960s, they dwarf spending for national defense.

Several things result from this pattern of expenditure. First, and perhaps contrary to common belief, most benefits of the American welfare state do not go to the poor. The lion's share of social insurance benefits go to Americans who were fully employed during their working lives, had the highest incomes, and paid the maximum level of Social Security taxes. Second, because social insurance benefits go mainly to those who are retired, the elderly fare much better than the young. One result is a significant decrease in the poverty rate among the elderly over the past two decades and an increase in the poverty rate among children.[22] (The child poverty rate fell, however, from 1998 through 2001.)

Social Security and Other Social Insurance Programs

Social insurance programs that guard against loss of income due to old age, disability, and illness are the largest, most popular, and fastest-growing parts of the American welfare state.[23]

Components of Social Insurance

There are a number of social insurance programs designed to meet different contingencies.

Old Age, Survivors, and Disability Insurance (OASDI)   This is the largest of the social insurance programs and the full, technical name of Social Security. OASDI is funded by a payroll tax on employees and employers under the Federal

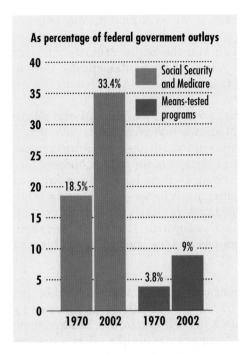

As percentage of federal government outlays

FIGURE 17.6 Comparing the Size of Social Insurance and Means-Tested Programs, 2002

Social insurance programs, such as Social Security and Medicare, receive many more federal dollars than means-tested programs, such as public assistance, food stamps, and Medicaid. Recently, the relative advantage of social insurance over means-tested programs has become even more pronounced.

Source: Office of Management and Budget, *The Budget of the United States, 2003.*

Insurance Contributions Act (the familiar FICA on your weekly or monthly pay stub). Theoretically, these tax revenues are deposited in a Social Security trust fund; in fact, this is a paper transaction only, with payroll taxes treated as simply another component of the government's general revenue stream. (There is, in fact, no "locked box" where payroll taxes remained protected.) Because the program is paid for to a substantial degree by those who are currently working, the net effect is to redistribute income across generations.

Many Americans worry that Social Security funds will run out before they can begin collecting benefits. Presently, Social Security takes in more in payroll taxes than it pays out in benefits each year, so its trust fund shows a strong positive balance. However, because the population is aging, there will come a point in time when the fund will be paying out at a faster clip than it is being replenished. Especially troublesome to many is the sizable baby-boom generation, whose first members will reach retirement age in 2010. Recent estimates by the actuary of the Social Security trust fund say that the fund will not move into the red until the year 2041. Of course, Americans can decide long before then to solve the trust fund problem by raising payroll taxes, cutting back benefit levels, or raising the retirement age.[24] Policymakers can also decide, as some have suggested, to fully or partially privatize the system, depending more on individual stock market accounts. The public supports this innovation in principle but seems less sure when reminded that stock prices can fall as well as rise. The terrible stock market performance of 2002, highlighted by the collapse in Enron, Qwest, and WorldCom share prices, substantially cooled public enthusiasm for privatization.

Generally, Democrats think the system is in good health, and only requires some tinkering to solve emerging problems. Republicans, on the other hand—including President George W. Bush and the Social Security advisory panel he created in 2001—believe the system to be fundamentally flawed, with major overhauls being the only way to save it.

Medicare   Medicare pays for a substantial portion of the hospital and doctor bills of retirees and the disabled. Since Medicare was created in 1965, it has grown into one of the largest federal programs in total dollar expenditures; more than $226 billion was spent in 2002, about 11 percent of the federal budget.

Paying for Medicare is a recurring problem. Outlays have been growing at about 10 percent a year for the past 15 years, much faster than those for other federal programs and much faster than Medicare revenues are coming in. And waiting in the wings, again, is the baby-boom generation. It is no wonder, then, that the issue of controlling Medicare costs has become one of the constants of recent American politics.

Unemployment Insurance   Unemployment insurance is administered by the states under federal guidelines, assisted by federal subsidies. It is financed by federal and state taxes on employers for each of their employees. Studies show that the program is not very popular with Americans (unlike other social insurance programs, such as Medicare), perhaps because employees do not contribute to the fund and perhaps because of the importance of work in American culture. Physically able people who are not working do not seem "deserving" to many Americans.[25] The level of benefits is set by the states, and there are wide variations among them.

Do Social Insurance Programs Work?   In an era when it is fashionable to deride the ability of government to do anything well, it is important to know about the relative success of America's social insurance programs.

Successes   Social Security and Medicare work beyond the wildest dreams of their founders. Although the benefits do not allow people to live luxuriously, they provide an income floor for the retired and pay for costly medical services

Web Exploration
Reforming Social Security

Issue: There has been a great deal of talk lately about reforming, even "saving," Social Security.

Site: Access Public Agenda Online on our Website at **www.ablongman.com/greenberg**. Go to the "Web Explorations" section for Chapter 17, select "reforming social security," then "proposals." Select "Social Security" from the list on the left side of the page, then select "framing the debate." Read the "Perspectives in Brief."

What You've Learned: Which of the competing proposals for reforming Social Security appeals to you the most? Why?

HINT: Your answer will probably depend on how much confidence you have in the present system and how much risk you can tolerate in the stock market.

that, before 1965, were as likely as not to impoverish those who had serious illnesses and long hospital stays.

Their effectiveness is shown in a 1989 Census Bureau study on the effects of government taxing and spending programs on income inequality and poverty. The principal finding was that Social Security (including Medicare) "is the Federal government's most effective weapon against poverty and reduces the inequality of Americans' income more than the tax system and more than recent social welfare [means-tested] programs."[26] In fact, Social Security and Medicare have helped reduce the elderly poverty rate from about 48 percent in the mid-1950s to just under 10 percent today.[27] (To learn how the government determines the number of poor people in the United States, see "By the Numbers: How many Americans are poor?")

Problems Despite these successes, many problems remain. Social Security and Medicare have remained viable, for instance, only because Congress has steadily raised payroll taxes to pay for them. FICA and Medicare taxes now take a larger bite out of the paychecks of a majority of Americans than the personal income tax. For those who generally oppose taxes, this trend is cause for concern.

Many also worry about the fiscal viability of Social Security and Medicare. The problem is serious, to be sure, but it is certainly solvable, as we suggested earlier.

Means-Tested Programs (Welfare)

Means-tested programs, popularly referred to as *welfare,* account for only a small part of the annual federal budget but have attracted more criticism than virtually anything else government does. While Social Security and Medicare enjoy widespread support, means-tested welfare programs have long been an object of scorn.[28]

For most Americans, the traditional welfare program (we will talk about the new form of welfare later) seemed to contradict such cherished cultural values as independence, hard work, stable families, and responsibility for one's own actions. Public opinion polls consistently showed that Americans believed that welfare kept people dependent; didn't do a good job of helping people stand on their own two feet; and encouraged divorce, family disintegration, and out-of-wedlock births.[29]

The government offers several means-tested programs designed to assist low-income Americans. Let us look at the five most important ones.

Food Stamps This program is available to most Americans who fall below a certain income line. About 8 percent of Americans presently receive food stamps. Food stamp benefit levels are set by the individual states under general federal guidelines, and states vary substantially in their generosity. Stamps can be used only for food; they cannot be used for alcohol, cigarettes, or gambling, despite rumors to the contrary. The program seems to have made a significant dent in the prevalence of malnutrition in the United States, even though the average benefit has never exceeded 80 cents per person per meal.[30]

Medicaid The federal government allocates matching funds to the states to provide medical assistance for their indigent citizens in this rapidly growing program (expenditures grew from $30 billion in 1988 to $147 billion in 2002). Except for the requirement that they provide Medicaid for all public assistance recipients, the states formulate their own eligibility requirements and

By the Numbers

How many Americans are poor?

Though the Bible says, "For you will have the poor with you always" (Matthew 26:11), it does not tell us how many of the poor will be with us at any given time.

Why It Matters: Knowing how many poor there are, and being relatively confident in the validity and reliability of that number, is extremely important for a number of reasons:

- Comparing the number who are poor in the United States over time gives us an indication of how well we are doing as a society.
- Comparing the number who are poor in the United States over time lets us know the dimensions of a serious social problem that may require government action or the mobilization of private charities, or both.
- The number of people living in poverty helps determine the size (and thus the cost) of many government programs, including food stamps, Medicaid, rent supplements, and the Earned Income Tax Credit.

Interestingly, if the numbers are to be believed, we have recently made important progress in diminishing the incidence of poverty in the United States. The Census Bureau reports, for example, that 11.3 percent of Americans lived below the poverty line in 2000, a drop from 11.8 percent in 1999. This represents the lowest rate in 21 years and is close to matching the lowest rate for poverty ever recorded in the United States (11.1 percent in 1973). The poverty rate crept back up to 11.7 percent in 2001, however, reflecting troubles in the U.S. economy as a whole.

The Story Behind the Poverty Measure: But what is poverty and how can we measure it? Most would probably agree that poverty involves living in dire circumstances; that is, being poorly housed, underfed, and without adequate medical care. But we might have a harder time agreeing on the exact dividing line between adequate and inadequate living standards. To get around this, government statisticians use *income* as a proxy for calculating poverty. Rather than collect information about how people live—what their homes and apartments are like, for example—the Census Bureau collects information about how much money they earn. The assumption, of course, is that in an economy such as ours, what one earns is directly related to how one lives and consumes.

Calculating the Poverty Line: The poverty line was first calculated in 1964 by Census Bureau statisticians. They started with the Department of Agriculture's determination of what it would cost a family of four to buy enough food to survive (called the "emergency food budget"). Then, because it had been determined that the average American family in 1964 spent one-third of its after-tax income on food, the statisticians multiplied the Agricultural Department's emergency food budget figure by three to determine the official government poverty line. They then adjusted this income number for family size, creating poverty line numbers for single persons living alone, two-person families, and so on.

This 1964 baseline figure is used to the present day. Starting in 1965, and every year since then, the poverty line from the previous year is adjusted for inflation, taking into account different family sizes. The table on p. 525 shows the official poverty line thresholds for 2000. To be under the line is to be officially poor.

set their own benefit levels. The eligibility rules are complex and tend to exclude those who are not extremely poor, blind, disabled, or children of out-of-work parents. The problem of noninclusion is serious; only about 40 percent of the nation's officially designated poor are covered by Medicaid, and the remainder are without medical benefits or protection.

Criticisms of the Poverty Line Measure: As with most official statistics, the poverty line calculation has its critics.

- Because the typical American household today spends a much lower proportion of its income on food than in 1964, the "emergency food budget" figure from the Agriculture Department should be multiplied not by three, as has been since the beginning, but by five or six, to calculate the poverty threshold, say some critics. This would result in a substantial increase in the number of people officially designated as poor.
- If poverty is really about lifestyles and consumption patterns, argue conservatives, then household income calculations should include the income equivalents of non-cash government benefits such as public housing, rent supplements, Medicaid support, and food stamps. Doing this would reduce the number of people officially living in poverty.
- By calculating a single, national poverty threshold, the Census Bureau fails to take into account the substantial differences in the cost of living that exist across states and communities. A family of four earning $17,000, for example, could no doubt stretch its dollars farther in rural Alabama than in San Francisco.

What to Watch For: All government statistics are built on a set of assumptions, some of which are

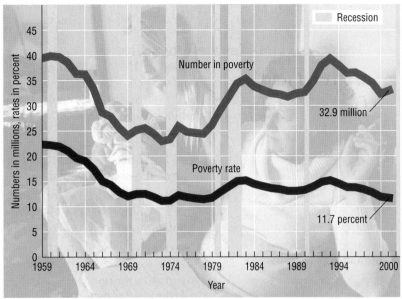

Poverty in the United States

sensible and some of which defy common sense. Be aware of such assumptions when you use official statistics. Luckily, every government agency describes in detail how it collects and calculates statistics, so you can figure it out once you read the documentation.

What Do You Think? With all its problems, should we continue to depend on the Census Bureau's poverty line calculation? Do the virtues of simplicity, consistency, and comparability across the years of the present way of calculating poverty trump its several problems? Or would you rather see poverty rates calculated in some other way? What do you think should be included and excluded from such a calculation?

1 Person	2 People	3 People	4 People	5 People	6 People	7 People	8 People	9 or More People
$8,794	$11,239	$13,738	$17,603	$20,819	$23,528	$26,754	$29,701	$35,060

Supplemental Security Income Supplemental Security Income (SSI) is a program created in 1974 that provides cash benefits to the elderly, blind, and disabled poor when social insurance programs are insufficient to elevate them above the poverty line. The program is relatively small and getting smaller.

Head Start   This is by far the most popular means-tested social welfare program. It reaches about 300,000 children per year (only about 20 percent of those who are technically eligible) in an effort to prepare poor preschool children for entrance into public schools.

Welfare Block Grants   The Temporary Assistance to Needy Families Act (TANF), passed in 1996, created an entirely new system of public assistance. The new welfare system is extremely complex and only in its earliest stages, so how it will eventually develop or how effective it will be is unknown at this time. Its major features are as follows:

- The status of welfare assistance as a federal entitlement has been ended. The families of poor children are no longer guaranteed assistance by the federal government.
- The design and administration of welfare programs have been turned over to the individual states. In the end, the United States will have 50 different welfare systems.
- States receive block grants from the federal government to help them finance the welfare systems they devise. States can use up to 30 percent of the grants on noncash benefit programs for the poor (such as child care, training, transportation, and the like).
- The head of every family receiving welfare is required to work within two years of receiving benefits and is limited to a total of five years of benefits. States are allowed to impose even more stringent time requirements. Connecticut, for example, has set the limit at 21 months. States are also allowed to use their own funds (not federal block grant money) to extend the two-year and five-year limits.
- Unmarried teenage parents can receive welfare benefits only if they stay in school and live with an adult.
- States must provide Medicaid to all who qualify under current law.

Proponents of the legislation suggest that the new welfare system will end welfare dependence, reestablish the primacy of the family, improve the income situation of the poor as they enter the job market, and help balance the federal

Because of limits on how many years people can be on welfare under the 1996 welfare reform legislation, many families, including this one, will soon find their benefits running out.

budget. Opponents of the legislation say that the new system will lead to more poverty, homelessness, and hunger, especially among children once recipients use up their time limits.

Only time will tell which of these scenarios will prevail over the long run. In the short run, however, the results have been surprisingly good,[31] probably because of the spectacular performance of the American economy in the late 1990s, which allowed many former recipients to move into paying jobs. Most dramatically, welfare rolls have declined almost everywhere: 60 percent nationally between 1994 and 2001. Moreover, about two-thirds of those people who left welfare during this period now work at least 20 hours per week.[32] And, at least midway through 2001, there was no evidence that homelessness increased. On the other hand, about 20 percent who left the welfare roles during these boom years eventually returned to them. And, because pay levels for entry-level jobs are so low, only a handful of former welfare recipients have been able to cross the official **poverty-line** threshold.[33]

Though welfare reform had generally good outcomes during the economic good times of the late 1990s, poor economic performance in 2001–2002 put great strains on the system. Many people returned to the welfare rolls in 2002 after losing jobs in the depressed economy. Others reached their five-year benefit limit and were supposed to leave the welfare system, but were unable to find jobs. Trying to avoid undue hardships, a number of states took advantage of a

Participation
Making a Difference: Social Welfare Reform

poverty line

The federal government's calculation of the amount of income families of various sizes need to stay out of poverty.

Web Exploration
Making It on Welfare

Issue: Is it possible to live a decent life under the new welfare system? Find out by preparing your own family budget and comparing it with the welfare benefits available in your state.

Site: Access the Green Book of the House Ways and Means Committee and look at the maximum TANF family payment for your state on our Website at **www.ablongman.com/greenberg**. Go to the "Web Explorations" section for Chapter 17, select "making it on welfare," then "benefits." In Section 7, look carefully at Table 7.9 on "maximum benefits" for each state.

What You've Learned: Imagine you are a welfare recipient living in your present community. Pretend that you have two children. Prepare a monthly budget for what it would cost you to live at a minimum level of decency. Be sure to account for housing costs, including utilities, food (you will pay about half, with food stamps covering the other half), transportation (used car, with insurance and gas) or public transportation, school supplies for your children, some modest entertainment, some clothes, personal hygiene and beauty care products, and whatever else you believe to be essential. Don't worry about medical care; you'll be covered by Medicaid.

How does your budget compare with the maximum monthly benefit paid in your state? Do you believe it is possible for you and your hypothetical family to live a decent life under TANF? Is there anything you could eliminate from your budget to make it leaner?

HINT: Most students find that what they consider to be necessary for minimum decency is far above what is allowed to welfare families.

USING THE FRAMEWORK: **Welfare Reform**

Why did our welfare system change so suddenly in 1996?

Background: America's traditional welfare system, created in 1935 almost as an afterthought to Social Security, had grown to the point that it provided cash payments to families of one in nine children in the United States by 1995. Although it did not pay very much to individual families, and represented but a tiny portion of the federal government's budget, the program was never very popular with the public, grew even less popular in recent decades, and was replaced by a radically new program in 1996. Examining structural, political linkage, and governmental factors that contributed to a dramatic change in welfare policy will make the story clearer.

Governmental Action

The Temporary Assistance to Needy Families Act becomes law in 1996.

Governmental Level

- The Republican-controlled Congress delivered on its promise in the Republican Contract with America to pass a bill to radically transform welfare. →

- President Clinton, himself a believer in welfare reform (he had promised to "end welfare as we know it"), signed the bill into law near the beginning of the 1996 presidential campaign.

Political Linkages Level

- The Democratic Party lost a substantial number of blue-collar, unionized workers, concerned about "wasteful spending" on welfare, from their electoral base. →
- "New Democrats" also embraced welfare reform. →
- Republican consevatives won control of the House and Senate in the 1994 elections.

- Conservative intellectuals and think tanks attacked the AFDC welfare system during the 1980s on the grounds that it killed individual initiative and created dependency, destroyed families, and rewarded immorality. →
- Public opinion became more critical of welfare in the 1970s and 1980s. →
- The Republican Party used the "welfare mess" issue with great effect in election campaigns, winning the presidency in 1980, 1984, and 1988 and the Senate for much of the 1980s.

Structural Level

- The American political culture celebrates competitive individualism, small government, and self-reliance, and denigrates handouts to the "undeserving" poor. →
- Competitive pressures from the global economy in the 1990s pushed governments in all of the rich democracies to make their welfare states more efficient. →
- The fall of communism and the post–Cold War boom in the United States enhanced the attractiveness of conservative ideas in America. →
- Federalism allowed states to experiment with alternative modes of welfare delivery.

provision of TANF that allows states to exempt a portion of their recipients from the five-year rule. In the state of Washington, for example, the governor ordered permanent exemptions from the effects of the five-year limit rule for almost all of the 3,200 recipients who came up against the time limit in 2002.[34]

Fierce partisan debate accompanied congressional efforts to reauthorize the TANF program in 2002. Though most Republican and Democratic representatives and senators believed that welfare reform was working, they disagreed sharply about President Bush's proposals to strengthen work requirements for recipients and to provide funding to encourage marriage among them. Democrats proposed child care and health care benefits for legal immigrants, something that Republicans and the president strenuously opposed.

The Earned Income Tax Credit   The working poor benefit greatly from a provision in the U.S. Tax Code that allows low-income individuals with at least one child to claim a credit against taxes owed or, for some, to receive a direct cash transfer from the IRS. This provision of the Tax Code benefits more than 50 million low-income Americans without much bureaucratic fuss.[35]

How the American Welfare State Compares with Others

Although all of the industrialized democracies are also social welfare states, not all social welfare states are alike. Welfare states range from low-benefit types, where beneficiaries are narrowly targeted (e.g., the poor and the elderly), to high-benefit types, where beneficiaries include most people in the society. The former are sometimes called *minimal* or *liberal* (in the free market, limited-government sense of the word *liberal*) welfare states; the latter are called *developed* or *social democratic* welfare states.[36] The United States is very close to the minimal end of the spectrum. How you feel about where the United States fits on the spectrum depends on your values. For those who believe that small government is always better than big government, it is a very good thing. Others may disagree, believing that government should play a more significant role in protecting and sustaining its citizens.

Longman
Participate.com
2.0
Comparative
Comparing Social Welfare Policy

How the United States Differs   How does our welfare state compare with those of the other rich democracies?

- *The U.S. welfare state developed later than the others.* Generally, social insurance programs were introduced in America much later than elsewhere.[37] National health insurance was introduced in Germany in the late nineteenth century; it was available in almost all Western European nations by 1950. Medicare for the elderly and Medicaid for the indigent didn't happen in the United States until the 1960s.

- *The American welfare state is smaller than most.* Despite complaints about its size and cost, ours is one of the smallest of the social welfare states.[38] Among the rich democracies, only Japan and Australia spend relatively less than we do on social welfare, and the former is well known for the generosity of company benefits to workers.

- *The American welfare state covers fewer people than other welfare states.* Welfare states near the developed end of the spectrum blanket their entire populations with benefits. Family allowances in such places as Austria, the Netherlands, Norway, and Sweden, for instance, go to all citizens who have children. Medical coverage is universal in most of the OECD nations. In the United States, in contrast, social welfare provision

Medicare pays for a substantial portion of the health care costs of elderly Americans. Before Medicare, those over 65 depended on private health insurance or paid out-of-pocket for medical care.

is a patchwork, and many citizens are not protected or covered. More than 40 million Americans, for example, have no health insurance coverage at all.

- *The elderly do considerably better than the young in the American welfare state.* Medicare and Social Security, already the largest parts of social welfare in the United States, continue to outstrip the rate of growth of programs that benefit the nonelderly poor, especially children.[39] In most other welfare states, family allowances and universal medical coverage keep benefit distributions more balanced.[40]

- *The American welfare state requires less of private employers.* All Western European welfare states require that employers help employees with their parenting obligations. All require employers to offer maternity and parenting leaves (now required for workers in firms with 50 or more employees in the United States under the Family and Medical Leave Act), with pay (not required here); all require that work schedules be adjusted for parenting needs. German mothers receive six weeks' paid leave before giving birth and eight weeks' after. All Western European governments mandate four to six weeks of paid vacation.

- *The American welfare state does not include universal health care.* The OECD countries either provide health services directly (the National Health Service in Great Britain is an example), offer universal health insurance coverage (e.g., the Canadian system), or use some combination of the two. In the United States, Medicare provides health insurance coverage for the elderly, Medicaid provides coverage for the poor, and the Veterans Administration covers costs for veterans of the military and their dependents. Other Americans must depend on private insurance, pay out-of-pocket, or do without.

Why the American Welfare State Is Different

How to explain the special character of the American welfare state? Here we identify structural and political linkage factors that influence the kind of social welfare state we have.

Constitutional Rules Federalism is one of the reasons social welfare programs were introduced here so late. Until the 1930s, it was not clear where the main responsibility for social welfare was constitutionally lodged. It was not generally accepted that the national government had any authority at all on social welfare matters until the U.S. Supreme Court belatedly relented and accepted the New Deal. Federalism is also responsible for the incredible administrative complexity of our social welfare state and for the great unevenness in program coverage. Our system takes into account the needs and interests of each of the states. The result is great variation among the states in benefits, eligibility requirements, and rules. The only large-scale programs that are universal in the European sense (uniform, comprehensive, and administered and funded by the national government) are Social Security and Medicare.

Racial and Ethnic Diversity It is often argued that Europe's greater propensity toward welfare states with universal coverage is a result of the ethnic and racial homogeneity of their societies. In homogeneous societies, the argument goes, voters are willing to support generous welfare programs because recipients are felt to be very much like themselves: neighbors who are down on their luck.[41]

Whether or not this argument is valid—the growing diversity within European countries will eventually allow us to test this idea—it is apparent that racial and ethnic tensions influence the shape of the American welfare state. Some of the hostility toward AFDC, for instance, was probably related to the fact that African-Americans made up a disproportionately large share of AFDC recipients (although less than a majority of all recipients), and that media stories about welfare recipients focused almost entirely on African-Americans.[42]

Political Culture Almost every aspect of the American political culture works against a generous and comprehensive welfare state. The belief in competitive individualism is especially important. Voters who believe that people should stand on their own two feet and take responsibility for their lives are not likely to be sympathetic to appeals for help from able-bodied, working-age people.[43]

Antigovernment themes in the political culture also play a role. Generous and comprehensive welfare states, such as those in Europe, are almost always large and centralized states supported by high taxes. Being deeply suspicious of politicians, centralized government, and taxes, Americans are strongly resistant to welfare state appeals.

Business Power Business plays a disproportionately powerful role in American politics (see Chapter 7). Almost without exception, the business community has opposed the creation of a welfare state along European lines. It has been a voice for low taxes and limited benefits and for voluntary efforts over government responsibility. We can see this stance in the area of medical care. Ours is a patchwork quilt that combines social insurance for the elderly (Medicare), a means-tested program (Medicaid) for *some* of the poor, private insurance (Blue Cross/Blue Shield, Prudential, etc.) for many Americans, and a multitude of for-profit hospitals and nursing homes. Doctors, hospital corporations, insurance companies, and nursing home owners are major players in the American system of interest group politics, and they continuously press politicians to maintain this system of mixed government–private enterprise medical care.

HOW DEMOCRATIC ARE WE?
Economic and Social Policy and the American People

PROPOSITION: The economic and social policies that the government in Washington produces are very far from what the people want. Americans don't get the kinds of economic and social policies that satisfy them.

AGREE: The discontent expressed by the public about government—it's too big, spends and taxes too much, and cannot be trusted to do the right thing—is largely related to the fact that government actions do not come very close to what the public wants it to do. Elected leaders are largely unaffected by elections and mainly pay attention to what special interests want, so our economic and social policies are tilted in ways that satisfy them. The tax law, for instance, is riddled with provisions that reward powerful interests.

DISAGREE: In broad outline, the American public gets what it wants from government in terms of economic and social policy, although, to be sure, they continue to complain about government. Even though these policies do not satisfy many conservative and liberal critics, democracy is served to the extent that policies closely match what the majority wants from government. For example, Americans want a level of government spending and taxing that is lower than that of the other rich democracies, which it gets. It wants a government that provides only minimal cash support and services for people who seem able but unwilling to help themselves, which it also gets. In the post–Cold War arena, it wants funds shifted from the defense sector to domestic needs, which elected leaders have done. It has demanded that the federal budget be balanced, which happened in the late 1990s. The public wants a government that mostly allows the free market to operate on its own, but that also pays attention to issues of consumer safety and environmental protection. Economic policies reflect these seemingly contradictory desires.

THE AUTHORS: It is certainly the case that in broad outline, economic and social policies match what the majority of Americans want. In this sense, popular sovereignty is served. However, we would hasten to add that the hand of special interests may be found in abundance in the details of many of our economic and social policies. This is the case for spending, for example, where commitments to specific priorities and projects, from weapons systems procurement to direct business subsidies, are hammered out in a legislative process in which special interests dominate. This is the case for taxation, where the detailed provisions of the Tax Code are the outcome of the efforts of special interests—who are also the main beneficiaries. This is also the case in regulatory policy, where far too many regulatory agencies remain "captured" or heavily influenced by those they are charged with regulating. This is the case as well in social welfare policy, where business and interest groups representing the professions and the elderly play a prominent role, while the poor play almost no role at all. And, finally, it is the case in monetary policy, where the Federal Reserve Board is especially sensitive to the needs of large investors and financial institutions.

Weak Labor Unions   Countries in which the working class is organized and exercises significant political power have extensive welfare states; countries in which the working class is not well organized and fails to exercise significant political power have minimal welfare states.[44] American labor unions have never been very strong or influential when compared with labor unions in other Western capitalist societies, as you learned in Chapter 7.

Summary

The federal government plays an important role in national economic affairs and in providing social welfare for its citizens. Both roles arise from problems created by a dynamic free enterprise market economy and the demand by people in a democratic society that government lend a helping hand.

With respect to macroeconomic policy, the government uses both fiscal and monetary tools to try to encourage economic growth and low inflation. The annual budget fashioned by the president and Congress is the main tool of fiscal policy; decisions by the Federal Reserve Board that affect the supply of money in the economy serve as the main tool of monetary policy. Monetary policy has become increasingly important as problems in controlling the budget deficit have made fiscal policy less effective and less attractive.

The federal government also subsidizes essential infrastructure that would otherwise not be made available by private enterprise and plays an important regulatory role. The origins of the government's role may be found in market failures and diseconomies that triggered popular and business pressures on government. Despite the deregulation efforts of recent years, the regulatory responsibilities of the federal government are likely to remain substantial.

Economic policies are fashioned by the president, Congress, and the Federal Reserve Board. But others are involved as well. Interest groups play a particularly central role. Political parties are also important: Democrats and Republicans take different approaches to economic questions and support different policies when in power.

The social welfare commitment of the federal government has grown substantially since the 1930s, with the most important recent growth occurring in social insurance programs such as Social Security and Medicare. Public assistance grew less slowly and accounted for a much smaller portion of the federal government's social welfare budget. Public assistance was unpopular, however, and in 1996, it was replaced by a block grant program in which the states were given wide latitude to design their own programs.

The American welfare state is very different from others. Ours is smaller, less comprehensive, less redistributive, and more tilted toward the benefit of the elderly. Structural and political linkage factors explain most of the differences.

Suggestions for Further Reading

Cantril, Albert H., and Susan Davis Cantril. *Reading Mixed Signals.* Washington, D.C.: Woodrow Wilson Center Press, 1999.
> *A report on public ambivalence about the role and responsibilities of government in managing the economy and providing social welfare.*

Eisner, Marc Allen. *Regulatory Politics in Transition,* 2nd ed. Baltimore: Johns Hopkins University Press, 2000.
> *Argues that regulatory policies are best understood in terms of the historical periods in which they were introduced.*

Gilens, Martin. *Why Americans Hate Welfare.* Chicago: University of Chicago Press, 1999.

> *A very provocative book that suggests that low popular support for welfare is based on unflattering stereotypes about African-Americans.*

Kuttner, Robert. *Everything for Sale: The Virtues and Limits of Markets.* New York: Knopf, 1997.

> *A careful examination of areas where free enterprise and free markets advance human welfare and where they do not and why government has a role to play in compensating for the latter.*

Noble, Charles. *Welfare as We Know It: A Political History of the American Welfare State.* New York: Oxford University Press, 1997.

> *A comprehensive, sophisticated, and lively discussion of why we have the kind of welfare state we have in the United States and why the establishment of a European-style welfare state remains out of the question here.*

Page, Benjamin I., and James R. Simmons. *What Government Can Do: Dealing with Poverty and Inequality.* Chicago: University of Chicago Press, 2000.

> *A passionate, articulate, and empirically supported argument in favor of a larger role for government in alleviating poverty and making the United States a more equal society.*

Peters, Guy B. *American Public Policy: Promise and Performance,* 6th ed. New York: Chatham House/Seven Bridges Press, 2002.

> *A comprehensive examination of the formation and content of American public policies.*

Internet Sources

American Enterprise Institute   **www.aei.org**
> *A prominent conservative think tank with information about social policy.*

Budget of the United States   **www.whitehouse.gov/omb/budget/index.html**
> *The budget of the United States, with numbers, documentation, and analyses.*

Electronic Policy Network   **www.epn.org/**
> *Reports from liberal think tanks on social welfare issues.*

Fedstats   **www.fedstats.gov**
> *Links to statistics and data from a broad range of federal government agencies, including those most relevant for economic and social welfare policy in the United States. These include the Federal Reserve Board, the Bureau of Labor Statistics, the Social Security Administration, the Bureau of the Census, the Bureau of Economic Analysis, and Administration for Children and Families.*

Public Agenda Online   **www.publicagenda.org/**
> *A nonpartisan site with comprehensive information about government policies, alternative proposals to solve societal problems, and what the public thinks about existing and alternative policies.*

Notes

1. Arnold J. Heidenheimer, Hugh Heclo, and Carolyn Teich Adams, *Comparative Public Policy: The Politics of Social Choice in America, Europe, and Japan,* 3rd ed. (New York: St. Martin's Press, 1990), p. 137.

2. Fred C. Pampel, *Age, Class, Politics, and the Welfare State* (New York: Cambridge University Press, 1989), p. 16; Harold Wilensky, *The Welfare State and Equality* (Berkeley, CA: University of California Press, 1975).

3. Robert E. Goodin, "Reasons for Welfare," in J. Donald Moon, ed., *Responsibility, Rights, and Welfare: The Theory of the Welfare State* (Boulder, CO: Westview Press, 1988); and Wilensky, *The Welfare State and Equality*. See also Clark Kerr, John T. Dunlop, Fredrick H. Harbison, and Charles A. Myers, *Industrialism and Industrial Man* (New York: Oxford University Press, 1964).

4. This discussion is based largely on B. Guy Peters, *American Public Policy: Promise and Performance,* 5th ed. (New York: Chatham House, 1999), pp. 187–199.

5. Steven Pearlstein, "The Market, the Economy and the Fed," *The Washington Post National Edition* (March 26–April 1, 2001), p. 18.

6. Statistical information in this section is from *The Budget of the United States, 2003* (Washington, D.C.: Office of Management and Budget, 2002).

7. *The Budget of the United States, Fiscal 2003.*

8. U.S. Bureau of the Census, *Statistical Abstract of the United States, 2001.* (Figure is an estimate.)

9. Peters, *American Public Policy,* pp. 229–230.

10. Richard W. Stevenson, "Fed Chairman Says Tax Cuts Should Follow Debt Reduction," *The New York Times* (January 25, 2002), p. A1. (Data on tax effects in the article are from Citizens for Tax Justice.)

11. Benjamin Friedman, *Day of Reckoning: The Consequences of American Economic Policy Under Reagan and After* (New York: Random House, 1989), p. 90.

12. George J. Stigler, "The Theory of Economic Regulation," *Bell Journal* 2 (Spring 1971), pp. 3–21. Also see Gabriel Kolko, *The Triumph of Conservatism* (Chicago: Quadrangle, 1967); James Weinstein, *The Corporate Ideal in the Liberal State* (Boston: Beacon Press, 1968).

13. See Richard Harris and Sidney Milkis, *The Politics of Regulatory Change* (New York: Oxford University Press, 1989); Marc Allen Eisner, *Regulatory Politics in Transition* (Baltimore: Johns Hopkins University Press, 2000).

14. See G. William Domhoff, *The Higher Circles* (New York: Random House, 1970); Edward S. Greenberg, *Capitalism and the American Political Ideal* (Armonk, NY: Sharpe, 1985); Kolko, *The Triumph of Conservatism;* Weinstein, *The Corporate Ideal in the Liberal State.*

15. Frances Fox Piven and Richard A. Cloward, *Poor People's Movements* (New York: Vintage, 1979).

16. Marver Bernstein, *Regulation by Independent Commission* (Princeton, NJ: Princeton University Press, 1955); Grant McConnell, *Private Power and American Democracy* (New York: Vintage Books, 1966); Theodore J. Lowi, *The End of Liberalism,* 2nd ed. (New York: Norton, 1979).

17. David Vogel, *Fluctuating Fortunes: The Political Power of Business in the United States* (New York: Basic Books, 1989), pp. 59, 112.

18. James Buchanan and Gordon Tullock, "Polluters, Profits and Political Responses: Direct Control versus Taxes," *American Economic Review* 65 (1975), pp. 139–147; L. Lave, *The Strategy of Social Regulation* (Washington, D.C.: Brookings Institution, 1981); Murray Weidenbaum, *The Costs of Government Regulation of Business* (Washington, D.C.: Joint Economic Committee of Congress, 1978).

19. See Thomas Byrne Edsall, *The New Politics of Inequality* (New York: Norton, 1984); Vogel, *Fluctuating Fortunes;* Kevin P. Phillips, *The Politics of Rich and Poor: Wealth and the American Electorate in the Reagan Aftermath* (New York: Random House, 1990); Thomas Ferguson and Joel Rogers, *Right Turn: The Decline of the Democrats and the Future of American Politics* (New York: Farrar, Straus & Giroux, 1986).

20. Stephen Labaton, "Bush is Putting Team in Place for a Full-Bore Assault on Regulation," *The New York Times* (May 22, 2001), p. A1.

21. As reported in Vogel, *Fluctuating Fortunes,* pp. 262–263, 278–279.

22. Eugene Smolensky, Sheldon Danziger, and Peter Gottschalk, "The Declining Significance of Age in the United States: Trends in the Well-Being of Children and the Elderly Since 1939," in John L. Palmer, Timothy Smeedling, and Barbara Boyle Torrey, eds., *The Vulnerable* (Washington, D.C.: Urban Institute, 1988); and *Poverty in the United States, 1998,* U.S. Bureau of the Census.

23. See Merton C. Bernstein and Joan Brodshaug Bernstein, *Social Security: The System That Works* (New York: Basic Books, 1988), pp. 13–14; Peters, *American Public Policy,* ch. 11.

24. Benjamin I. Page and James R. Simmons, *What Government Can Do: Dealing with Poverty and Inequality* (Chicago: University of Chicago Press, 2000), ch. 3.

25. Fay Lomax Cook and Edith J. Barrett, *Support for the American Welfare State: The Views of Congress and the Public* (New York: Columbia University Press, 1992), ch. 7.

26. "U.S. Pensions Found to Lift Many of the Poor," *The New York Times* (December 28, 1989), p. A1. See also Theodore R. K. Marmor, Jerry L. Mashaw, and Philip L. Harvey, *America's Misunderstood Welfare State* (New York: HarperCollins, 1990), ch. 4.

27. U.S. Bureau of the Census, *Statistical Abstracts of the United States, 2001.*

28. Hugh Heclo, "The Political Foundations of Anti-Poverty Policy," in Sheldon Danziger and Daniel Weinberg, eds., *Fighting Poverty: What Works and What Doesn't?* (Cambridge, MA: Harvard University Press, 1986); Cook and Barrett, *Support for the American Welfare State.*

29. David T. Ellwood, *Poor Support: Poverty in the American Family* (New York: Basic Books, 1988); Martin Gilens, *Why Americans Hate Welfare: Race, Media, and the Politics of Antipoverty Policy* (Chicago: the University of Chicago Press, 1999).

30. John E. Schwarz, *America's Hidden Success: A Reassessment of Public Policy from Kennedy to Reagan* (New York: Norton, 1988), p. 37.

31. Robert Pear, "White House Releases Glowing Data on Welfare," *The New York Times* (August 1, 1999), p. 12; Jason DeParle, "States Struggle to Use Windfall Born of Shifts in Welfare Law," *The New York Times* (August 28, 1999), p. 1.

32. Carey Goldberg, "Most Get Work After Welfare," *The New York Times* (April 16, 1999), p. 1.

33. Jared Bernstein and Mark Greenberg, "Reforming Welfare Reform," *The American Prospect* (January 1–15, 2001), pp. 10–16; Robin H. Rogers-Dillon, "What Do We Really Know About Welfare Reform?" *Society* (January/February, 2001), Vol. 38, no. 2, pp. 7–15.

34. Peter T. Kilborn, "Recession is Stretching the Limit on Welfare Benefits," *The New York Times* (December 9, 2001), p. A28.

35. Peters, *American Public Policy,* p. 207; Christopher Howard, *The Hidden Welfare State* (Princeton, NJ: Princeton University Press, 1997), ch. 3.

36. Gosta Esping-Andersen, "The Three Political Economies of the Welfare State," *Canadian Review of Sociology and Anthropology* 26 (1989), pp. 10–36; Norman Furniss and Timothy Tilton, *The Case for the Welfare State* (Bloomington, IN: Indiana University Press, 1977); Walter Korpi, *Democratic Class Struggle* (New York: Routledge, 1983).

37. Christopher Pierson, "The 'Exceptional' United States: First New Nation or Last Welfare State," *Social Policy and Administration* 24 (1990), p. 188.

38. Vincent A. Mahler and Claudio J. Katz, "Social Benefits in Advanced Capitalist Countries: A Cross-National Assessment," *Comparative Politics* 21 (1988), pp. 37–50. See also Heidenheimer, Heclo, and Adams, *Comparative Public Policy;* Stein Ringen, *The Possibility of Politics: A Study in the Political Economy of the Welfare State* (New York: Clarendon Press, 1987).

39. Smolensky, Danziger, and Gottschalk, "The Declining Significance of Age in the United States."

40. Fred C. Pampel and Paul Adams, "Demographic Change and Public Support for Children: Family Allowance Expenditures in Advanced Industrial Democracies," working paper, Department of Sociology, University of Colorado, Boulder, 1990.

41. Nathan Glazer, *The Limits of Social Policy* (Cambridge, MA: Harvard University Press, 1988), pp. 187–188. See also W. Sombart, *Why There Is No Socialism in the United States* (Armonk, NY: Sharpe, 1976).

42. Gilens, *Why Americans Hate Welfare.*

43. See Louis Hartz, *The Liberal Tradition in America* (New York: Harcourt Brace, 1955); G. V. Rimlinger, *Welfare Policy and Industrialization in Europe, America and Russia* (New York: Wiley, 1971); Marmor, Marshaw, and Harvey, *America's Misunderstood Welfare State;* Wilensky, *The Welfare State and Equality.*

44. See David Cameron, "Social Democracy, Corporatism, Labor Quiescence, and the Representation of Interests in Advanced Capitalist Society," in John H. Goldthorpe, ed., *Order and Conflict in Contemporary Capitalism* (New York: Clarendon Press, 1984); Francis G. Castles, *The Impact of Parties: Politics and Policies in Democratic Capitalist States* (Newbury Park, CA: Sage, 1982); Gosta Esping-Andersen, *Politics Against Markets* (Princeton, NJ: Princeton University Press, 1985); Korpi, *Democratic Class Struggle;* John Stephens, *The Transition from Capitalism to Socialism* (London: Macmillan, 1979).

Chapter 18
Foreign Policy and National Defense

In This Chapter

- What structural level factors are responsible for U.S. superpower status
- What new problems are emerging in the post–Cold War world
- What national security means today
- How foreign and defense policies are made
- How the democratic process affects foreign and defense policies

The Triumph of Unilateralism?

In his "State of the Union" address on January 29, 2002, President George W. Bush announced a dramatic shift in American foreign policy. In addition to the war on terrorism, which he vowed to continue regardless of how long it might take and how much it might cost, the president also indicated that the United States was committed to an even more ambitious foreign policy goal:

> Our . . . goal is to prevent regimes that sponsor terror from threatening America or our friends and allies with weapons of mass destruction. Some of these regimes have been pretty quiet since September the 11th. But we know their true nature. . . .
>
> North Korea is a regime arming with missiles and weapons of mass destruction, while starving its citizens. . . . Iran aggressively pursues these weapons and exports terror, while an unelected few repress the Iranian people's hope for freedom. . . . Iraq continues to flaunt its hostility toward America and to support terror. . . . States like these, and their terrorist allies, constitute **an axis of evil** [emphasis added], arming to threaten the peace of the world. By seeking weapons of mass destruction, these regimes pose a grave and growing danger. . . .
>
> We'll be deliberate, yet time is not on our side. I will not wait on events, while dangers gather. I will not stand by, as peril draws closer and closer. The United States of America will not permit the world's most dangerous regimes to threaten us with the world's most destructive weapons.[1]

Bush indicated that these countries must be prevented from developing and deploying weapons of mass destruction. The means for doing so, he implied, would depend on the countries themselves. Matters might be settled through negotiations, and in cooperation with our allies and international organizations, or they might be settled in the end by unilateral military action by the United States.

> My hope is that all nations will heed our call. . . . But some governments will be timid in the face of terror. And make no mistake about it: If they do not act, America will.[2]

Bush's articulation of a new and vigorous foreign policy, later reaffirmed in a "National Security Strategy" document that called for preemptive attacks against those who threaten the United States, was miles apart from what he had said during the election campaign. The United States should "be humble, but strong," he said, sparing in its use of military power, and cautious about imposing its values and policies on others. Seeing himself as the leader of a country

that needed to get its domestic house in order, he was loath to commit the country to ambitious, expensive, and dangerous foreign policy adventures. Nine-Eleven and the subsequent victory of American arms against the Taliban and al Qaeda in Afghanistan, transformed George W. Bush's outlook and gave him the popular support he needed to fashion more ambitious goals.

Though talk of a struggle against the "axis of evil" played fairly well in the United States, American allies expressed alarm. None had been consulted. None thought that lumping these three countries into a single axis made intellectual or policy sense. None thought it would work. None were happy: The German Foreign Minister complained that Bush was treating the allies like mere "satellites"; the French Foreign Minister dismissed Bush's goals as "simplistic"; Christopher Patten, the foreign affairs minister of the

European Union, worried aloud about the "absolutist" nature of the president's thinking, and protested that allies were being treated as "an optional extra"; China warned of "serious consequences" if war were carried to Iraq; the German foreign minister warned that "success of future actions . . . will not lie in . . . policies of lonely decision-making"; and even Canada said that America's unilateral action in the next phase of the war "will go nowhere."[3]

What most concerned American allies, as well as many home-grown critics of the Bush approach, was the apparent shift to "unilateralism" as the guiding principle of American foreign policy. Advocates of unilateralism, such as Defense Secretary Donald Rumsfeld and Vice-President Richard Cheney, argue that the United States must be engaged in the world to protect its security, its interests, and its values—it cannot be isolationist, that is to say—but it must do so on its own terms, without asking leave of international organizations or allies. To critics, the "axis of evil" talk was distressingly similar to other Bush administration actions that smacked of "unilateralism": the refusal to be part of the Kyoto treaty on global warming; the announcement that the

United States would go ahead with the testing and deployment of a missile defense shield, even if it meant withdrawal from the 1972 Anti-Ballistic Missile treaty; and the administration's refusal to grant prisoner-of-war status to Taliban and al Qaeda captives taken in Afghanistan.[4] For the most part, these allies, as well as many Americans, had hoped that the president would have chosen a more multilateral approach to American foreign policy—namely, a state of affairs in which policies are arrived at in concert with a broad range of countries and carried out in cooperation with them and with international agencies.

The debates in the United States and abroad about whether American foreign policy *is* unilateralist or multilateralist in character, and whether it *should be* unilateralist or multilateralist, will be with us for some time to come. How we ultimately choose to deal with other peoples and countries, as we try to protect our security, interests, and values in the world, will be enormously consequential for us and for others. One can only hope that our political system operates in a fashion that allows a wide range of Americans to be engaged in the deliberations that decide the issue. ■

Thinking Critically About This Chapter

This chapter is about American foreign and military policies, how these policies are made, and how they affect Americans and others.

Using the Framework   You will see in this chapter how foreign and military policies are the product of the interaction of structural factors (such as American economic and military power, the collapse of the Soviet Union, and "globalization"), political linkage level factors (such as the choices the media make about foreign news coverage, public opinion about what the U.S. role in the world ought to be, and what various interest groups want the government to do), and governmental factors (such as the objectives and actions of presidents, members of Congress, and important executive branch agencies such as the Central Intelligence Agency and the Joint Chiefs of Staff).

Using the Democracy Standard   Using the evaluative tools you learned in Chapter 1, you will see that foreign policy is not always made with the public as fully informed or as involved as in domestic affairs. You will see why this is so, ask whether policies would be better if they were made more democratically, and investigate how the public might play a larger role. ◄

Foreign Policy and Democracy: A Contradiction in Terms?

Making U.S. foreign policy has traditionally been different from making domestic policy. For one thing, presidents and the executive branch tend to play a much more important part than they do on domestic issues. In the perpetual tug-of-war between presidents and Congress on international matters, presidents usually prevail in the midst of diplomatic or military crises. Also, the ordinary political factors, such as public opinion and interest groups, are sometimes set aside in favor of considerations of the **national interest,** as defined by a small number of national security advisers and other executive branch officials.

national interest
What is of benefit to the nation as a whole.

Foreign policy is not always purely the result of democratic processes, as we understand democracy. Public opinion, for example, is sometimes reshaped or ignored. In crisis situations, the public often "rallies 'round the flag," accepting the president's actions, at least as long as the results seem good and there is little dissent among political leaders. (When things go wrong, however, domestic politics can return with a vengeance, as it did in the case of the Vietnam War.) Also, much of foreign policy is influenced by *structural* factors, such as the power and resources of the United States, its economic interests abroad, and the nature and behavior of other nations.

Several features of foreign affairs tend to limit the role of ordinary citizens in policymaking. The sheer complexity of international matters, their remoteness from day-to-day life, and the unpredictability of other countries' actions all tend to make the public's convictions about foreign policy less certain and more subject to revision in the light of events. In military matters, the need for speed, unity, and secrecy in decision making and the concentration of authority in the executive branch mean that the public may be excluded and that government policy sometimes shapes public opinion rather than being shaped by it.

At the same time, however, the exclusion of the public is far from total. The American public has probably always played a bigger part in the making of foreign policy than some observers have imagined, and its role is increasingly important in such foreign policy issues as trade, immigration, global environmental protection, and corporate behavior abroad. Note, for example, the very high involvement of the public in general, and interest groups in particular—labor unions, environmental organizations, corporations, business trade associations, and the like—in the struggle over ratification of the North American Free Trade Agreement (NAFTA) and in the debate over granting China normal trade status and membership in the WTO. Public involvement was high because what was decided in these cases was certain to have important effects on jobs, wages, and environmental quality. Just how big the role of the public should be is a matter of dispute, an object of the ongoing struggle for democracy.

The United States as a Superpower: History and Structure

In the autumn of 1990, the United States sent more than half a million troops, 1,200 warplanes, and six aircraft carriers to the Persian Gulf region to roll back Iraq's invasion of Kuwait. In 1996, U.S. troops were deployed in Bosnia as part of a NATO peacekeeping operation. The warring parties signed the peace agreement after the United States consented to be the guarantor of the agreement, backed by troops on the ground in Bosnia. In 1999, the United States supplied almost all the pilots, airplanes, ordinance, supplies, and intelligence for the NATO bombing campaign to force the Serb military out of Kosovo province. And, in less than three months following 9/11, American armed forces routed the Taliban and al Qaeda in Afghanistan. In 2002, the United States turned its attention to Iraq and began to build up military forces in the Persian Gulf. These examples reflect the status of the United States as a **superpower,** a nation strong enough militarily and economically to project

superpower
A nation armed with nuclear weapons and able to project force anywhere on the globe.

its power into any area of the globe. Indeed, since the collapse of the Soviet Union, the United States is the world's *only* military superpower and its pre-eminent economic power.

The Cold War

Longman Participate.com 2.0 Timeline From Stand-alone to Superpower: The Evolution of Foreign Policy

When World War II ended with Japan's surrender on August 15, 1945, Germany and Japan, devastated by the bombing of their cities and industries, found themselves occupied by Allied forces. Britain and France, great powers of the past, had also suffered severe damage and were losing their colonial empires to nationalist revolutions. But the United States emerged with its homeland intact, its economy much larger than before the war (accounting for more than half the manufacturing production of the entire world), its military forces victorious around the globe, and—for a few years, at least—with monopoly control of nuclear weapons.[5]

The only serious challenge to the power of the United States came from the Soviet Union, which had been terribly damaged in the war (suffering perhaps 20 to 25 million deaths) but which retained a large population and military and occupied most of Eastern Europe. The United States and the Soviet Union soon found themselves in a series of confrontations.

American foreign and military policy was focused, for more than 40 years, on the **Cold War** struggle (so-called because the adversaries never actually fought each other during these years) against the Soviet Union. In an odd sort of way, this made matters relatively simple for policymakers both here and in the Soviet Union. Relationships with allies; efforts to win the support of newly independent poor countries in Africa, Asia, and Latin America; and what weapons systems to develop were all measured against what the other side was doing or likely to do.

American policy was based on the doctrine of **containment,** meaning that foreign and military policy was designed to halt the spread of the Soviet state and the influence of communism.[6] The policy was first put into effect when the

Cold War

The period of tense relations between the United States and the Soviet Union from the late 1940s to the late 1980s.

containment

The policy of resisting expansion of the Soviet Union's influence by diplomatic, economic, and military means.

During the Cold War, the United States and the Soviet Union were locked in a nuclear stalemate in which each side had the power to destroy the other, even after absorbing a first strike from its adversary. Here Soviet nuclear missiles are prominently displayed in a military parade in Moscow during the height of the Cold War.

United States agreed to give military aid to the Greek government so that it could prevent a communist takeover. President Truman invoked what came to be known as the **Truman Doctrine**—the idea that the United States would help "free peoples" resist "armed minorities or outside pressures"—when he introduced the Greek-Turkish Aid bill to Congress in 1947.

In the decades that followed, the struggles between the United States and the Soviet Union, and between liberal capitalism and communism, played themselves out in alliance-building by each side, small but hot wars fought by surrogates, counterinsurgency and terror directed against the opposing alliance, and efforts to win over Third World nations. The United States began with **Marshall Plan** aid to rebuild Europe; the formation of the Federal Republic of Germany out of the parts of the old Germany controlled by the United States, Britain, and France; and the creation of **NATO** (the **North Atlantic Treaty Organization**), an anti-Soviet military alliance. For its part, the Soviets installed puppet governments in the Eastern European countries, and with them, formed the **Warsaw Pact** to oppose NATO on the military front. Sharply drawn boundaries divided Eastern from Western Europe.[7]

In retrospect, we can see that the Cold War essentially stalemated or stabilized in the early 1950s after the Korean War—in which the United States and South Korea fought North Korea and China—with most of the world divided into two opposing camps that had fairly fixed boundaries and a reasonably stable balance of power. For some 35 years afterward, both sides spent immense resources—perhaps $12 trillion—on huge armies that faced each other across the stable boundaries in Europe, never fighting but deterring attack and helping keep their own countries' allies in line. Elsewhere in the world, the many covert operations, skirmishes, and civil wars between pro- and anticommunist forces had important (sometimes devastating) effects on the local people involved, but they had little real impact on the great powers or on the shape of the Cold War world.

One crucial reason for this stalemate was the presence on both sides of powerful nuclear weapons. Both the United States and the Soviet Union built large numbers of strategic bombers that could drop nuclear warheads on the other country, and both began ballistic missile programs. Eventually, both sides attained a sort of nuclear parity, or rough equality. A surprise attack by either side would result in the devastation of both countries. This situation, which came to be called **mutually assured destruction (MAD),** deterred either side from launching a nuclear attack. The balance of terror was threatened only once, during the Cuban Missile Crisis in 1962, when President Kennedy forced the Soviet Union to remove intermediate-range missiles from Cuba. Sobered by the threat of mutual nuclear destruction, the United States and Soviets eventually agreed to a Strategic Arms Limitation Treaty (SALT I).

Vietnam was the great exception to the relative peace that Americans enjoyed for more than three decades after the Korean War. As we saw in Chapter 5, the Vietnam War, fought in an effort to prevent a communist takeover of South Vietnam, was a major setback for American foreign policy. The war's cost (about $179 billion, in 1990 dollars) and casualties (47,355 battle dead, 153,303 wounded),[8] as well as the social disruption and moral unease that accompanied it and the economic difficulties that followed it, discouraged intervention abroad for a while. Nervousness about military involvement in Somalia, Bosnia, Kosovo, and Haiti in the 1990s stemmed from memories of the Vietnam War and its effects.

Truman Doctrine

President Truman's policy that the United States should defend non-communist countries from outside pressure and internal rebellion from communists.

Marshall Plan

The program of U.S. economic aid set up to rebuild Europe after World War II.

North Atlantic Treaty Organization (NATO)

An alliance of the United States, Canada, and Western European countries for defense against the Soviet Union.

Warsaw Pact

An alliance of the Soviet Union and Eastern European communist countries.

mutually assured destruction (MAD)

A situation of nuclear balance in which either the United States or the Soviet Union could respond to a surprise attack by destroying the other country.

These casualties from the 1968 Tet Offensive added to the total of more than 47,000 Americans killed and 150,000 wounded during the Vietnam War.

The End of the Cold War

The Cold War ended with unexpected suddenness in 1989, symbolized by the fall of the Berlin Wall. The Soviet Union, demoralized by military failure in Afghanistan, weakened and humbled by the failure of its economy (especially when compared with the booming economies of the United States, Western Europe, Japan, and the so-called Asian Tigers, including Hong Kong, Taiwan, and Singapore), unable to compete in military technology, and unable to keep up with renewed American spending on defense, was ready for radical reform when Mikhail Gorbachev came to power in 1985. He introduced policies to foster greater use of the "market" in economic affairs (*perestroika,* or "restructuring") and more political freedom (*glasnost,* or "openness"). He also refused to intervene militarily, as the Soviet Union had done on numerous occasions in the past, when anticommunist regimes came to power in Poland, Czechoslovakia, and Hungary and asked the Soviets to withdraw behind their own borders. In November 1989, Berliners tore down the wall that had long separated them from their friends, family, and countrymen, and the process was under way that would eventually lead to the absorption of the former communist East Germany into the German Federal Republic.

The final collapse of the Soviet Union followed a failed coup against Gorbachev in August 1991 by hard-line communists. Boris Yeltsin, president of the Russian Republic—the first popularly elected official in Russian history—led the resistance to the coup in Moscow and Leningrad. The coup plotters, winning little popular or military support, quickly gave up. Gorbachev was restored to office. But the central government rapidly disintegrated. The Communist party, which Gorbachev had tried to reform, lost all legitimacy and was temporarily banned in most of the Soviet Union. The Soviet Union itself fell apart as the Baltic republics (Estonia, Latvia, and Lithuania) became completely independent, and virtually all the other 12 republics, even the crucial Ukraine and Russia, then insisted on independence.

Although many Russians saw NATO expansion as a threat to their struggling nation, President Yeltsin was unable to prevent former Warsaw Pact

With the reunification of Germany after the collapse of communism in Eastern Europe, there was no longer a reason to garrison Soviet troops in East Germany. Here, Soviet tanks are loaded on a train for shipment out of Germany.

members Poland, Hungary, and the Czech Republic from joining it. His successor, Vladimir Putin, positively embraced NATO as a way to forge stronger ties with the West. In 2002, Russia entered into a formal partnership agreement with NATO. Putin also signed a treaty with the United States in 2002 requiring both countries to cut their nuclear arsenals by two-thirds.

The Structural Bases of American Superpower Status

A nation's place in the international system is largely determined by its relative economic, military, and cultural power. At the beginning of the new century, the United States is particularly advantaged in all three areas. Together, they make the United States the world's only superpower, so preeminent that leaders and commentators are searching for new language to describe it (the French have started to use the term "hyper-power").

Economic Power In early 2002, the United States had a population of about 285 million people—considerably fewer than China's 1.3 billion or India's roughly 1 billion—but enough to support the world's largest economy, with an annual gross domestic product (GDP) of more than $10.2 trillion. The GDP of the United States is more than twice that of China (but nine times larger on a per capita basis); more than two-and-a-half times that of Japan; more than five times that of Germany; seven times that of Great Britain; and fourteen times that of Russia.

By all indications, the relative strength of the American economy has been increasing, even taking the 2001–2002 economic troubles into consideration. While Asia, Japan, and Europe's economic performance at the end of the twentieth century and beginning of the twenty-first were inconsistent and uncertain, the U.S. economy grew steadily as its companies established preeminence in the economic sectors that count the most in the new global economy: telecommunications, mass entertainment, biotechnology, software, finance, e-commerce, business services, transportation, and computer chips.

American corporations are increasingly global, a fact that affects our foreign policy. For the largest of them, a substantial portion of their revenues comes from sales abroad, much of their manufacturing takes place in other countries, and many of the parts for items manufactured domestically are imported. And in industries such as oil and petrochemicals, many of the sources of raw materials are outside our borders. Because American businesses can be found almost anywhere, American national interests can be said to be found almost anywhere as well. It follows that American officials must be attentive to potential trouble spots around the globe. Today, they must be especially attentive to the problem of terrorism, directed at both government installations, such as embassies and bases, and private American companies and their employees.

Longman
Participate.com
2.0
Visual Literacy
Evaluating
Defense
Spending

Military Power   This enormous economic strength enables the United States to field the most powerful armed forces in the world. The United States spent roughly $396 billion in 2002 on national defense. This is, by far, the largest national defense budget in the world: 6 times more than Russia, 9 times more than China, almost 12 times more than Britain, 27 times more than India; it is also bigger than the combined spending of the next 25 largest national defense spending countries (see Figure 18.1). This level of spending allows the United States to support a large and flexible armed force made up of 1.4 million men and women on active military duty; a strategic force (strategic bombers, land-based **intercontinental ballistic missiles,** and nuclear missile submarines) of more than 1,000, capable of delivering 6,000 nuclear warheads; and 18 aircraft carriers and their associated battle groups. Moreover, the United States has order-of-magnitude advantages over other countries in sea and airlift capac-

intercontinental ballistic missiles (ICBMs)

Guided missiles capable of carrying nuclear warheads across continents.

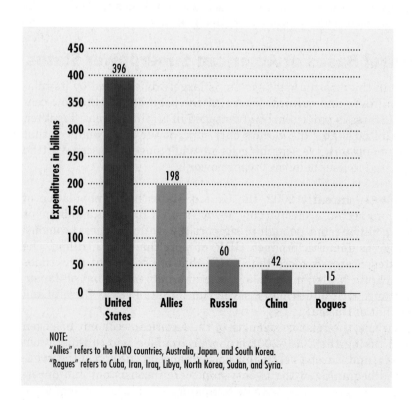

FIGURE 18.1 Expenditures for National Defense, 2001–2002

The national defense budget of the United States is orders of magnitude higher than those of friends and foes alike. The continuing war on terrorism will likely push U.S. defense spending even higher in the years ahead.

Source: Center for Defense Information, Washington, D.C., 2002.

The F-117A Stealth fighter-bomber, a star of the Persian Gulf War and the air war in Kosovo, represents just a small part of U.S. military strength.

ity for moving forces to distant locations, in the ability to collect intelligence from satellites and unmanned drones, and in high tech and intelligent weapons systems. Advances on the last have been particularly noteworthy. During the Gulf War, about 10 percent of bombs dropped were of the "**smart**" variety, with each costing about $1 million. In the Afghanistan conflict, about 90 percent were "smart," with each costing about $18,000.[9]

smart bombs
Bombs capable of being guided precisely to their targets.

No other country in the world comes close to matching the power of the U.S. armed forces. Russia, after the breakup of the Soviet Union, with its economy and once-proud military in disarray, has renounced most foreign adventures, given up on its opposition to the eastward expansion of NATO, and proceeded to cut its nuclear and conventional arms under international treaties. Although it retains a formidable nuclear arsenal, Russia's ability to use force abroad (except on its immediate periphery, in former Soviet republics) is now very much in doubt.

China has a fast-growing economy, millions of military personnel, and some strategic nuclear missiles, but it is much weaker than it looks on paper. Most of China's arms consist of old Soviet-style weapons that the Iraqis found inadequate when they were decisively defeated by U.S. airpower, smart bombs, and missiles in the Persian Gulf War. China's recent efforts at modernizing its weapons have not yet gotten very far. (This may change as its economy becomes richer and more sophisticated.)

The rich countries of Western Europe (Great Britain, Germany, and France) together have relatively small military establishments and a relatively small number of nuclear weapons. They do produce, deploy, and operate very sophisticated military technologies, however, usually under the umbrella of NATO in which the United States plays the leading role. During the Kosovo bombing campaign, European military and political leaders became uncomfortably aware, however, that they were heavily dependent on the United States for laser-guided bombs, strategic reconnaissance, and aircraft, and they began to talk publicly about the need for a new, joint European military command, bolstered by substantially enhanced defense spending by the European states.[10] For the most part, very little has happened on this front.

"Soft Power" Although the effect of "Americanization" is often decried by critics here and abroad—the spread of McDonald's, Kentucky Fried Chicken, Disney theme parks, Hollywood movies, and television sitcoms and dramas take the brunt of the criticism—we should not underestimate the influence of what some have called "soft power," the attractiveness of a nation's culture, ideology, and way of life for people living in other countries. As political scientist

Joseph Nye has pointed out, it is important for the U.S. position in the world that more than half a million foreign students study in American colleges and universities; that people in other countries flock to American entertainment and cultural products; that English has become the language of the Internet, business, science, and technology; and that the openness and opportunity of American society is admired by more than would perhaps care to admit it.[11] And, if it is this very openness and opportunity that allows the United States to be in the best position to prosper in the new global, information-based economy—which many believe to be the case—then the United States's soft power enhances its harder economic and military powers.[12]

None of this is meant to deny the uncomfortable fact that various strains of anti-Americanism also exist in the world, something American foreign policymakers must take into account. Some berate the U.S. for failure to live up to its own standards of freedom; others are troubled by past and present support for various dictatorial regimes. Still others find their ways of life and well-being threatened by economic and cultural globalization, and vent their anger at the United States, the leading advocate and practitioner of globalization. Many no longer see the American business culture as something to emulate or the United States as a good place to invest money after the debacles at Enron, WorldCom, Arthur Andersen, and other firms. More than a few resent what they perceive to be American unilateralism and even arrogance, as the United States exercises its vast power in its own national self-interest. Europeans were especially alarmed at president Bush's announcement of a new policy of "preemption" in which the United States would strike first against those groups or nations threatening American security. Finally, there are many in countries that have been left behind in the global race for development who simply resent the dynamism, wealth, and power of the United States.

Problems of the Post–Cold War World

While the United States is the world's preeminent superpower, it is not entirely clear what the American public and its leaders want to do with this power, though the Bush administration seems to have some very strong ideas about what is required. As the country struggles with this issue, debate tends to be organized around three traditional views about what America's role in the world should be:

isolationists

Those who believe the United States should defend itself behind formidable defensive walls and avoid foreign military and diplomatic entanglements.

- **Isolationists** would have the United States arm itself for self defense, avoid getting ensnared in "entangling alliances" (as suggested by George Washington), and let other countries solve their own problems. Isolationism was in the saddle when the U.S. Senate refused to ratify the Versailles Treaty at the end of the First World War. In the late 1930s, "America First" organizations were influential in trying to keep the United States out of the growing European conflict that would become the Second World War. More recently, Pat Buchanan articulated isolationist views during each of his political campaigns.

unilateralists

Those who believe the United States should vigorously use its military and diplomatic power to pursue American national interests in the world, but on a "go it alone" basis.

- **Unilateralists** would have the United States actively engage in the world, based on the belief that what goes on elsewhere around the world cannot help but affect American interests, but would have the United States do so on its own terms, without asking the permission of others or binding itself under restrictive international treaties. The existence of such a theme in American foreign policy may better explain the United States's unwillingness to sign treaties on the establishment of an international criminal court and on the banning of land mines. Unilateralism seems to be the foreign policy stance favored by many in the Bush administration, including Defense Secretary Donald Rumsfeld and Vice President Richard Cheney. An example was administration promises in 2002 that the United States would go it alone in Iraq if the United Nations failed to support strong measures against Saddam Hussein.

- **Multilateralists** would vigorously protect American interests in the world but, recognizing that the United States is not all-powerful, would seek to work in cooperation and collaboration with other nations. This theme in our foreign policy can be seen in our participation in the international agreement that created the World Trade Organization, and the anti-terrorism coalition President George W. Bush forged in the months following the attacks on the World Trade Center and the Pentagon. The existence of an anti-terrorist coalition, as well as unanimous Security Council support for the U.S. resolution on inspections in Iraq, suggest that the Bush team has not been entirely unilateralist.

multilateralists
Those who believe the United States should use its military and diplomatic power in the world in cooperation with other nations and international organizations.

Even as Americans grapple with the problem of what stance to take toward the world, a whole series of new foreign policy problems has arisen.

New Security Issues

The most frightening possibility of the past—a Soviet-led invasion of Western Europe that could lead to a nuclear Armageddon between the superpowers—has completely vanished. But threats to American security remain.

Terrorism   The issue of terrorism moved front-and-center in the minds of political leaders and the public after the September 11, 2001, attacks on the World Trade Center and the Pentagon. The attacks on the Taliban regime and al Qaeda in Afghanistan are likely to be but the opening rounds in a long war on terrorism. This war is likely to involve a wide range of activities, some done in cooperation with others, some done unilaterally. At a minimum, American policymakers will try to enhance intelligence-gathering capabilities, create rapid strike armed forces to attack terrorist cells, and fashion credible policies that will make other countries less likely to offer aid and sanctuary to terrorist organizations.

The fight against terrorism is likely to be a major element of American foreign policy for a long time to come. Here, people in Nairobi, Kenya, haul away victims of the 1998 bombing of the U.S. Embassy by elements of the al Qaeda terrorist organization.

Russia and the Former Soviet Union

The collapse of the centralized communist regime threw into question the fate of the vast Russian and former Soviet armed forces, with their millions of troops and many nuclear weapons—more than 10,000 of them. Could these weapons fall into the hands of warring ethnic factions, criminal organizations, terrorist groups, or rogue states such as Iraq, creating new dangers and instability? The United States worked out agreements for drastic reductions in Russian, Ukrainian, and Kazakh nuclear weaponry. Ukraine and Kazakhstan have renounced nuclear weapons altogether, but their stockpiles of weapons remain large and central control appears shaky. There is some evidence of Russian nuclear materials showing up on the international black market, raising dangers of **nuclear proliferation,** or the spread of nuclear weapons. A high-priority task for American foreign policy has been to prevent proliferation.

nuclear proliferation

The spread of nuclear weapons to additional countries or to terrorist groups.

The Middle East

The Middle East is a tinder box. There is the unending conflict between Israel and the Palestinians, which stirs passions in the Arab and Muslim worlds and feeds anti-Americanism. There are the restless populations of the Arab countries—saddled with undemocratic governments, stagnant economies, mass unemployment, and historical resentments about the decline of Islam relative to the West[13]—that threaten the stability of the region and access by the United States and the other rich democracies to its vast oil reserves. (Saudi Arabia sits on 25 percent of the world's known oil reserves.) Such restless populations, it must be said, also provide many of the foot soldiers and much of the financial support for terrorism.

The Balkans

What about the countries of the Balkans? Bitter ethnic and national tensions have arisen in this area, most notably among the Serbs, Croats, and Muslims of the former Yugoslavia. The United States brokered a peace agreement between the warring factions in Bosnia and sent troops to help enforce it. In Kosovo, the United States and NATO waged an air campaign to get the Serb military and paramilitary out of the province. American policymakers are struggling still, however, on what role we should play in the Balkans. Some say that the Balkans are a European problem, and the European powers should worry about the area. Others believe the Balkans to be a problem of world order that only the world's single remaining superpower can handle.

Anti-American sentiment is widespread in the Middle East, heightened in recent years by the Arab-Israeli conflict and the United States's fight against terrorism. This sentiment of the so-called "Arab street" must be taken into account by American foreign policymakers.

The Indian Subcontinent The United States must also be concerned about the possible outbreak of war between India and Pakistan, each armed with nuclear weapons. The issues between the two will not be easily resolved, given the history of enmity between them, past military conflicts, and the struggle over the future of Muslim Kashmir. The situation is complicated for the United States by the fact that Pakistan is crucial to the fight against terrorism and al Qaeda in Afghanistan, and that India has appropriated American rhetoric about punishing states that train and harbor terrorists to bring pressure on Pakistan for its aid to Kashmiri terrorists.

China China, with its huge population, fast-growing economy, and modernizing military may pose a long-time threat to the United States. Some Americans have warned of a great "clash of civilizations" between the West and "Confucian" China.[14] Disputes over fair trade, alleged nuclear spying, threats against Taiwan, and human rights disputes periodically cloud U.S.–Chinese relations. But China also joined the anti-terrorism coalition that George W. Bush created in the wake of 9/11, and the United States and China cooperated on anti-terrorist intelligence gathering during and after the Afghanistan conflict.

Weapons of Mass Destruction As we related in the chapter opening story, President George W. Bush designated Iraq, Iran, and North Korea as nations both capable of creating weapons of mass destruction—chemical, biological, and/or nuclear—and using them against neighbors, American allies, or the United States itself. The problem of the spread and use of weapons of mass destruction, whether by axis or other so-called rogue nations, by factions within disintegrating nations, or by terrorists, is surely real, though how to go about addressing this danger is not entirely obvious. Some suggest direct action whenever the threat of such weapons becomes apparent. Others think that the judicious use of sanctions, coupled with UN weapons inspections, would be a safer and more effective approach.

The Developing World American policymakers and the public must decide how large a role they want to play in the developing world, even when the United States is not directly threatened. One example concerns humanitarian intervention. When the government of a country is violating basic human rights and taking the lives of segments of its own population—Rwanda and Chechnya come to mind—should the United States intervene or stay out? If it intervenes, should it do so on its own or under the auspices of the United Nations or NATO?

And what about poverty and misery in the Third World? Does the enormous gap between rich and poor nations pose a long-term security threat to the United States in terms of illegal immigration, terrorism, or armed conflicts? How can or should the United States encourage economic growth and democracy in poor countries?

Economic and Social Dilemmas

It is apparent, then, that America's exalted status as the world's only military superpower and its preeminent economic power has not made U.S. foreign policy problems go away. In fact, national security has taken on new and broader meanings and encompasses new problems.

Globalization Issues Globalization, or the integration of much of the world into a single market and production system, with the United States playing the leading role, has raised a number of new issues for American policymakers and American citizens to address.

General Agreement on Tariffs and Trade (GATT)

An international agreement that requires the lowering of tariffs and other barriers to free trade.

trade deficit

An excess of the value of the goods a country imports over the value of the goods it exports.

European Union (EU)

A common market formed by Western European nations, with free trade and free population movement among them.

North American Free Trade Agreement (NAFTA)

An agreement among the United States, Canada, and Mexico to eliminate nearly all barriers to trade and investment among the three countries.

World Trade Organization (WTO)

An agency designed to enforce the provisions of the General Agreement on Tariffs and Trade and to resolve trade disputes between nations.

Trade   At the peak of its economic dominance after World War II, the United States presided over a world regime of free trade in which many countries negotiated lower tariff barriers through the **General Agreement on Tariffs and Trade (GATT).** Because the United States was the world's most powerful trading state, this reduction was very advantageous for U.S. exports and investments, which continued to grow.

By the late 1960s, however, the rebuilt economies of Germany and Japan began to turn out goods that challenged American products abroad and in the United States, beginning with automobiles and moving on to consumer electronics. Additional competition came from newly industrialized countries (NICs), such as South Korea, Taiwan, Singapore, and Hong Kong, and from the increasingly integrated Economic Community (EC) of Europe. By the mid-1980s, Americans were importing many more goods than they were exporting, creating a multibillion dollar **trade deficit**.

Reacting to this competitive pressure, the United States during the 1980s pressured other countries—especially Japan and the EC, now known as the **European Union (EU)**—to lower hidden barriers and subsidies that hurt American exports while at the same time arranging voluntary quotas and other policies to control imports to the United States. Next, U.S. policymakers negotiated the **North American Free Trade Agreement (NAFTA)** with Canada and Mexico, which was finally implemented after a 1993 vote in Congress resolved a bitter political conflict over its implications for U.S. jobs.[15] The Clinton administration also concluded a comprehensive free trade agreement with 116 countries, under the Uruguay Round of GATT. The agreement, signed in 1994, set up the **World Trade Organization (WTO)** for enforcement. U.S. negotiators hoped that the new agreement would open more markets to American agricultural products and halt the piracy of patented and copyrighted goods such as software and films. The massive anti-WTO demonstrations in Seattle in late 1999, and others that followed, helped focus public attention on the WTO.

Though verbally committed to free trade, the United States does not always live up to its own rhetoric. The United States, for example, retains duties on many agricultural and textile products from poor Third World countries, presumably to

Web Exploration
What Direction for U.S. Foreign Policy?

Issue: Although the United States is unequaled in military and economic power, Americans are not entirely sure how they want to use that power.

Site: Access Public Agenda Online on our Website at **www.ablongman.com/greenberg**. Go to the "Web Explorations" section for Chapter 18. Select "what direction for U.S. foreign policy," then "U.S. role." Select "America's global role," then look in the section "Major Proposals."

What You've Learned: See what the public thinks about the United Nations, humanitarian intervention, and foreign assistance. After looking at the poll results, would you conclude that Americans are isolationists, unilateralists, or multilateralists?

HINT: You might be surprised to learn how many Americans lean in a multilateral direction.

protect American producers. In 2002, moreover, President Bush announced the imposition of new tariffs on steel imports.

A crucial question about growing international trade, and about the increased ability of U.S. and other firms to produce goods cheaply abroad, is whether it brings prosperity to all Americans or tends to push American workers' wages down. If free trade hurts U.S. wages—a matter about which economists are deeply divided[16]—what can be done, short of inefficient protectionism?

Corporate Behavior Abroad U.S.-based corporations operating abroad find themselves being scrutinized for their behavior on a variety of fronts.[17] Some activists, NGOs (non-governmental organizations), journalists, and government officials have focused the international spotlight on matters of pay and working conditions, including such issues as "sweatshop" production, child labor, the absence of labor rights in many places, and gender equities. Others have focused on the effects of corporate production practices on local environments. Still others have focused on the purported homogenizing effects of global products on local cultures—think here of McDonald's and Hollywood—among others.

Intellectual Property Rights How strongly should our foreign policy attempt to protect the intellectual property rights of American companies and citizens? The issue is fairly straightforward when it comes to the "piracy" of movies, music tapes and CDs, and software in places like China; Americans generally support policies that are aimed at ending these practices. Protection of patents for life-saving drugs—anti-malarial and anti-AIDS medications are good examples—is another matter. Many Americans believe that companies ought to provide such drugs at low prices or allow poor countries to find or produce generic substitutes, ignoring the patent protections of western pharmaceutical companies.

Economic Instability What role should the United States play in stabilizing global financial markets, and in rescuing countries on the verge of economic collapse? A strong American role is probably inevitable—we are the leading player and financial supporter of the International Monetary Fund and the World Bank, and our own economy is affected by what happens elsewhere—but precisely how to respond to crises is not clear. No consensus has emerged among American leaders. In 1982 and 1995, for example, the United States helped Mexico emerge from its debt crisis and financial collapse; in 2001–2002, the United States offered only modest assistance to Argentina (in the form of an IMF loan) as it tried to recover from a devastating financial collapse.

Foreign Aid The world is divided rather starkly into rich nations and poor nations. Rich nations, whether for humanitarian or security reasons, have given assistance to poor countries in an effort to improve living standards. Although the United States contributes to World Bank developmental loans for poor countries and has programs such as Food for Peace, the Peace Corps, and technical and educational assistance programs, our spending for foreign aid is very low and has been declining relative to the size of the total federal budget and to the size of the American economy; it now stands at about 1.9 percent of the federal budget, and 0.1 percent of U.S. GDP.[18] In relative terms, what we spend on foreign assistance is much lower than that of such countries as Denmark, Norway, Sweden, and France (see Figure 18.2), though George W. Bush proposed in 2002 to increase foreign aid by 50 percent over three years. Moreover, only about two-thirds of U.S. foreign aid goes for assistance for economic development and humanitarian relief; the remainder is linked to military and security objectives or to encourage the sale of American goods and services abroad.

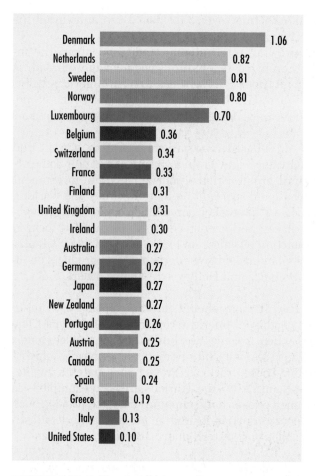

FIGURE 18.2 Foreign Aid as a Percentage of GDP, 2000

Although Americans often complain about how much aid we give to other countries, a comparison with other donor countries shows that we give very little as a percentage of GDP.

Source: Organization for Economic Cooperation and Development, 2002.

Arms Sales The United States sells many weapons to other countries. During the Cold War, we shared dominance of the international arms market with the Soviet Union. After the breakup of the Soviet Union, however, Russian arms sales fell sharply, and most countries clamored to buy American weapons. Now we are by far the biggest arms exporter in the world, with $18.6 billion in sales in 2000. Russia was second, with $7.7 billion, followed by France ($4.1 billion) and Germany ($1.1 billion).[19]

The Global Environment Increasingly, Americans realize that environmental problems cross national borders. The United States and Canada have worked out a joint approach to reduce acid rain; the United States has signed on to agreements on oil spills, the exploitation of Antarctica, and the protection of the ozone layer. The United States is also a signatory to the biodiversity treaty. Global warming is a different story, however. Though the Clinton administration was involved in hammering out the details of the Kyoto Protocol to limit greenhouse gases, George W. Bush refused to join the agreement, even after the Environmental Protection Agency issued a report in 2002 confirming

AIDS is devastating many countries of Sub-Sahara Africa. Anti-AIDS activists there and in the West are demanding that global pharmaceutical firms relax their patents on AIDS drugs so that they can be made widely available at low cost to those suffering from the disease.

global warming and its mainly human origins. The president was concerned that the treaty imposed no pollution controls on large, fast-growing economies among the developing countries, such as China and India, and that it would do irreparable harm to the American economy.

Environmentalists express particular concern about the rapid cutting and burning of tropical rain forests, which removes oxygen-producing trees and at the same time pours smoke and carbon dioxide into the atmosphere. However, such countries as Brazil strongly resist any restrictions on their economic development unless they get substantial compensation. Various possible solutions have been discussed, including land purchases or forgiveness of debts to U.S. banks in return for preservation of the rain forests.

The Drug Trade   U.S. relations with nations south of its border are also complicated by the flow of enormous amounts of marijuana and cocaine from Peru, Bolivia, Haiti, Colombia, and Mexico into the United States and by the inability or unwillingness of those countries to stop the profitable drug trade. U.S. responses have included assistance with law enforcement (not always fully welcomed), crop eradication (bitterly resented by poor peasant farmers), and crop replacement (very costly). Some military strategists have proposed using U.S. armed forces to seize drug shipments and eradicate production, but that would threaten other countries' sovereignty and raise the specter of Vietnam-like drug wars in which the United States might be pitted against local populations. The United States is now heavily involved, for example, in a program to train and equip the Colombian military to wage war on drugs in its country.

Part of the problem in eradicating the drug trade is that demand for drugs is very high in the rich countries, including the United States. Additionally, many of the technologies and organizational strategies that make it possible for corporations to operate on a global scale also help criminal drug organizations do the same thing. Such organizations have easy access to e-mail, express package service, air freight, global banking services, and high-speed telecommunications to enhance the efficiency of their operations.

An official dumps cocaine seized on a freighter from Latin America. Stopping the flow of illegal drugs, which brings huge profits to exporting countries, is a major U.S. foreign policy challenge.

Immigration Throughout history, people have migrated to other lands, seeking a better way of life for themselves and their families. In the emerging global economy, where manufacturing and associated jobs are highly mobile and where the revolution in transportation makes movement of people easier,

Web Exploration
What Does the Future Hold?

Issue: A number of new and serious challenges are emerging in the post–Cold War world that will command the attention of the American public and its political leaders.

Site: Access the *Which World?* site on our Website at **www.ablongman.com/greenberg**. Go to the "Web Explorations" section for Chapter 18. Select "what does the future hold," then "challenges." Select "Explore the Site," then "Trends."

What You've Learned: Which problems are emerging as the most important ones in the new century? Is it population growth? Increasing inequality of living standards? Environmental degradation? Arms proliferation? Are you optimistic or pessimistic about the future? Do you think that the United States can help alleviate the major problems you have identified, or should we leave that to others?

HINT: What you think can and should be done about emergent problems will probably depend on whether you are an isolationist, a unilateralist, or a multilateralist.

cheaper, and more efficient, people in search of improvements in their standards of living are increasingly mobile. Especially noteworthy is the migration of people from poor Third World countries to the rich democracies of the West. Where poor countries lie adjacent to rich countries—for example, Mexico and Central America are close to the United States, the world's richest country—immigration pressures are especially strong.

In recent years, immigration from abroad—especially illegal immigration—has become a major political issue in the United States, because many Americans perceive pressure on their jobs, wages, and tax-supported social benefits, as well as worries about cultural conflict. Government leaders have responded, focusing on tightening the borders and denying government benefits to illegal immigrants. See Chapter 4 for more on the political response to immigration.

Who Makes Foreign Policy?

The president and members of the executive branch are the chief governmental decision makers on most foreign policy issues most of the time, particularly those involving crisis situations, **covert operations,** or the waging of war, as in Afghanistan and the war on terrorism. But Congress has always been involved in decisions about international trade, foreign aid, military spending, immigration, and other matters that clearly and directly touch constituents' local interests, and it is seeking a larger voice in diplomatic and military affairs. Public opinion, the mass media, and organized interest groups affect what both Congress and the executive branch do.

Different types of foreign policy are made in very different ways. Crisis decision making, for example, involving sudden threats, high stakes, and quick action, or covert operations, belongs mostly to the executive branch—often, just a small, unified group of top national security officials. The major decisions on the military response to the September 11 terrorist attacks on the United States, for example, were made by the president in consultation with a small handful of

covert operations

Secret or semisecret activities abroad, often involving intelligence gathering, influence on other countries' politics, or the use of force.

Though presidents are the main decision makers regarding American foreign policy and national defense, they depend on a wide range of experts and advisors for information and advice. Here President Bush confers with top military, intelligence, and foreign policy members of the National Security Council and the Cabinet regarding the military campaign against the Taliban regime in Afghanistan.

staffers and executive branch officials, including Vice-President Richard Cheney, Defense Secretary Donald Rumsfeld, National Security Advisor Condoleezza Rice, CIA chief George Tenet, and Secretary of State Colin Powell. Congress, the public, interest groups, and others usually do not play much part, except to the extent that executive decision makers consult a few key members of Congress and try to anticipate the public's reactions.

Broader issues of defense policy—including treaties on arms control or military alliances, participation in major wars, and the amount of money spent on defense—involve much greater participation by Congress, the general public, interest groups, and others. Here, too, the executive branch ordinarily takes the lead, but it must either respond to domestic political forces or change those forces, as in the debate over Iraq. Decisions about military bases and procurement contracts involve congressional committees and interest groups, especially local businesspeople dependent on bases and weapon-producing corporations. Foreign trade, international economic policy, and immigration also sometimes provoke substantial political conflict.

The President and the Executive Branch

Longman
Participate.com 2.0
Simulation
You Are the President: Policy Toward Iran

Because the Constitution gives the principal diplomatic and war powers to the president—the power to appoint and receive ambassadors, to negotiate treaties, and to be commander in chief of the armed forces—the president is the top decision maker on foreign policy and military issues. He has help from many people and government units. In the Bush administration, Vice-President Dick Cheney plays an especially important role in foreign policy.

One of the president's most important White House staff members is the *national security adviser,* head of the *National Security Council (NSC),* who meets with the president nearly every day on matters of defense and foreign policy. The NSC can brief the president on any part of the world or on any military or intelligence matter at a moment's notice.[20]

The *State Department,* headed by the Secretary of State, is the president's chief arm for carrying out diplomatic affairs. The Department is organized along both functional lines—economic affairs, human rights, counterterrorism, and refugees—and geographic lines with "country desks" devoted to each nation of the world. There are 270 embassies and missions that carry out policy abroad and advise the department on new developments.[21] Attached to the State Department are the Arms Control and Disarmament Agency, the U.S. Information Agency, and the Agency for International Development, which oversees foreign economic aid. As issues of trade, U.S. corporate investment in other countries, and protection of intellectual property rights (patents and copyrights) become more important in the global economy, both the *Department of Commerce* and the *Office of the U.S. Trade Representative* have become more important.

The *Department of Defense (DOD),* housed in the **Pentagon,** is also influential in shaping foreign and military policies. The DOD is headed by a civilian *secretary of defense,* who has authority over the entire department and reports directly to the president. Civilian secretaries are in charge of the Departments of the Army, Navy, and Air Force and report to the secretary of defense. Each service also has a military command structure headed by people in uniform: the army and air force chiefs of staff, the chief of naval operations, the commandant of the marine corps, and their subordinates. The uniformed chiefs of each branch serve together in a body called the **Joint Chiefs of Staff (JCS),** headed by the chairman of the Joint Chiefs, who reports not only to the secretary of defense but also directly to the president.

Pentagon

The building in Arlington, Virginia, that contains the offices of the military chiefs and top officials of the Defense Department.

Joint Chiefs of Staff (JCS)

The military officers in charge of each of the armed services.

These B-52 bombers, destroyed by the United States as part of the Strategic Arms Limitations Treaty, must be left in their dismembered state for 90 days so that Russia can confirm their destruction with satellite photos. Satellite photography is used by the United States and other nations to confirm arms control measures and as a strategic device to monitor activities around the world.

A large intelligence community is also involved in the fashioning and implementation of foreign and military policy. This community is made up of a number of specific agencies. The **National Security Agency (NSA)** is responsible for intercepting and monitoring electronic messages from around the world, and the **National Reconnaissance Office (NRO)** is responsible for satellite reconnaissance. Each of the armed services has a separate tactical intelligence unit. Most important is the **Central Intelligence Agency (CIA),** which was established in 1947 to advise the National Security Council, to coordinate all U.S. intelligence agencies, to gather and evaluate intelligence information, and to carry out such additional functions as the NSC directs.

Congress

Congress has generally played a less active role in foreign than in domestic policy. Members of Congress believe that their constituents care more about policies that are close to home than those that are far away. Moreover, the executive branch, with its vast intelligence and national security apparatus, has far more information, expertise, and control of events. Still, Congress has shown signs of more activity since the end of the Cold War. Because the military threat to the United States seemed to have declined with the collapse of the Soviet Union, members of Congress during the 1990s did not feel as compelled as before to defer to the commander in chief on any but the most dangerous situations. Also, on a range of foreign policy issues that now directly affect the everyday lives of

National Security Agency (NSA)

The federal government agency that intercepts and decodes electronic messages and secures U.S. communications around the world.

National Reconnaissance Office (NRO)

The government agency in charge of surveillance by satellite photography and other technological means.

Central Intelligence Agency (CIA)

The organization that coordinates all U.S. intelligence agencies; it also gathers and evaluates intelligence itself and carries out covert operations.

their constituents—immigration, drug trafficking, and corporate investment abroad—members of Congress are less willing than in the past to leave matters to the president. Congress became especially assertive during Bill Clinton's second term when animosity between the president and the Republican-controlled Congress was intense and no apparent foreign military threat was evident. The House of Representatives, for example, passed a bill in early 2000 that mandated more direct ties between the United States and Taiwan military, much to the dismay of President Clinton, who was trying to forge stronger relations with China, whose leadership sees Taiwan as one of its own provinces. Many of President Clinton's appointments of ambassadors, to take another example, were held up for months as a result of his dispute with Senator Jesse Helms over the organization of the State Department and U.N. dues.

After the terrorist attacks on the United States in 2001, however, Congress once again took a back seat to the president on foreign and military policy. None of its leaders was about to take on George W. Bush, given the crisis situation and the president's extraordinary popularity.

The Constitution gives Congress the power to declare war and to decide about any spending of money. It also gives the Senate the power to approve or disapprove treaties and the appointment of ambassadors. At times, Congress has used its treaty or spending powers to challenge the president on important issues: trying to force an end to the Vietnam War, creating difficulties over the Panama Canal treaty and the SALT II arms control treaty, defeating the Nuclear Test Ban Treaty, resisting the Reagan administration's aid to the Nicaraguan Contras, and barely acquiescing to military and peacekeeping operations in Bosnia and Kosovo.

Public Opinion and the News Media

It was once thought that public opinion on foreign policy was so uninformed, unstable, and weak that it could not possibly have much effect on policymaking. As we saw in Chapter 5, however, that picture is not correct. It is now clear that public opinion does, in fact, have substantial effects. Historical studies of such issues as arms control and foreign aid indicate that policymakers have often taken public opinion into account in making their decisions.[22]

Still, the executive branch has considerable leeway. Seldom does public opinion demand that particular actions be taken abroad. More often, the public more or less goes along with what the president does, at least until the results begin to come in. If the results look bad (as in the Vietnam War), the public tends to punish the administration with low popularity ratings and rejection at the polls. If the results look good, as in the Persian Gulf War and in the Afghanistan conflict, the public rewards the administration.

As indicated in Chapter 10, this system of electoral reward and punishment creates incentives for presidents to do things that will please the public in the long run, but there is leeway in the short run, and presidents sometimes miscalculate how things will work out. Moreover, with many foreign policies that are secret or barely visible, the moment for reward or punishment never comes, and the administration can act without being called to account. On some issues, however, the public is so clear about its preferences that a president must tread carefully. For example, the public's reluctance to accept combat casualties when no national security threat is evident convinced President Clinton to rule out the use of ground forces to drive Serb troops out of Kosovo and end "ethnic cleansing." (See the "Using the Framework" feature.)

According to political scientist V. O. Key Jr., public opinion mainly sets up "dikes" that confine policy to certain broad channels. Within those channels,

News media reporting of foreign events can often sway public opinion about distant places. Here, a horde of television cameras document the plight of Muslim refugees fleeing ethnic cleansing in Kosovo. This news coverage helped pressure American and NATO leaders to initiate military action against the Serb-dominated Yugoslav government of Slobodan Milosevic as a way to halt the expulsion of Kosovars from their homes.

the president and the executive branch largely determine the flow.[23] This view may have to be altered slightly to take account of the increasingly important role the news media play in placing issues on the agenda and framing the debate about them. When the plight of Kosovar Muslims at the hands of the Serbs dominated the news broadcasts, the president, the executive branch, and Congress were forced to pay attention. Other human rights tragedies receiving less attention—as in the early stages of the Rwanda atrocities—did not lead to significant U.S. intervention.

Corporations, Interest Groups, and Social Movements

American corporations are among the most active players in the global economy, producing, marketing, and selling goods and services around the world. Naturally, these corporations with a considerable global presence have good reasons to care about U.S. foreign policy. Companies such as Microsoft want the government to aggressively fight software piracy in places such as China and Russia. Many multinational firms seek free trade policies and diplomatic or military protection abroad. Other firms, especially those relying on U.S. markets but threatened by foreign competition (e.g., in automobiles, steel, clothing, and consumer electronics), have sought government subsidies, tariffs, or quotas against foreign goods.

The defense budget involves big money as well. Arms manufacturers such as Lockheed Martin, Boeing, Raytheon, TRW, and General Dynamics play a significant part in decisions about the development and selection of weapons systems.

Ethnic groups also can affect U.S. foreign policy. This is most obvious in the case of U.S. policy toward Israel, in which widespread public sympathy toward that country is reinforced by the efforts of the American-Israel Public Affairs Committee (AIPAC) and by various organized groups representing Jewish Americans. Palestinian-American organizations are becoming more active in an effort to counteract this tendency in U.S. foreign policy. Similarly, African-American groups strongly opposed apartheid in South Africa and military rule in Haiti, and Cuban-American groups have insisted on tough policies against Fidel Castro's Cuba.

USING THE FRAMEWORK: Air War in Kosovo

Why did we depend entirely on air power in Kosovo? Why no ground forces?

Background: Americans strongly supported the use of American ground forces in Afghanistan following the September 11, 2001, terrorist attacks on the United States, and tell pollsters they are willing to have ground forces used in a widened war against terrorism. Apparently, the American people are willing to use troops and to accept casualties when threats to the national security of the United States are clear. This has not been the case in other recent conflicts.

Announcing his plan to rely solely on an air bombing campaign to try to halt the Serb "ethnic cleansing" campaign in the Yugoslavian province of Kosovo in 1999, President Clinton renounced the use of ground combat troops. Many critics, including several of our NATO allies, believed that only troops on the ground could protect Kosovar Muslims from being forced from their homes. Air power eventually prevailed, forcing a Serb withdrawal, but it took time, and the human toll was high. Why, then, did President Clinton avoid sending ground troops? Taking a broader look at how structural, political linkage, and governmental factors affected President Clinton's decision to only use air power in Kosovo will help explain the situation.

Governmental Action

President Clinton orders air strikes against Serb forces in Yugoslavia and Kosovo.

Governmental Level

- The president and his advisors believed that Serb aggression threatened the stability of the Balkans and that some form of military intervention in Kosovo was essential. →
- Congress was uneasy about the use of ground troops and voted a (nonbinding) resolution against their use. →
- The Joint Chiefs and other military leaders did not want to get bogged down in a Balkan quagmire.

Political Linkages Level

- Recently, the news media have "individualized" and "personalized" American military action so that virtually every American combat death receives extensive coverage. →
- The public was not inclined to accept American casualties in humanitarian interventions where the perceived threat to the United States was low. →
- The public came to believe that air power was both effective and saved American lives.

Structural Level

- As commander-in-chief, the president had the constitutional power to put American military forces into action. →
- As the leading military power in the world, the United States had the resources to wage any form of military campaign in Kosovo it wished. →
- The United States had, near at hand, especially at various locations in Europe, sufficient air assets to wage a bombing campaign.

HOW DEMOCRATIC ARE WE?

The American Public and the Making of Foreign Policy

PROPOSITION: Foreign and military policymaking is not and should not be very democratic.

AGREE: Americans care more about what is going on in the United States that affects them directly than they do about issues and developments in distant places. They also know more about what is going on in the United States—whether health care, living standards, or the environment—than they do about what is happening elsewhere, particularly in the poor countries that get very little media news coverage. Additionally, to be effective, many foreign and military policies must be made in secret, so citizens often do not have the information that is necessary to be politically effective. Given all of this, it is clear that Americans are more competent as citizens when faced with domestic matters than with military and foreign affairs. Therefore, for the most part, Americans give political, diplomatic, and military leaders a relatively free hand in making foreign and military policy.

DISAGREE: While it is true that citizens play a smaller role in deciding foreign policies compared with domestic policies, they are not powerless. Citizens do, in fact, give their leaders a great deal of freedom in deciding what to do in foreign and military affairs, but these leaders are ultimately answerable to the people, and they know it. Presidents and members of Congress pay very close attention to public opinion and worry about the next election, so they are careful to avoid actions that may eventually prove unpopular. In addition, if Americans play a lesser role than required by democratic theory, it is something we ought to work on improving. If we are to be a democracy at all, citizens must be engaged in helping to decide all important policies, whether these policies are about health care or nuclear proliferation.

THE AUTHORS: It is true that Americans know less and care less about foreign affairs than they do about domestic affairs. It is also true that some secrecy is required in fashioning and conducting foreign and military policies and that speed is sometimes of the essence. However, it is also probably the case that Americans are becoming more informed about other places, whether through the mass media or the Internet, and are coming to recognize the interconnectedness of our fate with the fates of others, something that 9/11 made evident to all. Americans are paying increasing attention to and learning more about international trade and competitiveness, human rights violations abroad, terrorism threats, and global warming and other environmental problems, to take only a few examples. They are becoming more competent as citizens and seem to be paying closer attention to what our political leaders do in these policy areas and holding them accountable. This is all to the good, in our view, because democracy involves popular control of government leaders and the policies they make.

As the single-minded focus on the Cold War has receded and other foreign policy issues with domestic implications come to the fore, an increasing number of public and private interest groups have been drawn into the politics of foreign policymaking. Labor unions, for example, have become very active in the politics of trade agreements, pushing hard for wage guarantees and worker safety provisions so that jobs at home are not lost to cheap labor abroad. Farm organizations in 2000 successfully lobbied Congress to allow food exports to Cuba. Conservative religious groups and human rights organizations became involved in the fight over the trade status of China because of

Longman
Participate.com
2.0
Participation
Economic
Sanctions and
Cuba

that regime's ill-treatment of Christians (see the Chapter 7 opening vignette). The incipient antiglobalization movement made its presence felt in the streets of Seattle in late 1999 where it clashed with police during demonstrations against the World Trade Organization, causing President Clinton and some other world leaders to consider including labor standards and environmental protections in global trading rules.

Summary

The United States has become the world's only military superpower, with a much larger economy and much more powerful armed forces than any other nation. The United States's advantages in high tech and smart weapons, aerial reconnaissance, and the ability to deploy large forces to world trouble-spots are particularly important.

Longman
Participate.com
2.0
Comparative
Comparing Foreign and Security Policies

For more than 40 years, American foreign policy was focused around the tense Cold War with the Soviet Union, competing for influence in Europe, fighting Soviet allies in Korea and Vietnam, and skirmishing over the Third World. When the Soviet Union collapsed, attention turned to other issues, including regional and ethnic conflicts, international economic competition, efforts at transition to democracy and free markets in Russia and Eastern Europe, problems of world poverty, and the global environment.

Foreign policy has traditionally been made mostly in the executive branch, where the president is assisted by a large national security bureaucracy, including the National Security Council, the Department of Defense, the Department of State, and various intelligence agencies. Congress has been little involved in crises or covert actions and has generally gone along with major decisions on defense policy; it has asserted itself chiefly on matters of foreign trade and aid, military bases, and procurement contracts. Public opinion affects policy, perhaps increasingly so, but this influence is limited by the executive branch's centralization of decision making, secrecy, and control of information. How large a part interest groups and corporations play is disputed, but it is probably substantial. Structural factors, including U.S. economic and military strength and the nature of the international system, strongly affect what policies seem feasible or desirable.

Suggestions for Further Reading

Ambrose, Stephen. *Rise to Globalism,* rev. ed. New York: Penguin Books, 1997.
Describes the rise of the U.S. military, economic, and political power in the twentieth century.

Greider, William. *One World, Ready or Not: The Manic Logic of Global Capitalism.* New York: Simon & Schuster, 1997.
A pessimistic analysis of trends in global capitalism; describes the future as one of economic instability, growing inequality, and corporate control.

Huntington, Samuel P. *The Clash of Civilizations: Civilizations and the Remaking of World Order.* New York: Simon & Schuster, 1997.
Suggests that the post–Cold War world will be organized along the lines of competing civilizations and that one of these civilizations, Islam, presents the greatest danger to a stable world order.

Johnson, Chalmers. *Blowback: The Costs and Consequences of American Empire.* New York: Metropolitan Books, 2000.
A controversial but thought-provoking book which suggests that American global preeminence will not make it safer, especially if the nation's leaders continue to act arrogantly and unilaterally in world affairs.

La Feber, Walter. *America, Russia, and the Cold War, 1945–1990*. New York: McGraw-Hill, 1991.
> *A clear, brief history of the Cold War.*

Nye, Joseph. *The Paradox of American Power: Why the World's Only Superpower Can't Go It Alone*. Oxford: Oxford University Press, 2002.
> *A passionate argument for a multilateral rather than a unilateral foreign policy.*

Russett, Bruce M. *Controlling the Sword: The Democratic Governance of National Security*. Cambridge, MA: Harvard University Press, 1990.
> *Argues that public opinion is much more important in making foreign policy than was previously thought.*

Sen, Amartya Kumar. *Development as Freedom*. New York: Knopf, 1999.
> *The Nobel Prize winner in economics argues that freedom is the basis for the development of poor countries, a fact that should inform the foreign policies of the rich countries.*

Internet Sources

Amnesty International   **www.amnesty.org**
> *Reports and documents from the international human rights organization.*

Center for Defense Information   **www.cdi.org**
> *Analyses of the defense budget, weapons systems, and national security threats.*

Defense Link   **www.defenselink.mil/**
> *The home page of the Department of Defense.*

Fedworld   **www.fedworld.gov**
> *Links to the home pages of all federal departments and agencies involved in foreign affairs and national defense, including the State Department, the Central Intelligence Agency, the Commerce Department, and the Defense Department.*

International Herald Tribune Online   **http://www.iht.com/**
> *Complete international news with a much broader perspective than that found in most U.S. newspapers and other media outlets.*

National Security Website   **www.nationalsecurity.org**
> *Essays and news about foreign and military policy, sponsored by the Heritage Foundation, from a conservative point of view.*

Peacenet   **http://www.peacenet.apc.org**
> *A Website devoted to peace, social and economic justice, and human rights; information on all of these subjects as well as links to organizations working in these fields.*

Statistical Resources on the Web: Military and Defense
www.lib.umich.edu/govdocs/stats.html
> *A vast statistical and information compendium on military and national security issues; covers the United States and other countries.*

United Nations   **www.un.org**
> *Home page of the United Nations; links to a wealth of statistics, documents and reports, UN departments and conferences, and information on reaching UN officials.*

Notes

1. President George W. Bush, The State of the Union Address, The United States Capitol, Washington, D.C. (January 29, 2002).

2. Ibid.

3. Steven Erlanger, "Europe Seethes as the U.S. Flies Solo in World Affairs," *The New York Times* (February 22, 2002), p. A10; David E. Sanger, "Allies Hear Sour Notes in 'Axis of Evil' Chorus," *The New York Times* (February 17, 2002), p. A1.

4. Ibid.

5. Paul Kennedy, *The Rise and Fall of the Great Powers* (New York: Random House, 1987).

6. "X" (George F. Kennan), "The Sources of Soviet Conduct," *Foreign Affairs* 25 (1947), pp. 566–582; Lawrence S. Wittner, *American Intervention in Greece, 1943–1949* (New York: Columbia University Press, 1982).

7. Walter La Feber, *America, Russia, and the Cold War, 1945–1990* (New York: McGraw-Hill, 1991).

8. U.S. Bureau of the Census, *Statistical Abstracts of the United States, 1992* (Washington, D.C.: U.S. Government Printing Office, 1992), pp. 341, 344. Some authorities give a figure of 58,000 for total U.S. *war-related* deaths in Vietnam.

9. Thomas E. Ricks, "A New Way of War," *The Washington Post* (December 10–16, 2001), p. 6.

10. Roger Cohen, "Europe Seeks a New Parity," *The New York Times* (June 15, 1999), p. A1.

11. Joseph S. Nye Jr., "Redefining the National Interest," *Foreign Affairs* (July/August, 1999), pp. 22–35.

12. Thomas L. Friedman, *The Lexus and the Olive Tree* (New York: Farrar, Straus, Giroux, 1999).

13. Bernard Lewis, *What Went Wrong? Western Impact and Middle Eastern Response* (Oxford: Oxford University Press, 2001).

14. Samuel P. Huntington, "The Clash of Civilizations," *Foreign Affairs* 72 (1993).

15. Mario F. Bognanno and Kathryn J. Ready, eds., *The North American Free Trade Agreement: Labor, Industry, and Government Perspectives* (Westport, CT: Praeger, 1993).

16. Jagdish Bhagwati and Marvin H. Kosters, eds., *Trade and Wages: Leveling Down Wages?* (Washington, D.C.: AEI Press, 1994).

17. Jerry Mander and Edward Goldsmith, eds., *The Case Against the Global Economy* (San Francisco: Sierra Club Books, 1996).

18. *Budget of the United States, 2003;* Organization for Economic Cooperation and Development (OECD), *International Development Statistics, 2002.*

19. Congressional Research Service, *Conventional Arms Transfers to Developing Nations, 1993–2000* (Washington, D.C., 2001).

20. Charles W. Kegley Jr. and Eugene R. Wittkopf, *American Foreign Policy: Pattern and Process,* 4th ed. (New York: St. Martin's Press, 1991), p. 387.

21. Donald M. Snow and Eugene Brown, *Puzzle Palaces and Foggy Bottom: U.S. Foreign and Defense Policy-Making in the 1990s* (New York: St. Martin's Press, 1994), p. 96.

22. Bruce M. Russett, *Controlling the Sword: The Democratic Governance of National Security* (Cambridge, MA: Harvard University Press, 1990); Richard Sobel, ed., *Public Opinion in U.S. Foreign Policy: The Controversy over Contra Aid* (Lanham, MD: Rowman & Littlefield, 1993).

23. V. O. Key Jr., *Public Opinion and American Democracy* (New York: Knopf, 1961), p. 552.

Appendix

- The Declaration of Independence
- The Constitution of the United States
- *The Federalist Papers,* Nos. 10, 51, and 78
- Presidents and Congresses, 1789–2005
- Chief Justices of the Supreme Court, 1789–2003

The Declaration of Independence

When in the Course of human events, it becomes necessary for one people to dissolve the political bands which have connected them with another, and to assume among the Powers of the earth, the separate and equal station to which the Laws of Nature and of Nature's God entitle them, a decent respect to the opinions of mankind requires that they should declare the causes which impel them to the separation.

We hold these truths to be self-evident, that all men are created equal, that they are endowed by their Creator with certain unalienable Rights, that among these are Life, Liberty and the pursuit of Happiness. That to secure these rights, Governments are instituted among Men, deriving their just powers from the consent of the governed, That whenever any Form of Government becomes destructive of these ends, it is the Right of the People to alter or to abolish it, and to institute new Government, laying its foundation on such principles and organizing its powers in such form, as to them shall seem most likely to effect their Safety and Happiness. Prudence, indeed, will dictate that Governments long established should not be changed for light and transient causes; and accordingly all experience hath shown, that mankind are more disposed to suffer, while evils are sufferable, than to right themselves by abolishing the forms to which they are accustomed. But when a long train of abuses and usurpations, pursuing invariably the same Object evinces a design to reduce them under absolute Despotism, it is their right, it is their duty, to throw off such Government, and to provide new Guards for their future security.—Such has been the patient sufferance of these Colonies; and such is now the necessity which constrains them to alter their former Systems of Government. The history of the present King of Great Britain is a history of repeated injuries and usurpations, all having in direct object the establishment of an absolute Tyranny over these States. To prove this, let Facts be submitted to a candid world.

He has refused his Assent to Laws, the most wholesome and necessary for the public good.

He has forbidden his Governors to pass Laws of immediate and pressing importance, unless suspended in their operation till his Assent should be obtained; and when so suspended, he has utterly neglected to attend to them.

He has refused to pass other Laws for the accommodation of large districts of people, unless those people would relinquish the right of Representation in the Legislature, a right inestimable to them and formidable to tyrants only.

He has called together legislative bodies at places unusual, uncomfortable, and distant from the depository of their Public Records, for the sole purpose of fatiguing them into compliance with his measures.

He has dissolved Representative Houses repeatedly, for opposing with manly firmness his invasions on the rights of the people.

He has refused for a long time, after such dissolutions, to cause others to be elected; whereby the Legislative Powers, incapable of Annihilation, have returned to the People at large for their exercise; the State remaining in the mean time exposed to all the dangers of invasion from without, and convulsions within.

He has endeavoured to prevent the population of these States; for that purpose obstructing the Laws of Naturalization of Foreigners; refusing to pass others to encourage their migration hither, and raising the conditions of new Appropriations of Lands.

He has obstructed the Administration of Justice, by refusing his Assent to Laws for establishing Judiciary Powers.

He has made Judges dependent on his Will alone, for the tenure of their offices, and the amount and payment of their salaries.

He has erected a multitude of New Offices, and sent hither swarms of Officers to harass our People, and eat out their substance.

He has kept among us, in times of peace, Standing Armies without the Consent of our legislature.

He has affected to render the Military independent of and superior to the Civil Power.

He has combined with others to subject us to a jurisdiction foreign to our constitution, and unacknowledged by our laws; giving his Assent to their acts of pretended legislation:

For quartering large bodies of armed troops among us:

For protecting them, by a mock Trial, from Punishment for any Murders which they should commit on the Inhabitants of these States:

For cutting off our Trade with all parts of the world:

For imposing taxes on us without our Consent:

For depriving us in many cases, of the benefits of Trial by Jury:

For transporting us beyond Seas to be tried for pretended offences:

For abolishing the free System of English Laws in a neighbouring Province, establishing therein an Arbitrary government, and enlarging its Boundaries so as to render it at once an example and fit instrument for introducing the same absolute rule into these Colonies:

For taking away our Charters, abolishing our most valuable Laws, and altering fundamentally the Forms of our Governments:

For suspending our own Legislature, and declaring themselves invested with Power to legislate for us in all cases whatsoever.

He has abdicated Government here, by declaring us out of his Protection and waging War against us.

He has plundered our seas, ravaged our Coasts, burnt our towns, and destroyed the lives of our people.

He is at this time transporting large armies of foreign mercenaries to compleat the works of death, desolation and tyranny, already begun with circumstances of Cruelty & perfidy scarcely paralleled in the most barbarous ages, and totally unworthy the Head of a civilized nation.

He has constrained our fellow Citizens taken Captive on the high Seas to bear Arms against their Country, to become the executioners of their friends and Brethren, or to fall themselves by their Hands.

He has excited domestic insurrections amongst us, and has endeavoured to bring on the inhabitants of our frontiers, the merciless Indian Savages, whose known rule of warfare, is an undistinguished destruction of all ages, sexes and conditions.

In every stage of these Oppressions We have Petitioned for Redress in the most humble terms: Our repeated Petitions have been answered only by repeated injury. A Prince, whose character is thus marked by every act which may define a Tyrant, is unfit to be the ruler of a free People.

Nor have We been wanting in attention to our British brethren. We have warned them from time to time of attempts by their legislature to extend an unwarrantable jurisdiction over us. We have reminded them of the circumstances of our emigration and settlement here. We have appealed to their native justice and magnanimity, and we have conjured them by the ties of our common kindred to disavow these usurpations, which, would inevitably interrupt our connections and correspondence. They too have been deaf to the voice of justice and of consanguinity. We must, therefore, acquiesce in the necessity, which denounces our Separation, and hold them, as we hold the rest of mankind, Enemies in War, in Peace Friends.

We, therefore, the Representatives of the united States of America, in General Congress, Assembled, appealing to the Supreme Judge of the world for the rectitude of our intentions, do, in the Name, and by Authority of the good People of these Colonies, solemnly publish and declare, That these United Colonies are, and of Right ought to be Free and Independent States; that they are Absolved from all Allegiance to the British Crown, and that all political connection between them and the State of Great Britain, is and ought to be totally dissolved; and that as Free and Independent States, they have full Power to levy War, conclude Peace, contract Alliances, establish Commerce, and to do all other Acts and Things which Independent States may of right do. And for the support of this Declaration, with a firm reliance of the Protection of Divine Providence, we mutually pledge to each other our Lives, our Fortunes and our sacred Honor.

John Hancock,

Josiah Bartlett, Wm Whipple, Saml Adams, John Adams, Robt Treat Paine, Elbridge Gerry, Steph. Hopkins, William Ellery, Roger Sherman, Samel Huntington, Wm Williams, Oliver Wolcott, Matthew Thornton, Wm Floyd, Phil Livingston, Frans Lewis, Lewis Morris, Richd Stockton, Jno Witherspoon, Fras Hopkinson, John Hart, Abra Clark, Robt Morris, Benjamin Rush, Benja Franklin, John Morton, Geo Clymer, Jas Smith, Geo. Taylor, James Wilson, Geo. Ross, Caesar Rodney, Geo Read, Thos M:Kean, Samuel Chase, Wm Paca, Thos Stone, Charles Carroll of Carrollton, George Wythe, Richard Henry Lee, Th. Jefferson, Benja Harrison, Thos Nelson, Jr., Francis Lightfoot Lee, Carter Braxton, Wm Hooper, Joseph Hewes, John Penn, Edward Rutledge, Thos Heyward, Junr., Thomas Lynch, Junor., Arthur Middleton, Button Gwinnett, Lyman Hall, Geo Walton.

The Constitution of the United States

We the people of the United States, in Order to form a more perfect Union, establish Justice, insure domestic Tranquility, provide for the common defence, promote the general Welfare, and secure the Blessings of Liberty to ourselves and our Posterity, do ordain and establish this constitution for the United States of America.

Article I

Section 1 All legislative Powers herein granted shall be vested in a Congress of the United States, which shall consist of a Senate and House of Representatives.

Section 2 The House of Representatives shall be composed of Members chosen every second Year by the People of the several States, and the Electors in each State shall have the Qualifications requisite for Electors of the most numerous Branch of the State Legislature.

No person shall be a Representative who shall not have attained to the Age of twenty-five Years, and been seven Years a Citizen of the United States, and who shall not, when elected, be an Inhabitant of that State in which he shall be chosen.

Representatives and direct Taxes shall be apportioned among the several States which may be included within this Union, according to their respective Numbers, which shall be determined by adding to the whole Number of free Persons, including those bound to Service for a Term of Years, and excluding Indians not taxed, three fifths of all other Persons. The actual Enumeration shall be made within three Years after the first Meeting of the Congress of the United States, and within every subsequent Term of ten Years, in such Manner as they shall by Law direct. The Number of Representatives shall not exceed one for every thirty Thousand, but each State shall have at Least one Representative; and until such enumeration shall be made, the State of New Hampshire shall be entitled to chuse three, Massachusetts eight, Rhode-Island and Providence Plantations one, Connecticut five, New-York six, New Jersey four, Pennsylvania eight, Delaware one, Maryland six, Virginia ten, North Carolina five, South Carolina five, and Georgia three.

When vacancies happen in the Representation from any State, the Executive Authority thereof shall issue Writs of Election to fill such Vacancies.

The House of Representatives shall chuse their Speaker and other Officers; and shall have the sole Power of Impeachment.

Section 3 The Senate of the United States shall be composed of two Senators from each State, chosen by the Legislature thereof, for six Years; and each Senator shall have one Vote.

Immediately after they shall be assembled in Consequence of the first Election, they shall be divided as equally as may be into three Classes. The Seats of the Senators of the first Class shall be vacated at the Expiration of the second Year, of the second Class at the Expiration of the fourth Year, and of the third Class at the Expiration of the sixth Year, so that one-third may be chosen every second Year; and if Vacancies happen by Resignation, or otherwise, during the Recess of the Legislature of any State, the Executive thereof may make temporary Appointments until the next Meeting of the Legislature, which shall then fill such Vacancies.

No Person shall be a Senator who shall not have attained to the Age of thirty Years, and been nine Years a Citizen of the United States, and who shall not, when elected, be an Inhabitant of that State in which he shall be chosen.

The Vice President of the United States shall be President of the Senate, but shall have no vote, unless they be equally divided.

The Senate shall chuse their other Officers, and also a President pro tempore, in the absence of the Vice President, or when he shall exercise the Office of the President of the United States.

The Senate shall have the sole Power to try all Impeachments. When sitting for that purpose, they shall be on Oath or Affirmation. When the President of the United States is tried, the Chief Justice shall preside: And no person shall be convicted without the Concurrence of two thirds of the Members present.

Judgment in Cases of Impeachment shall not extend further than to removal from Office, and disqualification to hold and enjoy any Office of honor, Trust, or Profit under the United States: but the Party convicted shall nevertheless be liable and subject to Indictment, Trial, Judgment, and Punishment, according to Law.

Section 4 The Times, Places and Manner of holding Elections for Senators and Representatives, shall be prescribed in each state by the Legislature thereof; but the Congress may at any time by Law make or alter such Regulations, except as to the Places of Chusing Senators.

The Congress shall assemble at least once in every Year, and such Meeting shall be on the first Monday in December, unless they shall by Law appoint a different Day.

Section 5 Each House shall be the Judge of the Elections, Returns and Qualifications of its own Members, and a Majority of each shall constitute a Quorum to do Business; but a smaller number may adjourn from day to day, and may be authorized to compel the Attendance of absent Members, in such Manner, and under such Penalties, as each House may provide.

Each House may determine the Rules of its Proceedings, punish its Members for disorderly Behavior, and, with the Concurrence of two thirds, expel a Member.

Each House shall keep a Journal of its Proceedings, and from time to time publish the same, excepting such Parts as may in their Judgment require Secrecy; and the Yeas and Nays of the Members of either House on any question shall, at the Desire of one fifth of those Present, be entered on the Journal.

Neither House, during the Session of Congress, shall, without the Consent of the other, adjourn for more than three days, nor to any other Place than that in which the two Houses shall be sitting.

Section 6 The Senators and Representatives shall receive a Compensation for their Services, to be ascertained by Law, and paid out of the Treasury of the United States. They shall in all Cases, except Treason, Felony, and Breach of the Peace, be privileged from arrest during their Attendance at the Session of their respective Houses, and in going to and returning from the same; and for any Speech or Debate in either House, they shall not be questioned in any other Place.

No Senator or Representative shall, during the Time for which he was elected, be appointed to any civil Office under the Authority of the United States, which shall have been created, or the Emoluments whereof shall have been increased, during such time; and no Person holding any Office under the United States shall be a Member of either House during his continuance in Office.

Section 7 All Bills for raising Revenue shall originate in the House of Representatives; but the Senate may propose or concur with Amendments as on other bills.

Every Bill which shall have passed the House of Representatives and the Senate, shall, before it become a Law, be presented to the President of the United States; If he approve he shall sign it, but if not he shall return it, with his Objections, to that House in which it shall have originated, who shall enter the Objections at large on their Journal, and proceed to reconsider it. If after such Reconsideration two thirds of that House shall agree to pass the bill, it shall be sent, together with the objections, to the other House, by which it shall likewise be reconsidered, and if approved by two thirds of that House, it shall become a Law. But in all such Cases the Votes of both Houses shall be determined by Yeas and Nays, and the Names of the Persons voting for and against the Bill shall be entered on the Journal of each House respectively. If any Bill shall not be returned by the President within ten Days (Sundays excepted) after it shall have been presented to him, the Same shall be a Law, in like Manner as if he had signed it, unless the Congress by their Adjournment prevent its Return, in which Case it shall not be a Law.

Every Order, Resolution, or Vote to which the Concurrence of the Senate and House of Representatives may be necessary (except on a question of Adjournment) shall be presented to the President of the United States;

and before the Same shall take Effect, shall be approved by him, or being disapproved by him, shall be repassed by two thirds of the Senate and House of Representatives, according to the Rules and Limitations prescribed in the Case of a Bill.

Section 8 The Congress shall have Power

To lay and collect Taxes, Duties, Imposts and Excises, to pay the Debts and provide for the common Defence and general Welfare of the United States; but all Duties, Imposts and Excises shall be uniform throughout the United States;

To borrow money on the credit of the United States;

To regulate Commerce with foreign Nations, and among the several States, and with the Indian Tribes;

To establish a uniform Rule of Naturalization, and uniform Laws on the subject of Bankruptcies throughout the United States;

To coin Money, regulate the Value thereof, and of foreign Coin, and fix the Standard of Weights and Measures;

To provide for the Punishment of counterfeiting the Securities and current Coin of the United States;

To establish Post offices and post Roads;

To promote the Progress of Science and useful Arts, by securing for limited Times to Authors and Inventors the exclusive Right to their respective Writings and Discoveries;

To constitute Tribunals inferior to the Supreme Court;

To define and punish Piracies and Felonies committed on the high Seas, and Offences against the Law of Nations;

To declare War, grant Letters of Marque and Reprisal, and make Rules concerning Captures on Land and Water;

To raise and support Armies, but no Appropriation of Money to that Use shall be for a longer Term than two Years;

To provide and maintain a Navy;

To make Rules for the Government and Regulation of the land and naval forces;

To provide for calling forth the Militia to execute the Laws of the Union, suppress Insurrections and repel Invasions;

To provide for organizing, arming, and disciplining the Militia, and for governing such Part of them as may be employed in the Service of the United States, reserving to the States respectively, the Appointment of the Officers, and the Authority of training the Militia according to the discipline prescribed by Congress;

To exercise exclusive Legislation in all Cases whatsoever, over such District (not exceeding ten Miles square) as may, by Cession of particular States, and the acceptance of Congress, become the Seat of Government of the United States, and to exercise like Authority over all Places purchased by the Consent of the Legislature of the State in which the Same shall be, for the Erection of Forts, Magazines, Arsenals, dock-Yards, and other needful Buildings;—And

To make all Laws which shall be necessary and proper for carrying into Execution the foregoing Powers, and all other Powers vested by this Constitution in the government of the United States, or in any Department or Officer thereof.

Section 9 The Migration or Importation of such Persons as any of the States now existing shall think proper to admit, shall not be prohibited by the Congress prior to the Year one thousand eight hundred and eight, but a tax or duty may be imposed on such Importation, not exceeding ten dollars for each Person.

The privilege of the Writ of Habeas Corpus shall not be suspended, unless when in Cases of Rebellion or Invasion the public Safety may require it.

No Bill of Attainder or ex post facto Law shall be passed.

No capitation, or other direct, Tax shall be laid unless in Proportion to the Census or Enumeration herein before directed to be taken.

No Tax or Duty shall be laid on Articles exported from any State.

No Preference shall be given by any Regulation of Revenue to the Ports of one State over those of another: nor shall Vessels bound to, or from, one state, be obliged to enter, clear, or pay Duties in another.

No Money shall be drawn from the Treasury, but in Consequence of Appropriations made by Law; and a regular Statement and Account of the Receipts and Expenditures of all public Money shall be published from time to time.

No Title of Nobility shall be granted by the United States: And no Person holding any Office of Profit or Trust under them, shall, without the Consent of the Congress, accept of any present, Emolument, Office, or Title, of any kind whatever, from any King, Prince, or Foreign State.

Section 10 No state shall enter into any Treaty, Alliance, or Confederation; grant Letters of Marque and Reprisal; coin Money; emit Bills of Credit; make any Thing but gold and silver Coin a Tender in Payment of Debts; pass any Bill of Attainder, ex post facto Law, or Law impairing the Obligation of Contracts, or grant any Title of Nobility.

No State shall, without the Consent of the Congress, lay any Imposts or Duties on Imports or Exports, except what may be absolutely necessary for executing its inspection Laws: and the net Produce of all Duties and Imposts, laid by any State on Imports or Exports, shall be for the Use of the Treasury of the United States; and all such Laws shall be subject to the Revision and Control of the Congress.

No State shall, without the Consent of Congress, lay any duty of Tonnage, keep Troops, or Ships of War in time of Peace, enter into any Agreement or Compact with another State, or with a foreign Power, or engage in War, unless actually invaded, or in such imminent Danger as will not admit of delay.

Article II

Section 1 The executive Power shall be vested in a President of the United States of America. He shall hold his Office during the Term of four years, and, together with the Vice President, chosen for the same Term, be elected, as follows:

Each State shall appoint, in such Manner as the Legislature thereof may direct, a Number of Electors, equal to the whole Number of Senators and Representatives to which the State may be entitled in the Congress; but no Senator or Representative, or Person holding an Office of Trust or Profit under the United States, shall be appointed an Elector.

The Electors shall meet in their respective States, and vote by Ballot for two persons, of whom one at least shall not be an Inhabitant of the same State with themselves. And they shall make a List of all the Persons voted for, and of the Number of Votes for each; which List they shall sign and certify, and transmit sealed to the Seat of the Government of the United States, directed to the President of the Senate. The President of the Senate shall, in the Presence of the Senate and House of Representatives, open all the Certificates, and the Votes shall then be counted. The Person having the greatest Number of Votes shall be the President, if such Number be a Majority of the whole Number of Electors appointed; and if there be more than one who have such Majority, and have an equal Number of Votes, then the House of Representatives shall immediately chuse by Ballot one of them for President; and if no Person have a Majority, then from the five highest on the List the said House shall in like Manner chuse the President. But in chusing the President, the votes shall be taken by States, the Representation from each State having one Vote; a quorum for this Purpose shall consist of a Member or Members from two-thirds of the States, and a Majority of all the States shall be necessary to a Choice. In every Case, after the Choice of the President, the Person having the greatest Number of Votes of the Electors shall be the Vice President. But if there should remain two or more who have equal votes, the Senate shall chuse from them by Ballot the Vice President.

The Congress may determine the time of chusing the Electors, and the Day on which they shall give their Votes; which Day shall be the same throughout the United States.

No person except a natural-born Citizen, or a Citizen of the United States, at the time of the Adoption of this Constitution, shall be eligible to the Office of President; neither shall any Person be eligible to that Office who shall not have attained to the Age of thirty-five years, and been fourteen Years a Resident within the United States.

In Case of the Removal of the President from Office, or of his Death, Resignation, or Inability to discharge the Powers and Duties of the said Office, the same shall devolve on the Vice President, and the Congress may by

Law provide for the Case of Removal, Death, Resignation, or Inability, both of the President and Vice President, declaring what Officer shall then act as President, and such Officer shall act accordingly, until the disability be removed, or a President shall be elected.

The President shall, at stated Times, receive for his Services a Compensation, which shall neither be increased nor diminished during the Period for which he shall have been elected, and he shall not receive within that Period any other Emolument from the United States, or any of them.

Before he enter on the execution of his Office, he shall take the following Oath or Affirmation:—"I do solemnly swear (or affirm) that I will faithfully execute the Office of President of the United States, and will, to the best of my Ability, preserve, protect, and defend the Constitution of the United States."

Section 2 The President shall be Commander in Chief of the Army and Navy of the United States, and of the Militia of the several States, when called into the actual Service of the United States; he may require the Opinion, in writing, of the principal Officer in each of the executive Departments, upon any subject relating to the Duties of their respective Offices, and he shall have Power to Grant Reprieves and Pardons for Offences against the United States, except in Cases of Impeachment.

He shall have Power, by and with the Advice and Consent of the Senate, to make Treaties, provided two thirds of the Senators present concur; and he shall nominate, and by and with the Advice and Consent of the Senate, shall appoint Ambassadors, other public Ministers and Consuls, Judges of the supreme Court, and all other Officers of the United States, whose Appointments are not herein otherwise provided for, and which shall be established by Law: but the Congress may by Law vest the Appointment of such inferior Officers, as they think proper, in the President alone, in the Courts of Law, or in the Heads of Departments.

The President shall have Power to fill up all Vacancies that may happen during the Recess of the Senate, by granting Commissions which shall expire at the End of their next Session.

Section 3 He shall from time to time give to the Congress Information of the State of the Union, and recommend to their Consideration such Measures as he shall judge necessary and expedient; he may, on extraordinary occasions, convene both Houses, or either of them, and in Case of Disagreement between them, with respect to the Time of Adjournment, he may adjourn them to such Time as he shall think proper; he shall receive Ambassadors and other public Ministers; he shall take Care that the Laws be faithfully executed, and shall Commission all the Officers of the United States.

Section 4 The President, Vice President and all civil Officers of the United States, shall be removed from Office on Impeachment for, and Conviction of, Treason, Bribery, or other high Crimes and Misdemeanors.

Article III

Section 1 The judicial Power of the United States, shall be vested in one supreme Court, and in such inferior Courts as the Congress may from time to time ordain and establish. The Judges, both of the supreme and inferior Courts, shall hold their Offices during good Behaviour, and shall, at stated Times, receive for their Services, a Compensation, which shall not be diminished during their Continuance in Office.

Section 2 The judicial Power shall extend to all Cases, in Law and Equity, arising under this Constitution, the Laws of the United States, and treaties made, or which shall be made, under their Authority;—to all Cases affecting ambassadors, other public ministers and consuls;—to all cases of admiralty and maritime Jurisdiction;—to Controversies to which the United States shall be a Party;—to Controversies between two or more States;—between a State and Citizens of another State;—between Citizens of different States,—between Citizens of the same State claiming Lands under Grants of different States, and between a State, or the Citizens thereof, and foreign States, Citizens or Subjects.

In all Cases affecting Ambassadors, other public Ministers and Consuls, and those in which a State shall be Party, the supreme Court shall have original Jurisdiction. In all the other Cases before mentioned, the supreme Court shall have appellate Jurisdiction, both as to Law and Fact, with such Exceptions, and under such Regulations as the Congress shall make.

The trial of all Crimes, except in Cases of Impeachment, shall be by Jury; and such Trial shall be held in the State where the said Crimes shall have been committed; but when not committed within any State, the Trial shall be at such Place or Places as the Congress may by Law have directed.

Section 3 Treason against the United States, shall consist only in levying War against them, or in adhering to their Enemies, giving them Aid and Comfort. No Person shall be convicted of Treason unless on the testimony of two Witnesses to the same overt Act, or on Confession in open Court.

The Congress shall have power to declare the Punishment of Treason, but no Attainder of Treason shall work Corruption of Blood, or Forfeiture except during the Life of the Person attained.

Article IV

Section 1 Full Faith and Credit shall be given in each State to the public Acts, Records, and judicial Proceedings of every other State. And the Congress may by general Laws prescribe the Manner in which such Acts, Records and Proceedings shall be proved, and the Effect thereof.

Section 2 The Citizens of each State shall be entitled to all Privileges and Immunities of Citizens in the several States.

A Person charged in any State with Treason, Felony, or other Crime, who shall flee from Justice, and be found in another State, shall on demand of the executive Authority of the State from which he fled, be delivered up, to be removed to the State having Jurisdiction of the crime.

No Person held to Service or Labour in one State, under the Laws thereof, escaping into another, shall, in Consequence of any Law or Regulation therein, be discharged from such Service or Labour, but shall be delivered up on Claim of the Party to whom such Service or Labour may be due.

Section 3 New States may be admitted by the Congress into this Union; but no new State shall be formed or erected within the Jurisdiction of any other State; nor any State be formed by the Junction of two or more States, or parts of States, without the Consent of the Legislatures of the States concerned as well as of the Congress.

The Congress shall have Power to dispose of and make all needful Rules and Regulations respecting the Territory or other Property belonging to the United States; and nothing in this Constitution shall be so construed as to Prejudice any Claims of the United States, or of any particular State.

Section 4 The United States shall guarantee to every State in this Union a Republican Form of Government, and shall protect each of them against Invasion; and on Application of the Legislature, or the Executive (when the Legislature cannot be convened) against domestic Violence.

Article V

The Congress, whenever two-thirds of both Houses shall deem it necessary, shall propose Amendments to this Constitution, or, on the Application of the Legislatures of two-thirds of the several States, shall call a Convention for proposing Amendments, which, in either Case, shall be valid to all Intents and Purposes, as part of this Constitution, when ratified by the Legislatures of three-fourths of the several States, or by Conventions in three-fourths thereof, as the one or the other Mode of Ratification may be proposed by the Congress; Provided that no Amendment which may be made prior to the Year One thousand eight hundred and eight shall in any Manner affect the first and fourth Clauses in the Ninth Section of the first Article; and that no State, without its Consent, shall be deprived of its equal Suffrage in the Senate.

Article VI

All Debts contracted and Engagements entered into, before the Adoption of this Constitution, shall be as valid against the United States under this Constitution, as under the Confederation.

This Constitution, and the Laws of the United States which shall be made in Pursuance thereof; and all Treaties made, or which shall be made, under the Authority of the United States, shall be the supreme Law of the Land; and the Judges in every State shall be bound thereby, any Thing in the Constitution or Laws of any State to the Contrary notwithstanding.

The Senators and Representatives before mentioned, and the Members of the several State Legislatures and all executive and judicial Officers, both of the United States and of the several States, shall be bound by Oath or Affirmation to support this Constitution; but no religious Test shall ever be required as a qualification to any Office or public Trust under the United States.

Article VII

The Ratification of the Conventions of nine States shall be sufficient for the Establishment of this Constitution between the States so ratifying the same.

Done in Convention by the Unanimous Consent of the States present the Seventeenth Day of September in the Year of our Lord one thousand seven hundred and Eighty seven, and of the Independence of the United States of America the Twelfth. In Witness whereof We have hereunto subscribed our Names.

Go. Washington, President and deputy from Virginia; Attest William Jackson, Secretary; Delaware: Geo. Read,* Gunning Bedford, Jr., John Dickinson, Richard Basset, Jaco. Broom; Maryland: James McHenry, Daniel of St. Thomas' Jenifer, Danl. Carroll; Virginia: John Blair, James Madison, Jr.; North Carolina: Wm. Blount, Richd. Dobbs Spaight, Hu Williamson; South Carolina: J. Rutledge, Charles Cotesworth Pinckney, Charles Pinckney, Pierce Butler; Georgia: William Few, Abr. Baldwin; New Hampshire: John Langdon, Nicholas Gilman; Massachusetts: Nathaniel Gorham, Rufus King; Connecticut: Wm. Saml. Johnson, Roger Sherman,* New York: Alexander Hamilton; New Jersey: Wil. Livingston, David Brearley, Wm. Paterson, Jona. Dayton; Pennsylvania: B. Franklin,* Thomas Mifflin, Robt. Morris,* Geo. Clymer,* Thos. FitzSimons, Jared Ingersoll, James Wilson, Gouv. Morris.

Articles in Addition to, and Amendment of, the Constitution of the United States of America, Proposed by Congress, and Ratified by the Legislatures of the Several States, Pursuant to the Fifth Article of the Original Constitution.

Amendment I [1791]

Congress shall make no law respecting an establishment of religion, or prohibiting the free exercise thereof; or abridging the freedom of speech, or of the press; or the right of the people peaceably to assemble, and to petition the Government for a redress of grievances.

Amendment II [1791]

A well regulated Militia, being necessary to the security of a free State, the right of the people to keep and bear Arms shall not be infringed.

Amendment III [1791]

No Soldier shall, in time of peace, be quartered in any house, without the consent of the Owner, nor in time of war, but in a manner to be prescribed by law.

Amendment IV [1791]

The right of the people to be secure in their persons, houses, papers, and effects, against unreasonable searches and seizures, shall not be violated, and no Warrants shall issue, but upon probable cause, supported by Oath or affirmation, and particularly describing the place to be searched, and the persons or things to be seized.

Amendment V [1791]

No person shall be held to answer for a capital or otherwise infamous crime, unless on a presentment or indictment of a Grand Jury, except in cases arising in the land or naval forces, or in the Militia, when in actual service in time of War or public danger; nor shall any person be subject for the same offence to be twice put in jeopardy of life or limb; nor shall be compelled in any criminal case to be a witness against himself, nor be deprived of life, liberty, or property, without due process of law; nor shall private property be taken for public use, without just compensation.

Amendment VI [1791]

In all criminal prosecutions, the accused shall enjoy the right to a speedy and public trial, by an impartial jury of the State and district wherein the crime shall have been committed, which district shall have been previously ascertained by law, and to be informed of the nature and cause of the accusation; to be confronted with the witnesses against him; to have compulsory process for obtaining witnesses in his favor, and to have the Assistance of Counsel for his defence.

Amendment VII [1791]

In suits at common law, where the value in controversy shall exceed twenty dollars, the right of trial by jury shall be preserved, and no fact tried by a jury, shall be otherwise reexamined in any Court of the United States, than according to the rules of the common law.

Amendment VIII [1791]

Excessive bail shall not be required, nor excessive fines imposed, nor cruel and unusual punishments inflicted.

Amendment IX [1791]

The enumeration in the Constitution, of certain rights, shall not be construed to deny or disparage others retained by the people.

Amendment X [1791]

The powers not delegated to the United States by the Constitution, nor prohibited by it to the States, are reserved to the States respectively, or to the people.

Amendment XI [1798]

The Judicial power of the United States shall not be construed to extend to any suit in law or equity, commenced or prosecuted against one of the United States by Citizens of another State, or by Citizens or Subjects of any Foreign State.

Amendment XII [1804]

The Electors shall meet in their respective States and vote by ballot for President and Vice President, one of whom, at least, shall not be an inhabitant of the same State with themselves; they shall name in their ballots the person voted for as President, and in distinct ballots the person voted for as Vice President, and they shall make distinct lists of all persons voted for as President, and of all persons voted for as Vice President, and of the number of votes for each, which lists they shall sign and certify, and transmit sealed to the seat of the government of the United States, directed to the President of the Senate;—The President of the Senate shall, in the presence of the Senate and House of Representatives, open all the certificates and the votes shall then be counted;—The person having the greatest number of votes for President, shall be the President, if such number be a majority of the whole number of Electors appointed; and if no person have such majority, then from the persons having the highest numbers not exceeding three on the list of those voted for as President, the House of Representatives shall choose immediately, by ballot, the President. But in choosing the President, the votes shall be taken by states, the representation from each state having one vote; a quorum for this purpose shall consist of a member or members from two-thirds of the states, and a majority of all the states shall be necessary to a choice. And if the House of Representatives shall not choose a President whenever the right of choice shall devolve upon them, before the fourth day of March next following, then the Vice President shall act as President, as in the case of the death or other constitutional disability of the President.— The person having the greatest number of votes as Vice President, shall be the Vice President, if such number be a majority of the whole number of Electors appointed, and if no person have a majority, then from the two highest numbers on the list, the Senate shall choose the Vice President; a quorum for the purpose shall consist of two-thirds of the whole number of Senators, and a majority of the whole number shall be necessary to a choice. But no person constitutionally ineligible to the office of President shall be eligible to that of Vice President of the United States.

Amendment XIII [1865]

Section 1 Neither slavery nor involuntary servitude, except as a punishment for crime whereof the party shall have been duly convicted, shall exist within the United States, or any place subject to their jurisdiction.

Section 2 Congress shall have power to enforce this article by appropriate legislation.

Amendment XIV [1868]

Section 1 All persons born or naturalized in the United States, and subject to the jurisdiction thereof, are citizens of the United States and of the State wherein they reside. No State shall make or enforce any law which shall abridge the privileges or immunities of citizens of the United States; nor shall any State deprive any person of life, liberty, or property, without due process of law; nor deny to any person within its jurisdiction the equal protection of the laws.

Section 2 Representatives shall be apportioned among the several States according to their respective numbers, counting the whole number of persons in each State, excluding Indians not taxed. But when the right to vote at any election for the choice of electors for President and Vice President of the United States, Representatives in Congress, the Executive and Judicial officers of a State, or the members of the Legislature thereof, is denied to any of the male inhabitants of such State, being twenty-one years of age, and citizens of the United States or in any way abridged, except for participation in rebellion, or other crime, the basis of representation therein shall be reduced in the proportion which the number of such male citizens shall bear to the whole number of male citizens twenty-one years of age in such State.

Section 3 No person shall be a Senator or Representative in Congress, or elector of President and Vice President, or hold any office, civil or military, under the United States, or under any State, who, having previously taken an oath, as a member of Congress, or as an officer of the United States, or as a member of any State legislature, or as an executive or judicial officer of any State, to support the Constitution of the United States, shall have engaged in insurrection or rebellion against the same, or given aid or comfort to the enemies thereof.

But Congress may by a vote of two-thirds of each House, remove such disability.

Section 4 The validity of the public debt of the United States, authorized by law, including debts incurred for payment of pensions and bounties for services in suppressing insurrection or rebellion, shall not be questioned. But neither the United States nor any State shall assume or pay any debt or obligation incurred in aid of insurrection or rebellion against the United States, or any claim for the loss or emancipation of any slave; but all such debts, obligations, and claims shall be held illegal and void.

Section 5 The Congress shall have the power to enforce, by appropriate legislation, the provisions of this article.

Amendment XV [1870]

Section 1 The right of citizens of the United States to vote shall not be denied or abridged by the United States or by any State on account of race, color, or previous condition of servitude—

Section 2 The Congress shall have power to enforce this article by appropriate legislation.

Amendment XVI [1913]

The Congress shall have power to lay and collect taxes on incomes, from whatever source derived, without apportionment among the several States, and without regard to any census or enumeration.

Amendment XVII [1913]

The Senate of the United States shall be composed of two Senators from each State, elected by the people thereof, for six years; and each Senator shall have one vote. The electors in each State shall have the qualifications requisite for electors of the most numerous branch of the State legislatures.

When vacancies happen in the representation of any State in the Senate, the executive authority of such State shall issue writs of election to fill such vacancies: Provided, That the legislature of any State may empower the executive thereof to make temporary appointments until the people fill the vacancies by election as the legislature may direct. This amendment shall not be so construed as to affect the election or term of any Senator chosen before it becomes valid as part of the Constitution.

Amendment XVIII [1919]

Section 1 After one year from the ratification of this article the manufacture, sale, or transportation of intoxicating liquors within, the importation thereof into, or the exportation thereof from the United States and all territory subject to the jurisdiction thereof for beverage purposes is hereby prohibited.

Section 2 The Congress and the several States shall have concurrent power to enforce this article by appropriate legislation.

Section 3 This article shall be inoperative unless it shall have been ratified as an amendment to the Constitution by the legislatures of the several States, as provided in the Constitution, within seven years from the date of the submission hereof to the States by the Congress.

Amendment XIX [1920]

The right of citizens of the United States to vote shall not be denied or abridged by the United States or by any State on account of sex.

Congress shall have power to enforce this article by appropriate legislation.

Amendment XX [1933]

Section 1 The terms of the President and Vice President shall end at noon on the 20th day of January, and the terms of Senators and Representatives at noon on the 3d day of January, of the years in which such terms would have ended if this article had not been ratified; and the terms of their successors shall then begin.

Section 2 The Congress shall assemble at least once in every year, and such meeting shall begin at noon on the 3d day of January, unless they shall by law appoint a different day.

Section 3 If, at the time fixed for the beginning of the term of the President, the President elect shall have died, the Vice President elect shall become President. If a President shall not have been chosen before the time fixed for the beginning of his term, or if the President elect shall have failed to qualify, then the Vice President elect shall act as President until a President shall have qualified; and the Congress may by law provide for the case wherein neither a President elect nor a Vice President elect shall have qualified, declaring who shall then act as President, or the manner in which one who is to act shall be selected, and such person shall act accordingly until a President or Vice President shall have qualified.

Section 4 The Congress may by law provide for the case of the death of any of the persons from whom the House of Representatives may choose a President whenever the right of choice shall have devolved upon them, and for the case of the death of any of the persons from whom the Senate may choose a Vice President whenever the right of choice shall have devolved upon them.

Section 5 Sections 1 and 2 shall take effect on the 15th day of October following the ratification of this article.

Section 6 This article shall be inoperative unless it shall have been ratified as an amendment to the Constitution by the legislatures of three-fourths of the several States within seven years from the date of its submission.

Amendment XXI [1933]

Section 1 The eighteenth article of amendment to the Constitution of the United States is hereby repealed.

Section 2 The transportation or importation into any State, Territory, or possession of the United States for delivery or use therein of intoxicating liquors, in violation of the laws thereof, is hereby prohibited.

Section 3 This article shall be inoperative unless it shall have been ratified as an amendment to the Constitution by conventions in the several States, as provided in the Constitution, within seven years from the date of the submission hereof to the States by the Congress.

Amendment XXII [1951]

No person shall be elected to the office of the President more than twice, and no person who has held the office of President, or acted as President, for more than two years of a term to which some other person was elected President shall be elected to the office of the President more than once.

But this Article shall not apply to any person holding the office of President when this Article was proposed by the Congress, and shall not prevent any person who may be holding the office of President or acting as President, during the term within which this Article becomes operative from holding the office of President or acting as President during the remainder of such term.

Amendment XXIII [1961]

Section 1 The District constituting the seat of Government of the United States shall appoint in such manner as the Congress may direct:

A number of electors of President and Vice President equal to the whole number of Senators and Representatives in Congress to which the District would be entitled if it were a State, but in no event more than the least populous State; they shall be in addition to those appointed by the States, but they shall be considered, for the purposes of the election of President and Vice President, to be electors appointed by a State; and they shall meet in the District and perform such duties as provided by the twelfth article of amendment.

Section 2 The Congress shall have power to enforce this article by appropriate legislation.

Amendment XXIV [1964]

Section 1 The right of citizens of the United States to vote in any primary or other election for President or Vice President, for electors for President or Vice President, or for Senator or Representative in Congress, shall not be denied or abridged by the United States or any State by reason of failure to pay any poll tax or other tax.

Section 2 The Congress shall have the power to enforce this article by appropriate legislation.

Amendment XXV [1967]

Section 1 In case of the removal of the President from office or his death or resignation, the Vice President shall become President.

Section 2 Whenever there is a vacancy in the office of the Vice President, the President shall nominate a Vice President who shall take the office upon confirmation by a majority vote of both houses of Congress.

Section 3 Whenever the President transmits to the President pro tempore of the Senate and the Speaker of the House of Representatives his written declaration that he is unable to discharge the powers and duties of his office, and until he transmits to them a written declaration to the contrary, such powers and duties shall be discharged by the Vice President as Acting President.

Section 4 Whenever the Vice President and a majority of either the principal officers of the executive departments, or of such other body as Congress may by law provide, transmit to the President pro tempore of the Senate and the Speaker of the House of Representatives their written declaration that the President is unable to discharge the powers and duties of his office, the Vice President shall immediately assume the powers and duties of the office as Acting President.

Thereafter, when the President transmits to the President pro tempore of the Senate and the Speaker of the House of Representatives his written declaration that no inability exists, he shall resume the powers and duties of his office unless the Vice President and a majority of either the principal officers of the executive departments, or of such other body as Congress may by law provide, transmit within four days to the President pro tempore of the Senate and the Speaker of the House of Representatives their written declaration that the President is unable to discharge the powers and duties of his office. Thereupon Congress shall decide the issue, assembling within 48 hours for that purpose if not in session. If the Congress, within 21 days after receipt of the latter written declaration, or, if Congress is not in session, within 21 days after Congress is required to assemble, determines by two-thirds vote of both houses that the President is unable to discharge the powers and duties of his office, the Vice President shall continue to discharge the same as Acting President; otherwise, the President shall resume the powers and duties of his office.

Amendment XXVI [1971]

Section 1 The right of citizens of the United States, who are 18 years of age or older, to vote shall not be denied or abridged by the United States or any state on account of age.

Section 2 The Congress shall have the power to enforce this article by appropriate legislation.

Amendment XXVII [1992]

No law varying the compensation for the service of Senators and Representatives shall take effect until an election of Representatives shall have intervened.

The Federalist Papers

The Federalist Papers is a collection of 85 essays written by Alexander Hamilton, John Jay, and James Madison under the pen name Publius. They were published in New York newspapers in 1787 and 1788 to support ratification of the Constitution. Excerpts from Federalist Nos. 10, 51, and 78 are reprinted here.

JAMES MADISON: Federalist No. 10

Among the numerous advantages promised by a well constructed Union, none deserves to be more accurately developed than its tendency to break and control the violence of faction. The friend of popular governments never finds himself so much alarmed for their character and fate as when he contemplates their propensity to this dangerous vice. He will not fail, therefore, to set a due value on any plan which, without violating the principles to which he is attached, provides a proper cure for it. The instability, injustice, and confusion, introduced into the public councils, have, in truth been the mortal diseases under which popular governments have everywhere perished; as they continue to be the favorite and fruitful topics from which the adversaries to liberty derive their most specious declamations. The valuable improvements made by the American constitutions on the popular models, both ancient and modern, cannot certainly be too much admired; but it would be an unwarrantable partiality, to contend that they have as effectually obviated the danger on this side, as was wished and expected. Complaints are everywhere heard from our most considerate and virtuous citizens, equally the friends of public and private faith, and of public and personal liberty, that our governments are too unstable; that the public good is disregarded in the conflicts of rival parties; and that measures are too often decided, not according to the rules of justice, and the rights of the minor party, but by the superior force of an interested and overbearing majority. However anxiously we may wish that these complaints had no foundation, the evidence of known facts will not permit us to deny that they are in some degree true. It will be found, indeed, on a candid review of our situation, that some of the distresses under which we labor, have been erroneously charged on the operation of our governments; but it will be found, at the same time, that other causes will not alone account for many of our heaviest misfortunes; and, particularly, for the prevailing and increasing distrust of public engagements, and alarm for private rights, which are echoed from one end of the continent to the other. These must be chiefly, if not wholly, effects of the unsteadiness and injustice, with which a factious spirit has tainted our public administrations.

By a faction, I understand a number of citizens, whether amounting to a majority or minority of the whole, who are united and actuated by some common impulse of passion, or of interest, adverse to the rights of other citizens, or to the permanent and aggregate interests of the community.

There are two methods of curing the mischiefs of faction: The one, by removing its causes; the other, by controlling its effects.

There are again two methods of removing the causes of faction: the one, by destroying the liberty which is essential to its existence; the other, by giving to every citizen the same opinions, the same passions, and the same interests.

It could never be more truly said, than of the first remedy, that it was worse than the disease. Liberty is to faction what air is to fire, an aliment, without which it instantly expires. But it could not be a less folly to abolish liberty, which is essential to political life because it nourishes faction, than it would be to wish the annihilation of air, which is essential to animal life, because it imparts to fire its destructive agency.

The second expedient is as impracticable, as the first would be unwise. As long as the reason of man continues fallible, and he is at liberty to exercise it, different opinions will be formed. As long as the connection subsists between his reason and his self-love, his opinions and his passions will have a reciprocal influence on each other; and the former will be objects to which the latter will attach themselves. The diversity in the faculties of men, from which the rights of property originate, is not less an insuperable obstacle to a uniformity of interests. The protection of those faculties is the first object of government. From the protection of different and unequal faculties of acquiring property, the possession of different degrees and kinds of property immediately results; and from the influence of these on the sentiments and views of the respective proprietors, ensues a division of the society into different interests and parties.

The latent causes of faction are thus sown in the nature of man; and we see them everywhere brought into different degrees of activity, according to the different circumstances of civil society. A zeal for different opinions concerning religion, concerning government, and many other points, as well of speculation as of practice; an attachment to different leaders, ambitiously contending for preeminence and power; or to persons of other descriptions, whose fortunes have been interesting to the human passions, have, in turn, divided mankind into parties, inflamed them with mutual animosity, and rendered them much more disposed to vex and oppress each other, than to cooperate for their common good. So strong is this propensity of mankind, to fall into mutual animosities, that where no substantial occasion presents itself, the most frivolous and fanciful distinctions have been sufficient to kindle their unfriendly passions, and excite their most violent conflicts. But the most common and durable source of factions has been the various and unequal distribution of property. Those who hold, and those who are without property, have ever formed distinct interests in society. Those who are creditors, and those who are debtors, fall under a like discrimination. A landed interest, a manufacturing interest, a mercantile interest, a moneyed interest, with many lesser interests, grow up of necessity in civilized nations, and divide them into different classes, actuated by different sentiments and views. The regulation of these various and interfering interests forms the principle task of modern legislation, and involves the spirit of party and faction in the necessary and ordinary operations of government.

No man is allowed to be a judge in his own cause; because his interest will certainly bias his judgment, and, not improbably, corrupt his integrity. With equal, nay, with greater reason, a body of men are unfit to be both judges and parties at the same time; yet what are many of the most important acts of legislation, but so many judicial determinations, not indeed concerning the rights of single persons, but concerning the rights of large bodies of citizens? And what are the different classes of legislators, but advocates and parties to the cause which they determine? Is a law proposed concerning private debts? It is a question to which the creditors are parties on one side, and the debtors on the other. Justice ought to hold the balance between them. Yet the parties are, and must be, themselves the judges; and the most numerous party, or, in other words, the most powerful faction, must be expected to prevail. Shall domestic manufactures be encouraged, and in what degree, by restrictions on foreign manufactures? are questions which would be differently decided by the landed and the manufacturing classes; and probably by neither with a sole regard to justice and the public good. . . .

It is in vain to say, that enlightened statesmen will be able to adjust these clashing interests, and render them all subservient to the public good. Enlightened statesmen will not always be at the helm; nor, in many cases, can such an adjustment be made at all, without taking into view indirect and remote considerations, which will rarely prevail over the immediate interest which one party may find in disregarding the rights of another, or the good of the whole.

The inference to which we are brought is, that the causes of faction cannot be removed; and that relief is only to be sought in the means of controlling its effects.

If a faction consists of less than a majority, relief is supplied by the republican principle, which enables the majority to defeat its sinister views, by regular vote. It may clog the administration, it may convulse the society; but it will be unable to execute and mask its violence under the forms of the constitution. When a majority is included in a faction, the form of popular government, on the other hand, enables it to sacrifice to its ruling passion or interest, both the public good and the rights of other citizens. To secure the public good, and private rights, against the danger of such a faction, and at the same time to preserve the spirit and the form of popular government, is then the great object to which our inquiries are directed. Let me add, that it is the great desideratum, by which alone this form of government can be rescued from the opprobrium under which it has so long labored, and be recommended to the esteem and adoption of mankind.

By what means is this object attainable? Evidently by one of two only. Either the existence of the same passion or interest in a majority, at the same time must be prevented; or the majority, having such coexistent passion or interest, must be rendered, by their number and local situation, unable to concert and carry into effect schemes of oppression. If the impulse and the opportunity be suffered to coincide, we well know, that neither moral nor religious motives can be relied on as an adequate control. They are not found to be such on the injustice and violence of individuals, and lose their efficacy in proportion to the number combined together; that is in proportion as their efficacy becomes needful.

From this view of the subject, it may be concluded, that a pure democracy, by which I mean a society consisting of a small number of citizens, who assemble and administer the government in person, can admit of no cure from the mischiefs of faction. A common passion or interest will, in almost every case, be felt by a majority of the whole; a communication and concert, results from the form of government itself; and there is nothing to check the inducements to sacrifice the weaker party, or an obnoxious individual. Hence it is, that such democracies have ever been spectacles of turbulence and contention; have ever been found incompatible with personal security, or the rights of property; and have, in general been as short in their lives, as they have been violent in their deaths. Theoretic politicians, who have patronized this species of government, have erroneously supposed that by reducing mankind to a perfect equality in their political rights, they would, at the same time, be perfectly equalized and assimilated in their possessions, their opinions, and their passions.

A republic, by which I mean a government in which the scheme of representation takes place, opens a different prospect, and promises the cure for which we are seeking. Let us examine the points in which it varies from pure democracy, and we shall comprehend both the nature of the cure and the efficacy which it must derive from the union.

The two great points of difference, between a democracy and a republic, are, first, the delegation of the government, in the latter, to a small number of citizens elected by the rest; secondly, the greater number of citizens, and greater sphere of country, over which the latter may be extended.

The effect of the first difference is on the one hand, to refine and enlarge the public views, by passing them through the medium of a chosen body of citizens, whose wisdom may best discern the true interest in their country, and whose patriotism and love of justice, will be least likely to sacrifice it to temporary or partial considerations. Under such a regulation, it may well happen, that the public voice, pronounced by the representatives of the people, will be more consonant to the public good, than if pronounced by the people themselves, convened for the purpose. On the other hand, the effect may be inverted. Men of factious tempers, of local prejudices, or of sinister designs, may by intrigue, by corruption, or by other means, first obtain the suffrages, and then betray the interests, of the people. The question resulting is, whether small or extensive republics are most favorable to the election of proper guardians of the public weal; and it is clearly decided in favor of the latter by two obvious considerations.

In the first place, it is to be remarked, that however small the republic may be, the representatives must be raised to a certain number, in order to guard against the cabals of a few; and that however large it may be, they must be limited to a certain number, in order to guard against the confusion of a multitude. Hence, the number of representatives in the two cases not being in proportion to that of the constituents, and being proportionally greatest in the small republic, it follows that if the proportion of fit characters be not less in the large than in the small republic, the former will present a greater option, and consequently a greater probability of a fit choice.

In the next place, as each representative will be chosen by a greater number of citizens in the large than in the small republic, it will be more difficult for unworthy candidates to practice with success the vicious arts, by which elections are too often carried; and the suffrages of the people being more free, will be more likely to center in men who possess the most attractive merit, and the most diffusive and established characters. . . .

The other point of difference is, the greater number of citizens, and extent of territory, which may be brought within the compass of republican, than of democratic government; and it is this circumstance principally which renders factious combinations less to be dreaded in the former, than in the latter. The smaller the society, the fewer probably will be the distinct parties and interests composing it; the fewer the distinct parties and interests, the more frequently will a majority be found of the same party; and the smaller the number of individuals composing a majority, and the smaller the compass within which they are placed, the more easily they will concert and execute their plans of oppression. Extend the sphere, and you take in a greater variety of parties and interests; you make it less probable that a majority of the whole will have a common motive to invade the rights of other citizens; or if such a common motive exists, it will be more difficult for all who feel it to discover their own strength, and to act in unison with each other. . . .

Hence, it clearly appears, that the same advantage, which a republic has over a democracy, in controlling the effects of faction, is enjoyed by a large over a small republic—is enjoyed by the union over the states composing it. Does this advantage consist in the substitution of representatives, whose enlightened views and virtuous sentiments render them superior to local prejudices, and to schemes of injustice? It will not be denied, that the representation of the union will be most likely to possess these requisite endowments. Does it consist in the greater security afforded by a greater variety of parties, against the event of any one party being able to outnumber and oppress the rest? In an equal degree does the increased variety of parties, comprised within the union, increase this security? Does it, in fine, consist in the greater obstacles opposed to the concert and accomplishment of the secret wishes of an unjust and interested majority? Here, again, the extent of the union gives it the most palpable advantage. The influence of factious leaders may kindle a flame within their particular states, but will be unable to spread a general conflagration through the other states; a religious sect may degenerate into a political faction in a part of the confederacy; but the variety of sects dispersed over the entire face of it, must secure the national councils against any danger from that source; a rage for paper money, for an abolition of debts, for an equal division of property, or for any other improper or wicked project, will be less apt to pervade the whole body of the union, than a particular member of it; in the same proportion as such a malady is more likely to taint a particular country or district, than an entire state.

In the extent and proper structure of the union, therefore, we behold a republican remedy for the diseases most incident to republican government. And according to the degree of pleasure and pride we feel in being republicans, ought to be our zeal in cherishing the spirit, and supporting the character of Federalists.

JAMES MADISON: Federalist No. 51

To what expedient then shall we finally resort, for maintaining in practice the necessary partition of power among the several departments, as laid down in the constitution? The only answer that can be given is, that as all these exterior provisions are found to be inadequate, the defect must be supplied, by so contriving the interior structure of the government, as that its several constituent parts may, by their mutual relations, be the means of keeping each other in their proper places. . . .

In order to lay a due foundation for that separate and distinct exercise of the different powers of government, which, to a certain extent, is admitted on all hands to be essential to the preservation of liberty, it is evident that each department should have a will of its own; and consequently should be so constituted, that the members of each should have as little agency as possible in the appointment of the members of the others. . . .

It is equally evident, that the members of each department should be as little dependent as possible on those of the others, for the emoluments annexed to their offices. Were the executive magistrate, or the judges, not independent of the legislature in this particular, their independence in every other would be merely nominal.

But the great security against a gradual concentration of the several powers in the same department, consists in giving to those who administer each department, the necessary constitutional means, and personal motives, to resist encroachments of the others. The provision for defense must in this, as in all other cases, be made commensurate to the danger of attack. Ambition must be made to counteract ambition. The interest of the man must be connected with the constitutional rights of the place. It may be a reflection on human nature, that such devices should be necessary to control the abuses of government. But what is government itself, but the greatest of all reflections on human nature? If men were angels, no government would be necessary. If angels were to govern men, neither external nor internal controls on government would be necessary. In framing a government, which is to be administered by men over men, the great difficulty lies in this: You must first enable the government to control the governed; and in the next place, oblige it to control itself. A dependence on the people is, no doubt, the primary control on the government; but experience has taught mankind the necessity of auxiliary precautions.

This policy of supplying by opposite and rival interests, the defect of better motives, might be traced through the whole system of human affairs, private as well as public. We see it particularly displayed in all the subordinate distributions of power; where the constant aim is, to divide and arrange the several offices in such a manner, as that each may be a check on the other; that the private interest of every individual, may be a sentinel over the public rights. These interventions of prudence cannot be less requisite to the distribution of the supreme powers of the state.

But it is not possible to give to each department an equal power of self-defense. In republican government, the legislative authority necessarily predominates. The remedy for this inconvenience is, to divide the legislature into different branches; and to render them by different modes of election, and different principles of action, as little connected with each other, as the nature of their common functions, and their common dependence on the society will admit. It may even be necessary to guard against dangerous encroachments, by still further precautions. As the weight of the legislative authority requires that it should be thus divided, the weakness of the executive may require, on the other hand, that it should be fortified. An absolute negative on the legislature, appears, at first view, to be the natural defense with which the executive magistrate should be armed. But perhaps it would be neither altogether safe, nor alone sufficient. On ordinary occasions, it might not be exerted with the

requisite firmness; and on extraordinary occasions, it might be perfidiously abused. May not this defect of an absolute negative be supplied by some qualified connection between this weaker department, and the weaker branch of the stronger department, by which the latter may be led to support the constitutional rights of the former, without being too much detached from the rights of its own department?

There are, moreover, two considerations particularly applicable to the federal system of America, which place that system in a very interesting point of view.

First. In a single republic, all the power surrendered by the people is submitted to the administration of a single government, and the usurpations are guarded against by a division of the government into distinct and separate departments. In the compound republic of America, the power surrendered by the people is first divided between two distinct governments, and then the portion allotted to each subdivided among distinct and separate departments. Hence a double security arises to the rights of the people. The different governments will control each other, at the same time that each will be controlled by itself.

Second. It is of great importance in a republic not only to guard the society against the oppression of its rulers, but to guard one part of the society against the injustice of the other part. Different interests necessarily exist in different classes of citizens. If a majority be united by a common interest, the rights of the minority will be insecure. There are but two methods of providing against this evil: the one by creating a will in the community independent of the majority—that is, of the society itself; the other, by comprehending in the society so many separate descriptions of citizens as will render an unjust combination of a majority of the whole very probable, if not impracticable. The first method prevails in all governments possessing an hereditary or self-appointed authority. This, at best, is but a precarious security; because a power independent of the society may as well espouse the unjust views of the major, as the rightful interests of the minor party, and may possibly be turned against both parties. The second method will be exemplified in the federal republic of the United States. Whilst all authority in it will be derived from and dependent on the society, the society itself will be broken into so many parts, interests and classes of citizens, that the rights of individuals, or of the minority, will be in little danger from interested combinations of the majority. In a free government the security for civil rights must be the same as that for religious rights. It consists in the one case in the multiplicity of interests, and in the other in the multiplicity of sects. The degree of security in both cases will depend on the number of interests and sects; and this may be presumed to depend on the extent of country and number of people comprehended under the same government. This view of the subject must particularly recommend a proper federal system to all the sincere and considerate friends of republican government, since it shows that in exact proportion as the territory of the Union may be formed into more circumscribed Confederacies, or States, oppressive combinations of a majority will be facilitated; the best security, under the republican forms, for the rights of every class of citizens, will be diminished; and consequently the stability and independence of some member of the government, the only other security, must be proportionately increased. Justice is the end of the government. It is the end of civil society. It ever has been and ever will be pursued until it be obtained, or until liberty be lost in the pursuit. In a society under the forms of which the stronger faction can readily unite and oppress the weaker, anarchy may as truly be said to reign as in a state of nature, where the weaker individual is not secured against the violence of the stronger; and as, in the latter state, even the stronger individuals are prompted, by the uncertainty of their condition, to submit to a government which may protect the weak as well as themselves; so, in the former state, will the more powerful factions or parties be gradually induced, by a like motive, to wish for a government which will protect all parties, the weaker as well as the more powerful. It can be little doubted that if the State of Rhode Island was separated from the Confederacy and left to itself, the insecurity of rights under the popular form of government within such narrow limits would be displayed by such reiterated oppressions of factious majorities that some power altogether independent of the people would soon be called for by the voice of the very factions whose misrule had proved the necessity of it. In the extended republic of the United States, and among the great variety of interests, parties, and sects which it embraces, a coalition of a majority of the whole society could seldom take place on any other principles than those of justice and the general good; whilst there being thus less danger to a minor from the will of a major party, there must be less pretext, also, to provide for the security of the former, by introducing into the government a will not dependent on the latter, or, in other words, a will independent of the society itself. It is no less certain than it is important, notwithstanding the contrary opinions which have been entertained, that the larger the society, provided it lie within a practical sphere, the more duly capable it will be of self-government. And happily for the republican cause, the practicable sphere may be carried to a very great extent, by a judicious modification and mixture of the federal principle.

ALEXANDER HAMILTON: Federalist No. 78

We proceed now to an examination of the judiciary department of the proposed government.

In unfolding the defects of the existing confederation, the utility and necessity of a federal judicature have been clearly pointed out. It is the less necessary to recapitulate the considerations there urged; as the propriety of the institution in the abstract is not disputed; the only questions which have been raised being relative to the manner of constituting it, and to its extent. To these points, therefore, our observations shall be confined.

The manner of constituting it seems to embrace these several objects: 1st. The mode of appointing the judges; 2nd. The tenure by which they are to hold their places; 3rd. The partition of the judiciary authority between courts, and their relations to each other.

First. As to the mode of appointing the judges: This is the same with that of appointing the officers of the union in general, and has been so fully discussed . . . that nothing can be said here which would not be useless repetition.

Second. As to the tenure by which the judges are to hold their places: This chiefly concerns their duration in office; the provisions for their support; the precautions for their responsibility.

According to the plan of the convention, all the judges who may be appointed by the United States are to hold their offices during good behavior; which is conformable to the most approved of the state constitutions. . . . The standard of good behavior for the continuance in office of the judicial magistracy is certainly one of the most valuable of the modern improvements in the practice of government. In a monarchy, it is an excellent barrier to the despotism of the prince; in a republic, it is a no less excellent barrier to the encroachments and oppressions of the representative body. And it is the best expedient which can be devised in any government, to secure a steady, upright, and impartial administration of the laws.

Whoever attentively considers the different departments of power must perceive, that, in a government in which they are separated from each other, the judiciary, from the nature of its functions, will always be the least dangerous to the political rights of the constitution; because it will be at least in a capacity to annoy or injure them. The executive not only dispenses the honors, but holds the sword of the community. The legislature not only commands the purse, but prescribes the rules by which the duties and rights of every citizen are to be regulated. The judiciary, on the contrary, has no influence over either the sword or the purse; no direction either of the strength or of the wealth of the society; and can take no active resolution whatever. It may truly be said to have neither force nor will, but merely judgment; and must ultimately depend upon the aid of the executive arm for the efficacious exercise even of this faculty.

This simple view of the matter suggests several important consequences: It proves incontestably, that the judiciary is beyond comparison, the weakest of the three departments of power, that it can never attack with success either of the other two: and that all possible care is requisite to enable it to defend itself against their attacks. It equally proves, that, though individual oppression may now and then proceed from the courts of justice, the general liberty of the people can never be endangered from that quarter; I mean so long as the judiciary remains truly distinct from both the legislature and executive. For I agree, that "there is no liberty, if the power of judging be not separated from the legislative and executive powers." It proves, in the last place, that as liberty can have nothing to fear from the judiciary alone, but would have everything to fear from its union with either of the other departments; that, as all the effects of such a union must ensue from a dependence of the former on the latter, notwithstanding a nominal and apparent separation; that as, from the natural feebleness of the judiciary, it is in continual jeopardy of being overpowered, awed or influenced by its coordinate branches; that, as nothing can contribute so much to its firmness and independence as permanency in office, this quality may therefore be justly regarded as an indispensable ingredient in its constitution; and, in a great measure, as the citadel of the public justice and the public security.

The complete independence of the courts of justice is peculiarly essential in a limited constitution. By a limited constitution, I understand one which contains certain specified exceptions to the legislative authority; such, for instance, as that it shall pass no bills of attainder, no ex post facto laws, and the like. Limitations of this kind can be preserved in practice no other way than through the medium of the courts of justice, whose duty it must be to declare all acts contrary to the manifest tenor of the constitution void. Without this, all the reservations of particular rights or privileges would amount to nothing.

Some perplexity respecting the right of the courts to pronounce legislative acts void, because contrary to the constitution, has arisen from an imagination that the doctrine would imply a superiority of the judiciary to the legislative power. It is urged that the authority which can declare the acts of another void, must necessarily be superior to the one whose acts may be declared void. As this doctrine is of great importance in all the American constitutions, a brief discussion of the grounds on which it rests cannot be unacceptable.

There is no position which depends on clearer principles than that every act of a delegated authority, contrary to the tenor of the commission under which it is exercised, is void. No legislative act, therefore, contrary to the constitution, can be valid. To deny this would be to affirm, that the deputy is greater then his principal; that the servant is above his master; that the representatives of the people are superior to the people themselves; that men, acting by virtue of powers, may do not only what their powers do not authorize, but what they forbid.

If it be said that the legislative body are themselves the constitutional judges of their own powers, and that the construction they put upon them is conclusive upon the other departments, it may be answered, that this cannot be the natural presumption, where it is not to be collected from any particular provisions in the constitution. It is not otherwise to be supposed that the constitution could intend to enable the representatives of the people to substitute their will to that of their constituents. It is far more rational to suppose that the

courts were designed to be an intermediate body between the people and the legislature, in order, among other things, to keep the latter within the limits assigned to their authority. The interpretation of the laws is the proper and peculiar province of the courts. A constitution is, in fact, and must be, regarded by the judges as a fundamental law. It must therefore belong to them to ascertain its meaning, as well as the meaning of any particular act proceeding from the legislative body. If there should happen to be an irreconcilable variance between the two, that which has the superior obligation and validity ought, of course, to be preferred; in other words, the constitution ought to be preferred to the statute, the intention of the people to the intention of their agents.

Nor does this conclusion by any means suppose a superiority of the judicial to the legislative power. It only supposes that the power of the people is superior to both; and that where the will of the legislature declared in its statutes, stands in opposition to that of the people declared in the constitution, the judges ought to be governed by the latter, rather than the former. They ought to regulate their decisions by the fundamental laws, rather than by those which are not fundamental. . . .

It can be of no weight to say, that the courts, on the pretense of a repugnancy, may substitute their own pleasure to the constitutional intentions of the legislature. This might as well happen in the case of two contradictory statutes; or it might as well happen in every adjudication upon any single statute. The courts must declare the sense of the law; and if they should be disposed to exercise will instead of judgment, the consequence would equally be the substitution of their pleasure to that of the legislative body. The observation, if it proved anything, would prove that there ought to be no judges distinct from the body.

If then the courts of justice are to be considered as the bulwarks of a limited constitution, against legislative encroachments, this consideration will afford a strong argument for the permanent tenure of judicial officers, since nothing will contribute so much as this to that independent spirit in the judges, which must be essential to the faithful performance of so arduous a duty.

This independence of the judges is equally requisite to guard the constitution and the rights of individuals, from the effects of those ill-humors which are the arts of designing men, or the influence of particular conjunctures, sometimes disseminate among the people themselves, and which, though they speedily give place to better information, and more deliberate reflection, have a tendency, in the meantime, to occasion dangerous innovations in the government, and serious oppressions of the minor party in the community. . . . Until the people have, by some solemn and authoritative act, annulled or changed the established form, it is binding upon themselves collectively, as well as individually; and no presumption, or even knowledge of their sentiments, can warrant their representatives in a departure from it, prior to such an act. But it is easy to see, that it would require an uncommon portion of fortitude in the judges to do their duty as faithful guardians of the constitution, where legislative invasions of it had been instigated by the major voice of the community.

But it is not with a view to infractions of the constitution only, that the independence of the judges may be an essential safeguard against the effects of occasional ill-humors in the society. These sometimes extend no farther than to the injury of the private rights of particular classes of citizens, by unjust and partial laws. Here also the firmness of the judicial magistracy is of vast importance in mitigating the severity, and confining the operation of such laws. It not only serves to moderate the immediate mischiefs of those which may have been passed, but it operates as a check upon the legislative body in passing them; who, perceiving that obstacles to the success of an iniquitous intention are to be expected from the scruples of the courts, are in a manner compelled by the very motives of the injustice they meditate, to qualify their attempts. . . .

That inflexible and uniform adherence to the rights of the constitution, and of individuals, which we perceive to be indispensable in the courts of justice, can certainly not be expected from judges who hold their offices by a temporary commission. Periodical appointments, however regulated, or by whomsoever made, would, in some way or other, be fatal to their necessary independence. If the power of making them was committed either to the executive or legislature, there would be dan-

ger of an improper compliance to the branch which possessed it; if to both, there would be an unwillingness to hazard the displeasure of either; if to the people, or to persons chosen by them for the special purpose, there would be too great a disposition to consult popularity to justify a reliance that nothing would be consulted but the constitution and the laws.

There is yet a further and a weighty reason for the permanency of judicial offices, which is deducible from the nature of the qualifications they require. It has been frequently remarked, with great propriety, that a voluminous code of laws is one of the inconveniences necessarily connected with the advantages of a free government. To avoid an arbitrary discretion in the courts, it is indispensable that they should be bound down by strict rules and precedents, which serve to define and point out their duty in every particular case that comes before them; and it will readily be conceived, from the variety of controversies which grow out of the folly and wickedness of mankind, that the records of those precedents must unavoidably swell to a very considerable bulk, and must demand long and laborious study to acquire a competent knowledge of them. Hence it is, that there can be but few men in the society, who will have sufficient skill in the laws to qualify them for the stations of judges. And making the proper deductions for the ordinary depravity of human nature, the number must be still smaller, of those who unite the requisite integrity with the requisite knowledge. . . .

Presidents and Congresses, 1789-2005

Year	President and Vice-President	Party of President	Congress	Majority Party — House	Majority Party — Senate
1789–1797	**George Washington** John Adams	None	1st 2nd 3rd 4th	Admin. Supporters Federalist Democratic-Republican Federalist	Admin. Supporters Federalist Federalist Federalist
1797–1801	**John Adams** Thomas Jefferson	Federalist	5th 6th	Federalist Federalist	Federalist Federalist
1801–1809	**Thomas Jefferson** Aaron Burr (to 1805) George Clinton (to 1809)		7th 8th 9th 10th	Democratic-Republican Democratic-Republican Democratic-Republican Democratic-Republican	Democratic-Republican Democratic-Republican Democratic-Republican Democratic-Republican
1809–1817	**James Madison** George Clinton (to 1813) Elbridge Gerry (to 1817)	Democratic-Republican	11th 12th 13th 14th	Democratic-Republican Democratic-Republican Democratic-Republican Democratic-Republican	Democratic-Republican Democratic-Republican Democratic-Republican Democratic-Republican
1817–1825	**James Monroe** Daniel D. Tompkins	Democratic-Republican	15th 16th 17th 18th	Democratic-Republican Democratic-Republican Democratic-Republican Democratic-Republican	Democratic-Republican Democratic-Republican Democratic-Republican Democratic-Republican
1825–1829	**John Quincy Adams** John C. Calhoun	National-Republican	19th 20th	Admin. Supporters Jacksonian Democrats	Admin. Supporters Jacksonian Democrats
1829–1837	**Andrew Jackson** John C. Calhoun (to 1833) Martin Van Buren (to 1837)	Democratic	21st 22nd 23rd 24th	Democratic Democratic Democratic Democratic	Democratic Democratic Democratic Democratic
1837–1841	**Martin Van Buren** Richard M. Johnson	Democratic	25th 26th	Democratic Democratic	Democratic Democratic
1841	**William H. Harrison** (died a month after inauguration) John Tyler	Whig			
1841–1845	**John Tyler** (VP vacant)	Whig	27th 28th	Whig Democratic	Whig Whig
1845–1849	**James K. Polk** George M. Dallas	Democratic	29th 30th	Democratic Whig	Democratic Democratic

Year	President and Vice-President	Party of President	Congress	Majority Party House	Majority Party Senate
1849–1850	**Zachary Taylor** (died in office) Millard Fillmore	Whig	31st	Democratic	Democratic
1850–1853	**Millard Fillmore** (VP vacant)	Whig	32nd	Democratic	Democratic
1853–1857	**Franklin Pierce** William R. King	Democratic	33rd 34th	Democratic Republican	Democratic Democratic
1857–1861	**James Buchanan** John C. Breckinridge	Democratic	35th 36th	Democratic Republican	Democratic Democratic
1861–1865	**Abraham Lincoln** (died in office) Hannibal Hamlin (to 1865) Andrew Johnson (1865)	Republican	37th 38th	Republican Republican	Republican Republican
1865–1869	**Andrew Johnson** (VP vacant)	Republican	39th 40th	Unionist Republican	Unionist Republican
1869–1877	**Ulysses S. Grant** Schuyler Colfax (to 1873) Henry Wilson (to 1877)	Republican	41st 42nd 43rd 44th	Republican Republican Republican Democratic	Republican Republican Republican Republican
1877–1881	**Rutherford B. Hayes** William A. Wheeler	Republican	45th 46th	Democratic Democratic	Republican Democratic
1881	**James A. Garfield** (died in office) Chester A. Arthur	Republican	47th	Republican	Republican
1881–1885	**Chester A. Arthur** (VP vacant)	Republican	48th	Democratic	Republican
1885–1889	**Grover Cleveland** Thomas A. Hendricks	Democratic	49th 50th	Democratic Democratic	Republican Republican
1889–1893	**Benjamin Harrison** Levi P. Morton	Republican	51st 52nd	Republican Democratic	Republican Republican
1893–1897	**Grover Cleveland** Adlai E. Stevenson	Democratic	53rd 54th	Democratic Republican	Democratic Republican
1897–1901	**William McKinley** (died in office) Garret A. Hobart (to 1901) Theodore Roosevelt (1901)	Republican	55th 56th	Republican Republican	Republican Republican

Year	President and Vice-President	Party of President	Congress	Majority Party	
				House	Senate
1901–1909	**Theodore Roosevelt** (VP vacant, 1901–1905) Charles W. Fairbanks (1905–1909)	Republican	57th 58th 59th 60th	Republican Republican Republican Republican	Republican Republican Republican Republican
1909–1913	**William Howard Taft** James S. Sherman	Republican	61st 62nd	Republican Democratic	Republican Republican
1913–1921	**Woodrow Wilson** Thomas R. Marshall	Democratic	63rd 64th 65th 66th	Democratic Democratic Democratic Republican	Democratic Democratic Democratic Republican
1921–1923	**Warren G. Harding** (died in office) Calvin Coolidge	Republican	67th	Republican	Republican
1923–1929	**Calvin Coolidge** (VP vacant, 1923–1925) Charles G. Dawes (1925–1929)	Republican	68th 69th 70th	Republican Republican Republican	Republican Republican Republican
1929–1933	**Herbert Hoover** Charles Curtis	Republican	71st 72nd	Republican Democratic	Republican Republican
1933–1945	**Franklin D. Roosevelt** (died in office) John N. Garner (1933–1941) Henry A. Wallace (1941–1945) Harry S Truman (1945)	Democratic	73rd 74th 75th 76th 77th 78th	Democratic Democratic Democratic Democratic Democratic Democratic	Democratic Democratic Democratic Democratic Democratic Democratic
1945–1953	**Harry S Truman** (VP vacant, 1945–1949) Alben W. Barkley (1949–1953)	Democratic	79th 80th 81st 82nd	Democratic Republican Democratic Democratic	Democratic Republican Democratic Democratic
1953–1961	**Dwight D. Eisenhower** Richard M. Nixon	Republican	83rd 84th 85th 86th	Republican Democratic Democratic Democratic	Republican Democratic Democratic Democratic
1961–1963	**John F. Kennedy** (died in office) Lyndon B. Johnson	Democratic	87th	Democratic	Democratic
1963–1969	**Lyndon B. Johnson** (VP vacant, 1963–1965) Hubert H. Humphrey (1965–1969)	Democratic	88th 89th 90th	Democratic Democratic Democratic	Democratic Democratic Democratic

Year	President and Vice-President	Party of President	Congress	Majority Party	
				House	Senate
1969–1974	**Richard M. Nixon** (resigned office) Spiro T. Agnew (resigned office) Gerald R. Ford (appointed vice-president)	Republican	91st 92nd	Democratic Democratic	Democratic Democratic
1974–1977	**Gerald R. Ford** Nelson A. Rockefeller (appointed vice-president)	Republican	93rd 94th	Democratic Democratic	Democratic Democratic
1977–1981	**Jimmy Carter** Walter Mondale	Democratic	95th 96th	Democratic Democratic	Democratic Democratic
1981–1989	**Ronald Reagan** George H. W. Bush	Republican	97th 98th 99th 100th	Democratic Democratic Democratic Democratic	Republican Republican Republican Democratic
1989–1993	**George H. W. Bush** J. Danforth Quayle	Republican	101st 102nd	Democratic Democratic	Democratic Democratic
1993–2001	**Bill Clinton** Albert Gore Jr.	Democratic	103rd 104th 105th 106th	Democratic Republican Republican Republican	Democratic Republican Republican Republican
2001–2005	**George W. Bush** Richard Cheney	Republican	107th 108th	Republican Republican	Democratic Republican

Notes

1. During the entire administration of George Washington and part of the administration of John Quincy Adams, Congress was not organized in terms of parties. This table shows that during these periods the supporters of the respective administrations maintained control of Congress.

2. This table shows only the two dominant parties in Congress. Independents, members of minor parties, and vacancies have been omitted.

Chief Justices of the Supreme Court, 1789-2003

Chief Justice	Appointing President	Dates of Service
John Jay	Washington	1789–1795
John Rutledge	Washington	1795–1795
Oliver Ellsworth	Washington	1796–1800
John Marshall	J. Adams	1801–1835
Roger Brooke Taney	Jackson	1836–1864
Salmon Portland Chase	Lincoln	1864–1873
Morrison Remick Waite	Grant	1874–1888
Melville Weston Fuller	Cleveland	1888–1910
Edward Douglass White	Taft	1910–1921
William Howard Taft	Harding	1921–1930
Charles Evans Hughes	Hoover	1930–1941
Harlan Fiske Stone	F. Roosevelt	1941–1946
Frederick Moore Vinson	Truman	1946–1953
Earl Warren	Eisenhower	1953–1969
Warren Earl Burger	Nixon	1969–1986
William Hubbs Rehnquist	Reagan	1986–

Glossary

agenda setting Influencing what people consider important.

amicus curiae Latin for "a friend of the court"; describes a brief in which individuals not party to a suit may have their views heard.

Anti-Federalists Opponents of the Constitution during the fight over ratification.

appellate courts Courts that hear cases on appeal from other courts.

appropriation Legal authority for a federal agency to spend money from the U.S. Treasury.

balance of payments The annual difference between payments and receipts between a country and its trading partners.

beat The assigned location where a reporter regularly gathers news stories.

bias Deviation from some ideal standard, such as representativeness or objectivity.

bicameral As applied to a legislative body, consisting of two houses or chambers.

bill of attainder A governmental decree that a person is guilty of a crime that carries the death penalty, rendered without benefit of a trial.

Bill of Rights The first ten amendments to the U.S. Constitution, concerned with basic liberties.

block grants Federal grants to the states to be used for general activities.

blue-collar worker A skilled, semiskilled, or unskilled worker in industry.

briefs Documents setting out the arguments in legal cases, prepared by attorneys and presented to courts.

budget deficit The amount by which annual government expenditures exceed revenues.

capital crime Any crime for which death is a possible penalty.

capture A situation in which a regulated industry exercises substantial influence on the government agency regulating it.

casework Services performed by members of Congress for constituents.

categorical grants Federal aid to states and localities clearly specifying what the money can be used for.

caucus A meeting of party activists to choose delegates to a national presidential nominating convention.

Central Intelligence Agency (CIA) The organization that coordinates all U.S. intelligence agencies; it also gathers and evaluates intelligence itself and carries out covert operations.

checks and balances The constitutional principle that government power shall be divided and that the fragments should balance or check one another to prevent tyranny.

chief of staff A top adviser to the president who also manages the White House staff.

circuits The 12 geographical jurisdictions and 1 special court that hear appeals from the federal district courts.

civil disobedience Intentionally breaking a law and accepting the consequences as a way to publicize the unjustness of the law.

civil liberties Freedoms found primarily in the Bill of Rights that are protected from government interference.

civil rights Guarantees by government of equal citizenship to all social groups.

civil servants Government workers employed under the merit system; not political appointees.

civil service Federal government jobs held by civilian employees, excluding political appointees.

class action suit A suit brought on behalf of a group of people who are in a situation similar to that of the plaintiffs.

cloture A vote to end a filibuster or a debate; requires the votes of three-fifths of the membership of the Senate.

Cold War The period of tense relations between the United States and the Soviet Union from the late 1940s to the late 1980s.

collective public opinion The political attitudes of the public as a whole, expressed as averages, percentages, or other summaries of many individuals' opinions.

concurring opinion The opinion of one or more judges who vote with the majority on a case but wish to set out different reasons for their decision.

conditions Provisions in federal assistance requiring that state and local governments follow certain policies in order to obtain federal funds.

confederation A loose association of states or territorial divisions formed for a common purpose.

conference committees Ad hoc committees, made up of members of both the Senate and the House of Representatives, set up to reconcile differences in the provisions of bills.

Connecticut Compromise Also called the *Great Compromise*; the compromise between the New Jersey and Virginia plans put forth by the Connecticut delegates at the Constitutional Convention; called for a lower legislative house based on population size and an upper house based on equal representation of the states.

conservative The political position that holds that the federal government ought to play a very small role in economic regulation, social welfare, and overcoming racial inequality.

constituency The district of a legislator.

constituent A citizen who lives in the district of an elected official.

constitution   The basic framework of law that prescribes how government is to operate.

constitutional courts   Federal courts created by Congress under the authority of Article III of the Constitution.

containment   The policy of resisting expansion of the Soviet Union's influence by diplomatic, economic, and military means.

convention   A gathering of delegates who nominate a party's presidential candidate.

conventional participation   Political activity related to elections (voting, persuading, and campaigning) or to contacting public officials.

cooperative federalism   Federalism in which the powers of the states and the national government are so intertwined that public policies can happen only if the two levels of government cooperate.

cost-benefit analysis   A method of evaluating rules and regulations by weighing their potential costs against their potential benefits to society.

Council of Economic Advisers (CEA)   An organization in the Executive Office of the President made up of a small group of economists who advise on economic policy.

covert operations   Secret or semisecret activities abroad, often involving intelligence gathering, influence on other countries' politics, or the use of force.

dealignment   A gradual reduction in the dominance of one political party without another party supplanting it.

delegate   According to the doctrine articulated by Edmund Burke, an elected representative who acts in perfect accord with the wishes of his or her constituents.

democracy   A system of rule by the people, defined by the existence of popular sovereignty, political equality, and political liberty.

depression   A severe and persistent drop in economic activity.

devolution   The delegation of power by the central government to state or local bodies.

direct democracy   A form of political decision making in which the public business is decided by all citizens meeting in small assemblies.

discharge petition   A petition signed by 218 House members to force a bill that has been before a committee for at least 30 days while the House is in session out of the committee and onto the floor for consideration.

discount rate   The interest rate the Federal Reserve charges member banks to cover short-term loans.

dissenting opinion   The opinion of the judge or judges who are in the minority on a particular case before the Supreme Court.

disturbance theory   A theory that locates the origins of interest groups in changes in the economic, social, or political environment that threaten the well-being of some segment of the population.

divided government   Control of the executive and the legislative branches by different political parties.

dual federalism   Federalism in which the powers of the states and the national government are neatly separated like the sections of a layer cake.

due process clause   The section of the Fourteenth Amendment that prohibits states from depriving anyone of life, liberty, or property "without due process of law," a guarantee against arbitrary or unfair government action.

economic conservatives   People who favor private enterprise and oppose government regulations on spending.

economic liberals   People who favor government regulation of business and government spending for social programs.

economic liberty   The right to own and use property free from excessive government interference.

elastic clause   Article I, Section 8, of the Constitution, also called *the necessary and proper clause;* gives Congress the authority to make whatever laws are necessary and proper to carry out its enumerated responsibilities.

electoral college   Representatives of the states who formally elect the president; the number of electors in each state is equal to the total number of its senators and congressional representatives.

electoral competition model   A form of election in which parties seeking votes move toward the median voter or the center of the political spectrum.

electoral reward and punishment   The tendency to vote for the incumbents when times are good and against them when times are bad.

electors   Representatives who are elected in the states to formally choose the U.S. president.

entitlements   Government benefits that are distributed automatically to citizens who qualify on the basis of a set of guidelines set by law; for example, Americans over the age of 65 are entitled to Medicare coverage.

enumerated powers   Powers of the federal government specifically mentioned in the Constitution.

equal protection clause   The section of the Fourteenth Amendment that provides equal protection of the laws to all citizens.

Equal Rights Amendment (ERA)   Proposed amendment to the U.S. Constitution stating that equality of rights shall not be abridged or denied on account of a person's gender.

equal time provision   The former requirement that television stations give or sell the same amount of time to all competing candidates.

establishment clause   The part of the First Amendment to the Constitution that prohibits Congress from establishing an official religion; the basis for the doctrine of the separation of church and state.

European Union (EU)   A common market formed by Western European nations, with free trade and free population movement among them.

ex post facto law   A law that retroactively declares some action illegal.

exclusionary rule   A standard promulgated by the Supreme Court that prevents police and prosecutors from using evidence against a defendant that was obtained in an illegal search.

Executive Office of the President (EOP)   A group of organizations that advise the president on a wide range of issues; includes the Office of Management and Budget, the National Security Council, and the Council of Economic Advisers.

executive privilege   A presidential claim that certain communications with subordinates may be withheld from Congress and the courts.

externalities   The positive and negative effects of economic activities on third parties.

faction   Madison's term for groups or parties that try to advance their own interests at the expense of the public good.

fairness doctrine   The former requirement that television stations present contrasting points of view.

federal   Describing a system in which significant governmental powers are divided between a central government and smaller units, such as states.

federalism   A system in which significant governmental powers are divided between a central government and smaller units, such as states.

Federalists   Proponents of the Constitution during the ratification fight; also the political party of Hamilton, Washington, and Adams.

filibuster   A parliamentary device used in the Senate to prevent a bill from coming to a vote by "talking it to death," made possible by the norm of unlimited debate.

fiscal policy   Government's actions affecting spending and taxing levels; affects overall output and income in the economy.

framing   Providing a context for interpretation.

franchise   The right to vote.

franking privilege   Public subsidization of mail from the members of Congress to their constituents.

free exercise clause   That portion of the First Amendment to the Constitution that prohibits Congress from impeding religious observance or impinging upon religious beliefs.

free rider   One who gains a benefit without contributing; explains why it is so difficult to form social movements and noneconomic interest groups.

General Agreement on Tariffs and Trade (GATT)   An international agreement that requires the lowering of tariffs and other barriers to free trade.

general revenue sharing   Federal aid to the states without any conditions on how the money is to be spent.

gerrymandering   Redrawing electoral district lines to give an advantage to a particular party or candidate.

grand juries   Groups of citizens who decide whether there is sufficient evidence to bring an indictment against accused persons.

grandfather clause   A device that allowed whites who had failed the literacy test to vote anyway by extending the franchise to anyone whose grandfather had voted.

grants-in-aid   Funds from the national government to state and local governments to help pay for programs created by the national government.

grass roots   The constituents, voters, or rank-and-file of a party.

Great Depression   The period of economic crisis in the United States that lasted from the stock market crash of 1929 to America's entry into World War II.

gross domestic product (GDP)   Monetary value of all goods and services produced in a nation each year, excluding income residents earn abroad.

habeas corpus   The legal doctrine that a person who is arrested must have a timely hearing before a judge.

hearings   The taking of testimony by a congressional committee or subcommittee.

hopper   The box in the House of Representatives in which proposed bills are placed.

ideology   A system of interrelated attitudes and beliefs.

in forma pauperis   Describing a process by which indigents may file a suit with the Supreme Court free of charge.

incorporation   The gradual use of the Fourteenth Amendment by the Supreme Court to make the Bill of Rights and other constitutional protections binding on the states.

independent expenditures   Money spent on behalf of candidates by interest groups and individuals who are not connected to a candidate's campaign organization.

Industrial Revolution   The period of transition from predominantly agricultural to predominantly industrial societies in the Western nations in the nineteenth century.

inflation   A condition of rising prices.

infotainment   The merging of hard news and entertainment in news presentations.

institutional presidency   The permanent bureaucracy associated with the presidency, designed to help the incumbent of the office carry out his responsibilities.

integration   Policies encouraging the interaction of different races, as in schools or public facilities.

intercontinental ballistic missiles (ICBMs)   Guided missiles capable of carrying nuclear warheads across continents.

interest group   Any private organization or association that seeks to influence public policy as a way to protect or advance some interest.

interest group liberalism   A political regime in which interest groups help formulate and carry out government policies.

intermediate scrutiny   A legal test falling between ordinary and strict scrutiny relevant to issues of gender; under this test, the Supreme Court will allow gender classifications in laws if they are *substantially* related to an *important* government objective.

iron triangle An enduring alliance of common interest among an interest group, a congressional committee, and a bureaucratic agency.

isolationism The policy of avoiding involvement in foreign affairs.

isolationists Those who believe the United States should defend itself behind formidable defensive walls and avoid foreign military and diplomatic entanglements.

Jim Crow Popular term for the system of legal racial segregation that existed in the American South until the middle of the twentieth century.

Joint Chiefs of Staff (JCS) The military officers in charge of each of the armed services.

joint committees Congressional committees with members from both the House and the Senate.

judicial activism Actions by the courts that go beyond the strict role of the judiciary as interpreter of the law and adjudicator of disputes.

judicial review The power of the Supreme Court to declare actions of the other branches and levels of government unconstitutional.

Keynesians Advocates of government programs to stimulate economic activity through tax cuts and government spending.

laissez-faire The political-economic doctrine that holds that government ought not interfere with the operations of the free market.

legislative courts Highly specialized federal courts created by Congress under the authority of Article I of the Constitution.

liberal The political position that holds that the federal government has a substantial role to play in economic regulation, social welfare, and overcoming racial inequality.

literacy test A device used by the southern states to prevent African-Americans from voting before the passage of the Voting Rights Act of 1965, which banned its use; usually involved interpretation of a section of a state's constitution.

lobby An interest or pressure group that seeks to convey the group's interest to government decision makers.

macroeconomic policy Having to do with the performance of the economy as a whole.

majority-minority districts Districts drawn to ensure that a racial minority makes up the majority of voters.

majority rule The form of political decision making in which policies are decided on the basis of what a majority of the people want.

majority tyranny Suppression of the rights and liberties of a minority by the majority.

mandate A formal order from the national government that the states carry out certain policies.

markup The process of revising a bill in committee.

Marshall Plan The program of U.S. economic aid set up to rebuild Europe after World War II.

mass mobilization The process of involving large numbers of people in a social movement.

means-tested Meeting the criterion of demonstrable need.

median household income Household income number at which one-half of all households have more income and one-half have less income; the mid-point of all households ranked by income.

median voter Refers to the voter at the exact middle of the political spectrum.

monetarists Advocates of a minimal government role in the economy, limited to managing the growth of the money supply.

monetary policy Government's actions affecting the supply of money and the level of interest rates in the economy.

multilateralist The stance toward foreign policy that suggests that the United States should seek the cooperation of other nations and multilateral institutions in pursuing its goals.

multilateralists Those who believe the United States should use its military and diplomatic power in the world in cooperation with other nations and international organizations.

mutually assured destruction (MAD) A situation of nuclear balance in which either the United States or the Soviet Union could respond to a surprise attack by destroying the other country.

national debt The total outstanding debt of the federal government.

national interest What is of benefit to the nation as a whole.

National Reconnaissance Office (NRO) The government agency in charge of surveillance by satellite photography and other technological means.

national security adviser A top foreign policy and defense adviser to the president who heads the National Security Council.

National Security Agency (NSA) The federal government agency that intercepts and decodes electronic messages and secures U.S. communications around the world.

National Security Council (NSC) An organization in the Executive Office of the President made up of officials from the State and Defense Departments, the CIA, and the military, who advise on foreign and security affairs.

nationalist position The view of American federalism which holds that the Constitution created a system in which the national government is supreme, relative to the states, and that granted to it a broad range of powers and responsibilities.

nationalizing The process by which provisions of the Bill of Rights become incorporated. See *incorporation*.

nativist Antiforeign; applied to political movements active in the nineteenth century.

necessary and proper clause Article I, Section 8, of the Constitution, also known as the *elastic clause*; gives

Congress the authority to make whatever laws are necessary and proper to carry out its enumerated responsibilities.

New Deal The programs of the administration of President Franklin D. Roosevelt.

New Deal coalition The informal electoral alliance of working-class ethnic groups, Catholics, Jews, urban dwellers, racial minorities, and the South that was the basis of the Democratic party dominance of American politics from the New Deal to the early 1970s.

New Jersey Plan Proposal of the smaller states at the Constitutional Convention to create a government based on the equal representation of the states in a unicameral legislature.

newsworthy Worth printing or broadcasting as news, according to editors' judgments.

normal vote The proportion of the votes that each party would win if party identification alone affected voting decisions.

North American Free Trade Agreement (NAFTA) An agreement among the United States, Canada, and Mexico to eliminate nearly all barriers to trade and investment among the three countries.

North Atlantic Treaty Organization (NATO) An alliance of the United States, Canada, and Western European countries for defense against the Soviet Union.

nuclear proliferation The spread of nuclear weapons to additional countries or to terrorist groups.

nullification An attempt by states to declare national laws or actions null and void.

objective journalism News reported with no evaluative language and with any opinions quoted or attributed to a specific source.

obscenity As defined by the Supreme Court, the representation of sexually explicit material in a manner that violates community standards and is without redeeming social importance or value.

Office of Management and Budget (OMB) An organization within the Executive Office of the President that advises on the federal budget, domestic legislation, and regulations.

open-seat election An election in which there is no incumbent officeholder.

opinion A written explanation of judicial reasoning that accompanies a Supreme Court decision.

opinion of the Court The majority opinion that accompanies a Supreme Court decision.

ordinary scrutiny The assumption that the actions of elected bodies and officials are legal under the Constitution.

original intention The doctrine that the courts must interpret the Constitution in ways consistent with the intentions of the framers rather than in light of contemporary conditions and needs.

original jurisdiction The authority of a court to be the first to hear a particular kind of case.

participation Political activity, including voting, campaign activity, contacting officials, and demonstrating.

partisan A committed member of a party; seeing issues from the point of view of the interests of a single party.

party caucus An organization of the members of a political party in the House or Senate.

party identification The sense of belonging to one or another political party.

party platform A party's statement of its positions on the issues of the day.

Pentagon The building in Arlington, Virginia, that contains the offices of the military chiefs and top officials of the Defense Department.

petit (trial) juries Juries that hear evidence and sit in judgment on charges brought in civil or criminal cases.

plaintiff One who brings suit in a court.

pluralist A political scientist who views American politics as best understood in terms of the interaction, conflict, and bargaining of groups.

plurality More votes than any other candidate but less than a majority of all votes cast.

pocket veto Rejection of a bill if the president takes no action on it for ten days and Congress has adjourned during that period.

policy preferences Citizens' preferences concerning what policies they want government to pursue.

political action committee (PAC) A private organization whose purpose is to raise and distribute funds to candidates in political campaigns.

political efficacy The sense that one can affect what government does.

political equality The principle that says that each person carries equal weight in the conduct of the public business.

political liberty The principle that citizens in a democracy are protected from government interference in the exercise of a range of basic freedoms, such as the freedoms of speech, association, and conscience.

poll tax A tax to be paid as a condition of voting; used in the South to keep African-Americans away from the polls.

popular sovereignty The basic principle of democracy that the people ultimately rule.

pork Also called *pork barrel;* projects designed to bring to the constituency jobs and public money for which the members of Congress can claim credit.

poverty line The federal government's calculation of the amount of income families of various sizes need to stay out of poverty.

precedents Rulings by courts that guide judicial reasoning in subsequent cases.

presidential approval rating A president's standing with the public, indicated by the percentage of Americans who tell survey interviewers that they approve a president's "handling of his job."

presidential popularity The percentage of Americans who approve a president's handling of his job.

pressure group An interest group or lobby; a group that brings pressure to bear on government decision makers.

primary elections State elections in which delegates to national presidential nominating conventions are chosen.

prior restraint The government's power to prevent publication, as opposed to punishment afterward.

privatization The process of turning over certain government functions to the private sector.

privileges and immunities clause The portion of Article IV, Section 2, of the Constitution that states that citizens from out of state have the same legal rights as local citizens in any state.

proportional representation The awarding of legislative seats to political parties to reflect the proportion of the popular vote each party receives.

prospective voting model A theory of democratic elections in which voters decide what government will do in the near future by choosing one or another responsible party.

public goods Products and services that citizens want but the private sector does not provide, such as national defense and pollution control.

public opinion Political attitudes expressed by ordinary citizens.

pundits Somewhat derisive term for print, broadcast, and radio commentators on the political news.

random sampling The selection of survey respondents by chance, with equal probability, to ensure their representativeness of the whole population.

realignment The process by which one party supplants another as the dominant party in a political system.

reapportionment The reallocation of House seats among the states, done after each national census, to ensure that seats are held by the states in proportion to the size of their populations.

recession Two straight quarters of declining economic activity.

reciprocity Deferral by members of Congress to the judgment of subject-matter specialists, mainly on minor technical bills.

red tape Overbearing bureaucratic rules and procedures.

redistricting The redrawing of congressional district lines within a state to ensure roughly equal populations within each district.

regulations The issuing of rules by government agencies with the aim of reducing the scale of negative externalities produced by private firms.

remedy An action that a court determines must be taken to rectify a wrong.

representative democracy Indirect democracy, in which the people rule through elected representatives.

republicanism A political doctrine advocating limited government based on popular consent, protected against majority tyranny.

reservation clause The Tenth Amendment to the Constitution, reserving powers to the states or the people.

responsible party A political party that takes clear, distinct stands on the issues and enacts them as policy.

retrospective voting A form of election in which voters look back at the performance of a party in power and cast ballots on the basis of how well it did in office. Voting on the basis of past government performance.

rule of four An *unwritten* practice that requires at least four justices of the Supreme Court to agree that a case warrants review by the Court before it will hear the case.

sample survey An interview study asking questions of a set of people who are chosen as representative of the whole population.

scope of conflict The number of groups involved in a political conflict; few groups mean a narrow scope of conflict, and many groups mean a wide scope of conflict.

secularization The spread of nonreligious values and outlooks.

select committees Temporary committees in Congress created to conduct studies or investigations. They have no power to report bills.

selective incorporation The U.S. Supreme Court's gradual and piecemeal making of the protections of the Bill of Rights binding on the states.

senatorial courtesy The tradition that judicial nominations for federal district court appointments be cleared by the senior senator of the president's party from the relevant state.

seniority Length of service.

separate but equal doctrine The principle articulated in *Plessy* v. *Ferguson* (1896) that laws prescribing *separate* public facilities and services for nonwhite Americans are permissible if the facilities and services are *equal* to those provided for whites.

separation of powers The distribution of government legislative, executive, and judicial powers to separate branches of government.

sit-down strike A form of labor action in which workers stop production but do not leave their job site.

smart bombs Bombs capable of being guided precisely to their targets.

social conservatives People who favor traditional social values; they tend to support strong law-and-order measures and to oppose abortion and gay rights.

social insurance Government programs that provide services or income support in proportion to the amount of mandatory contributions made by individuals to a government trust fund.

social liberals People who favor civil liberties, abortion rights, and alternative lifestyles.

soft money Expenditures by political parties on general public education, voter registration, and voter mobilization.

spoils system The practice of distributing government offices and contracts to the supporters of the winning party; also called patronage.

standing Authority to bring legal action because one is directly affected by the issues at hand.

standing committees Relatively permanent congressional committees that address specific areas of legislation.

stare decisis The legal doctrine that says precedent should guide judicial decision making.

states' rights position The view of American federalism which holds that the Constitution created a system of dual sovereignty in which the national government and the state governments are sovereign in their own spheres.

stay acts Enactments postponing the collection of taxes or mortgage payments.

strict construction The doctrine that the provisions of the Constitution have a clear meaning and that judges must stick closely to this meaning when rendering decisions.

strict scrutiny The assumption that actions by elected bodies or officials violate constitutional rights.

suffrage The right to vote.

Sun Belt States of the Lower South, Southwest, and West, where sunny weather and often conservative politics prevail.

superpower A nation armed with nuclear weapons and able to project force anywhere on the globe.

supremacy clause The provision in Article VI of the Constitution that the Constitution itself and the laws and treaties of the United States are the supreme law of the land, taking precedence over state laws and constitutions.

suspect classification The invidious, arbitrary, or irrational designation of a group for special treatment by government.

test case A case brought to force a ruling on the constitutionality of some law or executive action.

think tanks Nonprofit organizations that do research on public policy issues and distribute their findings through a variety of outlets. Although formally nonpartisan, most have an identifiable ideological stance.

trade deficit An excess of the value of the goods a country imports over the value of the goods it exports.

Truman Doctrine President Truman's policy that the United States should defend noncommunist countries from outside pressure and internal rebellion from communists.

trustee According to the doctrine articulated by Edmund Burke, an elected representative who believes that his or her own best judgment, rather than instructions from constituents, should be used in making legislative decisions.

trusts Large combinations of business corporations.

turnout The proportion of eligible voters who actually vote in a given election.

tyranny The abuse of power by a ruler or a government.

unanimous consent Legislative action taken "without objection" as a way to expedite business; used to conduct much of the business of the Senate.

unconventional participation Political activity in the form of demonstrations or protests.

unilateralist The stance toward foreign policy that suggests that the United States should "go it alone," pursuing its national interests without seeking the cooperation of other nations or multilateral institutions.

unilateralists Those who believe the United States should vigorously use its military and diplomatic power to pursue American national interests in the world, but on a "go it alone" basis.

unitary system A system in which a central government has complete power over its constituent units or states.

veto Presidential disapproval of a bill that has been passed by both houses of Congress. The president's veto can be overridden by a two-thirds vote in each house.

Virginia Plan Proposal by the large states at the Constitutional Convention to create a strong central government with power in the government apportioned to the states on the basis of population.

Warsaw Pact An alliance of the Soviet Union and Eastern European communist countries.

watchdog The role of the media in scrutinizing the actions of government officials.

welfare state The set of government programs that protects the minimum standard of living of families and individuals against loss of income.

whip A political party member in Congress charged with keeping members informed of the plans of the party leadership, counting votes before action on important issues, and rounding up party members for votes on bills.

whistle-blowers People who bring official misconduct in their agencies to public attention.

white-collar worker A person working at a service, sales, or office job.

white primaries Primary elections open only to whites.

World Trade Organization (WTO) An agency designed to enforce the provisions of the General Agreement on Tariffs and Trade and to resolve trade disputes between nations.

writ of certiorari An announcement that the Supreme Court will hear a case on appeal from a lower court; its issuance requires the vote of four of the nine justices.

writ of mandamus A court order that forces an official to act.

yellow journalism Sensational newspaper stories with large headlines and, in some cases, color cartoons.

Credits

Text, Figures, and Tables

Page 61: Box map, "Educated Guesses: Sampling Is Taboo, But the Census Does Plenty of 'Imputing'—It Fills in Missing Answers on Race, Sex, Age—Even Postulates Whole People—Whatever the Neighbors Say" by Glenn R. Simpson, *The Wall Street Journal,* August 30, 2001. Reprinted by permission of *The Wall Street Journal,* Copyright © 2001 Dow Jones & Company, Inc. All Rights Reserved Worldwide. License number 562821481997; **p. 73:** Figure 3.5, Morris P. Fiorina and Paul E. Peterson, *New American Democracy,* Second Edition (New York: Longman Publishers, 2001), p. 81. Reprinted by permission of Pearson Education, Inc.; **p. 79:** Figure 3.6, used with the permission of the Center for American Woman and Politics (CAWP), Eagleton Institute of Politics, Rutgers University; **p. 225:** Table 8.1, reprinted with the permission of Simon & Schuster Adult Publishing Group from *America in Black and White* by Stephan Thernstrom and Abigail Thernstrom. Copyright © 1997 by Stephan Thernstrom and Abigail Thernstrom; **p. 288:** Table 10.1, "Comparing Major Party Convention Delegates to Other Americans" from *The New York Times*/CBS News Poll, *The New York Times,* August 14, 2000. Reprinted by permission of *The New York Times;* **p. 427:** Figure 14.3, from *Storm Center: The Supreme Court in American Politics,* Fourth Edition, by David M. O'Brien. Copyright © 1996, 1993, 1990, 1986 by David M. O'Brien. Used by permission of W. W. Norton & Company, Inc.; **p. 506:** Figure 17.1, "American GDP Change on Previous Quarter," *The Economist* (October 28, 1995), p. 89. Copyright © 1995 The Economist Newspaper Ltd. All rights reserved. Reprinted with permission. Further reproduction prohibited. **www.economist.com.**

Photos

Page abbreviations are used as follows: **(T)** top, **(B)** bottom, **(L)** left, **(R)** right.

Page 4: AP/Wide World Photos; **p. 7:** The Granger Collection, New York; **p. 10:** Alan Diaz/AP/Wide World Photos; **p. 11:** Bob Daemmrich/The Image Works; **p. 13:** The Granger Collection **p. 13:** The Granger Collection; **p. 17:** AP/Wide World Photos; **p. 27:** The Granger Collection; **p. 30 (L):** The Granger Collection; **p. 30 (R):** Library of Congress; **p. 34:** Pete Souza/Folio, Inc.; **p. 37:** Art Resource, NY; **p. 39:** © The Illustrated London News/February 16, 1861; **p. 48:** Rick Reinard; **p. 55:** Tyrone Turner/Stockphoto.com; **p. 58:** AP/Wide World Photos; **p. 62:** Contact Press Images; **p. 64:** Stephanie Maze/Corbis; **p. 68:** Franklin Delano Roosevelt Library; **p. 72:** Lyndon Baines Johnson Library & Museum; **p. 75:** P. Jorden/Corbis Sygma; **p. 76:** Sam Sweeny/Stock Boston, Inc.; **p. 78:** John Nordell/The Image Works; **p. 80:** Anneal Vohra; **p. 85:** Axel Koster/Corbis Sygma; **p. 89:** S. Kelly, ©1995 San Diego Union-Tribune, Copley News Service; **p. 93:** Rob Crandal/The Image Works; **p. 97:** Joe Sohm/Chromosohm; **p. 101:** Bettmann/Corbis; **p. 102:** Liaison Agency/Getty Images; **p. 105:** Boris Yurchenko/AP/Wide World Photos; **p. 106:** Mikhail Metzel/AP/Wide World Photos; **p. 108:** Diego Goldberg/Corbis Sygma; **p. 117:** C. Simonpietri/Corbis Sygma; **p. 120:** Bob Daemmrich/The Image Works; **p. 121:** Bettmann/UPI/Corbis; **p. 126:** Wally McNamee/Corbis Sygma; **p. 127:** Doug Mills/AP/Wide World Photos; **p. 132:** Ron Coppock/Liaison Agency/ Getty Images; **p. 136:** Corbis; **p. 137:** Tony Freeman/PhotoEdit; **p. 139:** Folio, Inc.; **p. 143:** Robert Trippett/SIPA Press; **p. 151:** Haviv/Corbis Saba Press; **p. 153:** © Reprinted by permission Tribune Media Services; **p. 155 (L):** © New York Journal, February 7, 1898; **p. 155 (R):** Colorado Historical Society; **p. 156:** Chenet/Liaison Agency/Getty Images; **p. 157:** AP/Wide World Photos; **p. 159:** Peter Cosgrove/AP/Wide World Photos; **p. 161:** Ben Van Hook; **p. 163:** Folio, Inc.; **p. 169:** CNN/Corbis Sygma; **p. 174:** © By permission of Mike Luckovich and Creators Syndicate; **p. 175:** The Image Works; **p. 179:** Michael L. Abramson/TimePix; **p. 185:** Fritz Hoffman/The Image Works; **p. 187:** Library of Congress; **p. 191:** Library of Congress; **p. 192:** Mark Peterson/Corbis Saba Press; **p. 193:** Dennis Brack/Black Star/Stockphoto.com; **p. 195:** Paul Conklin/PhotoEdit; **p. 198:** Allan Tannenbaum/Corbis Sygma; **p. 205:** AP/Wide World Photos; **p. 215:** The Granger Collection; **p. 219:** Hulton/Archive/Getty Images; **p. 220:** David Butow/Corbis Saba Press; **p. 223:** McCartney/Photo Researchers, Inc.; **p. 224:** Elaine Thompson/AP/Wide World Photos; **p. 226:** Peter Lennihan/AP/Wide World Photos; **p. 227:** Stephen Jaffee/Reuters/Getty Images; **p. 228:** Bettmann/Corbis; **p. 229:** AP/Wide World Photos; **p. 232:** David Burnett/Contact Press Images; **p. 239:** AP/Wide World Photos; **p. 241:** Edward Greenberg; **p. 243:** Pearson Education U.S. ELT/Scott Foresman; **p. 245:** AP/Wide World Photos; **p. 249:** William Waldron/The Image Works; **p. 251:** AP/Wide World Photos; **p. 253:** Mark Peterson/Corbis Saba Press; **p. 254:** Impact Visuals; **p. 255:** Mathieu/Corbis Sygma; **p. 256:** AP/Wide World Photos; **p. 267 (L):** AP/Wide World Photos; **p. 267 (R):** AP/Wide World Photos; **p. 271:** David Burnett/Contact Press Images; **p. 275:** Rob Crandall/The Image Works; **p. 277:** The St. Louis Art Museum. Gift of Bank of America; **p. 280:** AP/Wide World Photos; **p. 282:** Black Star/Stockphoto; **p. 285:** Rusty Burroughs/AP/Wide World Photos; **p. 286:** Porter Gifford/Getty Images; **p. 287 (L):** Bettmann/Corbis; **p. 287 (R):** Arnold Zann/Black Star/Stockphoto.com; **p. 289:** David J. & Janice L. Frent Collection/Corbis; **p. 295:** Michael Samojeden/AP/Wide World Photos; **p. 307:** Reuters NewMedia Inc./Corbis; **p. 310:** Mike Wintroath/AP/Wide World Photos; **p. 314:** Jeffrey Markowitz/Corbis Sygma; **p. 324:** Getty Images; **p. 325:** Courtesy Congresswoman Rosa DeLauro; **p. 330:** Brad Markel/Getty Images; **p. 331 (B):** Joe Marquette/AP/Wide World Photos; **p. 331 (T):** Trippett/SIPA Press; **p. 333:** AP/Wide World Photos; **p. 335:** Susan Ragan/AP/Wide World Photos; **p. 337:** Ron Sachs/Corbis Sygma;

Index

ABC, 156
ABC/Cap Cities, 159
Abolitionist movement, 215, 218
Abortion. *See also* Pro-life movement
    public opinion on, 131
    right to, 491–493
    social movements and, 220, 227
    stem cell research and, 122
    Supreme Court and, 49, 430, 431,
        439, 442
Absentee voting, 279, 299
Accountability, 241
Accused, rights of. *See* Rights of
    accused
ACT-UP, 220
Adams, John, 65
    Declaration of Independence and, 30
    judicial appointments of, 422, 429
Adams, John Quincy, 244, 300
Adams, Samuel, 43
Adams, Sherman, 361
Adarand Construction v. *Peña,* 477, 488
Adjudication, 398
Advertising
    by interest groups, 199
    regulation of campaign, 292
    on television, 289–290
Aetna Insurance, 186
Affirmative action
    function of, 486–487
    origins of, 485–486
    present state of, 488
    public opinion on, 135, 487
    Supreme Court and, 488–490
    University of California and, 89, 477
Afghanistan
    American policy in war in, 106, 126,
        162, 175, 359, 376, 407, 541
    cost of conflict in, 504
    military equipment used in, 547
AFL-CIO, 192
African-Americans. *See also* Minorities
    affirmative action and, 485–490 (*See
        also* Affirmative action)
    civil rights and, 217, 477, 478,
        483–490 (*See also* Civil rights;
        Civil rights movement)
    in civil service jobs, 400
    in Congress, 312, 313
    congressional districts and, 317
    discrimination and, 484
    income of, 96
    in military service, 17, 19
    northern migration of, 19
    political participation and, 233,
        280–283
    poverty among, 97
    pre–Civil War era and, 478–480
    presidential election of 2000 and,
        134, 293
    public opinion and, 134–135

as Supreme Court justices, 428
voting rights for, 3–4, 11, 67, 109,
    276–277, 480–481
Age
    political participation and, 283
    public opinion and, 141
    voting rights and, 277
Agencies, 392
Agency for International Development,
    390, 558
Agenda setting, 172
Aggregate demand, 509
Agriculture Department, 388
Agriculture industry
    lobbying efforts of, 192
    population shifts and, 90, 91
AIDS/HIV. *See* HIV/AIDS
Aid to Families with Dependent
    Children (AFDC), 55, 477, 531
Airbus, 185
Airline Passenger Fairness Act (Senate
    Bill 383), 196
Airline Security Act, 392
Alien and Sedition Acts, 65, 174
Amazon.com, 102
Amendments, 43, 44, 48–49. *See also*
    Constitution, U.S.; *specific amend-
    ments*
American Civil Liberties Union
    (ACLU), 456–457, 471
American Conservative League (ACU),
    200, 201
American Dairy Association, 192
American Dental Association (ADA), 192
American Enterprise Institute, 165
American Federation of Teachers, 291
American-Israel Public Affairs
    Committee (AIPAC), 561
Americanization, 547–548
American Medical Association (AMA),
    192
American Revolution, 27, 29
Americans for Democratic Action
    (ADA), 200, 201
Americans for Fair Drug Prices, 198
American Spectator, 169
Americans with Disabilities Act, 70,
    437, 494–495
American Wheat Growers Association,
    192
American Woman Suffrage Association
    (AWSA), 215–216
Amicus curiae briefs, 197, 432, 442
Ancient Greece, 6, 7
Anthony, Susan B., 215, 216
Anthrax outbreak, 386
Anti-Americanism, 548, 550
Anti-Ballistic Missile Treaty, 360, 540
Anti-Federalists, 46, 47, 385
Antiglobalization movement
    explanation of, 220, 224

Green party and, 249
World Trade Organization and, 377,
    378
Anti-Vietnam War movement, 219. *See
    also* Vietnam War
AOL/Time-Warner, 103, 104, 158
Apartheid, 561
Appellate courts, 426
Appropriations, 406
Arab Americans, 485. *See also* Muslims
Argentina, 553
Armey, Dick, 330, 331
Arms Control and Disarmament
    Agency, 558
Arms market, 554
Arthur Andersen, 103, 206, 518
Articles of Confederation
    presidency under, 354
    provisions of, 32, 39, 42, 44
    shortcomings of, 27–28, 33, 36, 45
    time period of, 29
Ashcroft, John, 342, 401, 405, 464–465
Asian-Americans
    discrimination and, 484
    income of, 96
    internment of Japanese, 437, 438,
        442
    political participation and, 283
    public opinion and, 136
Asian tigers, 102, 544
Assisted suicide, 464–465
Associated Press (AP), 154, 160
Atkins v. *Virginia,* 471
Atlantic Monthly, 155
Atomic Energy Commission, 390
AT&T, 202
AT&T Broadband, 159
Austria, 529
"Axis of evil," 539, 540

Baker, James, 340, 361
Balance of payments, 507–508
Balkans, 550
BankAmerica Corp, 103
Bank of the United States, 66, 110, 354
Barr, Bob, 471
Barron v. *Baltimore,* 452, 454
Bauer, Gary, 193, 285
Beard, Charles, 37
Beat, 162
Bell Atlantic, 103
Bennett, Lance, 160
Benton Harbor, Michigan, 98
Berlin Wall, 544
Bernstein, Carl, 162
BET, 156
Bicameralism, 309–310
Bill of attainder, 309, 450
Bill of Rights. *See also* Civil liberties;
    specific amendments
    capital punishment and, 468–471

Congress members ratings by, 199–201

disturbance theory and, 190

diverse types of, 189

economic policy and, 518

explanation of, 186

foreign policy and, 561

functions of, 198–199

government organization and, 189–190

grass roots mobilization by, 197–198

incentives for, 190–191

lobbying function of, 194–197 (See also Lobbying)

nominations and, 254

politics and, 208

presidents and, 376

private, 191–193

public, 193–194

representational inequities and, 200

representing business, 191–192, 200–201, 204–205

resource inequities and, 200–203

social movements vs., 217

statistics regarding, 189

Interior Department, 388

Intermediate scrutiny, 490–491

Internal Revenue Service (IRS), 342, 390, 402, 406

International Monetary Fund, 553

International Relations Committee, House, 340

Internet

campaign Websites and, 157

government regulation and, 177–179

news coverage on, 157–158, 160

political participation and, 6

pornography on, 459–460, 518

reliability of information on, 158

use of, 156–157

Interstate Commerce Act of 1887, 68

Interstate highway program, 73

Iran

as "axis of evil," 539, 551

hostage crisis in, 128, 168, 295

Iran-Contra Affair, 357, 363

Iraq

as "axis of evil," 539, 551

European Union and, 107

George W. Bush and war with, 308, 352, 359, 540, 541, 549

invasion of Kuwait by, 127, 358, 369, 376, 541

Iron triangle, 203–204

Isolation, 134

Isolationism, 104

Isolationists, 548

Israel, 152, 247, 561. See also Mideast conflict

Jackson, Andrew

accomplishments of, 354

Bank of America and, 110, 354

election of 1824 and, 244, 300

Japan

economic issues and, 102, 359

political culture in, 108

post–World War II, 542

unitary system in, 57

World War II and, 104

Japanese American internment, 437, 438, 442

Jay, John, 46

Jefferson, Thomas

accomplishments of, 354

Constitution and, 43, 45

Declaration of Independence and, 30

dual federalism and, 64

election of 1800 and, 364

Marbury v. Madison and, 422

party formation and, 244

Supreme Court and, 426

Jeffords, James, 258, 327, 351

Jews

presidential election of 2000 and, 137, 293

public opinion held by, 137

as Supreme Court justices, 428

Jim Crow, 19, 480

Job Corps, 72

Johnson, Andrew, 342

Johnson, Gregory, 457–458

Johnson, Lyndon

approval rating for, 127

civil rights and, 360

election of 1964 and, 294

Great Society program and, 69, 72, 73, 413, 485

legislative skills of, 370, 371

as majority leader, 332, 333

Vietnam War and, 117, 289, 372–373

voting rights and, 17

War on Poverty and, 395–396, 413

Joint Budget Committee, 334

Joint Chiefs of Staff (JCS), 558

Joint committees, 334

Jordan, Barbara, 79

Jordan, Vernon, 151

Journalism. See also Media

objective, 164–165

yellow, 154

Joyce, James, 460

Judges

appointment of, 427–430

impeachment of, 423–424

salaries of, 424

Judicial activism, 439–440

Judicial review

democracy and, 423

explanation of, 49, 66, 439

power of, 421–423

Judicial system. See also Supreme Court, U.S.

appointments and, 427–430

constitutional provisions and, 423–424

federal district courts and, 424–425

lobbying, 197

U.S. Courts of Appeal and, 425–426

Judiciary Act of 1789, 422, 423

Judiciary Committee, Senate, 428

Juries, 424

Justice Department, 388, 392, 393, 441

Kaelin, Kato, 163

Kashmir, 551

Kazakhstan, 550

Kemp, Jack, 413

Kennedy, Anthony, 432, 496

Kennedy, John F.

accomplishments of, 357, 358

civil rights and, 228

Cuban Missile Crisis and, 366, 543

election of 1960 and, 95, 299

Kennedy, Robert, 365

Kenney v. Tamayo-Reyes, 468–469

Kenya, 549

Key, V. O., Jr., 560–561

Keynes, John Maynard, 509

Keynesians, 509

King, Martin Luther, Jr., 228, 477, 484, 486

Kissinger, Henry, 361

Knight-Ridder, 158

Knowles v. Iowa, 467

Korean War

African-Americans in, 17, 19

as campaign issue, 295

MacArthur and, 366

Truman and, 376

Korematsu v. United States, 437, 438

Kosovo, 106, 132, 162, 164, 172, 358, 369, 541, 543, 547, 550, 561, 562

Kuwait, 162, 541

Kyllo v. United States, 467

Kyoto Protocol, 351, 360, 540, 554

Labor Department, 388–389

Labor movement

explanation of, 218

party system and, 248

repression of, 230

sit-down strikes and, 227, 228

Labor Relations Act, 435–436

Labor unions

Democratic party and, 253

function of, 192–193

presidential election of 2000 and, 139

social welfare programs and, 533

Lady Chatterley's Lover (Lawrence), 460

Laissez-faire, 435, 443

LAPS test, 460

Latinos. See Cuban-Americans; Hispanics

Latvia, 544

Lawrence, D. H., 460

Lay, Kenneth, 342

League of Conservation Voters (LCV), 200, 201

Lee, Richard Henry, 47

Lee v. Weisman, 463

The Left Wing Manifesto (Gitlow), 455–456

Legislation

committee action on, 340–341

conference committee action on, 341

floor action on, 341

introduction of, 340

pathway for, 338, 339

presidential role in, 341, 359

Legislative courts, 423